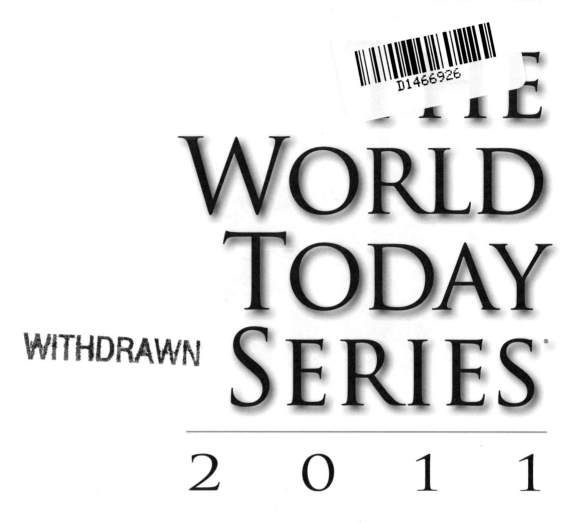

THE
WORLD
TODAY
SERIES®
2 0 1 1

CANADA

WAYNE C. THOMPSON

27TH EDITION

Wayne C. Thompson . . .

Prof. Thompson taught politics at Washington and Lee University; Professor Emeritus of Political Science, Virginia Military Institute; Ohio State University (B.A. in Government); Claremont Graduate School (M.A. and Ph.D. with distinction). He did further graduate study at the University of Göttingen, Paris/Sorbonne and Freiburg im Breisgau, where he was subsequently a guest professor. He has studied and researched in Europe for many years as a Woodrow Wilson, Fulbright, *Deutscher Akademischer Austauschdienst* (DAAD) and Alexander von Humboldt Fellow. The Canadian government, through its Embassy in Washington, awarded him a Faculty Enrichment Grant to do research in Canada. During the 1995–1996 academic year he was a Fulbright Professor in Estonia, and from 1999–2000 he was a visiting professor at the Air War College in Montgomery, Alabama. In 2001 he was a Fulbright Professor at the College of Europe in Bruges, Belgium, and continued for seven years to teach at that graduate institution. He has authored or edited ten books and many articles and book reviews on politics, history and political theory.

Making its debut as *Canada 1985*, and annually revised, this book is published by

Stryker-Post Publications
An imprint of the Rowman & Littlefield Publishing Group, Inc.
4501 Forbes Blvd., Ste 200
Lanham, MD 20706

International Standard Book Number: 978–1–935264–19–4

International Standard Serial Number: 0883–8135

Library of Congress Catalog Card Number: 2011932750

Cover design by: nvision Graphic Design

Cartographer: William L. Nelson

Typography by Barton Matheson Willse & Worthington
Baltimore, MD 21244

The World Today Series has thousands of subscribers across the U.S. and Canada. A sample list of users who annually rely on this most up-to-date material includes:

Public library systems
Universities and colleges
High schools
Federal and state agencies
All branches of the armed forces and war colleges
National Geographic Society
National Democratic Institute
Agricultural Education Foundation
ExxonMobil Corporation
Chevron Corporation
CNN

Great Bear Lake, N.W.T.   Courtesy: Michael J. Hewitt   **Vancouver: Canada Place, harborfront site of the Canada Pavilion at Expo 86**

ACKNOWLEDGEMENTS

I wish to thank several institutions and individuals who helped me while I was preparing this book. The Canadian government, through its embassy in Washington, D.C., gave me a Faculty Enrichment Grant, which enabled me to spend an entire summer in Canada, conducting interviews and research in nine of the ten provinces, and especially in Ottawa and Quebec. The staff of the Canadian Embassy library in Washington was generous and helpful to me when I used their well-organized materials.

I thank the *Liberal Party* of Canada for arranging numerous interviews for me in Ottawa, providing me with many materials and inviting me to attend its leadership conference in June 1984. The former *Progressive Conservative Party* also gave me much useful material and kindly permitted me to attend its 1983 leadership conference. I discovered that one can learn more about Canadian politics in a few days of party congresses, at which the country's prime minister and opposition leaders are chosen, than in months of library work abroad. The headquarters of the *New Democratic Party* in Ottawa welcomed me cordially. Its staff patiently answered my many questions and provided me with reading material which I found to be very beneficial. Too, it arranged my visit to its provincial office in Winnipeg, Manitoba. Finally, I am grateful to the staff at the party headquarters of the *Parti Québécois* in Montreal for being so generous with its time and for providing me with reading and campaign materials, which I needed for this book.

Professors Richard Beach, Martin Lubin and the late Jeanne Kissner of the State University of New York, Plattsburgh, accepted me as a participant in several of its Annual Quebec Summer Seminars in Montreal and Quebec City in 1983. I thus had the opportunity to gain a deeper understanding of the changes which Quebec has experienced since the early 1960s and to discuss Quebec's future with them and with many political and opinion leaders, such as Lise Bissonnette, Robert Bourassa, Roch Carrier, Gerald Godin, Roger Landry and Henry Milner.

The Association of Canadian Studies in the U.S. (ACSUS) and the Mid-Atlantic and Southeastern Associations of Canadian Studies helped me pursue my interest in Canada by sponsoring conferences at which I could familiarize myself with many diverse aspects of Canada which are not within my field of specialization. My former Canadian students at the College of Europe, Miriam Bekkouche, Jarrett Reckseidler and Denis Poirier, gave me good advice on Canadian politics. I am particularly grateful to Denis, who works in the Privy Council Office in Ottawa, for sending me campaign materials, newspapers and results related to the 2004 and 2006 federal elections; I used these extensively in updating this book.

I would like to thank many unnamed Canadians whom we met in places as diverse as camp grounds, folk festivals and political rallies. Many of their insights, comments, opinions, and concerns have found their way into the lines of this book. Washington and Lee University's Office of Special Programs frequently invited me to give lectures to their travelers in Canada. These study tours enabled me to travel to the Canadian North and West, as well as to Quebec, Nova Scotia, and Newfoundland and Labrador. I am grateful for these unique opportunities. I owe special thanks to Michael Nix from Mississauga, Ontario, who carefully read every word of this book to correct style and typographical errors. I thank my partner at Stryker-Post Publications, David T. Wilt, for getting many newer and better photographs for this and my two other books in the World Today Series and for his help in many other aspects of my work.

Finally, I wish to thank my wife, Susie, and my two daughters, Juliet and Katie, for sharing my enthusiasm for Canada and for assuring me in many ways that my effort to prepare, write, and annually update this book is worthwhile.

W.C.T.

Lexington, Virginia, July 2011

Bilingual Canadian students at the College of Europe

CONTENTS

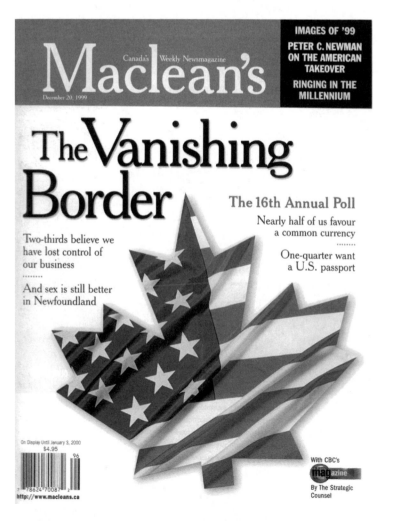

Canada's Weekly Newsmagazine

Maclean's
December 20, 1999

IMAGES OF '99
PETER C. NEWMAN
ON THE AMERICAN
TAKEOVER
RINGING IN THE
MILLENNIUM

TheVanishing Border

The 16th Annual Poll

Nearly half of us favour
a common currency
....
One-quarter want
a U.S. passport

Two-thirds believe we
have lost control of
our business
....
And sex is still better
in Newfoundland

On Display Until January 3, 2000
$4.95

96

7 76824 70087 3

http://www.macleans.ca

With CBC's
magazine
By The Strategic
Counsel

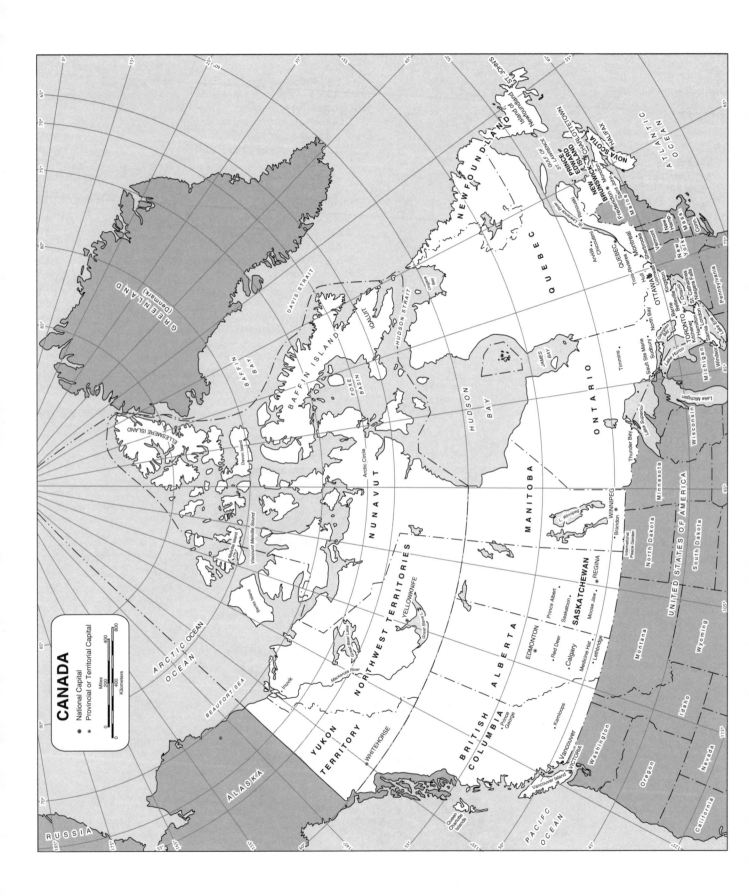

CANADA

Her Majesty Queen Elizabeth II

The Rt. Hon. Stephen Harper
Prime Minister of Canada

His Excellency The Rt. Hon. David Johnston
Governor General of Canada

Aerial view of Parliament

Canadian Prime Ministers since Confederation

Rt. Hon. Sir John A. Macdonald (2)	(C)	July 1867–Nov. 1873
Hon. Alexander Mackenzie (11)	(L)	Nov. 1873–Oct. 1878
Rt. Hon. Sir John A. Macdonald (2)	(C)	Oct. 1878–June 1891
Hon. Sir John J. C. Abbott (17)	(C)	June 1891–Nov. 1892
Rt. Hon. Sir John S. D. Thompson (10)	(C)	Dec. 1892–Dec. 1894
Rt. Hon. Sir Mackenzie Bowell (19)	(C)	Dec. 1894–Apr. 1896
Rt. Hon. Sir Charles Tupper (16)	(C)	May 1896–July 1896
Rt. Hon. Sir Wilfrid Laurier (3)	(L)	July 1896–Oct. 1911
Rt. Hon. Sir Robert L. Borden (7)	(C)	Oct. 1911–Oct. 1917
Rt. Hon. Sir Robert L. Borden (7)	(U)	Oct. 1917–July 1920
Rt. Hon. Arthur Meighen (14)	(U–L & C)	July 1920–Dec. 1921
Rt. Hon. Wm. Lyon Mackenzie King (1)	(L)	Dec. 1921–June 1926
Rt. Hon. Arthur Meighen (14)	(C)	June 1926–Sept. 1926
Rt. Hon. Wm. Lyon Mackenzie King (1)	(L)	Sept. 1926–Aug. 1930
Rt. Hon. Robert B. Bennett (12)	(C)	Aug. 1930–Oct. 1935
Rt. Hon. Wm. Lyon Mackenzie King (1)	(L)	Oct. 1935–Nov. 1948
Rt. Hon. Louis Stephen St. Laurent (4)	(L)	Nov. 1948–June 1957
Rt. Hon. John G. Diefenbaker (13)	(C)	June 1957–Apr. 1963
Rt. Hon. Lester B. Pearson (6)	(L)	Apr. 1963–Apr. 1968
Rt. Hon. Pierre Elliott Trudeau (5)	(L)	Apr. 1968–June 1979
Rt. Hon. Charles Joseph Clark (15)	(C)	June 1979–Mar. 1980
Rt. Hon. Pierre Elliott Trudeau (5)	(L)	Mar. 1980–June 1984
Rt. Hon. John Napier Turner (18)	(L)	June 1984–Sept. 1984
Rt. Hon. Martin Brian Mulroney (8)	(PC)	Sept. 1984–June 1993
Rt. Hon. Kim Campbell (20)	(PC)	June 1993–Nov. 1993
Rt. Hon. Jean Chrétien (9)	(L)	Nov. 1993–Dec. 2003
Rt. Hon. Paul Martin	(L)	Dec. 2003–Feb. 2006
Rt. Hon. Stephen Harper	(C)	Feb. 2006–present

(C)	Conservative
(L)	Liberal
(U)	Unionist
(PC)	Progressive Conservative

Note: The number in parentheses immediately following their names reflects the relative effectiveness of the Prime Minister as rated by Canadian scholars in 1997. The categories are Great (1–3), Near Great (4), High Average (5–7), Average (8–13), Low Average (14–15) and Failure (16–20).

Canada Today
Against All Odds

It has often been said that Canada is a "geographic improbability" a huge, sparsely-settled country whose diverse people have in common only a map and a preference not to be absorbed by the United States. As poet Al Purdy put it, it is "an opposite nation talked into existence." Because of Canadians' enormous differences in language and cultural heritage, it is difficult to call them a "nation." Nor is it politically correct, in the opinion of journalist Andrew Coyne: "The very idea that we are a nation . . . has disappeared. The Parliament of Canada may be so bold as to recognize 'the *Québécois*' as a nation, but it would not dare to say the same of Canada. We are a superstructure, a federation, perhaps a country—but never a nation."

Nevertheless, Canadians have shaped a democratic, peaceful and prosperous country seemingly against all odds. Canada was created in the middle of the last century from those remnants of the British empire in North America which had managed to escape America's momentous revolution in the 18th century and exuberant "Manifest Destiny" in the 19th century, that American dream of the "Stars and Stripes" flying all over North America. It was a country born of patience and compromises, not of violent revolution, and its unity has been preserved through the years by forbearance and concessions, not by civil war.

For Americans, Canada is no longer a region for expansion or merely for recreation, but a vibrant sovereign country with a British governmental system and characteristics that should be studied and understood. Canada is a neighbor, and a very desirable neighbor at that. Former Prime Minister Brian Mulroney was right when he said a couple of weeks after his 1984 election victory that "if I were the President of the United States, I'd wake up in the morning and probably look at the events around the world—Americans under attack here, U.S. Embassy attacked there, acts of terrorism and violence—I'd look at all that, and I'd look at Canada and say, 'Thank God I have Canada for a neighbor. Now, what can I do for Canada today?'" The two countries conduct the world's largest bilateral trade and are each other's best trading partners. They are each other's most preferred country for foreign investments. They share the world's longest *undefended* border and are close allies in the North Atlantic Treaty Organization (NATO) and the North American Aerospace Defense Command (NORAD).

What other country but Canada would have harbored American diplomats who had escaped from the American Embassy in Teheran, Iran, on that fateful day in 1979 when scores of Americans were taken hostage and held captive for more than a year? At great risk to their own diplomatic personnel, the Canadians worked with the Central Intelligence Agency in devising an escape plan, issued diplomatic passports to the Americans, closed their embassy in the Iranian capital and escorted the nervous Americans through the checkpoints and controls onto an airplane bound for home. America's gratitude was accurately conveyed when a sign was put on a giant billboard overlooking the border into Canada reading, "Thank you, Canada!"

After the September 11 terrorist attacks that claimed the lives of 24 Canadians as well as over 3,000 Americans, hundreds of flights were diverted to Canada, where communities housed and fed the stranded Americans. More than 100,000 Canadians gathered on Parliament Hill to honor the victims, the largest gathering there ever known, and the American embassy was deluged with flowers. Charter buses carried several thousand to New York for a grand "Canada Loves New York" weekend in December 2001. Vancouver firefighters raised $535,000 for their fallen comrades, and a fourth of them traveled to New York at their own expense to pay their respects at funerals. Only two weeks after the tragedy, more than 60 skilled tradesmen from Ontario and Alberta went to help rebuild the stricken city. New Yorkers on the sidewalks stopped to shake their hands, and one businessman spoke for an entire nation when he told them:

"This has been so hard for us all, but because of people like you, we'll all get through it. You have no idea what this means to us. As your neighbor, I thank you." Then Prime Minister Jean Chrétien was given the "Statesman of the Year Award" in New York the following year.

John F. Kennedy said about Canada: "Geography made us neighbors. History made us friends. And economics made us partners." A quarter century later, President Ronald Reagan made no secret about his reasons for meeting with the Canadian prime minister in March 1985, a practice that is usually repeated twice a year: "No other country in the world is more important to the United States than Canada, and we are blessed to have such a nation on our northern border." In both his terms in office, his first foreign trips were to Canada, as was President Barack Obama's first foreign outing in February 2009. The first foreigner to fly into space with American astronauts was a Canadian, Marc Garneau. He worked at NASA the rest of the century and flew his third shuttle mission in 1999. Other Canadians served in the space station (Julie Payette, who made a return visit in May 2009) or walked in space (Chris Hadfield).

Canada is the only foreign country that is permitted to locate its embassy on Pennsylvania Avenue. Former Canadian Ambassador Derek Burney had this to say about the modern building, opened in 1989 and situated halfway between the White House and the Capitol: "It conveys the message that I want to convey: Canada counts." Ottawa extended the same privilege to the United States by allowing it to open its new embassy in 1999 on the last vacant lot on Parliament Hill. The site

---

Area: 3,849,670 sq. mi. = 10,693,528 sq. km.
Population: 33.2 million.
Capital City: Ottawa (Pop. 715,000, estimated).
Other Principal Cities: Toronto (4.6 million), Montreal (3.12 million), Vancouver (1.6 million), Edmonton (680,000), Calgary (620,000), Winnipeg (605,000).
Climate: Varying climatic regions from moderate to bitterly cold Arctic, with generally mild summers in the southern areas and long, cold winters.
Neighboring Countries: The United States of America.
Official Languages: English and French.
Other Tongues: A broad spectrum of languages spoken by immigrants from Europe and Asia. Smaller groups speak native Indian and Inuit dialects.
Principal Religions: Christianity (Roman Catholic, 54%; Protestant, 40%).
Chief Commercial Products: Canada is a highly industrialized nation producing a wide variety of sophisticated goods; it is also rich in natural resources. Its leading exports are natural resources, especially crude petroleum and natural gas, metal ores, diamonds, wheat, lumber, paper and pulp.

Also automobiles and parts, machinery and equipment, and high technology products.
Major Trading Partners: The United States (77.7% of exports and 52.4% of imports), EU (7.5% of exports and 12.5% of imports), Japan (2.1% of exports and 3.5% of imports), China (2.3% of exports and 9.8% of imports), Mexico (4.1% of imports), and the United Kingdom (2.7% of exports).
Currency: Canadian Dollar (roughly at parity with U.S. dollar in 2010). Its nickname is the "loonie" ("toony" for two-dollar coin) because of the aquatic bird depicted on it.
National Holiday: Canada Day (July 1). In Quebec the main holiday is June 24, the Fête Nationale, formerly called St-Jean Baptiste Day.
Head of State: Her Majesty Queen Elizabeth II of Great Britain.
The Queen's Representative: His Excellency The Rt. Hon. David Johnston, Governor General of Canada (since October 2010).
Head of Government: The Rt. Hon. Stephen Harper, Prime Minister (Leader of the Conservative Party), since February 2006.
National Flag: A stylized red maple leaf on a white square flanked by red bars one half the width of the square.

Canada

is prominent on Sussex Drive, the ceremonial parade route between Parliament and the Prime Minister's residence. For the first time a sitting president left the U.S. to open an embassy. The architecture of the bomb-resistant, four-story steel and concrete structure with 3-inch glass, situated near the National Gallery and Chateau Laurier Hotel, was not universally praised by aesthetically-minded Canadians.

The United States and Canada are different countries, but perhaps no two other nations in the world need to remind themselves so often of that fact. Canada has a population of 33.2 million, and the U.S. is the world's sole superpower with a population (308 million) and economy ten times larger, but in a land area 10% smaller, than Canada's. The relationship between the two countries is therefore lopsided and difficult for the smaller of the two. Former Prime Minister Pierre Elliott Trudeau once remarked that sharing a border with the United States is like "sleeping with an elephant. No matter how friendly or even-tempered is the beast, if I may call it that, one is affected by every twitch and grunt!"

Because of its economic, political and military weight, the United States' policies and moods cannot help from affecting Canada more than the other way around. Canadians are sometimes offended that Americans are often unaware or unconcerned about their impact on Canada. Mulroney said only half-jokingly that to get a mention down in Washington, you have to be either Wayne Gretzky [the great Canadian hockey star] or a good snowstorm." Canadians sometimes sense that the United States takes advantage of its greater power and influence. This is at least partly true some of the time. In the words of Brian Mulroney, because "the equation is unequal," Canada "must always be vigilant. And, if we must be vigilant, the Americans must always be fair."

Nevertheless, Canada is that country in the world with which the U.S. is most successful at settling differences; the frictions that exist between them are always manageable. The most important reason for this is the common-sense and good will which they are inclined to show toward the other. Americans and Canadians are well practiced at "splitting the difference."

CULTURE

Canadians tend to focus on the differences between them and Americans, although, as Pierre Berton admitted, they are often "tongue-tied" when asked to define them. "We know we're not the same

Corporal Doug Ford and Constable Diane Bérubé of the Royal Canadian Mounted Police

but we can't express it succinctly." Americans are inclined to emphasize the similarities. Canadians do not appreciate Americans' habit of viewing Canadians as "just like us" and of not considering Canada to be a foreign country. There is, to be sure, an extraordinary degree of military and economic interdependence between the two countries. According to a 2005 SES Research poll, Canadians and Americans still find their countries to be defined more by their similarities than by their differences. Asked which country in the world is most like Canada in terms of human rights, Canadians chose the U.S. more than any (43%), while 51% of Americans chose Canada. Two thirds of Canadians (67%) had a generally positive attitude toward the U.S., even if 58% said they disapproved of former President George W. Bush. The sincere and constant references to Canada as America's "partner" and "good neighbor" help erase in Americans' minds the sharp line that usually appears between "us and them."

Perhaps the main reason why Americans consider Canadians to be "just like us" is that at least visually their northern neighbors do bear many striking resemblances. The turn-of-the-century *Maclean's* CBC poll, presented in a cover story on December 20, 1999, entitled "The Vanishing Border," revealed that half of Canadian respondents believed Canadians had become more like Americans in the past decade. Half "feel the same" as Americans, while half "feel different"; 71% described the two cultures as "mainly" or "essentially the same." One in three agreed with the prediction that Canada and the U.S. will become one country within the next quarter century. A fifth (vs. 28% of *Québécois*) actually supported political union with the U.S. In a 2002 poll, 63% opposed adopting the U.S. dollar as Canada's currency, but 70% seemed reconciled to the idea that it would be Canada's currency in 30 years. A year later, two-thirds favored integrating environmental policies, but only one-third would meld energy policies and a mere fourth would merge banking. One detects a mixture of pragmatism, a desire for a little more distance and recognition that Canadian values are distinct and worth preserving: 42% of Canadians wanted to become less like the U.S. in the

future, whereas 48% wanted no change in the relationship.

The American traveling in Canada sees people who dress almost exactly as he does. Canadians wear baseball caps, jeans, jogging shoes, sweatshirts and T-shirts with writing on them—basically the same things that are in style in the United States.

The American also meets people who, by and large, speak English as he does except those 22% who speak French as a mother tongue and who therefore might speak English with a French accent. The English that Canadians speak much more closely resembles that spoken in the United States than in the United Kingdom. This is understandable in an age of radio and television, quick travel and strong trade ties. A few British usages do linger on. Most say "aluminium," with the accent on the third syllable, "controversy" with the accent on the second syllable, and "schedule," as if there were no "c" in the word. "Been" is pronounced like "bean," and "again" like "a-gane." A "lieutenant" is addressed as "leftenant." Also, the "i" in the last syllable of words ending in "-ile" is likely to be pronounced distinctly, rather than to be swallowed, as most Americans do. "Out" and "house" are spoken more like "ute" or "whuse."

Perhaps the most distinctive sign that a Canadian is speaking, though, is the "eh?" (pronounced as a long "a"), which is frequently tacked onto the end of sentences.

Totem poles at Museum of Anthropology, University of British Columbia
Credit: Province of British Columbia

There is a rough French equivalent in Quebec: *hein*. Their writing is also slightly different: not all Canadians have dropped the "u" when writing such words as "labour" or "colour." "Centre," "cheque," "theatre" and "connexion" are not American spellings, and the word "defense" is still spelled with a "c," as is the custom in Britain.

French-speakers (now called "francophones" in Canada, in contrast to "anglophones"—English-speakers) have opened the gates to let in hundreds of English words, such as le *fun, dialer* ("to dial"), *la potate* ("potato"), *le smoked beef, le hamburger, les king pins, le brake drum, un party,* or *une shop*. Notice, for example, the following advertisement for an *Atelier Mecanique-Machine Shop Crankshaft* which once appeared in the yellow pages of the Montreal telephone book: *Moteur nettoyé et testé. Moteur grindé all surfaces. Crankshaft nettoyé et testé with sonoflux process. Crankshaft grindé with micro finish.*

The mixture of the two languages to form what is often derisively referred to as "Franglais" or "Frenglish" has perhaps reached its height among Acadians in New Brunswick. One francophone from Moncton provided *Maclean's* with an example of the "chiac" dialect: *J'ai drivé mon friend à l'airport, but la plane a také off à dix minutes de quatre. Too bad que j'avais pas findé ça out avant.* The French spoken elsewhere in New Brunswick sounds little different from that in Poitou and Brittany, France, from where their ancestors hailed. The pronunciation and slang of the French spoken on the streets of Quebec and Acadia are intriguingly different from Parisian French.

In recent years, there has been a tremendous improvement in the quality of French spoken in Quebec as a result of the province's governmental legislation on the use of French on Radio Canada; TV is also a good example of international French. Nevertheless, Candice Bergen's French-language Sprint ads were taken off the air in 1995 because her French was "too Parisian."

Americans also find that most Canadians know far more about the United States than Americans know about Canada. For instance, a 1995 Louis Harris poll revealed that a mere 1% of Americans knew that Jean Chrétien was prime minister. Only 11% of American university students surveyed in 1989 knew which city is Canada's capital; only 1% knew the name of the premier of Quebec, a province much larger than Texas, bordering on several New England states, and the United States' sixth-largest trading partner in the world. Only 12% knew that Canada is America's largest trading partner, and only 57% had heard of the Free Trade Agreement, vs. 97% of the Canadians.

Margaret Atwood was referring to this ignorance when she described the 49th parallel as the world's biggest one-way mirror. Entertainer Rick Mercer became famous by producing TV specials, *Talking to Americans*, that brought howls of laughter to Canadians. He asked people on the streets of America, including Congressmen and Harvard professors, ludicrous questions to show just how little they knew about their northern neighbor.

Canadians watch more American television than Canadian, and what Canadian news programs they watch bring incomparably more news about the United States than American newscasts bring about Canada, despite the penetration into the American broadcasting elite of such Canadians as ABC's anchorman Peter Jennings, Kevin Newman (formerly of ABC's Nightline), and CBS's Morley Safer. Controversial talk-show hostess Jenny Jones hails from Canada, as does Robert MacNeil of the earlier MacNeil-Lehrer Report. He has a summer home in his native Halifax, the setting of the first of his several novels, *Burden of Desire*. He confesses to "a sense of sentimental curiosity" about Canada, but admits: "The Canada I grew up in was white bread, dominated by Anglo-Scots and Quebec. Now Canada is a wondrously multi-coloured, multilingual country. It's fascinating, but it's not the Canada I grew up in." That is why he became an American, as he described in *Looking for my Country. Finding Myself in America*.

Canadians often read such American newsmagazines as *Time* and *Newsweek*, whereas few Americans have ever even held a Canadian magazine, such as *Maclean's*, in their hands, let alone read one. Since 88% of all Americans live farther than 100 miles from the Canadian border and cannot see or hear Canadian programs by simply switching on their dial, Americans must make a more concerted effort to become informed about Canada, and few do. Even Fox News from the United States was expanded into Canada in 2011 under the name Sun TV.

This is changing somewhat. Major American newsmagazines and newspapers are carrying much more news about

Canada

Pamela Anderson

Canada. In 1970 only 89 American institutions offered Canadian studies courses; by 1995, over 250 colleges and universities offered 1,100 courses on Canada, with a total enrollment of 23,000. Also, the Association for Canadian Studies in the United States (ACSUS) has grown considerably, with well over 1,100 members by 1995. The *Toronto Star* even complained: "Curse those Americans. They are taking away one of our great Canadian preoccupations. They are not ignoring us any more." In any case, the American visitor can still chat with Canadians about a wide variety of American subjects ranging from the president's difficulties with Congress and midwestern farmers' financial problems to the World Series, Superbowl and Academy or Grammy Award nominations, forgetting in the process that he is talking to a foreigner.

The popular culture on both sides of the border is strikingly similar. One hears rock, country-western and gospel music (in rock or traditional form) either blaring out from car radios or softly channeled into Canadian ears by omnipresent walkman earphones. Paul Anka, Percy Faith, Hank Snow, Neil Young, Anne Murray, Bryan Adams, Michelle Wright, Buffy Sainte-Marie, a native North American who wrote the Oscar-winning theme song for the film, "An Officer and a Gentleman," Sarah McLachlan (who has starred both as rock singer and women's rights advocate), rhythm and blues diva Deborah Cox, jazz pianist and singer Diana Krall from Nanaimo, British Columbia (BC), the rock groups Crash Test Dummies and Barenaked Ladies (a fun-loving male quintet), are all Canadians popular on both sides of the border.

An immigrant tailor's son from London, Ontario, Guy Lombardo, was dubbed in 1945 by *Time* magazine as "America's No. 1 long-time dance-band leader." His saxophone arrangement of *Auld Lang Syne* is still synonymous with New Year's Eve. On his 80th birthday in 2005, jazz maestro Oscar Peterson had the honor of being the only living Canadian to have a special stamp issued by Canada Post. In 1997 Ottawa rocker, Alanis Morissette, won the favorite album and female artist awards at the American Music Awards. Nobody gets American tiny boppers screaming more loudly than Canadian teenage crooner Justin Bieber (whose name in German aptly means "beaver"). Before his seventeenth birthday on March 1, 2011, he had already made a world tour, topped the charts in 17 countries and sold more than six million CDs.

Ontario native, Shania Twain, was named best female country artist. Her "The Woman in Me" surpassed "Patsy Cline's Greatest Hits" as the best-selling female country album ever. By 1999 she had become history's top-selling country singer and was named the entertainer of the year at the 2000 Academy of Country Music Awards. Quebec superstar, Céline Dion, who is the top-selling singer of all time in France, won top album and best pop album Grammys in 1997. In 1998 Dion, who claims to be "very proud" of being both a Quebecer and a Canadian, was inducted into the prestigious Order of Canada and Order of Quebec. By 2007, she had sold 200 million records, and her Las Vegas show, "A New Day," had grossed more than US$400 million during its four-year run. Because Morissette, Dion and Twain each won two Grammy awards in 1999 and Joni Mitchell of Saskatchewan received the U.S. National Academy of Recording Arts and Sciences lifetime achievement award in 2001, few persons disputed *Maclean's* claim that "Canadian divas virtually rule the world of female pop."

Men in both countries admire the same beauty, gazing at the British Columbian sex goddess Pamela Anderson, who was discovered in 1989 wearing a tight-fitting Labatt's T-shirt at a B.C. Lions football game. In a 1995 cover story, *Maclean's* called her "the most famous Canadian on the planet."

Canadians laugh at the same comedians, such as Dan Aykroyd, Bob and Doug McKenzie, Jim Carrey and "Wayne's World" star Mike Myers—all Canadians. The biggest box office hit in the history of screen comedy, *Ghostbusters*, was a product of Canadian filmmaker Ivan Reitman. His Montreal-born son, Jason Reitman, directed one of 2008's hottest movies,

Nia Vardalos in *My Big Fat Greek Wedding*

Juno, which was filmed in Vancouver and starred two Canadians—Ellen Page and Michael Cera. Two years later, his football film, *The Blind Side*, was a blockbuster; its female lead, Sandra Bullock, won the best actress Oscar. Even Warner Brothers was founded by Canadians.

Quebec's cinema is thriving, and Quebecers produce excellent French-language films which are of a different style than those viewed by Americans. An example is *Maria Chapdelaine*, based on Louis Hemon's classic 1914 novel, a moving portrait of the restricted life led by Quebec women in the frontier.

Americans and anglophone Canadians usually go to the same movies, however. Canadians watch more Hollywood films than films produced in Canada, and English Canadian filmmakers must search hard for an audience. In fact, only 2% of box office revenues are derived from Canadian films. Canadians have far less money to spend. Montreal filmmaker, Philippe Falardeau, defined a Canadian film as "one with less means and no star system. Canadian films talk about universal things." Producers have trouble getting some of their films shown on Canadian screens since American companies largely control distribution of movies in Canada. To stimulate the industry an annual Whistler Film Festival awards prizes for promising Canadian feature films.

Some films to which Americans flock are Canadian, often unbeknownst to Americans. Winnipeg's Nia Vardalos took the cinema world by storm in 2002 with her award-winning film, *My Big Fat Greek Wedding*, which was filmed in Toronto and was the year's fifth-highest grossing movie. Norman Jewison, one of the world's most successful directors as a result of such blockbusters as *Fiddler on the Roof* and *Moonstruck* (much of which was filmed in Toronto), is Canadian. In 1999 he was granted a special Academy Award for lifetime achievement. He founded the Canadian Film Centre in north Toronto, an elite institution for ten highly selected filmmakers annually and the only film school in the world that produces its own features.

James Cameron, born in Kapuskasing, Ontario, and raised near Niagara Falls, studied physics at university. He specializes in gargantuan high-tech films of mass destruction, such as *The Terminator*, *Judgment Day*, *Aliens*, *The Abyss*, *True Lies*, and *Titanic*. In 2010, his three-dimensional *Avatar* broke all records for box office receipts. In the words of Fox's president, Cameron "has taken Hollywood by the throat and they do what he says."

The 1997 Academy Award for best film was given to *The English Patient*, based on the best-selling novel by Canadian author Michael Ondaatje. He had been assisted in his research by a grant from the Canada Council. In 1992, he shared the Booker Prize, the world's most prominent English-language literary award. His *Anil's Ghost* won him both the Governor-General's Award and the Prix Médicis, France's highest prize for a foreign novel, in 2000. In 2007 his *Divisadero* won him his fifth Governor General's Literary Award for English-language fiction, which tied the record of the late Hugh MacLennan.

In 2004 Canadian director Denys Arcand made history when his film, *The Barbarian Invasions*, became the first Canadian movie to win an Oscar for best foreign-language film. In 2007 Indian-born Canadian director, Deepa Mahta, won a best foreign-language Oscar nomination for her extraordinarily successful Hindi-language film, *Water*. This was the first non-French Canadian film to receive such an honor. In the same year, her *Partition* opened, depicting the tragic carnage following the division of India in 1947.

Many American films are being shot in Canada. With the average cost of making a film in the U.S. soaring to $76.9 million by 2000, it is small wonder that producers are attracted to Canada, with its generous provincial and federal tax breaks to foreign and domestic film companies, its able film crews and, until recently, the low Canadian dollar. To lure more American filmmakers back to Ontario in the wake of a rising loonie, which has scared off some Hollywood productions, the province offered even greater tax inducements.

Toronto has become the third-largest film-producing center in North America after Los Angeles and New York City. CBS's *Due South*, starring an impeccably polite do-right Mountie in Chicago, was filmed in Toronto. For authenticity, garbage was trucked in to make the city look dirty; it lasted only one season. The "Superman" movies were filmed in Alberta. Two of the 2006 Oscar nominations were filmed in the Canadian West: *Brokeback Mountain* near Calgary and *Capote* in

Historical dress in an Acadian village

Winnipeg. U.S. TV networks, including ABC and CBS, buy Canadian police serials like "Rookie Blue" and "Flashpoint" at the discount rate of $350,000 per episode, far cheaper than the typical license fee of well above $1 million an episode. The CTV creative president, Susanne Boyce, commented: "For years we've been bringing in fantastic programs from the U.S. It's nice to do the reverse."

Vancouver and Montreal also attract more and more American moviemakers. British Columbia boasts of $1 billion annual revenues from film production, two-thirds of which comes from the U.S. This can also cause problems for Canadian filmmakers since high-cost American productions inflate the prices that Canadian film crews charge. However, the "runaway productions" are an unmistakable boon for Canadian film people. Some union actors in the U.S. call Canada a scab country for aggressively courting American film, television and advertisement production with tax rebates and other incentives. Kenneth W. Ferguson, president of the Toronto Film Studies, remarked: "We're not used to people hating Canadians."

Films feature such familiar stars as Glenn Ford, Walter Pidgeon, Raymond Burr, Genevieve Bujold, Margot Kidder, Christopher Plummer, Lorne Greene, Rod Cameron, Jay Silverheels ("Tonto" in *The Lone Ranger*), William Shatner, Raymond Massey, Michael J. Fox (the "all-American boy"), Keanu Reeves, and Donald Southerland, all Canadians. Even many soap opera stars are from Canada, such as Gordon Thompson, Jean LeClerc, Shawn Thompson, Domini Blythe, Teri Austin and Shannon Tweed.

Canadians and Americans read much of the same literature, by such authors as Jack Kerouac, Will Durant, Saul Bellow, Arthur Hailey, Robertson Davies, Mordecai Richler, Brian Moore, Morley Callaghan and Alice Munro, all of whom are Canadians. In 2004 Munro, who hails from southern Ontario, won her second Giller Prize for her collection of eight stories entitled *Runaway*, which appeared on the *New York Times'* bestseller list as well as on Canada's. In 2009 she became the first short-story writer to win the Man Booker international prize. Her stories focus on Canadians and their peculiarities. Both countries also sometimes forbid the same books. In 2005 Nova Scotia's education department banned Harper Lee's *To Kill a Mockingbird*.

Other authors focus on their native Canada and are read and admired in both countries. Perhaps the best known Canadian author is Lucy Maud Montgomery, whose precocious, pert, and lovable Anne of Green Gables has delighted children and adults from scores of nations for three-quarters of a century. Hugh Mac-

Canada

Lennan's *Two Solitudes* is the classic study of the separate worlds in which the *Québécois* and anglophone Canadians have lived. In 2001 Alistair MacLeod became the first Canadian to win the world's richest literary prize, the International IMPAC Dublin Literary Award, for his debut novel, *No Great Mischief*, translated into 14 languages. Pierre Berton was perhaps Canada's most prolific writer, producing best-selling books on the country's history and people almost on an annual basis. When he died in 2004, writer June Callwood said of him: "It's as if the biggest tree has fallen down."

Margaret Atwood writes about the lives and challenges of modern women. In her view, "survival" is the "single unifying and informing symbol . . . which holds the country [Canada] together and helps the people in it for common ends." She also points to the search for identity: "Canadians are forever taking the national pulse like doctors at a sickbed; the aim is not to see whether the patient will live well but simply whether he will live at all. . ." By 1989 one of her novels had sold 40,000 hardback and 200,000 paperback copies in Canada, an amazing accomplishment in a country with little more than 20 million fluent English-speakers. Her ninth novel, *Alias Grace*, a mystery about a murder, was a global sensation in 1996, winner of the Giller Prize.

By 1997, many of her 41 books had been translated into 22 languages. In 2000 she became only the second Canadian to win Britain's highly competitive Booker Prize for *The Blind Assassin*, an epic tale about a once-wealthy family in Ontario. Her sly, operatic and feminist retelling of *The Odyssey* from the perspective of the dutiful wife of Homer's hero in her 2005 work, *The Penelopiad: The Myth of Penelope and Odysseus*, was an instant success. Her 2009 *Year of the Flood* is a story of a totalitarian dystopia. By 2006 her popularity had become such that that she started using an electronic pen that could activate a remote robotic arm to replicate her autograph for fans thousands of miles away.

In 2002 Canadian Yann Martel beat out two other Canadians on the short list, Rohinton Mistry and the late Carol Shields, to win the Booker Prize with his novel, *Life of Pi*, a magical fable of a young man ship-wrecked with a Bengal tiger. Clearly Canada's book business is thriving.

Stephen Leacock was one of the most famous Canadians of his time and in his heyday from 1910 to 1925 was the world's best-selling English-language humorist. His stories bring alive the early Ontario of his childhood. Rudy Wiebe's writings, including The Temptations of Big Bear and The Scorched-Wood People, describe with great vision and understanding the lives of Indians, Métis and white settlers in the Canadian West. Northrop Frye, who hailed from Ontario and taught his entire career at the University of Toronto, is widely acclaimed to be the greatest literary critic of our time. American-born Carol Shields, who moved to Canada in 1957, won the 1995 Pulitzer Prize for her novel about sexual and family values, *The Stone Diaries*. She died in 2003.

Quebec also boasts authors of international renown. Anne Hebert, who now lives in Paris, became famous in 1970 through her great novel, *Kamouraska*, which was later made into a film in Quebec. Gabriele Roy wrote Quebec's first urban, socially aware novel, *Bonheur d'Occasion* (known to anglophones as *The Tin Flute*), just after the Second World War. This novel, like *Maria Chapdelaine*, deals with survival and a young girl's rejection of a glamorous lover who could have taken her out of the narrow French Canadian world in which she lived. Also like *Maria Chapdelaine*, *The Tin Flute* was made into a movie in Quebec in 1983.

Roch Carrier has written perceptively and humorously about the gulf between the *Québécois* and anglophone Canadians. In *La Guerre, Yes Sir* he describes Quebecers' negative attitudes about fighting in the two world wars. In a short story, "The Hockey Sweater," the mother of a young boy in rural Quebec orders a Montreal Canadiens hockey shirt from a Montreal department store, which by mistake sends a Toronto Maple Leafs jersey instead. The boy is panic-stricken. But with no other hockey shirt to wear, he goes out to play with his friends, only to be shunned by his pals and ordered from the ice by the parish priest. The boy is devastated and goes to the parish church and prays that moths will descend from heaven and consume the shirt so that his mother will buy him another. In an interview with *Maclean's*, Carrier implied that the wall which once separated Quebec from anglophone Canada has become much more porous: "When my books were first translated, everybody felt it was a kind of treason, giving my books to the rest of the country. But today everybody wants to be on the other side of the frontier."

Translation into English can today be indispensable for a French-language novel, as Gil Courtemanche discovered. His first novel, *A Sunday at the Pool in Kigali*, was a modest success in Quebec when it was published in French in 2000. But after being translated by Knopf into English in 2003, the book quickly won him international fame and was translated into 13 more languages. How many more nuggets might there be in the Quebec literary scene?

If an American does not want to go to a film, read a book or listen to music, he can simply sit at home and immerse himself in Americana by playing "Trivial Pursuit," a game invented by two Canadians, Chris Haney and Scott Abbott. Or he can pick up the telephone, invented by Canadian Alexander Graham Bell in Canada before moving to the U.S. If he is hungry, he can go to McDonalds, founded by Canadians. One gradually begins to wonder whether what is sometimes called the "Americanization" of Canadian culture might, in some cases, be better called the "Canadianization" of American culture.

American films, television and radio broadcasting, reading material, music, slang and styles do continue to pour northward across the border because most Canadians themselves are attracted to them. Canadians are usually the first to admit that American culture is produced primarily for domestic consumption and that no American ever forced it upon Canadians. Nevertheless, they are nervous about the massive influx of American customs and usages. It is therefore Canadian policy to encourage and to subsidize Canadian cultural products in order to avoid being engulfed by American culture and to make it possible for talented Canadians to work in Canada rather than seeking their fame and fortune in the United States. The government wishes to help offer the population an alternative.

About 2% of the federal government's budget is devoted to culture, although the sums are lower than in most western European countries and were slashed by the Mulroney and Chrétien governments. These cuts came at a time of intense upheaval in many spheres of the arts. A communications minister in the federal cabinet disperses money through a variety of institutions which enjoy a high degree of autonomy from the federal government and which have become powerful lobbying groups when their freedom or budgets are trampled upon: the National Film Board and Telefilm financially support Canadian cinema. In 1997 public funding for television amounted to $200 million, which helps make Canada the world's second-largest exporter of TV shows after the U.S. Only $50 million is allotted to feature films. Provincial governments also help finance the production of films, and their censorship can prevent "X-rated" movies from being shown in Canadian theaters.

The Canadian film industry has created an Academy Awards ceremony of its own called the "Genie Awards." The National Arts Centre in Ottawa contains several stages of various sizes and puts on more than 900 performances and entertains almost 800,000 persons each year. The semi-independent Canada Council dispenses grants to a wide variety of professional artists and organizations. They include writers, publishers, translators, musicians and composers, dancers, painters, sculptors, photographers and film makers. Government money was instrumental in building and maintaining the National Ballet Company in Toronto, *le Theatre du Nouveau Monde* and *les Grands Ballets Canadiens* in Montreal, the Canadian Opera Company, the Stratford Shakespearean Festival in Ontario, and more than 160 theater groups across the country.

Canadians, most of whom live along the American border, listen freely to American radio and watch much American television. Canada is the most heavily cabled country in the world. Canadians are among the most generous donors to American public television stations along the U.S. border. The Canadian governments do nothing to prevent their citizens from tuning in to American stations, but they do go to great expense and effort to provide Canadian alternatives and to reinforce a sense of Canadian community by making it possible for Canadians everywhere in the country to learn about each other.

A failure in information control occurred in the course of the Liberal Party's "sponsorship scandal" in 2005. Judge John Gomery ordered that testimony given at a Montreal inquiry into alleged kickbacks and criminal conspiracy be kept secret because one of the witnesses was to be tried for fraud a month later. Such revelations could harm his right to a fair trial. However, an American across the border put the details of the testimony on his Web site, which was easily accessed by thousands of Canadians, thereby forcing the judge to release sensational evidence that ultimately brought ex-Prime Minister Paul Martin's Liberal government down in 2006.

The Canadian Broadcasting Corporation (CBC—called *Radio Canada* in Quebec) operates radio and television networks in French and English, as well as in many native languages, in the entire country. CBC sponsors a 24-hour all-news channel in English—*Newsworld*—while *Radio Canada* does the same in French through RDI. Among the rapidly proliferating are two privately-operated networks: Canadian Television (CTV) in anglophone Canada and *Reseau de Television* (*TVA*) in francophone Canada. Since 1998 TVA, Quebec's most popular French-language TV network, must be included in the mandatory cable-TV selection across Canada. In 1997 CTV launched Canada's first round-the-clock headline news service—CTV News 1. In covering the 2006 election, it outdrew CBC by 1.5 million viewers to 1.2 million. It also outbid CBC for the 2010 and 2012 Olympic Games. There are many private radio stations and a proliferation of spe-

Typical road sign in English and French

cialty channels on cable. In 1994 three Canadian channels began beaming into American homes through DirecTV, setting a trend that brings more Canadian programming to U.S. viewers.

Public money enables the CBC to offer more elevated and experimental programming. But it is not freed from the constant battle over ratings as the country entered a 500-channel universe. Between 1989 and 1996 it lost a fourth of its TV audience; it dropped all its U.S. commercial programming. Its budget and personnel are being steadily reduced while suffering the indignity of attracting fewer than half as many viewers for its *Prime Time News* as do popular American programs. The beleaguered service has tried to compete with private broadcasters by imitating their programming in some ways, but this has weakened the public's willingness to continue to support it. By 2006 polls indicated that the percentage of Canadians who believed that CBC and Radio-Canada were "very important to being Canadian," had fallen since 1984 from 34% to 18% (and in Quebec from 43% to 13%). It seems that only the lucrative *Hockey Night in Canada* keeps them alive. They face a continual identity crisis: do CBC and Radio-Canada offer a service or a product?

To ensure that Canadian networks, private or public, do not simply buy cheaper American programs, the Canadian Radio-Television and Telecommunications Commission establishes "Canadian Content" guidelines. "Canadian Content" is defined by means of a complicated formula involving whether the cast, singers, songwriters or production team are Canadian citizens. The exact quotas change according to the political winds. Radio stations must devote 30% of their airtime to Canadian music, even though only 13% of music purchased in record stores is Canadian. Ownership of TV and radio stations, newspapers and magazines is restricted to Canadians or Canadian companies.

Despite these efforts, Canadian television programs claimed only a 34% audience share in 1998. Canadian viewers and listeners do not seem to like these restric-

tions, according to a 2002 poll: fewer than half feel it is very important to protect the arts, culture, TV and radio, and 61% outside of Quebec want federal regulations on TV to be dropped. Only one in five Canadians felt they have a national culture that is distinct from American culture, according to a 2002 *National Post* poll.

Americans may find such regulations to be like a hand of "Big Brother," but they should bear two important things in mind: first, there is no attempt to prevent Canadians from receiving broadcasts or any other cultural influences from the U.S.; Canadians are free to watch or listen to any broadcasts they like, even if they offend some Canadians. In 1997 the Canadian Broadcast Council criticized New York "shock jock" Howard Stern, who in broadcasts to Toronto and Montreal called francophones "scumbags" and claimed that the only things Canada produces are "hockey players, whores and William Shatner." His Canadian audience ratings soared, and his talk show was not banned.

Second, Canada does have a culture of its own, and it is not easy to preserve it when such a culturally magnetic country is so close. About 80% of magazines on newsstands, more than 60% of books, 90% of recordings, 64% of TV programs, and 94% of films are foreign, overwhelmingly American.

In order to "have the means to communicate with our own people," in the words of ex-Prime Minister Chrétien, Canada insists on exempting cultural industries from its two free-trade agreements with the U.S. Such Canadian governmental decisions as slapping an 80% excise tax on *Sports Illustrated Canada* and other "split-run" magazines (which have Canadian editions and advertising, but mostly American editorial content) and withdrawing Country Music Television's broadcasting license and awarding it to a Canadian-owned country channel, are bound to antagonize Americans. In 1997 the U.S. sought and won a ruling from the World Trade Organization: Canadian punitive taxes on split-run magazines, as well as postal subsidies to Canadian magazines, violate international trade rules. The dispute was resolved in 1999.

Canada's next moves were to convene a summit meeting of 20 culture ministers (excluding Americans) to discuss international misgivings about the "onslaught" of U.S. films, TV and music. Then in 1999 Parliament passed legislation prohibiting Canadians from advertising in split-run magazines; negotiations between Ottawa and Washington were commenced to head off a conflict, and the dispute was resolved. For the first time, the U.S. accepted the principle that countries can take steps to limit imports in order to protect the viability of local culture. The Canadians agreed

Canada

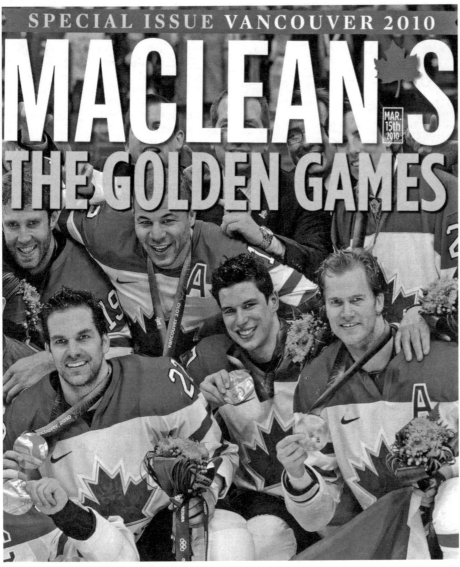

MACLEAN'S
THE GOLDEN GAMES

MAR. 15th 2010

Olympic Gold in 2010!

tion, and fears were openly expressed that half the Canadian teams might not exist a year later. Nevertheless, during the 2007 NHL season, five out of the top seven teams in terms of attendance were Canadian, and the sixth, Edmonton, was able to sell 98% of its tickets.

Canada produced the first woman in the NHL, Mamon Rhéaume, backup goalie for the Nashville Knights. One had to admire a 122-lb Québécoise wearing size 5 skates and children's-sized equipment, who shared the ice with players almost twice as big as she. Along with other female national team stars like Nancy Drolet, Rheaume helped inspire thousands of Canadian girls to take up ice hockey. In the 2002–03 season a record 61,000 females registered for teams across Canada, 7,000 more than the previous season and five times more than a decade earlier. In rural areas some former boys-only squads are filling their rosters with girls. The payoff came in the 2006 Olympic Games in Turin, where the Canadian women took gold; they repeated this feat in the 2010 Vancouver Games.

American teams are well-stocked with Canadian players; in fact, 52% (down from 96.7% in 1967) of the National Hockey League's (NHL) players are Canadian. Priceless hockey property such as Wayne Gretzky, the "Great One" who retired in 1999 and later became coach of the Phoenix Coyotes, is known and admired almost as much in the United States as in Canada and helped make professional hockey so popular in the U.S. One mystery remains unexplained in this cross-border sport: most Canadian players (including Gretzky) shoot left-handed, while most Americans shoot right-handed.

The 2010 Winter Olympics in Vancouver brought Canada glorious victories over the Americans in both men's and women's hockey, a sport many Canadians think they own. After all, what other country in the world puts the sport on its currency? The five-dollar bill shows kids playing hockey on a pond with a quotation from Roch Carrier's beloved short story, "The Hocky Sweater": "The winters of my childhood were long, long seasons. We lived in three places—the school, the church and the skating rink—but our real life was on the skating rink."

Even Canadian troops in Afghanistan put down their weapons to view their teams' triumphs. They were joined by 85% of Canadians at home who reportedly watched their men's hockey team defeat the American players 3–2 in a sudden-death overtime thriller in the last event of the games. Sidney Crosby, captain of the NHL's Pittsburgh Penguins and the youngest captain ever to lift the Stanley Cup in victory, fired the magic

to allow American publishers to produce special Canadian editions as long as less than 18% of its advertising pages are from Canadian advertisers aimed at Canadian readers. The Canadian government would provide annual operating subsidies to the Canadian magazine industry. In cultural terms, the border is not undefended. In 2005 Canada approved in UNESCO the first international treaty designed to protect music, movies and other cultural treasures from foreign competition; the U.S. found itself in a minority of two.

The American sports fan notices a few unfamiliar sports in Canada, such as curling, but most are strikingly similar. Ice hockey, reportedly invented at Kingston's Tete du Pont Barracks on a Christmas day in 1855 by a group of bored soldiers, who tied blades to their boots and used field hockey sticks and an old lacrosse ball, is a Canadian export to the world. Most fans

on both sides of the border know the name of hockey legend Maurice Richard, who in 2005 was immortalized by the most expensive film ever produced in Quebec, bearing his name (in English Canada: *The Rocket*).

The National Hockey League is, in fact, *international*, with more professional teams in the U.S. than in Canada. Six Canadian teams face serious financial difficulties and threaten to relocate in the U.S. The Winnipeg Jets left in 1995, and the Quebec Nordiques went to Denver a year later. In 2001, 80% of the fabled Montreal Canadiens, once known as *Les Glorieux*, and all of the Molson Centre where they play were bought by a Colorado businessman, George Gillett. Fortunately the Canadiens remain in Montreal, and Gillett respects the Canadiens' spirit, which he calls "truly a religion and a passion." In 2003 the Ottawa Senators filed for bankruptcy protec-

shot. This was Canada's eighth Olympic men's hockey gold medal since 1920, and it ignited an outburst of Canadian patriotism few people could have ever imagined in this divided country. There were red maple leafs all over, on flags, signs and clothing, and *O Canada* could be heard everywhere. Even many normally modest Canadians were taken aback by their own public outpouring of pride in their athletes, who won the most gold medals any country had ever won in any Winter Olympic Games—fourteen. They took home medals in nine different sports.

Their success was the result of a program to finance the Olympic athletes' preparation to the tune of $117 million. The motto was controversial: "Own the Podium." Some found this too arrogant, too boastful, yes, too American. But it worked. The Vancouver Games was a smashing success from beginning to end. Three billion persons watched the opening ceremonies, and 3.5 billion tuned in to the Games at some point during the 17 days to see what a winter sport superpower Canada had become.

A troubling aspect of professional hockey in Canada came to light in 1997. To claw their way into the NHL, many adolescent Canadian boys enter an intense and regimented system, which has deep roots in Canada. It culminates in 49 "major junior" teams divided into three leagues and lumped together under an umbrella organization called the Canadian Hockey League (CHL). Talented players as young as ten are drawn into the system, and beginning at age 14 top prospects hire agents and are aggressively pursued by the top clubs. At age 16 or 17 they often move away from home and are billeted with families paid by the clubs. Attending unfamiliar high schools where they do not play on school teams, they become so dependent upon their all-power-

ful coaches that they are easy prey for abuse, sexual and otherwise. The NCAA considers CHL teams to be professional, so its players are barred from college athletics on both sides of the border.

Fifty-six percent of NHL players come through the CHL system, and over the years it has produced more professional hockey players than any other organization in the world. Only 10% come from college or high school teams although 30% of NHL players went to college. But since only 6% of players coming out of major junior or college teams ever play in the NHL, more and more young players weigh their options between the CHL and intercollegiate hockey that results in a college education. Those who do not survive the CHL are unable to continue playing on American or Canadian university teams. Unlike their American counterparts, Canadian universities do not offer athletic scholarships.

It is no wonder that enrollment in the CHL system is declining steeply. Even the number of Canadian kids playing hockey is going down, and more now play soccer than hockey. It is a problem that the high costs of maintaining ice rinks have caused

a distressing number of them to close. One way to deal with this is the introduction at some rinks of artificial ice made with a plastic polymer. Nobody is happy with this alternative since it makes stopping and turning harder, and experts admit it is only "80% like a real ice surface." One small aboriginal community in northern Alberta, Fort Chipewyan, opened the first such rink.

Although two-thirds of Canadians say that hockey is important for the country, according to a 1999 poll, 60% think the player development system needs change; 85% believe the sport needs to be overhauled. One player put it this way: "There's too much emphasis on size and hitting, and not enough on finesse and skill." A March 6, 2000, *Maclean's* cover story was entitled "Blood Sport," and the magazine reported in 2003 that a third of the 33,000 referees in minor-league hockey quits every year because of abuse from parents, players and coaches. Its message: "Relax, it's just a game."

One would not have known that in 2004 when the NHL's Todd Bertuzzi brutally attacked Steve Moore from behind and broke his neck in an internationally televised game. Although Bertuzzi was banned for the rest of the season, the NHL cannot bring itself to ban fighting or to draft tougher rules on violence; regrettably, fighting seems to sell tickets. It is said only half in jest that the only time Canadians' politeness ends is when they strap on skates. Rules are selectively enforced, and frontier justice of revenge and retribution is encouraged, not just tolerated.

That "rink rage" is a continuing problem was demonstrated in 2006 when a father, who was furious that his son had been benched, choked the coach until the latter lost consciousness. Another dad slammed a referee's head against a metal door, while a mother threw coffee in the face of a player who had cross-checked her son from behind. Forgiving judges gave them all light fines and temporary bans from rinks.

Canadian women take Olympic hockey gold in 2006 and again in 2010. Source: *Maclean's*

Canada

On January 2, 2009, the inevitable happened: York University student Donald Sanderson was killed when his head slammed against the ice after his helmet came off during the fight. Although 60% of Canadians said in the aftermath of the tragedy that they favored banning fighting in amateur hockey (and 54% opposed fighting in the NHL), it takes a long time to change the rules in a sport that Canadians have long claimed teaches values like respect, discipline and grace under pressure. A 2009 poll revealed that while 61% of Canadians said they want to get fighting out of the game, 63% opposed such a ban, and 62% said that it is a "significant part" of the sport. In 2011, 60% thought pro hockey had become more violent in the past five years, and four out of five (79%) believed the NHL had not done enough to protect its players from head injuries. But only a minority (41%) thought that hockey would be better off if fighting were banned. One exasperated Canadian said: "I can see a time when hockey will be like a Roman circus: no referees and lots of body bags."

It remains to be seen if automatic ejections, escalating fines and suspensions, and prohibitions on removing helmets and gloves become a part of Canadian hockey. A small but welcome step was taken in 2010 to ban blindside hits to the head in order to curb the many concussions in the NHL. Also head injuries are no longer treated on the bench with mere smelling salts, but any player suspected of having a concussion will be removed from the game and evaluated by a doctor. Putting pressure on the NHL clubs to do more to protect its players are some powerful corporate sponsors, such as Air Canada, which threatened to end its sponsorship arrangements.

Asked in 1996 what professional sports they preferred, 60% of Canadian respondents said hockey, 16% baseball, and only 6% basketball. Ten years later that had changed remarkably: 19% preferred Canadian football and only 13% favored hockey, 13% baseball and 7% basketball. Nevertheless, the unique contribution that hockey makes to national identity is that it bridges English-and French-speakers, native and non-natives, eastern and western Canadians. The NHL teams are in some economic trouble despite a US$50.3 million team salary cap. Overall their profit margin is a razor-thin 4%. But by 2011 sponsorship revenues were up by a third, and the NHL signed seven-year deal for $400 million with Molson Coors making it the "official beer" on both sides of the border.

Canadians also play basketball, although as a winter sport it must always take the back seat to hockey. One NBA team remains in Canada, the Toronto Raptors, after the Vancouver Grizzlies moved to Memphis. Americans can thank a Canadian, Dr. James Naismith, who devised this game in a Springfield, Massachusetts, YMCA in 1891 as a more interesting indoor alternative to calisthenics. Canada reached its basketball pinnacle in 2006 when Steve Nash, a dazzling point guard who came from Victoria, BC, and starred at Santa Clara before joining the Phoenix Suns, won the NBA's most-valuable player award two consecutive years. This put him in the company of such greats as Michael Jordan, Magic Johnson, Larry Bird, Wilt Chamberlain and Bill Russell.

Football was also first played in Canada and brought to the United States about a century ago when a group of McGill University students came down to Harvard to teach a few of its people the new game. With team names like, "The Blue Bombers," (Winnipeg), the "Ottawa Rough Riders," the "Calgary Stampeders" or the "B.C. Lions," and with Americans composing 45% of the professional players on the nine Canadian teams, American football fans feel right at home in Canada (at least until they count 24 players on the field, notice scores on the board like "four to one," and see teams punting on third down from the fifty-three yard line!) Even the cheering sections chant familiar yells, such as "Give me a 'B," an 'l,' a "u," an "e," "what do you have?! . . ."

Canadians were asked in a 1999 poll which icons and institutions helped most to define Canada. The Canadian Football League placed third behind the Order of Canada and the beaver and just ahead of health care, maple syrup and beer. Polls in 2006 indicated that more Canadians (19%) preferred their professional football than their pro hockey (13%).

Due to insurmountable financial difficulties, the American teams in the Canadian Football League (CFL) disappeared. Some Canadian teams in the league teeter on the brink of bankruptcy. Despite average annual salaries of only $50,000 and team salary caps, American players still play in the cash-strapped CFL. With no mandatory drug testing, the CFL attracts many American players who have the talent to play in the NFL.

Baseball and softball are played everywhere in Canada. Even the legendary Babe Ruth hit his first home run in organized baseball in Toronto's Hanlan's Point Stadium on September 5, 1914, and blasted his longest homer (600 feet) at Montreal's Guybourg Grounds in a 1926 exhibition game. His first wife (Helen Woodford) was from Halifax, and his favorite hunting and fishing destinations were New Brunswick and Nova Scotia. Jacky Robinson first broke the sport's race barrier in Montreal's de Lorimier Grounds with the Royals in 1946.

Although the Expos packed their bags in 2005 for a move to Washington D.C., with a new name—The Nationals, major league teams still play "America's favorite pastime" against the Blue Jays in Toronto. Canadian professional teams in all sports face daunting financial problems which drive more and more of them south. They are usually located in smaller towns that are not as willing as American cities to subsidize stadiums and arenas or to reduce property taxes. The popular resentment against millionaire players discourages governments from assisting clubs.

Fans at Blue Jays home games are treated with the usual major league fare: hot dogs, peanuts, cokes and beer, organ music and comic figures both on huge electronic boards and in costume running around the sidelines and into the crowd. Games are begun, though, by playing two national anthems, not just one. In 1985 New York Yankees fans booed when *O Canada* was heard in Yankee Stadium

O Canada

O Canada!
  Our home and native land!
True patriot love
  in all thy sons command.
With glowing hearts
  we see thee rise,
The True North
  strong and free!
From Far and wide,
  O Canada,
We stand on guard
  for thee.
God keep our land
  glorious and free!
O Canada,
  we stand on guard for thee.
O Canada,
  we stand on guard for thee.

Ô Canada

Ô Canada!
  Terre de nos aïeux,
Ton front est ceint
  de fleurons glorieux!
Car ton bras
  sait porter l'épée,
Il sait porter
  la croix!
Ton histoire
  est une épopée
Des plus
  brillants exploits.
Et ta valeur,
  de foi trempée,
Protegera nos foyers
  et nos droits,
Protégera nos foyers
  et nos droits.

The Canadian National Anthem

RCMP mourning death of four comrades

Source: *Maclean's*

prior to a game against the Toronto Blue Jays. That incident was so embarrassing that the American ambassador in Ottawa formally apologized to the Canadians. During the 1992 World Series the President of the United States himself had to do the same after a Marine honor guard unfurled Canada's flag upside down in a pre-game ceremony. Within days T-shirts could be seen all over Canada bearing the inverted Stars and Stripes and the words, "Sorry, eh?"

Horrified Canadians had sweet revenge when the Blue Jays captured the series in a six-game thriller. To rub salt in the wounds, the Blue Jays won again in 1993. In 1997 Larry Walker of the Colorado Rockies became the first Canadian to win the National League's most valuable player award. The next year he led the league in batting and won the Lionel Conacher Prize. In 2003 the Blue Jays ace, Roy Halladay, was the American League's Cy Young winner, while Montreal's Eric Gagné won the National League's Cy Young Award for best pitcher. The National League's Most Valuable Player in 2010 was Toronto-born first baseman for the Cincinnati Reds, Joey Votto. He was the third Canadian to win an MVP award in "America's favorite pastime." In the 2006 season, 21 Canadians played in the major leagues, double the number only a decade earlier.

The American fan was confronted with intriguing language differences when attending a home game of the Montreal Expos. In Montreal *O Canada* had to be sung in two languages. Announcers used both languages, and the American experienced such play-by-play accounts as this: "The situation is tense for the Expos; there are already two *retraits* (outs). The *frappeur* (batter) steps up the plate. The *lanceur* (pitcher) receives the signal from the *receveur* (catcher) and uncorks a mighty pitch. The *frappeur* is undaunted, though. He swings and, hurray, slams a *circuit* (home-run)!" This vocabulary is no longer needed in Washington D.C.

The American motorist also notices few differences, except that road signs show distances in kilometers, are in French in Quebec and are often in both French and English outside of the French-speaking regions. The chances are that he will not notice that he is paying more for gasoline (though not as much as if he were driving in most other foreign countries), since it is measured in liters (spelled "litres" in Canada), not in American gallons. Even when a Canadian speaks in terms of "gallons," he means an imperial gallon, which contains a fifth more than an American one. Canada has already adopted the metric system, although many Canadians still talk in terms of inches, feet, miles, pints, quarts, pounds and tons. It cannot be denied that a system of measurement which makes a mile equal the distance a Roman legion could march in 1,000 double steps, a yard equal to the distance from Henry I's nose to his fingertips and an inch as equal to the width of three barleycorns laid side-by-side, is not as logical as the metric system.

Canadian roads are quite good, unless, of course, he wants to drive deeply into the northern parts of the country. He sees American-looking cars and pickup trucks everywhere. In 1995 the young racing sensation, Jacques Villeneuve, became the first Canadian to win the Indianapolis 500, snatching victory in the final laps from another Canadian, Scott Goodyear. In 1997 he became the first Canadian to clinch the world Formula One championship. In 2011 another Canadian race driver, Alex Tagliani, won the pole position at the Indianapolis 500.

What the American may not know is that all major North American automotive producers have plants in Canada and that completely free trade in automotive vehicles and parts exists between the two countries. In 2004, for the first time, Ontario produced more vehicles than Michigan. The American tourist may, in fact, be driving a Canadian car, rather than an American one.

Most cities have a North American look, with the full rundown of fast-food chains, gasoline stations and convenience stores. There are some charming exceptions, such as Quebec City and Victoria, BC. There are far fewer slums and less litter and graffiti; concern grows over the noticeable increase of homeless Canadians in its chilly cities. But the cores of cities remain vital and have been largely spared the kind of urban deterioration that has afflicted some American cities.

Canadian cities are still somewhat safer than their American counterparts. In a 2003 World Health Organization report, five Canadian cities were listed as among the safest in the world—Sault Ste. Marie, Brockville and Rainy River in Ontario, as well as Calgary and Fort McMurray in Alberta. The chances of being murdered are lower than in a U.S. city. A 2002 Internet definition of a Canadian is not far off the mark: "An unarmed American with health insurance."

Although there was a decline in violent crime in Canada from the mid-1990s, homicides jumped by 4% in 2005, but declined in 2007. The overall crime rate in 2009 was falling and was at a 30-year low. Nearly as many Canadians reported encountering violent crime as did Americans (21% to 26% in 2007). Fear of street violence is widespread: a third (36%) of Canadians (and half the women) said in 2006 that they "would not walk alone at night within one kilometer of my own home." The percentage is down from 40% in 1975 and about the same for American respondents.

Since the mid-1990s there has been a threefold growth in gang-related killings. It is not only rising, but it is overwhelming authorities. One out of five persons killed in Canada is the victim of a gang hit, and there are few arrests and very few convictions. Vancouver has the spotlight, but Saskatoon, Winnipeg and Regina are the cities most plagued by violent crime. It is often connected to the drug trade. This trade is not only in organic drugs, such as cocaine and heroin, but increasingly also in synthetic drugs, such as methamphetamine and ecstasy. It has become North America's leading producer and exporter of these synthetic substances.

Quebec experienced one of the longest and bloodiest gang wars in North American history as the Hell's Angels showed shocking brutality in seeking to gain control of the province's drug trade. More than 160 had died by 2003. In May 2009 a long

Canada

overdue OperationSharQc, planned for four years and involving more than 1,200 police officers from 20 different forces, arrested 111 Hell's Angels and their hangers-on in Quebec. This ended the infamous biker club's stranglehold on Quebec's drug trade. Admitted illegal drug use in Canada is high, according to the UN's "World Drug Report 2007": it has the highest percentage of marijuana users among developed countries (16.8% in 2004 vs. 6.1% in the Netherlands), and 2.3% use cocaine.

The omnipresence of potential violence was seen in tragic killing rampages in schools since 1999. In that year a ninth-grade dropout terrorized a rural high school in Taber, Alberta, killing one student and seriously wounding another with a 22-caliber rifle. A year later three teenage boys were shot and wounded by a fellow student at a Toronto high school, Emery Collegiate Institute. Some argued that Canada's tighter gun control measures made these senseless attacks less deadly: instead of accumulating an arsenal of guns and explosives, as in Columbine, Colorado, the Taber boy could only get his hands on his father's rifle. But in 2006 a young man was able to arm himself with a Baretta semi-automatic rifle, a Glock .45 pistol, a shotgun and a tote bag with 1,000 rounds of ammunition. He walked into Montreal's Dawson College, the province's biggest junior college, and proceeded to kill one student and wound 19 others before turning his gun on himself. Only a brilliant police response prevented the carnage from being much worse.

Guns are increasingly used in such violence; they were involved in two-thirds of Toronto murders in 2005, twice the rate from previous years. Police gun seizures in British Columbia rose by 50% from 2002 to 2005. Controls on the sale of handguns are stricter than in the U.S., but they are not banned, and their use is rising. In 2008 the number of guns per 100 people was 30 in Canada and 90 in the U.S. The overall murder rate per 100,000 persons was 1.9 in Canada and 5.7 in America, and gun murders per 100,000 was 0.6 in Canada and 3.4 in the U.S.

Many of the guns used in the kind of violent incidents that are now alarming Canadians are smuggled in from the U.S. Canadian crime experts claim that half come from south of the border, a figure that American authorities dispute although nobody denies that many guns find their way north into Canada. Canadian border agents seized 5,400 firearms from the U.S. in the five years since 2000, and that is only a fraction of the true number. Canadian gun orders reached such a high volume in 2000 that the U.S. federal government suspended the export of handguns, rifles and ammunition to Canada. Canada had been at the center of one of the largest firearms-smuggling operations in North American history. In 2000 nearly 23,000 vintage U.S. military guns, which are legal in Canada but not in the United States, were seized in Toronto and Montreal gun shops before they could be shipped south of the border.

High-powered hunting guns, including semiautomatics, are widely available. A fourth of all households possess firearms. In 1995 the Liberal government enacted a stricter gun law, banning some small handguns and requiring registration of firearms. In 2000 it tightened the law by requiring registration of all guns by the end of 2002. There is a powerful lobby against gun registration, including by six provinces and two territories that contend that this is an unconstitutional intrusion into their authority. The federal auditor-general criticized its large cost, and the four Western provinces and Newfoundland opted out of administering the program. But the Supreme Court of Canada ruled in June 2000 that both laws had been "passed in the spirit of protecting the public" and were therefore valid.

At the same time that gun- and gang-related crime is dangerously increasing, there are worries that the legendary Royal Canadian Mounted Police (RCMP) is no longer up to the job of maintaining peace and order. The RCMP is a federal force that is contracted by 200 cities and every province and territory but Quebec and Ontario (which have their own provincial police forces) to help enforce the law. It also patrols the Great Lakes and St. Lawrence River. Thus it is caught between the need to meet the growing demand for sophisticated federal policing services, such as immigration, weapons enforcement, counter-terrorism and commercial and white-collar crime, and the "contract policing" at the provincial and local level, which requires that well-trained officers patrol the streets of small towns and answer citizens' calls. It is not performing either duty as effectively as it could.

The force is in deep crisis and is struggling to cope with the challenge of replacing many baby-boom officers while fewer young Canadians are interested in law-enforcement careers. There are only 195 policemen per 100,000 people, compared with 222 in the U.S. and 270 in Britain. The force is too understaffed to put two officers in every control car. Its performance is declining, especially in the kind of detailed investigations that one expects of an elite agency. Burn-out is so serious that one in eight members receives disability pay, increasingly for psychological damage. A major drug bust fell apart in 2007 when five officers could not testify because they were on stress leave. Only half the policemen feel "respected and trusted" and believe they are being treated fairly by the RCMP. Confidence in their leaders is at an all-time low.

The eight provinces and three territories that use the Mounties' services have little interest in creating their own police forces since Ottawa pays up to 30% of the policing tab, 10% for municipalities. By and large, Canadians still trust the RCMP so much that its occasional use of phone buggings, wire-tappings, break-ins, use of general search warrants, forgery of income-tax forms, mail tampering, planting of incriminating evidence on innocent persons and harassing left-wing political groups—actions that would seldom be tolerated by American courts or the public if they were known—are generally accepted by Canadians. However, the public's tolerance has its limits. This was shown in November 2007 when four RCMP officers at Vancouver International Airport killed an innocent, unarmed, and

Dinnertime at the Royal Military College of Canada

distressed Polish traveler who spoke no English by shooting him with a taser stun gun when he did not understand and respond to their orders. This lamentable incident was captured on video. Two years later a 200-page report concluded that such use of the electronic weapon was both premature and inappropriate.

Canadians go about their daily lives in a way similar to Americans, with a few minor differences. As in the U.S., schools are run by local school boards under the overall authority of the individual provinces. Their aim is now mass education in comprehensive schools, not academically tracked education in separate schools, as in most European countries. Depending on the particular province, children begin school at age six or seven and generally attend elementary school for six years, junior high school for three and senior high school for three. In Quebec pupils enter a two- to three-year *college d'enseignement general et professionnel* (college of general and professional instruction) to prepare either for the university or a specific occupation.

Canadian pupils score very well in international comparisons. For example, in the 2010 PISA survey of several dozen developed countries, Canadians were ranked sixth in science, fourth in reading and eighth in mathematics, far ahead of their American cohorts. On the darker side, there is an alarmingly high dropout rate for black high school pupils: at 40% it is almost double the rate for the student population as a whole.

A lower percentage of Canadians (ca. 42%) attend universities than in the U.S. (over 50%); this percentage is much higher for Asian students (ca. 70%) but lower for Caribbean (12%). Canadian universities have strictly meritocratic admission policies, and Canadian-born and foreign Asian students have the reputation for studying the hardest and having the most success. The immigration process attracts highly educated parents, who pass on their high aspirations to their children.

More students are being admitted, and over the decade before 2003 university enrollment increased by 20%. Following a trend also noticeable in the U.S., 57% of undergraduates in Canadian universities are women, and this can be as high as 79% at such institutions as Mount Saint Vincent University in Halifax. This is especially pronounced in medicine: the majority of students at 13 of Canada's 17 medical schools are women, and at the Université Laval the percentage rises to 70%. No wonder 52% of doctors under age 35 are women. More graduate programs have been created. Also, the institutions have been expanded to include more vocationally relevant courses, as has always been true of American universities.

Those who wish to study have a wide variety of universities from which to choose. There are elite research universities, such as McGill, University of Alberta, University of Toronto, University of British Columbia and Université de Montréal. These five institutions alone enroll 22% of undergraduates and produce 45% of doctorates. They receive 46% of all the public monies distributed for research and innovation. By 2010 Waterloo had been placed first in *Maclean's* annual ranking of best overall universities 17 out of 20 years. In the global Shanghai rankings of the top 100 universities, four Canadian institutions and 54 American ones are included. There are also fine primarily undergraduate institutions, such as Mount Allison, Brandon, Mount Saint Vincent, St. Thomas, Moncton, Acadia, Bishop's, St. Francis Xavier, Wilfrid Laurier and the Royal Military College of Canada (RMC).

These universities and colleges, all public with a few exceptions in Ontario, are not as expensive as equivalent American institutions. Tuition in 2008 cost an average of Can$4,724, and it ranged from $5,932 in Nova Scotia to $2,167 in Quebec. Students also pay annual compulsory fees of $695 ($827 in Nova Scotia and $423 in New Brunswick).

In 2007 Quest University Canada, Canada's first private, non-profit secular liberal arts and sciences college, opened its doors in Squamish BC, costing between Can$25,000 to Can$30,000 in tuition, room and board. It hopes ultimately to attract half its 160 to 640 students from Canada and half from the U.S. and abroad.

Canadian institutions are severely cash-strapped and overcrowded because the federal government reduced its transfer payments to the provinces. In 1999 Canadian universities spent 60% per pupil of what large public universities do in the U.S. In the final five years of the century state allocations to U.S. universities increased by 28% (50% in California) while they dropped by 6% in Canada.

In a 2010 survey, two-thirds of parents said they could not afford the four-year average cost of $60,000 to send their children to university. Three-fifths of all students have to take loans to finance their studies, and the average debt upon graduation stood at $26,680 in 2010, roughly the same as the average college debt in the U.S. Canadian universities are learning how to raise private funds, but it will be years until they catch up with their American counterparts. For example, the university with the largest endowment is Toronto, with only $1.3 billion, less than one-twentieth of that of Harvard and Yale.

In 2005, 28,140 Canadians went to the U.S. for their post–secondary education, and that number is growing. They consti-

tute the largest group of foreigners at Harvard (150 or 2.3%). This educational migration is particularly true of Ph.D. students. The word that many would-be professors hear in Canada is that an American Ph.D. may give one an edge. American-trained professors are in the majority in many departments, especially at leading Canadian research universities. Canada confers fewer than 10% as many doctorates as does the much larger U.S. Nevertheless, Canadians still earn five times as many Ph.D. degrees in Canada as they do in America.

Only 3,000 Americans choose to attend Canadian universities. The latter are aggressively recruiting American high school students, promising gun-free schools, good ski possibilities and quality education for less tuition. Today 12% of McGill's students are Americans. Also popular are branch campuses of American universities in Canada, primarily for teachers and other professionals. By 1990 seven U.S. universities (including Niagara and Central Michigan) offered extension programs for about 500 students in Ontario alone, and such operations are expanding in Alberta and British Columbia. Despite the higher tuition costs, these programs offer study opportunities at night and on weekends.

Five provinces provide state support for religiously affiliated schools. Also, the federal government is directly responsible for educating Indians and Inuit children and indirectly involved in education through financial support for higher education and bilingual teaching throughout Canada. Canadian public schools, which 95% of children attend, are suffering under the strain of funding cuts, labor strife and the needs of an increasingly diverse student body. Since 1995 the percentage of provincial wealth spent on education has declined dramatically.

Americans are quick to recognize Canadians as a friendly, open and pragmatic people. Canadians are a bit more reserved than Americans. As Pierre Berton noted, "we are not a back-slapping race" and Canadians themselves admit to being somewhat embarrassed by public displays of emotions. A publication of the Royal Bank once capsulated how many Canadians react to their more ebullient neighbors: Americans are "much given to travel, colourful clothing, gadgets, hand-held foods, and striking metaphoric variations on the English language. They prefer first to second names, and, in conversation, they seem to use yours in every sentence or two . . . They belong to clubs and lodges named after animals. They talk to strangers on street corners and at lunch counters. As they themselves would put it, they're friendly as hell."

Polls consistently reveal that Americans have a far more positive impression of

Canada

Alberta's lake and mountain landscape.

Canadians than vice versa. Asked in 2000 to describe the other country in one word, Canadians' top choices were: snobs, arrogant, aggressive, greedy, selfish and ignorant. In 2005 they added "rude" and "violent" to this list of complimentary adjectives. Americans answered: friendly (29%), peaceful, polite, helpful. In 2004 that had changed little, with the words "arrogant" and "patriotic" first coming to Canadians' minds. More said "dangerous" than "compassionate." Americans use the words "tolerant," "compassionate" and "funny" to describe Canadians. Only 1% of Canadians think Americans are "funny" or "humorous."

A December 2007 *Maclean's* poll to determine which people in the world have the most knowledge of Canadian affairs determined that Americans do, with the British, of all people, knowing the least. Although they made some mistakes (eg. half the American respondents thought that Canadian soldiers were fighting in Iraq), the southern neighbors are relatively familiar with Canada and like what they see. Asked in an earlier poll what countries they like most, Americans began with Canada, favored by 90%, followed by Britain. Only 3% had a negative view of Canada. A quarter of Canadians and Americans indicated that they would accept citizenship in the other country, and a third of *Québécois* said they would accept an offer to become U.S. citizens. A resounding 91% of Americans agreed in 2007 that they would have a better quality of life if they moved to Canada.

Many people argue that there is no such thing as Canadian patriotism because there is no such thing as a Canadian nation. Whatever patriotism exists is far lower-keyed than in America. "It embarrasses us . . . to love our country out 'loud,'" Berton observed. Although Canadians are patriotic, they feel uncomfortably American when they display it too much in public. In his 1988 book, Peter C. Newman wrote that "becoming a Canadian never required conversion to a burning faith or even a salute, since we had no distinctive flag during the first 98 years of our existence." The mass flag waving and outpouring of national pride that greeted Canada's gold-medal-winning team in the 2010 Winter Olympics in Vancouver revealed that there may be more overt patriotism than one had ever imagined.

The two countries' standing in the world is very different. Reflecting on the differences between his Canadian and American students, Northrop Frye said: "American students have been conditioned from infancy to think of themselves as citizens of one of the world's great powers. Canadians are conditioned from infancy to think of themselves as citizens of a country of uncertain identity, a confusing past and a hazardous future." Toronto academic Abraham Rotstein argued that the problem with having the U.S. as a neighbor is that its "instinctive imperialism" is an all-pervasive force of nature that "envelops us as a mist, penetrating every sphere of our cultural, political and social environment." Asked in 2006 which country is the greatest threat to theirs, 37% of Canadians and 46% of Mexicans said the U.S.; a quarter of Americans agreed. In 2007 a quarter (26%) of Canadians said the U.S. is the greatest threat to global stability; 23% of Americans agreed. However, these opinions are significantly shaped by the popularity of the sitting American president.

Former *New York Times* bureau chief in Toronto, Andrew H. Malcolm, reported an example of the differing manifestation of patriotism. At the start of a stock car race in Calgary, the announcer asked the crowd to stand for the national anthem. A few seconds after a record of "O Canada" had begun to play, he stopped the music with a wrenching scratch and said, "You all know the rest," as the racecars' engines began to roar. Such an incident would be unthinkable in the United States.

Against such an anti-jingoist background, the extreme popularity in 2000 of a patriotic chant, known as "the Rant," is stunning. It appeared in a 60-second Molson beer commercial that won a major international prize, the Bronze Lion, at the Cannes film festival. Performed on TV and at a Stanley Cup game in Toronto by a 28-year-old Nova Scotia actor, Jeff Douglas, it poked fun at Americans' clichés about Canadians and expressed the kind of pride in Canada that young people appeared to want to hear shouted from the rooftops: "I'm not a lumberjack or a fur trader. I don't live in an igloo, eat blubber or own a dogsled. I don't know Jimmy, Suzie or Sally from Canada, although I'm certain they're very nice. I have a prime minister, not a president. I speak English and French, not American. And I pronounce it 'about', not 'a-boot.' I can proudly sew my country's flag on my backpack. I believe in peacekeeping, not policing; diversity, not assimilation. And that the beaver is a proud and noble animal. A tuque is a hat, a chesterfield is a couch. And it's pronounced zed. Okay? Not zee. Zed. Canada is the second-largest land mass, the first nation of hockey and the best part of North America. My name is Joe and I am Canadian!"

Drinkers in bars and audiences in movie theaters stopped talking and recited the words when the ad came on. Molson set up a special "I AM Canadian" Web site (www.iam.ca) that provided unlimited replays and a chat room for countless other ranters. Such un-Canadian flag-waving caught many Canadians by surprise. Charles Gordon, a columnist with *The Ottawa Citizen,* wrote: "there is good news and bad news about Canadian nationalism. The good news is that it exists. The bad news is that the proof of its existence lies largely in beer commercials." Former *National Post* (now *Maclean's*) columnist, Mark Steyn, concluded: "If you drink enough Molson, eventually even Canada makes sense." It is ironic that in 2004 Molson's consumated a marriage with Coors of Colorado to shore up its sales.

Perhaps most characteristically Canadian is the fact that the Rant was endlessly spoofed and parodied throughout Canada. For example, in Alberta: "I speak flawless English and gripe to the store manager about French labels on cereal boxes." From an English-language radio station in Quebec delivered with a French accent: "I believe in language police, not equal rights. I believe Club Supersex is an appropriate place for my wife and I to celebrate our *anniversaire*. The land where everybody is shacking up and the legal drinking age is just a suggestion. *Je m'appelle Guy*—and I am not *Canadien!*" Further, "Newfoundland is the second island province, the first nation of drinking and the best party in North America! My name is Baz, and I am Newfie!"

Asked at the end of the century about factors that are important parts of what makes them Canadian, 80% named the flag (60% in Quebec) and only 41% named the British Queen (20% in Quebec). Nevertheless, rather than pledging allegiance to the flag, most Canadian pupils make their pledge to the Queen. In May they are released from school for a day in order to celebrate Victoria Day, in honor of Queen Victoria, despite the fact that she never visited Canada during her long reign. The birthday of Canada's "founding father," Sir John A. Macdonald, is not a federal holiday, but school children observe Martin Luther King Jr. Day in January. Thanksgiving comes the second Monday in October, almost six weeks earlier than in the United States. Also, there is certainly no Fourth of July celebration in a country which remained loyal to Britain during the American Revolution and which was a haven for Loyalists who either left or were driven out of the Thirteen Colonies. Canadian school children still learn about such heroic men of principle as *Benedict Arnold*, who demonstrated their devotion to order and the English sovereign. Canadians' national holiday is July First, the day on which both the country's constitutions were enacted in 1867 and 1982.

Canada has its own history, has been shaped by more challenging geographical conditions, has different cultures and languages, and has a different political heritage. Its political system is British by origin, even though it has been powerfully influenced by political practices in the United States. And Canadians have tended to place a greater emphasis on order than have Americans, who tend to treasure liberty above all else. Canadian-born sociologist, Seymour Lipsit, gave an example: "Canadians were told to go metric and they did. Americans were told to go metric and they didn't."

Canada's first constitution, the British North America Act (BNA) of 1867, set up

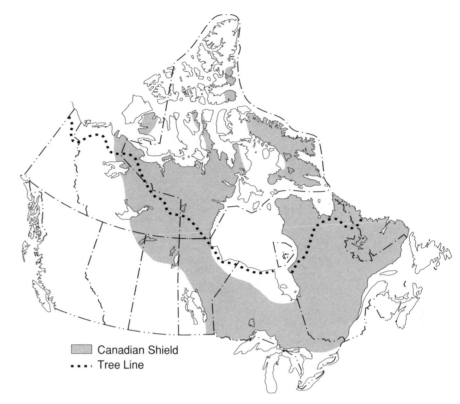

Canadian Shield
• • • • Tree Line

the objectives of "peace, order, and good government" rather than "life, liberty and the pursuit of happiness." Canada never had a "wild West" because, unlike in America, organized society in the form of the mounted policeman, the railway agent, the bank manager, the missionary and agents of the Hudson's Bay Company usually arrived before or along with the settlers. Therefore, there has always been less violence and greater respect for authority in Canada than in the United States. What other country in the world uses a policeman (the Mountie) as a national symbol?

Canadians know that their emphasis on order makes them seem boring to the rest of the world. In a "boring headline" contest held in 1986 by the U.S. magazine, *The New Republic*, the winner was: "Worthwhile Canadian Initiative." In an interview with *The Economist* in 2003, one Canadian compared Canada to a "boring party where the guests are too polite to leave." The book titles of two earlier bestsellers were: *Canada on the World Stage: Is Anyone Listening?* and *The Future of Canada: Does Nationalism Even Matter?* Australians call Canadians "frozen Yanks." Nevertheless, when asked in which country they would rather live other than their own, Australia was Canadians' first choice (18%), followed by the U.S. (14%).

In a 1992 editorial, "Boring, and proud," *The Globe and Mail* countered: "The reason Canada is considered boring is because nothing apocalyptic ever happens here—no civil wars, no nuclear disasters, no famine.

On a global scale, Canada just can't cut it when it comes to violence and tragedy. We discuss our possible national break-up over lunch beside a lake. Blame our Canadian forefathers for the cruel hand we've been dealt. Didn't they realize that when they founded this country on the principles of Peace, Order, and Good Government that it would never make CNN?"

Although they are changing, Canadians have tended to be less assertive of their rights than have Americans. For instance, in a restaurant if a customer was quarreling about the bill, it was generally assumed that the person was probably an American rather than a Canadian. Peter Newman put it this way: "In dramatic contrast to the individualism of the United States, the idea was to be careful, to be plainly dressed, quiet-spoken and, above all, close with one's money and emotions . . . You could immediately spot a Canadian at any gathering: he or she was the one who automatically chose the most uncomfortable chair."

The *Maclean's*/CBC end-of-century poll provided ample evidence that Canadians believe they have a unique identity, separate and distinct from all other countries, as 90% of respondents indicated. Fully 77% believe it is based on a strong sense of their own history and appreciation of what they have accomplished as a nation, rather than simply a desire not to be American; 81% hold the view that they can thrive in the twenty-first century by keeping their own values and not trying

Canada

to become more like Americans. A subsequent *Maclean's* poll published on July 1, 2006, concluded that the endless and mostly futile search for a single national identity and vision had been replaced by a growing sense that Canada's greatest asset is its diversity of lifestyles, beliefs and opinions. Former Prime Minister Jean Chrétien expressed this confidence: "We are North Americans but not Americans. We are different because of history and geography, but basically we have built a different society."

Events from the 1960s on tended to sharpen Americans' and Canadians' awareness of the differences between their countries and objectives. The United States' seemingly endless involvement in the Vietnam War became unpopular in Canada, where an estimated 50,000 or more Americans fled to avoid military service; all but 20,000 returned to the U.S. after a 1977 amnesty. Those who stayed include several judges, scores of university professors, a popular radio host, a music promoter, a well-known film critic and numerous politicians. Less known is the fact that as many as 40,000 Canadians fought in that war, and more than a hundred Canadians' names are etched on the Vietnam Memorial in Washington, D.C.

In 2004 four American soldiers deserted their Iraq-bound units and fled to Canada, where they requested refugee status. But unlike in 1969, when Prime Minister Pierre Elliot Trudeau declared his country to be "a refuge from militarism," the Canadian government, backed by a board that hears refugee cases, opposed their applications, arguing that they were not persecuted and that the war was not illegal. Canada is no longer an open-armed sanctuary despite the fact that three in five Canadians think American deserters should be granted permanent residency. Parliament approved nonbinding resolutions in 2008 and 2009 to stop the deportation of deserters, but the government refused to do so. In July 2008 the first American soldier was deported, and more followed. There are still more Canadians serving in the U.S. military forces than any foreign nationality.

From 1968 to 1984 Trudeau felt freer to criticize American foreign policy in public, and many Canadians agreed with him. Also, racial violence in America and the disillusionment stimulated by the Watergate scandal dulled the image of America in Canadian eyes. Further, Canadians began to feel a surge of nationalism and sought to lessen their country's economic dependence upon the United States in ways that greatly irritated American businessmen and the U.S. government.

More and more Americans began to take notice of the fact that Canada is a sovereign country that defines its own interests. As Americanized as Canadians might have become, they seem determined to be a different kind of society, which tries to avoid the kinds of problems the United States faces. One young Canadian, Neil Bishop, noted: "It's not that U.S. civilization is bad; on the contrary, it is truly great. But one U.S.A. is surely enough."

GEOGRAPHY

Canada is the second-largest country in the world; only Russia is larger. Covering almost four million square miles, it is 10% larger than the United States (including Alaska) and 40 times bigger than Great Britain; it is roughly the same size as the entire European continent and occupies 46.6% of North America. It is bracketed by huge islands, such as Newfoundland, Vancouver and Baffin, the world's fourth largest island, with 16,000 miles of crinkled coastline.

Canada stretches 4,545 miles east to west and almost 3,000 miles north to south, and it spans one fourth of the world's time zones. Its three coasts, when combined, are the world's longest coastline, with an enormous store of offshore riches. Inland Canada has more than a million rivers, streams and lakes, containing over a fifth of the world's fresh water supply. In Manitoba alone there is one lake for every 10 inhabitants. It also shares with the U.S. the world's largest body of fresh water: the Great Lakes. Canada possesses a fourth of the world's wetlands and 15% of its forests. Even though it occupies the "winter half" of North America, it has a wide range of climates, and there are regions in Canada which experience one-hundred degree drops of temperature in the wintertime.

Almost one-half of Canada is located on a massive shield of ancient Precambrian rocks hewed and scraped by a gigantic prehistoric glacier. It covers the bulk of six provinces and most of the Northwest Territories. It is a sparsely-populated physical environment of forests, wilderness, lakes and rocks jutting from the earth. This landscape differs remarkably from the lowlands south of it and keeps Canadians hemmed in close to the U.S. border, where most of them live. This Shield has always been a formidable barrier to settlement, to the building of roads and railways and to the movement of Canadians from east to west or from south to north.

Since it is practically uninhabitable, it has prevented Canada from having a Midwest comparable to that found to the south in the United States. A thousand miles of rocks, eroded mountain chain and bogs placed a wall between the Prairie provinces (the West) and the settled portion of Ontario, which belongs to Canada's East, even though Toronto is closer to such Midwestern cities as Cleveland, Detroit and Chicago, than to New York and Boston. It has always threatened to cut off the Canadian West from the East and has contributed to a greater feeling of separation from each other on the part of westerners and easterners than is felt in the United States.

It has helped to create and perpetuate a western dependence on eastern financial power that has always been resented in the West. Finally, it has strengthened Canadians' reliance upon government and has helped shape the Canadian character. As Pierre Berton wrote, "if we are a solemn people, it is partly because the Shield and the wilderness bear down upon us, a crushing weight, squeezing us like toothpaste along the borders of your country."

Nevertheless, the rugged Shield also contains treasures that help make Canada

Peggy's Cove, Nova Scotia   Courtesy: Michael J. Hewitt

a natural resource powerhouse. It was an ideal habitat for beavers, which had almost single-handedly attracted European attention to Canada three centuries ago and provided the first important economic stimulus to Canadian settlement. One result is that Canada is the only country in the world with a rodent for its national animal: the beaver. Its image was on the first Canadian postal stamp in 1851 and is on today's nickel.

This amazing creature, which can cut down 216 trees a year with its bare teeth, suffered a horrible indignity in January 2010. In 1920 the Hudson Bay Company had founded a journal of popular history called *The Beaver*. On its ninetieth birthday, the editors felt compelled to change its name to the dull *Canada's History* because the iconic animal's name had become a slang carnal term referring to a certain location on a woman's body. The death knell was rung by the internet. If spam filters did not bury it, users of its website were often disappointed to discover that the content was history rather than something else, and they clicked out on average after only eight seconds. Editors hope the publication's new name will expand its 50,000 circulation.

Today, much of the Shield is richly endowed with nickel, cobalt, zinc, copper, gold and silver; it is the source of 40% of Canada's mineral production. It contains the trees that make Canada one of the two major pulp and paper producers in the world, the uranium mines in northern Saskatchewan and the huge Ungava iron ore deposits. It is a major source of waterpower, which supplies Canada with 70% of its electricity and enables it to export hydroelectricity to the United States, especially to the Northeast.

The Shield's rugged landscapes, scenery and wildlife, particularly multitudes of birds including millions, even billions, of ducks and geese, have inspired some of Canadians' best painting, especially since the 1920s, when seven talented Canadian artists (known as the "Group of Seven") captured its majestic beauty on their canvases. It also attracts vacationers from all over North America and helps to perpetuate that erroneous image which some Americans have of modern Canadians: as lumberjacks or rugged frontiersmen who carve a precarious living out of a beautiful, but hostile, land. As we shall see, Canadians are predominantly city-dwellers who have learned to exploit the riches of the Shield in order to create and maintain a comfortable standard of living similar to that enjoyed by most Americans.

Canada is a very sparsely settled land, with an overall population density of only six persons per square mile, compared with 60 in the United States. Even Saudi

Former Governor General visiting Parliament in Ottawa

Arabia has a higher population density than does Canada. Its climate and geography have powerfully influenced settlement patterns. The Shield and climate compressed Canadians to close proximity to the U.S. border. There were further incentives to settle in the extreme south. Many settlers to Canada came from the United States and wanted to remain close to that country. Many Canadian manufacturing facilities were owned by Americans or were intentionally located close to the American market, which is the world's largest and the target for 85% of Canadian exports. Also, in the level plains between the southern rim of the Shield and the U.S. border are fertile farmlands and a fortuitous string of lakes and rivers connected in places by canals that provide inexpensive transportation and waterpower.

The result of these forces is that three-fourths of all Canadians live within 100 miles of the U.S. border, and 90% live within 200 miles. In fact, three-fourths of all Canadians live *south* of the northernmost point of the 48 contiguous United States. By contrast, most Americans live far away from Canada, and only 12% of them live within 100 miles of the Canadian border. This percentage is decreasing as more and more Americans move south within the U.S.

If one regards only population distribution, Canada more closely resembles the snake-shaped country of Chile, rather than the well-proportioned geographic configuration that Canada is. It could be seen as a country 4,545 miles wide and a hundred miles tall, albeit with a hinterland which stretches straight to the per-

mafrost, the ice pack and the North Pole. Even within this thin band of settlement, Canadians are not dispersed evenly. Four out of five Canadians live in cities; 31% live in the three largest—Toronto, Montreal and Vancouver—and half of new immigrants settle in these three cities. One-third of Canadians live in communities with fewer than 10,000 inhabitants. Political pollsters detect an urban-rural split on such issues as gun control and gay rights, and the economic disparity is growing. Differing lifestyles are also reflected in the facts that rural Canadians are more likely to smoke, drink underage, and be obese.

Urban concentrations are strung out from east to west, "an archipelago of population islands walled off from each other by the terrifying obstacles of Precambrian rock, muskeg (bogs), mountain barriers, storm-tossed waters," to quote Pierre Berton. The bulk of Newfoundland's people have to cross the Gulf of St. Lawrence to get to the Canadian mainland. French-speaking Acadia and Quebec separate anglophones in the east from those in Ontario. Distance and the southern extremity of the Shield, which juts through western Ontario, separate most inhabitants of Ontario, the most populous Canadian province, from the prairie provinces of Manitoba, Saskatchewan and Alberta. Finally, the Rocky Mountains provide a majestic separation of the prairie region from British Columbia.

These sharply divided regions are, in many ways, northward thrusts of the North American continent. Indeed, a serious challenge to Canada has always been that only man-made barriers separate Ca-

Canada

nadian from American regions, whereas daunting natural barriers divide most of Canada's regions from each other. This has made the forging of unnatural east–west links and the overcoming of the natural north–south ties absolutely essential if Canada were to become and to remain a unified country. A closer look at these distinct regions will demonstrate why this has always been difficult and why author Arthur Malcolm described Canada as a "puzzling collection of frequently feuding fiefdoms."

THE ATLANTIC PROVINCES: In the East are the Atlantic Provinces, composed of the three Maritime provinces of Nova Scotia, Prince Edward Island (Canada's smallest province although twice the size of Rhode Island) and New Brunswick (40% of whose population is French-speaking Acadian) plus Newfoundland and Labrador, Britain's first overseas colony. Officially renamed Newfoundland and Labrador in 2001, this is Canada's most recent province. Not until 1949 did it join Canada, after a very close vote by its people. It still remains remote from the rest of the country and even has its own time zone 30 minutes ahead of the Maritime provinces. Less urbanized than Ontario and Quebec, this region is covered by forested hills and low mountains. Water is everywhere. These provinces are largely encircled by rocky coastlines, coves, isolated fishing villages and port cities, such as St. Johns and Halifax.

With only 2.3 million inhabitants, 7% of the country's population, Atlantic Canada is the most ethnically homogeneous region of Canada. There are Acadians, remnants of those ten thousand hardy pacifist folks brutally rooted out and resettled by the British in 1755 for trying to stay neutral in the war between England and France. They were immortalized in Longfellow's moving poem, "Evangeline." No longer discriminated against because of their French language, they now live along New Brunswick's northern border and eastern shore and are sprinkled around in other parts of the region, especially in the southwest corner of Prince Edward Island and on Cape Breton in

Nova Scotia. On August 15, 2005, thousands of them assembled at the site of their ancient village of St. Pré in the heart of their lost homeland to celebrate their survival of that deportation 250 years earlier, now referred to as *le grand dérangement* (the Big Inconvenience).

About 80% of the Atlantic Provinces inhabitants are of British descent (higher in Newfoundland), especially Scottish, from whom Nova Scotia, meaning "New Scotland," got its name. Perhaps the most famous Scotsman to grow up and live here was Alexander Graham Bell, who invented the telephone. It is reported that more people speak Gaelic in Nova Scotia today than in Scotland itself. One still hears a distinctive Scottish burr when many Nova Scotians speak English, especially in Cape Breton, which is experiencing a revival of Gaelic cultures and language.

This predominantly British population has long valued its transatlantic ties with Great Britain, and it has always maintained thriving trading relations with the northeastern seaboard cities south of the border. Because of its window to the Atlantic, it has always been strategically important. During the two world wars its ports were assembly points for convoys of ships carrying troops and supplies from North America to Europe. It is no surprise that Canada's small navy is headquartered in this part of the country. In fact, Halifax, the capital of Nova Scotia, is the home of Canada's largest defense establishment, which provides employment for almost a fourth of the city's work force.

Despite their strategic location, the Atlantic Provinces have always been the poorest of Canada's provinces. They have been excessively reliant upon fishing and timbering. A greater percentage of their jobs are dependent upon the extraction of primary resources and increasingly upon tourism, and this has resulted in a large number of single-industry towns. They have too little arable land, population and industry to have a more balanced economy and to be prosperous on their own. They are just now finding reliable alternatives to their former economic mainstays of fishing, lumber and military bases. Average wages were until recently only two-thirds of the national figure, but they are now rising.

Their present economic hopes and success stem from discoveries of natural gas and oil off the coasts of Nova Scotia and Newfoundland and Labrador. These capital-intensive industries do not generate many jobs directly, nor do they spread cash around as cod fishing once did. But they boost government resources and trickle down to others. The importance of these discoveries explains the history of

bitter struggles with Ottawa over the question of who owns or controls these valuable resources: Canada or the individual provinces. The people in these provinces are proud of their more relaxed, less urbanized life, but they have also tended to resent the economic and political domination of Canadian life by provinces to the west. In 2000 the region's four premiers formed a joint council to lobby in Ottawa. By 2009 Newfoundland had become a "have" province, sending more financial assistance to other provinces than it receives from them.

Although the region lacks a very large urban center, Halifax is an important and interesting city. With a population of around 280,000, it is a showcase of 19th century architecture with the leisurely air of a small, tree-lined community. Its significance as Atlantic Canada's most important port city suffered with the opening of the St. Lawrence Seaway, which enabled ships to by-pass Halifax and churn their way directly into the Great Lakes.

ST. LAWRENCE LOWLANDS: The two provinces of Quebec and Ontario form the heartland of the Canadian Confederation. They were formerly two separate colonies, called Lower Canada (Quebec) and Upper Canada (Ontario). Their merger in 1840 signaled the imperfect wedding of Canada's "two founding peoples" in one country. Although very large portions of these two provinces are covered by the Canadian Shield, they share in the south the St. Lawrence Lowlands, which form the most heavily populated, most industrialized and, therefore, richest part of Canada. It contains 60% of Canada's entire population. It has more cities of over 100,000 inhabitants than any other region, and it includes Canada's two largest cities, Toronto and Montreal, as well as the federal capital, Ottawa.

About three-fourths of the total value of Canada's manufactured goods are produced in this region. Its moderate climate and excellent agricultural lands attracted many settlers in the 18th and 19th centuries, and farms here still help feed the country's most densely populated region. A further blessing for this region is the waterway formed by the St. Lawrence River, the Great Lakes and connecting canals and locks, the last of which were completed in 1959. The economic importance of the Great Lakes cannot be underestimated: the eight American states and Ontario that share the lakes account for 30% of North America's employment and output and 36% of manufacturing jobs.

This entire waterway is ice-free about nine months a year and gives this inland area enviable access to the Atlantic Ocean and from there to the rest of the world. For example, although located 1,000 miles from the sea, the port of Toronto receives ocean-going ships and is the same shipping distance from Britain as is New York City. Also, many vessels can travel almost 2,000 miles from the Atlantic Ocean all the way westward to Thunder Bay, the railhead for products and grain from the West and located on the northern shore of Lake Superior, and then return to the high seas.

QUEBEC: While the St. Lawrence Seaway binds the eastern half of Canada, it could never erase the crucially important cultural differences of the people who live close to its banks. This Canadian heartland is sharply divided into francophones in Quebec and anglophones in Ontario. With a land area three times larger than France, Quebec is Canada's largest province and is as wide at its widest point as the distance between Dallas and Washington, D.C.

It is a French-speaking island in the midst of an anglophone sea in which francophones are outnumbered by fifty to one. According to the 2001 census, Quebec's population had shrunk to 24.1% of Canada's total, from 27.9% three decades earlier. Now about 87% of Quebec's 7.4 million people speak French as a mother tongue, 7% speak English at home, 6% speak another native language, and 16% of the total population is fluent in a third language. Fifty-eight percent of the francophones speak only French, especially those living outside the larger cities of

IRAK
Un proche de Bush sera chargé
des privatisations
Page A 7

VACHE FOLLE
Exportation de bœuf:
Washington jette du lest
Page C 1

● www.ledevoir.com ●

LE DEVOIR

Vol. XCIV N° 178 ●   LES SAMEDI 9 ET DIMANCHE 10 AOÛT 2003   1.95$ · TAXES · 2.25$

Mariages gays: l'intervention du Vatican choque les élus québécois

HÉLÈNE BUZZETTI
DE NOTRE BUREAU D'OTTAWA

La vaste majorité des députés fédéraux du Québec sont d'accord pour étendre le mariage aux couples de même sexe, comme entend le faire Ottawa. Bon nombre d'entre eux se sont même indignés de ce que l'Église ait tenté de les influencer, rappelant que la Révolution tranquille a justement servi à placer une distance entre les religieux et les élus.

C'est ce qui ressort de la trentaine d'entrevues effectuées par *Le Devoir* cette semaine sur cette question. Tous les 75 élus ont été approchés, mais plusieurs étaient en vacances ou n'ont pas rappelé. Des 37 députés et ministres interrogés par *Le Devoir*, 28 ont indiqué qu'ils sont d'accord pour permettre aux gais et lesbiennes de se marier civilement comme les couples hétérosexuels, et six se disent contre. Trois ont soutenu ne pas s'être fait une opinion sur le sujet. Le *Globe and Mail*, qui a interrogé seulement les députés libéraux, ajoute à cette liste de Québécois deux partisans du changement, quatre opposants et sept indécis ou discrets. Les ministres québé-

« Moi, ma religion en est une d'ouverture, de générosité, d'égalité des êtres humains. C'est une

Oui, je le veux...

Le Tout-Montréal se bat pour sauver son Grand Prix

■ *Ecclestone nie que l'épreuve a été annulée*

■ *Legault reste sur sa position*

BRIAN MYLES
LE DEVOIR

La bataille pour sauver le Grand Prix du Canada est en marche. Une coalition représentant le tout-Montréal touristique — forte de 70 000 emplois, de deux milliards de dollars en retombées économiques et de l'appui du maire Gérald Tremblay — a demandé hier à Québec et Ottawa de s'ali-

Montreal and Quebec City. In Montreal two-thirds speak both French and English. The *Québécois*, as they are now called most of the time even outside of francophone Canada, have a distinctive language, culture and heritage.

In the past they tended to consider themselves more as *Québécois*, than as Canadians. In the 1994 *Maclean's*/CTV poll, only 45% of Quebec respondents identified themselves as "Canadian." By 2001 that figure had risen to 75%, and in *Maclean's* 2003 year-end poll an unprecedented 69% claimed they were "proud to be Canadian." That percentage continues to go up: *La Presse* published a poll in 2007 showing that 85% were proud to be Canadian, a 20-year high. Due largely to a serious Liberal Party scandal in Quebec, the number of *Québécois* who considered themselves "very proud to be Canadian" fell from 65% in 1985 to only 32% in 2006 (in Anglophone Canada the percentage fell from 80% to 61%). Nevertheless, a former separatist (PQ) premier, Bernard Landry, said in 2007 that "being Canadian isn't dishonorable." That was high praise from a man who once called the Canadian flag "a piece of red rag." In the wake of Canada's superb Olympic performance in 2010, fewer than one-third of *Québécois* supported the notion of having their own Olympic team.

Québécois still regard themselves as a nation, even though they are linked polit-

ically with the rest of Canada. For the first time the Canadian parliament gave this formal expression by declaring in November 2006 that *Québécois* are "a nation within a united Canada." Constituting almost a fourth of all Canadians, they have always doggedly resisted assimilation with the English-speaking world around them. They have successfully asserted their right to manage most of their own affairs and largely to determine their own destiny. They have their own national day on June 24, a week earlier than Canada Day on July 1. The Quebec government officially renamed it the Fête Nationale, but *Québécois* still refer to it as Fête de la St-Jean-Baptiste, or "La St-Jean."

A dramatic change had taken place by 2004. *Québécois* seem to accept Canada more than they used to. Only 2% of them considered national unity a major issue. As the most socially liberal Canadians, *Québécois* like the social experimentalism they see in Canada, such as gay marriage, abortion and legalization of marijuana: 69% endorsed the statement that they are proud of what Canada is becoming "because it shows what a socially progressive and diverse country we live in." The figure in the rest of Canada was 54%.

They also now share anglophone Canadians' views on Canada's place in the world. *Québécois* were more critical of the 2003 war in Iraq; 90% opposed it, and

Canada

some of the world's largest anti-war rallies had been held in Montreal. Thus, from being the most pro-American Canadians, *Québécois* have become perhaps the most skeptical of the foreign and social policies pursued by the United States—60% said their attitude toward the U.S. had become more negative in recent years, compared with just under half of Canadians as a whole. A broad dislike for President George W. Bush and the war in Iraq had much to do with this. A final reason for this unprecedented *Québécois* embrace of common Canadian values is the confidence *Québécois* now have that their language and culture are more firmly entrenched than ever before.

A third of all *Québécois* live in metropolitan Montreal, a city of over three million people and the world's third-largest French-speaking city after Paris and Kinshasa, Congo. This city dominates the economic and cultural life of Quebec. Quebec's major newspapers are published here: the one with the largest circulation is the unabashedly sensational tabloid, *Le Journal de Montreal*. *Le Devoir* is the influential French-language daily. *La Presse* occupies the middle ground between those two dailies and is the voice for Canadian unity. The *Montreal Gazette* is the major English-language daily. The newsmagazine, *L'Actualité*, the French-language sister of *Maclean's* is published in Montreal. All major Quebec political parties have their headquarters in the city, even though the provincial political capital is Quebec City.

At one time Montreal was the cultural and economic heart of Canada. Its population doubled from 1941 to 1971. Most of that growth came from the migration of unilingual Quebecers from the solidly-French countryside into this city, which offered hope for advancement and a better standard of living. Urbanization greatly changed the culture and outlook of the Quebecois and brought about a "Quiet Revolution" in the 1960s and 1970s. The influx also greatly altered the city of Montreal by bringing unilingual Quebecers to live side by side with anglophones, who dominated the city's economy. Nowhere else in the province was there such contact. Montreal became more and more French and again became the focus of Canada's most divisive debates, as it had been during the conscription controversies in both world wars.

It has experienced terrorism, so rare in Canadian-history, and serious political tension resulting from the vigorous assertion of French-language rights. An increasing number of anglophones and major corporate headquarters abandoned the city, and investments in the city dwindled. During the 1970s its economy and population declined, as Toronto overtook it as

Canada's major city. Although that economic and population decline was halted in the mid-1980s, Montreal's position as Canada's primary city was lost perhaps forever. Today it is corruption and organized crime that drive Montrealers into the suburbs and head offices elsewhere. In the six years to 2008, more than 20,000 city residents left for the suburbs.

In the 21st century Montreal has become a leading high-tech center. A 2000 PricewaterhouseCoopers study of large North American metropolitan areas ranked the city fourth in concentration of high-tech jobs on a per-capita basis. Wired magazine also singled it out as the only Canadian city on a list of 46 global high-tech hubs to watch. Bombardier Aerospace, which built the high-speed train for the Washington-Boston run in 2000 and produces rail engines and cars for the European market, is in Montreal.

ONTARIO: In the middle of the 19th century Queen Victoria located the federal capital of Ottawa on the banks of the Ottawa River, presumably because it was a safe distance from the United States (the War of 1812 was still a fresh memory) and because it was on the boundary separating English and French Canada. Today Ottawa is still Canada's most determinedly bilingual city. It is a pretty, comfortable city of only 310,000 inhabitants. However, it is surrounded by 26 communities that bring the total population to over 800,000, making Ottawa Canada's fourth largest metropolitan area. It is distinguished by its scenic drives, the Rideau Canal, its colorful downtown market district, and, of course, its stately gothic architecture which houses Parliament, the Supreme Court and other government institutions. This capital city is resplendent with pomp and pageantry, with scarlet-coated Mounties guarding Parliament Hill on horseback and Canada's Guards wearing bearskin hats, red coats and black trousers performing rituals before Parliament and the residence of the Governor-General.

Bruce Phillips, a television correspondent and former aide to the prime minister, remarked: "most people who live out-

side Ottawa see it as a place peopled with fat-cat civil servants with bulletproof jobs." Some Canadians look down on Ottawa as a boring, bureaucrats' city with little nightlife (except that which takes place in the bars and nightspots in Hull, across the river in Quebec, after Ottawans have gone to bed). A typical crack at the town was made by one of Trudeau's ministers, who contended, "the best thing about Ottawa is the train to Montreal." Some people also complain that the cultural life is not what one would expect in a federal capital. That is now changing, and, to quote Phillips again, "the city is sprouting a few cultural wings." In 2008 a *Maclean's* cover story named Ottawa Canada's "smartest city" and the fourth "most cultured" after Calgary, Victoria and Gatineau, Quebec.

Ottawa has long had a National Arts Centre near parliament, which houses a chamber orchestra, theaters and facilities for touring opera companies and shows. In 1988 a dramatic neo-Gothic glass and granite palace for the National Gallery, with a panoramic view of the city and Ottawa River, was opened. Designed by the Israeli-born Montreal architect Moshe Safdie, this gigantic magnificent edifice, which is a third larger than the National Gallery in Washington, finally relieves a major embarrassment of having a national collection of art, established in 1880, with no permanent home for it. In 1988 a new structure for the Canadian Museum of Aviation was also completed. In 1989 a Museum of Civilization opened across the river in Hull, connected to the Ottawa side and the National Gallery by a footbridge. The construction of two connecting museums in English and French Canada symbolizes the strengthening of fragile bonds that tie together Canada's two founding nations. In 2005, on the 60th anniversary of VE Day, a remarkable War Museum

Railway magnate William Van Horne points westward, Banff, Alberta

opened on the LeBreton Flats, a short distance from Parliament. Its primary architect, Raymond Moriyama, is a Japanese-Canadian who was interned in Canada during the Second World War.

The economic and cultural power of Toronto reflects the weight of Ontario within Canada. This province alone is three times as large as Japan. It occupies the entire northern shores of the Great Lakes, while eight American states are washed by their southern shores. No American state has such a commanding position within the American republic as does Ontario within the Confederation. Its predominance would be even greater if Quebec were ever to separate from Canada; Ontario would then become half of Canada, and it is uncertain whether any federal state could bear this. Because of the leading rank that Ontario has traditionally enjoyed, this province tends to be most satisfied with the status quo. Just as some Americans once believed that "what is good for General Motors is good for America," people in Ontario tend to believe that "what is good for Ontario is good for Canada."

With 11 million inhabitants, Ontario is not only the most populous province, but it is ethnically the most diverse. About 5% of its population, concentrated basically in the eastern part of the province, speaks French as a mother tongue, and in 1989 Bill 8 improved government services to Ontario's half million francophones. Non-British immigrant groups from a variety of European and Asian countries have settled here.

Greater Toronto has 5.6 million inhabitants and lively ethnic neighborhoods, restaurants and small businesses that are reminiscent of New York or Chicago a half century ago. The idea of neighborhood is strong, and in 1996 Forbes magazine rated Toronto as the best place in the world to balance work and family. Of its residents, half are immigrants, and Toronto is the favorite urban destination for newcomers to Canada. A fourth of the country's immigrants live there. A fifth of its people arrived in Canada after 1981 and a tenth after 1991. By 2007, 49% of its population had been born outside the country, the second highest figure in the world after Miami. Almost half (43%) of the overall population belongs to a visible minority. In fact, Toronto at the turn of the century was home to 42% of Canada's non-whites.

Since 1967 the largest Caribbean festival in North America, Caribana, takes place in Toronto. A tenth of the population is either Chinese or Filipino by ethnic origin. The airwaves are filled with a Babel of foreign languages; one radio station beams programs in 30 languages, while one television station shows films in many different languages.

Flatiron Building and CN Tower, Toronto, Ontario   Courtesy: Tourism Canada

The city government prints official notices in six languages, including Portuguese, Italian, Greek and Chinese. Drivers' tests are given in 12 languages. Half the children in state schools speak a native language other than English. Nevertheless, Ontario has maintained a fundamentally British air and sentiment. Its provincial flag still has a Union Jack prominently in the upper left-hand corner, and the word "Loyalist" has wholly positive connotations here.

Along with Alberta and British Columbia in the West, Ontario is one of Canada's high growth areas. Indeed, that cluster of cities around the western end of Lake Ontario extending from Niagara Falls and St. Catharines (north of Buffalo, New York) westward through Hamilton and Oshawa (the center of Canada's automotive industry) to Windsor (Detroit's twin-city) is called Canada's "golden horseshoe." While Canada's population between the 1996 and 2001 census takings grew by 4%, the population of the "golden horseshoe" had increased by 9.2%; 59% of Ontario's people and 22% of Canada's live there. Here is the center of gravity for Canadian industry, and its heart is Toronto, the country's capital of finance, culture, publishing and fashion. It is home to one out of seven Canadians, and almost 10 million

people live within 75 kilometers (50 miles) of Toronto. The city has not only been spared the mountains of litter, the hundreds of square miles of graffiti and a high crime rate, but it has remained freer of the racial tensions which have plagued some American, British, and Canadian cities.

Some observers have described Toronto as like "New York without the dirt." There has been a long-simmering feud with Michigan over the trucking of Toronto's trash to dump sites south of the border. Even presidential candidate John Kerry, fishing for votes in that important swing state, declared in 2004: "It's time to end the Canadian trash-dumping in Michigan!" He was supported by the Canadian-born governor of Michigan, Jennifer M. Granholm. The U.S. Supreme Court has repeatedly ruled that garbage is a commodity that is as subject to free trade as any other product. It also travels on a two-way street. An American company, Clean Harbors Environmental Services, operates a hazardous-waste landfill incinerator in Ontario that treats the contaminated remains primarily from U.S. auto plants around the Great Lakes. In fact, the trucks pass each other at the border.

Toronto did not have the European sophistication of Montreal or the natural beauty of Vancouver, and for a long time it was called "Hogtown." That has all changed now. Profiting from the shift of wealth from Montreal and fighting off the challenge of Calgary in the West, Toronto remains the financial heart of Canada. Its Bay Street is the equivalent of Wall Street in America, even though the Toronto Stock Exchange and most brokers and investment houses have moved to more spacious, modern quarters on other streets. Toronto is the home of the University of Toronto (Canada's largest and most renown). The headquarters of ten of the 20 leading corporations are domiciled there. The next in order are Calgary (6), Vancouver and Montreal. It is the center for hundreds of suburbs and satellite towns which are involved in a broad range of economic activities and which economically nourish and are nourished by Toronto.

Asked in a 1989 Gallup poll "which province has the greatest future?" half of Canadian respondents said Ontario. That is changing as economic and political influence is moving westward, especially toward oil-rich Alberta. A 2010 poll revealed how uncertain Ontarians have become: half believed that Ontario's influence in national affairs is declining and that the province is not treated with the respect it deserves.

Most of Canada's leading English-language publications are produced in Toronto. The Toronto Star had the country's largest circulation in 1999, with 458,000

Canada

daily and 703,400 on Sunday, as well as the largest advertising base. It also introduced a weekly section of articles from the *New York Times*, as well as a reduced version of the *Times Book Review*. Next is a tabloid, The *Toronto Sun* (daily 240,000 and Sunday 407,500). The *Globe and Mail* (ca. 250,000 daily) is owned by Canada's richest man, Ken Thomson and is one of Canada's most influential dailies. In 2010 it introduced a slightly smaller size and became the first major daily Canadian newspaper to print high-quality color on every page.

To compete with it, Conrad Black founded the somewhat rebellious *National Post* (ca. 170,000 daily), which is willing to sneer at some of Canada's traditional values. Started in 1998, the *National Post* still survives despite the determined efforts of the *Globe and Mail* to crush it. The *Post* is deeply in debt and has never made a profit. It filed for bankruptcy in October 2010, but it emerged from it and competes in the market. The *Financial Post* is the equivalent of the *Wall Street Journal* in the U.S. Other dailies in Canada are regional newspapers, with the exception of the *Ottawa Citizen*. Unlike their counterparts in the U.S., Canadian papers have largely avoided precipitous financial decline and have not been quite as overwhelmed by digital competitors.

By century's end Black already controlled more than half of Canada's dailies from his corporate headquarters in Toronto, and he was the world's third-largest newspaper publisher. But he sold most of them, including his 50% stake in the *National Post*. That left most major English-language newspapers in the hands of five TV or telecom giants. CanWest, owned by Canada's most powerful media mogul, Izzy Asper, bought the *National Post* and 135 other daily newspapers from Black for $2.2 billion. This was the largest media deal in Canadian history. University of Toronto journalism professor, Vince Carlin, asserted, "This is not a healthy situation. There is competition in the United States. There is no competition here." Nevertheless, a 2002 press study by Reporters Without Borders found that Canada ranked fifth in the world in terms of press freedom; the U.S. placed seventeenth.

Canada's second oldest magazine and most-read news magazine with three million readers, *Maclean's*, is produced in Toronto and moved in to fill the void. It emphasizes Canadian news, but it gives considerable coverage to events in the U.S. as well. Reacting to slumping sales, it overhauled its management in 2005 and became livelier and more provocative. It seeks to avoid the criticism often leveled at the Canadian press and broadcasters that they are bland and politically correct. Also published in Toronto is *Saturday Night,* a monthly that covers a multitude of subjects and is perceptive and well informed. It closely resembles *Harper's* and *Atlantic* in the United States. Finally, the women's monthly, *Chatelaine,* whose English- and French-language editions sell about 1.3 million copies, is produced in Toronto.

Toronto is filled with art galleries, museums, opera houses and more than 40 independent theater companies. It is a frequent location for first-run openings, and the Toronto Film Festival is a major event in North America. Its major league baseball team, the Blue Jays, and other athletic teams play in the SkyDome, renamed in 2005 the Rogers Centre, a 60,000-seat indoor-outdoor stadium with a unique retractable roof. By century's end, it was insolvent, but for a while it symbolized a new era of urban dynamism, as did the CN Tower, which is twice as high as the Eiffel Tower. Torontonians no longer have to say that the best thing about their town is that it is close to New York City.

PRAIRIE PROVINCES: Manitoba, Saskatchewan and Alberta could generally be described with the words "flat, prairie, wheat and petroleum." They form a region of new economic opportunity and wealth. The West is the fastest growing part of Canada. The discovery of oil and natural gas primarily in Alberta in 1947 greatly helped to diversify the prairie economy. This region always was and still is Canada's "breadbasket." Half of its area is covered by forest, but much of the other half is occupied by large farms, which are responsible for making Canada the world's second largest exporter of grain, behind the U.S.

The Prairie provinces have a very diverse ethnic mix. A resilient knot of francophones, some of them descendants of the Métis (a mixed race of French and Indian), have survived in Manitoba. Although they constitute only 6% of that province's population, they have been very successful recently in reasserting their rights to be schooled and to be spoken to in French. In this region a quarter of the population is made up of non-Anglo-Saxon immigrants from Germany, Eastern Europe, the Ukraine and Russia. Entire villages or sections of towns are inhabited by persons whose every-day language is other than English, and one sees almost as many onion-shaped domes of Russian and Greek Orthodox churches in this region as grain elevators.

This region was never a frontier area, as was the American West, because of the different ways in which the two Wests were won. The American West was won by "six-shooters" and by settlers advancing before the American flag and the forces of "law and order." The Canadian West was largely organized by Mounted Police. Settlers attracted by governmental policies and land-grants traveled to their new homesteads on transcontinental rail-ways, rather than in covered wagons.

Nevertheless, Canada's Westerners are an independent-minded people, who have a strong sense of regional identity. They long felt that Ottawa's policies favored central Canada, whether that favoritism be expressed in dictated freight rates on the railways, high interest rates set by banks headquartered in Montreal or Toronto, the high price tags on goods manufactured in the East which result from protective tariffs and federal subsidies, or attempts to force bilingualism on a people who, despite the many different languages they speak at home, wish to see English remain as Canada's only official language.

These Westerners have been confidently assertive in federal-provincial relations during the past couple of decades. In 1979, for the first time, a westerner (Joe Clark, leader of the Conservative Party) became prime minister although he remained in office less than a year. They have been inclined to form protest parties, such as the New Democratic Party (NDP), the Social Credit Party, or the Reform Party (renamed in 2000 the Canadian Alliance and in 2004 the Conservative Party, whose leader, Stephen Harper, became prime minister in February 2006). All have played very important roles in both regional and federal politics. Thus, one sees in the Prairie provinces a bastion of both conservative politics and of Canada's brand of socialism.

Since cities in the prairies were settled mainly in the 20th century, they have a slightly different appearance than those in the East. They have fewer old buildings and narrow winding streets, but newer construction and broad thoroughfares. They also are very spread out, as are many cities in the American West. Winnipeg, the capital of Manitoba, resembles Denver, although the air is noticeably cleaner. Here is Canada's commodity exchange, where buyers and sellers determine the price of grains. One can hear French spoken in the streets, especially in the suburb of St. Boniface. Also, one can visit the monu-

Vancouver, B.C.

ment to and home of Louis Riel, the leader of the French-speaking Métis. He led a rebellion against Ottawa in 1885, but is now given a hero's homage because he fought for the rights of francophones in the West.

Another major metropolis in the prairies is Calgary. Perhaps no city in Canadian history ever experienced such a boom as this city. In 1947 large reserves of oil were discovered. The Leduc oilfield was North America's largest at the time. The world energy crisis beginning in 1973 made Alberta's oil extraordinarily precious, and the entire province's economy felt the immediate benefit of swollen oil revenues. Almost overnight, Calgary became Canada's second-largest head office city, and easterners moved westward in one of the country's most massive migrations.

At one point, Calgary was growing at the astonishing rate of 2,500 newcomers a month. Americans joined this massive influx and now constitute a fifth of the city's population. Practically no new construction was necessary to accommodate the 1988 Winter Olympics in Calgary. With the recovery of Alberta's oil industry in the 1990s, prosperity returned to the city. In the twenty-first century it is a magnet for high tech companies and corporate head offices.

It has displaced Montreal and Vancouver as Canada's biggest business and financial center after Toronto. Indeed Alberta, with a population of 3.2 million, is a magnet for residents of other provinces. Some speak of "an internal brain drain to Alberta," and the vice-president of the Business Council of British Columbia noted: "It's almost as if we are creating a small version of the United States built right here into Canada."

The Calgary-Edmonton corridor has become the fasting growing economic region in Canada, boasting a per-capita GDP 40% higher than the national average. The Prairie provinces and BC have replaced Ontario as the engine of Canada's economic growth. The West's combined GDP surpassed that of Ontario for the first time in 2008. Taken together, Alberta and British Columbia now have a higher population (ca. 7.5 million) than Quebec. Statistics Canada projects that the West will have almost a third of Canada's total population by 2031. The West is younger, has more babies, attracts more migrants, is more open to change, displays a higher degree of egalitarianism and shows less deference to authority.

With the election of Albertan Stephen Harper as prime minister in January 2006, the country's political and commercial centers of gravity have shifted westward. Half of the Members of Parliament in his government are from the West. In 2008 the Conservatives took 52.5% of the votes and 75% of the seats west of Ontario. His winning strategy in the May 2011 elections was to continue the Conservative domination of the West, supported by Ontario, thereby achieving his goal of a majority government. In 11 elections since 1979, only once have western voters given the Conservatives fewer than 48% of the popular votes; usually it is more than 50%.

BRITISH COLUMBIA: This is Canada's window to the Pacific and the Far East, with which Canada maintains a growing volume of trade. In fact, the city of Vancouver, Canada's largest port, is 350 miles closer to Tokyo than to Halifax. British Columbia (or "BC," as it is called) is a third larger than Texas. It is cut off from the rest of Canada by the Rocky Mountains, whose various ranges cover most of the province, forcing three-fourths of the province's people into the southwest corner around Vancouver. Because of its isolation and great distance from the rest of Canada, British Columbia has an even more pronounced sense of regional pride than do the Prairie provinces. It shares the Canadian West's traditional distrust and hostility toward the East. It also has traditionally felt a certain kinship with the northwestern states in America, which it considered joining in the 19th century and with which it does a large volume of trade. The unnaturalness of east-west ties is felt more strongly in BC than in any other Canadian province. A cross-border alliance, called "Cascadia," encompasses an array of cooperative links between BC and the states of Washington and Oregon.

BC, with a population of 3.8 million, is a relatively prosperous province within the Canadian Confederation. It has very little arable land, but it possesses a panoply of mineral resources, almost unlimited hydroelectric power and huge forests, which provide its major product: timber. Its waters also produce a rich harvest of fish, including salmon. However, one does not see the countless quaint fishing villages along its coast, as one does in the Maritimes. The introduction of modern, long-range fishing vessels, and the existence of a few major processing and canning plants along a few rivers, especially the Fraser and the Skeena, have enabled the province's fishing industry to become centralized. BC's broad resource base has enabled the province to have considerable industrial growth and diversified production.

The capital of BC is Victoria, located on Vancouver Island. It is a city with a dis-

Canada

tinctive British air, complete with red double-decker buses and statues of the great 19th century queen for whom it was named. In 2010 *Maclean's* placed it on top of its ranking of Canada's "smartest" and most cultured cities. With only 78,000 inhabitants, it has two universities and two smaller colleges, its citizens are well-read, half its residents visit local museums, and it sustains a symphony, two ballets, an opera and a philharmonic choir.

The most important city in this province is Vancouver, which with 1.8 million residents in the metropolitan area is Canada's third largest city. It has a very mild climate, by Canadian standards, and is, without question, one of the world's most beautiful cities. It boasts a magnificent physical setting of mountains and sea, and it has a dazzling city center and Canada's first domed stadium. In 2008 Mercer's Quality of Living Survey ranked Vancouver fourth in the world (after Zurich, Vienna and Geneva) in terms of quality of life. No U.S. city was in the top 25, but Toronto, Ottawa, Montreal and Calgary joined Vancouver in that category. A 2009 examination by *Maclean's* named Vancouver the best-run city in Canada, and the Economist Intelligence Unit's business travel index placed it first in the world as a desirable business meeting location, followed by Toronto. Its image is being tarnished by rising brutal gang violence and drug and gun trade.

Vancouver is truly a world city. One fifth of its residents work for American companies. It has an ethnically diverse population, 30% of whom are immigrants and 40% of whom are of Asian origin. Half of the Asians are Chinese, giving rise

to one of the city's nicknames: Hongcouver. With only 13% of Canada's population, BC absorbs almost a fourth of all immigrants; 80% of those are Asian. Non-Whites comprised more than 40% of the city's population by 2005. It is one of the world's most integrated cities with 13% of young couples being inter-racial.

Its school system must struggle with the problem of teaching 55,900 pupils, 61% of whom speak a first language other than English. Almost half the school children in 1997 required English as a Second Language (ESL) courses. Such ESL instruction demands a growing share of shrinking education budgets. Pupils in Vancouver's Richmond School District represent 75 distinct languages and cultures. In Lord Strathcona Elementary School, 90% of the children are of Asian descent, and Chinese Cantonese interpreters must be present at PTA and parent-pupil meetings. In Grandview/ Uuqinak'uuh Elementary School, 52% of the students are First Nations (Indians), and 30% are recent immigrants or refugees.

With the Chinese community comprising a fifth of the population, Vancouver has Canada's most vibrant Chinatown, covering eight square blocks. This concentration has made the Chinese-language media—four newspapers, three radio stations and two TV stations—influential players in provincial and national politics.

All eyes were on Vancouver in February 2010 when half the world's population (3.5 billion) tuned in to some portion of the Winter Olympic Games. Canada emerged with more gold medals than any other country. These Games were a grand success by any definition.

THE NORTH: The Yukon, Northwest Territories, and Nunavut are vast, covering about 40% of Canada's land area. They are wild, cold, isolated, ruggedly beautiful and almost entirely uninhabited. Its few residents have to adjust to long, dark winters and short summers. The northern parts are Arctic regions of packed ice, frozen fjords, icebergs, countless islands and a hardy people, whom Americans call "Eskimo," meaning "meat-eaters," but who prefer to be called "Inuit," meaning "the people." About 51,000 of the world's Inuit live in Canada. Their communities tend to be located on bays, river mouths, inlets or fjords; this reflects the fact that their lives were always tied to hunting, fishing and gathering.

During the past quarter century, the isolation of the Inuit has been decreasing, and mainstream Canadian life-styles have penetrated their communities. Traditional hunting and fishing activities are not as important for their economy as they once were. The Inuit have grown dependent upon the comforts and conveniences of Canadian life: kayaks and dog sleds have by and large been replaced by canoes, motorized toboggans, snowmobiles, trucks and airplanes as their major means of transportation. Electricity, oil stoves and furnaces, schools, hospitals, films, television and radio (which beam some programs in their language—Inuktitut, which has more than 40 words for "snow") have greatly changed life in the extreme North. Unfortunately, some of these changes have so disturbed or destroyed traditional roles and ties within the communities that alcoholism, drug abuse and suicide have become frighteningly commonplace among the Inuit.

South of this Arctic area is a vast region of tundra and permafrost, covered by forests, filled with wild animals, and inhabited mainly by Indians, called aboriginals in Canada, who value their traditional identity. There are few roads and railways running northward into these areas, and the few cities there, such as Whitehorse, Yellowknife and Iqaluit, are small frontier towns, whose residents must become accustomed to paying high

Baffin Island, Nunavut, with stone marker ("Inukshuk") at left built by the Inuit
Courtesy: Michael J. Hewitt

Canada

prices and having all but air links severed during much of the bitter winter.

As a whole, the Canadian North contains important natural resources. These are not distributed evenly over the entire area. The extremely high costs of extraction and transportation, as well as the impact of mining and drilling on native cultures, greatly limits the extent to which they can be exploited. The oil and natural gas in the Arctic Sea are significant for the country's energy needs.

That this vast, sparsely populated northern expanse had to be defended necessitated close defense links with the United States. American defense planners were well aware that Canada lies directly between the U.S. and Russia. They were therefore more than willing to cooperate with the Canadians in creating NORAD and in maintaining a costly Distant Early Warning (DEW) line of radars in the Canadian North in order to be able to detect any hostile penetration of North American airspace. The shortest distance between U.S.-based missiles and the strategic cities of the former Soviet Union—and vice-versa—was via Canada over the North Pole. This route is only 3,600 miles versus 8,000–10,000 miles parallel to the Equator.

To ensure that Arctic concerns are given a higher priority, the Chrétien government appointed the first aboriginal ambassador of Circumpolar Affairs, Mary May Simon, a longtime Inuit activist, to spearhead federal efforts to protect Arctic ecology. In 1996 an eight-nation Arctic Council was created, consisting of Canada, the United States, Russia, Denmark (Greenland), Finland, Iceland, Norway and Sweden. In addition, full membership in the council with the same status of sovereign states has been granted to the Inuit Circumpolar Conference (ICC), a non-governmental group that draws together Inuit representatives from Alaska, Greenland, Canada and Russia every three years to develop common policies. In 1989 it agreed to develop a standardized script. In April 2009 the ICC declared "sovereignty" over the Arctic's natural resources.

The ICC has become a vigorous lobby and has resisted efforts by the U.S., Russia, Norway and environmental groups to declare the polar bear an endangered species. It argues that this would hurt the local economies by, among other things, deterring American hunters from paying millions of dollars a year for the right to shoot them. The killing continues in Canada and Greenland. Two-thirds of the world's estimated 25,000 polar bears roam the Canadian Arctic.

The Arctic Council also includes the Sami Council (representing Scandinavian aboriginals), the Association of Indigenous Peoples of the North of Russia, and

Population Density

☐ Less than 6 people per square mile
▨ 6-45 people per square mile
■ Over 45 people per square mile

the Aleuts on the islands between Alaska and Russia. The first foreign ministers' meeting of the members was held in Nunavut's capital, Iqaluit, in 1998. Canada is implementing its goal of a "Northern dimension" to Canadian foreign policy that strives to gain input from the peoples of the North rather than imposing "southern" values on them. Simon noted, "Northerners are really the pioneers of circumpolar cooperation."

PEOPLE

Unlike the United States, Canada is often described as a "mosaic," rather than a "melting pot." In many ways, this is accurate. In Canada there are many population groups which speak different languages or which are ethnically distinct from one another. Many vigorously resist assimilation with other Canadians; they are less inclined to lose their former identity in a larger "Canadianism," than have been most ethnic groups in the United States. The Canadian government recognizes this diversity by having an official policy of multiculturalism administered by a minister of state with cabinet rank.

Given the specific conditions of the country, this is an enlightened approach. It should be recognized, though, that this policy makes a virtue out of a necessity. Few British Canadians in the 18th and

early 19th centuries foresaw that French Canadians would struggle so successfully against assimilation and that one day ambitious anglophone children would be flocking to French-immersion schools in order to get a leg up on those who cannot speak French. Multiculturalism in Canada grew out of the need to conciliate francophones and has been broadened to include other ethnic groups as well. Many francophones were uneasy about such broadening because it seemed to undercut their view of Canada as a union of *two* peoples, rather than as a collection of ethnic minorities in which francophones are merely one of many. Yet it was Quebec nationalism that necessitated the official policy of multiculturalism, which is of such benefit to other minorities as well.

Some Canadians need reminders that Canada is multicultural and multilingual whether they like it or not. When in 1983 the unilingual John Crosbie challenged the completely bilingual Brian Mulroney and Joe Clark for leadership of the Conservative Party, he declared that Canada's 3.7 million bilingual Canadians should not regard themselves as "some sort of aristocracy" from which the country's prime ministers would be drawn. The fact is, though, that no unilingual Canadian does have the chance to become prime minister any more. Crosbie's unfortunate utterance completely destroyed his bid for leadership; Canada never was, is not and

Canada

Chinese-Canadians in Vancouver

will not become a homogeneous, wholly English-speaking country.

Of course, terms like "mosaic" and "melting-pot" are over-simplifications in the case of both neighbors, even though they are not "myths," as some persons claim. Some suggest that Canada is really a "mosaic of mosaics." The goal has never been to transform Canada into a land of isolated communities, but to accommodate cultural differences in a way that newcomers can be integrated into a shared civic space.

Since the 1960s many countries have experienced ethnic revivals, including the United States. The number of black, brown and yellow faces, "hyphenated Americans," bilingual schools and Spanish-language documents and signs reveal the limits of cultural and ethnic assimilation in the United States. American blacks have successfully demanded *group* rights for people of their race, as opposed to the traditional American emphasis on *individual* rights, which has been an American creed since the country's founding. Thus, the United States has also moved in the direction of a "mosaic" society.

Any implication that each "stone" in the Canadian "mosaic" shares equally in the overall product is misleading. To use Orwellian language, some Canadians "are more equal than others." A Canadian's race, language and/or ethnic background are still socially relevant. For instance, only slightly over 3% of all Canadian marriages and common-law unions are mixed race, and most of them are likely to be between Asian-Canadians and Caucasians.

Political, economic and social power is still held by people of European heritage. For example, of the 200 top corporate chief executives surveyed by the *Financial Post* in 1997, only seven were non-white, and they were all Asian.

Nevertheless, there is something remarkable about the way the parts stick together. Former Saskatchewan Premier Roy Romanow described it this way: "Each province, territory and region, plus our many cultures and different stories, can be likened to individual pearls making up a beautiful necklace, connected to each other by the strand of shared destiny. That strand, however, is fragile and requires constant attention."

Population Groups

The largest and historically most privileged "stone" in the "mosaic" is the British one. By the mid-1980s Canadians of British ancestry made up a little more than 40% of the total population, a proportion which has steadily decreased over the years, even though 76% of all Canadians claimed in the 1981 census to have at least one British ancestor. By 1997 the UK had fallen to tenth place as a source country for Canadian immigrants. Of course, this grouping is not as homogeneous as it might seem at first glance: it includes Scots and Welsh, who are not English, and it encompasses Irish Protestants from Ulster and Catholics from the rest of Ireland, groups which are by no means interchangeable.

The second largest "stone" is the French one, which makes up 22.9% of the total population (2001) and is declining. The French were the first Canadians, and they now constitute the overwhelming majority of Quebec's population, about 40% of New Brunswick's, 6% of Ontario's, and 6% of Manitoba's. Because of Quebec nationalism since the 1960s and the federal government's response to it, francophones' opportunities within the entire Canadian Confederation have been markedly improved. Because its oil-based economy attracts immigrants from all over Canada, Alberta is experiencing the country's greatest growth in francophone population—12.6% each year. It is the only province since 1996 to experience an increase in francophone children under age 5.

The third largest group of Canadians is of German ancestry, constituting 3.3% of the total. This group is perhaps the most fully assimilated minority in all of Canada, although there is a notable exception to this generalization: the Hutterites in the Prairie provinces, who came to Canada from South Dakota during the First World War because of their refusal to serve in the armed forces. They are a religious sect similar to the Amish and Mennonites, except that they believe in the communal

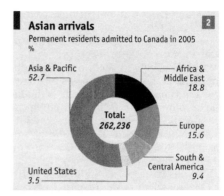

Asian arrivals
Permanent residents admitted to Canada in 2005 %

Asia & Pacific 52.7
Africa & Middle East 18.8
Europe 15.6
South & Central America 9.4
United States 3.5

Total: 262,236

Source: *The Economist*

ownership of property and rearing of children. They shun contact with the outside world as much as possible. Then come Italians, who make up 2.8% of the population and whose numbers have grown enormously since the Second World War. One Canadian citizen, Gino Bucchino, even won a seat in the Italian parliament in 2006.

In fifth place are Ukrainians, who make up 1.5% of all Canadians. Canada has the world's third-largest Ukrainian population after Ukraine itself and Russia. During the First World War about 5,000 Ukrainian Canadians were interned in a fit of ethnic fear, their property was confiscated, and many were forced to perform hard labor. Former Prime Minister Paul Martin acknowledged that this was "a dark day in Canadian history" and offered both a formal apology and $25 million to Ukrainians and other groups for educational exhibits and memorials. Roy Romanow, whose father left Ukraine in the 1920s, remembered growing up in Saskatoon: "Our family's universe was comprised of the Ukrainian hall, St. George's Ukrainian Greek Catholic Cathedral, our schools, and the shopping area of 20th Street just a few blocks away. We could go to church, visit friends and neighbours and buy our necessities without using either one of Canada's two official languages." The same was true of many other immigrants, including Icelanders, whose descendants in Canada outnumber the population of Iceland itself. The largest congregation of Finns outside of Scandinavia live in Canada, especially in Thunder Bay, Ontario.

Canada was always a land of immigration. Today there are over 200 immigrant groups there, and a fifth of Canadians were born outside the country; the figure is 12.2% in the U.S. and 4.8% in the United Kingdom. Forty members of the 2006 parliament were born outside Canada. The 2001 census confirmed that Canada now has the highest proportion of foreign-born persons since 1931. Immigrants, only 44% of whom come with the ability to speak English or French, were responsible for the 4% growth of the Canadian population between 1996 and 2002. Nevertheless, Canada's population is aging: 37% are over 45, increasing to 43% in 2011. By 2016 all of Canada's labor growth will have to come from outside the country.

An important demographic trend in Canada is the decreasing percentage of citizens of European heritage, from 79.7% in 1971 to only 66.9% in 1981. The reason for this is a decreasing birth rate (1.66 children per woman in 2011) and a change in the composition of immigrants to Canada. In the 1960s the Canadian Parliament liberalized the country's immigration policy, opening the door to Asians, Africans, Caribbean islanders, Latin Americans and other groups from the third world, which make up more than three-fourths of all immigration to Canada. Their percentages of Canada's total population changed noticeably from 1971 to 1981: Asians grew from 4.2% to 14%. In 2006 Asia accounted for 52.7% of new arrivals, while 15.6% were from Europe, 18.8% from Africa and the Middle East, 9.4% from Latin America and the Caribbean, and only 3.5% from the U.S. Those coming from the Caribbean have fallen sharply.

The top countries of origin for immigrants today are China, India, the Philippines and Pakistan. China and India alone account for 60,000 per year. They bring with them much university education and potential for high-paid occupations.

By 1996 the number of European immigrants had for the first time fallen below 50% of the total immigrant population. The magnets are Toronto (49% immigrant in 2007), Vancouver (17.7%) and Montreal (11.8%), making these three metropolitan areas increasingly distinct from the rest of Canada. Only 6% of newcomers chose to live outside major urban areas, and Canada's immigration policy seeks to attract young, large foreign families to rural Canada. Toronto is now home to 62 different ethnic groups numbering more than 10,000 people and 15 groups with more than 100,000. Geography professor Larry S. Bourne of the University of Toronto admits: "We just don't know how a Toronto of the future, which is 60 percent nonwhite with 110 different ethnic groups and languages, is going to relate to the rest of Canada."

The first Chinese came to Canada in 1858 to work as laborers in the gold mines that had begun to be opened during the Fraser River gold rush. From 1881 to 1884 they were used as laborers to construct the Canadian Pacific Railway. Many died doing their dangerous work, and from 1923 to 1947 they were banned from entry altogether. By 2004 they constituted 16% of Canada's immigrants and more than 3% of the total population (1.1 million). China is now Canada's largest source of immi-

grants, followed by India. Chinese wield considerable political and economic influence, and they form a crucial link in the country's growing trade with China. Acceding to a long-standing demand in 2006, the Canadian government offered both an apology and compensation for their past mistreatment.

Thousands of Japanese also immigrated, and during the Second World War they were suspected of disloyalty and received the same undignified treatment as Japanese-Americans: the 22,000 Japanese-Canadians, 17,000 of whom had Canadian citizenship, were forced to resettle in internment camps deep in the interior of the country, "to safeguard the defences of the Pacific coast of Canada." Their property was disposed in an attempt to prevent them from returning.

Most Canadians today regret that action, which Brian Mulroney called "one of the greatest blots on civil liberties ever inflicted on citizens of this country," and in 1988 the government agreed to pay about $291 million in compensation. From 1933 to 1945 Canada accepted only 5,000 Jewish refugees from Nazi Germany, compared with 200,000 by the U.S. and 15,000 by Bolivia.

Asians poured in from war-torn Indochina, including thousands of "boat-people" from Vietnam. At the end of the 1990s an organized attempt to smuggle Chinese into the country sparked angry

Canada

Miss Universe Natalie Glebova

demands for tighter controls. Chinese-based gangs receive down payments of up to $60,000 to drop Chinese onto Canada's shores. They are moved through an underground network to eastern Canada or the United States, where they are forced to work off their debts through low-paying jobs or prostitution. Canada's large Chinese community denounces these illegal Chinese as queue-jumpers.

In the past, Canadians have viewed each successive wave of immigration with suspicion; however, the fact that most newcomers are now non-white makes their reception even frostier. Pollster Allan Gregg noted, "you do not have to scratch too deep to find racist views." Despite Canadians' growing uneasiness about the goal of a "cultural mosaic," Ottawa passed a multiculturalism act in 1988 making Canada "in essence a microcosm of the world." Officials talk about Canada as a "community of communities," and the government provides more money to ethnic societies than it spends to encourage immigrants to become Canadians.

Polls in 1994 indicated that 72% of Canadian respondents believed at that time that the multicultural mosaic was not working and should be replaced by an American-style cultural melting pot, which insists that immigrants put their ethnic differences aside and embrace American values and customs. Some Canadians fear that the waves of newcomers will alter their way of life.

An example of this attitudinal change was the outcry against the decision to permit male Sikhs, who are required to wear turbans, to continue wearing them after becoming Mounties, as Sikhs were already allowed to do in the Canadian armed forces, unless safety is an issue. In 2006 the Supreme Court of Canada struck down the Montreal school board's ban on Sikh ceremonial daggers (kirpans), citing freedom

of religion. It did allow the boards to restrict the size of such daggers and require that they be sheathed and out of sight.

In 2007 a debate broke out in Quebec over the issue: how specific are Canadians willing to be in giving advice and setting rules and guidelines concerning how immigrants should live? Some Canadians argue that one should be able to expect "reasonable accommodation" of newcomers, especially Muslims, in adapting to the language, attitudes and lifestyles of the majority population. A 2007 SES poll found that a mere 18% of Canadians thought "it is reasonable to accommodate religious and cultural minorities," whereas 53% believed immigrants should "adapt fully to culture in Canada." A further 37% thought there should be no accommodation at all in schools and hospitals, and 45% believed the same about the work place. There were geographic differences: 77% of Quebecers thought that immigrants should fully adapt, compared with 49% in Ontario. These results were confirmed two years later, in 2009, when 62% of Canadians believed that laws and norms should not be modified to accommodate minorities (74% in Quebec). The Quebec government sponsored a long series of sometimes inflammatory public hearings on the subject and concluded that conflicts between lifelong *Québécois* and immigrants are rare, even if highly publicized in the media. Nevertheless, in 2010 the Quebec government passed legislation requiring woman to take off their veils and show their faces when receiving government services. Bill 94 was the first legislation in North America to ban face coverings in any government building, including schools and universities. A poll revealed that 95% of Quebecois and three-fourths of non-Quebecers approved of the law. Support for accommodation was highest in the Atlantic provinces, the Prairies and Alberta.

There are some doubts as to whether the traditional pattern of assimilation works any more. In the past, immigrants tended to congregate in enclaves, and then their children and grandchildren mastered English or French, moved out and integrated with Canadians. That does not always work these days. Incomes and employment rates are lower for immigrant families, and offspring of visible minorities reportedly tend to feel less Canadian and experience more racism than their parents.

The numbers of immigrants allowed to enter Canada each year has risen from 84,000 in 1985 to a quarter of a million today. More than half are skilled workers and their dependents picked for their potential contribution to the economy. Family reunification accounts for 28% of immigrants (compared with almost two-thirds in the U.S.). The country now takes in .8% of its

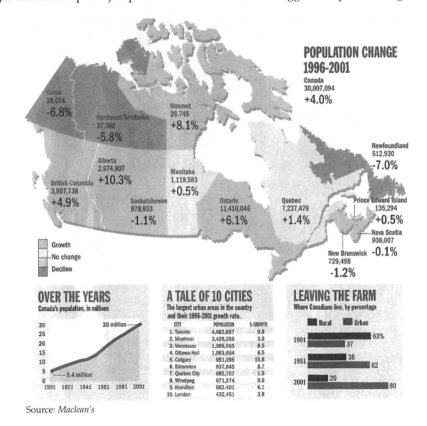

Source: *Maclean's*

population in new immigrants every year (compared to .6% for Australia and fewer for the U.S.), and most of them head for the three largest cities: Toronto, Vancouver and Montreal. Most learn a good deal about Canadian history, politics, culture and geography. This was tested in 2009 by the Dominion Institute: given a mock examination that mirrored the citizenship test, 70% of immigrants passed it, but only 40% of Canadians were able to do so. Asked what Canada's defining symbols were, both immigrants and Canadians ranked the maple leaf and hockey at the top.

A majority of immigrants now admitted are members of visible minorities, particularly Asians, Arabs and blacks. They join the 13.4% of Canada's population that, according to the 2001 census, were visible minorities. This varied from 21.6% in BC, 19.1% in Ontario (where some communities, such as Markham, had as many as 53%) and 11.2% in Alberta to only 7% in Quebec, .9% in PEI and .8% in Newfoundland.

Fears and intolerance prompted the Canadian government to admit fewer ref-

ugees, order more foreigners to leave, make generous welfare and health services less available to refugee-applicants, levy a $360 fee on such applicants and a $975 landing fee for other immigrants, and impose stiff penalties on airlines that bring passengers to Canada with false or incomplete documentation. The government ordered that greater priority be given to immigrants with high job skills and competence in English or French than to those joining families.

In 2002 a point system was introduced that assigned points for such things as years in school, numbers of university degrees, age, working experience and language skills. This created problems since foreigners with trade skills needed in the labor market often do not qualify. This made certain labor shortages even worse and sparked discussion on how to made immigration reflect the country's new economic and demographic needs. Also some who get in through the point system have difficulties applying their education due to discrimination, language handicaps or

**National Chief Phil Fontaine
Assembly of First Nations**

the problem of having their credentials recognized.

One category that fell through the cracks was exotic dancers from Eastern Europe, especially Romania. Because of their high education and minimal demands for public services, 552 Romanian strippers (out of 661 nude dancers) were selected to receive work permits. This ended when it came to light that Immigration Minister Judy Sgro had given preferential visa treatment to one of them who did volunteer work in her reelection campaign. Critics cried that the program had turned Canada into a pimp, and immigration officials were ordered to stop spending tax dollars to justify a labor shortfall of exotic dancers. She also allegedly offered a visa to a person who was a donor to her Liberal Party, a charge she denied. Sgro was forced to resign in 2005 but was soon exonerated. Canada offers visa-free travel to more than 50 countries (but not Mexico) compared with the U.S. list of just 35 countries.

A stunning and successful immigrant is Natalie Glebova. As a shy 12-year old who got off the plane from Russia in 1994 speaking only a few words of English, she settled with her family in Toronto and graduated in IT from Ryerson University. In 2005 she was crowned Miss Universe. She is the second Canadian to wear that crown after Karen Baldwin in 1982.

The July 2006 war in Lebanon prompted a lively discussion over what it means to be a citizen and what responsibilities Canada has toward its dual citizens living abroad; 15,000 Canadian passport holders were evacuated from that war-torn country to safety at a cost to the Canadian taxpayer of almost $100 million. How is it that 50,000 "Canadians" lived in Lebanon? They constitute about 1.3% of the total population and more citizens than the

Indians in ceremonial dress, Calgary, Alberta

Canada

An Eastern Orthodox church, Thunder Bay, Ontario

U.S., Britain and Germany combined have living there.

Canada permits dual citizenship since 1977. Among the best known dual citizens is former Governor General Michaëlle Jean (Haitian). All that is required to get a Canadian passport is three-years of residency. Many then leave the country and become what critics call "Canadians of convenience," with no ties to the country except an additional passport. Indeed, 40% of the Chinese who went to Canada in their working years during the late 1990s left the country for higher-paying jobs in Hong Kong or the U.S. Many Indo-Canadians also moved on. As many as half the Canadians who move to the U.S. are born outside of Canada.

They can vote in overseas elections, as well as in Canadian. Unlike American citizens, Canadians are not required to pay Canadian taxes no matter where they live. Therefore, Ottawa has no idea how many dual citizens live abroad, or even inside of Canada. The Asia Pacific Foundation of Canada calculates that there are 2.7 million overseas passport holders, roughly 9% of the population. That would represent proportionally the world's fourth-largest Diaspora, and it includes some of Asia's wealthiest people. An estimated quarter of a million reside in Hong Kong alone. Close to a million live in the U.S.

In 1986 the UN High Commission for Refugees awarded Canada its prestigious Nansen Medal; this was the first time the prize had ever been awarded to an entire nation. But Canada faces a tormenting dilemma about what kind of help it can offer to the world's 21.5 million political refugees and who precisely is a "political refugee." The backlog of individual applicants for visas, the increase in the number of refugees around the globe, and the

tighter immigration controls in other nations all contributed to an illegal stampede to Canada.

Every year about 25,000 persons claim refugee status in Canada. Once the claim is made, the newcomers are entitled to all the legal rights and benefits of Canadian citizens. They are allowed to work for at least four years and receive free medical care and social assistance for years while their cases are processed and appealed. As in the U.S., more than half of refugee claims are approved, compared with only about 15% in most countries. Even if they are ultimately rejected, they have a good prospect of never being removed. In 2007 there was a backlog of about 50,000 unexecuted deportation orders. All Canadians agree that they need an orderly and selective infusion of immigrants in order to keep their country strong and healthy. But critics are divided over whether too many or too few illegal newcomers are being permitted to stay. Many Canadians think

that the country's present immigration system is unable to handle the problem.

Attitudes hardened after the September 11, 2001, terrorist attacks in New York and Washington. They destroyed the prior assumption that all newcomers to Canada shared its fundamental values. Ottawa expanded police powers and the use of preventive arrests to deal with immigrants or refugees who might be involved in terrorist activities. These measures especially worry Canada's diverse population of more than 600,000 Muslims (about 2% of the population) from dozens of nationalities, upwards to 44 different ethnicities, and many different languages, cultures, economic and political backgrounds. Roughly half were born in Canada. Of those born abroad, about a third is Arab-Muslim, and another third is from Pakistan and India. More than 148,000 speak Arabic as their mother tongue.

One third of Canada's Muslims said in 2004 that their lives had changed for the worse after September 11, while 22% thought their lives had changed for the better because they now have the opportunity for greater dialogue and debate. An opinion survey in April 2009 revealed that 45% of Canadians believed that mainstream Islam encourages violence. B'nai Brith Canada reported that an unfortunate consequence of the post-September 11 tension was an increase in anti-Semitic violence usually involving young Arab and Muslim men.

In 2011 voters in Calgary elected Naheed Nenshi, a visible-minority Muslim academic as the first Muslim mayor of a major Canadian city. The son of immigrants, he won a scholarship to do graduate study at Harvard after graduating from the University of Calgary. This city's dynamic economy and cosmopolitan character have attracted more immigrants per capita than Montreal; one out of four inhabitants is a visible minority.

Rural Nova Scotia

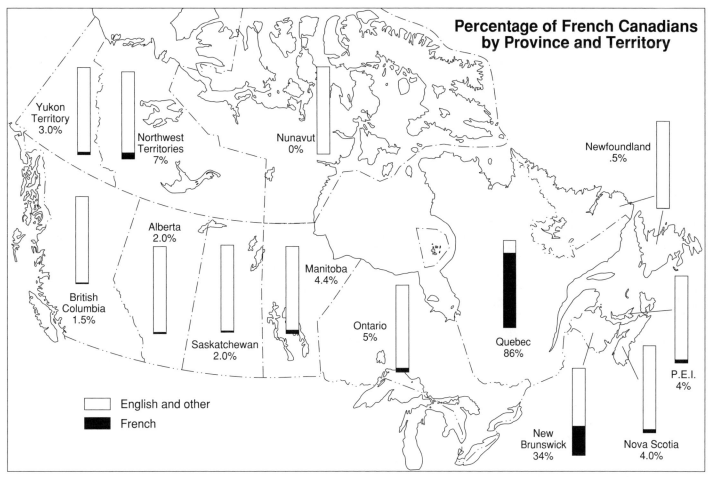

Percentage of French Canadians by Province and Territory

Yukon Territory 3.0%

Northwest Territories 7%

Nunavut 0%

Newfoundland .5%

Alberta 2.0%

Manitoba 4.4%

British Columbia 1.5%

Saskatchewan 2.0%

Ontario 5%

Quebec 86%

P.E.I. 4%

New Brunswick 34%

Nova Scotia 4.0%

☐ English and other
■ French

Hate crimes are also rising against Muslims, even at universities. Sometimes compromises would lessen tensions. An example was the request by Muslim art students at the University of Western Ontario to be given an alternate assignment instead of having to sketch nude models. The university rejected this. At the same time, more than 80% of respondents in a 2007 CBC poll of the Muslim community said they are broadly satisfied with their lives in Canada; 73% were "very proud" to be Canadian, and only 17% sensed that Canadians were hostile to Islam. In another poll, a mere 6% of Canadians claimed to be uneasy about the idea of a Muslim living next door. Rapid change is often most difficult to absorb. From 1991 to 2001 Canada's Muslim population doubled. This makes Islam the country's fifth largest religion and the second largest in every big city except Vancouver.

One immigrant group that is shrinking in Canada is Americans; from 1971 to 1981 their percentage of the Canadian population dropped from 9.3% to 8.06%. Canada's immigration laws make it more difficult to enter. In the 1980s two times more Canadians moved to the U.S. than *vice versa*. Nevertheless, Canada remains the favorite destination for American expatriates, followed

by Mexico and Britain. In 2006 the number of Americans settling in Canada—11,000— hit a 30-year high; this was a 20% increase over 2005. Their challenges in adjusting were such that the first American ex-pat support group was formed in Vancouver. The 60 or so regular members not only socialize with each other but discuss Canadian pet peeves, such as Americans' habits of talking loudly and neglecting to take off their shoes when entering a Canadian's house.

A visible portion of those former Americans is black. While it is true that the Underground Railway before the American Civil War extended all the way into Canada and that abolitionism was strong in Canada during the first half of the 19th century, slavery did exist there for more than 200 years. It had been introduced in New France in 1628 and was not abolished until the British Emancipation Act of 1833.

Even after emancipation, blacks in Canada continued to suffer discrimination and tended to be confined to all-black ghettos in the larger cities. Further black immigration from the United States was never officially barred, but blacks were normally prevented from crossing the border on all kinds of specious grounds, such as disease or inability to withstand Can-

ada's harsh climate. Discrimination has declined now, but it still exists in employment and housing, and racial prejudice has not been purged from Canadian social life. Festering racial tension in Montreal, Halifax and Toronto confirm that. Of course, not all Canadian blacks, who make up 4% of the population, are from the United States. Many have poured in from Africa, the U.K., and the Caribbean. Some, such as Haitians, do not speak English, and those who settled in Montreal have had difficulties in becoming equal citizens in Quebec society. Such diversity has meant that blacks remain the least cohesive of Canada's minority groups; they form distinct communities whose members arrived at different times.

Individuals can rise to prominence. Leading examples are Ontario's ex-Lieutenant General, Lincoln Alexander, son of Caribbean immigrants, and Governor General Jean. The stunning world record in the 100-yard dash set by Ben Johnson in 1987 focused attention on Canadian blacks. An immigrant from Jamaica, he especially did Canadians' hearts good by beating the brash, flag waving American, Carl Lewis, whose cocky manner epitomized that which irks many Canadians about Americans. However, Olympic gold turned to

Canada

dust when a urine test following his 1988 victory revealed that the now-disgraced Johnson had used performance-enhancing steroids. The 1996 Olympic Games produced a new hero: Donovan Bailey, who won the 100-meter sprint without the aid of drugs. He did manage to ignite a national furor when he said to a *Sports Illustrated* interviewer that Canada is as racist as the U.S.

Aboriginal Peoples

One minority of particular importance to Canadians and their governments is the native Inuit and Indian population, which constitute only 1.5 million (about 4.8%) of all Canadians. No one questions the fact that they were the first humans to settle what is now Canada, having migrated at least 12,000 years ago over the Bering Strait, a narrow stretch of water, about 50 miles wide, separating Siberia from Alaska. The Inuit remained in the Arctic North, while other tribes moved southward to the more temperate climate. Anthropologists still do not agree upon exactly when they came and how they crossed the Bering Strait, nor can they find any lingual connection between the 58 Indian languages and dialects spoken in Canada and languages spoken in Asia today.

When the first Europeans began to settle Canada in the 16th century, there were already an estimated 200,000 Indians and a few thousand Inuit living rather evenly distributed there. Culturally none had advanced beyond the stone-age. Most sustained themselves by hunting and fishing, but a few tribes, such as the Iroquois, had begun to establish semi-permanent settlements and had begun to derive a part of their livelihood from agriculture. They were indispensable to the first Europeans, teaching them how to survive in the rugged and cold North American setting.

There are about 553,000 "Status Indians" (also called "First Nations people") registered under the Indian Act of Canada. They belong to 609 different bands (tribes, averaging 650 persons, with the largest numbering 18,600—the Six Nations of the Grand River in Ontario), and about 326,000 of them live on 2,300 reservations, which are largely self-governing. Ontario has the largest native population, and BC has the greatest number of bands—197. There are also about 405,000 "Non-Status Indians," who do not enjoy special benefits. Many women married non-Indians, and other Indians gave up their status as Indians. Of registered Indians living off reservations who have children, 70% have their kids with non-status partners thereby relinquishing their registration entitlements.

The Canadian government's policy since 1970 of encouraging Indians to assimilate

with Canadian society has led to no dramatic changes. Since the birth rate on reservations is about the same as the number of Indians who leave, the reservations' populations are remaining stable. Forty-four percent of natives live in cities. Because of their high birth rate (twice the national average), aboriginals are Canada's youngest and fastest-growing ethnic group and are expected to increase by 25% before 2020. In 2002 nearly two-thirds were younger than 35, and half were under 25.

By 2004 one in four schoolchildren in Manitoba and Saskatchewan were aboriginal. The high school graduation rate for aboriginals was almost half that of non-natives. Compared with the national average in 2004, aboriginals on reservations have only half the national average income, a lower life expectancy (68 years vs. 75 for men, 75 vs. 81 for women), and greater dependence upon social assistance; 40% are on welfare. Canada as a whole is always ranked toward the top of the UN's annual Human Development Index, but its aboriginals alone would rank only 63rd. Nevertheless, comparisons of the 1981 and 2001 census figures show that there has been some improvement in the social conditions of urbanized aboriginals. More attend and graduate from institutions of higher learning, more are employed, and fewer depend on welfare assistance. From a half to two-thirds of aboriginal youths age 15 to 24 attended school in 2001, as opposed to only a third to a half two decades earlier.

Not only do Indians occupy huge tracts of Canadian territory, but they have a wide variety of special relations, both by treaty and by legislation, with the rest of Canada. About half the registered Indians, mainly those living in the three Prairie provinces and Ontario, receive treaty payments as a result of prior agreements with the British Crown. Still, the Canadian government continues to face difficult challenges from Indian and Métis (French-Indian) groups stemming from unsettled claims, the problems of defining who should be considered as a registered Indian, and what precisely the natives' rights should be. So controversial are some of these questions that Canadians were not yet prepared in 1982 to spell out native rights in their new constitution.

Native frustration exploded in 1990, only weeks after the rancorous Meech Lake debate designating Quebec as a "distinct society" had already laid bare the inter-communal fractures in Canadian society. It had failed to be ratified because a Cree Indian representative in Manitoba's legislative assembly, Elijah Harper, had single-handedly prevented that body from voting for it because it ignored native rights.

In Oka, Quebec, located 18 miles west of Montreal, Mohawk Indians from the nearby Kanesatake reserve, joined by warriors from the United States, protested a proposed expansion of a local golf course into what they claimed was their ancestral land. Ottawa agreed to buy the land and turn it over to the Mohawks, but militants seized upon the situation to publicize wider native grievances, including demands for sovereignty. Mulroney categorically stated that "native self-government does not now, and cannot ever, mean sovereign independence."

A fatal clash on July 11, 1990, was tinder for a massive escalation, as the violence moved to Montreal, where Mohawks blocked the Mercier Bridge, one of the main arteries connecting the island of Montreal with the southern shore of the St. Lawrence, creating immense inconveniences for commuters. All over Canada, Indians showed their support by mounting demonstrations and blockades of roads and rail lines. The Quebec police were unable to control the violence, and the provincial government requested Ottawa to send troops to quell the uprising. After 90 days of skirmishes and negotiations, the Indians surrendered, leaving Canadians perplexed about how to deal with the dilemma of native claims to more than half of Canada's land.

After that standoff, the Quebec police, RCMP and politicians stayed out of the Kanesatake community of 2,000 Mohawks, located at the far edge of northwest Montreal. This left a void that, according to elected Grand Chief James Gabriel, was filled by three dozen or so organized criminals, who traffic in cigarettes, alcohol, drugs, weapons and illegal immigrants. Mohawks do not regard themselves as Canadian. In 2010 they evicted 25 non-natives from their reserve just south of Montreal. First Nations have the right to determine who can live on their reserves.

Natives demand respect in symbolic ways as well. They blocked the naming of a road in Whitehorse, Yukon, after the author Jack London, who had once traveled in the territory. He was charged with having written insulting observations about aboriginals and having advocated white supremacy, charges that some literary experts dispute. In 2006 violence again erupted, this time in Caledonia, 80 km (50 miles) southwest of Toronto. When a new housing development broke ground on land claimed by the Six Nations Iroquois Confederacy, aboriginals occupied the site.

As a whole, Indians and the estimated 153,000 surviving Métis are among Canada's poorest citizens despite various forms of state assistance. They are plagued by unemployment, and many live on welfare. Their alcoholism rate is 13 times that among whites, their life expectancy is eight years less, infant mortality is twice as high, and their suicide rate is three times higher (five times among youth). Aboriginals account for as much as 8% of HIV infection, a higher percentage than any other ethnic group. About a quarter of new cases involve the native population. One reason is the large numbers of young Aboriginals who travel from inner cities to rural communities and reservations carrying infections back and forth. They are also disproportionately represented in prisons, a known breeding ground for disease. Only half of all Métis reach the ninth grade in school. Métis males are eight times more likely to be jailed than non-Métis. Winnipeg's growing problem of gang violence stems largely from Métis and native youths.

In 1992, a breakthrough occurred in native (called "aboriginal") standing. Aboriginals were admitted to the negotiating table to work out a new constitution and were granted the "inherent right of self-government." The Canadian government is attempting to settle the hundreds of land claims made by native groups. It spends C$9 billion each year on aboriginal programs. But the problems are mind-boggling. The 553,000 status Indians and 51,000 Inuit have different demands than the half million Métis and non-status Indians, who have no land base and often live in inner-city poverty.

The Assembly of First Nations (AFN), led from 2000–03 by Matthew Coon Come, an outspoken and savvy former grand chief of the Quebec Cree, is divided between moderates and radicals. They disagree on how to respond to settlement offers, and native groups' land claims often overlap each other. Come is known for his fierce and successful battle to rescue Cree lands from a large Hydro Quebec project. He canoed with a group of Cree and Inuit to New York City to denounce it and thereby eventually helped to thwart the $13-billion Great Whale undertaking. A product of residential schools for aboriginals and McGill Law School, he is not a man given to quiet diplomacy, as was his predecessor and successor, Phil Fontaine, who was reelected National Chief in 2003.

Self-government is difficult to define, especially before the thorny issue of boundaries is settled. Native leaders demand that aboriginals live only under their own laws, but this would create a patchwork of differing legal zones across Canada. Finally, women in the male-dominated bands might have fewer rights than those guaranteed them by the Charter of Rights and Freedoms.

In 1997, the Canadian Supreme Court ruled that native people can have clear, definable title to their land based on their oral histories and that governments have

a moral duty to negotiate with them. This ruling has profound ramifications, especially in British Columbia, where most native groups have never signed land treaties and where more than 230 of them are pursuing land claims that cover the entire province.

On January 7, 1998, the Canadian government apologized to all aboriginal peoples for decades of mistreatment. The "Statement of Reconciliation" dealt with an array of offenses, including the hanging of Métis leader Louis Riel in 1885. Finally, the statement was linked to a federal initiative called "Gathering Strength" to work with the provinces, territories and aboriginal groups to give native peoples more control over their land, government, and economic development. Hundreds of land claims throughout the country are being negotiated. The federal government claimed in 2007 that there were 790 outstanding claims, but the AFN said the number is 1,100. Around eight are settled every year.

The "Statement of Reconciliation" included earlier policies that had sought to stamp out native culture through "aggressive assimilation" by confining Indian children to government schools. Beginning in 1920 attendance at such schools was mandatory for Indian children between ages 7 and 16. About 150,000 were forced to do so. Most were closed by the mid-1970s, and the last one shut its doors in 1996. They were secluded from their families and forbidden from speaking their own languages. About 100,000 native children also were separated from their parents to attend a hundred or so residential schools operated by the major Christian churches all over Canada from the 1880s to 1996; 60% were run by Catholic orders. The children were often poorly fed and clothed, compelled to work long

hours, whipped if they spoke their native languages, and sometimes subjected to physical or sexual abuse. The national chief of the Assembly of First Nations, Phil Fontaine, claims that he had suffered sexual mistreatment.

A royal commission documented these offenses in 1996, and by 2000 more than 6,200 aboriginals had sued the federal government and the churches. The government has settled out of court and paid a few hundred claims. The churches, which publicly apologized and begged forgiveness, the last one being the Catholic Church during the pope's April 2009 visit, fear bankruptcy if they are pressed too far. Native leaders show little sympathy. They blame the traumatic experiences in those schools for much of the alcoholism, sexual abuse, suicide and divorces in their communities. One in seven of the 90,000 former students still alive has launched abuse claims against Ottawa and various churches, and new claims continue to pour in.

In 2002 the federal government and the Anglican Church of Canada agreed to divide liability for the increasing number of abuse claims by Indians, capping the Church's liability at $16 million and thereby saving it from insolvency. In 2006 the federal government announced $2 billion in payments to 80,000 natives who were abused in these residential schools. The sum includes about $120 million for a foundation to promote traditional native healing therapies and finance a "truth and reconciliation commission" to hear victims' testimony. The churches involved also agreed to open up their archives.

In June 2008 Prime Minister Stephen Harper offered a second public apology: "Today we recognize that this policy of assimilation was wrong, has caused great harm and has no place in our country."

Quebec recruits immigrants from Europe

Canada

The apology was combined with an agreement to pay $Can1.9 billion to the surviving students. In a seldom break with tradition, native leaders were permitted to speak from the House of Commons floor, some in their native languages.

In 1998, Ottawa, BC and native leaders initialed the Nisga'a land claim. The settlement, approved the following year by Parliament, gave that northern British Columbian tribe self-government, land, resource rights, and $253 million over 15 years. Fifty other BC claims are under negotiation.

In 1999, the Federal Court of Appeal handed the Mi'kmaq of New Brunswick a victory by ruling that the National Energy Board had not satisfactorily dealt with native interests when it granted a private company rights to build the Sable Island natural gas pipeline. There have been numerous cases where the tide is turned by aboriginal insistence that their rights be acknowledged and that there be assurances of job creation, revenue-sharing, and land ownership before industrial development is permitted to proceed. Companies put pressure on governments to reach a deal.

Only a month earlier, the Supreme Court of Canada had decided that a 1760 treaty gave the Mi'kmaq and other Maritime natives year-round fishing rights. The Mi'kmaq thereupon claimed the right to control their own lobster fishing. This sparked conflict and violence with non-native fishermen, who are obligated to observe limitations on their fishing. Shots were fired,

boats were rammed, and fishing traps were destroyed in the months of scuffling. Finally in 2000 the Mi'kmaq agreed to remove a substantial number of their lobster traps from the water, to shorten their fishing season, and to cooperate with federal authorities to maintain peace.

Demographic Characteristics

The 2001 census and subsequent demographic surveys provide a good snapshot of Canadians today. Canadians are one of the few peoples in the world who are even more mobile than are Americans. Almost one out of three Canadians changed provinces during the 1970s, and many more move either from one city to another or from the city centers to the suburbs or small towns. Canada is heavily urban today, with 80% living in towns of more than 10,000 people (compared with 56% in 1956). In fact, in the 21st century the most visible division in Canada is not between francophones and anglophones, but between five large urban areas that are dynamic, successful and appealing and the rest of Canada that is mainly rural with declining economies, high unemployment and heavy dependence on federal assistance.

The most noticeable regional shift is from the East to the West, a movement that continues in the 21st century. The Calgary-Edmonton corridor in Alberta has seen its population grow by 12.3% since 1996 and now has more people than the four Atlantic provinces combined. These shifts in population also brought a west-

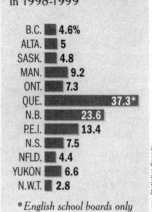

ward shift in economic and political power. Central Canada has lost some of its economic pre-eminence. Since seats in the House of Commons are distributed according to population, those regions that increased in population grew in political clout. The Atlantic Provinces have slipped significantly, and Ontario, where more than half of immigrants have settled since 1996 (two-thirds of whom in Toronto), has increased. The biggest gains in political power were made in Alberta and British Columbia.

The efficient distribution of medical services and the amenities of life enable Canadians to live longer (79.2 years for men and 83.6 for women) and to lower the infant mortality rate to 10.4 per 1,000, compared with 12.5 per 1,000 in the United States. Their family lives have also changed dramatically. Social changes, a decline in religious beliefs and liberalized divorce laws have meant that the proportion of marriages ending in divorce was frighteningly approaching one-half by the mid-1980s. Therefore, more Canadians are living alone than used to be the case.

It can hardly be doubted that the decline in religious belief is one contributor to the growing divorce rate. In a 2006 *Maclean's* Canada Day poll, only 34% of Canadians admitted that they attended a religious service "once a month or more," down from 41% in 1975. It is lowest in Quebec and BC. Two years later, only one in five Canadians identified themselves as "regular churchgoers."

Nevertheless, God is not dead in Canada: 81% believe in God, 62% in heaven, 62% in angels, and 48% in hell. Two-thirds believe Jesus Christ is God's divine son. A third believes earthlings can communicate

Stanley Park, Vancouver, BC   Credit: Province of British Columbia

with the dead. Three out of ten (28%) say "religion plays an important part in my life" (down from 61% in 1992), compared with 60% in the U.S. (down from 83%). In the 2005 annual *Maclean's* poll, almost a third of Canadians defined themselves as born-again Christians or evangelicals, but two thirds also said that political leaders should never use their religious beliefs to guide their actions. Only 3% claim to be out-and-out atheists (1% in the U.S.).

Sociologist Seymour Martin Lipset noted from diverse polling results, Americans are more inclined to believe in God, attend church regularly or adhere to religious beliefs than are either anglophone or francophone Canadians. They are also more inclined to apply their religious beliefs to politics than are Canadians. Canadians therefore often perceive American political views as too moralistic and uncompromising. This may seem surprising, given the fact that although Canada has officially separated church and state, the state in Canada does provide more support to religious institutions, particularly schools. Such support is understandable in the Canadian context, however; unlike the majority of Americans, most Canadians have belonged to the Roman Catholic or Anglican churches, both of which are hierarchically organized and historically linked with and supportive of the state.

According to the last published census numbers on belief, Catholicism is the biggest denomination, with 43% or 11.2 million members, followed by the United Church of Canada (formed in 1925 by the merger of the Presbyterian, Methodist, and Congregational churches, 3.8 million), the Anglican Church (2.5 million), and a myriad of conservative Christian denominations (2 million), the largest being the Pentecostal Assemblies of Canada, with a quarter million adherents. In all, Protestants account for 29%. The Eastern Orthodox Church claims 1.5%, most of Ukrainian ancestry, while 1.1% of Canadians are Jewish, a percentage that is growing slowly. Roughly 1% each are Hindus, Sikhs or Buddhists. Muslims make up 2%, while 16% of Canadians claim no religion.

Women are leaving their homes in large numbers to enter the work force. In 1951, 24% of Canadian women worked; in 2004 the figure was 57% (63% of mothers with children under age 3). Although the most blatantly discriminatory laws have been off the books for years and though Canada's new constitution spells out equality before the law, women in the work force still earned only about 60% as much money as males. This is in part because 28% of working women are part-timers compared with 11% of working men. This wage differential does not exist to any extent, however, in the professions and man-

agerial positions into which women have poured. Since 1971 the number of female lawyers increased six-fold, engineers five-fold and accountants three-fold. Three-fourths of female executives in 2004 believed that commitments to family hinder advancement. Nevertheless, in its gender equality rankings in 2005, the World Economic Forum placed Canada seventh in the world, ahead of the U.S. in 17th place.

Despite the fact that the Canadian population had steadily grown to 33.2 million by 2009, the Canadian birth-rate has declined rapidly. In 1971 the average woman who was past childbearing age had statistically given birth to 3.2 children. In 2011 that figure was down to 1.66, well below the 2.1 needed to maintain a constant population (and which the U.S. maintains). These changes in birth-rate differed regionally. In the Atlantic Provinces it remained high, whereas it was lowest in British Columbia and Quebec.

In Quebec, where families used to be large because of the strength of Catholicism and because of the determination to maintain the Quebec nation in the face of a perceived anglophone threat, the birth-rate plummeted, reaching 1.5 children per woman past childbearing age in 1992, below the country's average and below the 2.1 necessary to maintain Quebec's 6.5 million population in 1990. In an attempt to reverse this downward trend, the Quebec government adopted policies in 1988 and 1989 to create 60,000 more day care spaces and to make tax-free cash payments to parents of $500 for the first child, $1,000 for the second, and $4,500 for each additional child. These measures have helped raise Quebec's birth rate since 2001. Upon taking office in February 2006,

Prime Minister Stephen Harper promised parents $1,300 in cash annually to help defray the costs of day care.

Fewer women are marrying in their teens. The average marrying age for a Canadian woman was 28.5 in 2008 (compared with 25.1 in the U.S.). More are waiting to have their first child. The proportion of Canada's population under age 15 has decreased and over age 65 has increased. The result of this drop in births is noticeable in declining school enrollments. More and more parents are not marrying at all: in 2008, 25.6% of children (38.5% in the U.S.) were born out of wedlock. This figure was higher in Quebec, where 30% of all couples have common-law relationships, compared with 14% in Canada as a whole. More Canadians cohabit (18.4% of all couples) than Americans (7.6%).

The low birth-rate does not help Canada deal with the consequences of the baby-boom of the 1950s and 1960s, described by John Kettle in his book, *The Big Generation*: "Something extraordinary happened in Canada between 1951 and 1966. It has already wreaked havoc in our lives and will go on echoing down the years into the middle of the next century, disrupting and reshaping and rebuilding most of our society and economy in the process." This boom, which poured large numbers of young people into the job market in the early 1980s was more than the Canadian job supply could bear. It is a major factor in Canada's unemployment problem.

Although this swollen younger generation has gradually worked its way through the employment bottleneck, it will ultimately cause a different kind of problem in the 21st century. As a result of the declining birth-rate now, by the year 2030 there will

Hockey game at the Royal Military College, Annual Classic against West Point. Begun in 1923, the standing in 2004 was West Point 37, RMC 28.

Canada

be one pensioner for every two Canadians in the work force. The country's 240,000 immigrants each year help to boost the fertility rate in the short term, but they will not be able to solve the problem in the long run. This future reality cannot help from putting pressure on Canada's pension and social welfare system. To help alleviate this in 2007, the federal government eliminated the mandatory retirement age, but only 6% work past age 65.

Despite the problems with employment, the work ethic remains essentially intact. Canadians want to work, but they are compelled to find jobs in an economy that is changing and modernizing. Fewer and fewer Canadians are working on the land or in factories, and more and more are working in the service sector, including the public service.

Bilingualism
According to the 2001 census, Canada is an increasingly multilingual society, with more than five million inhabitants having a mother tongue other than English or French. Called "allophones," these people now constitute one out of six Canadians, up 12.5% from 1996. More than 100 languages are spoken in the country. The proportion of Canadians speaking English as a native language is 59.1% although 67.5% say they use it most often at home. French is the mother tongue of 22.9%, with 22% saying they speak it most often at home. Chinese is the third most common native language, spoken by 1.1 million people, up by a fifth from 1996. Next in order come Italian, German, Punjabi (from India) and Spanish.

One change since the early 1970s is that more Canadians have become bilingual in both of the languages proclaimed to be equal by the country's Official Languages Act in 1969: French and English. Today 17.7% of the population (9.4% of anglophones and 43.4% of francophones) has become bilingual in French and English, up from 13.5% in 1971. Traditionally the great majority of bilingual Canadians were francophones who needed to learn English in order to get ahead in an anglophone country. Even in the mid-1980s, 60% of bilingual Canadians were francophones. But the remarkable development is the percentage increase of anglophones who had acquired French: 56.7% for English as opposed to 13.4% for French speakers. In other words, anglophones are becoming bilingual at a quicker pace than are francophones. Westerners, who have shown considerable resentment to the conversion of Canada into a country with two official languages, have led the way toward bilingualism. In 2001, 43.4% of francophones reported in the census that they were bilingual, compared with 9% of anglophones.

In Quebec, where most francophones live, the percentage of anglophones has steadily declined since the 1960s and now numbers 750,000 representing less than 10% of the population; 83% and rising are francophones, 11% speak English at home, and 6% speak other languages as their mother tongue (and are referred to as "allophones"). Those anglophones who have remained in Quebec are now far more likely to be able to speak French and therefore feel more comfortable in their surroundings; 61% and rising of Quebec's anglophones now consider themselves to be functionally bilingual (up from 36% in 1971); 32% of Quebec francophones are bilingual (up from 26%).

A minority of anglophones in Quebec has even begun to speak French at home. This means that for the first time in Canada's history, English-speakers are assimilating into the French-speaking world. By 2005 a surge in marriage and coupling outside the communities was underway: 40% of anglophones have non-anglophone partners, and a fourth have paired with a francophone. There are economic incentives as well. Without French, an anglophone in Quebec is twice as likely to be unemployed; if employed he would earn only two-thirds as much as if he were bilingual. Enrollment in English-language schools has declined by 60% since the 1960s, and they are closing or switching to French instruction by the dozens. This has significant implications for Quebec politics since the fortunes of the independence movement were always dependent upon language tensions that are now slowly disappearing.

An "estates general" set up by the Quebec government in 2001 concluded that French is no longer under threat in the province. Although it did not recommend any loosening of the language laws, it saw no need to make them stricter. The problem, it found, was the poor quality of French spoken in Quebec. Perhaps that was embarrassingly demonstrated in 2001 when 20% of 8,055 prospective French-language teachers failed a written French test that is a prerequisite for employment by most francophone school boards.

This assimilation has affected the English which Quebec anglophones speak. So many French words, such as *depanneur* (convenience store) have seeped into their English that some worried observers are warning against "Frenglish." The Montreal *Gazette* decided to test the extent to which this process has gone by printing an article filled with Frenglish: "The work conflict has been a long one and the main revendications of the syndical militants have been for lower cotisations, more subventions for prestation beneficiaries and better social advantages." In standard English, this means: "The strike lasted a long time, and the prin-

cipal demands by union representatives were for lower dues, more grants for social benefit programs and better working conditions." For better or worse, all readers understood the report perfectly.

To strengthen its French character, Quebec spends almost twice as much per capita on cultural activities as does Ontario. Despite the outcry against the policies of the Quebec government during the past quarter of a century designed to protect and strengthen the French-speaking character of the province, Quebec remains the only province in Canada that requires the study of a second language in school. Beginning in 2001 francophone pupils started English in Grade 3 instead of Grade 4 in order to improve their skills. Although 98% of *Québécois* children study English, there are no English-immersion schools in Quebec; 37.3% of anglophone children in the province educated under the authority of English school boards were registered in French immersion by the year 2000.

A 1993 study of secondary education in Montreal concluded that anglophone Quebecers are leaving school more or less competent in both languages, while most francophones are not. Even though a majority of *Québécois* still speaks French only, there are a fifth more bilingual francophones in Quebec than there were in 1971. Quebec nationalists encourage individual bilingualism while opposing institutional bilingualism. A perfectly bilingual Jacques Parizeau proclaimed in 1992: "By God, I'll boot the rear end of anyone who can't speak English. A small people like us must speak English."

How have so many Canadians become bilingual so quickly? Some have buckled down and learned French out of necessity. Over a quarter of the federal civil service jobs now require *both* languages, and that percentage slowly rises every year. Thus, government employees have taken advantage of state-financed extra language courses. Also, many of the top jobs in politics, the judiciary and some of the professions, including journalism, public relations and economics, require proficiency in both languages. The federal capital of Ottawa has been proclaimed a bilingual city, so almost *any* job that involves dealing with the public demands facility in both tongues. The result, complained Mark Steyn, is that about 83% of Canadians are ineligible for the country's most prominent jobs. Therefore, night schools and crash language courses have experienced a boom.

Perhaps the most significant innovation in the long run is French-immersion schools for the children of English-speaking parents. They are largely funded by the provinces, which control education. During the 1990s Ottawa reduced its contribution by half, leaving it to the provinces to pick up the slack. In these schools anglophones learn all or part of their subjects totally in French. The programs vary, but most enrollees study exclusively in French for two to four years and then take about half their courses in French as long as they remain in the program. They enter "early" immersion beginning in kindergarten or "late" immersion, usually starting in the sixth or seventh grade.

This concept is sweeping the country, and the supply of such state-financed schools and qualified teachers cannot keep pace with the demand. Some ambitious parents reportedly wait in line through the night in order to get their children signed up for such programs. One such parent was former PEI premier Joe Ghiz, who himself took French lessons in 1988 to improve his prospects for higher federal office. He and 122 other applicants stood in line all night in 1989 to enroll his daughter in French-language kindergarten. The tired premier grumbled: "There must be a better way to get your child into French immersion." His favor for his child is bound to help young Robert's political career; at age 29 he led his father's Liberal Party in the 2003 PEI provincial elections.

These schools hardly existed before the 1970s. By 1979, they had an enrollment of 38,000, a figure that topped the 100,000 mark by 1983 and 317,000 by 2000. It is still rising, thanks in part to the fact that Ottawa remains a major booster of the program. Its annual budget for official-language education grew to $219 million in 2000, and it requires provinces to develop a formal action plan for such schooling. By 1989 immersion teaching and conventional French instruction reached roughly half of all anglophone elementary and high school pupils.

The stampede to such schools has tended to drown out the criticism that has been leveled against them. Some purists claim that these schools make pupils "little butchers of French." While it is true that many of the graduates of these schools do not speak French perfectly, they understand it and are wholly functional in standard (called "international") French, that form which is spoken and written by educated *Québécois* and Acadians in business, schools, newspapers and on the air. Acadian and Quebec dialects, such as *Joual*, that French spoken in the streets of Montreal and which contracts syllables and drops sounds, remain largely incomprehensible to outsiders, even to visitors from France; in fact, English-language films dubbed in Quebec must be re-dubbed for audiences in France. Other critics claim that these schools contribute to the creation of a "new cultural and economic elite."

The kinds of children who tend to enroll in these schools already come from middle-class or upper-income families, and their acquisition of French language competency in a country which lays so much stress on that enhances even further the social and economic advantages they already had. A survey in 1997 to determine the reasons parents chose early French immersion for their children revealed that the chief motives were "future employment enhancement," "a more stimulating learning environment," and "a better student-teacher ratio," in that order.

To some extent they serve the same purpose as private schools in other countries, such as the U.S. In other words, the social gap between Canadians from upwardly mobile families and those who are not becomes even wider. Statistics bear this point out: bilingual graduates entering the work force, especially the professions, do earn more than their unilingual counterparts. Most Canadians find the value of bilingualism indisputable. In a 2000 poll, 87% of respondents said they believe the ability to speak a second language is important. Employers agree. Some Canadians see bilingualism, not as a cultural fetish, but as the glue for a unified Canada. Nuclear physicist, John Madden, asserted: "If you believe in Canada as an entity, then you speak both of its official languages. It's as simple as that."

It is possible that Quebec's influence in Anglophone Canada will diminish over time. Given the composition of immigration to Canada, each future generation of francophone Canadians living outside of Quebec and Acadia will be half the size of the previous one. Among the fourth of all Canadians outside of Quebec who speak a different mother tongue than English, there are almost as many who speak Chinese as speak French. Soon the Chinese-speakers will surpass the francophones. This is already the case in British Columbia, where they outnumber French-speakers 15 to 1. With francophones shrinking as a minority outside of Quebec and Acadia, their claims for special treatment might become weaker.

Despite intense efforts and expense by the federal government, only 17.7% of Canadians are truly bilingual, and even fewer use both languages on the job. The truth is that few Canadians outside Quebec need French because its use has not spread appreciably. In Ontario dozens of communities have declared themselves as officially English-only, sending a powerful symbolic message across Canada and reflecting the deep divisions between the country's two language communities.

Nevertheless, one cannot speak of the failure of bilingualism. In fact, support for it reached an all-time high by 2006: 64% of Canadians support it, while 89% of *Québécois* do. Support continues to grow, rising to 49% in British Columbia and 47% in the Prairies. Only 12% of Canadians consider the state of English-French relations as a very serious problem, and the percentage that thinks Quebec will one day separate from Canada has fallen to 8% (25% in Quebec).

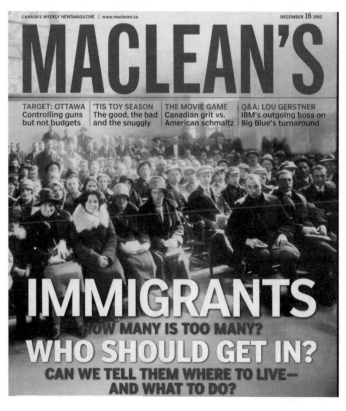

Canada

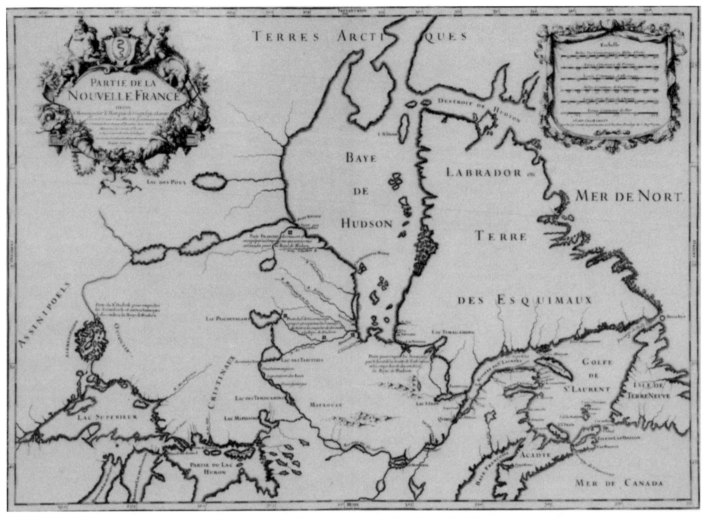

17th century French map of eastern Canada—*New France*
Public Archives Canada/C42132

HISTORY

Identity, Unity, Survival

Canadian history has been decisively influenced by three concerns: identity, unity and survival. The problem of identity, of defining what it means to be Canadian, has never been satisfactorily resolved. Is there such a thing? Right up into the 20th century, anglophone and francophone Canadians tended to regard each other as "racially" different.

Québécois still view themselves as a separate nation, and they refer to their provincial parliament as the "*National* Assembly." In any case, the concept of nationhood is very problematic in a country that makes a virtue out of necessity by describing itself as a "mosaic," rather than a "melting pot."

To what extent does being Canadian mean being distinct from being British? Francophones always resented the English connection, and for a long time, anglophones were ambivalent about how much they should share in Britain's institutions and destiny. In past wars any call to go to the aid of Britain, the "mother country," inevitably divided Canadians severely. In 1982 Canadians severed most of their formal ties with Britain when they finally revised and "Canadianized" their constitution. Nevertheless, the British monarch is still the head of state in Canada, and the country's political system continues to resemble that of Great Britain more than that of any other nation.

Canadians are more inclined than Americans to try to define their own identity as a people. Most Canadians tend to describe themselves in terms that contrast themselves to Americans. When asked what it means to be a Canadian, many preface their answer with such words, "well, unlike Americans, we . . ." Even Pierre Berton's book, *Why We Act Like Canadians. A personal exploration of our national character*, is written in the form of letters to an American friend named "Sam." The Canadian state took shape in a context of distrust toward the American Revolution and republicanism. As Northrop Frye once said, "historically, a Canadian is an American who rejects the revolution." Looking south, many Canadians saw too much democracy, which seemed to create unacceptable instability and violence. While Canadians can all agree that they are not Americans, such a negative definition of their own identity is barely strong enough to withstand the forces of division that often plague Canada. But at the same time, many Canadians have always felt themselves to be irresistibly attracted to certain aspects of the United States and have come to resemble Americans more than they might have wished.

The second concern in Canadian history is unity. Canada has often been accurately described as a "geographic improbability." Distance and rough terrain have always made communication and transportation difficult. It was settled by many different peoples with differing national backgrounds, languages and cultures. Geography aided them in preserving these differences. Regional diversity was always a salient fact in Canadian life, and politics was always characterized by a tug-of-war between the center and the provinces, which have often regarded themselves almost as separate kingdoms.

Finally, Canadian history has been shaped by the continual struggle for survival. But Canadians have viewed the threat as having different sources. For the *Québécois, la survivance* meant the survival of their language and culture, which they feared were vulnerable to the ever-growing power of anglophone culture in Canada. The powerful melting pot to the south also potentially threatened to destroy the Quebec nation. Anglophones, who always have been a minority within the province of Quebec, have felt their survival to be threatened by the francophone majority, especially since the 1960s.

Anglophone Canadians have usually perceived the primary threat as emanating from the United States. At every step in Canadian history, the dynamic, expanding, populous and economically powerful U.S. was a challenge and entered mightily into Canadian deliberations. Canadian governments were always on guard against potential annexation or loss of some far-

flung territory. At the same time, American culture threatened to overwhelm and to destroy whatever distinctive characteristics existed in Canadian culture. In the past, Canada's leaders have often been so busy maintaining their country's independence from the United States that they had little inclination to count their blessings at having such a democratic, tolerant and basically friendly country with which to share their 5,524-mile border.

Canada's first inhabitants were, of course, the Inuit and Indians. The white man's presence in the new world permanently changed the lives of Canada's native population.

In the 10th and 11th centuries the first white men had set foot on Canadian shores. Norsemen such as Leif Ericson set out from Iceland and Greenland to explore the uncharted West, and after perilous sailing sighted the Labrador coast. For 30 harsh years off and on, a small winter base-camp of Vikings eked out an existence at L'Anse aux Meadows in what is now Newfoundland. Its main purpose was to supply the larger Viking settlement of about 500 persons in Greenland. They struck out from L'Anse aux Meadows as far as what is now New Brunswick. This is known because the butternuts they brought back were only to be found there. Based on archeological excavations, these temporary Viking settlers averaged five-

feet ten-inches, which was very tall by the standards of their time. The European average was only five-feet five-inches. They wore cone-shaped helmets, not the horned models one sees in Hollywood films. Despite their reputation for fighting and pillaging, they mainly survived by raising livestock and cutting hay. They were also innovative shipbuilders and skilled artists who decorated woodwork and cast-metal ornaments with sophisticated designs.

Lacking both numbers of potential settlers and fire-arms necessary to subdue the Indians, the Norsemen withdrew from North America. A millennium later, in 2000, a replica of a Viking ship, accompanied by a flotilla of other Viking vessels, sailed from Iceland for a six-week voyage to L'Anse aux Meadows on the northern tip of Newfoundland. There they were greeted by hundreds of onlookers who remain fascinated by the mysterious Nordic mariners.

The New World remained hidden in Norse legend until three Spanish galleons under the command of the Italian mariner Christopher Columbus bumped into a Caribbean island in 1492 while searching for a passage to the riches of China and India. As soon as Columbus reported his discovery to an enthused Europe, a stream of hardy French and English explorers began steering their ships toward Canada. In 1497 the Italian seaman John Cabot

Champlain trading with the Indians
Public Archives Canada/C103059

Canada

Quebec in 1640
Public Archives Canada/06492

(who lived in England) rediscovered Newfoundland. In a series of three daring voyages in 1534, 1535 and 1541, Jacques Cartier sailed into the Gulf of St. Lawrence and up the St. Lawrence River as far as the present city of Montreal. On one such voyage, he reportedly went ashore to inquire as to his whereabouts. Believing that he was asking about their village, the Indians answered "Kanata," which was the Huron-Iroquois term for "a small fishing village." Upon returning to France, Cartier used this word to refer to the land he had seen, and the name, "Canada," stuck. In 1610 the Englishman Henry Hudson discovered the Hudson and James Bays, gigantic waterways that gave the English relatively easy and inexpensive access to the very heart of the vast Canadian half-continent. Between 1609 and 1615 Samuel de Champlain penetrated what is now eastern Ontario and pointed in the direction where the lucrative fur trade would develop.

These explorers were driven by a burning spirit of gain. Even though they did not succeed in finding a direct sea route to China, the fur trade provided fortunes for anyone who could move beaver pelts from the dense North American forests to the chic shops of London and Paris. Following in the wake of these explorers and frontier entrepreneurs came a different brand of Europeans: settlers.

NEW FRANCE

The first permanent European settlers to move to this new land were French, and they dominated most of what is now Canada until 1760. In 1604 they established a short-lived settlement on the island of St. Croix, and one year later French pioneers established a community at Port Royal (now Annapolis on Nova Scotia). But the explorer and soldier, Samuel de Champlain concluded that these two early sites were too exposed militarily and too unpromising economically. Therefore, he moved up the Gulf of St. Lawrence to the narrows guarded by the imposing cliffs of Cape Diamond. Here he founded the city of Quebec and befriended the Algonquin Indians. He thereby established a secure and well-placed base in the heart of the continent. Soon thereafter an outpost was established up the river at Trois Rivières.

In 1642 a Catholic mission to the Indians was established at Montreal. This outpost was situated on an island near the points where the Ottawa and Richelieu rivers flow into the St. Lawrence. It was subjected to constant Indian attacks. The fiercest assault occurred in 1660, but was stopped by Adam Dollard and a small band of Jesuit followers in a legendary struggle to the death. Once secured, Montreal became the natural control point for the fur trade and for westward expansion. Because of a brief but vigorous French governmental immigration policy initiated in 1666, the number of inhabitants in New France rose to 6,705 by the year 1672, when the French court ceased supporting emigration. It ultimately climbed to between 60,000 and 70,000 by 1760, when the English conquered the French in North America.

The French settlers' motives were varied. The Reformation in Europe had divided Europeans religiously, and the intolerance that had resulted led Europeans into some of the most bestial and bloody conflicts known to civilized man. Thousands escaped religious persecution by coming to the New World. Others, especially the Jesuit Order, came to North America in order to try to preserve the French Catholic tradition and to convert the Indians to Catholicism. From 1625, when the first Jesuits landed at Quebec, right up until the 1960s, Quebec province was a hostile place for French Protestants. No Huguenots were permitted to emigrate to New France. Thus, not only were some of the most industrious and imaginative elements of French society kept out, but the French population in the New World remained religiously homogeneous and conservative.

Settlers were also attracted to Canada by the longing for a new life and for economic gain. The northern half of America possessed all the basic economic resources for settlement: fish, furs, timber and agricultural land. Throughout the 17th and 18th centuries the most important of these resources by far was the fur trade, which ultimately provided the financial basis for the government and the church. From their bases in the north and south, the British hemmed in the French fur trade in the 17th century. In 1670 the British monarch, Charles II, had granted to the Hudson's Bay Company not only a trade monopoly but also the privilege of ruling all the land draining into that gigantic bay.

The British trading posts, which were established along the edge of the most lucrative fur-producing territory, had the enormous advantage of being supplied by sea and were therefore very economical. To the south of New France, the British had replaced the Dutch in the Hudson River Valley and had established a powerful base in Albany. Having inherited the Dutch alliance with the Iroquois Indians, the British could challenge the French bid for control of the Ohio Valley fur trade.

The English pincers to the north and south forced the French to push into the interior of the continent in search of the beaver. They forged into the Great Lakes and into the Saskatchewan and Mississippi Valleys. The Jesuit priest Jacques Marquette and the trader-explorer Louis Jolliet joined efforts in 1673 and paddled from Green Bay on Lake Michigan all the way down the Mississippi to the confluence with the Arkansas River. In 1682 Robert Cavalier de la Salle pressed on to the mouth of the Mississippi River, and in 1699 the French founded a colony on the Gulf of Biloxi, close to what is now the Gulf of Mexico. Thus, by the dawn of the 18th century, French *voyageurs* had established a far-flung network of trading posts embracing the entire Mississippi Valley and Great Lakes region. *Coureurs de bois*, (literally "runners of the woods") gathered furs from the Indians deep in the Ohio Valley, and as far north as Hudson Bay, and as far west as the plains.

This huge fur trading network brought great wealth to New France, but it also created severe problems. The French had

to build a string of forts over a massive area in order to protect their share of the fur trade from the English. This called for large expenditures for soldiers, and the long supply lines into the interior were both vulnerable and expensive to maintain. Also, the fur trade retarded development in other economic sectors and prevented New France from diversifying its economy. Perhaps worst of all, it forced the French to make territorial claims which continually brought them into conflict with the British, whose population in the New World soon far exceeded that of New France. From the early 17th century on, the French and English were rivals for control of North America. The undefined borders between their colonies were a constant source of war.

From 1627 New France was governed by private, chartered companies, such as the Company of New France, which performed governmental services in return for trade monopolies and control of land. In 1663 its status changed, and it became a royal French province, with all the trappings of French provincial law and government. In typical French fashion, all institutions—from the government and church to the fur trade—were highly centralized. The government was dominated by three offices: the governor was usually a military man and was appointed by the King to oversee defense and foreign relations. The *intendant,* a lawyer and administrator, was appointed by the King to maintain royal power, regulate the economy and administer justice. For a while, these persons were assisted by an ap-

pointed council, but its influence shrank quickly. New France was unable to develop an effective form of representative government at any level, as the British had done. The third pillar of power was the Catholic Church. Due largely to the personality and force of the first Bishop of Quebec, Francois Laval, no major governmental decisions were made without the influence of the Bishop being felt.

At the communal level, the two top leaders were the *curé,* ("pastor") who represented the Church, and the *seigneur,* ("Lord") a powerful and wealthy figure appointed by the governor. The *seigneur* was not necessarily a nobleman, but he had control over a feudal estate. Under him, peasants rendered feudal services in the form of rents and work.

The system was not as rigid as in France because of the peasants' possibility of escaping by merely running away into the woods. Also, since the captain of the militia provided military protection, the *seigneur* did not bear the feudal responsibility for protecting the peasants. Nevertheless, this communal order left important legacies for French Canada. The form of land ownership which was granted by the governors under the influence of the Church, and which was *not* bought and sold in a free market, greatly irritated and thereby limited English settlers to Quebec, who desired the kind of freer economic activity to which they had become accustomed in the British colonies. Second, politics in Quebec involved from the very beginning a close link between Church and state.

Montreal in 1720
Public Archives Canada/06497

Canada

View of Louisbourg in 1731
Public Archives Canada/C23082

Slavery existed for almost two centuries in Canada until it was abolished in the 19th century. During French rule, about 1,500 black slaves were imported, and 2,000 more were brought north by loyalists fleeing the American Revolution. Most slaves belonged to urbanized elites.

THE CONQUEST
(LA CONQUÊTE)

While the French established an early permanent presence in what is now Canada, the English first settled in what is now the United States. But the line between French and British America was not clearly defined, a factor which was the cause for continuous tension. Because New France was unified, and British North America was divided up into many separate colonies, New France could mobilize its resources more effectively and compete well, even though by 1760 it had only 10% of the British colonial population. Nevertheless, throughout the 18th century Britain whittled away at the French possessions in North America. The origins of the conflicts were often to be found in momentous events in Europe. For instance, the War of the Spanish Succession (1702–13) brought skirmishes in North America that influenced the Treaty of Utrecht in 1713.

That settlement required the French to renounce their claims to the Hudson Bay, Newfoundland (except the French shore) and all of Acadia (except Isle Royale, now known as Cape Breton Island). Acadia had been an area of French settlement that encompassed at that time most of the present-day provinces of Nova Scotia and New Brunswick. The British were also granted the right to trade with the western Indian tribes. The scales were thus tipped in favor of the British, and only their inability to coordinate an effective attack against Quebec enabled the French to survive in North America for another half century.

Determined to prevent further losses of territory to the British and to try to secure their vital exits from the St. Lawrence, the French built a further series of forts, including the magnificent Louisbourg. This elegant and imposing fortress was constructed on Isle Royale according to plans drawn up by the great French military engineer, Sebastien Vauban, and could accommodate 1,400 regular soldiers, the governor and his retinue, merchants, craftsmen and fishermen. The British seized the fort in 1745 during the War of Austrian Succession, only to give it back reluctantly to the French at the Peace of Aix-la-Chapelle in 1748 in exchange for Madras in far-away India. The French diplomatic victory was a short-lived one, though. The British became determined to rid North America of their perennial French rival.

The decisive conflict soon began in the Ohio Valley, which the French regarded as crucial for maintaining communications with their colony in Louisiana and for protecting their fur trade in the west. In 1753 the French sent a force into the Ohio Valley. Virginia responded by sending a wealthy planter by the name of George Washington to inform the French that they were treading on British territory. Rebuffed, Washington returned with an army in 1754, but his army was defeated at Ft. Necessity. Establishing Fort Duquesne (now Pittsburgh), and successfully conducting guerrilla warfare with their Indian allies, the French were resolved to make good their claim to the Ohio and to prevent the restless Virginians from pressing into the western side of the Allegheny Mountains.

Of four principal attacks upon New France in 1755, only one succeeded—that against French positions in French-speaking Acadia. The 13,000 Acadians had announced their decision to remain neutral in all struggles between the British and French and not to swear loyalty to the British Crown, even though they had fallen under British rule in 1713. Equally disturbing to the British was the fact that a few Acadians helped the French to construct a fort on the isthmus separating Nova Scotia and mainland Acadia (what is now New Brunswick).

A jittery British colonial government in Nova Scotia decided in 1755 to deal with this looming danger in a brutally effective way. This reflected just how serious the British were to eliminate their French rival from the New World: they hunted Acadians down in Nova Scotia, expelled them from their towns and villages and dispersed 10,000 of them to France and among the English-speaking colonies to the south. In his moving poem, "Evangeline" Longfellow immortalized this tragic diaspora, remembered as "*le Grand Dérangement*" (The Big Inconvenience). It was also the inspiration for Antonine Maillet's play, *La Saguine*. A few Acadians escaped expulsion and hid in the forests, fled to the French islands of Saint-Pierre and Miquelon, or took refuge in New Brunswick along the Restigouch and Miramichi rivers and along the shores of the Bay of Chaleur. Some returned from exile in the late 1700s and joined those Acadians who had fled to New Brunswick.

In northern Nova Scotia and northwestern New Brunswick, their offspring and those of some Quebecers who immigrated to New Brunswick more than a century later, continue to form a French-speaking minority distinct from the Quebecers and still noticeably neutral in the present debates between Quebec and the rest of Canada. In its final cabinet meeting in December 2003, the government of former Prime Minister Jean Chrétien approved a proclamation acknowledging the historic wrongs done by the British Crown between 1755 and 1763 when about 10,000 Acadians were expelled from the Maritimes.

Hostilities in the New World broadened rapidly, and both contenders were set on a collision course when in 1756 the Seven Years War erupted in Europe between the two mother countries. Known in North America as the French and Indian War, this grave struggle demonstrated the extent to which the colonial conflict was influenced by events in Europe as much as by concerns of the North Americans themselves. Determined to crush the French in the New World, William Pitt, the British minister of war, sent fresh land and naval reinforcements to America. The French court could send their colony little more than feeble moral support after 1756. One fortress after the other around the Great Lakes and Lake Champlain and along the Ohio River fell to the British onslaught. The most significant prize was Louisbourg, whose capture in 1758 opened up the St. Lawrence to Britain's formidable naval power.

In the summer of 1759 British ships entered the St. Lawrence and set their sights on the cornerstone of French power in America: the commanding fortress at Quebec City. After a nerve-wracking siege and a prolonged military cat and mouse game around Quebec, the British commander, General James Wolfe, succeeded in landing his army in the darkness of night. It scaled the cliffs to appear on the Plains of Abraham, just outside the fortress walls in the early morning light of September 13, 1759. The surprised French commander, the Marquis de Montcalm,

Newfoundland

Saint-Pierre & Miquelon
(France)

hastily assembled his army to face the British army outside the security of the fortress.

For the first time during the entire French and Indian War, the French unwisely decided to engage the British ac-

cording to the European rules of battle, rather than employing the irregular manner of guerrilla warfare, which had often been so successful. Within ten ferocious minutes of fateful fighting, both armies had suffered more than 2,000 casualties, including both the commanding generals. The French army was routed but not captured. Not until it was crushed at Montreal a year later did the final British "conquest," as French Canadians have called it ever since, occur.

The financial cost to Britain of the Seven Years War was so high that Britain had to raise taxes on its American colonies, thereby ultimately precipitating the American revolution 17 years later. Thus the foundations of both Canada and the U.S. were laid that day on the Plains of Abraham. Further, the terms of surrender drafted by General Wolfe, who died on the battlefield, established the protection of Quebec's unique culture, language, law and religion that has since become the hallmark of modern Canada's identity. But the memory of the *Conquête* has continued to nourish and invigorate French Canadian nationalism. In 2009 the long-scheduled re-enactment on the occasion of the 250th an-

General Wolfe mortally wounded on the Plains of Abraham, September 1759
Public Archives Canada/C12248

Canada

niversary of the most important battle ever fought on Canadian soil had to be canceled because Quebec separatist groups, some hinting at violence, claimed such an event would be "humiliating" and evidence of "federal propaganda." Canadian history has been politicized.

In the Treaty of Paris, the French lost to Britain all their North American holdings east of the Mississippi, except the two small islands of Saint-Pierre and Miquelon, which were needed as stations for the French naval and fishing fleets and which remain in French possession to this day. The French also relinquished to Spain all their holdings west of the Mississippi. In 1801 Napoleon secretly forced Spain to cede these western lands to France. But before he repossessed them, he sold them to the United States for $15 million in the Louisiana Purchase of 1803.

BRITISH NORTH AMERICA

By 1763, the British were in control of all land east of the Mississippi, but the magnitude of the problems facing them soon cut short their celebration of this great imperial victory. They faced the problem of how to rule the newly conquered French citizens in Quebec (which at that time was called "Canada"). Some of the leading French political leaders returned to France, but there was no mass French exodus from Quebec. The Catholic clergy remained, and, in the absence of the former French political leadership, the Catholic Church retained a leading position in Quebec life that lasted for two centuries. British law and administration, which was introduced, forbade Catholics from holding public office. Therefore those citizens who clung to that faith were barred from participation in the political life of the province.

The new masters viewed the application of this law as an incentive for the French to give up their language and religion. Hoping that many French would emigrate and that those remaining would be swallowed up by an influx of English-speaking Protestants, the British assumed that the new French minority would be simply digested into British North America. The French viewed this design as a dangerous threat to their culture and identity, and to this day they have never lost their fear of such assimilation. This danger made them more resistant than ever and continues to harden the backbone of the *Québécois* when facing anglophone Canadians.

By 1774 the British realized that their earlier hopes for a rapidly Anglicized Quebec had been naive and that it would be necessary to deal with a resilient French-speaking community through the

leaders who remained: the *seigneurs* and the clergy. The Quebec Act of 1774 reflected this realization by declaring that: 1) French Canadians need not take an anti-Catholic oath; 2) the Church could continue to take tithes; 3) French civil law could be practiced, although criminal law had to be English; 4) the seigneurial land system would be permitted, in contrast to the British free-holding system; 5) Quebec would be governed through an appointed council, as opposed to a representative council, as in other British colonies; 6) the boundaries of Quebec would be extended to include much of the old French empire between the Ohio and Mississippi Rivers, where Montreal fur traders continued to dominate the economy.

This act was good news to most French leaders, who saw it as protecting many of their former practices. However, it stimulated nervousness or downright anger in the minds of many Americans to the south, who saw it as evidence of shaky British commitment to representative government. They also viewed it as an unacceptable limitation on their westward expansion. As a response to that nervousness, two American armies led by Richard Montgomery and Benedict Arnold marched on Canada in 1775 and captured Montreal and besieged Quebec City before withdrawing in 1776. But the year 1776 was only the beginning of the major threat to British North America posed by the American Revolutionary War.

In that struggle few Quebecers took up arms for the British, a refusal which, as we shall see, was to be repeated in later conflicts, including the two world wars in the 20th century. However, very few French Canadians supported the American war effort either, even though France had openly sided with the Americans. The United States clearly had its eye on all the British holdings to the north. The Americans convened a *Continental* Congress, and their Articles of Confederation contained a section that was a door through which other British North American colonies could enter the newly independent country.

In the peace treaty of 1783 Britain retained its holdings north of the Thirteen Colonies while granting the Americans a peace so conciliatory that many Canadians still consider it an "astonishing giveaway" which allegedly severely crippled Canada's prospects for future growth. In the peace talks the American negotiator, Benjamin Franklin, asked for Quebec, Nova Scotia, Newfoundland and the Hudson Bay territory. The British negotiator did not consider this proposal to be unreasonable. But he was overruled by George III and parliamentary leaders in London, who insisted upon maintaining

in Halifax and Quebec a rampart against the northern expansion of the United States, as well as a refuge for loyalists from the Thirteen Colonies. Thus, the northern half of the continent was to remain separate from the southern half.

The British were probably inclined to make a lenient peace with the United States in order to woo the Americans away from their alliance with France. The British conceded the entire Ohio country, that great triangle west of the Appalachian Mountains between the Mississippi and Ohio Rivers, even though it was still controlled by the British and even though that area was a traditional dependency of Canada which, when populated, could ultimately have entirely changed the power and economy of Canada.

The northern boundary was also generous to the new nation, following the St. Lawrence River where it intersects with the 45th parallel, through the Great Lakes to the Lake of the Woods, from which it aimed straight westward to the Mississippi River. That boundary was imprecise at important points and provided a constant source of tension between Britain and the U.S. This was especially so because Britain decided to maintain its string of forts, such as Michilimackinac, Detroit, Niagara and Oswego, which were located on territory granted by the treaty to the new nation. Also, some Indian tribes refused to recognize the new boundaries and looked to the British to back up traditional Indian claims. Finally, the Americans were given access to the inshore fisheries of Nova Scotia and Newfoundland.

There were many consequences of the peace settlement of 1783 that helped shape the future development of Canada. First, Canada's contacts with the far West could no longer run through the Great Lakes and the shorter and less hostile lands to the south. Instead they had to be maintained over the rugged terrain of the Precambrian Shield north of Lake Superior. This ultimately necessitated the construction of a coast-to-coast railway in order to weld together the different parts of Canada.

Second, 32,000 loyalists, mainly city-dwellers from the eastern seaboard who had sought refuge in New York, Charleston and Savannah, sailed in British ships from the newly independent U.S. into Nova Scotia, trebling the population there and ultimately prompting the founding of New Brunswick. Many of the 8,000 free blacks, who had gained their freedom by fleeing their patriot owners for the British promise of emancipation for those who took up arms for the king, settled in Nova Scotia. A smaller number of loyalists, who were to form the nucleus of what would later become Ontario, trekked across the wilderness of northern New York to Niagara and Kingston and across the northern shore of Lake Ontario. Some even penetrated into the valley of the Ottawa River.

As loyalists, they brought with them an aversion to the particular American variety of republican democracy. But they were former Americans who still had emotional and personal links with the United States. Like the rebels, they too desired a new relationship between the colonies and the mother country. They later pressed successfully for the expansion of representative assemblies and democratic reforms in what became Canada.

About 8,000 loyalists, chiefly from Pennsylvania and New York, moved into Quebec north of the St. Lawrence, Lake Erie and Lake Ontario, creating for the first time a sizable English-speaking minority in that province and demanding to live under British political institutions. They received support from London after the French Revolution in 1789. The momentous changes wrought by that first democratic revolution in Europe stiffened British views on the subject of representative democracy.

At the same time, most French-speaking Canadians were critical of the democratic revolution in France, which led to a bloody onslaught against the Catholic Church and clergy there. That revolution drove a powerful wedge between revolutionary France and conservative Quebec. Not until the 1920s did Quebecers begin to look again toward Paris. A final important consequence of the French Revolution was that it ultimately produced a European war that so loosened the ties which France had to the New World that the United States was able to acquire the huge Louisiana territory from Napoleon Bonaparte in 1803. This ultimately greatly enlarged and strengthened the energetic and ambitious southern neighbor.

With a very mixed population in British North America, London saw a need in 1791 to divide Quebec into two separate provinces: Upper Canada (later Ontario) and Lower Canada (present-day Quebec—then called "lower" because it was closest to the point where the St. Lawrence met the Atlantic Ocean). English common law and freehold land tenure were established in Upper Canada. Thus, in that new province, considerable tension arose between small freeholders and an elite around the governor. On the other hand, Quebec was permitted to retain French civil law. That was a decision which infuriated the largely English-speaking merchants in Montreal, who nevertheless continued to control the economic life of the province and who forged close links with the senior clergy and wealthy seigneurs.

British General Sir Isaac Brock enters Queenston, 1812
Public Archives Canada/C46958

This "Chateau Clique," which included some anglophones, stimulated French nationalist opposition from the bulk of ordinary Quebecers. Thus, the Canada Act of 1791 left both new provinces with simmering social and political tensions. It also left to the north of the United States a variety of British colonies with no links to each other. Separated by geographical barriers, language and customs, each had its own governor or lieutenant governor, an appointed council and an elected legislative assembly with limited powers.

THE WAR OF 1812

The British masters of these loosely connected colonies continued to have tense relations with the young and restless United States. The flashpoints were many: the British possession of such forts as Niagara and Detroit on American territory continued to be a bone of contention, until the British finally relinquished the western posts in Jay's Treaty of 1794–5. Continuous Indian wars in Indiana and Ohio kept alive American suspicions that the British were actually encouraging and supporting the Indians. The American defeat of some western tribes in 1795 enabled the state of Ohio to be founded in 1803. However, even after the Americans, led by future president William Henry Harrison, defeated at Tippecanoe in 1811 an alliance of Indian tribes forged by the prodigious Shawnee orator, warrior and chief, Tecumseh, and his brother, the Prophet, Americans living in the West continued to be convinced that there were many Canadian traders and British officials who were prepared to stir up and arm the Indians for profits and politics. Finally, Americans

Canada

Bytown in 1830, later renamed Ottawa
Public Archives Canada/C607

strongly objected to British violations of neutral rights on the high seas, involving the boarding of American ships and the conscription of sailors on the grounds that they were still British subjects.

For a while these disputes could be settled peacefully, but that possibility diminished as time passed. Any armed struggle between the United States and Britain could only be fought on Canadian or American soil, and Canada was very vulnerable. It had only a fraction of the American population; by 1812 there were a half million persons living in British North America, compared to 7.5 million in the U.S. Also, many loyalists had emigrated from the United States after the Revolutionary War, and subsequently many more Americans had emigrated to Canada, especially to what is now Ontario, for economic, not political, reasons. Therefore, it could not be known at that time how enthusiastically many Canadians would fight for Britain. Further, British hands were tied by the struggle in Europe against Napoleon, and they could spare few troops and material for a war in North America. The 5,000 British troops in North America would have to be used primarily to defend Quebec and Montreal, while the areas to the West seemed to lie wide open to attack.

By 1812 many Americans in the western part of the country saw the British colonies as ripe pieces of fruit waiting to be picked. They prevailed upon President James Madison and a majority in Congress to declare war on Britain. A confident Henry Clay declared that "I verily believe that the militia of Kentucky are alone competent to place Montreal and Upper Canada at your feet." The American war effort was, indeed, mainly a Ken-

tucky affair, and two-thirds of the American casualties were from that state. But Clay soon learned how badly mistaken he had been. The U.S. was very poorly prepared for the War of 1812 and from the beginning there was little enthusiasm for actually conducting it.

Most state militiamen refused to fight outside the borders of their own states, and the New England states refused even to participate in the war. They kept their ports open to British shipping throughout the conflict and regularly traded with the enemy. Thus, the British did not even have to mount a defense for a large portion of the frontier separating the U.S. and their colonies to the north and could therefore concentrate on American attacks in the west.

The American campaigns into Canada in 1812, 1813 and 1814 were dispersed and very ineptly conducted. American hopes that French-speakers and settlers from the U.S. would side with them were in vain. The American forces were composed largely of Indian fighters and backwoodsmen, who did not fight according to the "rules of the game." Instead of standing shoulder-to-shoulder and advancing politely and openly toward the enemy, they ran through the woods with their squirrel rifles and hid behind rocks and trees. Frustrated British regulars screamed, "Show us our enemy!" This was a different kind of American than the easy-going farmers who had immigrated earlier into Canada, and they helped change Canadians' image of Americans.

Nevertheless, the well-trained British regulars, supported by Indians, blunted all American attempts to seize and hold territory. American forces did gain control of the Great Lakes, and they captured and burned to the ground the capital at York

(Toronto). This act prompted the British in 1814 to seize the American capital of Washington and to burn much of it in retaliation. Only the specter in Europe of a Napoleonic resurgence in 1814 saved the Americans in the nick of time. It inclined the British to accept a quick peace settlement with the United States, which confirmed the 1783 boundaries between British North America and the United States.

The War of 1812 was the last American attempt to expand northward into Canada east of the Rocky Mountains, but it was also very significant for the two countries' relationship in other ways. The war stimulated among most Canadians a sense of distinctiveness and separateness from the American nation and created the beginnings of a definite, though still weak, Canadian identity. To make sure that there would always be an alternative route between Toronto and Montreal in case the Americans ever seized control of the St. Lawrence, Canadians dug by hand the 123-mile Rideau Canal with 47 locks between Kingston and what is now Ottawa. By 1832 it was completed, after only six years of work, and it is one of the first examples of the state-sponsored mega-projects which have helped to build and to bind Canada together. Fortunately, it never had to be used for military purposes and today is a beautiful placid waterway flowing right through the middle of Ottawa.

The memory of the War of 1812 also ultimately led in 1858 to Queen Victoria's decision to establish the Canadian national capital in Ottawa, a tiny backwoods lumber town called Bytown, which grew into the "city of saws and laws." It was located on the Ottawa River, which now separates the provinces of Ontario and Quebec. It was therefore a symbolic cord linking Canada's two founding peoples. More important, though, it was safely located out of reach of possible American attacks. The war stimulated on both sides a desire for more peaceful relations. One of the first steps in that direction was the Rush-Bagot convention of 1817, which limited naval armament in the Great Lakes to police vessels. This was an important beginning for the establishment of what is now the longest undefended border in the world.

Diplomatic machinery was also set up to facilitate the peaceful settlement of disputes among the neighbors, and that machinery has functioned ever since. An 1818 convention established the northwestern boundary along the 49th parallel all the way to the Rockies. Unfortunately this convention was unable to settle conflicting claims on the Pacific Coast and provided for joint occupation of that area for the time being. Tempers were again to flare over this territory a quarter of a century later, with some Americans defiantly screaming "Fifty-four forty or fight!", meaning that the United States should have all the land west of the Rockies up to the fifty-four forty parallel. But after 1814 these neighbors were never to fight again over disputes, and this boundary was firmly established in 1846 along the 49th parallel, with only a minor southward dip to the Strait of Juan de Fuca so that Vancouver Island would remain entirely within British North America. After the northern border had been agreed upon, the United States could concentrate upon its western destiny, and Canada could turn its attention to creating a unified nation in the less hospitable northern part of the American continent.

THE ROAD TO INDEPENDENCE

The period from 1815 to the rebellions of 1837 was one of adjustment to rising demands for more democracy and for responsible government (government responsible not to a monarch or his governors, but to a popularly elected legislature). The revolutions in America and France had contradictory effects on many Canadians. These convulsions caused some Canadians to fear instability resulting from too much democracy; Canadians tended to see British institutions as the best bulwark against such instability and saw American democracy as offering too little order, an impression later greatly strengthened by the American Civil War. At the same time, those revolutions fanned the desire for more representative self-government in British North America.

During those years the immigration patterns changed so that the make-up of the Canadian population also changed. Following the War of 1812 the British showed less tolerance toward American immigration into their Canadian colonies. Therefore, the influx of Americans practically stopped until the end of the century. At the same time, economic and social distress in the British Isles led to a flood of emigration to the New World. Most went to the United States, but between 1815 and 1850 approximately 800,000 went to Canada. About 100,000 settled in the Maritime Provinces, strengthening the British character of that area. However, most moved into the uncleared portions of what is now Ontario, whose population by 1850 had practically reached a million.

These settlers left a motherland which herself was experiencing significant reform movements, and some of the settlers brought British progressive ideas with them and enthusiastically supported democratic reform in Upper and Lower Canada, such as William Lyon Mackenzie and Louis-Joseph Papineau. Both were admirers of British institutions, but both opposed aristocratic rule and favored the popular election of executive officers, as had long been practiced in the United States.

In 1837 followers of both men rebelled in Toronto and Montreal, but their uprisings were promptly crushed. Both leaders were forced to make hair-raising escapes to the United States. There they hoped to gain the support of the American government for their causes, but American leaders were not willing to risk conflict with Britain by granting assistance. Canadians have never experienced as much domestic violence as their American neighbors. But the rebellions of 1837 were among the few incidents of political violence in Canada. Although they failed in the short term, they did succeed in prompting the British to sit up and take notice of political conditions in Canada. They wisely launched an investigation that ultimately led in 1867 to a largely independent Canada.

The British remembered the futility of attempting to erect dams against the democratic tide in the United States six decades earlier. In 1838 they dispatched John Lambton, the first Earl of Durham, to Canada to serve as Governor General of all the provinces and to investigate the grievances of the rebels. Because of his hand in the passage of the Great Reform Bill in Britain in 1832, he had earned the nickname of "Radical Jack." Very soon after his debarkation at Quebec City, he became embroiled in quarrels with his home government. He returned to England only five months later and submitted his now famous Durham Report early in 1839. The report dealt with a wide range of North American problems. His most important

recommendations were the establishment of responsible government, the union of Upper and Lower Canada (ultimately aiming toward the union of all British North American provinces), and the practice of permitting the provincial governments to make most decisions, while reserving only a few important matters, such as defense and foreign policy, for the imperial government.

Ultimately all of Lord Durham's proposals were enacted and it became a major milestone in the transformation of the British Empire into a Commonwealth of self-ruling nations and in the evolution of democratic government in Canada. In 1841 the provinces of Upper and Lower Canada were united as the first step toward a unified Canada. A single legislature was created with each former colony having equal representation, even though initially only English could be spoken in the debates. By the end of the decade responsible government had been established.

Durham noted the gulf that divided anglophones from francophones: "I found two nations warring within the bosom of a single state; I found a struggle, not of principles, but of races." However, he had developed a very low opinion of French Canadians, believing them to be "an utterly uneducated and singularly inert population . . . destitute of all that can invigorate and elevate a people." He therefore believed it to be a "vain endeavor to preserve a French-Canadian nationality in the midst of Anglo-American colonies and states." Unity would ultimately anglicize the French, he mistakenly believed. Such remarks understandably stung French Canadians who openly opposed the Durham Report. These remarks and attitudes also hardened their determination to resist assimilation at all costs and to survive as a cultural entity. They were determined to demonstrate that Canada could not be ruled *without* French cooperation. However, through toleration, solidarity and constructive parliamentary work, the French showed in the years that followed

Canada

Letter dated October 3, 1840, in the hand of the Governor of Nova Scotia, Viscount Lucius Bentinck Cary Falkland (1840–46), to a London merchant requesting lamps plus sherry and claret glasses, ending the hasty request with "I am, gentlemen, your obed[ient] servant, FALKLAND."

that Canada could be ruled *with* French collaboration.

The political union of the two provinces proved to be quite cumbersome, and the result was frequent elections and changes of government. By the 1850s it was clear to many persons that a new and different kind of political framework, still linked with Britain, would ultimately be neces-

sary in order to enable Canada to face the challenges posed by economic development and the ever-present dynamism of the United States. The need to compete with the U.S. for business investments and immigrants, as well as to ward off the powerful American force of manifest destiny, stimulated Canadian determination to develop the West, to improve trans-

portation within the colonies, and to steer toward national unity.

The growing pressures for self-government also pointed toward greater unity. While the American political experience helped to whet many Canadians' own appetite for self-rule, the actual American political model had considerably less appeal. In Canadian eyes, the American

Canada

The Charlottetown Conference, September 1, 1864
Public Archives Canada/C733

Civil War (1861–1865) revealed serious weaknesses in the decentralized regime with excessively powerful states and no mature mother country to act as a stabilizer. More and more Canadians wanted self-rule, but very few wanted complete independence from Britain. What the reformers who were ultimately successful wanted was a large measure of self-rule under the British constitution and within the British Empire. The war also again stimulated some talk in America of acquiring Canada. For years some Americans had been angry about the fact that Canada had been the last station of the "Underground Railway" for run-away slaves. Others had been irritated by the fact that Britain had tolerated Confederate raids on the northern states launched from Canadian soil during the Civil War. President Lincoln's Secretary of State, William H. Seward, was reported to have been an interested listener to talk about taking possession of Canada. However, Lincoln turned a deaf ear to it.

CONFEDERATION

By 1864 the forces supporting Canadian unity really began to gain momentum. Legislative deadlock had been created over such explosive issues as "representation by population" (or "Rep by Pop" for short), which would have awarded legislative seats according to the size of population, thereby discriminating against Quebec. The reformist governing coalition since 1854 led by John A. Macdonald, who came to dominate Canadian politics until his death in 1891, and by the *Québécois*, George-Etienne Cartier, could no longer rule. In 1864 they helped form a broader coalition which initiated discussions among the colonies and London aiming toward some form of confederation.

It is very characteristic of Canadian politics that this coalition rejected all forms of coercion to muscle unwilling provinces into a new confederation, or to maneuver any province into a situation where it could simply be outvoted by the majority. Canada is very much a compact among powerful provinces, and even today many important political problems are dealt with in semi-annual "summit conferences" involving the prime minister and the ten provincial premiers.

The "Fathers of Confederation," as they later came to be known, found the greatest resistance to union in Quebec and the Maritimes. In September 1864 representatives of the Maritime provinces assembled in Charlottetown, Prince Edward Island, to discuss the possibility of uniting the four Atlantic provinces. This Charlottetown Conference is reverently regarded in Canada as the first step toward Canadian unity.

But it was only a first step because the astute John A. Macdonald mobilized a delegation to go to the conference and to persuade the Maritimers to consider a larger vision of Canadian unity. The latter agreed to postpone their decision and to attend a conference of all provincial leaders in Quebec City in October. There they met behind closed doors for two weeks. They thoroughly discussed the ever-explosive Canadian question of the relationship between provincial and central authority. They tried to find a way to create a central government sufficiently strong to hold the confederation together and to block possible American northward expansion without being so strong that it could crush the important cultural differences in the individual provinces.

In the end the delegates could agree on the general shape of confederation, and the "72 Quebec Resolutions" were a de-

tailed outline of the structure of government and the division of powers and financial responsibilities which became the basis for Canada's first constitution in 1867. Obtaining the approval of all the provincial legislatures proved to be considerably more difficult. There was relatively little opposition in what is now Ontario, the most populous part of Canada and well poised to benefit economically from westward expansion that was sure to follow unification.

Francophone Canadians were much more skeptical, fearing that union would make them an even smaller minority and therefore threaten their survival as a distinct cultural entity. Cartier was able to persuade a slim majority of *Québécois* that they would face a greater danger of extinction by remaining outside, rather than inside, the new union. He pointed out that a solitary Quebec would risk annexation by the United States. There the force of the "melting pot" would surely destroy French Canadian culture, as was actually demonstrated subsequently in the case of most French Canadian emigrants to the United States. He stressed that confederation would leave the provinces authority over educational and religious matters, that French civil law would remain in Quebec and that French would be one of two official languages in both the federal parliament and the province. Most important of all, confederation would recreate the separation of Lower from Upper Canada and create a province of Quebec in which there would again be a French-speaking majority.

The greatest resistance, though, was found in the Atlantic provinces. These had always had closer ties with Britain and New England than with the provinces farther west. They viewed the new constitutional scheme as favoring the more popu-

49

Canada

lous and economically powerful central Canada. Prince Edward Island and Newfoundland rejected union, and the latter colony did not reconsider this decision until 1949, when its people chose in a close referendum to become a part of Canada. But Britain at this time also wanted a united Canada and put great pressure on Nova Scotia and New Brunswick. Both finally decided to join, although Nova Scotia almost backed out of the union nine years later.

The next step took place in London in 1867, where a delegation of Canadians met British leaders to draw up the British North America Act (BNA). This act differed little from the Quebec Resolutions, except that it contained some compromises sought by the Maritimes. The BNA was accepted by the British Parliament without serious opposition, and it served as Canada's constitution until 1982. The differences in the way Canada and the United States adopted their first constitutions is revealing. There was no constitutional convention in Canada, and there was much less haggling over details.

Some of its terms or concepts were stated in very general terms, and, in good British style, some important political practices were left entirely unwritten. It explicitly provided that Canada should have "a constitution similar in principle to that of the United Kingdom." But it also revealed an awareness of the special difficulties of ruling a vast federation with sharp racial, cultural and regional differences. It left much room for the Canadian political system to evolve and to adapt to such a diverse and far-flung country. On July 1, 1867, the Dominion of Canada, composed of Ontario, Quebec, Nova Scotia and New Brunswick, came into existence. That date remains Canada's main national holiday. To soothe *Québécois* feelings after the 1960s, the federal government officially renamed the holiday "Canada Day," but some Canadians still call it "Dominion Day."

Canadians did not regard themselves as being independent of Great Britain, but only as being self-governing in their own domestic affairs. Indeed, as Pierre Berton noted, "we did not separate violently from Europe but cut our ties cautiously in the Canadian manner—so cautiously, so imperceptibly that none of us is quite sure when we actually achieved our independence." The tie with Britain, insofar as foreign and defense policy were concerned, was still considered to be of great importance in assisting this loose collection of provinces in defending their interests against the more powerful and self-confident American republic, which, Canadians feared, still had territorial ambitions north of their border. They saw evidence of this only four months

ANNO TRICESIMO

VICTORIÆ REGINÆ.

CAP. III.

An Act for the Union of *Canada*, *Nova Scotia*, and *New Brunswick*, and the Government thereof; and for Purposes connected therewith.

WHEREAS the Provinces of *Canada*, *Nova Scotia*, and *New Brunswick* have expressed their Desire to be federally united into One Dominion under the Crown of the United Kingdom of *Great Britain* and *Ireland*, with a Constitution similar in Principle to that of the United Kingdom:

And whereas such a Union would conduce to the Welfare of the Provinces and promote the Interests of the *British* Empire:

And whereas on the Establishment of the Union by Authority of Parliament it is expedient, not only that the Constitution of the Legislative Authority in the Dominion be provided for, but also that the Nature of the Executive Government therein be declared:

And whereas it is expedient that Provision be made for the eventual Admission into the Union of other Parts of *British North America*:

Be it therefore enacted and declared by the Queen's most Excellent Majesty, by and with the Advice and Consent of the Lords Spiritual and

The British North America Act, July 1, 1867
Public Archives Canada/C104073

before the Confederation was founded in 1867 when the United States purchased Alaska from Russia.

A *transcontinental* Canadian confederation was visibly taking shape, despite formidable obstacles. One of the first hurdles cleared was the Canadian government's purchase in 1869 of the Hudson's Bay Company's charter and trade monopoly in the West and Northwest. That company had, in a sense, held the Canadian West in trust until Canada became ready to develop it. It relinquished a huge expanse of land with a settled population of only about 7,000 persons, concentrated mainly around Fort Garry (now Winnipeg), in the Red River Colony (now Manitoba).

The Canadian acquisition of the Hudson's Bay charter was not good news to most of the inhabitants of the Red River Colony. Most of them were Métis, a racial mixture of Indians and French and British fur traders, who spoke both French and English. The Métis had very few contacts with or interest in Eastern Canada, and over the years they developed a strong sense of their own identity. They feared that their traditional way of life would be destroyed. There were unfortunate clashes with the new government in Ottawa, and under the leadership of the legendary Louis Riel, the Métis formed a provisional government and prepared to resist Ottawa's authority.

The Canadian government was torn over how to respond. In Ontario there was outrage at Riel's order to execute a Canadian official who had been sent to the colony. On the other hand, Quebecers sympathized with the French-speaking Métis. Faced with such differences, the infant Canadian government developed a two-pronged strategy: it sent troops to Fort Garry, forcing Riel to flee to Montana, where he became a poverty-stricken school teacher for the next 15 years. It also received in Ottawa a delegation from the Red River Colony to discuss terms for entry into the Canadian federation.

Ottawa conceded all the essential rights which Riel had demanded, especially demands for religious schools and the equality of French and English as official languages. The Colony entered the federation as the province of Manitoba in 1870, but, as we shall see, the problems of insuring the French language rights that were granted in 1869 continue to plague Manitoba and Ottawa today.

The next step in building Canada was to induce the colony of British Columbia to join the federation. It was heavily attracted to the United States, and not until 1869 did the sentiment to join Canada outweigh the inclination to enter the American union. Finally, in 1871 Ottawa struck a deal with British Columbia. As a price for the colony's entering Canada, Ottawa promised to assume its accumulated debt and to build a railway all the way to the Pacific. This latter promise proved an exceedingly difficult one to keep. In 1871 British Columbia entered Canada. In that same year the new country entered into difficult negotiations with the United States in which many specific disputes were settled. The major significance of this Treaty of Washington, though, was that the U.S. officially recognized the facts that the American continent north of Mexico was forever to be divided between the two countries, and that Canada was a federation extending from coast to coast. In 1873 Prince Edward Island, which saw union as the only solution to its desperate financial problems, joined Canada.

Ottawa skillfully hammered together a unified Canada by enticing wavering colonies into the federation through promises of economic benefit. This tool was particularly important and effective because of a severe world-wide economic downturn which began in 1873 and lasted until the mid-1890s. This seemingly endless economic depression was the longest and worst the modern world has ever known. It greatly hampered the construction of a northern transcontinental railway which the Canadian government promised the new provinces in the East and West. The crucial importance of that

railway, which would staple together all the far-flung provinces of Canada and attract investments and immigrants from Europe, was revealed in a letter which Prime Minister Macdonald wrote to London: "Until this great work is completed, our Dominion is little better than a geographical expression."

TIGHTENING THE EAST–WEST LINK

Short railways had begun to be built in the 1840s and 1850s to link trading terminals and to connect with the rail networks which were being constructed in the U.S. But Macdonald knew that in order to prosper, Canada had to establish an East–West transportation and trade axis that could counteract the more natural North–South trade axis. Voted back into power in 1878, Macdonald proclaimed a "national policy," which called for raising the protective tariff to shelter Canadian companies from excessive competition by bigger and financially stronger American firms. Such protectionist economic measures were vigorously debated at that time.

One of the ironies of such a lasting protectionist policy is that American companies circumvented it by establishing their own subsidiaries in Canada. They thereby created what many observers and critics would later call the "Americanization" of the Canadian economy. Indeed, the large degree of foreign (especially American) ownership of the economy remains an unsolved and perhaps insoluble dilemma.

Macdonald's policy also called for the fulfillment of the Dominion's promise to British Columbia to complete the railway to the Pacific. He was also determined that this railway be constructed entirely within Canada, rather than to extend partly through the less foreboding Ameri-

can landscape. This was a daunting task. Because of Canada's immense size, formidable terrain, extremely variable climate and sparse population, economic development has depended far more on gigantic projects and close cooperation between the government and business leaders than was ever considered necessary or desirable in the United States. This pattern of a large governmental hand in the nation's economy continues to this day.

In order to persuade British and Canadian businessmen to take the great risks of building a transcontinental railway, the government offered an assortment of cash subsidies, special privileges and huge land grants in the unsettled areas through which the rail lines would run; much of this land is still owned by the Canadian Pacific Railway Company (CPR). The opposition Liberal Party strongly criticized the generosity of the contract offered to the CPR. Every dollar the CPR could lay its hands on was needed to build the railway through the twisted, rocky countryside of western Ontario, across the Prairies and though the treacherous Kicking Horse Pass in the Rocky Mountains. On November 7, 1885, Macdonald received a telegram informing him that the railway had finally been completed.

The central government in Ottawa moved energetically to secure order and to enlarge its powers throughout Canada. The Royal Canadian Mounted Police (RCMP) controlled the western settlements much more tightly than was the case in the U.S., so the shooting iron and the violence that characterized much of life in the early American West were largely absent. Hollywood helped to create a myth about the Royal Canadian Mounted Policeman that is misleading. Pierre Berton noted in his book, *Hollywood's Canada*, that Hollywood made 575 movies about Canada between 1907 and 1975, and in 256 of them the "Mounty" always "got his man" (a name and a slogan the RCMP dislikes today).

Although his guns blazed in the movies, he, in fact, seldom drew his weapon. He did enforce the law, but he also dispensed social services, helped persons get to faraway hospitals, tried to secure food for the settlers and Indians in his area in time of need, and sometimes even sorted and delivered the mail. His patient, tactful paternalism helped to prepare Canadians' receptivity to the idea of the state as the generous dispenser of social services like family allowances and universal medical treatment. This is a notion less firmly implanted in the minds of most Americans.

Trying to avoid the bloody Indian wars the American settlers had experienced, the Canadian government negotiated what it thought at the time were fair treaties with

Rt. Hon. John A. Macdonald
Public Archives Canada/C5327

Canada

Lord Strathcona drives in the last spike completing the Canadian Pacific Railway, November 1885

Public Arcvhives Canada/C3693

the Indians, and some allowed themselves to be relocated on reservations. Indeed, there were fewer Indian wars and massacres of natives in Western Canada than in the United States. However, in the late-20th century Indians began to challenge many of those treaties, as well as their status as second-class citizens in modern Canadian society.

The last two decades of the 19th century were not a golden age of harmony for the young dominion. Most of the provinces resented the growth of Ottawa's power, and there was one crisis after the other. Western farmers resented both the high freight prices, which resulted from the CPR's monopoly, and the high price of goods manufactured in the East, which resulted from

the country's high tariff policy. In the territory that is now Alberta and Saskatchewan, the mainly Indian and Métis inhabitants resented the intrusion of government agents into their lives. They feared a radical disruption of their traditional way of life. The great Cree Indian chief, Big Bear, was attempting to unify the Indians to renegotiate the treaties with the white men. Also, the Métis in the Saskatchewan River Valley were pressing for surveys of their land claims in order not to be dispossessed of their farms again, as they had been in Manitoba after the government had allegedly broken its promises to them. In short, the region was ripe for a rebellion.

Because the Macdonald government showed little interest in these concerns, the

Métis in 1884 asked Louis Riel to return from his American exile in order to lead them in their resistance to Ottawa. He proclaimed the provisional government of Saskatchewan on March 19, 1885. Aided by his able adjutant general, Gabriele Dumont, he led an ill-fated uprising, known as the Northwest Rebellion of 1885, which pitted a guerrilla force of 600 Métis and Plains Indians against a poorly-trained Canadian army of 8,000 men. The war opened with a Métis victory at Duck Lake, with Riel, a self-proclaimed "Prophet of the New World," riding unarmed within range of the Canadians waving a crucifix and yelling, "Fire! In the name of the Son and the Holy Ghost! Fire!"

But the brave natives were ultimately defeated by the railway, which carried thousands of green Canadian troops to the West in 10 days. After 51 days of fighting that included an indecisive battle at Fish Creek and a stinging loss at Batoche, the uprising was crushed. The last human barriers to white settlement of the West were thereby eliminated.

Dumont escaped and fled to the United States where he later joined Buffalo Bill's Wild West Show as a sharpshooter on horseback and the "hero of the half-breed revolution." Riel was captured, and despite vigorous protests by Quebecers, who regarded him as a staunch defender of French and Catholic rights, he was hanged on November 16, 1885, in the Mounted Police barracks at Regina, Saskatchewan. Canada, Macdonald (who said that "Riel shall hang, though every dog in Quebec bark in his favor"), and his Conservative Party suffered greatly from that

Louis Riel in front of Manitoba's legislature

act, which was one of the most significant events in Canadian history. English Protestants at the time viewed Riel as a common criminal, but francophones saw him differently. His execution reignited French Canadian nationalism and exacerbated the animosities between anglophones and francophones. The debate over Riel was the first time since Confederation that anglophones and francophones were diametrically opposed. It paved the way for the Liberal Party's acquisition of national power in 1895, five years after Macdonald's death, and was the beginning of the Conservative Party's almost complete political exclusion from Quebec, which continues right up to the present time. Quebec has consistently reacted to any perceived attack on the rights of French speakers anywhere in Canada in the same way as it did to Riel's execution.

In 1985, the centennial of the Northwest Rebellion, many Canadians were still uncertain that a war had to be fought in order to deal with the Métis' and Indians' grievances. That struggle seems to symbolize the basic tensions that still exist in Canadian life: the struggle for minority rights and for regional autonomy. With the resurgence in the 1970s of various forms of nationalism in Canada, many Western Canadians came to regard Riel as a defender of Western interests; socialists see him as a staunch opponent of imperialism, and francophones continue to view him as the champion of French language rights. Riel's home and grave in Winnipeg are maintained as befitting a hero, not a rebel to be despised. It is an irony that Riel is perhaps Canada's only real hero today.

In 1992 the House of Commons, which was desperately trying to keep Quebec in Canada and placate the West, officially recognized Riel's "unique and historic role as a founder of Manitoba." This act was, in former Prime Minister Joe Clark's words, "an indication that we have matured as a nation." In 1998 the Canadian government apologized to all aboriginal peoples for past mistreatment and offenses, including the hanging of Riel. Nevertheless, the Métis National Council regretted that the apology fell short of an official pardon. The fact that most Canadians want Riel exonerated was revealed in a 1999 poll that showed Riel as the most popular Canadian politician; his "approval rating" was 75%, the same percentage of respondents who believe it was wrong to hang him as a traitor. In 1999 the first overt political act of Governor General Adrienne Clarkson was to attend a ceremony honoring Riel. She called him "the founder of Manitoba" who "played a key, vital role in opening up Canada's West."

Within months after leading his party to electoral victory 1891, John A. Macdonald

Louis Riel addresses the jury before his conviction, Regina, Saskatchewan, 1885
Public Archives Canada/C1879

died, and five years later the era of Conservative Party dominance in Canada came to an end. In the three decades of that era, Canada had survived the initial challenges of self-government. It had expanded its borders from coast to coast. As a young country with only four million citizens in 1885, it had tied the country from East to West with a railway; the U.S. had completed its first transcontinental railway a quarter of a century earlier, but America's population and market were ten times larger than Canada's at that time, and its terrain is much more amenable to railroad construction than is that of its neighbor to the north. Canada had survived the effects of the world-wide recession which had begun in 1873 and which had seemed interminable. It had worked out a national economic policy, which had foreseen not only the expansion of the railways, but also increased immigration and the erection of a tariff barrier to encourage the growth of Canadian manufacturing.

In 1896 Sir Wilfrid Laurier led the Liberal Party to victory in the federal elections and launched practically a century of almost continuous Liberal Party rule in Canada. Laurier was a handsome, urbane, superbly educated man, who was equally articulate and elegant in both his native French and in English, which he spoke with an appealing French touch. He was regarded as a master of rationality and compromise. His skill at finding the middle ground enabled him to govern as prime minister for 15 years. He helped to unify both French and English concerns, calling on all his countrymen to remember that "your duty is simply and above all to be Canadians." He gave his party something of a basic philosophy. He believed that his party was heir to British, not continental European liberalism; therefore cultural tol-

eration should be a guiding rule, and anti-clericalism (the view that organized churches have no place in political affairs) should have no part. He did expect the Catholic Church to restrain itself, though.

By the time Laurier became prime minister, Canada had already begun to pull out of the economic crisis; indeed, for decades the Liberal Party benefited from this fortunate coincidence of gaining power at the threshold of a long period of prosperity and development. The Conservative Party would not be so lucky; as we shall see, it would have to bear much of the blame for the suffering that the First World War and the Great Depression of the 1930s would inflict on Canadians.

Canada was beginning to take full advantage of the world-wide rise in grain prices. Canadian wheat began to represent in the economy what fur had once been in the French Canadian economy: it played the dominant role until well into the 1930s. Gold was discovered in the Yukon in 1898, followed by rich mining strikes elsewhere in Canada. This was also a time of robust industrial development; the net value of manufacturing production grew by more than two and one-half times from 1901 to 1911. A new mood of optimism had been created which began to attract hundreds of thousands of immigrants from the United Kingdom, continental Europe and the United States. Most came to the Canadian West where there was still free land to be had. By the 1890s most of the free land in the United States had already been claimed. With the practical closing of the American frontier, Canada had become the place for landless people with dreams. In 1896, almost 17,000 immigrants came, but by 1913 this inflow became a flood-tide of a half million annually. From 1896 to 1911 over two million

Canada

persons poured into Canada. From 1897 to 1930 almost a million and a half American farmers from Minnesota, the Dakotas and other border states crossed the line into the Prairie provinces.

Such an explosive migration into Canada was an important boon to the young country. Nevertheless, it did bring certain social, political and economic changes that would trouble Canada. A multitude of new, relatively short railroads were constructed west of Winnipeg to provide transport for the produce of new farms which were opening up. The financing of these lines, obtained in Canada, New York and London from private sources, was a very high risk, as the investors would find out within a few decades. Almost none of the immigrants came from France; thus, despite the higher birth-rate in Quebec, the percentage of French in the overall Canadian population continued to decline. This decline was aggravated by the steady stream of French Canadians who left Quebec and the Maritimes for New England during the second half of the 19th century. Today at least two million of their descendants live in Maine, New Hampshire, Vermont and Massachusetts. These population trends and patterns disturbed Quebec's leaders, who were angrily watching French language rights being whittled away not only in Manitoba but also in Saskatchewan and Alberta, which had become provinces in 1905. Despite legal assurances to francophones in 1875, separate French Catholic schools and the status of French as an official language alongside English were largely abolished. French Canadians have often shown that they have long memories, and the recollection of these actions at the end of the 19th century would in the 1970s and

1980s again spark bitter conflict over French language rights in Manitoba.

More than a fourth of the newcomers came from Central Europe and the Ukraine. Settling in the prairies, they faced ethnic and cultural condescension and resentment from settlers of British descent. As the visitor can see today, these Central European and Ukrainian people have had and still have an important cultural influence in the West, but they were forced to earn the respect they now enjoy. Distressing to the Quebecers was the fact that when these non-British immigrant groups finally became integrated, they integrated into English, not French language and culture, whether they settled in Quebec or not. With this phenomenon in mind during the 1970s, the Quebec government required by law that immigrant children in Quebec province be schooled in French, not English. Almost none of the immigrants stayed in the Maritime Provinces, and the economic boom of this era touched these provinces less than elsewhere, thereby helping to deepen the economic distress that still exists there. Also, the journey of some of the less fortunate immigrants stopped in the urban slums of major cities in Quebec and Ontario, and their restlessness for social and economic improvement brought ferment into urban politics and labor union activity.

LOOSENING THE APRON STRINGS

The 1898 Yukon gold rush in the Klondike fields sparked another of many border disputes with the United States. This one involved the eastern border of the Alaska Panhandle, through which supplies to the Klondike had to pass. Rus-

sia had obtained Alaska from Britain in 1825 and had sold it to the United States in 1867. The U.S. insisted upon the border that had been recognized in 1867. The British government wanted at the time to defuse disputes with the U.S. It agreed to have the question adjudicated in 1903 by a commission composed of three Americans, two Canadians and one Englishman. When the Englishman sided with the three Americans in accepting the American claim, Canadians were incensed, against both the U.S. and Britain.

This incident in 1903 was a helpful reminder to Canadians that their interests were by no means identical to those of the U.S., and that Britain could no longer be relied upon energetically to back up Canadian demands in the face of American opposition. Of course, this realization had not come suddenly. Macdonald had believed that Canada's independence in the face of "American Manifest Destiny" depended upon its ties with Britain, but he also was convinced that the colonial apron strings must gradually be cut if Canada were to fully mature as a nation. He began sending ambassadors to London after 1880. Despite a strident Quebec nationalist stance early in his career, Laurier was a great admirer of many things British, and he accepted a knighthood. Nevertheless, he, like many of his countrymen, had feared a more active British imperial policy in the world, and he had staunchly opposed the creation of a permanent Imperial Council, which could have imposed tariff and military measures on all the colonies. Even before the end of the 19th century, the Canadian government had secured the right to negotiate, though not sign, treaties.

This and the entire series of negotiations since 1867 with the Americans on a wide variety of issues ranging from commerce, fishing, waterways and boundary lines persuaded both neighbors that an International Joint Commission (IJC), composed of three representatives each from the U.S. and Canada, would be a very useful permanent body to settle bilateral disputes, particularly ones dealing with waterways. This commission has worked effectively since its creation in 1909. That same year the Canadians also decided that because Canada had to look out for its own interests, it should create a Department of External Affairs through which a Canadian foreign policy could be conducted. It began as little more than an archive, and it would be more than a decade before Canada could truly handle its own foreign affairs.

Foreign policy disputes had created a rather strong anti-American sentiment in Canada, which boiled to the surface in the federal elections of 1911, when voters rejected the aging Laurier because he had

Panning for gold in the Yukon, 1898
Public Archives Canada/C16459

dared to negotiate tariff reductions with Washington. Anti-British feeling had also become a greater force to be reckoned with, as Canada's leaders were painfully to discover at the time of the outbreak of the First World War in 1914.

THE FIRST WORLD WAR

When Britain decided to enter the war in September 1914, many Canadians and most Britons considered Canada automatically to be at war also. However, there were many Canadians, particularly francophones, who saw this matter very differently. An early warning of francophones' reaction to a British war effort had already been given 15 years earlier when the Boer War had broken out in South Africa. The Laurier government had been faced in 1899 with emotional demands from English-speaking Canadians to stand by Britain during this conflict, but francophones made equally forceful demands that their sons should not be called upon to die for Britain in far-away wars, unrelated to the defense of Canada itself. Laurier's compromise that volunteers could be sent to fight for Britain prompted his brightest follower in Quebec, Henri Bourassa, to break with him.

Bourassa became a rallying point for dissident francophones. In 1907 he declared: "There is Ontario patriotism, Quebec patriotism or western patriotism, but there is no Canadian patriotism." He laid the groundwork in Quebec for the bitter resistance to Canada's participation in the First World War.

As a member of the British Empire, Canada found itself legally at war in 1914. Canada was sparsely peopled, overwhelmingly rural, mired in an economic recession, and divided by language, faith and region. A majority of Canadians favored Canada's involvement, but the willingness to sacrifice Canadian blood and resources for a European dispute was not equally felt by all Canadians. This was revealed in the makeup of the First Canadian Contingent that was raised and sent overseas within two months of the war's outbreak. Of its 36,267 volunteers, only 1,245 were francophones, only 10,880 had been born in Canada, and over 23,000 were British-born with close ties to the old country. Many anglophones felt deep loyalty to Britain. But *Québécois*, who represented three of the eight million Canadians at the time, neither shared that loyalty nor felt a sentimental attachment to France, where the bloodiest battles of the war were fought. The France of the 20th century was no longer the France to which the *Québécois* ancestors had belonged. The French Revolution had beheaded the king and his family, proclaimed a republic, de-

capitated 25,000 persons and brutally attacked the Catholic Church. The Jacobin regime had even gone so far as to briefly to proclaim a worship of reason, instead of God, renaming the Cathedral of Notre Dame the "Temple of Reason."

During the entire 19th century the controversy over the role of the Church in French society had been a dominant issue in French politics. This was shocking to a people like the *Québécois*, who until the 1960s were a deeply Catholic people and who accepted the Church's active hand in politics. Also, French society had become socially experimental in ways that shocked many Quebecers, who until the 1960s were socially conservative. As McGill historian Pierre Boulle noted: "The name of Quebec as a special, protected entity—very different from nasty revolutionary France—essentially existed until the 'Quiet Revolution' in the 1960s." In short, *Québécois* did not regard Frenchmen in 1914 as brothers in distress who should be saved.

The turmoil that followed entry into the "Great War" in 1914 indicated that there was absolutely no unanimity concerning how much Canada should be integrated in the British Empire and how much Canadians should contribute to the war effort. The uneasiness about the war increased as casualties began to pile up and as Canadians began to realize that this war was going to be much longer than they had initially thought.

On Easter morning, April 9, 1917, the Canadian Corps fought together under their own commanders for the first time. It was also the first time that all four divisions of the Canadian Army came together. They defeated the Germans at Vimy Ridge after suffering terrible casualties: 3,598 killed and 7,004 wounded. Many argue that the Canadian nation was born on that day. The victory also made the Canadians the sharp point of the Allied spear. Joined by the Australians, they broke through the German lines at Amiens on August 8, 1918, and helped set off the drive that would win the war three months later. This ugly four-year conflict would claim more than 60,000 Canadian lives (12,000 more than the U.S.) and would call 619,636 Canadians to arms, all but 75,000 of whom for overseas duty. Canadian troops performed very well and showed themselves and the world that their country was capable of things undreamed of before 1914. The last Canadian veteran of this "Great War," John Babcock, died in February 2010 at age 109. Prime Minister Stephen Harper called him "the last living link" to a conflict "which in so many ways marked our coming of age as a nation."

After the war had bogged down in the trenches, unimaginative mass suicidal assaults against the well-entrenched enemy

claimed more and more lives. The demands on Canadian man-power became so great that a politically explosive crossroads was reached. Recruiting declined dramatically in 1916, endangering the Canadian commitment to maintain four divisions on the Western front. Therefore, in 1917 the Canadian government felt compelled to present legislation to introduce conscription, just as the Americans had done upon entering the conflict in April of that year. This decision ushered in the greatest threat to Canada's internal harmony since confederation almost a half century earlier.

The most prominent French Canadian politician, Sir Wilfrid Laurier, vigorously opposed the draft, although he continued to support the war effort. Other Quebec leaders had greater difficulty understanding why the Canadian government felt justified in calling for greater sacrifices. After all, a considerable number of *Québécois* had volunteered for military service, and with a few exceptions, they had served in English-speaking units. A notable exception was the highly decorated Twenty-Second Regiment of Quebec (called the "Vandoos"). In the midst of the struggle, an affront that deepened the antagonism was the elimination of bilingual schools in Manitoba and severe restrictions on French-language instruction in Ontario. The actual introduction of conscription in June 1917 ignited intense emotions in Quebec, and many Quebecers openly protested the measure or went into hiding to avoid the recruiters. In March and April 1918 serious riots protesting Canada's war policy took place in Quebec City.

The conscription issue split the Liberal Party. Quebec Liberal membership was solidly opposed to the measure. In a bitter and virulently racist federal electoral campaign in December 1917 over the issue of conscription and the formation of a united government (one which would include all the country's major parties), the Liberal Party won all but three seats in Quebec, but it won only 20 seats outside of Quebec. The Conservative Party, under Prime Minister Robert Borden, won the hard-fought contest. His majority Unionist government introduced measures that would have been unthinkable a few years earlier: the vote for women, railway nationalization, the income tax, and prohibition. But this election decisively altered party alignment and effectively banished the Tory Party to English Canada for decades. Not until the federal elections of 1984 were there signs that the Liberal Party lock on *Québécois*' votes in federal politics had been broken.

Borden and his Conservatives, which had been in office throughout the war, paid a high price for its willing aid to the victorious allies. It had widened the gulf

Canada

Rt. Hon. William Lyon Mackenzie King
Public Archives Canada/C86772

between English and French-speaking Canadians. The bill was presented to them in the first post-war election on December 6, 1921: they were dealt a stinging defeat, winning only 49 seats, 37 of which were in Ontario alone. Thus, the Conservative Party, which in 1917 had been practically eliminated from Quebec politics, now had been banished to the wilderness in federal politics as well.

THE INTERWAR YEARS

The end of World War I saw a problem identical in both Canada and the United States. Almost all railroads had gone broke. In the U.S., they went into receivership under the Railroad Administration, later to be returned to private ownership. In Canada, all but the Canadian Pacific were bankrupt. The government, which had made generous grants of land and money for their construction held the first mortgage, with priority over the private sector investors. Ultimately it took permanent control of these lines in 1923, combining them into the Canadian National, which remains as government property today. It includes what used to be the venerable Grand Trunk Railroad, running from Portland, Maine (via its subsidiary, the Central of Vermont) and the Grand Trunk Pacific, with a line to Prince Rupert, British Columbia. A few privately owned lines remained in operation, but the government was permanently in the railroad business. It combined lines it already owned into a massive system stretching from the Maritime Provinces to Vancouver and Prince Rupert.

The 1921 election ushered in a long era of Liberal Party domination in federal pol-

itics, first under the leadership of William Lyon Mackenzie King, who ruled Canada for most of the rest of his life, until his death in 1950. He had received a Ph.D. from Harvard and had served for years as an industrial relations consultant for the Rockefellers in the United States. He remained a bachelor all his life, and is widely regarded as the strangest (but largely respected) politician in Canadian history. He was deeply immersed in spiritualism, had a kind of psychopathic devotion to his deceased mother, and thought he had worked out a way to talk to her. That might sound odd, but a *Maclean's* poll on Canada Day 2006 revealed that half (55%) of Canadians still believed in psychic powers, and a third thought that earth-bound human beings can communicate with the dead. Despite all his personal quirks, though, he was responsible for making the Liberal Party an effective and attractive "all-things-to-all-men" grouping which could gather together Canadians of many different persuasions.

In addition to renewed Quebec nationalism and division between anglophones and francophones, the First World War brought other important changes to Canada. The heavy demand for military production stimulated Canadian industry. With Britain's hands tied, Canadians turned to the United States for investment capital. New York replaced London as Canada's chief source for outside capital, and during the war American investment in Canada increased by more than threefold. The rate of such investment grew steadily thereafter, until it became a matter of grave concern to Canadians after the Second World War. The war also sparked a renewed wave of immigration from Europe into Canada. Finally the "Great War" boosted the feeling of Canadian nationalism and the determination to become an entirely self-ruling country. During the war the Canadian government had made an important assertion of independence by insisting that a Canadian, Sir Arthur Currie, *not* an Englishman, command Canadian troops. It also demanded that Canada be treated as an ally, not as a colony. Accordingly, in 1917 all the prime ministers of the dominions (British colonies settled primarily by whites) were included in the Imperial War Cabinet.

At the 1919 Versailles Conference, which patched Europe together again, Canada was represented as a separate country, and it signed the treaty as an independent land. Professor Margaret MacMillan, great-granddaughter of British Prime Minister Lloyd George and former Trinity College provost at the University of Toronto, described the conference in her prize-winning study, *Paris 1919: Six Months that Changed the World*. Asked how

she could be so even-handed in her treatment, she answered: "When you're a Canadian, you're looking at great events from a distance."

Unlike the U.S., Canada joined the League of Nations, which had sprung from the imagination of American President Woodrow Wilson. Like the United States, though, Canada remained largely aloof from European affairs during the interwar years, and it was not actively supportive of the League.

There was much disagreement within Canada about how quickly the country should move toward autonomy from Britain, but while the debate was going on, the government took several concrete steps. In 1922 Prime Minister King indicated to Britain that Canada could no longer be committed in advance to military actions on the basis of its association with the British Empire. In 1923 it assumed the right to negotiate and *sign* treaties and to make its own foreign policy. It did promise Britain the courtesy of keeping it informed about what Canada was doing. In 1927 Canada sent its first ambassador to the United States.

At a large gathering of nations within the British Commonwealth in 1926, leaders of Britain and the dominions proclaimed that they were "equal in status and in no way subordinate one to another." This understanding became law with the passage by the British Parliament of the Statute of Westminster in 1931. This statute formally deprived the British Parliament of the right to legislate for the dominions. There remained a few apron strings, though. In Canada's case, the British Parliament retained the exclusive right to amend Canada's constitution, the British North America Act (BNA), whenever the issue involved the distribution of political powers between the central government and the provinces. Canada would probably have obtained this right also if the various provincial governments in Canada could have agreed upon a formula for doing that. But it was not until 1982 that agreement could be reached regarding constitutional amendments on all subjects. Finally, the Judicial Committee of the Privy Council, which is lodged in the British House of Lords, remained the highest court of appeal for Canadians until 1935 for criminal cases and until 1949 for civil cases.

Despite the fact that the decade following the end of the war was a relatively prosperous one, compared with the 1930s, it was a time of political radicalization. Canadians were confronted with a wave of labor agitation and strikes throughout the land. Canadian labor unions had doubled their membership during the war, but with returning veterans vying for jobs, unemployment grew and union leaders feared that their power and influence would become weakened. Employers were especially resistant to demands for collective bargaining, and workers resented what they saw as employers' excessive profiteering and conspicuous consumption. Frustration was increased by the high inflation, which had been stimulated during the war, and by the perennial perception on the part of Westerners that the government in Ottawa, supported by industrial and financial powers in Eastern Canada, regulated the economy to the advantage of the East and at the expense of the West. On top of this catalogue of concrete economic grievances, some labor leaders espoused socialist convictions and syndicalism (radical trade unionism to achieve political objectives).

The unrest came to a dramatic crescendo in the Winnipeg General Strike, which lasted from May 15 until June 25, 1919. At first, only workers in the building and metal trades struck to protest their employers' refusal to grant either higher wages or collective bargaining. But a couple of weeks later the Winnipeg Trades and Labour Council also struck in sympathy, paralyzing the economic life of the city within a few hours. Unionists in Vancouver and other Western cities joined the strikers. For a while the strike remained free of violence, but many employers and members of the federal and provincial government were inclined to see the strike as a deliberate attempt by Bolsheviks to undermine the democratic order in Canada. In the United States a similar "Red Scare" was afoot in 1919. The Canadian government had sent 4,400 troops to Russia after the overthrow of the czar in 1917. Although public opinion and the government turned against this deployment, it was not until April 1919 that the last Canadians were withdrawn from Soviet Russia.

A particularly unfortunate event occurred when Mounties and militia troops in Winnipeg broke up a banned march by strikers. In the confused situation that developed, one person was killed and 30 were injured. This tragic development prompted the government to arrest the leaders of the strike on charges of sedition and to patrol the streets of Winnipeg with soldiers. Finally, on June 25 the strike was called off after the government promised to look into the underlying causes of the strike. A governmental commission did indeed conclude that the aim of most of the strikers had been to achieve collective bargaining and better working conditions.

Nevertheless, the jailed union leaders were tried and convicted of seditious activities and were given jail sentences from six months to two years. This strike created

bitterness in Winnipeg and elsewhere that took decades to remove, and it stimulated the creation of protest sentiments and movements, which, through many twists and turns, continue to survive today.

Canada's social and economic problems became desperate in the aftermath of the New York stock market crash in 1929. Canada was very vulnerable to the severe and prolonged worldwide economic depression that set in. The country had always been dependent upon foreign capital and upon the exportation of raw materials to industrial nations, which now could no longer buy the things that Canada had to sell. By 1933 almost a fourth of the country's labor force was unemployed, and one was confronted everywhere with the same images as in the United States: bankruptcies and evictions, farm foreclosures, tent cities, soup-kitchens and itinerant Canadians desperately looking for work. Much of the government's attention was spent on maintaining law and order. The terrible economic situation sparked bitter labor unrest, and the government responded by sending in Mounties to disperse demonstrations, infiltrating union meetings with agents and censoring literature the government perceived to be radical.

Such a charged political atmosphere was an ideal greenhouse for diverse populist protest parties. They were heirs to the defunct Progressive Party, which had reared up against the dominance of the eastern financial centers, but which had lost all its strength by the early 1930s. Two of these parties, which still have a role in Canadian politics, sprang up in the West. The Social Credit Party, headed by a fiery radio evangelist, William Aberhart, aimed its appeal to ranchers and farmers and excoriated the eastern bankers, who allegedly manipulated credit, freight rates

and tariffs for their own selfish interests. This party won the Alberta provincial elections in 1935. Although most of its anti-banking legislation was struck down by the Supreme Court, it managed to establish a foothold in Albertan politics which remained firm for decades. It always rejected socialism and became an increasingly conservative party, which seeks to protect "the little guy" and Western Canadian interests. Today the party rules in British Columbia, and it cooperates with the Conservative Party in federal politics.

A second party that was from its very beginning a socialist party was the Cooperative Commonwealth Federation (CCF). It set out to organize laborers and farmers in order to "eradicate capitalism and put into operation the full programme of socialized planning which will lead to the establishment in Canada of the Cooperative Commonwealth," as its Regina Manifesto proclaimed in 1933. As doctrinaire as its program seems to be upon first reading, the party never sought an abolition of private property; it promised the "security of tenure for the farmer upon his farm." Also, unlike many radical parties, the CCF strongly favored parliamentary government and reform by legal, nonviolent means. It gained ground among urban intellectuals and trade unionists and became a permanent fixture in Canadian politics, although it never established firm roots in Atlantic Canada or Quebec. Its electoral fortresses were always in the West, and in 1944 it became the ruling party in Saskatchewan. In 1961 it changed its name to the *New Democratic Party (NDP)*.

A third party that rose up at this time was the Union Nationale in Quebec. In 1935, under the leadership of the former Quebec Conservative party leader, Maurice Duplessis, it gathered together the

Winnipeg General Strike, June 10, 1919
Public Archives Canada/C26782

Canada

The Great Depression: unemployed men board a train for Ottawa, June 1935
Public Archives Canada/C29461

scraps of that province's Conservative and Liberal parties. As in almost all times of adversity, Quebec nationalism flared up again during the depression. No doubt it was aggravated by the fact that almost all of the major employers in the province were anglophones, while an overwhelming majority of unemployed were francophones. Charging that the provincial government was ridden with corruption and that reform was needed in Quebec, Duplessis became premier in 1936. Despite repeated charges that he and his ruling clique were as corrupt as the leaders they replaced and that they were not genuine reformers, the *Union Nationale* gained a hold on Quebec politics that would not be broken until 1970. It pursued a conservative policy and maintained close relations with the Church. It also opened the door widely to foreign investment. Until it was finally swept aside by a new breed of Quebec nationalists and reformers who gained momentum in the late 1960s, it could always reap a rich harvest of votes by championing Quebec provincial rights in opposition to the government in Ottawa.

Economic depressions often spark energetic governmental intervention in the economy, especially in Canada, where the state's role in the economy has always been larger than in the United States. In the midst of so much anxiety and human misery, a *Conservative Party* government was elected. The new prime minister was R.B. Bennett, a lawyer from Calgary. He was energetic and competent, but he was

also an authoritarian manager. He was elected by promising social welfare and employment for hard-pressed Canadians.

In January 1935 Bennett introduced to Parliament a far-reaching "New Deal," which proposed no less than "modifications of the capitalist system to enable that system more effectively to serve the people." He advocated state-supported farm credit, unemployment insurance, minimum wages and maximum hours of work. Bennett's program stunned many of his fellow Conservatives. His Liberal opponents charged that the measures were unconstitutional on the grounds that they infringed upon provincial powers, a charge which the Supreme Court largely upheld in an important decision a year later. The prime minister had already become so unpopular that he and his party were thrown out of power by a landslide in October 1935; the Liberal Party won a stunning 171 seats to the Tories' 39, and Mackenzie King again assumed the helm.

The discredited Conservative Party, which had had the misfortune of being in power during the depression, was banished to the political wilderness for most of the next half century. Nevertheless, the strides which Bennett had taken were not repudiated by his party in the long run; the Conservative Party in Canada today still advocates a wider social welfare net and a more activist government than do most Americans, Democrat or Republican. Also, the federal government's intervention in the economy continued, despite

the 1936 Supreme Court decision. In 1934 the Bank of Canada had been established, and in 1938 it became fully nationalized. In 1935 the Wheat Board was established, a body which still exists to stabilize prices. The Canadian Radio Broadcasting Commission was created; it was renamed the Canadian Broadcasting Corporation (CBC) in 1936 and continues to provide and regulate radio and television broadcasting with a heavy Canadian content. The Bennett government also began the process of establishing a state-controlled air transport system, which in 1937 became the Trans-Canada Air Lines, a nationalized ("Crown") corporation and forerunner to Air-Canada. It had become clear that the government's hand was in the economy to stay.

THE SECOND WORLD WAR

Canadian economic life remained wretched throughout the 1930s. However, in 1939 an event came which not only led Canada out of the depression, but ushered in momentous political, diplomatic and military challenges and changes for Canada: the outbreak of the Second World War. Canada had pursued a basically isolationist foreign policy during the 1920s and 1930s. It had resisted any efforts to involve itself in any collective security arrangement stemming from its membership either in the League of Nations or the British Empire. It remained neutral in the Spanish Civil War from 1936–9 although 1,700

Canadians defied the law and formed the Mackenzie-Papineau Battalion to fight on the republican government's side; over 400 were killed. Canada also had done very little to keep up the size and quality of its armed forces. Therefore, by 1939 it was quite unprepared for war.

Unlike in 1914, when Canada had become automatically involved in the war upon Britain's entry, in September 1939 the Canadian government and Parliament deliberated for a week after fighting had commenced before declaring war on Britain's side. Also, the King government felt free to negotiate a defense agreement with the U.S. at Ogdensburg in 1940. In August 1940 Prime Minister King and President Roosevelt agreed to a Permanent Joint Board on Defense, which could design defense arrangements for the North American continent. In 1941 these two leaders also penned the Hyde Park Declaration, which provided for the sharing of defense production and for increased trade in defense equipment. These were measures that deepened the meshing of the two countries' economies. These agreements were a clear indication that Canadian defense was no longer linked exclusively with that of the British Empire.

The war created a potentially dangerous domestic political situation for Canadians and threatened to open up the terrible wounds of 1914–18. Parliament adopted the declaration of war almost unanimously, but support from French-speaking Canadians stemmed largely from the King government's promise not to draft Canadians into the armed forces for service abroad. Most Canadians understood that their country's contribution was to be mainly economic. Canada was indeed a crucial source of supplies for Britain in the 27 months before the United States entered the war. Throughout the war its eastern ports continued to be important points of origination for convoys that churned back and forth across the submarine-infested Atlantic bringing indispensable supplies to the Allies.

The government assured Canadians that their fighting forces would be composed exclusively of volunteers. The contribution of these soldiers was considerable during the war: almost a million Canadians served admirably in all theaters of operation. Following the disaster on the Belgian beaches at Dunkirk, Canadian soldiers formed the primary armed forces defending Britain, while that island nation caught its breath and reequipped itself for the onslaught which lay ahead. They bore many casualties in the unsuccessful attempts to defend Hong Kong from the Japanese in December 1941.

On August 19, 1942, 5,000 Canadians led an allied force that included 1,000 British to probe the European coastal defenses at Dieppe. The object was to demonstrate that a fortified port could be seized from the sea, but the attack was a disaster: 907 Canadians were killed and 1,154 were wounded, while 1,954 were captured. Three months after D-Day 1944, the 2nd Canadian Division liberated Dieppe. Canadian divisions were heavily involved in the invasion of Sicily in 1943 and subsequently the liberation of Italy. An elite integrated Canadian-American commando unit, the First Special Service Force (FSSF), fought at the bloody Anzio beachhead. Canadian soldiers played an important role at the Normandy beaches in 1944. Numbering 14,000 they dominated the landing at Juno Beach. One can still visit the fortified beaches in northern France which they were assigned to conquer and see why Canadian casualties were higher than any other units during the critical Normandy invasion. One out of ten soldiers who went ashore on June 6 was Canadian, as were 375 of the 2,500 Allied dead on that day. A further 7,600 Canadians were killed liberating the Netherlands in the closing months of the war, something the Dutch have never forgotten. To this day schoolchildren tend the graves of fallen Canadians. By war's end, 42,000 Canadians had lost their lives.

A further Canadian contribution was its development and administration of the British Commonwealth Air Training Plan, which provided airfields and training schools on Canadian soil for more than 131,500 airmen and air mechanics from Britain and the Dominions. Canadian pilots flew in Britain's Royal Air Force and in 41 Canadian squadrons which protected the sea lanes and which joined in the air attack against Germany.

It is scarcely surprising that the massive Canadian participation in the world war would put intense pressure on the government's commitment not to draft soldiers into the armed forces. Conscription for duty inside Canada had already begun in the summer of 1940. However, by April of 1942 the mounting casualties and the lagging of volunteers from Quebec forced the government to hold a controversial plebiscite asking Canadians whether they would free the government of its pledge not to introduce conscription for overseas duty. The results of the vote revealed very clearly how divided the country was over this historically explosive issue. In English Canada 80% of the voters said "yes," but 72% of *Québécois* said "no."

Even though France had been occupied and controlled by Germany, French-speaking Canadians were inclined to perceive the conflict as a "British war." Two *Québécois* who would later become prominent in Canadian politics were among the

Recruitment poster for World War II
Public Archives Canada/C87427

many French-speaking Canadians who avoided military service. Pierre Elliott Trudeau managed to avoid ever putting on a uniform, and René Lévesque served as a public information officer in the American army and wore an American uniform. Prime Minister King unmistakably sensed the danger, and he resisted sending conscripts to war zones until November 1944, when he finally ordered 16,000 draftees overseas. Angry riots broke out in Quebec province, and some *Québécois* came close to mutiny in some military bases. However, victory in Europe in May 1945 fortunately defused this gathering domestic political storm, and a relieved Canada proceeded to demobilize its draftees as quickly as possible.

In 1997 a panel of 25 scholars of Canadian history evaluated and ranked Canada's 20 prime ministers. They especially valued a leader's coherent vision of the country and well-articulated goals in domestic and foreign policy. In their opinion, William Lyon Mackenzie King was the best. They were impressed by his great political skills, his devotion to unity, his establishment of Canada's international identity, his steps towards establishing the social welfare safety net, and the brilliant way he ran Canada's enormous war effort. On May 8, 2005, the sixtieth anniversary of Victory in Europe (VE) Day, a spectacular new War Museum was opened on LeBreton Flats upriver from Parliament Hill in Ottawa to commemorate the sacrifices of Canadian soldiers.

Canada

AFTER 1945

The Second World War and its aftermath changed the face of Canada and its people. The end of the most destructive war the world has ever known churned up a wave of immigration into Canada, as millions of persons in war-torn Europe sought security and a more promising life in this huge and sparsely populated land. The massive influx helped to more than double the country's population from 11.5 million in 1941 to 25 million in 1985. These modern immigrants tended to settle in cities. They joined the masses of native-born Canadians who were leaving the countryside, changing Canada almost overnight into a predominantly urbanized country. Only a third of the newcomers were of British stock. The result is that citizens of British heritage no longer constitute a majority of the total population, falling to less than 45% in the 1990s.

It is true that the newcomers, who often continued to speak a wide variety of languages in their homes and churches, almost invariably decided to adopt English, not French, as their new language, even if they chose to settle in the province of Quebec. This distressed francophones, who already had dramatically lowered their own birth-rate; their percentage among the Canadian population dropped from 31% in 1945 to under 23% today. While these demographic shifts meant that *every* Canadian had become a member of a minority within Canada, they stimulated an anxiety in francophone Canada that would ultimately find a Quebec nationalist expression.

While the Canadian population underwent significant alteration, other developments that had been set in motion in the 1930s and 1940s were to demand much of the country's attention right into the 1980s. First, the economic depression and the war had brought a significant enlargement of the powers of the central government at the expense of the provincial governments. Second, the war had demonstrated Canada's almost total independence from the apron strings of the mother country and had made even more glaring the anachronism of having to request a foreign parliament to amend some important parts of its constitution. It seemed to more and more Canadians that a country that still could not amend all of its own constitution was not yet entirely sovereign.

Third, Canada had accumulated far more wealth than it had expended during the war. It had become even more highly industrialized and had emerged from the war as one of the world's major industrial and trading nations. The war had fostered a more intense interrelationship between the economies of Canada and the United States, and, as had been the case in 1918,

had brought another burst of American capital investments across the border. Canadians did absolutely nothing to stem that flow, and in the 1960s they woke up to find that much of their economy and natural resources were in the hands of a single foreign country—its neighbor to the south. Fourth, despite ugly riots which had taken place in Quebec in the closing months of the war, Canada had emerged from the armed struggle far more unified as a country than it had in 1918.

All four developments sparked further changes in the post-war era. The provinces energetically reasserted themselves and challenged Ottawa's hold on a wide variety of powers, from taxing to the pricing of natural resources extracted within their borders. As we shall see, the long and bitter disputes over the shape of the new constitution revealed just how muscular the provinces are. The result of those prolonged disputes was a new constitution, which was signed in 1982 by the British Queen and the Canadian prime minister and which left Canadians as the undisputed political masters in their own house. The only symbolic link with the mother country that remains is that the British monarch is still formally the Canadian head of state.

Canada had fought with its allies in the Korean War (1951–53), and 309 of its soldiers were killed. However, the war in Vietnam (1965–1974) forced Canadians to reexamine their relationship with the United States. Canada's participation in the International Control Commission in Indochina from 1954 until 1973, along with Poland and India, caused some friction when American leaders sometimes thought that the Canadians, who had been appointed with the expectation that they would be biased toward the American view (Poland was selected to provide the opposite bias), did not show enough sympathy toward the U.S. position. There was evidence that these charges were untrue most of the time, but the Vietnam War was indeed a landmark in Canadians' appraisal of America's leadership in the world.

As was true of many of the United States' other allies, Canadians were uneasy about American policy in Indochina, even though up to 40,000 Canadians served as volunteers in the American armed forces in Southeast Asia. They were more skeptical of containment of communism based on military force and were more inclined to see the roots of third-world instability in poverty and social problems, rather than in Soviet or Chinese meddling.

Prime Minister Lester Pearson spoke for most of his countrymen when he delivered a speech at Temple University in 1965

calling for a bombing halt in North Vietnam. President Lyndon B. Johnson was livid. What angered him was not only that Canada had departed from its usual quiet diplomatic style to criticize the United States publicly in a time of crisis. Its prime minister had done so *on American soil*. Johnson put it unofficially in his typically crude way: Pearson had "pissed on my rug."

Pearson was the best diplomat Canada had ever produced. He played a pivotal role in creating NATO and the United Nations, and he was elected president of the UN General Assembly in 1952. For his negotiation skills, he was awarded the Nobel Peace Prize in 1957. More than any other, he popularized the image of Canadians as an understated, compassionate and peacemaking people.

Perhaps he was wrong to deliver such a speech in Philadelphia. Perhaps also Canadians do not fully appreciate the difficulties of America's position as a superpower. But the speech and Canadians' general support of its basic message indicated at least two things: Canadians do view the world somewhat differently than do Americans, and no Canadian government could support every American policy, regardless of what it is. Since the Vietnam conflict Canadians have had doubts about the quality of American leadership, which were evident in the 1960s and 1970s. There is some doubt (shared by the United States' other allies and friends) about whether American leaders truly understand today's myriad global challenges and whether they know how to use power wisely.

Canada experienced a birth or rebirth of two forms of nationalism in Canada: first, Canadians grew nervous about the extent to which foreigners controlled their economy. An economic nationalism asserted itself in response to such domination. This sentiment was strongest in English Canada. The economic nationalism visible in Quebec was directed as much against English Canada's penetration of the Quebec economy as against that of the United States. Second, the dramatic assertion of political and cultural nationalism in Quebec from the 1960s on represented the greatest threat to Canadian unity since confederation in 1867. At times, one could not be sure that Canada as a country would survive into the 21st century.

THE "QUIET REVOLUTION" IN QUEBEC

The "French fact" had, of course, existed in Canadian life for more than two centuries, despite the illusions of many anglophones that the *Québécois* would become absorbed into the Anglo-Saxon mainstream, as had been so many other groups in North America. All too often, *Québécois* were viewed condescendingly "as priest-ridden, traditional-bound, backward, clannish and occasionally sullen or riotous," in the words of sociologist Jane Jacobs. Francophones resented what they interpreted as an arrogant sense of superiority on the part of anglophones, who indeed did dominate much of Quebec's economy, and who, in the opinion of many *Québécois* sought to destroy their culture. In times of crisis, Quebecers had repeatedly shown that they could not be expected to react as anglophones thought they should. Quebecers were Canadians, but they were distinct and intended to remain that way. Profound disagreements could always be papered-over by compromise. But each side often felt that the necessary compromises had been foisted on it by the other, and these feelings intensified resentment and became the fodder for yet other grievances.

Quebecers had always proved to be an extraordinarily resilient people who would never permit their language and culture to die. The French nobleman and politician, Alexis de Tocqueville, had discovered their traditional secret for survival during his trip to North America in 1831–1832, a journey that resulted in a seminal book, *Democracy in America*. The *Québécois*, he noted, "is tenderly attached to the land which saw his birth, to his church tower, and to his family." Traditionally, Quebecers turned their backs on the cities, which threatened the family and society and which placed them at the mercy of English employers and customs. For a long time, they tended to remain in rural areas, where the Catholic Church shielded them from alien influences, provided a firm guiding hand and administered an educational system which shunned commercial and technical subjects and which reinforced traditional values and French language and society.

Finally, the Québécois were prodigious procreators, responding to the threats, often described vividly from the pulpit, presented by an almost total absence of immigrants from France and by a constant emigration to northeastern United States of young Quebecers who were unable to find farmland or employment in their own province. Between 1851 and 1931 over 700,000 left for the melting pot south of the border. To help stem this tide, the Church sponsored colonization drives to channel Quebecers into the formerly anglophone Ottawa Valley and Eastern Townships or into the Quebec interior around Lac St. Jean and in the Laurentian Mountains. The best defense, though, was the *revanche des berceaux* ("revenge of the cradles")! Until the post-1945 era, Quebe-

Rt. Hon. Louis St. Laurent, 1949
Public Archives Canada/C20048

cers maintained the highest birth-rate in Canada.

Like all Canadians, Quebecers have always been concerned with survival. But theirs was a different kind of survival from that of their English-speaking compatriots. For English Canadians it meant survival of the Canadian union against the hostile forces of geography, climate, internal diversity and the dynamic southern neighbor, with a population ten times the size of Canada's. It meant coping with these challenges and reconciling the diversities in order to preserve the whole. For the *Québécois, la survivance* meant

the preservation of their separate *nation*, against domination or, worse, absorption by anglophones in *both* English Canada and the United States. An important motto in Quebec has been *Exister c'est survivre!* ("To exist is to survive!"). This nation has always been held together by a common memory of Quebecers' past and a separate language and culture. On every Quebec license plate today are the words, *Je me souviens* ("I remember"). They are an allusion to a poem with the bitter line, "I remember that I was born under the *fleur-de-lis* and grew up under the [English] rose." They underscore the importance of Quebec's past for the present values and feeling of community. Survival as Quebecers' goal cannot be denied. The question now is how it can be guaranteed when the traditional supports of religion, rural isolation and educational and economic backwardness have broken down.

As we have seen, Quebec nationalism was very visible during the Second World War, but it was prevented from boiling over by the timely end of the war, by the election of Maurice Duplessis, who had been returned to the Quebec premiership in 1944, and by the accession of a French Canadian Liberal, Louis St. Laurent, to the prime ministry of Canada upon the retirement of Mackenzie King in 1948. Upon the death in 1941 of King's chief lieutenant, Ernest Lapointe, the prime minister had appointed St. Laurent, a successful bilingual lawyer from Quebec City with close connections with the leading Montreal and Toronto businessmen. As a conservative French Canadian and as King's loyal lieutenant during the Second World War, he had gained the gratitude of many anglophones and the criticism of ar-

Flag of the Province of Quebec

Canada

dent Quebec nationalists, who accused him of "selling out" to the English. This well-educated, silver-haired statesman became so well liked in English Canada that he was dubbed "Uncle Louis" by the English-language press. He quickly came to symbolize Canada's post-war stability and affluence, thereby gaining respect in both anglophone and francophone Canada. Until his retirement in 1957 he provided a psychologically important French presence in Ottawa, even though he was a conservative French Canadian, much in the mold of Sir Wilfrid Laurier.

Another French-Canadian conservative, Maurice Duplessis, remained Quebec's premier until his death in 1959, and his *Union Nationale* ruled uninterruptedly for the next 16 years (and again for one last term from 1966 to 1970). Duplessis and his party resorted to Quebec nationalist rhetoric at every opportunity. In two important cases he followed his words with concrete steps: he introduced a provincial income tax to make Quebec somewhat less dependent financially upon Ottawa. Also, he adopted a new Quebec flag that underscores the province's French character: the *fleur-de-lis*, which portrays a white cross on a blue field and a white *fleur-de-lis* in each quadrant. This flag still flies over the *National* Assembly building in Quebec City and is far more visible throughout the province than the Canadian maple leaf flag, which had been adopted in the 1960s to placate Quebec sensitivities by purging all traces of the British heritage.

Nevertheless, his was an older, more conservative form of nationalism. By raising the specter of integration with English Canada, he maintained the support of the Catholic Church in the province, which in return retained its hold over the education of the Catholic French majority. But by the 1950s many Quebecers were beginning to call upon the government to follow the example of other provinces and to become more active in the fields of education, health and welfare, and even to wield the state's power in the economic sector in order to loosen anglophones' grip and to stem the inflow of investment capital and companies from English Canada and the United States.

Before the "conquest" of 1763, the state in New France had always intervened heavily in economic affairs. But for the next 200 years energetic state activity had not been a part of the Quebec political tradition. Under British rule, Quebecers were suspicious of the state, even including the province's political system, which had originally been modeled on British governmental practice.

They considered it to be safer to rely upon traditional French-Canadian institu-

Quebec Premier Jean Lesage, April 1964
Public Archives Canada/PA108147

tions, especially the Catholic Church, to educate the young and to provide any additional health or welfare assistance that individuals might need. Duplessis respected these traditions, and he still clung to the belief that the Quebec nation was and always would remain essentially rural and agrarian.

The Union Nationale merely papered over temporarily the momentous social, economic and attitudinal changes that were occurring in Quebec. Quebec was already becoming rapidly industrialized and urbanized; by 1945 less than a third of Quebecers lived in rural areas, as opposed to three-quarters in 1900. Also, the bitter Asbestos strike of 1949 revealed how militant some of Quebec's trade unions had become. As René Lévesque, who would later be Quebec's premier, noted, modern *Québécois* had become "city dwellers, wage-earners, tenants. The standards of parish, village, and farm have been splintered." More and more articulate reformers began to criticize the conservative and, they claimed, corrupt Quebec government and called for fundamental changes in the way Quebec was ruled. These critics were at first centered at Laval University and the University of Montreal.

Laval had been established in 1852 as an outgrowth of the Jesuit seminary of Quebec City. It had been inspired in part by the desire to have a French-language alternative to McGill, the venerated English-speaking university in Montreal. Later, the University of Montreal was cre-

ated, first as a French-language branch of Laval and then in 1920 as a university with its own charter.

No critic was more prominent than a young, brilliant and wealthy law professor at the University of Montreal, Pierre Elliott Trudeau. Born into a prominent Montreal family of a Scottish mother, from whom he learned to speak perfect English, and a *Québécois* father, Trudeau was given a first-rate classical education at the Jesuit-operated College Jean de Brebeuf in Montreal, and he rounded off his education at the University of Montreal Law School, the Sorbonne, the London School of Economics and Harvard University. He had deftly managed to elude the recruiters during the Second World War and, instead, had spent an enviable youth reading philosophy and traveling both to Europe and to exotic places, such as the Holy Land, China and Tibet, unreachable at the time to young people without sizable private means. Always an eccentric person, he often wore gaudy and intentionally inappropriate clothing, and he drove his sports car to the site of the 1949 Asbestos strike, to show his support for the strikers. Nevertheless, he always had at his disposal one of the most powerful minds ever produced in Canada.

In his many articles in the journal *Cite Libre* ("Free City"), for which he was the principal contributor and editor (along with Gerard Pelletier), he used his powerful logic and language to attack his fellow Quebecers' notions of authority. He called for the use of political power as a positive instrument of the people's will to bring about social and economic progress. He advocated a kind of social democracy, free from the Church and centered in the city, rather than in the villages and farms. He and increasingly more Quebec intellectuals wanted a modern, forward-looking Quebec, in step with the times, while retaining its French character.

The year 1960 was a watershed in Quebec history. In that year the Quebec Liberal party, under the leadership of Jean Lesage, toppled the conservative Union Nationale government and ushered in a wave of reform that unalterably changed the province and the attitudes of its people. So momentous were the changes that everyone began speaking of a *revolution tranquille* ("quiet revolution"). This term was first coined by an English Canadian journalist, but it suited very well the character of the people to whom it applied. René Lévesque, one of its most important proponents, explained that the word "quiet gives us to understand that Quebec could not change radically. Nonetheless this same old Quebec, where a system of values had broken down, was trying to organize itself to face the modern world."

The change was indeed revolutionary. From the early 1960s on, the most fundamental assumptions and beliefs of Quebecers about politics, religion, economics and society were being carefully scrutinized and, to a large extent, discarded. Rather than viewing technology, business, industrialization and urbanization as a threat to their unique culture, *Québécois* began to regard them as instruments for elevating and improving their people. Rather than turning to traditional social institutions, such as the Catholic Church, to protect them from the modern world, they became more secular in their outlook on the world and began to take a more positive view of the state as a tool to help Quebec develop itself and catch up with the rest of Canada.

During the "quiet revolution," Quebecers drew a much sharper boundary around their conception of the Quebec "nation" to fit the geographical boundaries of Quebec province. Although they were to remain sensitive to the treatment of francophones in other parts of Canada, Quebecers no longer felt a *national* link with them; the term "French Canadian" fell into disfavor in Quebec. Most important of all, *Québécois* gained the self-confidence that they could change things if they really wanted to. They acquired a mood of optimism that they could be progressive and modern, while still being completely French in outlook, institutions and language.

At first, these developments were greeted in anglophone Canada as signs that Quebecers were finally developing a pragmatic Anglo-Saxon outlook, which would help bring about a greater unity of Canada's two founding peoples. It was not long, though, until the very opposite became obvious. Rather than becoming more attached to Canada, Quebecers were becoming more attached to Quebec. They were developing the courage, not only fundamentally to challenge Canadian federalism, but perhaps even to challenge the very existence of Canada as a unified country.

The Liberal Lesage government was determined that Quebec would make more of its own decisions, and that meant that the Quebec government would have to wield many of the powers which had long been exercised by the federal government in Ottawa. This was a direct challenge to the prevailing distribution of powers between Ottawa and the provinces. It was a matter that no government in the country's capital could ignore because it went to the very core of the Canadian political system.

For a few years Ottawa did make some important concessions. It agreed to give Quebec, without strings or conditions, funds which the federal government would have used to administer and finance a program in the province. The province could then design and execute the policy in its own way. An example of this so-called "opting-out" possibility was the hard-fought Quebec Pension Plan, which protects Quebecers, while other Canadians are covered by the Canada Pension Plan. By aggressively seeking out political terrain into which exclusive Quebec governmental authority could be extended, the province's political leaders were able to take advantage of numerous such "opting out" opportunities in a variety of areas, including health, education and welfare. By doing this, Quebec had secured for itself a *de facto* special status within the Canadian federation.

The Lesage government, which was reelected in 1962 under the slogan *Maitres chez nous* ("masters in our own house"), was able to act particularly decisively in the field of education, which has always been a provincial prerogative. Although it had often been a controversial matter, Quebec schools had always been in the hands of the Church, which was regarded as the chief protector of Quebec's values and culture. But one of the most dramatic changes during the Quiet Revolution was the weakening of religious sentiments that occurred almost overnight. Quebec author Roch Carrier was living in France at the onset of the Quiet Revolution. He recalled that what surprised him most when he returned to Quebec in the early 1960s was that so few people seemed to go to church anymore.

Pope John Paul II, during a visit to the province two decades later went so far as to call Quebec a "dechristianized society." Polls in 1994 revealed that only 19% of *Québécois* attend religious services at least "once a week or so," the second lowest percentage among Canadian provinces; only 56% said that maintaining Christian values "is very important to me," the lowest percentage in Canada outside British Columbia. It had become secularized, and this fact was bound to affect the schools and almost everything else in Quebec society. One of few remnants of religion in the minds of some secularized *Québécois* is when he swears. Take heed when he angrily uses in French such words as "Oh tabernacle!" or "chalice," "host" or "baptism."

Many changes were introduced in rapid order, but perhaps the most important was the creation in 1964 of a provincial Ministry of Education and a non-denominational Advisory Committee to replace the separate Catholic and Protestant Committees. The practice of appointing only Catholic clergymen as rectors of Laval and the University of Montreal was done away with, and both universities completely severed their ties with the Church. In 1968 a new University of Quebec, with branches all over the province, was founded with no ties to the Church whatsoever. Tuition-free state high schools were created to compete with Catholic-operated schools and to break the Church's stranglehold on university admissions. This de-emphasis on religion and secularization of the province's schools occurred at all levels of the school system and dramatically affected the preparation and the attitudes of the students who emerged from Quebec schools to become a part in the modernized Quebec society. In 1997 the Quebec National Assembly voted to replace the denominational school boards with French and English ones.

This secularized school system produced a new kind of graduate: one with less knowledge of philosophy, French poets and Catholic scholasticism, but with more technical and business training. It produced a much larger middle class, with the kinds of technical skills that would enable young *Québécois* to operate in the province's business elite and to enter the civil service. Because a very large portion of those graduates was unable to find jobs in the private economy, they became employees of the state, either as teachers, civil servants or managers in newly nationalized corporations. During the Quiet Revolution, the public sector swelled, as the Quebec state took on more and more responsibilities. This "state middle class," as it was often called, became the motor and backbone for the continuing Quiet Revolution and, as we shall see, for that separatist party which gained power in 1976: The *Parti Québécois (Quebec Party—PQ)*.

The activism of the Quebec state was very apparent in the province's economy. The basic rationale was that if Quebecers were to be "masters in their own house," they would have to have more influence within the economy, which was largely controlled by anglophone Canadians and Americans. The Lesage government tackled this objective head-on by creating and expanding state economic enterprises. The most successful of these, Hydro-Quebec, created in 1962, was the project of one of Lesage's cabinet ministers, René Lévesque. This new state-owned enterprise integrated Quebec's many hydro-electric facilities and became Quebec's largest employer. Its cheap electricity became essential for the industrial rebirth and revival of business confidence in Quebec during the late 1980s and 1990s. More important for Quebec nationalists was the fact that the working language within Hydro-Quebec was made exclusively French. This insured that the management of the enterprise would be solely in the hands of francophones. To demonstrate further that successful economic un-

Canada

France's President de Gaulle: "Vive le Québec libre!"
Public Archives Canada/C6013

dertakings need not be directed by anglophones, French was made the exclusive working language of the Manicougan Dam construction, the largest such structure in the world, even though the capital for this mega-project had to be raised in the United States. French was also the working language of the later massive hydro-electric project at James Bay in the 1970s. Even though francophone ownership of and management positions within the economy grew by leaps and bounds in the 1960s and 1970s, the goal of wresting control over the province's economy from anglophone hands never succeeded.

In 1966 the *Union Nationale* defeated the Liberal Lesage government and experienced its last chance to hold the reins of Quebec provincial power before disappearing from the political scene. The event most remembered during this four-year period was the Montreal Exposition in 1967. The federal government in Ottawa gave full support for this world fair, which was held in the centennial of the founding of the Canadian confederation in 1867. This massive event was to underscore the success in creating a unified Canada. But the aftermath of this Expo would reveal and widen the rifts that existed in that confederation.

The Expo 67, which was arguably the most successful of all world fairs, became a source of great pride for Quebecers, one-third of whom live in Montreal. It displayed to the world that they could manage successfully a large, glittering project the people of many nations could enjoy. It attracted the world's attention to the accomplishments and the aspirations of a province that had changed so much in less than a decade. It also called the world's attention to a festering wound right in the heart of Canada.

The unpredictable French president, Charles de Gaulle, traveled to Montreal to visit the Expo. There were signs of trouble when his cruiser dispensed with the customary naval courtesy of flying the Canadian flag. His enthusiasm was whetted during his 10-hour motor trip to Montreal through 22 communities along the St. Lawrence River. He noted: "I have encountered an atmosphere the same as at the Liberation" (of France in 1944–5). He gave an unforgettable speech from the balcony of Montreal's City Hall in which he repeated the separatist slogan: *Vive le Québec libre* ("Long live free Quebec"). This utterance unleashed chants among the thousands of Quebecers who heard it: *Québec libre! Oui, Oui, Oui! De Gaulle l'a dit! Oui, oui!* ("A free Quebec! Yes, yes, yes! De Gaulle said it! Yes, yes!"). The Canadian government immediately and indignantly announced that such support of the separatists on the part of a foreign chief of state was "unacceptable," and the proud Frenchman left the country within hours.

A decade later, René Lévesque admitted, "we owe him enormous recognition for having made us known throughout the world with this fortunate blunder." Yet Lévesque and other cooler heads were aware that such pronouncements could propel irresponsible forces that become very difficult to control and which thereby endanger, rather than facilitate, the achievement of important goals. It is important to note that it was not until two decades later, in 1987, that a French president again visited Canada. The tone of the visit was very different. President François Mitterrand made a point of arriving in Ottawa, not Quebec, and his toast to his Canadian hosts was: *Vive le Canada! Vive la France!*

The political developments and the violence that were taking place in Quebec toughened the will of the political leaders in Ottawa and Quebec to seek solutions that went to the very roots of the problem. The Liberal government in Ottawa intensified its efforts to so change Canada that francophones could not help but recognize Canada as a congenial home for all of them.

Pierre Elliott Trudeau is often incorrectly credited with having ushered in the kinds of changes in Canada that ultimately undercut the separatist movement in Quebec. He was later to lend his prestige and intellect to bridging the huge gulf that had developed between Quebec and the rest of Canada. But he had not yet joined the Liberal Party in 1963 when the new Liberal government of Lester Pearson appointed a Royal Commission on Bilingualism and Biculturalism to find and document the causes of the crisis and to propose ways of dealing with the serious frictions that existed between "the two founding races." The Commission's first report in 1965 left no doubt that francophones were severely handicapped in their efforts to advance economically and to preserve their language and culture. The report documented the fact that these two aspirations were linked. The conclusion was that "Canada, without being fully conscious of the fact, is passing through the greatest crisis of its history." Many of the reforms that followed were based on this ground-breaking report. Affectionately called "Mike," Pearson also played the leading role in introducing universal medicare, the Canada-U.S. Auto Pact, and the Canada Pension Plan. In 1965 he also ordered the new Canadian maple leaf flag to be run up parliament's Peace Tower. By getting rid of the remnants of the British flag on Canada's colors, he eliminated yet another potential irritant in Quebec's adjustment to Canada.

Pearson found an undeniably competent and effective lieutenant and ultimate successor in Trudeau, who joined the Liberal Party in 1965 and was elected to the House of Commons that same year. Trudeau wanted to demonstrate that the aspirations of francophone Canada could be furthered in Ottawa, as well as in Quebec City. He feared that the kind of Quebec nationalism that was emerging would not only destroy Canada, but would drive Quebec into isolation. Only a tolerant federalism could remedy the situation.

In 1966 he was appointed as Justice Minister, and he lent his support to enlarging what was called "cooperative federalism." This meant in practice that all ten provinces would be granted their full powers under the BNA and that Ottawa would return to the provinces all the powers that it had assumed during the 1950s. It also instituted periodic meetings and consultations between the governments in Ottawa and the ten provincial capitals, so that provincial concerns could be aired and influence on federal policy strength-

ened. These meetings are still a part of routine Canadian political practice. The Liberal Party government decided that it would be appropriate to remove a symbol from the country's flag which many francophones found to be insulting: the Union Jack, a reminder of Canada's imperial heritage. The debate over the design of the new flag was bitter and protracted. One proposal, to combine the Union Jack and the *fleur-de-lis,* was rejected. Finally, the present flag, with a single red maple leaf on a white field, was adopted.

Perhaps the most important measure the Liberal government took to quell the fears of francophones was to create a bilingual Canada, in which francophones would feel equal and at home everywhere. In 1969 the Official Languages Act made Canada officially a bilingual country. The brunt of this new law was felt most immediately in the federal civil service, where more and more jobs were reserved for bilingual Canadians. In coming years this law was to have a greater and greater impact on many dimensions of Canadian life. The move to transform Canada into a bilingual country was, however, not greeted in all quarters of Canadian society. Many anglophones, particularly in the West, found it to be an unnecessary and unjustified imposition, and many Quebecers found that it did not go far enough in protecting French language rights.

The policies which the Liberal governments of Lester Pearson and Pierre Elliott Trudeau introduced were in the long run very important for the salvation of Canada as a unified country. But in the 1960s and 1970s they were unable to satisfy the ardor of Quebec nationalism. No Canadian needed a reminder in the 1970s that his country was faced with dangers which

Trudeau and Lévesque

threatened to rip it asunder. It was clear that if a peaceful solution could not be found, then Canada could be buffeted by something rather rare in the Canadian experience: violence. In the early 1960s a rough separatist group emerged, the *Rassemblement pour l'Independence Nationale,* led by the young socialist firebrand Pierre Bourgault. A few bombing incidents occurred in Montreal in February 1963, and in October 1964 a visit by the British Queen to Quebec City to commemorate the 1864 Confederation Conference ignited frightening riots.

The stakes were raised considerably in the summer and fall of 1970, when an extremist separatist organization, the *Front de Liberation du Québec* (Front for the Liberation of Quebec—FLQ) perpetrated a series of violent deeds, beginning with bombings and robberies and culminating in the twin kidnapping of Richard Cross, senior British trade commissioner in Montreal, and Pierre Laporte, Quebec's minister of labor and immigration. A flurry of police and political activity could not defuse the crisis, so Premier Bourassa requested Ottawa to

War Measures Act: soldiers at the Palais de Justice (police headquarters), Quebec
Public Archives Canada/PA129838

Canada

Lighting the flame at the Summer Olympic Games, Montreal, July 1976
Public Archives Canada/PA115800

send in the army. In a now famous television confrontation on the steps of Parliament on October 13, Trudeau scornfully noted, "bleeding hearts just don't like to see people with guns and helmets. Go on and bleed. It is more important to keep law and order." When queried about how far he would go to maintain order, he snapped "just watch me!"

On October 16, Canadians held their breath as Prime Minister Trudeau proclaimed the War Measures Act and outlawed the FLQ and any organization that promoted the use of force. Extremists wasted no time in responding to Ottawa's sternness; the next day they murdered Pierre Laporte and left his bloodied body in the trunk of an abandoned car.

Political assassinations are very rare in Canadian history; only two have occurred since 1867. When they do occur, however, the federal government acts with an energy and determination to which Americans are unaccustomed. For instance, when the political leader, D'Arcy McGee, was assassinated on the steps of his Ottawa boardinghouse in 1868, the government suspended Habeas Corpus, arrested 70 suspects and held them for four months without charging them or permitting them to speak to lawyers.

A century later, Trudeau had the full support of his countrymen to respond to the Laporte murder by whatever means, and he signaled that he was willing to take full advantage of that support. After a wave of searches and arrests, Cross was located alive, and he was freed in return for allowing his kidnapers to fly off to Cuba. This frightening crisis reminded Canadians that they were not free of the scourge of violence that was afflicting other democratic countries at the time. But it also demonstrated the willingness of Canadian governments to act with great

energy and determination against any overt threats to undermine the constitutional order in Canada. Between 1963 and 1970, the FLQ ignited over 200 bombs in Montreal, killing at least five and wounding dozens. But terrorism never entrenched itself in the Quebec separatist movement.

From 1970 to 1976 Quebec was again ruled by the *Liberal Party* under the leadership of Robert Bourassa. He and his Liberal government sought to maintain many of the gains which had been made since the Quiet Revolution, but they were leery of that central assumption of the revolution that a continuing expansion of the government's powers and activities was necessary or good for Quebec. They were concerned that excessive confrontations with anglophones who were well-entrenched in the province's economy would damage the investment climate in the province and thereby hurt Quebecers more than help them. The premier was not convinced that much good could flow from Quebec's separation from Canada, and he therefore by and large supported Canada's federal system. Under his administration there were no major transfers of powers or resources from the federal capital to Quebec City. Critics contended that Bourassa had not pressed Quebec's demands energetically enough.

The Bourassa government did become the first Quebec government to pass comprehensive legislation dealing with the status of French in Quebec. His government did not believe that the federal Official Languages Act of 1969 was strong enough to shore up the French language in Quebec and to satisfy nationalist sentiments. Bill 22 declared that French alone is the province's "official language." This act was bitterly reviled by Quebec's anglophones, some of whom going so far as

to accuse the government of using "Nazi-like tactics" and committing "cultural genocide." Still, by the standards of language legislation that was to come later, Bill 22 was mild. For instance, it did not require that English-language schools in the province be restricted exclusively to children whose mother tongue was English. The majority of immigrant children continued to go to English-language schools. Therefore, many francophones viewed the bill as a farce that would not really change their status within Quebec.

On the occasion of the second gala event in Montreal within a single decade, the 1976 Olympic Games, the world again had the opportunity to witness the political and economic turmoil in a province so deeply in process of change. The opening of the games was preceded by bitter labor strikes and protests, which had strong Quebec nationalist overtones. Many labor union leaders and members had clearly become militant and nationalist. All was not in order in *la belle province*, and in 1976 very important challenges to Canadian unity were again on the horizon.

Both Ottawa and Quebec City had sought in very different ways to satisfy francophone desires. The result is a tug-of-war that will dominate Canadian politics for the rest of the century. Many *Québécois* remained frustrated, and political forces were emerging within Quebec that steered toward Quebec independence. In the 1960s a heterogeneous coalition of Quebecers who wanted to push the Quiet Revolution further, who wanted a fairer relationship between Quebec and the rest of Canada, or who wanted a totally separate Quebec, took shape. This diversity was never easy to manage, but for at least two decades it was held together by the only Quebecer who possessed the necessary charisma, political skill and patience to be its leader: René Lévesque.

The son of a French-speaking country lawyer in New Carlisle, a predominantly English-speaking town of about a thousand inhabitants surrounded by the French-speaking world of Quebec's Gaspé Peninsula, he grew up bilingually. Therefore, as an adult who could speak perfect English, he personally suffered neither discrimination for being a francophone nor the trauma of having to learn English as a foreign language. Nevertheless, he remembers the taunts exchanged by bands of French and English Canadians: "They used to call us 'pea-soupers'; we called them 'crawfish'." His Quebec nationalism flowered early; while a student in the Jesuit-run Garnier College (prep school), he wrote in one of his papers: "Never forget that you are French Canadians, that your own people have been stagnating for generations, and that if they, the people, *your* people do not act, they are lost!" In the early 1940s he abandoned his law studies, or, as he remembers it, "they began to abandon me."

Since it was wartime, he was under the threat of being drafted into the Canadian army. His attitude about this prospect was vintage *Québécois:* "Though I was willing to go overseas, I was not willing to go in the uniform of His Majesty. I therefore went to New York in 1943 and managed to join an information office, and then to be appointed war correspondent in the American Seventh Army. I went to war on a purely intuitive impulse." He sailed from Halifax to London early in 1944 on a ship that was not a part of a convoy, a voyage that understandably gave him ten days of "acute anxiety, especially during the night," as he recalls. At the age of 21, he edited and announced messages to occupied France, and in February 1945 he was attached to the Sixth Army and moved with this unit and the First French Army eastward through France to the Rhineland, Bavaria and Austria. He was present at the battle of Nuremberg, and he was among the first to discover the horrors of Dachau concentration camp a few miles outside of Munich and to speak with the liberated French leaders, including Edouard Daladier, Leon Jouraux, Paul Reynaud and General Weygand, whom the Germans had imprisoned in comfortable confinement in a castle. He saw Mussolini's mutilated body, and he was one of the few journalists to hear Hermann Goering a few minutes after his surrender.

After the war he became a political journalist, a job that took him across Canada and the United States, to Korea and back to Europe. In the mid-1950s he switched from radio journalism to become one of Canada's first TV journalists. His half-hour Sunday evening program, *Point de Mire*, ("Focal Point"), was first aired in October 1957 and made him a celebrity. It focused on international issues. At a time when most Quebecers had little schooling and exposure outside of French Canada, this became their window to the world. Because Radio-Canada (the Quebec equivalent to the Canadian Broadcasting Corporation) had a TV monopoly in Quebec at that time, he became extremely popular, and his ratings sometimes reached 100%. The show made his diminutive figure, his gravelly voice and his extremely well informed opinions familiar to millions of Canadians.

The program consisted of a study of one event or one problem occupying a central point in the news. This focus enabled him to make the transition from international problems, which had occupied him for more than a decade, to domestic politics. The federal government's rough handling of a 68-day strike at Radio Canada greatly angered him. "I was scared, even traumatized by that experience, so that sooner or later I felt I would have to enter politics."

He served in the Liberal Party cabinet of Jean Lesage for six years as the minister of natural resources and came to incorporate the aspirations of the Quiet Revolution. However, he gradually grew impatient with the Liberal provincial government, which, he believed, did not press vigorously enough for an independent Quebec. He was unable to persuade the Liberals to adopt a manifesto he had published calling for sovereignty for Quebec within a common market association with Canada. Therefore, he and a group of moderate, but disgruntled, Liberals left their party in 1967 and formed the *Mouvement Souverainete-Association* (Movement for Sovereignty-Association, MSA). A year later the *MSA* merged with a couple of other smaller separatist parties, the right-wing *Ralliement national (National Rally—RN)* and the somewhat demagogic, "grass roots" *Rassemblement pour l'independence nationale* (Rally for National Independence—RIN) to form the *Parti Québécois (PQ).* The precise objectives of these three parties were never the same, and the internal strains would always plague the party and would weaken and fragment it in the 1980s.

The PQ became a basket for a very diverse collection of Quebecers who wanted to see the Quiet Revolution carried on with greater energy (though they disagreed on how radical the political and economic changes should be) and who wished to see some kind of sovereign Quebec (though they could not agree upon just how sovereign). Only René Lévesque could hold such a movement together. He was a cautious leader who insisted that the party be democratic and respectable. His notion of sovereignty-association was a compromise around which party members could unify.

Although he was always careful not to define this notion too concretely, he said that "we do not want to end, but rather to radically transform, our union with the rest of Canada, so that, in the future, our relations will be based on full and complete equality." Quebec was only a "half-fledged state" in conflict with the rest of Canada; "in order to end once and for all the struggle of wills, the costly dividing up of energies and resources, the system must be replaced."

The finished product he envisaged was not a francophone nation that would completely turn its back on Canada. For him, sovereignty-association "means a sovereign State of Quebec which will accept, or rather offer in advance, new links of interdependence with Canada, but links which will this time be negotiated between equal peoples, as a function of their geographic and other unquestionable common interest." Thus, although the "obsolete constitutional links" would have to be cut, there would still be links of free trade, free travel without passports between Quebec and Canada, a common currency, a joint administration of the St. Lawrence Seaway and a military alliance with Canada, the United States and NATO.

Although Quebecers were not unified insofar as their precise expectations for a new relationship with Canada were concerned, many of them were drawn to the PQ, which appealed to all the diverse values which francophones in Quebec felt to be important. The reward was 30% of the popular vote in 1973 and a stunning electoral victory for the PQ in the Quebec provincial elections in November 1976. Lévesque's party won only 41% of the vote in Quebec, and as a government without a majority of the inhabitants behind it, he had to move cautiously. However, he had won an absolute majority of francophones' votes, winning in every region in Quebec

Young Quebecers with the provincial flag

Canada

except in the anglophone-dominated West Montreal. He drew votes from all classes of *Québécois*, but his showing was particularly strong among the young and the professional and semi-professional middle class, especially teachers.

With the support of a majority of francophones, Lévesque perceived that he had a mandate for change. However, the terms for that mandate were not clear. Those PQ voters who wanted sovereignty were not in agreement on exactly what form it should take. Many Quebecers voted for the PQ because they wanted "clean government," after the Bourassa government had been tainted by scandals. Their vote was by no means an endorsement of Quebec sovereignty. What most PQ voters did agree upon, though, was that the protections for the French language should be even tighter than those provided in Bill 22.

The result was Bill 101, which required that all public signs (including road signs) and every form of commercial advertising be exclusively in French. Thus, Eaton's and Ogilvy's department stores were compelled to remove the apostrophe from their name. In contrast, McDonald's has been able to survive in Quebec with its apostrophe. However, a greasy spoon diner in Montreal, "Irv's Light Lunch," had to be renamed "Chez Irv." Quebec's language officials ruled in 2000 that companies with English-language registered trademark names cannot be forced to use French versions in Quebec. They argued that international law protects the use of such names. This did not help Quebec-born race driver Jacques Villeneuve. He was reported to the language police in 2001 for naming his new Montreal restaurant "Newtown," the English translation of his last name and his nickname in racing circles. He responded to those who complained: "You have to look further than the tip of your nose. It's a big world!"

Second, access to English-language schools was restricted to children with at least one parent who had been educated in English *in Quebec*. That meant that not only immigrant children, but the offspring of anglophones from other Canadian provinces were required to attend French-language schools. Thanks to a decision by the Canadian Supreme Court, that last provision was softened to permit children with a parent who was educated in English anywhere in Canada to attend English-language schools. By 2007, 80% of immigrant children learn in French, and more than half of those whose mother tongue was neither French nor English can converse in both languages. However, in 2000 a Quebec Superior Court upheld legislation that prohibits francophone children from attending English schools. The judge ruled that Quebec has a respon-

The late Hon. René Lévesque

sibility to protect French. The Supreme Court of Canada by a vote of 7–0 came to the same conclusion in 2005.

Bill 101 went beyond Bill 22 by requiring that French alone be used for provincial legislation, public administration, the judicial system, most public institutions. It originally required that laws and tribunals would be in French only, but that was later struck down. Ultimately it would have to be used as the working language in all businesses within the province. Employers were required to write all communications to their employees in French, and they could not dismiss or demote an employee simply because he spoke no English.

A watch-dog *Office de la langue française* (Office of the French Language) was set up to settle disputes arising from this law. It could be anticipated that this office would be overly vigilant in protecting the French language. Perhaps the most widely publicized and most regrettable instance of overreaction was the 1983 case of an elderly patient in Montreal's St. Mary's hospital, who, it was determined, had been denied her "right to die in French." The official language commission investigator maintained that the patient's nurses spoke little or no French in the intensive care ward during 34% of the time she was dying. He waved off the hospital's objections that services were always *available* in French and argued that humane and legal treatment required that *every* contact and every sound uttered within hearing distance of a francophone patient had to be in French.

Bill 101 understandably antagonized many anglophones in Quebec. Their demand that the language rights of the minority be respected was dismissed by the

Lévesque government, which correctly pointed out that the language rights of the French minority in *other* provinces had never been effectively guaranteed. The law created new opportunities for francophones and forced the anglophone minority, not the francophone majority, to pay the economic price for unilingualism.

The *PQ* made little headway in bringing more of Quebec's economy under state domination and in wresting control from anglophones in the rest of Canada or the United States. Some members of his party were demanding that the government break the anglophone capitalists' hold over the province's economy, no matter what the costs would be. But Lévesque believed that the economic recession that led to growing unemployment in the 1970s made any such moves risky. Instead, he focused in the late 1970s on finding the right moment to fulfill a promise he and his party had made during the 1976 election campaign: to conduct a referendum in order to establish Quebec as a sovereign state. This finally happened in May 1980.

Remembering that the bloodiest war in American history was fought from 1861 to 1865 in order to deny states the right to secede from the Union, an American is likely to be amazed by the fact that a Canadian government would permit the citizens of a province to *hold a vote* over whether they wished to destroy the country's unity. It is true that the prime minister made a veiled threat that he would resort to force if Quebec tried anything "illegal," but he never clarified what action might be illegal. During the entire campaign, Lévesque and his party stressed the peaceful and democratic nature of their cause. He had amply demonstrated in the past that he wanted nothing to do with firebrands willing to depart from democratic terrain. In any case, the entire campaign proceeded without violence, and there is absolutely no evidence that any kind of fear of civil war influenced the outcome of the vote. This forbearance and absence of violence indicated how different the political temperaments of Canadians and Americans are.

Lévesque had always been aware of how sensitive the question of Quebec independence had always been. He knew very well that while many *Québécois* were dissatisfied with the federal structure as it existed, they were not in favor of complete independence. Lévesque therefore was ambivalent and hesitating. He preferred to proceed toward his goal in stages (which he termed *étapisme*), thereby reaping scorn from those separatists who wanted immediate and decisive action. The very wording of the referendum revealed Lévesque's sensitivity for a wavering francophone attitude about independence: "The Government of Quebec has made public its proposal to negotiate a new agreement with the rest of Canada, based on the equality of nations; this agreement would enable Quebec to acquire the exclusive powers to make its laws, levy its taxes and establish relations abroad—in other words, sovereignty—and at the same time, to maintain with Canada an economic association including a common currency; no change in political status resulting from these negotiations will be effected without approval from the people through another referendum; on these terms, do you give the Government of Quebec the mandate to negotiate the proposed agreement between Quebec and Canada?" Clearly, the premier feared a "once and for all" vote to secede and merely asked for the right to talk to Ottawa about some kind of new arrangement. By watering down the gravity of the choice, he hoped to gather in as large a flock of *Québécois* as possible.

The Trudeau government in Ottawa campaigned enthusiastically against the question, and it no doubt influenced the vote. For one thing, it was difficult for the *PQ* to argue persuasively that Quebecers were an exploited and degraded race within the Canadian federation when the government in Ottawa was led by a prime minister (Trudeau), a finance minister (Marc Lalonde) and a justice minister (Jean Chrétien), *all* of whom were Quebecers. Also, the long-standing differences in income and opportunity that had existed between anglophones and francophones in Quebec had largely disappeared. Further, the governments of Canada and of all other provinces announced that they would *not* negotiate any form of sovereignty-association with Quebec, including an economic common market. Finally, the Trudeau government promised that a *non* vote would result in the BNA's being replaced by a new constitution which could be amended at home and which would bring about a kind of "renewed federalism" which would be satisfactory to all of Canada's ten provinces.

The results of the vote stunned the *PQ*: 59.5% of Quebecers voted against Lévesque's proposal. As anticipated, an overwhelming majority of Quebec's anglophone population voted against the proposition. However, his followers were shocked that a narrow majority (52%) of francophone *Québécois* also voted *against* it. Quebecers under the age of 40 voted overwhelmingly for it, but their votes could not salvage the battered dreams of Quebec separatism. In provincial parliamentary elections on April 13, 1981 (less than a year later) 49% of Quebecers voted for the PQ, giving the party a majority of 80 of 122 seats in the Quebec National Assembly. Nevertheless, the road to a separate, sovereign Quebec had become hopelessly blocked. The 1980 referendum had brought a palpable change in Quebecers' political attitudes toward the *PQ* and separatism.

By the end of 1984 it had become clear to Lévesque that separatism had reached a dead end and that it would be disastrous for the *PQ* to make this issue the centerpiece of the next provincial election. Already, polls were indicating that only a fifth to a third of Quebecers would vote for the *PQ*. Since 1981 the party had suffered a distressing loss of members, down to 113,000 from an all-time high in 1982 of 300,000. Without the belief in Quebec sovereignty, which had united the party's faithful in the past, the PQ had increasingly become a loose coalition of social democrats and conservatives who had very little in common. A deep economic recession in 1982–3, which drove unemployment figures upwards to 15%, had prompted a series of severe government austerity measures that rolled back the salaries of provincial civil servants and halted labor negotiations in the public sector. These measures, to which Lévesque saw no alternative, eroded the *PQ's* image as a social democratic movement and alienated Quebec's public sector employees, labor union members and young people, who had been among the PQ's staunchest supporters. Also, a series of embarrassing scandals in the highest leadership levels of the PQ rocked the party's image as a party of honesty and clean government; these included the conviction of one leader on charges of sexually molesting young girls and of another for shoplifting in a Montreal department store.

Paradoxically, a major reason why separatism had ebbed temporarily as a mainstream political force was that the nationalist thrust had accomplished so much in the preceding quarter of a century. These successes convinced many Quebecers that they could advance their social and cultural causes within the Canadian Confederation. Because of the Official Languages Act of 1969, the use of French has been expanded throughout Canada, and the number of bilingual Canadians has greatly increased.

Québécois had also made gigantic strides that had become obvious to almost everyone. In the 1960s only 4% of them went to universities, compared with 20% in the 1980s. One in six of these students studies business or economics now, as compared with one in ten in the rest of Canada. Francophones have become more comfortable in the boardrooms of Quebec's businesses. In the 1960s they owned only 20% of the province's economy; by the 1980s that figure had doubled to 40%.

The government in Ottawa did, in fact, produce a new constitution for Canada after tireless discussions with provincial governments. The 1982 constitution spells out provincial rights more accurately than did the BNA, and it contains a bill of rights that can be invoked by those who perceive language discrimination anywhere in Canada.

Feeling that he had been out-maneuvered in the negotiations leading up to the new constitution, Lévesque refused to sign the new document. However, he indicated in 1984 that he would not require as a condition for his signature a Quebec veto over future amendments. His willingness to cooperate with Ottawa on this important issue was not only due to the fact that the air had gone out of the separatist balloon. He was then dealing with a prime minister in Ottawa, Brian Mulroney, who was a Quebecer himself, and whom Lévesque found much more con genial and sympathetic than he found Trudeau.

Bill 101 made French the sole official language and greatly expanded its use in all sectors of Quebec society, despite the judicial restrictions that have been placed on it. The bill prompted scores of anglophone firms, such as the Sun Life Assurance Company's huge corporate headquarters, and thousands of English-speaking citizens to leave the province, reducing the percentage of Quebecers who listed English as their mother tongue from 14.7 in 1971 to 12.7 in 1981. In fact, a University of Montreal demographer, Jacques Henripin, even predicted that if anglophones continued to leave the province at the rate that they did during the 1970s, the English community would disappear within 50 years. That result is unlikely.

But, just as Quebec City, which was once 40% English, is now almost wholly French, so Quebec province has become more French and will probably continue to do so. The problem remains in Montreal, though, where the percentage of French-speaking residents declined from 64% in 1951 to 60% in 1992. This is partly because 90% of all immigrants in Quebec settle there, and two-thirds of them do not speak French. The anglophone exodus opened new economic opportunities for francophones. Francophone businesses supplied 61.6% of the jobs in 1987, compared with 54.8% in 1978. It also opened up many formerly anglophone neighborhoods to francophones, a fact which helps break down the "Two Solitudes" which had long characterized these groups' lack of contact with each other.

Quebecers seemed to be tired of language battles, but have unmistakably heard the message that Quebec is a *French-speaking* province, at least on the surface. But numerous appeals to the Quebec and

Canada

Former Prime Minister Chrétien meeting with provincial premiers

Photo: J.M. Carisse

Canadian supreme courts progressively weakened the application of 101. At the end of 1986, the Quebec Court of Appeal declared that those parts of 101 that mandated French-only signs violated Quebecer's rights to freedom of expression and were therefore unconstitutional. This decision provoked a storm among nationalists just when the new premier (Bourassa) and new mayor (Jean Doré) were trying to put the linguistic wars behind them and revitalize Montreal as an international finance center. Businesses taking advantage of the new ruling faced a rash of bomb threats, window smashing and a fire-bombing. Language tension reentered *"la belle province."*

In the long run, more and more *Québécois* are becoming bilingual. One prominent advocate of English rights noted: "There is linguistic peace. . . . We have evolved from perceiving ourselves as part of the English-Canadian majority to learning to live naturally and willingly as a minority."

Even though polls in 1985 indicated that only four percent of Quebecers favored the complete independence of Quebec, the dream of such a future dies hard. The radical separatist and professor at the University of Quebec at Montreal, Pierre Bourgault, called this development an "end of a dream. End of an era . . . Today it is possible to see that all along Lévesque was on the wrong track with the wrong people. He was still pursuing the Quiet Revolution while his troops wanted something else . . . It all goes back to a very big mistake that happened at the beginning: separatists had an idea about Quebec and they incarnated it in René Lévesque. But he had different ideas at different times. The truth is that Lévesque flirted with separatism because the idea seduced him,

but in the end he lacked the guts to do it. And in the end he betrayed himself. What now?" Also, the Montreal playwright Michel Tremblay declared: "It took us 200 years to wake up, and now we seem to be going back to sleep. I don't even dare consider the future, things are so bad. We had promised our children a country, and we haven't delivered."

With an eye to Quebec's history, it would be safe to say that Quebec nationalism never dies; it just dies down temporarily. Nevertheless, Lévesque decided that the time was not ripe for independence. In 1984, at the end of a bitter intraparty debate that had raged since 1982, he declared that in the next provincial election "sovereignty must not be at stake, neither wholly nor in parts that are more or less disguised." This pronouncement prompted the resignation of seven of his cabinet members, and further resignations and by-election losses reduced his party's majority in the National Assembly from 80 to 65. But in an extraordinary *PQ* convention held in 1985, a majority of delegates (869 to 453) voted to shelve the issue of Quebec sovereignty. This caused such an uproar within the party that Lévesque himself announced his resignation in mid-1985.

At the end of 1985 the *PQ* handed the reins of power back to the man and the party from whom it had wrested them in 1976: Robert Bourassa and the *Liberal Party*. A freelance journalist, Benoit Aubin wrote: "Quebecers, for better or for worse, seem to have decided to join the rest of North America." But in 1989 separatism roared back on the political agenda when the *PQ*, led by Jacques Parizeau and running again on an independence platform, won 40% of the votes in the provincial elections. (See Quebec Politics.)

MEECH LAKE ACCORD

Therefore, 1987 appeared to be a good time for the Canadian government to take audacious steps toward securing language harmony and finally winning Quebec endorsement of the 1982 Constitution. It introduced legislation to revise and update the 1969 Official Languages Act. The aim was to bring it in line with the 1982 Charter of Rights and Freedoms by stating that federal services will be provided in both official languages where there is "significant demand." It also reached a ground-breaking "Meech Lake Accord" with the 10 provincial premiers at an isolated Quebec retreat north of Ottawa.

The agreement they struck would have become a part of the Constitution and would have made Quebec "a distinct society," explicitly recognized the coexistence of French and English language groups as "a fundamental characteristic of Canada," and given Parliament and the provincial legislatures the role of preserving—but not promoting—the francophone and anglophone character of Canada. The Prime Minister sought a settlement that, in his words, would reflect "a country organized and governed in a manner that corresponds to the diversity of the Canadian people" and end "Quebec's estrangement from the Canadian constitutional family, on terms that are good for Quebec, good for our other regions and good for Canada." It is no surprise that Quebec was the first province to ratify the accord.

What were good for all provinces were the decentralizing clauses which would permit them to opt out of shared-cost programs as long as their own conformed to "national objectives," had more say on the nomination of senators and Supreme Court justices, and determined their own immigration policy. Most importantly, each province would have an absolute veto on future constitutional amendments. This accord reflected Mulroney's belief in government decentralization, local initiative and power sharing, as well as his attachment to cultural and linguistic rights. There were many critics of the accord. The most noted was Pierre Elliott Trudeau, who feared a dangerous weakening of Ottawa's power: "Those Canadians who fought for a single Canada, bilingual and multicultural, can say goodbye to their dream." His close associate and later prime minister, Jean Chrétien, shared this view, and women and native peoples found in it no protection of their particular rights.

Constitutional expert Eugene Forsey called it riddled with "ambiguities and obscurities," which could actually limit the rights of linguistic minorities. His warning seemed to be borne out by events in Saskatchewan in the spring of 1988, which threatened to open wide the language wounds in Canada, which seemed to have been healed. The origin of this dispute goes back to 1980, when a francophone priest insisted on using French to enter his plea for a speeding ticket. This demand was based on Section 110 of the North-West Territories Act of 1886, which stipulated that both languages could be used in courts and assemblies and that all statutes had to be in both languages. The Canadian Supreme Court ruled in February 1988 that that statute was still valid in Saskatchewan, but that the province was free to repeal Section 110 of the act.

Faced with the same problem in 1985, Manitoba had chosen to comply by beginning the laborious and expensive process of translating all past and present laws. However, despite pleas from Prime Minister Mulroney, Saskatchewan's premier, Grant Devine, chose a different route. His government introduced legislation to repeal the bilingual provision of the old law. He argued that he had to pay attention to anglophone sentiment and to the budgetary strains that would result from translating thousands of prior laws for only 2.3% of the province's population that is francophone.

Minority language groups throughout all of Canada were incensed, despite Devine's promises to translate some of the more important laws and to provide some French-language services at an undetermined time in the future. Quebec Premier Bourassa supported Devine, but this did not quiet the storm. Coming at a time when the Meech Lake agreement was under growing attack, critics charged that Saskatchewan's actions made the agreement's commitment to "preserve" minority language rights worthless and made it clear that nobody knows exactly what the accord would do for minorities.

In 1989–90 the gulf of understanding between anglophones and francophones was widened in a way which endangered the delicate Accord. English Canadians reacted angrily in 1988 when Bourassa, faced with an intense resurgence of separatist sentiment in Quebec, decided to prohibit the use of English on outdoor commercial signs, an action that seemed to violate the rights of Quebec's anglophones. This struck critics as a foretaste of how Quebec would use the powers implied by the "distinct society" clause in the accord. It provoked a backlash and made bilingualism harder to sell in the rest of Canada. But the political storm increasingly focused on Meech Lake, as momentum against the accord gathered force in English Canada, especially in the West, New Brunswick, and Newfoundland. As the clock turned midnight on June 23, 1990, Meech Lake was dead.

In the Manitoba legislative assembly, the only native member, Elijah Harper, who wanted the accord to fail because it did not address native issues, stalled debate by procedural tricks and prevented a vote from being taken. Newfoundland's premier, Clyde Wells, objected to the "fabricated precipice" which the deadline created, and called off his own legislature's vote. Mulroney's feverish last-minute efforts to find a compromise merely antagonized opponents even more.

The outcome ignited a new wave of Quebec nationalism, which in turn stirred up even more anti-*Québécois* resentment in anglophone Canada. It helped nurture a new sense of alienation in the West and sparked native assertiveness throughout Canada. It left a legacy of polarization and volatility and brought to the surface stresses and strains in the very fabric of Canadian society. It put wind in the sails of a new party, the *Bloc Québécois*, and carried the *PQ* (which had opposed Meech Lake) to victory in the two succeeding Quebec provincial elections and perhaps more in the new century. A rising Reform Party (renamed the Canadian Alliance in 2000) thrived in the West. Because of Trudeau's and Chrétien's opposition to Meech, the federal *Liberals* became near pariahs in Quebec, but they became more popular in English Canada. Perhaps most important, it left Quebec's signature off the Canadian constitution and thereby rendered Canada vulnerable to calls for Quebec separation. It sent Mulroney's approval rating into the cellar (14%). One pollster noted in 1991 that in terms of popularity, he "is tied with Fidel Castro, but higher than Saddam Hussein." The conflict alienated him from his old friend, Lucien Bouchard, and from Chrétien, with whom he had had a courteous relationship. A cover story in *Maclean's* commem-orating the tenth anniversary of the Meech Lake Accord was entitled, "June 23, 1990: The Day that Changed Canada." Canada was never the same again.

A NEW CONSTITUTION FOR CANADA?

Many Quebecers interpreted the downfall of Meech Lake as a rejection of them by the rest of Canada, and they acted accordingly. Polls in 1991 indicated that more than two-thirds favored full sovereignty. Premier Bourassa named a "Belanger-Campeau Commission" to conduct four months of public hearings to gather opinions from Quebecers on the province's future. In March 1991 it issued its report, calling for a plebiscite no later than October 26, 1992, to determine its future status, unless the federal government can present an acceptable alternative. Bourassa favored continued links with Canada, but he envisaged a country that would leave the federal government with little more responsibilities than protecting the borders, managing the currency, and repaying the federal debt.

Seeing that his countrymen were unnerved, uncertain, and pessimistic, Mulroney asserted, "a sense of hurt over a constitutional failure—however real—is insufficient reason for Quebecers to give up on Canada." He promised that his government would put forward its own proposals for constitutional change to build "a new and stronger Canada. We have every intention of restructuring Canada. We have no intention of dismantling it." He added: "Let me be clear: Canada is not up for grabs. Either you have a country or you don't. You can't have it both ways."

His problem was to devise constitutional reforms far more comprehensive than the Meech Lake Accord in only 18 months that would satisfy both Quebec and all the other groups clamoring for greater autonomy from the central government. Remembering how many Canadians had resented the secretive way the Meech Lake talks had been conducted behind closed doors and the fact that they had focused on Quebec's demands, the government decided this time to open up the debate and negotiations to the public and interest groups and to include something for the anglophone provinces and native peoples as well. This was a radical shift in constitutional talks, which had always been tugs of war between Ottawa and the provinces over who controlled what. To sound out the wishes of all those groups and to try to understand the deep malaise in Canada, Mulroney created a Citizens' Forum on Canada's Future, led by Keith Spicer. It organized hearings throughout the land to hear the com-

Canada

plaints and suggestions of hundreds of thousands of Canadians, and it reported them to the government. Six provincial commissions were simultaneously holding traveling hearings.

In 1991 Mulroney turned to former Prime Minister Joe Clark to head a new Ministry for Constitutional Affairs and a cabinet committee which would produce a draft proposal for amending the constitution. The challenge, in Mulroney's words, was to come up with "a new, modern and dynamic Constitution that will be accepted by all the provinces." A bilingual Westerner, Clark's job was to turn around Westerners' and other anglophones' anti-Quebec sentiment and to get them to accept a constitutional plan that would also be compatible with Quebec's demands for recognition as a "distinct society." He had at the same time to offer Quebecers a palatable alternative to sovereignty. No one envied his task, but his performance gained him almost universal trust and respect. His secret was patience, fairness, and elegant, well-crafted speeches: "We can be the first generation of Canadians to pass on to the next less than was passed on to us. There is nothing automatic about this country. Canada was not here at the beginning of the last century. There is no logic that says it must be here at the beginning of the next. We have to work to keep it. We always have. This is a large and diverse country. Keeping it large without destroying its diversity has always been our challenge."

A process was set into motion that would have dramatically reduced the federal government's role in the country's affairs and enlarged the powers and responsibilities of the provinces. This was already taking place, but a constitutional change would have given added authority to the on-going shift in the balance of federal and provincial powers, which is reversing a decades-old trend toward an ever more powerful central government. The center seems no longer to be holding and the parts are defining the whole. Ontario's premier, Bob Rae, declared, "we cannot just turn the federal government into a post office. It leaves out the soul of Canada."

After two years of intense work, the premiers of the nine anglophone provinces, native leaders, and the prime minister agreed to the "Charlottetown Accord" on August 28, 1992. It included: 1. **Senate reform**: The existing appointed body would be replaced by a more powerful one elected by proportional representation at a different time than the House of Commons (in which Quebec would be guaranteed one-fourth of the seats). In response to Western demands, each province would have six seats. The territories, aboriginal groups, and women would also be represented. 2. **Aboriginal rights**: The inherent native right to self-government was accepted, subject to the Charter of Rights and Freedoms, with aboriginal governments recognized as one of three orders of government, alongside Ottawa and the provinces. 3. **Division of powers**: Ottawa would recognize the provinces' exclusive power over such areas as tourism, forestry, housing, and culture. Powers would be divided more efficiently. 4. **Social and economic issues**: Commitments to preserve universal health care, the equalization between richer and poorer provinces, and the free flow of goods, capital and services throughout Canada would be enshrined in the constitution. 5. **Quebec**: It would be recognized as a "distinct society," characterized by its language, culture, and civil-law tradition, and it would choose three Supreme Court justices. 6. **Minorities**: Anglophone communities in Quebec and francophone communities elsewhere would be protected.

Every mainstream political party and institution supported the package except the Reform Party, and the *Parti Québécois*. Former Prime Minister Trudeau also opposed it. On October 26, 1992, 54% of the voters, six provinces, and the Yukon Territory said no to the accord. Only Newfoundland, New Brunswick, Prince Edward Island, and, by the closest of margins, Ontario, said yes. Since the package needed the ratification of every province and the federal government, the rejection could not have been more decisive. One drinker in a Montreal bar reportedly called it "horrendously Canadian: a populist revolt in favor of the status quo." It was a popular vote against Canada's leaders. Westerners thought the accord gave too much to Quebec, and Quebecers thought it did not do enough for them. For Quebec separatists, the Western no-vote confirmed that Canada would never recognize Quebec's special character. Parizeau said, "with Meech they said no to Quebec; this time we said it to each other."

Looking back on his dramatic 1993 election victory, Prime Minister Jean Chrétien declared that the *Tories* had "spent too much time on constitutional affairs and not enough on the economy. So I want to do exactly the reverse." He did not have that luxury. Many Canadians seemed to sense an imminent challenge to their country's unity. Canadians saw the separatist *Bloc Québécois* functioning as the official opposition in the federal parliament and the *PQ* emerging victorious in the 1994 Quebec provincial elections.

PQ leader Jacques Parizeau ordered a referendum on October 30, 1995, to clear the way for an independent Quebec. This time, the separatists came closer to victory than ever before, winning 49.4% of the votes in a huge 94% turnout. This was a gain of 10 percentage points since 1980; 60% of Quebec's francophones voted "*oui*," while nearly all anglophones and immigrants voted *non*. Subsequent investigation revealed that many "no" ballots had been declared invalid for mysterious and trivial reasons, leading to charges of possible *PQ* election rigging. Nevertheless Quebecers had never displayed such deep dissatisfaction with the status quo. Regarding the outcome as a moral victory,

Quebec's Parliament Building

Quebec's new leader, Lucien Bouchard, evoked the memory of Lévesque by proclaiming: "Let us keep the faith. The next time will be the right one. And the next time may come sooner than people think." Parizeau, who resigned as premier after the disappointing defeat, was correct in saying that for many Canadians "this Quebec problem is like a never-ending visit to the dentist."

In the midst of the 1997 federal parliamentary elections Parizeau showed that he, himself, was that dentist. After Prime Minister Chrétien had called early elections to focus on the country's economic success and challenges, Parizeau published his memoirs, *For a Sovereign Québec*, in which he admitted that he had been prepared to declare Quebec's independence immediately after a yes-vote in 1995, not after negotiations with Ottawa, as his party had proposed during the referendum campaign. The PQ government had also set aside $17 million to buy up provincial bonds it feared nervous investors might dump on the market. This reminded Canadians that those who support Quebec sovereignty, though divided among themselves on tactics and on the definition of the term, are dead serious about Quebec independence. Quebec Premier Lucien Bouchard promised another referendum by the year 2000, but flagging interest in Quebec for complete separation has caused it to be postponed indefinitely. Polls continue to show that *Québécois* are divided on the question and that a majority continues to oppose independence. The uproar caused by Parizeau brought the issue of unity back into the center of Canadian politics

Chrétien had promised in 1995 to reexamine Quebec's constitutional demands. But resistance to that in anglophone Canada and in the *Reform Party*, as well as Premier Bouchard's and the *BQ's* rejection of another round of constitutional talks, limited the prime minister to a meaningless resolution in parliament recognizing the distinct nature of Quebec. His then finance minister, Paul Martin, and most of his closest advisers were *Québécois*, and he appointed Montreal political scientist Stéphane Dion as Canada's first minister of intergovernmental affairs.

Dion, who in 2006 became party leader, helped the *Liberal* government in Ottawa formulate a two-pronged approach to Quebec, known as "Plan A" and "Plan B." Plan A is a national unity strategy of economic growth and job creation that would benefit Quebec and win support throughout Canada for the notion that Quebec is a "distinct society." Plan B is hardball involving tough talk designed to disabuse *Québécois* of any illusions about what life would be like if they voted for indepen-

dence. They could not expect to continue using Canadian passports or money, to remain in NAFTA, or even retain all the territory within Quebec's current borders. In Chrétien's words, "if Canada is divisible, Quebec is divisible." Thus if anglophones, Indians or Inuit in Quebec want the areas in which they live to remain in Canada, they could do so. The end of 1997 he made it clear that any abrupt move by Quebec to secede, even after a big "Yes" vote to separate, would be illegal. "There will be a negotiation with the federal government . . . no doubt about that." Federal lawyers asked the Supreme Court in 1997 to rule on the legality of a unilateral Que-

bec secession. Dion emphasized: Plan A is "the plan is reconciliation"; Plan B involves "the rules of secession." "We are not governing an ordinary country. We are governing a great federation that is in danger of collapse."

On August 20, 1998, the nine Supreme Court justices issued a unanimous ruling: Quebec does not have the right under the constitution to declare independence unilaterally. Since it is not a victim of "alien subjugation" or an "oppressed people," it has no automatic right to self-determination under international law. Any referendum would have to offer a "clear question" (such as Chrétien's pro-

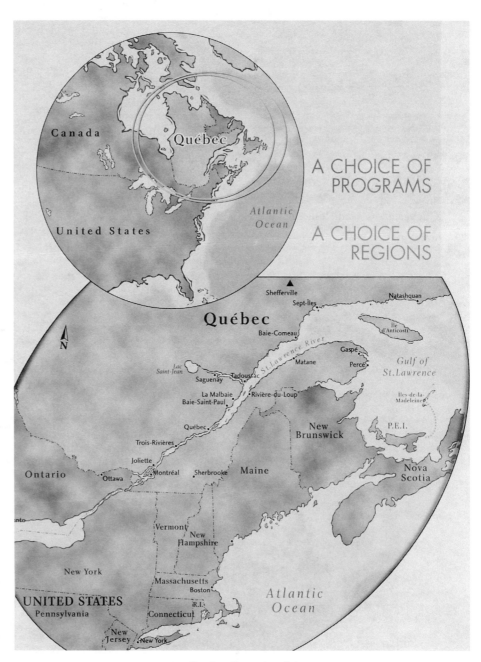

Quebec lures tourists

Canada

Quebec homestead along the St. Lawrence

posed "Do you want to separate from Canada?"). If a "clear majority" voted in favor of independence, then negotiations with the rest of Canada would be "necessary," and a constitutional amendment would be required. Federalists rejoiced at the ruling. The Quebec government unexpectedly joined the celebration. Seeing much room for interpretation, Bouchard emphasized the requirement that Ottawa negotiate with Quebec after a successful referendum and read the "clear majority" mandate narrowly. He pointed out that Newfoundland had entered Canada in 1949 with only 52% support in a referendum. In its headline the *Ottawa Citizen* summed up the differing interpretations: "One ruling, two solitudes."

After initially greeting the 1998 Supreme Court decision, the *PQ* let it be known in October 1999 that it no longer felt bound to follow an interpretation of a court whose judges were appointed by Ottawa. In the words of Joseph Facal, the *PQ's* intergovernmental affairs minister, "all rules governing the next referendum will be determined by the national assembly of Quebec." This declaration, along with polling results indicating that a third of those who had voted "Yes" in the 1995 referendum had thought that Quebec would still be a province of Canada even if the "Yes" side won, prompted the federal government to take the initiative over

the secession question for the first time in three decades.

Bill C-20, known as the "clarity bill," was introduced in December 1999. For the first time the legislation legitimizes the right of any province to hold a referendum on secession. But it establishes stringent conditions. First, the question would have to be direct and concise and make no mention of future economic or political partnerships with Canada. To insure that any future question would be sufficiently clear, it would first have to be vetted by the federal parliament and get its approval. Next any referendum majority itself must be clear. The bill does not clearly spell out what the word "clear" means, but only that the traditional 50%-plus-one would not be sufficient. Not until the House of Commons had determined that "a clear expression of the will of the population" had been given would the federal government enter negotiations about a secession agreement.

According to former Prime Minister Chrétien, "we are forcing them to be honest." It goes without saying that the *PQ* seethed over the clarity bill. However, voters in Quebec supported the concept. In a 1999 poll, seven out of ten believed 60% represents the clear majority required by the court; 93% favored a clear question, and 61% did not think the 1995 question was clear.

Quebec City

Constitution Act,
1867

Constitution Act, 1982

Canadian Charter of
Rights and Freedoms (1982)

POLITICAL SYSTEM

For a person interested in comparing different governmental systems, Canada is an extraordinarily intriguing case. As we have seen, Canada never rebelled from Britain. It became an independent country so gradually that Canadians cannot quite agree on exactly when it finally happened. In the 19th century a majority of Canadians wanted to retain some ties with Britain. Also, they wanted a governmental system modeled on that of Great Britain, not on that of the United States. The Canadian system of government has been influenced by the political experiences of the British, French and American nations. However, Canadians have adapted these experiences to their own special needs.

In 1867 the British Parliament passed the British North America Act (BNA), granting the Canadian government the authority "to make Laws for Peace, Order and Good Government." It was a short, sober, legalistic document, almost totally lacking in the kind of ringing, quotable

language one reads in the Declaration of Independence, penned almost a century earlier by Thomas Jefferson.

The BNA was written exclusively by Canadians at conferences that no British delegates attended. When it was presented to the British government for formal approval, the latter objected to only two minor points: it was nervous about calling the new country "the Kingdom of Canada," as the Canadians had wanted. The reason: such a name might be offensive to the Americans, who had reacted violently to the notion of monarchy 90 years earlier. The Canadians therefore settled on the word "Dominion," taken from the 72nd Psalm, "He shall have dominion also from sea to sea and from the river unto the ends of the earth." To the "Fathers of the Constitution," (as Canada's founders were called) this term, which had never been used before to describe a nation, embodied the monarchial principle so subtly that the Americans would not even notice it.

The second minor point on which the British insisted was a provision for breaking a deadlock between the two houses of parliament, a provision which has never been used. Other than these two points, the *BNA* was purely a Canadian creation. It prescribed "a Constitution similar in principle to that of the United Kingdom." That meant, without spelling it out, that Canada would have a parliamentary democracy in which the cabinet (which was called the "Privy Council") would be responsible to the House of Commons, not to the British monarch.

It also meant that custom and tradition would be an essential part of the country's constitution without having to be written down, as Americans had done. Thus, such fundamental constitutional principles and practices as "responsible government," "collective responsibility," "parliamentary supremacy," the fusion of executive powers and legislative powers (as opposed to "separation of powers"), "votes of confidence" for the government, the need for

Canada

the prime minister and cabinet (terms which do not appear in the document) to have seats in Parliament, were not written down in the *BNA* and are still not spelled out on paper.

The trappings of Canadian politics evoke the strong British heritage: Privy Council, governor general, the House of Commons, prime minister, Throne Speech, Parliament meeting only upon royal summons, and Crown corporations. After they arrest criminals, the Royal Canadian Mounted Police turn them over to Crown prosecutors to charge them. Officers are educated at the Royal Military College of Canada. All federal acts begin with the words: "Her Majesty, by and with the advice and consent of the Senate and the House of Commons, enacts as follows." Provincial laws commence with similar wording, and all bills need "Royal Assent," to be enacted. Even the Canada Act of 1982 requested "that Her Majesty may graciously be pleased to cause a Bill to be laid before the Parliament of the United Kingdom . . . by and with the advice and consent of the Lords Spiritual and Temporal, and Commons . . ." Immigrants who become citizens pledge their "loyalty and allegiance to Canada and Her Majesty Elizabeth II, queen of Canada."

While the vestiges of the British heritage are still visible, there have been recent reminders that Britain has only a limited hold on the hearts and minds of many Canadians. In 1965 Britannia's stripes were removed from Canada's flag, and a simple maple leaf replaced the Union Jack. In 1970 the "E II R" cipher, meaning "Elizabeth II Regina" was removed from Canadian mailboxes. In 1980 the country adopted a new anthem, "O Canada," which can be sung in two languages, to replace "God Save the Queen," which, it need not be said, was only sung in English. Shortly thereafter, the 12,000 member Monarchist League lost other battles: the country's major holiday, Dominion Day, celebrated July 1st, was rechristened "Canada Day," and even the British North America Act was renamed the "Constitution Act 1867." One member of the Royal Commonwealth Society rudely referred to each of these changes as a "sop to Quebec." A more accurate explanation is that each of those symbols rubbed salt in the unhealed wound with which Canada was born: the English-French division. Each was a brick in the wall that separated the majority of Canadians from that third of their countrymen who were francophones.

Perhaps no country in the world has been more successful than Canada in reconciling the claims of two founding peoples who are determined to preserve their languages and cultures. It has not been easy, but the English-speaking majority has recognized the "French fact" in Canada. Canadian politics has been significantly influenced by that fact. In Quebec itself, French civil law prevails, and Quebec's anglophones have accepted the necessity of speaking French in their native province. In other provinces, such as New Brunswick, French and English are both used in public life, and everywhere in Canada a francophone can deal with the federal government in French. In Ottawa, French and English are both used on the street and in Parliament. Every prime minister, governor general and speaker of the House of Commons, as well as at least three of nine Supreme Court justices, must speak both languages, and parliamentary debates are freely conducted in both.

Primarily because of the "French fact," Canada had to be created as a federal state. This means that law-making authority is divided between the central government and the provinces. It was unthinkable that Canada be a unitary state, as Britain is. Quebec's persistent assertion of provincial rights also benefited other provinces as well, especially in the West, which wanted to lighten Ottawa's hand on their shoulders. Further, Quebec prevented Canada from ever being a "melting pot," as the United States. Canada has adopted a policy of multiculturalism, overseen by a cabinet minister. In other words, other minority groups in Canada owe their special treatment largely to the efforts of the *Québécois*.

The influence of the British and French heritages on Canadian political life is obvious, but another nation has also had a powerful influence on Canada: the United States. As we have seen, much of the Canadian experience was an attempt to survive as a sovereign country and as a unique cultural product in the face of powerful challenges by the American neighbors. In 1812 the Americans were beaten back after a half-hearted attempt to spread America's "Manifest Destiny" northward. In 1837 the rebellions in Upper and Lower Canada, which resulted in the Durham Report and ultimate independence, were led by men infected by the idea of rule by the people. These were populist notions that had come alive again during the Jacksonian era of the 1830s. Canadians could learn about them right across the border in the U.S.

Canadians adopted federalism for reasons of their own size and diversity. However, their brand was shaped by their horror of the American Civil War, which seemed to have resulted from an exaggerated and destabilizing concept of states' rights. The "Fathers of Confederation" did create an upper house called a Senate, which was supposed to defend regional interests, something that it has utterly failed to do. Today, such things as the hoopla of Party conventions where the leaders are selected, the increasing observance of four years as a long enough time between national elections, a written bill of rights and a largely written constitution, are a few of many examples of America's impact on Canadian politics.

Despite heavy borrowing from the other countries' political traditions and practices, it has been Canadians themselves who have shaped their own political system. It is they who have adapted to their unique situation as a huge, regionally and culturally diverse country. The Canadian regime may be a hybrid, but the mix is uniquely Canadian. Its basic outline is as follows: voters elect 308 members of the House of Commons, the lower house of Parliament. The leader of the party that wins a majority of seats (or can get more votes in the House of Commons on important issues than any other party) becomes the prime minister, the most powerful political figure in the land. Queen Elizabeth II, the Queen of Canada, is the head of state, but neither she, nor her representative, the governor general, makes any important political decisions.

The prime minister selects other ministers, who are also experienced parliamentary leaders in the Party, to sit in the cabinet. Together, the prime minister and cabinet are called "the government," which rules "collectively." That is, all members of the government must publicly support its policies or resign from office. Also, the entire team assumes responsibility for the overall policy. The government rules as long as it maintains a majority in the House of Commons. In other words, it rules until it loses a "vote of confidence" on an important bill. The prime minister must call an election at least five years after the preceding election, but he can announce one earlier if that would be to his party's advantage.

Unlike in the United States, where both houses of Congress are equally powerful, the Canadian upper house, the Senate, has far less power than the House of Commons. Also unlike in the U.S., there is no "separation of powers" among the executive, legislative or judicial branches. Executive and legislative powers are fused, and the prime minister is *both* the chief executive and chief legislator of the land. Through his tightly disciplined party, he controls the House of Commons. Finally, as in the U.S., but unlike in Britain, some laws can be judged unconstitutional by the Supreme Court of Canada. In Canada "parliamentary supremacy" exists in theory, but not in fact, because of federalism and a constitution which stands above Parliament.

CONSTITUTION

Government in Canada is democratic, in that the people elect the representatives who govern them. It is also constitutional, in that it has certain rules which bind all political actors, which limit the exercise of governmental power, which impose obligations on the governments and which provide for the enforcement of the rules by courts of law. In a federal state like Canada, a constitution has an additional function: it distributes legal power to the central and the provincial legislatures; in the words of Canadian political scientist David Milne, it "forms a master power grid from which all the governmental players get their authority."

Thus, it is not surprising that any effort to change the constitution, such as took place in Canada in the early 1980s, would expose the very nerves of Canadian government; it would inevitably reveal the tensions and power struggles in federal-provincial, inter-provincial and ethnic group relations.

With regard to the form of its constitution, Canada stands between the United Kingdom and the United States. The British constitution is *unwritten*; it is a collection of clearly defined documents, such as the Magna Carta of 1215 and the Statute of Westminster of 1931, as well as of important customs and traditions that no government would dare violate. However, any portion of the constitution could be changed by Parliament, which is "supreme." At the other democratic extreme is the United States, which has a *written* constitution that spells out the rules of the game and the institutions of governments (with a few prominent omissions, such as political parties). The American document is extremely difficult to change and has been amended only 26 times in more than 200 years. Congress cannot change it; it, not the Congress, is "supreme." Unlike Britain and Canada, which had not experienced revolutions, the U.S. had fought for its independence. After successful revolutions, winners are far more inclined to put in writing the kind of guarantees and rights that had been denied them by the former ruler.

The *BNA* called for a political system like that of Britain. This included customs and traditions, such as the need for the prime minister to have the confidence of the House of Commons, or the understanding that the monarch "reigns but does not rule." In typical British fashion, these things were not written down, and most of them are still unwritten. But Canada's founding fathers had a challenge that could not be met by merely adopting British practices. They had to create a form of government that was sufficiently strong to hold such a huge, sparsely populated country together, while at the same time sufficiently decentralized to satisfy the aspirations of different regions and peoples. They could coax the various strong-willed colonies into the new union only by promising them that they could share with the central government the responsibility for ruling the country. They even used a misnomer to describe the new governmental structure: a "confederation," which means a loose alliance of sovereign nations. Actually, they had created a federation, which does not recognize the provinces as sovereign states, but which divides authority between the central and provincial governments.

Since 1867 the written portion of the *BNA* has been supplemented by other important documents that have constitutional standing. In all, 24 documents (called "organic laws") make up the constitution; there are 13 acts of the British Parliament (amendments to the *BNA*, also called British North America Acts), seven acts of the Canadian Parliament and four British orders-in-council (government declarations permitted by law). This collection includes such statutes as the acts admitting other provinces to Canada after 1867, provincial constitutions, the Supreme Court Act of 1875, the War Powers Act of 1914, the Statute of Westminster of 1931, the Elections Acts, the House of Commons Act, the Legislative Assembly Acts, the Public Service Acts, the Bill of Rights of 1960 and the Official Languages Act of 1969. With all these constitutional acts and the many customs that provided the ground rules for Canadian politics, one might think that all the bases had been touched and that Canadians could settle down and live by their voluminous, complicated constitution. But they could not. There were still some very important things missing.

The 1970s and 1980s were decades of both nationalist and regional resurgence in Canada. Many *Québécois* were demanding separation from Canada, or at least a radically different kind of federal structure that would enable them largely to rule themselves. Discontent was also reaching the boiling point in the energy-rich western provinces, which believed that their economic development was being seriously threatened by Ottawa's policy toward their natural resources. The western premiers banded together to form the first regional bloc in Canadian history that could seriously threaten the predominance of Ontario and Quebec. The Atlantic provinces had always resented Central Canada's dominance. They also feared that the federal government would find a way of depriving them of the benefits from the oil and gas that had been found off their shores and which, they hoped, could finally enable them to catch up economically with the rest of Canada.

On top of this regional turmoil, the Trudeau government in Ottawa had embarked upon a nationalist campaign to increase the Canadian hold over the country's own economy and energy resources. The very joints of the Canadian state began to creak under the weight of competing visions of federalism, nationalism and regionalism. Canada was in crisis, so its political and legal minds set out to find a constitutional solution that could save the country from tearing apart.

The result was the Canada Act, which served as the basis for the Constitution Act, 1982. Canada did not adopt an entirely new constitution. Instead it refined many existing arrangements and added some important provisions to the existing constitution. It was a compromise, but one that was reached only after an enormous hue and cry and some of the most determined political maneuvering in Canadian history. It was a high-stakes intergovernmental struggle among giants. In David Milne's words, "because the battle concerned the kind of state (or states) Canada was to be, it challenged every Canadian to define his sense of country more sharply than ever before. Predictably there was no consensus among Canadians as a whole."

The struggle involved many twists and turns before it was resolved; it also revealed how many power centers must be dealt with in Canadian politics. The Trudeau government, which had been voted back into power after a nine-month breather in February 1980, fought a successful battle against the *Parti Québécois'* effort to win a provincial referendum in May 1980 that could have paved the way to some form of separatism. In order to undercut the *PQ's* appeals during the campaign, Trudeau had promised a new federal arrangement. In July of that year, intergovernmental negotiations began but reached an impasse by September 13. On October 6, Trudeau placed a unilateral proposal before Parliament in order to force the provinces back into action. The latter wasted no time by challenging Trudeau's move in court. By November 1980, Britain's Select Committee on Foreign Affairs began to study the UK's role in the constitutional debate and concluded two months later that "Westminster cannot act as a mere rubberstamp on all requests coming from Parliament to Canada."

After months of further debate, deliberation and challenges in provincial high courts, the Supreme Court of Canada rendered a decision on September 28, 1981, which was somewhat puzzling but which nevertheless declared that Trudeau's reso-

Canada

lution in Parliament was legal and that a province did not have a veto over the entire process. This decision practically forced the premiers to reenter negotiations with the Canadian government. In November they culminated in a substantial agreement among all parties except Quebec. In December 1981 the constitutional resolution cleared through both houses of the Canadian Parliament, was signed by the governor general and delivered to Buckingham Palace in London.

Premier Lévesque, who felt betrayed and outmaneuvered by Trudeau and the other premiers, unsuccessfully appealed to Prime Minister Margaret Thatcher to delay the proceedings until Quebec's veto power could be established by the Quebec Court of Appeal. Also, Canadian Indians appealed unsuccessfully to the British Court of Appeals, claiming that their full rights had not been secured in the new agreement. In March 1982 the Canada Act breezed through both houses of the British Parliament. On April 17, 1982, while thousands of *Québécois* and Indians publicly protested and mourned, Queen Elizabeth proclaimed the Canada Act in a signing ceremony in front of the Canadian Parliament. This act terminated the British Parliament's power over Canada and transferred the entire Canadian constitution to the Canadians themselves. Bitter about having been deprived of an absolute veto power, the Quebec government never accepted the validity of this act. This is precisely the deadlock the 1987 Meech Lake Accord sought to resolve.

Under the terms of this Canada Act, the Canadian government was able to proclaim the Constitution Act, 1982. This act lumped together and renamed the *BNA* and all its amendments the "Constitution Acts, 1867–1975." Canada's major holiday, July 1, was renamed "Canada Day." Canada had entered a new age. Canadian government was changed in several important ways. Perhaps the most significant change was that Canada could now amend every part of its own constitution without having to secure British approval. This is surely a power that any truly sovereign country must possess. Because it is so important, Canadians spoke of the "patriation" (bringing home) of their constitution. In 1927 the first attempts had been made to secure this right. However, for more than a half-century all such efforts foundered on the inability of the federal and provincial governments to agree on a method of amendment. This inability should not be surprising if one remembers that the power to amend a constitution is the power to change the political rules of the game. It is therefore a matter of utmost importance.

The American constitution provides for only one amending process, but the Constitution Act, 1982, elaborates four different formulae or processes, depending upon the issue. Important changes dealing with such matters as the monarchy, the governor general, the use of the French and English languages in the federal government or the Supreme Court of Canada, require the ultimate approval of the House of Commons and *every* provincial legislature. In other matters, a single province would not have a veto; only two-thirds of the provinces need to approve. There are two prominent exceptions which reveal the extent to which provincial powers were respected: a proposed change that would affect only one or several provinces, but not such matters as boundary changes or the use of French or English in a particular province. In such cases, the affected provinces would have the right of veto. Also, a province can "opt out" of *any* amendment that takes away any of its powers, rights or privileges. A final amending formula deals with most changes in Canada's executive, Senate or House of Commons; in these cases, a change can be made by an ordinary act of Parliament.

A second important change brought by the Constitution Act, 1982, is that it "entrenches" certain parts of the written constitution, making it impossible for Parliament or any provincial legislature to change them by simple legislative acts. This applies to the monarchy, the governor general, the composition of the Supreme Court, or the amending formulae themselves. The existence of such "entrenched" portions of the constitution that are out of Parliament's reach is a conscious departure from the British doctrine of "parliamentary supremacy," which gives Parliament the right to decide anything in the political realm. In a third change, the provinces were granted more control over the taxing and exportation of their own natural resources. A fourth change was that the Constitution Act, 1982, included a Charter of Rights and Freedoms, in order to strengthen the liberty of individual Canadian citizens. This was also a break from the tradition in Britain, where individual liberties are considered to be adequately protected by common law and were therefore never written down, as they were in the American Bill of Rights in 1791.

The Constitution Act, 1982, was a carefully constructed compromise between the central and provincial governments and contained some very significant innovations. However, much of it consolidated and refined many existing arrangements in the political system. It left the main structure of government, including the division of powers between Ottawa and the provinces, intact.

Queen Elizabeth II signs the Canadian Constitution, 1982. Prime Minister Trudeau is seated at left. Public Archives Canada/PA/140705 Photo by Bob Cooper

78

Rideau Hall, residence of the Governor General

GOVERNMENTAL STRUCTURE

As in the United Kingdom, Canada distinguishes between a "formal executive," who is the head of state, and the "prime minister," who really wields the political power. Americans make no such distinction, and their president must not only be the chief policy maker, but he must also spend many hours meeting visiting heads of state on the White House lawn and dining with them, pinning badges on scouts, congratulating winning athletic teams, posing with handsome Thanksgiving turkeys and smiling at cameras while turning on Christmas tree lights. In Canada such ceremonial functions are performed by the representatives of that political figure in whom executive authority is still theoretically vested: the Queen of Canada, who spends most of her time being the British monarch.

The Monarch

She and her representatives, the governor general and the lieutenant governors in the 10 provinces, are surrounded by a glittering group of advisers known as the Queen's Privy Council in Canada. This is composed of all present and former prime ministers, cabinet members, speakers of both houses of Parliament, chief justices of the Supreme Court and various other prominent citizens. This large group of people rarely assembles and only at such ceremonial occasions as the accession of a new monarch. The only people among these advisers who actually wield any power are the present prime minister and cabinet, who in the constitution are referred to as "the Committee of the Privy Council." All cabinet decisions are issued as decisions of the Privy Council. Even though no federal or provincial bill could be enacted without Royal Assent, no monarch would make a decision without being told by the prime minister what to do. Despite the sweeping powers which the constitution seems to give her, she "reigns but does not rule."

If the Queen and her representatives have so little power, why has the monarchy been retained in Canada? Monarchs have often served useful functions in countries that have become democracies. In Britain, for example, the Queen symbolizes the unity of the nation and the continuous thread through English history. She is thus the focus of national pride. In Canada the monarch often symbolizes and exacerbates the disunity of the nation. *Québécois* have seldom revered the monarch of a nation that conquered New France in 1760, and when Queen Elizabeth II visited Quebec during the Quiet Revolution, her presence sparked serious riots. She and her family seldom set foot in the *"la belle province."*

In 1987 she made her first tour of the province in almost a quarter century and was greeted with polite indifference. To most Quebecers she is no longer a hated symbol of English oppression. As Pierre Bourgault, a former radical who organized the 1964 protests against her, noted: "Our problems are with the English in Quebec who still refuse to speak French, not with the Queen. She simply comes for a short visit, speaks French while she's here and then goes back to England." But in the tense weeks following the failure of Meech Lake in 1990, nationalists made it clear that she was not welcome in Quebec. Many young anglophone Canadians are no longer stirred by the monarch. One 18-year old who joined the crowd to see the Queen and her consort during a visit to Canada in 1984 confessed, "I'm here because she's famous, I guess." Quipped one young lady when Prince Andrew and Princess Sarah visited Canada in 1989, "I don't see why we should have to curtsy to a person who a few years ago was living with a race-car driver!" No doubt, some Canadians said the same about the prince.

In 1982 a CBC TV journalist dared not to curtsy before Her Majesty and continued her work unrepentant and unscathed. If one compares the yawning public response to that act with that toward another CBC interviewer in 1959, one can see just how much monarchical sentiments have weakened in Canada the last quarter of a century: when Joyce Davidson remarked on the air that "like most Canadians, I am indifferent to the Queen's visit," she required police protection from irate viewers and finally was forced to leave the country in order to find further employment. Today, almost all Canadians ignore Commonwealth Day (on differing dates in late winter or early spring), when the Queen traditionally gives a broadcast message. Prince Charles experienced the spirit of Canadian equality in 2001 when he was required to wipe his shoes on a special disinfectant mat like every other passenger when stepping off a plane from the UK, which was plagued by hoof and mouth disease.

In a poll after the Constitution Act, 1982, had been passed, three-fourths of the Canadian respondents thought that the importance of the monarchy is declining. Asked at the end of the twentieth century to name the symbols that are important for the Canadian nation, the monarchy was at the bottom of the list.

Canada

Only 41% of respondents cited it (34% of men and 48% of women); the figure in Quebec was 20%. While some historians argue that the splendid royal visit in 1939 (nostalgically reenacted by the Queen Mother in July 1989) helped solidify Canadian support for Britain when Hitler invaded Poland a few weeks later, it is unthinkable that British royalty could sway an important Canadian political decision today.

Nevertheless, the royal family can still electrify crowds. Many older anglophone Canadians regard the Queen as a regal symbol of Canadian patriotism. As one 60-year old Royal Canadian Air Force veteran in New Brunswick admitted, "Whenever a band plays 'God Save the Queen,' I drop my cigar and stand up straight as wood."

When the Queen Mother died in April 2002, a cry of disgust rang out throughout the country when the most widely read weekly Canadian newsmagazine, *Maclean's*, inadvertently placed the address labels across the photo of her face on the cover. The embarrassed editor had to send a letter of apology to all subscribers assuring them that the magazine meant no disrespect to the deceased monarch.

Warm crowds greeted Queen Elizabeth II wherever she went in Canada, including Nunavut, during her triumphant 12-day Jubilee tour in October 2002. However, the visit elicited a variety of public thoughts about the monarchy. The most prominent was then Deputy Prime Minister John Manley, who repeatedly expressed his preference for "an entirely Canadian institution" to replace the monarchy after Elizabeth's reign. Journalist Allan Fotheringham wrote: "She's a magnificent monarch. But she's not ours." Peter Donolo tactfully

suggested: "What better gift could we give ourselves on the occasion of this Golden Jubilee year than to give the Queen a hearty handshake, thank her for all her services, wish her the best, and do what any self-respecting nation does: choose our own head of state?" Her nine-day return visit in mid-summer 2010, her 22d official tour of Canada, elicited very little such commentary.

Elizabeth herself is well-liked: 84% of Canadians polled in 2005 thought she has done a good job. In 2010, 69% had a "mostly favorable" opinion of her. But in a March 2005 poll taken two months before her visits to the centennials in Alberta and Saskatchewan, 46% supported replacing the monarch as Canada's head of state, while 37% opposed it. At the same time, 49% believed she should remain the monarch until she dies. Only 6% thought she should abdicate in favor of Prince Charles, and 18% wanted her to cede the throne to Prince William.

The latter's glittering wedding to Kate Middleton on April 29, 2011, sent a current of excitement through Canada. The prime minister could not attend because he faced an election only a few days later. But Toronto's venerable King Edward Hotel opened its Sovereign Ballroom at 5 AM to broadcast the wedding live, accompanied by a "royal breakfast" costing $68 a head. When this event sold out, the overflow was invited to afternoon tea to watch a taped rebroadcast of the nuptial event, all for a fee of $69 per person. The handsome couple chose Canada for their first official foreign visit a couple of months later.

Another poll four years later on the eve of the first visit by Prince Charles and his second wife Camilla as a couple, found that 65% were in favor of cutting ties to the Crown and only 35% wanted her successor to rule Canada. The royal couple's unenthusiastic reception during this 10-day visit in November 2009 seemed to back up these polling figures. However, the constitutional difficulty of abolishing the monarchy ensures that this would not happen quickly or easily.

For some Canadians, the monarchy is still an emotional and nostalgic link with their country's and the British Empire's heritage. The Queen's photo adorns the currency and hockey rinks, and toasts are offered to her. As a democratic country without a revolutionary tradition, Canada has always taken an evolutionary view of the future and has never turned its back abruptly upon its past.

It is certain that the British monarch will remain in Canada's constitution, as well as on its currency, well into the 21st century. Even if a constitutional amendment were proposed, passage would require the unanimous consent of the federal govern-

ment, parliament and each of the ten provinces. Any sensible politician would prefer to jump off a cliff than to attempt to achieve such a degree of unanimity in a country like Canada.

The seamy details of the royal family's private lives weakened some Canadians' ties to the monarchy. *Maclean's* offered the following description of the average Canadian's ambivalence about it: "If pushed to come up with a definition, they seem to be comfortable with the idea that they live in a federation of frisky provinces with attitude issues, united by a cold climate and by parliamentary institutions under the politically disinterested Crown."

The Governor General

Inside Canada the Queen is represented by the governor general. The governor general normally holds office for five years, although the term can be extended for up to two years. For about 60 years, the British government decided who would occupy this post, but in 1926 the Canadian government assumed the right to select the person, and since 1952 the governor general has always been a Canadian. The position alternates between an anglophone and a francophone although by custom all must be bilingual. For example, an anglophone, Edward Schreyer, was succeeded by Madame Jeanne Sauvé. In 1990 she was followed by Ramon Hnatyshyn, who, in a break from the norm, was not fluently bilingual. His successor in 1995 was an Acadian francophone from New Brunswick, Roméo LeBlanc. In October 2010 anglophone David Johnston replaced Michaëlle Jean.

There is an equivalent of the governor general, called a lieutenant governor, in each of the ten provinces. This official is also nominally appointed by the Queen, but in fact he or she is selected by the prime minister after seeking the advice of the particular provincial government.

What is the job of the governor general? If one only looks at the written part of the Canadian constitution, one would have the impression that he or she wields enormous power: he must assent to all legislative acts, appoint the prime minister, hire and fire cabinet members, dissolve or convoke Parliament, decide when elections are to be held and, since 1947, command Canada's armed forces. Ex-Governor General Michaëlle Jean provided a reminder of this latter honor in the Remembrance Day ceremony in November 2009. Standing next to Prince Charles, she presided wearing a resplendent uniform. She visited Afghanistan twice and regularly attended repatriation ceremonies to honor those soldiers killed in combat.

The governor general has almost never exercised any of these powers above,

Queen Mother, an unintended cover up

which paradoxically exist only as long as they are never used. He normally acts only on the "advice" of the prime minister, which is a nice way of saying that he almost always does what he is told to do. Never in Canadian history has a governor general rejected a federal bill. When he delivers the Throne Speech laying out the government's policy at the beginning of each parliamentary session, he merely reads word for word a speech written by the prime minister and cabinet and put into his hands.

Yet, the governor general does perform a function that some Canadians still consider to be important. He does have a residue of powers (called "prerogative power") that could be used in times of crisis. For example, if a group might attempt to seize power unconstitutionally, he could serve as a rallying point for Canadians who support the democratic form of government.

He could also be useful in a time when no party leader could get enough support in the House of Commons to form a government (a collective term in Canada to refer to the prime minister and his cabinet, similar to what Americans mean when they speak of "the administration"). He would then be charged with finding a person who could gain such support or calling a new election. When there is a government, she invariably follows its advice; when there is none, he must act on his own. When the Conservative (Tory) government lost a vote of confidence in December 1979, Prime Minister Joe Clark went to the governor general to ask that a new election be called. Edward Schreyer discussed the various alternatives with Clark for almost an hour, and only informed him in a later phone call that he would approve of a new election.

This important role in the formation of government became the topic of intense discussion in 2004 when it became certain that no party would win a parliamentary majority. Suddenly Canadians realized that then Governor General Adrienne Clarkson's position could be more than mere pomp and ceremony. She became the one who would decide which party leader would be capable of commanding enough support in the House of Commons to conduct government business and win sufficient parliamentary votes for the longest possible time before new elections would be necessary.

If no party wins a majority of seats, it is normally the incumbent prime minister's privilege to approach the governor general first and explain why he would like to continue to rule and how he could do it. The prime minister would inform him of his plan and commitments from other parties for support. He could require that such commitments be in writing or set

Throne Speech 2006

conditions and a time limit for such commitments to be acquired.

Acting in a non-partisan way and stressing that his loyalty is to Parliament, not to any particular party, he could turn to the head of another party with fewer seats if he concluded that another leader would have a better chance of creating a stable government. Finally he can defer or refuse last-minute patronage appointments, such as ambassadorships or Senate seats, made by a prime minister before he leaves office.

In December 2008 Governor General Michaëlle Jean had to cut short a foreign visit and race home to deal with one of the biggest and most unexpected political crises in the country's history. Prime Minister Harper's minority government had strengthened its position in early elections in October 2008 only to face a possible vote of confidence on its budget because it contained no stimulus spending and sought to cut public financing for parties that the three opposition parties need more than the Conservatives. By tradition, a lost budget vote invariably leads to new elections. To prevent such a confidence vote, the prime minister sought the governor general's permission to prorogue parliament, meaning to prevent parliament from acting on bills or other business.

This was not unprecedented, and never in history has a governor general rejected a request to prorogue. However, this was the first time such a measure was used in the midst of a political crisis and over the objections of a majority in parliament. While a passionate constitutional debate throughout Canada ensued, she decided to allow the prime minister to do what he wanted. A month later the Liberals supported a revised Tory budget, and the crisis subsided.

This happened again on December 30, 2009, when Harper prorogued parliament for two months ostensibly to prepare the budget. But opponents charged that it was intended to end embarrassing inquiries into charges that Canadian soldiers had turned detainees over to Afghan authorities, who might have then tortured them. Such a shut down means that all committees in both houses are disbanded, and government bills die. This was a break with tradition since such proroguing usually occurs only after most of the legislative business has been completed. A letter signed by over 200 political and constitutional experts alleged that this measure en-

Their Excellencies the Rt. Hon. Adrienne Clarkson, former Governor General of Canada, and her husband, Mr. John Ralston Saul
Photo: Sgt. Michel Roy

Canada

Their Excellencies the Rt. Hon. Michaëlle Jean, Governor General of Canada, and her husband, Mr. Jean-Daniel Lafond, and daughter

abled the prime minister "to evade democratic accountability." A March 2010 poll revealed that 57% of Canadians thought parliament should limit the prime minister's powers. A further break in tradition was that the prime minister phoned the governor general to get her permission rather than appearing before her in person. This was interpreted as gravely insulting.

To perform his duties, the governor general has the same right as the British Queen "to be informed, to advise and to warn." As a rule, the prime minister will meet with him at least every other week to inform her of the political situation. Every three months he dutifully sends the Queen a report on the political and economic situation in Canada. The extent to which the governor general could influence the prime minister would, of course, depend upon the rapport he has with him. Sauvé was not a member of the same political party as Brian Mulroney and therefore was said to have had little influence. In one celebrated snub, she was even excluded from the ceremonies surrounding the American president's visit to

Quebec City in March 1985. By contrast, Hnatyshyn had been Mulroney's leader in the House of Commons from 1984–86 and his justice minister from 1986–88, when he lost his seat in parliament. He therefore had more influence on the prime minister.

Canadian governors general are usually leading politicians in their own right who have been appointed because of their political service to the country. Schreyer was one of the *New Democratic Party's* most successful politicians and had been the premier of Manitoba. He was the first westerner to be appointed, a symbol of the West's rising importance in Canadian politics. He was also a non-WASP (white Anglo-Saxon Protestant), and his appointment was a form of recognition that Canadians of British descent are a minority today.

Jeanne Sauvé was perhaps the most successful female politician in Canadian history. Her appointment in 1983 was greeted by all major parties. She was almost too good to be true: born in the francophone community of Prud'homme, Saskatchewan, she was the second westerner in a row to serve. She rose to prominence as a jour-

nalist and Liberal Party politician in Quebec, and in the 1970s she had held various portfolios in Trudeau's cabinet; she was only the third female and the first Quebec woman ever to sit in the cabinet. In 1980 she became the first woman ever to serve as speaker of the House of Commons. Her impartial and competent performance in that trying job marked her as an ideal candidate for the position of governor general. In 1988 she became the first governor general ever to make a state visit to France.

The governor general's most frequent role is a ceremonial one. He entertains important foreign dignitaries, supports many worthy causes and events, honors and awards many Canadians who have distinguished themselves in various walks of life, cuts ribbons and opens new hospitals and museums. For these functions, he is housed in Rideau Hall, an estate on 88 acres, across from the prime minister's residence at 24 Sussex Drive. It is "guarded" by red-coated soldiers wearing bearskin hats and is surrounded by woods, a park, a skating rink, toboggan slide, cricket field, tennis courts and three greenhouses. He conducts much of her business in the main ballroom underneath a 12,000-piece crystal chandelier with two massive paintings on each end of the room: one a portrait of Queen Elizabeth II and the Duke of Edinburgh and the other of the Fathers of Confederation, entitled *Charlottetown Revisited*. He also has a secondary residence inside The Citadel in Quebec City. He has a staff of 96 and a budget of almost five million dollars.

His ceremonial activities are a full-time job and unquestionably take a heavy burden from the shoulders of the prime minister. For instance, Adrienne Clarkson participated in 908 events during 2003, three times as many as her predecessors and an average of 17 per week. For some Canadians, though, his most important function is to link Canada with the majesty of its past.

Few people can fail to be impressed with the spectacle of the governor general riding in a brilliant carriage to Parliament. He proceeds with much fanfare to the throne in the ornate Senate chamber (in British tradition, he is not permitted to set foot in the House of Commons). He sends a messenger to the House to instruct it to choose a speaker. Later in the day he invites the Members of Parliament (MPs) to come to the bar of the door to the Senate to hear his speech in both English and French, even though everybody knows that it was written by the prime minister's staff. Queen's University historian David Mitchell argues that this job is actually harder than it looks since the governor general faces two contradictory expectations: if he presents himself royally, he appears to be embracing her lofty position too enthusiastically. But if he fails to read the Throne Speech with verve, he seems to be demeaning the institution.

At the conclusion of the speech, he leaves, and the MPs return to the House of Commons. There, again in accordance with three centuries of British parliamentary tradition, the prime minister promptly introduces a dummy bill, usually a "Bill Respecting the Administration of the Oaths of Office," which is then forgotten by all. This is done in order to prove that the House has the right to discuss anything it wishes, before it turns to the monarch's concerns. They then begin to discuss the points made in the governor general's speech.

A governor general is expected to be absolutely impartial, and this can be very frustrating for politicians. As one former incumbent, Earl Grey, once said, the essential task is walking "the tightrope of platitudinous generalities." *Maclean's* even wrote about "the governor of generality." Canada's 15th governor general, Lord Tweedsmuir, counted the days when he could again be "a free and independent politician," who could "liberate my mind on any subject, anywhere, at any time, at any length I please."

Schreyer had wanted to change this by speaking out on the country's pressing issues, but he found himself in a minefield every time he did it. His press conference in 1981, the first ever for a governor general, was not well received, and the Prime Minister's Office insisted on absolute control over any of his formal statements. When he indicated that he would have forced an election if Trudeau had attempted to ram his constitutional changes through Parliament in the face of provincial opposition, he was criticized by virtually everybody.

The idea that he might actually use any of his formal powers was unthinkable. Even Quebec Premier René Lévesque, who did not like at all what Trudeau was doing, told Schreyer in 1982 to return to his "normal occupation—sleeping." From every direction, he was consistently criticized for either not saying enough, for saying too much or for saying the wrong thing. As one of Schreyer's aides noted, the job would drive anyone "stark raving mad from boredom."

In a classic text, *The Government of Canada*, Professor R. MacGregor Dawson wrote that the governor general is "the social head of the country and has always been supposed to exercise moral leadership as well." It is difficult to exercise moral leadership when one is not permitted to express opinions. There is another problem in knowing what it means to be the "social head of the country." Canada is a predominantly middle-class country. Many Canadians preferred Schreyer's kind of

President Obama and Governor General Jean in Ottawa, February 2009

down-to-earth style, which did not restrain children and dogs from charging through the ballroom or which permitted him and his wife to invite ordinary Canadians, friends and family to Rideau Hall for a party or an overnight stay.

Richard Gwyn, columnist for the *Ottawa Citizen,* spoke for many Canadians when he said of all the regal glitter and dressy tea parties: *c'est magnifique, mais ce n'est pas le Canada!* ("It's magnificent, but it's not Canada!"). Others preferred the sophisticated elegance and impeccable propriety the gracious and polished Sauvé brought to Rideau Hall. The only certainty is that no matter what kind of style the governor general sets, it will not be right for all Canadians. After completing his "damned if you do, damned if you don't" job, Schreyer sardonically thanked all those who had given him "free advice" on his shortcomings as governor general and took his leave. One of his aides said, "the only person happier than Jeanne Sauvé right now is Ed Schreyer."

The next governor general, Roméo LeBlanc, was a former journalist, fisheries minister, Senate speaker, and political ally of ex-Prime Minister Jean Chrétien. One of seven children of subsistence farmers, he was the first Acadian to occupy the position. His appointment was intended to send a clear political message to *Québécois* at a critical juncture in Canadian history: Acadians and their culture have prospered *within* the Canadian Confederation.

In 1999 he was succeeded by the very embodiment of the immigrant success story: Adrienne Clarkson. Born in Hong Kong, she escaped with her family in 1942. She made her mark in Canada as a talented and strong-willed broadcaster, writer, publisher and diplomat. She is the first member of a visible minority to hold the position and only the second woman. In her inauguration, she described a Canada that is a work in progress. It was orig-

inally built on the French, English and aboriginal cultures, but it is now expanding to include all colors and religions, with immigrant parents like hers "dreaming their children into being Canadians."

Most agree that she performed her duties with elegance, intelligence, diligence, and a sense of purpose. She even criticized America in her regal style: "Our cold climate has created our character, that sense of solidarity. America isn't as cold as we are." In describing her performance in office, *Maclean's* called her "simply the best." At the end of her five-year term in October 2004 Prime Minister Paul Martin secured the Queen's consent and asked the much-loved governor-general to remain in office for an unusual sixth year. He wanted the experienced Clarkson on hand during the experiment with minority government after the June 2004 elections.

Canadians are somewhat ambivalent about the post of governor general; in a 2010 poll, a quarter of them considered the governor general "useless." It is difficult for the incumbent to exercise moral authority and leadership when the public questions the position's legitimacy. This is why outgoing Governor General Adrienne Clarkson proposed that the choice be subject to public review and ratification by Parliament. She suggested that the prime minister present a name to a parliamentary committee, which would study the candidate's suitability for the position. Then the committee's recommendation would be put to a vote of the entire Parliament. Without such a reform, there is no consultation or review; the prime minister simply decides whom he wants, and the Queen always approves.

In September 2005 a beautiful, young (48), charismatic, soft-spoken, multilingual (French, Creole, English, Spanish, Portuguese and Italian) former TV journalist in Quebec, Michaëlle Jean, became Clarkson's successor. The story of her life

Canada

Governor General David Johnston

is remarkable, coming to Quebec as a young Haitian refugee, working with battered women and supporting causes to improve the lot of the down-trodden.

She had some frantic explaining to do when a separatist magazine, *Le Québécois*, claimed that she and her controversial award-winning French film-maker husband, Jean-Daniel Lafond, had supported Quebec independence. The evidence came from one of his documentaries in 1991, *La Manière Nègre*, showing him and Jean toasting Quebec separatists. He also wrote in a book soon thereafter: "So, a sovereign Quebec? An independent Quebec. Yes, I applaud with both hands." Only after Jean issued a formal statement that she and her husband had "never belonged to a political party or the separatist movement" and were "fully committed to Canada" could majority public opinion accept her, and her appointment could move forward.

In her installation speech to parliament, she declared that the earlier "two solitudes" were over at last, and she called for an end to ethnic and linguistic divisions. The *Globe and Mail* applauded her for personifying "the free and open country Canada wants to be." She is a good listener, and in office she agreed to pass on to the prime minister concerns expressed to her by such advocacy groups as those supporting the homeless and subsidized housing in Quebec. Given her reportedly strained relationship with Prime Minister Harper, it is uncertain how this information was received.

Some Canadians questioned whether such activity is compatible with her largely neutral ceremonial role. But Queen's University constitutional expert Ned Franks argued that such actions are indeed within the bounds of the governor-general's func-

tions. In his words, he or she has the often ignored role "to represent Canada and Canadians to government."

On October 1, 2010, David Johnston was sworn in as governor general at age 69. Born in a small town in northern Ontario, he went on to become a two-time All-American and Hall of Fame hockey player at Harvard. He was also educated at Cambridge and Queen's Universities. The long-time principal (second in charge) of McGill University in Montreal and then president of another of Canada's best universities—Waterloo—he is regarded as one of Canada's leading advocates of higher education. He has 13 honorary degrees to prove it. In 1995 he took leave from McGill to head up the "no" campaign during the cliff-hanging Quebec referendum. "I guess I was driven by the sense of this marvelous country breaking up."

He is also a former law professor, which makes him especially qualified to deal with the kind of tough constitutional issues a governor general must now tackle: When is it legitimate for a prime minister to prorogue parliament? At what time can one say a government has lost the confidence of the House of Commons? Must a governor general always follow the prime minister's advice? His predecessor had to call in expert advice on these questions; Johnson is himself a constitutional expert.

To ensure that the new governor general would have unquestioned authority in the office and be independent of party, the Harper government appointed an independent expert committee to vet and recommend the best candidates. Political staffers were kept out of the process. Harper's spokesman made it clear: "This is not about politics." Commenting on the result, a former Liberal Justice Minister, Irwin Cotler, admitted: "I can't think of a

better choice." A near majority (49.3%) of respondents agreed that "he's an impeccable choice."

THE POLITICAL EXECUTIVE

On an official visit to Paris in October 2009, Governor General Jean twice referred to herself as Canada's "head of state." The Prime Minister's Office and the Monarchist League of Canada reminded her immediately that that title belongs to Queen Elizabeth II, not to the governor general. Surprisingly, a December 2008 poll had revealed that only 24% of Canadians knew this. Almost twice that percentage thought the prime minister was head of state, and one-third mistakenly thought it was the governor general. Almost a year later, 30% of respondents in another poll answered that they couldn't care less about such ceremonial titles.

In Canada there is obviously some confusion about the precise distinction between a formal executive ("head of state"), who has a largely ceremonial function, and a political executive ("head of government"), who actually makes policy and wields power. The confusion about these roles stems no doubt from the fact that it is the prime minister who is the undisputed nerve center of the entire Canadian political system. Within the government, the prime minister is far more than "first among equals," as he used to be called. He is the towering political figure. Indeed, in federal elections, many Canadians vote according to whom they want as prime minister, not according to whom they want as their local representative in the House of Commons. Most prime ministers serve a long time in office. Those who can survive the first few months have averaged eight

24 Sussex Drive, residence of the prime minister

Photo: J.M. Carisse

84

years; four were in power for 15 years or more.

Since 1951 the prime minister and his family are housed in an imposing residence at 24 Sussex Drive on the bluffs overlooking the Ottawa River. It was built in 1868 by a lumber baron named Joseph Merrill Currier, a member of parliament. Not having been built to house the country's top leader, it is said to oppress those who have to live there. It is drafty, has walls lined with asbestos, has no fire sprinklers and is in desperate need of repairs to the tune of $12 million. Not far away is Stornaway, the official residence of the opposition leader.

From what sources does the prime minister derive his immense power? First, he is the head of his party. Second, his party either has a majority of seats or more seats than any other party in the House of Commons. In the United States, it is possible for the president to be of one party and for one or both houses of congress to be controlled by the other party, a situation that reduces his ability to enact policy. This is never the case in Canada, where a person is prime minister *because* he leads the party which can get a majority of votes in the lower house. The majority in the House expresses confidence in him by voting in favor of his bills; if he loses "a vote of confidence," then he will be replaced or new elections will be held, and the problem will be settled within a matter of weeks.

The Canadian leader can control his party for several reasons. At election time the "coat-tails" effect is very strong in Canada, and many Members of Parliament (MPs) are elected because of the popularity of their leader. This was especially true in the 1984 elections in which virtually scores of Conservatives were swept into office by the popularity of Brian Mulroney. Many MPs elected that way depend upon the leader's success to advance their own political careers.

The prime minister, who by tradition must have a seat in the House of Commons or get one within a reasonable time, can also rely on "party discipline" to keep his party members in the House of Commons loyal to him. A government stands or falls depending upon whether it retains its majority in the House of Commons. Therefore, it is a very serious matter when an MP votes against his party on an important vote. The party could halt an MP's political advancement and deny him a variety of perks. Therefore, most MPs would never consider voting against their party. Historian Christopher Moore wrote: "The night they are elected you know what an MP is going to do for the next four years: vote how the government tells it, whenever it needs it. They should just fax in their votes if that's all they're going to do."

A third source of prime ministerial power is the fact that he is not only the country's chief executive, but its chief legislator as well. He and his cabinet draft all the important legislation the two houses of Parliament, the House of Commons and the Senate, consider. Until 2002 he could also appoint all committee chairmen. But in a rare backbench rebellion against Prime Minister Chrétien many in his own party supported an opposition motion to give MPs the right to elect committee chairmen of their own choice.

For Americans, who value the notion of "separation of powers" as a necessary safeguard against tyranny, the Canadian fusion of executive and legislative powers seems surprising. However, the benefit of such fusion, inherited from Britain, is a much greater degree of government efficiency. The kind of prolonged deadlocks between the president and congress are unknown in Canada, whose governments are given much power and are then expected to get on with their work. For example, if a prime minister's party could win as many votes as President Barak Obama did in 2008 (52.5%), his government could command a large majority of about 180 seats in Commons. It would be invincible and could easily achieve all its legislative goals. By contrast, the president's work with congress is infinitely more difficult.

A fourth source is the prime minister's power to appoint all senators, Supreme Court justices, federal judges, the governor general, the chief of the defense staff and the RCMP commissioner. He has the final approval over the placement of every senior public servant and controls thousands of appointments to public agencies and commissions. He has the exclusive right to deal with the governor general; any member of his government can have access to the formal executive only through him.

Further, the prime minister can determine when elections will be held, as long as such an election is held within five years of the last one and as long as the governor general approves, which is not necessarily automatic. Unlike in the U.S., where congressmen and senators are elected for fixed terms, in Canada nobody above the level of mayor is ever elected for a fixed term. In some cases, the cabinet can help influence a prime minister on when to call an election, as it did when John Turner announced an early election in 1984. However, the prime minister usually reserves this privilege for himself. It is a powerful weapon not only for keeping the opposition off guard, but also for securing the loyalty of his own party members in Parliament, who dread having to go on the hustings too often.

Prime Minister Stephen Harper was committed to democratizing governmental institutions. Supreme Court nominees were now supposed to be subject to review by a parliamentary committee, and he proposed filling vacant Senate seats by elections and limiting senatorial terms to eight years. He felt it expedient to violate these pledges.

Three months after taking office in February 2006, he announced bills allowing elections to take place at fixed four-yearly intervals, and this became law. This law did not amend the constitution, so it could always be changed. The prime minister could also call an election if he lost a vote of confidence. All parties supported this but the Liberals, who accused Harper of trying to make Canada be like the United States (always a potent charge). A majority of Canadians told pollsters they favored this reform. Three provinces had already adopted fixed election dates. However, Harper de-

Chamber of the House of Commons
Public Archives Canada/PA51823

Canada

Harper Crest 2006

cided on his own to strengthen his mandate by having new elections a year earlier, on October 14, 2008, and again on May 2, 2011. The 2006 election laws were no obstacle.

A fifth source of power is the fact that the prime minister is the center of publicity. Especially in the era of television, he is always in the limelight; in fact, the enormous growth of the modern prime minister's awesome political power has coincided with the advancement of television. No other political figure can begin to compete with him in terms of media exposure, except during election campaigns, which in Canada normally last only seven or eight weeks. Any successful prime minister today will learn to use television effectively and to cultivate his image carefully. Mulroney was reported to be particularly obsessed with and adept at this. He read dozens of newspapers and magazines each week and watched all national news broadcasts in both English and French to monitor what kind of image he was projecting.

A sixth reason for the prime minister's strength is that he dominates the cabinet, which is the real executive of Canada. Cabinet members are usually prominent political figures. Unlike in the United States, they do meet and decide on overall policy. Since they must be familiar with many different issues, from foreign, defense and economic policy, to the state's treatment of aboriginal peoples, they are normally "generalists," rather than specialists in only one field. Nevertheless, it is the prime minister who decides what the political agenda will be, and he determines what the sense of the cabinet is on a particular issue. He is free to take a vote or not in cabinet meetings.

Members of his cabinet cannot publicly criticize him because of the principle of "collective responsibility." This means that once a decision has been made, all members of the government are obligated to support it. The whole cabinet takes public responsibility for a policy, whether each individual member agrees with it or not. Even if a cabinet member were to resign voluntarily, he would not be permitted to reveal the grounds for his disagreement unless the prime minister freed him from the oath of secrecy he took upon assuming office. At the same time, each cabinet member is protected from removal by the House of Commons by the fact that if a single member were to lose the confidence of the House, then the *entire* government would have to resign. Only once in Canada's history (1896) has a cabinet ever forced a prime minister to resign.

Much more important, the prime minister hires and fires cabinet members. He can even determine how many members he wishes to have in his cabinet; in 1984 Mulroney chose 40. Kim Campbell greatly reduced this number during her brief prime ministry in 1993, and Prime Minister Jean Chrétien appointed only 22 ministers. He wanted to underscore his seriousness about tightening federal government operations. Paul Martin decided in July 2004 to appoint 39 ministers plus 28 parliamentary secretaries and a caucus whip. These totaled more than half the 135-member Liberal parliamentary caucus. Most of these were the heads of ministries, but some were ministers of state in charge of such areas as fitness, small business and tourism, multiculturalism and international trade. In other words, not all belonged to what is sometimes called the "inner cabinet."

The prime minister determines which assignments (called "portfolios") the cabinet members will receive, and his decisions can make or break political careers. A minister of state for fitness, for instance, will have far less visibility and influence than a justice minister. Also, some posts are extremely important, but are so exposed to public scrutiny and criticism that they are considered to be suicide posts. The most prominent of these is the Ministry of Finance. Few prime ministers were ever finance ministers. Recent exceptions were Liberal Party leaders, John Turner, who was prime minister for 80 days during the summer of 1984, Jean Chrétien, who had been entrusted with all major portfolios at one time or other during the Trudeau era, and Paul Martin.

Despite the prime minister's power to choose his own cabinet members, he must observe certain traditions which do restrict his choice somewhat. Canada's major parties are mass parties that include members of diverse ideological persuasions. Most prime ministers will try to include all such directions in their cabinets in order to maintain party unity. It is also a wise move to muzzle certain vocal critics from within the party by including them in the cabinet and thereby throwing the blanket of collective responsibility over their heads.

A far more important restraint, though, is the "representation principle." This is natural for a country as geographically and demographically diverse as Canada. Although there are no hard and fast rules, most regional, provincial, territorial, social and economic interests in the country are represented in the cabinet. Each province should have at least one representative, although tiny Prince Edward Island has often gone without one. If the ruling party did not elect a single MP in a particular province, as was the case for years with the *Liberal Party* in the West and in Nova Scotia in 1997, then Senators from those provinces can be included in the cabinet.

The two giants in the federation, Ontario and Quebec (which have two-thirds of the seats in the House of Commons), usually receive about ten cabinet seats. These members are chosen from different regions and cities from within those provinces in order that representation can be dispersed as much as possible. Major cities like Montreal and Toronto usually have more people in the cabinet than do all the Atlantic provinces put together. No cabinet is complete without some women, who are no longer visibly under-represented in Canadian political life.

For instance, in Jean Chrétien's cabinet, sworn in after his reelection victory in 1997, there were a total of 27 senior ministers and eight junior ministers, called secretaries of state. Twelve were from Ontario and four (plus Chrétien) from Quebec. He appointed four of the 11 Liberal MPs elected in Atlantic Canada. To reach out to the restless western provinces, he tapped nine of the 15 Liberal MPs elected in the West. Certain portfolios are traditionally reserved for particular regions: fisheries for someone from the Maritimes or British Columbia, agriculture for a westerner. The finance minister is usually from Ontario with good business connections, although since 1975 Canada has had three finance ministers from Quebec and one from Newfoundland.

In 2006 Stephen Harper named a cabinet of 27 ministers reflecting a broad geographic distribution rather than over-representing the West, from where the majority of his government's seats came. His Tory party did poorly in the Atlantic provinces, but he chose a foreign minister from there, Peter MacKay, who was also given the portfolio for the Atlantic Canada Operations Agency. He had no previous experience in foreign affairs and a year later was moved to the defense ministry. His replacement was one of the few high-profile Conservative MPs from Quebec, Maxime Bernier, who had been industry minister. Harper is desperately fishing for votes in Quebec. The Tories won none of the 48 seats in Montreal, Toronto and Vancouver. But he wanted someone in his cabinet from Montreal, so he appointed an unelected Tory co-chairman, Michael Fortier, to the Senate and brought him into his cabinet as public works minister. To have someone from Vancouver, he lured David Emerson from the preceding Liberal Party cabinet, pronounced him a Tory and made him minister for trade and the "Pacific Gateway." Harper selected six women and two Asian-Canadians for his cabinet.

The "representational principle" obviously has its advantages and disadvantages. In a country as diverse as Canada, every tool of unity is beneficial. Cabinet members are expected to support the interests of their region and social group. This is particularly important since the Senate cannot effectively perform this function. Some critics of Canadian government have argued that the provinces have far too little influence over federal politics; the cabinet is a place where at least some attention is paid to their interests.

At the same time, some cabinet members are named as "political ministers," charged with the responsibility to help organize the provincial parties and to oversee patronage appointments in the provinces. This means that the central government tries to influence the provinces, just as the provinces try to influence it. Disadvantages also include the growth of the cabinet to accommodate so many representatives. Some people fear that this makes the cabinets unwieldy. Finally, the prime minister is unable to choose the very best person for a particular job; it may be more important to

select a person for a ministry because he is an English-speaking Quebecer, rather than because he is an expert in the portfolio he is assigned.

A seventh source of prime ministerial power is his command of a multifaceted staff. Since Pierre Elliot Trudeau became prime minister in 1968, two offices have grown enormously in power: the Prime Minister's Office (PMO) and the Privy Council Office (PCO). Trudeau increased their size and importance in order to get policy recommendations independent of the more entrenched civil service. The PMO became the more powerful of the two. It is made up of the leader's major advisers and aides, who are political appointees, not civil servants. They do everything from answering mail and making travel arrangements to making policy recommendations and ensuring governmental unity.

Many Canadians, including Brian Mulroney, criticized the size and power of the PMO, charging that it was too costly and undercut the power of the cabinet and Parliament. Once in power, however, Mulroney made it even larger, costlier and more powerful. In 1985 it had 114 members, as opposed to 90 under Trudeau and 57 under John Turner. It included a special office and two aides for the prime minister's wife, Mila. More significant, the political operations of the office have been strengthened. It employed 13 policy advisers, instead of three under Trudeau. It had the added responsibility of reviewing all cabinet members' major press statements before they were released. It also cleared all patronage appointments and senior hiring by cabinet members. Some critics in the opposition and bureaucracy charged that this powerful center had become almost like a presidential White House staff.

The PMO lost none of its power under Prime Minister Jean Chrétien, whose popularity had always been bolstered by his image as a humble man of the people. Unique political circumstances—his *Liberal Party's* huge lead over a divided and weak opposition offering no viable national alternative—quelled any intraparty unrest toward him or his lieutenants in the PMO. A scandal stemming from his or his top PMO aides' alleged ordering Mounted Police officers to rough up and pepper spray student demonstrators at the 1997 Asia Pacific Economic Cooperation (APEC) summit in Vancouver (made worse by his dismissive comment that the protesters were lucky to have been sprayed instead of hit with baseball bats) was a catalyst for closer public scrutiny of his power. Former top civil servant, Gordon Robertson, who served prime ministers from Mackenzie King to Trudeau, ar-

gued in 1998, "the concentration of power in the hands of this prime minister is as great as I have ever seen it."

Traditionally, the Privy Council Office has been the clearinghouse and coordinating agency for proposals and ideas from the cabinet and various committees. The most important are "cabinet committees," which are smaller than the full cabinet. They can discuss matters more informally before they are brought to the attention of the full cabinet. The names, membership, precise organization and functions of these committees change with prime ministers. They usually deal with such matters as priorities and legislative planning, federal-provincial relations, economic and social policy and government operations.

Their work was normally supported by about 350 civil servants and employees in the PCO, who prepared and circulated documents to ministers and the committees. It also provides clerical and record-keeping back-up to ministers. It used to be almost exclusively responsible for briefing the prime minister on matters that were about to be discussed by the cabinet. Chrétien selected a bilingual microbiologist, Jocelyne Bourgon, to be clerk of the PCO. The first woman to hold the job, she was the boss of over 200,000 civil servants.

In addition to selecting his inner staff, the prime minister can make at least 3,500 "order-in-council" appointments, including about 500 high-level positions, such as ambassadors, senators, judges and heads of key government agencies. Prime ministers are technically free to hand out patronage appointments as they please, but both Trudeau and Mulroney were frequently criticized for their lavish handouts. Mulroney had made a campaign promise to give Parliament some say in the process, but only after much public grumbling about his own appointment practices did he consent to a procedure whereby all-party parliamentary committees would be permitted to review all appointees' qualifications.

The largest reservoir of support and information for the prime minister is the federal civil service, which has grown so fast in modern times that now one million Canadians, or one out of ten persons of working age, are employed by a government at some level. One of 50 Canadians works directly for a federal department or agency. Since Confederation in 1867, the Canadian population has increased sevenfold, while the civil service has increased a hundred-fold. This growth reflects the fact that Canadian government has become far more active in such fields as social welfare, the economy, education and language rights. Most people are skeptical that such a gigantic body of workers can be effectively controlled by anybody.

Canada

They are particularly skeptical about the possibility of controlling the many Crown corporations, which are wholly or partially owned by the state and whose directors are appointed by the prime minister and his government. Few would doubt, though, that the prime minister has more influence over the civil service than any other Canadian.

At the head of each of 22 departments is a cabinet minister. The minister brings with him some aides who are responsible to him. He is also assisted by some "parliamentary secretaries," who are MPs without cabinet seats. Since these latter positions are excellent opportunities for newer MPs to demonstrate their talent, the minister can usually count on good work from them. The second highest position within each ministry is the "deputy minister," who is a career civil servant at the top of his promotion ladder. They are so important that they are often referred to as "Mandarins," reminiscent of the wise and powerful advisers to the Chinese emperors.

The deputy minister is appointed and can be removed by the prime minister. However, they are supposed to serve any government, and they are usually nonpartisan, even though they are active participants in policy making. The deputy ministers have usually directed the day-to-day operations of the department for years, so their expertise is badly needed by the cabinet ministers, who are most often not specialists in the particular field for which they are responsible. When a government changes, every prime minister will replace a few deputy ministers. They are merely transferred to other civil service posts, since they cannot be fired. But the number of such changes is usually very low. For instance, after coming out of the wilderness of 16 years in opposition, the Conservatives, under Prime Minister Joe Clark, replaced only three deputy ministers. Far fewer heads roll in Ottawa after a parliamentary election than in Washington after a presidential election. There is no "revolving door."

Entry based on competitive examinations and promotion based on performance and bilingualism has placed severe limits on the spoils system. They have helped to produce civil servants who, by comparison with most other countries, are efficient, impartial and able. Civil servants are kept honest and incorruptible by being paid better than their counterparts anywhere else in the world. They have handsome fringe benefits, have almost complete job security and can retire as early as age 55 with pensions indexed to inflation. A sign of the high quality of Canada's civil service is shown by the fact that few Canadians propose radical changes in it, even

though some often complain, "government has gotten too big." Finally, to the disappointment of gossip columnists, financial and sexual scandals involving civil servants are almost unknown in Ottawa.

PARLIAMENT

Canada has a bicameral parliament, but unlike in the American system, both houses are not equal in power. The House of Commons is by far the more important chamber. In parliamentary elections, which must be held at least every five years, citizens who are at least 18-years old vote for an MP in each of 308 constituencies (called "ridings" and increased from 295 in 1997 and 301 in 2004 to 308 in 2006). Voters in Canada do not vote directly for a prime minister; only voters in his own constituency vote for him.

Counting the votes is not as complicated as in the United States, especially when compared to the disputed Florida tabulation in the 2000 presidential election. Canadians have a uniform voting system in the entire country. Citizens vote with pencil and paper, marking an "X" next to the name of the desired candidate. There are no chads, as there were in Florida. All votes are counted by hand, and the results are known within hours, not weeks.

The system of election is the single member district or "first past the post," an electoral method now used only in the UK, the U.S. and New Zealand. The candidate with the most votes in each riding is elected, even if he wins fewer than 50% of the votes. This electoral system has the advantage of preventing many parties from gaining seats in Parliament. It therefore enhances political stability. Since one or the other of the large parties usually has a majority in the House of Commons, there has never been the need for a coalition government to rule in Canada. Even if one party does not win a majority of seats, the custom is for the party with the most seats to form a "minority government." This leads a precarious existence for a while, relying on votes from another party.

Some critics rightly point out that this electoral system enables the two larger parties to win a far higher percentage of parliamentary seats than the percentage of votes they win nationally. Elections are usually won or lost by a three to four percent shift to one party or the other. If one focuses only on the parliamentary seats which are won or change hands, rather than on the popular vote, one gets an exaggerated impression of voter volatility; sweeps are seldom as massive as they seem. For instance, Mulroney's Tories barely received 50% of votes in all of Canada in September 1984, but won 211 out of the 282 seats in the House of Commons. In 1993 the PC Party won 16% of the votes, but received only two seats. The Reform Party won 18% of the votes, but captured 52 seats. The Liberals captured only 38% of the votes in 1997 but still won a

Canada

majority of seats (155). The same applied to the Conservatives in 2011, who won only 39.6% of the votes, but secured a parliamentary majority with 167 seats. In 2008, the Greens captured 6.8% of the votes but not a single seat.

The same thing can happen on the provincial level. In 1985 the Liberals won more votes than the Conservatives in the Ontario provincial elections. But because of the electoral system, the Conservative Party ended up with four more seats in the provincial legislature. Ontario's Liberals won only 46.5% of the votes in 2003, but they captured 70% of the seats. In the 1998 Quebec provincial elections: the Liberals won 43.7% of the votes, but captured only 48 of 125 seats. The PQ received 42.7% of the votes, but garnered 76 seats and remained the governing party.

Almost never does a governing party win more popular votes than the combined opposition. For example, in 2000 the Liberals won a landslide victory of 173 seats (57% of the total) by winning only 41% of the votes. If Canada had a proportional representation (PR) electoral system, the Liberals would have captured only 123 seats, which is not a majority. In June 2004 the Liberals won 36.7% of the votes and 135 seats (44% of the total); under PR it would have gotten only 116 seats. The newly formed Conservative Party captured 29.6% of the votes and was awarded 99 seats (32% of the total); under PR 92. The *Bloc Québécois* got 12.4% of the votes in Canada and received 54 seats (17.5%) since it dominated Quebec; under PR it would have had only 37. Things were worse for the New Democratic Party, which won 15.7% of the votes, but got a mere 19 seats (6% of the total); under PR it would have had 49. It is understandable that smaller parties do not like this system.

After the 2004 election the NDP, whose parliamentary votes the minority Liberal Party needed, was determined to push for proportional representation; after coming in second in the 2011 elections, it more easily accepts the present system. Precisely because the largest parties benefit from it, it is unlikely that the system will be changed.

The distribution of seats is based upon provinces' populations and is adjusted according to census figures. Only Quebec's 75 seats are always guaranteed, in order to protect the interests of the country's francophone minority. Ontario now has 108 seats, a third of the total. Added together, both provinces' have about two-thirds of all the seats. The remaining seats are distributed as follows: BC 36, Alberta 28, Manitoba 14, Saskatchewan 14, Nova Scotia 11, New Brunswick 10, Newfoundland 7, PEI 4, Northwest Territories 1, Yukon Territory 1, and Nunavut 1.

Hon. Gilbert Parent, former Speaker of the House of Commons, and the author, Wayne C. Thompson

Each province is represented fairly, but some ridings have more voters than others. For instance, cities, on the whole, are under-represented; in the 1979 election 81,000 persons voted in York–Scarborough, 45,000 in Vancouver Centre and only 28,000 in Gaspé, Quebec. The chief argument against making all districts equal in population is that some northern ridings would be even greater in size than they already are, thus making an MP's travel through the riding to keep in touch with his constituents almost impossible. In other words, some Canadians in such districts would be practically cut off from their government. The 1993 elections brought 54 women into the House (up from 38). They include the first black woman MP, Grenada-born Liberal Jean Augustine.

Election campaigns are much shorter and cheaper than in the U.S. For example, the 2000 campaign lasted only 36 days. Races are also more competitive. By 1990 the average cost of a House race was $29,500 in Canada and $268,000 in the U.S. ($2 million for the U.S. Senate), and the chances for reelection were 72.5% in Canada and 98% in the U.S. Candidates for a House of Commons seat face a spending limit of about $50,000, and each national party must restrict its spending to about $8.5 million. The Harper government reduced the amount that donors can give.

Pay for a member of the House of Commons in 2002 was $131,400 salary plus tax-free benefits and (in 2006) $122,700 for Senators. In 2002 the prime minister's salary rose to $263,000, and the opposition leader's pay was upped to $194,640. While money is often said to be the "mother's milk of politics," it cannot buy victories. In the 1993 federal parliamentary elections, the Tories spent $10.4 million to win two

seats, the Liberals $9.9 million for 177, the NDP $7.4 million for nine, the BQ $1.9 million for 54, and the Reform Party $1.5 million for 52.

The physical layout of the House is similar to the British House of Commons. The governing party sits to the right of the robed Speaker, directly across from the opposition parties. The government and the opposition leaders occupy the center seats in the front rows on each side of the aisles. The latter are known as the "shadow cabinet" since each cabinet member has a counterpart in the opposition. The "shadow cabinet" is ready to take office at any time. This is obviously different in the United States, where no one would have the slightest idea about the composition of the cabinet, if the other party were to occupy the presidency.

The fact that the two sides face each other across an aisle, which, by British tradition, is the width of two sword lengths, is intended to underscore the antagonistic relationship the government and the opposition have. The observer in the galleries notices, however, that this is only political, not personal, antagonism. MPs freely cross the aisle to chat with colleagues in other parties, and it is entirely normal for an MP to stand up and publicly wish a member of an opposite party good health after a serious operation or illness. This applies also to the parties' headquarters staffs, which maintain cordial relations with their counterparts in other headquarters and even provide each other with complimentary tickets to their party conferences. The fact that domestic political opponents are not regarded as enemies is one reason why democracy has functioned so well in Canada.

The prime minister recommends the Speaker of the House of Commons from among his party's MPs, and since 1985 he must be elected by the House. All MPs except party leaders and cabinet members are automatically considered to be standing for election unless they remove their names from the list. He or she is usually a prominent member of the governing party who was passed over for a cabinet post. The speakers in both chambers normally alternate between anglophones and francophones; in the House, the deputy speaker will always be a francophone if the speaker is an anglophone and vice versa.

By tradition, the prime minister and the opposition leader pretend to drag a resisting new Speaker down the aisle to the ornate Speaker's chair. This quaint custom was also inherited from Britain. From the 14th century for several hundred years the commoners' chosen spokesman risked the ire of the monarch and was sometimes even punished when he reported what the Commons wanted.

Canada

In Canada today, the Speaker is "punished" with a high salary ($134,800 in 1997), a rambling Kingsmere estate in the Gatineau Hills 15 kilometers (10 miles) from Ottawa, and a personal staff of about 15. This includes a chauffeur for his official limousine and a *maitre d'* to provide for the constant flow of visiting foreign members of Parliament who must be entertained. Most insiders would agree that he has to earn all his benefits, however. As Speaker, he is expected to referee parliamentary debates impartially, and even to call the prime minister and the government to order when they seem to be playing fast and loose with the rules. He sets the tone of the daily debates and decides whether they will be spontaneous and scrappy or formal and stiff.

Former Speaker Gilbert Parent described the House as "like a huge animal. Sometimes it lies dormant. Sometimes you prod it and it will jump up and bite you, and it's a wise Speaker who knows when to prod and when to let it sleep." Finally, he must manage the Commons' staff of 3,000 aides, pages, police and janitors. Along with the House leaders (who are usually different from the national party leaders in order that the latter can be absent from the Commons without disrupting the House's business) and whips, which each party selects, the Speaker is a crucial participant in shaping the House's law-making process.

He breaks tie votes in the House of Commons. On May 19, 2005, a no-confidence vote to determine whether then Prime Minister Paul Martin's government would fall resulted in a 152–152 tie. Speaker Peter Milliken, a Liberal, put the government over the top with his vote. This was the first time in Canadian history that a Speaker broke a tie in a vote of no-confidence. On October 12, 2009, Milliken became the longest-serving speaker in history. He stepped down June 2, 2011, after nine years in office when then Deputy Speaker Andrew Scheer of the Conservative party was selected as speaker following his party's victory in the May 2011 federal elections. At age 32, he is the youngest speaker in Canadian history and the first to hail from Saskatchewan.

The House is free to establish its own working procedures and it is carefully examining and changing the way it does its work. Many MPs travel to and from their ridings on Mondays and Fridays. Its number of sitting days has declined gradually from as many as 163 days in a year to a low of just 105 in 2008. Traditionally the average day would unfold something like this: when Parliament is in session, the usual day begins at 2 PM (11 AM on Fridays), when the Speaker takes the chair and the sergeant-at-arms lays the mace (a

Andrew Scheer, Speaker of the House

gold-plated war club and symbol of the House's authority) on the long table in front of the Speaker's chair.

After a few routine matters are completed, the question hour begins. This takes place from Mondays through Thursdays and is usually the liveliest part of the day, when the entire government and shadow cabinet are present, about 250 in all. This period (which lasts 45 minutes) is the most watched portion of each day in Ottawa. It is controlled by the opposition, which can pose any questions to any member of the government. Questions are intended to elicit information and often to embarrass the prime minister or cabinet members. One veteran MP confided, "the unwritten rule is never to ask a question unless you know the answer."

Sitting in his spectacular oak chair, the Speaker has a hidden computer screen in front of him with various camera angles to display the action in the House. He also has a countdown clock to help him limit questions and answers to 35 seconds and keep things moving briskly so that as many MPs as possible can get into the action. Most have no involvement, limiting their role to standing, clapping and cheering for their party and heckling and sneering at the other. So important is question hour for a government that Stephen Harper's cabinet became the first in history to meet every weekday after lunch to rehearse the ordeal together.

There are a few rules that are generally observed. MPs are never to be addressed by their family names and all remarks are technically directed to the Speaker. Sometimes civility does break down. Former Prime Minister Trudeau once was likened to Hitler, a comparison that prompted the prime minister to invite the MP to step outside for a fight (which the MP declined). He was also compared to an organ grinder, whose cabinet members are like monkeys. He was a past master at repartee, however. He dubbed opponents as

"nobodies" and as "the honorable stinker." MPs can ask questions in either English or French, and the answers should be given in the same language, if the cabinet member can manage it.

The overall purpose is to keep the government responsible and responsive to the opposition and to the country. The answers the government gives during question hour are widely reported in the press. Since 1977 question hour has been televised. It is broadcast live in Ottawa from 2:15 to 3 PM, and in many parts of the huge country it appears at prime time. News programs frequently show excerpts. It is an opportune time for MPs to impress the folks back home, and the government must prepare in advance for potentially damaging questions. Question hour can be raucous at times. Asked in a 2010 poll if it had become so uncivil that it needed to be reformed, two-thirds of respondents said "yes, it's a daily embarrassment"; 21% admitted they had stopped paying attention, and only 14% said "this is politics—it's not meant to be pretty."

MPs do not pose questions to members of their own parties. Backbenchers (MPs who are in neither the government nor the shadow government) have that opportunity only in the weekly party caucuses, which are held behind closed doors and in which genuine debate occurs. The question hour is usually cut off promptly at 3 PM, and the rest of day is devoted to bills before a mostly deserted House. Prime Minister Stephen Harper seldom bothers to speak in the House, except during question hour. Most bills have been introduced by the government and must survive three separate readings in the House before they are sent to the Senate for consideration. Debates are often lively and can be conducted in either English or French. Earphones with simultaneous translations are provided for MPs and spectators who need them. MPs are generally quite articulate and, as in Britain, feel free to bring humor into their remarks. About a third of them are lawyers, with many of the rest drawn from business and the professions.

An increasing amount of legislative work is done in committees. This is in response to the growing legislative workload. The "Striking Committee" decides on the committees' membership although it takes its cues from the assignments agreed upon by the parties themselves. There are "standing committees" which roughly correspond to the various cabinet portfolios. An example is the External Affairs and National Defence Committee. There are usually 20 MPs on each standing committee, and the composition is determined by parties' proportionate strength in the House. These committees help refine and improve legislation, and they often call in outside experts to testify or provide opinions. Until the rules were changed in 2002, they were never led by powerful and independent chairmen who could defy their party's leadership and prevent legislation from ever getting to the whole House. Chairmen are now elected by the whole House rather than being appointed by the prime minister.

The party leaders' control on all MPs is so strong and their claim to party discipline so sure that the government's legislation will survive all the legislative hurdles, no matter what. Debates in the whole House are lively, but the outcome of votes is seldom in doubt, so long as a government maintains its majority. If it does not, as was the case in 1979 during the Clark government, then the government can experience some real surprises. The Canadian political system hinges upon a government elected by the people which can legitimate its program in Parliament and then enact it until it is voted out of office.

Senate

The upper house of Parliament, the Senate, was designed in 1867 to serve two purposes: to serve as a check against "hasty or ill-considered legislation" coming from the House of Commons and to represent regional interests in the federal government. Its members do come from the various regions of Canada, and it does have the constitutional power to veto or amend legislation. It was not given the power to bring down a government by defeating a bill. However, as in so many other aspects of Canadian politics, powers on paper cannot always be exercised. In fact, the Senate has never performed the two functions given it in 1867. Canada's first prime minister, John A. Macdonald, swore that the Senate "will never set itself in opposition against the deliberate and understood wishes of the people." It has not dared veto legislation from the House of Commons since the Second World War. It has rarely amended a House bill in such a way that the principle of the bill is touched. Its legislative role has deteriorated, and its debates are seldom reported in the news media. It is not even held in high esteem. Why is this so?

First of all, it is an appointed, not an elected body. This means that its composition does not reflect the prevailing political power in the country. For example, in 1990 Liberals outnumbered Conservatives in the Upper House by two-to-one, even though the Liberals commanded only half as many seats in the House of Commons as the PC Party. Senators are appointed by the prime minister, not by the provincial

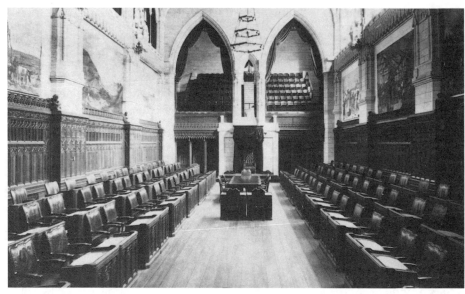

Senate Chamber
Public Archives Canada/PA34219

governments. Since the Liberals ruled almost constantly throughout the 20th century, they understandably packed the Senate with their own people. Appointments are almost invariably made on the basis of party loyalty and past services to the party in power.

The ruling party thus can dangle attractive patronage appointments to the Senate, which promise good pay until age 75 (or for life to those persons appointed before 1965) and work which need not be terribly taxing or time-consuming. The pay in 2006 was $122,700 in salary plus allowances, with a handsome pension indexed to inflation waiting at age 75. One reporter observed, "being named to the Senate in Canada is a lot like winning the cash-for-life lottery." Other cynics have called an appointment "a taskless thanks."

Liberal Senator Andrew Thompson demonstrated just how cushy the life of a Senator can be. Claiming that his health would be endangered by Ottawa's winter weather, he spent most of his time at his home in La Paz, Mexico, attending sessions only 12 times from 1990 to 1998. Astonished critics computed that his pay amounted to about $43,000 per appearance, more than his secretary earned in a year. Senate records in 1997 revealed rampant absenteeism on the part of about two dozen other members, and approximately a quarter of all Senators had missed at least 40% of the chamber's sessions. A furious Prime Minister Chrétien stripped Thompson of his office space, secretary, travel privileges, and seat in the Liberal caucus. But the truant legislator could not be fired.

Unlike an elected MP, a senator can seldom be held to account. An attempt was made in 2011 when a Liberal senator,

Raymond Lavigne, sent a staffer to chop down trees at his cottage and claimed more than $30,000 in work-related expenses during a three-month period in the preceding year. After years of resistance, every senator's expenditures are now posted online.

The trend has been to appoint people in the middle, rather than at the end of their careers. An example of a Trudeau appointment was Ann Cools, who had lost her bid for a seat in the House of Commons. A former student radical, who had spent time in prison for her part in the destruction of a university computer in Montreal in 1969, she was quickly pardoned before being named to the Senate. The government can also ease a cabinet member gracefully out of governmental business by appointing him to the Red Chamber (so named after the color of its interior decor). It can even appoint a member of the opposition party in order to free a *riding* of an unbeatable incumbent or to sow discord in the opponents' ranks. This does not mean that Senators are not talented people; it means that they need not be so as a condition of appointment.

Senators are chosen from the various regions of the country. The Fathers of Confederation gave equal representation of 24 members to Ontario, Quebec and the Maritime provinces (10 from Nova Scotia, 10 from New Brunswick, and 4 from PEI). Newfoundland was awarded six when it entered the Confederation in 1949. The West was also given 24 Senators (each of four provinces getting six). The Yukon and Northwest Territories have one each. Quebec's allotment must be selected from each of 24 senatorial districts. Unlike in the United States, where all states are rep-

Canada

resented equally in the Senate, a provision that gives enhanced power to the smaller states, in Canada, Senate seats are distributed to provinces roughly on the basis of population. Despite the fact that the appointees are residents of the various provinces, they cannot be said to "represent" those provinces because they were appointed by the prime minister on the basis of their service to his party. No doubt, it is the absence of a true provincial voice in the federal governmental institutions in Ottawa that has forced the provincial premiers to be so assertive about provincial rights and powers.

It cannot be said that the Senate performs no useful function. It does make minor amendments to bills that clarify some points. Some eminent lawyers or former premiers or cabinet members have the time to give a longer look at some bills in committee than the more harried MPs in the House have. Amendments made by the Senate are almost always accepted by the Commons, so long as those amendments are not seen as challenges to the deliberate will of the House. Senators are also invited to attend the weekly party caucuses with the MPs and try to influence their party's policies. The Senate has performed increasingly useful investigative work into a variety of topics ranging from defense policy to poverty and unemployment. It can thus sometimes produce useful reports much less expensively than could a Royal commission or task force, since its staff is already in place and Senators are already being paid. Finally, Senators are sometimes appointed to the cabinet.

Nevertheless, for a long time there have been many voices saying that the upper house must be reformed. Over a half century ago the Quebec nationalist, Henri Bourassa, quipped that demands for senatorial reform tend to break out "periodically, like other forms of epidemics and current fevers." The proposals have included allowing the provincial governments to appoint Senators, fixing the terms to, say, five or ten years, opening appointments up to a larger group of people than merely party loyalists, or changing its role in the legislative process. However, these reforms would not get around the problem that an appointed body simply cannot enjoy the same legitimacy in the citizens' eyes as an elected one. Also, an increase in its governmental role could diminish the power of the prime minister, the cabinet and the House of Commons; these present power centers cannot be expected to be very accommodating to any such proposals. This is especially true since there is nothing resembling a consensus concerning the functions the Senate could or should perform in the political system.

In 1984 the movement for senatorial reform began again to gain momentum. Trudeau's resignation that summer diverted attention from this reform. But his last-hour appointment of additional senators unleashed such indignation among the general public that it diminished his party's chances, under John Turner's leadership, of being reelected in 1984.

Controversies involving the Senate occur most frequently when different parties form a majority in each house. Thus, the public eye was again directed toward the Liberal-dominated Senate when it delayed approval of the Mulroney government's bills several times for months. A seriously miffed Mulroney demanded a curbing or abolition of the Senate even though each time its assent was finally given. His ire came to a boil in the fall of 1988 when John Turner instructed the Liberal majority in the Senate, led by Allan MacEachen, to reject the Free Trade Agreement that his government had negotiated with the U.S. Although the Liberal majority had shrunk through death or retirement since 1984 from 74 to 59, that was still enough to reject the bill. The Liberals knew that this would make it impossible for the Mulroney government to ratify the accord before the December 31, 1988, deadline and would therefore force the prime minister to call new elections, which would serve as a kind of referendum on that landmark agreement.

Although this maneuver was perfectly legal, some constitutional experts argued that it violated Parliament's unwritten conventions. There was no doubt about Mulroney's interpretation: "The leader of the Liberal Party has asked the Senate of Canada, a bunch of appointed people, to hijack the most fundamental rights of the Canadian House of Commons!" The tables were turned in 1994. The Conservatives, who had been reduced to only two seats in the House of Commons and whose only remaining federal power base was in the Senate, used their upper house majority to overturn legislation that would have prevented Canada's election boundaries from being revised before the next federal elections. Tories charged that this would have protected the seats of Liberal MPs.

In 1990 the question of whether an unelected Senate should have the power to veto legislation adopted in the elected House of Commons again grabbed headlines. When the Liberal-dominated Senate blocked passage of the government's highly unpopular value-added tax (GST), Mulroney appointed 24 new Tory senators in one month. This included Nova Scotia's Premier John Buchanan, who was under investigation for financial impropriety and who became the first sitting premier to leave provincial politics directly for a Sen-

ate seat. This raised the total number of senators to 112, eight more than normal. To do this, he invoked an almost forgotten loophole in the BNA, unused for 123 years, which empowers the British monarch, as Canada's head of state, to permit a prime minister to pack the Senate in order to break a legislative deadlock. The Queen said yes, and Mulroney got his majority.

The Liberal senators reacted with an angry walk-out, a filibuster while court challenges were prepared, and chaotic scenes on the floor of the dignified house which cast Canadians into disbelief: journalists were invited to enter the chamber floor; pandemonium reigned and vitriolic epithets were flung. One Liberal senator called his best friend across the aisle a "despicable little bugger." After cool heads were regained, he went to his friend, embraced him and apologized. Canadians rubbed their eyes and asked themselves again whether this institution, which many consider a constitutional relic, should be reformed or abolished. A poll at the time revealed that 80% favored reform.

Some provincial premiers, particularly those from the West and New Brunswick, have also called for the election of senators, but they often disagree on details. Alberta's ex-Premier Don Getty argued that western interests were being trampled by the Senate's central Canadian majority and called for a "Triple E" solution: an elected, equal and effective upper house, in which each province would have the same number of representatives. After a seat was vacated in 1987, Getty refused to nominate a replacement on the grounds that it should be filled by election. In 1989 his government organized the first-ever senatorial election, despite opposition from Ottawa. Mulroney took perhaps the most significant step. In the Meech Lake Accord of 1987 he struck a deal with the premiers by agreeing to give up his prime-ministerial prerogatives to appoint new senators and instead to select them on an interim basis from a list of candidates agreed upon with the provinces.

However, Meech Lake failed, as did the later Charlottetown accords. Because they failed spectacularly, Canadians shy away from attempting to change anything, including the Senate, by amending the constitution. Although 2004 polls showed that 84% of western Canadians and even 72% in Ontario still favored Senate reform, any change would have to be incremental.

Ex-Prime Minister Paul Martin mused in public about better ways to select senators, perhaps by allowing MPs to review Senate appointments. However, in 2004 he rejected Alberta Premier Ralph Klein's insistence that he appoint elected Alberta Senate nominees, arguing that reform must not be piecemeal. In 2006 his succes-

**Rt. Hon. Beverley McLachlin,
Chief Justice of the Supreme Court**

sor as prime minister, Stephen Harper from Alberta, violated the long-standing principle of his own western-based party by appointing unelected Michael Fortier to the Senate in order to have somebody from Montreal in his cabinet. But in the half year after that appointment he had left seven of the 105 seats vacant and vowed not to fill them until some kind of system for electing senators is devised.

Stephen Harper brought the upper house back into the heart of the debate over Canadian democracy. He proposed significant reform of the Senate in 2006. Triple E is history, but the notions of electing senators and limiting them to eight-year terms are not. He promised that his government would create "a new national process for choosing elected senators from each province and territory." He wanted to reform the body incrementally. His plan called for term-limits, the appointment of senators based on "consultative" votes, and the redressing of the kind of imbalance that allows New Brunswick and Nova Scotia to have 10 senators each, but provides mighty Alberta and British Columbia only six each. He favored offering Canadians a chance to vote for reform through a non-binding referendum.

Polls show that 73% of voters care who gets appointed to the Senate, and three-fourths would like to see it reformed. The prospects of successful reform are not good; all 13 attempts since 1900 to reform the Senate failed. Harper, who has called the Senate "a relic of the 19th century," admitted during the 2008 election campaign: "I'll be honest with you. I'm disappointed we haven't made at least some progress on Senate reform." He did appoint 27 new Conservative members in 2009 and five more in January 2010, finally giving his

party a majority in the upper chamber. He will enlarge that majority as more senators retire.

Any reform would require provincial approval. Premiers would almost certainly oppose a new and more powerful Senate because it would replace them in Ottawa as the main voices of the provinces and regions in national affairs. Premiers Dalton McGuinty of Ontario, Gordon Campbell of BC, ex-premier Lorne Calvert of Saskatchewan and ex-premier Gary Doer of Manitoba, as well as the New Democratic Party (NDP) and Bloc Québécois, favor abolishing the Senate altogether. In the complex mechanism of Confederation, it would diminish the importance of the provincial governments and those clubs of all premiers, the Conference of First Ministers (which includes the prime minister) and the Council of the Federation. There are many other problems: the convention that the upper house must normally pass bills the House sends to it would have to change. How would the transition work when the chamber would be a mix of appointed and elected members? Not until 2015 will forty-nine senators reach mandatory retirement age. Senate reform is not on the near horizon.

The Senate stepped up to tackle such important issues as defense, Canada-U.S. and Canada-Mexico relations, health care reform, and the legalization of marijuana. Finally granted $127,500 each for office and research expenses, senators increasingly treat their positions as full-time jobs. One committee chairman, Michael Kirby, noted: "People forget that there is a lot of talent in the Senate."

LAW AND COURT SYSTEM

Canadian criminal law is based upon English common law. This means that the law is derived from tradition, a slow developing of rules based on previous cases

or "precedents." It is law made by judge and jury, not by parliaments. Criminal law involves such things as murder and theft, which are considered to be crimes against the state even though they may be directed toward individuals. In Canada, criminal law is the same throughout the entire country. By contrast, "civil law" involves matters that are private to the individual citizen and have to do with property and civil rights. The federal and provincial governments share responsibility for civil law; it therefore differs from province to province. Quebec has retained its French Civil Code, which means that its property or civil rights were established by law-makers, rather than by precedents established by courts of law dealing with concrete cases that came to their attention. The other provinces have a civil code which comes from the English tradition of common law and which is therefore established by precedent.

Canada has a single court system organized hierarchically. There are three court levels: lesser provincial courts (such as family courts), provincial courts (composed of a provincial Supreme Court and superior, county and district courts) and federal courts (Supreme Court and Federal Court of Canada). This organization is not as simple as it appears on paper, though. The federal and provincial governments share judicial functions and responsibilities. The provinces have the power to determine the organization of their own court system, so there is considerable variation in the kinds of courts within the provinces. The appointment of *all* federal judges is made by the federal government, meaning the prime minister, with the assistance of the minister of justice. There is no parliamentary confirmation.

It should not be surprising to discover that the appointment of judges is, to some extent, based on political considerations. Any federal government would want to be

The Supreme Court Building in Ottawa

Canada

certain that an appointee shares its general view on, for instance, gay marriage, defendants' rights or the distribution of powers between the federal and provincial governments. There are Judicial Advisory Committees (JAC) in every province to vet nominees for the 1,100 federally appointed judge positions. During the Chrétien years, the Liberals filled these committees with their own party members. Judgeships have often been given to persons who had been active supporters or donors of the party in power. For example, half of the Liberal government's 2003 judicial appointments had donated to the party (60% of those appointed in Ontario, Alberta and Saskatchewan). The Harper government is determined to rebalance the benches. Despite such politicization of the appointment process, Canada's Supreme Court is not ideologically divided as is its American equivalent.

The Canadian selection process relies more heavily than the American on the advice of peers in the legal profession. Traditionally, before the prime minister makes the ultimate decision, the justice minister and ministry, Canadian Bar Association, law societies, and provincial governments are consulted. The result was an appointee's selection based more on judicial abilities and peer respect than on personal opinions.

That is changing. Former Prime Minister Paul Martin promised in 2004 more public and parliamentary scrutiny of judicial appointments. When he appointed two women from the Ontario Court of Appeal—Rosalie Abella and Louise Charron—to fill vacancies on the Supreme Court, the justice minister for the first time defended the nominations before a parliamentary committee although the appointees themselves were not present. Abella is a well-known and outspoken advocate of feminist, minority and gay rights causes. A judicial activist, she dismisses it as "unrealistic to say that judges should not impose their values or make law." It is "better to court controversy than to court irrelevance, and better to court criticism than to court injustice." Her appointment at a time of intense public discussion over same-sex marriage was significant.

Martin's last appointment to the Supreme Court before vacating office in February 2006 was Marshall Rothstein, a judge and former law professor at the University of Manitoba. He was renowned as the hardest working judge in the land, working seven days a week and refusing to hire clerks who did not do the same. For the first time in Canadian history, he was required to appear before an all-party panel of MPs for a televised grilling of his legal views. All was in English since he is the only justice who is not bilingual.

Prime Minister Harper wanted to strengthen the practice of allowing a parliamentary committee to interview potential justices. After all, justices are among the most powerful people in Canada, and prime ministers choose people who may in the long run turn out to be more important than he ever was. This is because of the way their decisions can change the country's social fabric; it is so immense that it throws into serious question the whole notion of parliamentary supremacy. Nevertheless, when Stephen Harper tapped bilingual Nova Scotia judge Tom Cromwell to fill a Supreme Court vacancy in September 2008, he decided there was no time for the procedures he himself had approved since he called an election two days later. He did not come back to it until he announced Cromwell's appointment on December 22. He was sworn in on January 5, 2009.

By 2016 Harper will have appointed at least five of the court's justices, so his government decided that an improved selection process should be firmly in place. Beginning in 2011, the justice minister invites members of the public to recommend candidates. A parliamentary panel composed of five MPs, including one each from the opposition New Democrat and Liberal parties, creates a short list of six candidates, from which the prime minister and justice minister pick two. These two finalists then answer questions before an ad hoc House of Commons committee, and the majority in parliament picks the winner. Prime Minister Harper explained that "overall, what you're looking for is record, experience, judgment, judicial temperament. These people sit on the bench a long time. We will choose very carefully."

One constitutional requirement with which few people quarrel is that three of the nine judges appointed to the Supreme Court of Canada, established in 1875, must be from Quebec. There is an unwritten tradition that the office of Chief Justice alternates between an anglophone and a francophone.

There was considerable controversy over Bill C-232, which parliament adopted in 2010, requiring all Supreme Court appointees to be fluent in both languages and be able to hear cases in both without the aid of an interpreter. The court had always been bilingual in the sense that anyone appearing before it could plead his case in either official language. Critics fear that this new requirement will dangerously reduce the pool of potential appointees, especially from the West.

In 1999 the first woman to be appointed chief justice was Beverley McLachlin. Born and educated in Alberta, she moved to British Columbia, where she became chief justice of the B.C. Supreme Court in 1988. She

was appointed to the Supreme Court of Canada a year later. Also in 1999 she was joined on Canada's highest court by Louise Arbour, who had won international recognition as head of the UN tribunal on war crimes. Arbour quit the Supreme Court in 2004 to become the UN High Commissioner for Human Rights.

McLachlin is universally acknowledged for her intellect, scholarship and persuasive powers, and her court produces an increasing number of unanimous decisions (82% in 2001). She takes a more cautious, centrist view of the law compared with her two predecessors, who were regarded as activists. She is more deferential to Parliament and less open to charges of judicial activism. In her words, "I'm not a politician. I'm not there to vote for this law or that. My job is to decide each case fairly, according to the law." Her formal powers are limited. The most important is to determine the size of the panel (five, seven or nine judges) that will hear a case. However, people speak increasingly of the "McLachlin court." She is more available to the media and open to defending the court's actions in public. As a relatively young judge, she could lead the court until 2018, when she reaches the mandatory retirement age of 75.

Despite the political nature of some appointments, Canada holds firmly to a basic legal principle: the independence of the judiciary, a tradition also inherited from Britain. This means that the government does not remove a judge, even if it dislikes the decision he rendered. Even though there are constitutional provisions for removing judges, no judge of any federal or provincial superior court has ever been removed since 1867. This principle of independence is also underscored by the appointment of judges until age 75.

Two other important principles are limited judicial review and judicial restraint. Canadian courts have the responsibility for delineating between federal and provincial jurisdiction. Therefore, the Supreme Court of Canada can determine which level of government has jurisdiction over which powers. It can rule that a parliament cannot enact a certain law because the authority for such issues resides with another legislature. That is, the court can overrule laws. The Canadian government can refer hypothetical questions to the Court concerning the constitutionality of Constitution Acts or of federal or provincial jurisdiction and powers. Ottawa did this in 1997 when it asked the Court whether Quebec had the right to declare independence from Canada unilaterally (the answer was "no"). Such advisory opinions are issued in the form of judgments that have always been treated as binding.

This referee role in federal-provincial jurisdiction is only a limited form of judicial review. It is more than British courts have, but less than that possessed by the United States Supreme Court, which can, under certain circumstances, rule any law null and void because it is in violation of the constitution. Former Chief Justice Antonio Lamer noted: "Since the charter came into effect, we no longer only rule on cases. Now, we rule on the laws themselves."

Until 1949 some cases could be appealed from the Supreme Court of Canada to the Judicial Committee of the Privy Council, the highest court in Britain. Now the Supreme Court of Canada is indisputably the last court of appeal for Canadians. The country's courts have had a long tradition of "legal restraint," meaning that they have been hesitant to use all the powers the constitution had granted them. But after 1949, the Supreme Court dealt increasingly with contentious issues, such as boundaries of free speech. Since the early 1970s, it has rendered important decisions such as: that hanging is not "cruel and unusual punishment," that offshore minerals belong to the central government, that the provinces are free to censor entertainment, and that Quebec's ban on the use of English in the courts was unconstitutional.

The influence of the American model is clear. As James Snell, a Canadian history professor at the University of Guelph, noted: "There is no doubt that the high profile of the Warren court in the United States did influence us in terms of what we expect from the court. Canadian citizens are now expecting them to make decisions that would before have been left to politicians." Former Chief Justice Brian Dickson also spoke about his American counterparts on the Supreme Court: "Increasingly, we look to their experience, not to follow it slavishly but simply as a starting point with which we may agree or disagree. They have made some mistakes that we don't have to make." There are two clear differences: unlike American high court justices, Canadian judges keep a low public profile, and they are far more scrupulous in avoiding visible ideological partisanship. Their decisions rarely give evidence of justices' personal philosophies.

The new Canadian Charter of Rights and Freedoms, enacted in 1982, gave the courts an additional watchdog role over citizens' rights. Some Canadians had thought that the tradition of "judicial restraint" would dissuade the judges from becoming fully immersed in the legally difficult issues of individual rights. They were badly mistaken. The Charter of Rights has, in fact, greatly stimulated the activity of the courts and significantly changed Canadian political life in the process.

About half of the Constitution Act, 1982, was devoted to basic civil and political liberties, and the popularity of these guarantees was shown by the massive public support for them. This Charter was a dramatic break from British and Canadian tradition. For a long time, Canadians believed that there was no need to write down basic individual rights, on the grounds that they were already adequately protected by Parliament and common law. There was therefore no mention of them in the BNA.

But there have been incidents in the past that made some Canadians wonder whether their rights were indeed adequately protected. The 1914 War Measures Act struck many persons as perhaps allowing the government too many sweeping powers. The government could rule by decree, usurping the powers of both federal and provincial parliaments. In 1917 naturalized citizens of German origin were prohibited from voting. Finally, in 1960 the federal government passed a Bill of Rights. However, this was a normal legislative act which applied only to the federal government and which could have been invalidated by another simple act of Parliament. Just how little it could restrain the federal government was demonstrated in October 1970 when shocking kidnappings by Quebec nationalists took place. The Trudeau government invoked the War Measures Act and made membership in the *Front de Liberation du Québec* (Liberation Front of Quebec) illegal. It then arrested those who had belonged to that group *before* it was a crime to do so.

In the wake of a wire tapping scandal in 1986 involving the deputy prime minister, a legal commission reported that twice as many wire taps are permitted by Canadian judges than by American judges. The report continued "It is astounding that this country has recorded on a per capita basis more than twenty times the number of authorizations [as] our massive American neighbor." Criticism of an overly—intrusive RCMP prompted the creation in 1984 of a special counterespionage agency, the Canadian Security Intelligence Service (CSIS), in order to reduce the RCMP's powers. In 1989 the second-ranking RCMP officer was forced to resign amid charges of political interference in two high-profile investigations involving a leak of the government's budget.

The Charter of Rights "entrenches" in the Constitution the rights that Canadian citizens have; that means that they cannot be done away with by a simple act of Parliament. The Charter, along with federalism, is yet another blow to the principle of "parliamentary supremacy." It applies to *all* levels of government. It also expands Canadians' rights to include such things as equality of women and the right to use either of the two official languages. It thereby gives constitutional status to the guarantees in the 1969 Official Languages Act. It spells out many of the same rights as are contained in the American Bill of Rights, which has been so important in the American political experience. Traditionally Canada has placed more emphasis on group rights than have Americans. But since the Constitution and Charter have been in place, legal scholars have noticed a convergence in the legal reasoning

---

Canada

CANADA'S NOT SAFE EITHER | GOING TRANS-FAT-FREE

MACLEAN'S

Canada's weekly newsmagazine | www.macleans.ca

MARCH 29 2004

GOT A PROBLEM WITH THIS?

Most Americans do—which is why gay couples are coming to Canada to tie the knot

JUST MARRIED: Nebraskans Michael Orr and Thomas Price at Niagara Falls, Ont.

of both countries' Supreme Courts when ruling on matters of rights.

As in the United States, the Canadian courts are the bodies that must decide what the various freedoms mean in practice. Judges have to give precise meaning to such phrases as "unreasonable search," "arbitrarily imprisoned," or "informed promptly." The Charter requires that any limitations on Canadians' rights must be "reasonable," but the courts will have to wrestle with the question of what kind of a line this draws. The Charter also affirms the existing aboriginal and treaty rights of native peoples, but the language in the document remained vague simply because there is no consensus in Canada as to what those rights are.

The courts have also found themselves in the middle of the emotionally-charged abortion question. In 1988 the Supreme Court struck down the restrictive federal abortion law as *unconstitutional* because it interfered with a woman's "bodily integrity." In July 1989 the Quebec Supreme Court countered by ruling that the *rights* of the father and the fetus, which it considered to be a human being entitled to the right to life, must be respected. But following passionate debate across the country the Supreme Court of Canada responded in August 1989 by permitting a Quebec woman to have an abortion (after she had had one anyway). Trying to take the issue out of the courts, the Mulroney government got parliamentary approval in November 1989 for a new law permitting abortion if one doctor believes the mother's health is threatened.

In 2003 the courts demonstrated how their interpretation of the Charter can affect sensitive social issues. The Supreme Court ruled that there is no constitutional right to smoke marijuana for recreational purposes. However, it left open the possi-

bility that parliament could decriminalize it. In November 2004 legislation was introduced to replace criminal sanctions with $150 fines for small amounts of marijuana (up to 15 grams or about a half ounce) and to lower penalties ($100) for those under age 18. In April 2005 Canada became the first country in the world to approve a marijuana-based painkiller for multiple sclerosis patients.

In June 2003 an Ontario appeals court had entered more controversial terrain by declaring that denying same-sex couples the right to marry violated their rights and offended "the dignity of same-sex relationships." The ruling took immediate effect, and hundreds of gay couples rushed to Ontario (one-third of whom from the United States) to marry. The then prime minister, Jean Chrétien, announced that the government would not appeal the decision, citing "an evolution in society."

In September then opposition party leader Stephen Harper introduced a motion in Parliament that had been overwhelmingly supported by the Liberals in 1999 defining marriage as the union of one man and one woman. However, this time it was narrowly defeated 137 to 132, a vote that accurately reflected the 50–50 split on the issue in Canadian society. Many Liberals said their switch had been influenced by the Ontario court decision. The prime minister sent draft legislation legalizing gay unions to the Supreme Court to get a ruling on the constitutionality of gay marriage. This elicited a rebuke to the government from Chief Justice Beverley McLachlin for referring the matter straight to the court, which usually rules only on appeals against lower court verdicts. Nevertheless, with the Liberals split on the issue and constituting only a minority in parliament, the prime minister left the matter in the Supreme Court and appointed two new justices who are likely to support same-sex marriages.

In October 2003 the highest court rejected requests by religious and family groups to appeal the Ontario court ruling, letting it stand as the law of the land. Within a year gay marriage was legal in a majority of provinces and territories. In December 2004 Canada's Supreme Court, acting on the government's request for a ruling on the constitutionality of eventual legislation, said that same-sex marriage is consistent with the constitution and did not violate the rights of religious Canadians who desire to uphold the traditional definition of marriage. The court did say that the guarantee of religious freedom protects clergymen from being forced to perform same-sex marriages. In sweeping language, the court pronounced that the constitution "is a living tree which, by way of progressive interpretation, accom-

modates and addresses the realities of modern life."

The Alberta premier threatened to invoke the "notwithstanding" (opt-out) provision to prevent it in his province. Nevertheless, the Martin government vowed to pass a law permitting gay marriage, with all MPs except cabinet members free to vote according to their conscience. However, when it came to a vote in April 2005, more than 30 Liberal MPs joined the opposition to reject the bill recognizing same-sex marriage. Many Canadians felt they had been railroaded on this. Still, polls indicated that those who opposed such marriages would overwhelmingly accept the Conservative opposition's alternative of civil unions granting gays the same rights, benefits and obligations as any married couple, with or without the title of marriage. However, by November 2009, two-thirds of Canadians accepted same-sex relationships.

To complicate matters even further, two Toronto women, who had been together for ten years before marrying in Ontario, filed for divorce in July 2004 after only five days of marriage. They were legally married, but Canada's Divorce Act did not provide for same-sex divorce. They got a ruling from a judge on the Ontario Superior Court of Justice declaring the current Divorce Act unconstitutional because it referred to a man and a woman. The divorce was then granted.

In 2009 the court turned its attention to another unconventional form of family: polygamy. British Columbia's government decided to seek to end polygamy practiced in its borders, especially in a Mormon commune called Bountiful, where one former "bishop" had 26 wives and 108 children. It was also confirmed that thousands of polygamous men in Ontario receive welfare payments for each of their wives. The court must determine if outlawing polygamy violates the constitutional guarantees of freedom of religion. Also, if gay marriage is permitted, on what legal grounds could polygamy be forbidden?

The Canada and Constitution Acts had to be careful compromises in order to gain the backing of the provinces, which for a hundred years had been unable to agree on these matters. Most provinces would agree to give the courts a clear mandate to strike down laws which violate the Charter only by securing a political safety-hatch in return. They wished to protect themselves from a flood of court cases attacking their laws. To minimize the dangers of "judicial lawmaking," the Charter contains a clause in Section 33 which says that Parliament or the legislature of a province may expressly declare that their law would still operate "notwithstand-

ing" (despite) the Charter's provisions. The legislature which disregards a provision of the Charter must, however, declare openly that it is doing so, and thereby bear whatever public onus such a declaration would cause. Such non-compliance could only last five years, although it could be renewed.

Many Canadians were convinced that provinces would be very hesitant to use this "notwithstanding" provision because that would be a public statement that they intended to deny rights guaranteed in the Charter. However, no sooner was the ink on the Charter dry, when Quebec, which for years has rejected the entire constitutional change and which fears that its efforts to make Quebec more French could be frustrated by the Charter, put a "notwithstanding" clause in *all* of its provincial laws. It invoked the clause again in December 1988 to invalidate a Canadian Supreme Court ruling restricting Quebec's French-only language legislation. Many critics understandably see this escape-hatch as a serious weakening of the Charter, but it should not be forgotten that without such compromises, there would have been no Canada and Constitution Acts in the first place. Americans should remember the unpleasant compromises that some of their Founding Fathers ac-

cepted, such as permitting slavery indefinitely and the slave trade for an additional 25 years, without which there would never have been a Constitution of the United States in 1787.

Since the Charter came into force in 1982, Canadian courts have been inundated with cases relating to individual rights. In the first two years alone, lower courts decided more than 1,000 Charter-based cases, covering issues ranging from an accused person's right to counsel and Parliament's authority to keep stores closed on Sundays to anglophones' right to have their own schools in Quebec. Thousands more such cases are on the dockets. Of the 100 cases heard annually by the Supreme Court, constitutional cases are usually the most time-consuming. Canada's former chief justice, Brian Dickson, said in 1984: "When there is a breach of the fundamental rights and freedoms under the Charter of Rights, we have been given the right, the duty and the responsibility to deal with it—and it is our duty to strike [the violation] down."

In 1985 Canada entered yet another era when the so-called "equity clauses" of Section 15 of the Charter took effect. This clause insures that every individual is equal before and under the law "without discrimination based on color, religion,

sex, age, or mental or physical disability." Such protection had been postponed three years from the enactment of the Charter to give the federal and provincial governments sufficient time to amend any discriminatory laws or regulations. Capital punishment is outlawed even though 53% of respondents said in 2009 that it was OK.

All governments were slow to respond to this task, in part because they were not sure what precisely constituted discrimination. Does it mean that age cannot be used to determine when a person may drive a car, consume alcohol, serve in the army, get married or be forced to retire? Could women be barred from combat roles in the military? Do people in insane asylums have the right to vote? What does "equal pay for equal work" mean? Section 1 of the Charter says that all of Canadians' rights and freedoms are subject "to reasonable limits prescribed by law," but what precisely does that mean in concrete cases? The social and legal consequences of Section 15 remain unclear, but one thing which is certain is the revolutionary power that has been given to the Canadian courts. In the words of Brian Dickson: "The Charter has replaced parliamentary supremacy with constitutional supremacy." No wonder Brian Mulroney

Canada

joked that one of the first things he intended to do with his new-born son was to enroll him in law school.

Ontario experimented with allowing Muslims to mediate some civil disputes by permitting tribunals that included imams, Muslim elders and lawyers to apply Islamic *sharia* law to family disagreements, inheritance, or business and divorce matters. This possibility was provided for under the Arbitration Act of the Province of Ontario, which gives religious and cultural groups the authority to resolve such disputes through private and binding arbitration. Catholics and Protestants never resorted to the act, but Jews had since 1991. By 2004 Muslim leaders had set up an Islamic Court of Civil Justice that had chosen arbitrators who had undergone training in *sharia* and Canadian civil law.

However, much of the Canadian public was dismayed and incensed that such courts could be permitted to operate in such a secular country. Even the Canadian Council of Muslim Women feared that they could undermine women's rights: "Sanctioning the use of religious laws under the Arbitration Act will provide legitimacy to practices that are abhorred by fair-minded Canadians, including Muslim women." In June 2005 Quebec banned Islamic law. In the words of Premier Jean Charest: "It's important to send a very clear message that there is one rule of law in Quebec." In September 2005 there were demonstrations in a dozen Canadian and European cities against Ontario's legal experiment. The government in Toronto quickly scrapped the use of *sharia* law and moved to outlaw religious tribunals by Christians and Jews.

FEDERALISM AND THE PROVINCES

In 1867 the Fathers of Confederation intended to create a federation in which the central government would be more powerful than the provinces. The BNA therefore granted the provinces only restricted powers that would enable them to maintain their cultural identity. They included powers over local government, property, social welfare, education, health, language and culture. These were not exclusive powers, though, because the federal government was given the power to protect the educational rights of religious minorities, which meant primarily the English Protestants in Quebec and the Catholic francophones outside of Quebec. The BNA even spoke of some "concurrent powers," such as agriculture and immigration, and it contained a "supremacy clause," which made the central government's claim on these shared powers supreme.

While the *BNA* granted a few specific powers to the provinces, it earmarked 29 kinds of powers for the federal government, such as defense, finance, criminal law, transportation, postal services, coinage of money, banking and Indians. It also granted Ottawa the most lucrative sources of revenue. Unlike in the U.S. Constitution, any powers not specifically granted to the provinces accrue to the central government in Canada. Further, the *BNA* contained a "declaratory power," which permitted the central government to usurp provincial powers if the reason for such action were "for the general Advantage of Canada or for the Advantage of Two or more of the Provinces." This power has been used very seldom.

Ottawa can also "disallow" a provincial law within a year of passage, or it can "reserve" such a law for federal governmental review before such a law goes into force. None of these powers has been exercised since 1961. The hefty central powers the founders built into the BNA explains why the regional units were called "provinces" rather than "states." The latter term denotes dignified sovereignty, whereas the word "province" implies a rural hinterland outside the limits of the metropolis. Almost everywhere else, "pro-vincial" is an insult. Yet over time, the provinces are entities that have drawn away some important powers from Ottawa and have become more powerful than American states.

Ottawa's power on paper is most impressive. However, as we have seen so many times, political practice in Canada can differ greatly from documentary powers. While the Fathers fully intended to create a Canada with a stronger central government and weaker provincial governments than the United States, the exact opposite has actually occurred: today, Canadian provinces are considerably stronger than are American states, and the provincial premiers are potentates, whose strength can hardly be exaggerated. While it is true that the courts, including the Judicial Committee of the British Privy Council, tended to judge more often in the provinces' favor than in Ottawa's, the strengthening of provincial rights has come primarily from the provincial leaders themselves. In good Canadian style, change has come chiefly by custom and convention. Today's reality is the result of political accommodation, not judicial decision and constitutional change.

The forces of decentralization and centralization are always at work in Canada. Author Peter C. Newman put it this way: "Few land masses of such outrageous dimensions can withstand the tensions of democracy. The stresses and strains of stretching the rule of law across 88 degrees of longitude and 42 degrees of latitude virtually guarantee inefficient central government. The powers of both levels of government have ebbed and flowed over the years. To summarize those evolutionary changes, the provinces were quickly dissatisfied with their limited powers, and they began almost immediately to strengthen their position through hard bargaining. However, two world wars, during which Ottawa ruled by means of expanded emergency powers, and the Great Depression in the 1930s brought a resurgence of cen-

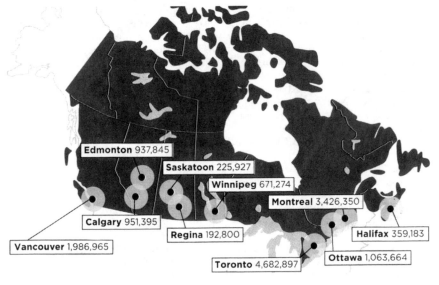

Edmonton 937,845
Saskatoon 225,927
Winnipeg 671,274
Montreal 3,426,350
Calgary 951,395
Regina 192,800
Halifax 359,183
Vancouver 1,986,965
Toronto 4,682,897
Ottawa 1,063,664

Source: *Maclean's*

tral powers. In the mid-1950s, though, the provinces reasserted themselves with a vengeance, first in Quebec, and then in the energy-rich West.

In the 20th century Canada had become a predominantly urbanized country, and provinces were faced with managing the growth of cities, which fell into their jurisdiction. The "minor powers" which they had been granted by the BNA, such as social welfare, health and education, became salient issues in a country that had become committed to expanding services in these areas. These now claim half the budgets of most provinces and require the provinces to put heavy pressure on Ottawa, with its greater taxing power, to help finance them. By the 1980s close to half of some provinces' budgets came from the federal government. By means of a system that some authorities have called "co-operative federalism," the two levels of government share the cost of many programs. The usual practice for such cooperation is that Ottawa sends financial support (for example, for health insurance or pensions) on the condition that the provinces' programs meet federal standards. Ottawa also sends some funds on an unconditional basis.

The dilemma remains: the constitution gives the provinces responsibility for most public services, including justice, education, health and the management of natural resources. But the central government has the most cash and can run up surpluses while the provinces struggle to provide the expensive services. Canadian politics is largely about chronic jurisdictional quarrels between different levels of government over transfers of money.

In the 1960s the provinces even challenged the federal government's exclusive power to conduct foreign relations. Quebec created a department of intergovernmental relations, which acts much like a foreign ministry and seeks to be represented in international conferences. It has opened trade and cultural missions in a variety of foreign countries, including the United States and France. Many other provinces rapidly followed suit, and Ontario alone maintains a dozen similar missions abroad. Prime Minister Trudeau set out to reverse the trend toward decentralization: the Constitution Act itself put some limits on the provinces' power to veto some constitutional amendments.

Of course, competition between Ottawa and the provinces is as old as the Confederation itself. The BNA granted the central government control over major 19th-century concerns, such as trade, banks, postal service and criminal law. However, the provinces were granted control over matters that rose to greater prominence in the late 20th and early 21st century, such as health care and education.

The provinces accept money from Ottawa but resist any federal intrusion into their jurisdictions. This is especially true of Quebec. But even Ontario has withdrawn from its traditional stance as the natural ally of Ottawa. Now that it is officially categorized as a "have-not" province, it complains like the other provinces that it is being cheated by Ottawa politically and economically. It is a messy process. But when asked in 2010 if federalism "has more advantages than disadvantages," 48% of respondents agreed (including in Quebec), and only 33% disagreed (42% in Quebec).

Contemporary Canadian federalism involves close and frequent cooperation and negotiation between provincial and federal governments. This has been called "executive federalism," because the executive branches facilitate the highly interpenetrated relationships. Civil servants from both levels meet and talk by phone daily, and cabinet members frequently meet to discuss common problems. Since the 1960s, the premiers and the prime minister meet in Conferences of First Ministers. These are convened and chaired by the prime minister.

Such "summit meetings" usually occur at least once a year although prime ministers often choose not to have them (eg. for several years from 2004). Much of the bargaining at these meetings occurs behind closed doors. To the participants it is known as "the Club," and civility is one of its most rigid conventions. According to one premier, "the clubby atmosphere of the gatherings puts tremendous pressures on each premier to conform." It discourages political head-on collisions although they sometimes occur. In 2004 the premiers began meeting semi-annually in the Council of the Federation, a forum that excludes the prime minister.

This form of "executive federalism" was seriously harmed by the failure of the Meech Lake Accord in 1990. Top leaders who were derisively dubbed "11 men in suits" made this agreement in relative secrecy. The result was a political disaster. Former Manitoba premier Gary Filmon learned the indelible lesson that if politicians indulge in top-down, brokerage politics, the voters will punish them. "When you look at the names and the faces that were associated with Meech Lake, every single person who signed that agreement was gone from office within a very few short years." Since 1990 federal-provincial agreements tend to be more painstakingly and publicly constructed over years of meetings and with much outside consultation.

The prime minister can decide if he wants more or fewer meetings with the premiers. Stephen Harper, who led minority governments from 2006–11, chose to be as conciliatory as possible with the powerful provincial barons. He bought peace by increasing transfer payments by billions of dollars and avoiding policy clashes. He was careful not to intrude on spheres chiefly under provincial jurisdiction.

The federal cabinet has a Standing Committee on Federal-Provincial Relations, and the Privy Council Office has a Federal-Provincial Relations Secretariat; both help prepare the prime minister and his retinue for meetings. In addition to these conferences, the premiers and territorial leaders hold an annual summer meeting among themselves, and frequently the Western or Atlantic premiers will gather. Starting in 2004 a Council of the Federation brings premiers and territorial leaders together twice a year. It has an Ottawa-based secretariat, and the federal government is not a member. Finally, bilateral meetings among premiers are a frequent occurrence.

Provincial Governments

The provinces themselves have governmental systems very similar to that of the federal government in Ottawa, except that none has an upper house. All have parliamentary systems. That means that the party leader with majority support in the legislative assembly forms the government, led by a powerful premier. Don Braid, political columnist for the *Edmonton Journal* once described the premiers: "They recall the medieval barons who armed against the king while demanding his protection. Their interests are purely regional, but fate has given them a huge role in the national melodrama. On this stage they cavort like off-Broadway Falstaffs shoved into King Lear's shoes. And yet, their subjects love them for it." Premiers are truly important movers and shakers in Canadian politics, but their strong regional power bases have always prevented them from rising to the pinnacle of Canadian political power in Ottawa. No premier has ever become prime minister of Canada.

There is a lieutenant governor appointed in each province by the prime minister on the advice of the provincial premier. He or she usually performs only ceremonial functions. In 2000 six of the ten lieutenant governors were women after then Prime Minister Chrétien appointed Myra Freeman, a sixth-grade Halifax teacher. She was the first woman and first member of Nova Scotia's Jewish community to serve as the Queen's representative in Nova Scotia.

The members of the legislative assembly (called "MLAs" in all provinces but Ontario, Newfoundland and Quebec,

Canada

where they are referred to as MPP, MHA and deputy respectively) are elected by the same kind of single-member district electoral system used in federal elections. There are, however, three exceptions: on Prince Edward Island, MLAs are elected in two-member districts, with each voter casting two votes. Also, Nova Scotia has three such two-member districts, and British Columbia seven. Three provinces have adopted fixed election dates. Each province establishes its own voter requirements for provincial elections. Thus, in BC one must be age 19 to vote, and in some provinces citizens of the British Commonwealth and the Republic of Ireland are permitted to vote.

One of the provincial government's main responsibilities is to oversee local governments. Because they are organized and granted authority by the provinces, their specific organization and responsibilities vary from province to province. All provide such services as elementary and secondary schools (to which 40% of the cities' budgets are devoted); such culture and recreation facilities as parks, pools and ice rinks, libraries and art galleries; health and welfare to include public health services, ambulances and welfare administration; housing for the aged and poor, and issuance of building permits, standards, planning and zoning; police and fire protection; public transportation and road repair; and a variety of utilities such as water, garbage and sewage and electricity.

The cities' demands for more powers to cope with their responsibilities have fallen on deaf ears in provincial capitals. Even though the provinces have successfully demanded more and more power from Ottawa, they have stubbornly refused to share any of theirs with local governments. Nevertheless, the mayors of major cities, such as Toronto, Montreal or Vancouver, can be powerful political figures in provincial and Canadian politics.

Of all the taxes Canadians pay, 50% goes to the federal government, 42% to the provincial governments, and 8% to the cities. To fund their activities, local governments rely primarily on provincial grants (44%), property taxes (34%), business taxes (4%) and sales and services (8%). As in the United States, cities find themselves continuously strapped for finances, made worse by central government budget cuts and high provincial debt. As demands for services have risen, property taxes can no longer cover municipal needs. With inadequate funding, cities, which generate most of the country's wealth, are experiencing deteriorating urban infrastructure and cuts in services. The debates over how to use limited funds does not seem to stimulate strong municipal electoral interest; voter turnout averages only 30% in city elections, versus 60.5% in the 2004 federal elections.

It has always been difficult to forge and maintain a unified country out of 13 so different provinces and territories. This is made particularly hard because Canada's major parties are highly decentralized and tend not to be strong in every part of the country. They can therefore do little to help hold the country together. Since the provinces have unique political scenes and problems and play such important roles in Canadian politics, let us look very briefly at each one of them.

NEWFOUNDLAND AND LABRADOR: This is Canada's most recent province, having entered the Confederation in 1949 after a close vote in a referendum. In 2001 it was officially renamed Newfoundland and Labrador to recognize the latter's importance. In 2003 decades of negotiations culminated in agreement on a 29,000-square mile new Inuit-governed territory created in Labrador, called Nunatsiavut ("our beautiful land").

Newfoundland has the lowest percentage of French-speakers in all of Canada. It also has its own dialect of English, having grown out of an archaic English spoken by seafarers and having been preserved by the province's relative isolation from the rest of Canada. So different is their language that a dictionary of Newfoundland English sells well. In it one can learn, for example, that a female companion was once called a "friendgirl." Heavily Irish, a third of Newfoundlanders is Roman Catholic. However, to raise the educational level, Newfoundlanders overwhelmingly voted in 1997 to replace all church-run schools with a state-run educational system.

The province has been confronted with knotty economic problems. The main one has been the devastated fishing industry, which was Newfoundland's main source of employment in the over 700 communities around its 6,000-mile coastline. How did this happen? In 1977 Canada declared a 200-mile limit in the sea and began subsidizing boats and fish processing plants, many of which now stand idle. Bowing to foreign and domestic political pressure, Canada banned the unrestricted killing of seals thereby enabling the seal population to triple since the 1970s. Each animal consumes an average of 45 pounds of fish a day. This, as well as overfishing, combined almost to destroy the fish stocks, especially cod. Seal hunting with clear quotas is permitted annually, and about 6,000 Canadians in outlying areas benefit from this part-time employment.

In 1989 Canada granted France the right to fish an extra 11,000 tons of cod from the waters off Newfoundland in return for France's agreement to submit to international arbitration a dispute about the mar-

Harbor outside St. John's, Newfoundland

itime boundaries around the French islands of St. Pierre and Miquelon, which have a population of only 6,000 and are located 16 miles off the coast of Newfoundland. In 1992 an international tribunal awarded France only a fourth of the area it had claimed. In 2009 France announced that it would file with the UN a new claim to an area of the continental shelf south of the two islands in an attempt to get some of the oil and gas that is enriching Newfoundland.

In the same year Ottawa slapped a moratorium on all northern cod fishing to allow the dwindling stocks to replenish themselves. This bitter decision sent thousands of fishermen and fishery workers into unemployment lines. Of the 42,000 who had once worked in the province's fishing industry, 27,000 were employed by 1999. Revenues from cod fishing had fallen from $136 million in 1988 to only $1 million a decade later. Former Premier Tobin acknowledged, "they know that the fish are gone, they know that the income support won't last forever." In April 2003 the federal fisheries minister announced the closure of most of the remaining Atlantic cod fishing industry because of the depleted stocks. Responding to ex-Premier Roger Grimes' angry demand for a constitutional change to give the province more control over the industry, former federal Liberal Party leader Stéphane Dion noted sadly: "No amendment would bring back the fish." There are some experts, such as George Rose of St. John's Memorial University, who think the cod will come back, but patience is needed.

There are some hopes that aquaculture, using the cold, unpolluted waters to raise seafood products such as scallops, salmon, mussels, whelk and sea urchins, can provide work for some of them. In 1998 huge increases in crab and shrimp catches pushed the value of fish landings to an all-time high. In 2004 alone the crab and shrimp catch was worth about $1 billion. But the industry employs far fewer people, about 2,000 in boats and 4,000 in processing plants, compared with about 18,000 in boats and up to 20,000 in plants earlier.

The EU agreed temporarily to suspend fishing in the area. When pirate fishermen from Europe continued to overfish the dwindling stocks, Canada decided in 1995 to act. It sent a frigate, fired a shot over the bow of a Spanish trawler outside the 200-mile fishing zone, boarded the vessel and ordered it to St. John's. There it found illegal nets on board and doctored records proving that the fishermen had indeed violated international agreements. After much acrimony, a settlement was reached calling for closer monitoring and enforcement of fish catches. The then Fisheries Minister Brian Tobin, a former TV anchor from New-

foundland, became a national hero overnight. A year later he was premier.

In October 2003 Conservative Danny Williams, a former Rhodes Scholar, crusading lawyer and multi-millionaire after selling his cable-TV business for $232 million in 2000, was elected premier with 34 of 48 legislative seats. He was scrappy, articulate and prone to the dramatic, and he has made a career out of tough talk and a knack for the well-chosen fight. His antics get Ottawa's attention. He faced a huge budget deficit, with $1 billion going annually to servicing a debt that amounts to $23,000 per person, Canada's largest. The population of 520,000 had shrunk by 10% from 1994–2003. His plans to trim the civil service by 14% or 4,000 jobs and to freeze civil servants' wages for two years sparked, in April 2004, the largest civil service strike in the province's history. In only three years he turned his province's fortunes around.

In the 1960s great reserves of off-shore oil and gas were discovered in the Grand Banks. The Hibernia field on the edge of this trove, 200 miles offshore, contains large quantities of oil. The province fought a furious battle with Ottawa over who owns and controls those reserves: Ottawa or St. John's. A Supreme Court decision in 1984 said that the federal government owns offshore resources. But in 1985, the Mulroney government signed an "Atlantic Accord" with Newfoundland, granting it most of the powers over the Hibernia field. In 1993, the federal government agreed to buy an 8.5% share in order that the project could continue and begin producing oil in 1997. The provincial government is trying to buy back that federal equity stake.

Kathy Dunderdale
Premier of Newfoundland

It is Canada's highest producing field and has helped make the province Canada's second-largest oil producer and one of the richer "have" provinces.

The Terra Nova field, 20 miles southeast of Hibernia, produced its first oil in 2000 although its output did not materialize as expected. White Rose (2006) and other fields followed. The southern extension of Hibernia was delayed. Nevertheless, Newfoundland expects to receive as much as $4.9 billion in oil revenues for the eight years following 2005.

Williams was determined to gain even more of the proceeds for his province, and he succeeded. In 2007 he risked a multi-billion-dollar deal with the oil companies by demanding a 4.9% ownership share in the Hebron offshore project and a generous royalty system. He signed a multi-year agreement with Chevron, ExxonMobil,

Government House, residence of the Lieutenant Governor of Newfoundland, St. John's

Canada

$1.75 Plus Tax

DOWNHOMER *Magazine*

FEBRUARY 1998 • VOL 10 - NO 9

• Polar Bears in Newfoundland and Labrador

• Ghosts in the hen house

• The life of the famous Captain of PT107 (aka Christmas Seal)

• The ghost of Foran's Hotel

• Newfoundlander youngest to win scholarship

• FEATURE: The Women's Institute

COVER PHOTO
Polar Bear
Photo-Hal Crews
See page 2

Shop the oldest street in North America
OPEN SUNDAYS DOWNHOMER *Shoppe & Gallery* • 303 Water Street, St. John's

Petro-Canada and StatoilHydro to develop Hebron, located south of the lucrative Hibernia fields. He was guided by his simple principle of "no more give-aways," and he won. He had tapped the Rock's sense of aggrieved nationalism and pledged to make the half a million Newfoundlanders "masters in our own house."

Voters rewarded him richly with a landslide reelection victory in October 2007. His party won almost 70% of the votes and all but four of the 48 seats. One NDP and three Liberal MLAs survived, but not Liberal leader Gerry Reid. This was not necessary good news for the federal Tories. Williams was the first premier to urge Canadians to vote for any other party but his own in federal elections. He believed a Conservative majority would be dangerous.

In 2002 a federal tribunal settled the 37-year boundary dispute between Newfoundland and Nova Scotia about 170 kilometers (ca. 105 miles) offshore. Newfoundland got 75% of the potentially oil-rich offshore region, known as the Laurentian sub-basin, which could hold nearly a billion barrels of oil. Nova Scotia was awarded only 16%, while the French islands of St. Pierre and Miquelon received 9%.

St. John's bargained hard for maximum benefits from one of the world's richest nickel deposits at Voisey's Bay in Labrador's rugged interior. The mine has the potential of supplying 13% of the world's nickel. After years of negotiations the provincial government and two Aboriginal peoples, the 5,000 Inuit and 1,500 Innu, agreed to allow nickel mining at an open-pit site starting in 2006, while a pilot processing plant is built at Argentia. The pro-

ject should create hundreds of permanent jobs, a hoped-for Can$11 billion in revenue for the government over 30 years, Can$255 million to the Inuit, who claim the land around the mine, and a percentage of the mine's profits to the two Aboriginal groups. Premier Williams revived an earlier plan to build an 11-mile (17-km) tunnel under the Strait of Belle Isle to connect Newfoundland and Labrador (population: 28,000).

The province was Canada's poorest and had its highest cost-of-living, lowest per capita income, and highest unemployment rate (13% in 2011—much higher than the national average of 7.6%). It also was heavily dependent upon Ottawa, which in 2002 was the source of 39% of the province's revenues. In 2004–5, the central government sent $674 million or $1,304 per person in the form of federal equalization payments.

That has changed for Newfoundland, considering its rising oil revenues. The rationale for equalization payments is that poorer provinces that are less able to afford basic services are given cash grants by Ottawa to bring them up to an established standard. In 2009 it joined Alberta, Saskatchewan and BC in not qualifying for such payments.

Williams quarreled with the federal government's view that Newfoundland's equalization payments should decline as revenues from offshore oil increase. He became very popular at home, with an astounding approval rating of 92% by the time of his retirement for health reasons in December 2010. His stand against big oil and his arguments that it's high time that Newfoundlanders be "masters of our own destiny" only heightened his popularity. However, he was unpopular everywhere else in Canada because of his insistence that Newfoundland receive every penny of its equalization funds while getting a bigger and fairer share of offshore oil wealth. He argued that this is its last and best chance to become a "have" rather than a perpetual "have-not" province. "This is our one shot. . . .We will invest in social programs, in infrastructure, we will lower our debt." He had already eliminated his province's budget deficit. But in 2009 the province still had a debt of $11.6 billion, the highest per capita in Canada.

Economic distress continues to stimulate some emigration annually from Newfoundland to more lucrative pastures in Canada although increasing prosperity at home and hard times in the West reduced such movement. Three-fourths of those departing are between the ages of 15 and 34. The 2001 census showed that 37% went to Ontario and 29% to Alberta. So many worked in the oil sand industry of Fort McMurray that locals jokingly called

their town Fort McNewfoundland. The out migration is particularly distressing since Newfoundland's birthrate is Canada's lowest despite polls at the turn of the century citing its people as the most sexually active Canadians. Almost a half million Newfoundland emigrés live in southern Ontario. They have their own monthly newspaper, The *Downhomer*.

An enduring irritant is the 65-year contract which Newfoundland's former Liberal premier, Joey Smallwood, signed with Quebec in 1969. He needed Quebec's support of development loans to construct one of the world's largest hydroelectric plants at Churchill Falls, in the wilderness of Labrador. In exchange, Newfoundland agreed to sell Quebec almost all the electricity produced by the plant for 65 years at 1969 prices. There was no provision for renegotiating the contract. No one anticipated the skyrocketing of energy prices following the 1973 energy crisis.

Today, Quebec buys the Churchill Falls electricity for one tenth the prevailing market price and turns around and exports it to New England for ten times what it pays Newfoundland for it. Newfoundland loses $800 million annually. Quebec claims that its exported electricity actually comes from its huge James Bay project, and that Quebec uses Newfoundland's electricity at home. Few Newfoundlanders can accept that argument.

To rub salt into the wounds, Newfoundland has had to construct four additional power plants to supply its own electrical needs since it receives only a very small portion of Churchill Falls' production. A much-trumpeted deal with Quebec to develop another hydroelectric project on the Lower Churchill River in Labrador collapsed in 2000. In 2005 Ontario and Quebec joined forces to bid for the development of the Lower Churchill River, one of the last remaining large untapped hydro-electricity sites in North America.

All efforts to renegotiate the original contract failed. The Supreme Court of Canada ruled that a deal is a deal. This issue seriously burdens relations with its western neighbor; it gives Quebec political leverage. For example, when Newfoundland's premier announced his opposition to the Meech Lake accord, Quebec Premier Robert Bourassa tartly responded that renegotiation of hydroelectric and other deals with Quebec would be easier in a climate of "cordial relations." Newfoundland continues to badger Quebec for a change, but to no avail.

That 1969 Churchill Falls deal still haunts the province. The boldness in negotiating high royalties and partial ownership in the Hebron field in 2007 offered the opportunity to put that painful and humiliating history behind them. The future holds even greater frustration regarding Churchill Falls. It was rediscovered that Quebec has the right to a 25-year extension of the contract at even lower pre-set rates after the current 44-year term runs out in 2016. Newfoundlanders groan that the new rate is "barely distinguishable from being free." A week before his successor took office in December 2010, the province signed a $6.2 billion deal for a hydro mega-project on the Lower Churchill.

Williams was succeeded by his former minister of natural resources, Kathy Dunderdale. Not only is she Newfoundland's first female leader, but she enters the fall 2011 provincial election as the favorite in a field consisting only of women: Lorraine Michaels of the NDP and Yvonne Jones of the Liberals. Born one of 11 children of a trawlerman in Placentia Bay, she never finished her degree at Memorial University in St. John's. She worked her way up the political ladder, starting as a Liberal before switching to the Tories, and became Williams' right-hand person. She is just as feisty as he is and may one day become almost as popular: in March 2011 she enjoyed Canada's second highest approval rating (55%) after Premier Brad Walls of Saskatchewan (63%).

Human residents share the island with 150,000 moose, which are increasingly making nuisances of themselves. Brought from the mainland a century ago to help attract tourists and hunters to the then British colony, they have no predators since the native wolf became extinct. They are unpredictable, can run 35 miles (56 kilometers) per hour, swim as fast as two grown men paddling a canoe, and worse, are inclined to wander out on highways at night and cause collisions.

The World Trade and Convention Centre, Halifax, Nova Scotia

ince's history and Canada's biggest construction project entering the 21st century. Delivery of gas began in 1999, with New England as the principal market. There were hopes of even more gas outside the Sable development, but they have been disappointed by a series of dry wells and expired exploration licenses. Many analysts now conclude that there is not as much gas as some had believed.

In 2002 Nova Scotia lost an offshore boundary dispute with Newfoundland over possession of potentially vast reserves of gas and oil. Newfoundland claimed it had never signed a 1964 deal drawing a line. The financial stakes were raised for Nova Scotia in 2001 when Ot-

tawa announced the closure of the Prince colliery, the island's last working underground coal mine.

In June 2009 the voters elected the first NDP government in Atlantic Canada after a decade of Tory rule. Led by Premier Darrell Dexter, the New Democrats won 45.26% of the votes and 31 seats. In the opposition are the Liberals, led by Stephen McNeil, who captured 27.22% of the votes and 11 seats, and the Conservatives, led by Rodney MacDonald, who slid to 24.52% and only 10 seats.

The son of a sheet metal worker who plays up his working-class roots, Dexter earned a journalism degree at the University of King's College and law and educa-

NOVA SCOTIA: Like Newfoundland, this province staked great hopes on an economic resurgence stimulated by offshore energy resources, especially on the natural gas reserves in the Sable Island area 180 miles east of Halifax. With both offshore and onshore facilities for producing and processing natural gas, it is the largest industrial undertaking in the prov-

Hon. Darrell Dexter

Canada

tion degrees at Dalhousie University. Before practicing law, he served as a naval sub-lieutenant. He has been an MLA since 1998 and led his party in two provincial election campaigns before winning the prize in 2009.

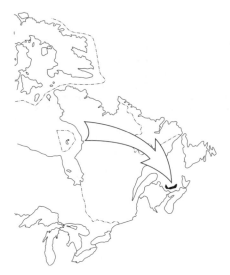

PRINCE EDWARD ISLAND: In this tiny, beautiful island, which strives to maintain its unique culture and pace of life, the Tories ended 10 years of Liberal rule in an electoral upset in 1996. Voters awarded the Tories 18 seats in the 27-seat Legislative Assembly. The Liberal Party, whose former leader, Catherine Callbeck, had been the first elected female premier in Canadian history, captured only eight seats.

Enjoying a 75% approval rating after three and one-half years, the Tories decided to call new elections in 2000. The results were staggering. Running on the slogan, "Let's continue," they captured 58% of the votes and 26 of 27 seats. The Liberals won 34%, but they were able to preserve only one seat, that of potato farmer Ron MacKinley. This was the Liberals' worst defeat in provincial history. Led the next time by Robert Ghiz, a political rookie whose father Joe had been premier from 1986 to 1993, the Liberals did better on September 29, 2003, the day Hurricane Juan swept through the province depriving two-thirds of households of power. Nevertheless, an astonishing 83% of eligible voters turned out to return the Tories to their third consecutive term. Voters again witnessed the effects of the single-member electoral system. With only 54% of the popular votes, the Tories won 23 seats, while the Liberals' 43% entitled them to only four seats.

The premier is Pat Binns. His success is especially remarkable on an island where family connections can make or break a political career. Binns was born in Wyburn, Saskatchewan, and grew up in

Hon. Patrick Binns

Lloydminster, Alberta. He first came to PEI in 1970 on a student exchange program and married a local girl. Returning in 1978, he became a bean farmer and plunged right into politics. One of his Tory colleagues noted: "Pat is the kind of politician they go for out here. He grew up on a farm, he always returns phone calls, he never loses his temper." He successfully met the unenviable task of helping PEI adjust to the shocks of steady reductions in transfer payments from Ottawa. Agriculture remains the island's main source of income, especially potato farming. Nevertheless, the number of family farms has declined from around 5,000 in 1970 to only 2,200 in 2001, and most islanders work in offices. PEI was also the first province to provide internet access in all schools and public libraries.

Within 24 hours of Binns' 1996 election, the last concrete span of the 13-kilometer (8-mile) Confederation Bridge was lowered into place. On May 31, 1997, the bridge opened. At a cost of about $25, cars can cross it in 12 minutes. This is PEI's first physical link with the outside world since the ice age. Fears of disrupting PEI's peaceful style of living had erupted in 1987 when plans for this bridge across the frigid waters of the Northumberland Strait from Borden, PEI, to Cape Tormentine, N.B., were announced. In a 1988 referendum on the issue, 59% of PEI voters approved the link with the mainland, despite protests from fishermen, ferry employees, and other islanders who feared that outsiders, particularly Americans, would be encouraged to buy up more land on their island.

To quiet that fear, legislation was passed forbidding non-islanders from purchasing more than five acres without cabinet approval or from having a shorefront more than 50 meters (165 feet). That has not stopped foreigners from buying. By 2001 Americans owned 30% of PEI's vacation properties, and non-residents hold 9% of all acreage. Some islanders believe that the bridge and foreign ownership threaten something fundamental to the PEI psyche: the sense that they are separate and different from the rest of Canada.

The Confederation Bridge attracts more tourists. In fact, PEI's new license plates feature the bridge instead of the pigtailed and freckled Anne of Green Gables, the island's most famous fictional resident and most popular tourist site. With a population of only 139,000 PEI already draws over one million tourists annually, outnumbering the islanders by almost ten to one.

Province House in Charlottetown, P.E.I., where the Canadian federation was born

NEW BRUNSWICK: In the 1987 provincial elections, ex-Premier Frank McKenna's Liberals captured *all* 58 seats, with 62% of the votes. McKenna wasted little time in selling the airplane that had been used to fly his predecessor around and in establishing a more austere style of government, including stringent personal spending guidelines for himself and the members of his government. Voters approved of his rule and awarded the Liberals impressive victories in the 1991 and 1995 elections.

One of the province's oldest political problems is how to accommodate the Acadian French minority, which numbers 242,000 (only 8% of whom no longer speaks French at home) and makes up 35% of its population. This is proportionately the biggest francophone community in any province outside Quebec. The Université de Moncton opened its doors in 1963 and rapidly became North America's largest French-speaking university outside of Quebec. For a while it was a hotbed of activism for bilingualism and equal rights for francophones. But as life for them improved, most of the anger disappeared. In 1969 New Brunswick became the only bilingual province in Canada, and the government moved to make the government, courts and public institutions bilingual. Francophone leaders, organized in such groups as the *Societé des Acadiens du Nouveau Brunswick*, pushed for faster progress.

The government's efforts to increase the number of bilingual (the bulk of whom are Acadian) civil servants aroused charges that unilingual anglophones can no longer be hired or promoted in government service, a charge that is incorrect. So angry were many anglophones that they press their demands through a New Brunswick Association of English-Speaking Canadians and a vocally anti-bilingual party, the Confederation of Regions (COR). In the 1991 provincial elections COR won a stunning eight seats, becoming the main opposition party in Canada's only officially bilingual province. Its capture of 30% of anglophone votes risked inflaming lan-

Hon. Shawn Graham

guage tensions. But in the 1995 elections it was wiped out of the legislature.

During an Acadian world conference in 1994 author Antoine Maillet, whose play, *La Sagouine*, portrays Acadian resilience, could boast that "we don't need to fight for survival any more, we did it." Ex-Prime Minister Jean Chrétien savored the opportunity to take a swipe at Quebec separatists

by complimenting Acadians for finding "concrete ways to live in harmony instead of remaining prisoners of old grudges." In 1999 he chose Moncton, which is on the verge of replacing St. John as the province's most vibrant economy, as the site for a Francophonie conference of leaders from 49 nations where a majority or sizable minority speak French. This was the first time a French president visited the nearly 290,000 Acadians spread out among the provinces of New Brunswick (242,000), Nova Scotia (35,000), PEI (5,500) and Newfoundland (2,300). In August 2005 tens of thousands of Acadians celebrated their survival of the deportation 250 years earlier.

The province's bilingualism is now regarded as an asset instead of a liability. The percentage of anglophone children enrolling in French immersion courses is an impressive 11%. This is Canada's highest rate of such enrollment at the grade school level. McKenna showed his sensitivity to the need to accommodate francophones by immersing himself in the study of French and by opposing the Meech Lake accord on the grounds that it might ultimately endanger the rights of language minorities in every province.

In an era of cynicism about government, McKenna retained an astonishing popularity. A self-deprecating down-to-earth workaholic with a personal life beyond reproach, he is credited with social and economic improvements while laboring in

Confederation Bridge linking Prince Edward Island with mainland New Brunswick

Canada

**Baking bread in New Brunswick:
an Acadian village woman
in traditional garb**

difficult times. Extolling New Brunswick's strengths—sophisticated telecommunications, bilingual workers, and low property and labor costs—he lured companies into the province to counterbalance jobs lost in forestry and mining.

Convinced that he had accomplished his political objectives for New Brunswick, McKenna stepped down in 1997. In the 1999 provincial elections, restive voters opted for change and swept the 12-year-old Liberal government from power. Led by their new young leader, Bernard Lord, the Progressive Conservatives took power. In the June 2003 elections Lord's inability to do anything about the high cost of auto insurance nearly ended the Tory government. Advocating a 25 percent drop in rates, Shawn Graham's Liberals almost overtook the Tories, capturing 26 seats to Lord's 28. He ultimately replaced Lord as premier.

The completely bilingual and bicultural Lord (Acadian mother and anglophone father) had worked his way through law school at the Université de Moncton as a Toyota car salesman. He pushed language reforms to guarantee francophones more powers and rights. They can attend French-language schools and receive health care in their mother tongue. He has not disappeared from the Canadian political scene. He is one of the favorites to play a leadership role in the federal Conservative party some day. His perfect French would help the party enlarge its foothold in Quebec.

QUEBEC: In 1985, nine years after it had ascended to power, the *Parti Québécois* had to relinquish it. In 2007 it suffered an especially devastating electoral defeat, surpassed by two other Quebec parties. In a way, it had been the victim of its own success. French language and cultural rights within the province had been secured, and Canada had been prodded to become bilingual. Quebec had also modernized itself almost beyond recognition. As "masters in their own house," *Québécois* were ready to turn their attention more to personal achievement and to the down-to-earth problems of unemployment and economic revival. The PQ itself became divided over whether to cling to the dream of sovereignty. Neither the Tories nor the New Democrats are political forces in Quebec provincial politics; therefore neither has seats in the assembly.

Commenting on the Liberals' 1985 election victory, Lysiane Gagnon, columnist for *La Presse* of Montreal wrote: "Quebecers changed governments the way one changes banks—without passion, as a business decision. There are neither dreams nor exultation nor broken hopes." But dreams

and passions were reawakened in 1987, when René Lévesque died of a heart attack. The emotional outpouring sparked comparisons of the charismatic spiritual father of the PQ and his successor, the aloof Pierre Marc Johnson. The latter's replacement in 1987 was future PQ premier, Jacques Parizeau, whose wit, energy, professorial air, and economic record were only outdone by his fervor for Quebec sovereignty.

The Quebec Liberals are staunchly pro-federalist, and Bourassa met many times with Brian Mulroney to negotiate the Meech Lake accord. In 1987 he broke with almost a quarter century of Quebec tradition and hosted a banquet for the Queen. He presided over an enviable improvement in the economy of Quebec.

Bourassa's party had promised to relax restrictions on bilingual signs. However, in office Bourassa did nothing because the courts were reviewing the issue. After a temporary respite from language tensions, the flames were rekindled in 1988. The Supreme Court of Canada ruled that Bill 101 violates the freedom-of-expression guarantees in Quebec's own charter of rights by banning the use of non-French words on commercial signs. Nationalist groups immediately rose up against the court decision, showing just how volatile the language issue still is. Wishing to avoid a confrontation with Quebec nationalists, Bourassa announced Bill 178, which prohibits English on outside signs while permitting it on inside signs, providing that French is used more prominently. He also invoked the so-called "notwithstanding clause" in the 1982 Constitution to prevent any further court challenge.

He saw this move as a compromise, but it pleased almost nobody and detonated the most serious English-French confronta-

Traditional Acadian garb

"The Rocks," Hopewell Cape near Monckton, which are about 200 feet high until partially covered by the ocean at high tide.

setback in 1992 when its development plans collided with environmentalists and native claims. The 13,500 Cree living in Quebec maintained that the project is on their land and would poison their fish. Indeed, in 1912 the federal government devolved present-day northern Quebec, known to Indians as Ungava, to the province as an administrative convenience.

The Crees' opposition to the James Bay project, which would reduce the flow in the Great Whale and other rivers, found support among American environmental groups. This resulted in New York State's cancellation of its power contract with Quebec. This was devastating news for Quebec. In 1994 Parizeau had to put the project on hold indefinitely. In 2002 the Cree agreed to drop their lawsuits against the hydro plans on the Rupert and Eastmain rivers in perhaps the most important treaty signed with an Aboriginal group. They opened up their territory to mining, logging and industrial development by Hydro-Québec. In return, Quebec paid the Cree a minimum of Can$3.5 billion over 50 years and granted them a say in any development in order to protect traditional hunting and trapping rights. This deal was calculated to create 8,000 jobs and increase electricity production by about 8%.

In 2011 the Quebec government announced an ambitious 25-year plan to develop a large part of its vast northern and Arctic region, an area where, in Premier Jean Charest's words, "we have every resource imaginable." While industrial activity will be banned in some of the region, mining and industry will be allowed in other parts, all in close coordination with the local aboriginal populations. Not

tion since 1980. Hard-line *Québécois*, who were infuriated that English could again be used on some signs, demonstrated and threw fire bombs into the Montreal offices of the English-rights lobby group called Alliance Quebec, which later imploded in 2005 when the federal government cut off its funds. One young man climbed the large cross on top of Montreal's Mount Royal and sat there for 13 freezing hours in protest. Three anglophone cabinet members resigned, including Clifford Lincoln, who asserted: "rights are rights are rights. There are no inside and outside rights." Anglophone Quebecers felt betrayed and became uneasy again, while Anglophones all over Canada protested. Fears of emigration were reawakened. During the nine-year PQ rule, 140,000 left Quebec, and more than 400,000 departed over a two-decade span from 1976 and 1996.

The Meech Lake accord was former Prime Minister Brian Mulroney's attempt to create harmony by granting Quebec the status of "a distinct society" and by protecting minority language rights everywhere in Canada; it also would have secured Quebec's ratification of the 1982 Constitution. Its rejection angered Quebecers and reignited powerful nationalist sentiments. A saddened Hugh MacLennan, whose 1945 novel *Two Solitudes* had chronicled the cultural divide between francophones and anglophones, mused in 1989, one year before his death, about his French-speaking countrymen: "I wish we could get along with them . . . I just don't know if they want us anymore." There remains much ignorance about Quebec. A 1989 study showed that only 5% of the

stories in CBC or the *Globe and Mail* came from Quebec.

In making an unambiguous appeal for final and complete separation from Canada and in rejecting federalism of any kind as an option (which is why he rejected Meech Lake), the self-confident Parizeau differed from the humble populist, Lévesque, who always couched his pitch for sovereignty in the context of an undefined association with the rest of Canada. Parizeau, who speaks perfect English and has a doctorate in economics from the London School of Economics, argued that new social and economic conditions make independence more viable now. "I can rely on new strengths that Quebec did not have 20 years ago, when it was not at all obvious that Quebec entrepreneurs were capable of competing internationally. Now it is."

By improving the province's access to American markets, the North American Free Trade Agreement (NAFTA) further reduces Quebec's economic dependence on the rest of Canada. An independent Quebec would have to negotiate with Canada, the U.S. and Mexico to gain entry into that trilateral agreement. As an independent country it would be the United States' sixth-largest trading partner.

Both supporters and opponents of sovereignty rest their plans on economic prowess in Quebec. There have been some setbacks. The complex and expensive James Bay project was to be financed largely by exporting electricity to northeastern U.S. in order to supply cheap energy to companies lured into Quebec. However, the province suffered a severe

Canada

since the northern Alberta oil sands were exploited has there been such a grandiose attempt to develop the sparsely populated north. Charest also argued that this "Plan Nord" will strengthen Canada's disputed claims to the Northwest Passage. It "is an affirmation of sovereignty."

An independent Quebec would have to face the prospect that the Cree and the Inuit, supported by Ottawa, would take back more than half the present province. Quebec's relations with its 60,000 aboriginal peoples, most of whom prefer to speak English, were already strained over their claims also to be a "distinct society." Quebec's aboriginals find their most compelling arguments in the PQ's rhetoric. Cree Grand Chief Matthew Coon Come asserts: "If Canada is divisible, so is Quebec," a concept endorsed by Prime Minister Chrétien in 1996.

Inuit leaders have also put Quebec on notice that "we are not coming with you on a journey toward independence," as Zebedee Nungak put it. The Inuit of the northern third of Quebec moved a step closer to self-government in November 1999. They signed a political accord with Ottawa and Quebec setting up a commission to facilitate discussions leading to a government in their region called Nunavik. There are no roads linking Nunavik to the rest of the province. To bring the two parts closer together, the Quebec government is working on plans to construct roads to a few Nunavik communities.

Numerous anglophone groups in Quebec, supported by the federal government, picked up on the idea of partition in the event that Quebec breaks away from Canada. Examples are the Quebec Committee for Canada and the Committee for a New Quebec. Both proposed that any area in which francophones are not prominent, including suburbs of Montreal, remain with Canada. PQ leaders dismissed such warnings and proposals as nonsense.

Parizeau shrewdly played on the frictions between Quebec and the rest of Canada in rejecting what he saw as a flawed federalism. His solution: a series of referenda to take over powers from Ottawa, on the way to a sovereign Quebec. The political equation was further complicated by the formation in the federal parliament of a *Bloc Québécois*, led initially by Lucien Bouchard. The PQ supported it in the 1993 federal elections rather than Mulroney's Tories, as it had done in the prior two elections. This cost Mulroney valuable backing in Quebec and enabled the *Bloc Québécois* to become the second-largest party and official opposition in Ottawa.

In 1994 Quebecers had their clearest choice ever. Gone was the fuzzy middle ground of "sovereignty-association" *à la Lévesque*. The PQ now called for nothing short of separation. It said that a victory would be interpreted as a mandate to have the National Assembly make a "solemn declaration" of Quebec's intention to become independent. It would then approach Ottawa to negotiate terms and put the result to Quebec voters within 10 months of the election. A narrow plurality of Quebec's voters decided to give the PQ that chance.

The PQ noted with uneasiness that it had received only 44.7% of the popular votes, compared with the pro-federal Liberals' impressive 44.3%. This bode ill for the referendum Parizeau had pledged to hold in 1995. Even if he could woo many of the 6.5% of voters who had supported the *Action Démocratique du Quebec (ADQ)*, led by Mario Dumont and composed of moderate ex-Liberals of a separatist tinge, he faced an uphill struggle. Bouchard, who had lost a leg in 1994 to a frightening flesh-eating disease, began to express his opinion publicly that the separatist option should include close ties with Canada.

Quebec and Canada had changed significantly since the referendum on Quebec sovereignty in 1980. The presence of the *Bloc Québécois* as the official opposition in the House of Commons gave separatism a new respectability and boost. Bouchard was able to persuade Parizeau and Dumont to agree on a "soft" referendum question calling for negotiating with Ottawa an economic and political partnership with an independent Quebec. The 1995 referendum results show that a majority of Quebec francophones supported that concept.

This is one reason why there was such an outcry throughout Canada in the midst of the 1997 federal parliamentary elections when Parizeau published his memoirs, *For A Sovereign Quebec*, in which he admitted that he had been prepared to declare Quebec's independence immediately after a yes-vote in 1995, not after negotiations with Ottawa, as his party had proposed during the referendum campaign. Many think he deceived Quebec voters. In 2004 he published a letter in *La Presse* demanding that referenda be done away with and that the next *PQ* electoral victory be considered a mandate in itself to prepare for succession. Even within the PQ such ideas are scorned.

In the campaign, Parizeau stepped aside to allow Bouchard to energize it. A charismatic master of lofty emotion, he became a hero and savior in Quebec, the most popular figure since Lévesque. His oratorical skill brought separatists within a whisker of victory, winning 49.4% of the votes in a huge 94% turnout. This was 10 percentage points higher than in 1980. As in 1980, the difference was made by anglophones and immigrants, who voted overwhelmingly against independence, while 60% of francophones voted "yes."

Until the final days before the October 30, 1995, referendum the then Prime Minister Jean Chrétien chose to stand aloof from the debates in Quebec over separation, declaring that "I was elected not to talk about the constitution" and that "everybody knows where I stand. I come from Shawinigan. My province is Quebec. My country is Canada. My language is French. And they are all compatible." This aloofness was a serious blunder that hurt him in Canadian politics. Jean Charest was correct in saying that "winning a referendum doesn't mean you have solved the problem."

A confident Bouchard, who took over the premiership of Quebec from Parizeau in 1996, promised a new referendum by the year 2000, but he had to back off from that. He defiantly rejected any option but sovereignty, asserting: "no one is going to get us into sterile discussions we've been having for 30 years. No longer will sovereigntists be begging for anything from the rest of Canada." This attitude guaranteed that Quebec would vigorously test Canada's fragile unity for many years. Perhaps his mother best captured the mood of many *Québécois* at that time: "I've never met an English-speaking Canadian. But I'm sure they are as nice as any other foreigners."

The Quebec economy, although vigorous in general, has Canada's highest per capita debt, highest tax burden (42.2% of GDP, vs. 37.2% elsewhere), shortest work week and oldest population, as well as aggressive unionization and a determined unwillingness to change its generous but expensive social system. The safety net used to be offered by the Church and large families, but that has been replaced by the

Cree lands

most interventionist government in North America. Quebec's GDP in 2007 was 20% below that of Ontario and ranked 54th out of 60 North American states and provinces. Business interests solidly oppose sovereignty, and many withheld investments in the province until its political future was clarified. While investment has grown by 2.7% annually in Quebec, the other provinces are experiencing a 4.2% rise. By 2007 Quebec's share of Canadian private investment had declined dramatically from 23% in 1987 to below 18%.

Quebec economist Pierre Cléroux lamented: "we are not going in the same direction as the other provinces." University tuition was frozen for 13 years until Premier Charest vowed in 2007 to raise it slightly. Despite the freeze, Quebec has the lowest university attendance and degree-completion record in all of Canada.

The governing PQ resurrected the Commission to Protect the French Language, abolished in 1993, derisively known among anglophones as the "language police" or "tongue troopers" because of their linguistic repression. It pledged to enforce language laws strictly, which had been diluted since 1993 because of constitutional standoffs in Canada's Supreme Court and international pressure, including from the U.N. English became permissible on outdoor signs, so long as it appears at half the size of the equivalent French words. A Quebec Superior Court upheld this law in 2000 when two anglophone storeowners erected signs featuring equal-sized French and English lettering.

English-speaking Canadians who move to Montreal can send their children to English-language schools, but francophone and immigrant parents are not permitted to do so. Just how secular Quebec has become, especially in Montreal, was demonstrated in 1999 when the province replaced its Catholic and Protestant confessional school boards with 60 French-language, nine English-language, and three aboriginal boards. A constitutional amendment makes its school system entirely secular.

This seems logical in a province where church attendance among Catholics stands at 15%, the lowest rate in North America. The average age of priests is nearly 65, with empty seminaries providing few replacements. While 88% of *Québécois* say they believe in God, less than a third say they believe in the God portrayed by the Church. Only 34% believe there is a hell, compared with 49% in the rest of Canada. The 1999 *MacLean's*/CBC Poll revealed that Quebecers value individual rights and freedom to define one's own morality more highly than other Canadians; 70% strongly believe no one has the right to impose morality on others (52% in the rest of Canada), and 29% say they would support a 17-year-old

Trompe l'oeil in Old Town Quebec

daughter's decision to have an abortion, compared with 15% elsewhere. Sexual permissiveness is widespread, with 53% of births out of wedlock.

The province's share of Canada's population has shrunk from 27.9% in the early 1970s to 24.1% in 2001. While Quebec has one of the lowest birth rates in the western world, its situation is improving, and the province has gained a reputation as "parent-friendly. The first step was "bucks for babies": parents were paid $500 and $1,000 for the first two offspring respectively; subsequent children brought in as much as $8,000. The next was 200,000 subsidized day-care places. This costs parents only $7 per day. A parental leave policy that allows parents to take almost a year off at up to three-quarters of their salary is North America's most generous. The results are impressive: an 8% increase in the birth rate in 2006, and 2.6% in 2007. The fertility rate has risen to 1.66, which is higher than the national average, even if still under the replacement rate of 2.1.

Former Language Minister Louise Beaudoin lashed out at what she called "rampant bilingualism" in the public service and proclaimed 30 new measures to send the message of "French first!" Civil servants are required to get permission from superiors before making speeches in English. They may speak only French in meetings with Quebec-based companies and in dealing with the public by telephone or in person. The government no longer deals with Quebec-based compa-

nies that do not meet French language requirements in the workplace. More than eight of 10 francophones and over half of anglophones in Montreal already speak French on the job. All computer software must be available in French unless no French version exists.

In 1998 a new challenge emerged: Jean Charest resigned as federal chairman of the Progressive Conservative Party to assume the leadership of Quebec's Liberals. It was not easy for him to fight in Quebec for the cause of a united Canada. He cannot be so aggressive as to alienate the province's "soft nationalists," those who regard Canada as a sensible arrangement but give their emotional attachment to French Quebec. They are the voters who make the difference in provincial elections and referenda.

In 2001 Bouchard resigned as premier saying that he had failed to accomplish the PQ's dream of making Quebec an independent country. A decade later, in 2010, he remained extremely popular, but he had given up on Quebec sovereignty: "There's no referendum in sight, and I don't want any more defeats. . . . It remains just a dream."

His successor was Bernard Landry. A former optometrist from Joliette, Quebec, Landry was drawn into the separatist movement by Lévesque's vision and charisma and has embraced the sovereigntist gospel most of his adult life: "I am convinced not only that Canada has no use, but that it has been harmful."

Canada

He vowed that his government's priority would be secession. However, he discovered that the province's foundering economy and a changed environment in North America made it necessary to put his pet project on the back burner. PQ party membership dropped to 65,000 although the party contends that the number is still close to 100,000.

In April 2003 a political earthquake occurred in Quebec. The PQ was buried in a Liberal landslide in provincial elections. Led by Jean Charest, the Liberals won 45.9% of the votes and 76 seats, a solid majority in the 125-seat National Assembly. The PQ under Landry, who had predicted in the campaign that Quebec would become a sovereign state within 1,000 days after his party's victory, fell to 33.2% and only 45 seats. It was hurt by Mario Dumont's ADQ, a center-right party that pledged to postpone referenda. Dumont described his party's goal as autonomy for Quebec while rejecting a complete rupture with Canada. "Old-fashioned separatism has little appeal for younger voters."

The turning point was a televised debate two weeks before the election in which Landry was unable to counter Charest's question why former Premier Jacques Parizeau was again blaming the loss of the 1995 referendum on "money and the ethnic vote," a code for Jews and immigrants. The PQ declined steadily thereafter.

Parizeau's reference to the importance of immigrants backfired, but it points to an important demographic development in Quebec that is distressing for the PQ. About one in ten voters in Quebec (compared with 27% in Ontario) is an immigrant, and roughly 90% live in Montreal. With the birthrate plummeting, they make up a growing segment of the province's population. Although Quebec has for decades exercised its power to select its immigrants and to require that their children be educated in French, they feel little sympathy for the PQ's nationalist strivings. They have no stake in the historic English-French divide. But they have difficulties finding jobs; their unemployment rate in 2007 was 17.8%.

Equally important is the fact that nearly 70% of the province's 918,000 anglophones are bilingual, an increase of roughly 12% since 1991. They do not fight against the language laws any more, and indeed the majority accepts them. They are willing to marry Quebecers outside their anglophone suburbs. However, they continue to support overwhelmingly the Liberal party, Quebec's only outright federalist party. At the same time more and more francophones believe that the goal to protect their language has been achieved. They are coming out of their Montreal ghettos. Teenagers are no longer inclined to speak the old *joual* dialect and often find English-sounding names for bars and restaurants "cool." The result is that more and more Quebecers are tired of the old passionate language disputes, and this affects politics.

The long-term result of Bill 101 is that two-thirds of anglophones in Quebec are now bilingual, and more than half of those persons whose mother tongue is neither French nor English can now speak both. Francophones are no longer underdogs. When the bill had first been introduced, the median income of anglophone households was 20% to 30% higher than the provincial average. Wealth is spread more evenly in today's Quebec. Sponsors of Bill 101 had thought it would generate momentum toward independence, but it has had the opposite effect. By demonstrating that such a radical reform was possible within Confederation, it has deflated the separatist movement more than any measure that Ottawa could have taken. The bill itself has disappeared from the headlines even though language remains a touchy subject in Quebec.

Charest exploited this language fatigue, knowing that a political system based on the former lingual divisions was overdue for a shakeup. He quickly pursued a conservative agenda, promising to "re-engineer" the way government operates. Nothing was sacred, and he let it be known that the time of state intervention, taken for granted after the Quiet Revolution of the 1960s, was over. He initiated tax cuts and reductions in subsidies and tax breaks.

The results were a disaster. His determination turned his opponents into enemies and jolted the powerful public-sector unions, which are closely tied to the PQ,

Hon. Lucien Bouchard

into protest and rebellion. By year's end, two-thirds of *Québécois* were displeased with him and his government, and support for secession began to rise again. Quebec voters are stubborn and insist on being led where they want to go. They had dismissed the PQ from office in the 2003 elections, not given Charest a mandate to run the province as he had tried to do.

Humbled and discredited, Charest was forced to change course. Rather than forging ahead with privatization and outsourcing, he held public forums to consult the people on the changes. He offered a budget heavy on welfare spending and announced an anti-poverty policy. He continued to pursue the streamlining of government and tax cuts in order to bring taxes down to the Canadian average.

He was not helped by a damaging federal Liberal scandal that provided tens of millions of dollars in taxpayers' money to friendly advertising companies in the province to sway Quebec opinion away from independence after 1995. Most of the money was simply pocketed by the businesses. But *Québécois* were insulted that anglophone Canadians, who accuse them often unfairly of blatant corruption, would engage in such sordid tactics themselves. Even though the *Bloc Québécois* assured Quebec voters that a vote for it was not a vote for independence, the party benefited from the scandal in the 2004 federal elections. It captured 54 of the province's 75 seats and forced the federal Liberals into a minority government. In 2006 it slipped to 51 seats and only 42% of the votes, far short of the majority it would need to secure independence for the province.

The January 2006 federal elections caused a political earthquake in Quebec. The Conservatives gained a foothold in the

Dr. Jacques Parizeau

province, rocketing from 9% to 24.6% of the votes (vs. the Liberals' 20.7%) and ten seats. By promising such things as flexible federalism, decentralization and Quebec's own representation in international organizations like UNESCO and by beginning practically every speech in Ottawa in French, Prime Minister Stephen Harper won a lot of support, not just in Montreal, but in the eastern hinterland, including Quebec City, where nationalists were traditionally strong. He moved the Conservatives into the broad middle ground that had formed after the federal Liberals and the separatists had radicalized their positions between centralizing federalism and outright separation. The separatists no longer have an easily identifiable enemy.

It is ironic that *Québécois*, who had been unhappy during a 39-year period when prime ministers from Quebec ruled them for 36 years, are now generally pleased with a western anglophone at the helm in Ottawa. Stephen Harper gave them much to be happy about. In 2006 he brought his entire cabinet to Quebec City to celebrate his close relationship with the people of Quebec; this was the first time since the 1950s that this had happened. Later in the year, he outmaneuvered both the *Bloc Québécois* and the federal Liberals to persuade an overwhelming majority in Parliament, including all four federal parties, to adopt a historic resolution declaring that Quebecers (not Quebec) "form a nation within a united Canada." It refers to a people, not a government or a state. Although this formulation has no constitutional significance and does not imply that Canada is indeed a union of "two founding peoples," it is the first time Ottawa has recognized the people of Quebec as a "nation."

Harper met with Premier Charest more frequently than with any other premier and more than any Canadian prime minister since the 1960s. His 2007 federal budget corrected what he called "fiscal imbalance" by awarding an extra $2.1 billion transfer payment to Quebec, which already received $2.2 billion more each year from Ottawa than it contributed. He also steered a $900 million Strategic Aerospace and Defence Initiative to Montreal and permitted Quebec the prestige of occupying its own seat at UNESCO.

In November 2005 the PQ elected a dashing young (39) André Boisclair as its new leader. He was the first PQ leader not belonging to the generation that had founded the party in the 1960s. But he advocated a radical program for a quick referendum after the PQ returns to power, followed "as soon as possible" by a unilateral "declaration of national sovereignty" in the event that even the barest majority says yes. He pledged to ignore the Clarity Act. He parted with the party's

former promises of a "partnership" with Canada and a year of negotiations leading to secession.

Such a radical program is out of sink with the province's majority. To make things worse for the PQ, two of Quebec's cultural icons, playwrights Michel Tremblay and Robert Lepage, admitted in 2006 to have lost some of their faith in the separatist cause. In Tremblay's words, "it was a beautiful dream, and one must respect such dreams, but it will never be more than a dream if we keep looking at it in economic terms first." He remembered that "the driving force was our pride in being the beacon of francophone culture in America—not the economy."

The uproar and panicked bickering that followed reveals a real dilemma for the PQ. It had indeed downplayed culture to broaden its appeal to include immigrant groups and not just francophones. Another way of expressing the PQ's dilemma is that it must assume power in order to achieve sovereignty. Yet it has to soften its platform in order to win that power. But then it lacks the strong mandate needed to proceed toward separation. It also competes in a greatly changed Quebec where language inequalities have been eliminated. The PQ and Boisclair had trouble finding new arguments to fire up supporters for a new push for secession. This was especially hard with a conciliatory prime minister and a *Québécoise* governor general in Ottawa. The smoother the relations between Ottawa and Quebec, the greater the decline for the separatists. Prime Minister Harper astutely adjusted his policy to the shifting ground in Quebec politics.

Noticing the PQ's disorientation and shaky leadership, the unpopular Premier

Premier Jean Charest
Leader, Quebec's *Liberal Party*

Charest called an early election in 2007. His Liberal party lost its majority, falling from 72 to 48 seats and from 46% to 33.1%; this produced Quebec's first minority government since 1878. But the PQ fared much worse, declining from 45 to 36 seats and only 28.3% of the votes (down from 33.2%). Both parties experienced their worst results since 1976 (in the case of the Liberals) and 1970 (for the PQ).

The primary victim of the PQ's electoral failure was Boisclair, who was promptly replaced as PQ leader by former social worker and ex-cabinet member in several PQ governments, Pauline Marois. Her condition for acceptance was that the party stop its squabbling over a timetable for a future referendum and get back in touch with the real-life concerns of many voters. A pragmatist, she argued that rad-

Quebec City in winter

Canada

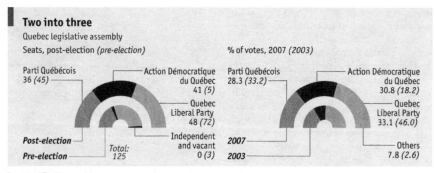

Two into three

Quebec legislative assembly

Seats, post-election (pre-election)

Parti Québécois 36 (45)

Action Démocratique du Québec 41 (5)

Quebec Liberal Party 48 (72)

Post-election

Pre-election

Total: 125

Independent and vacant 0 (3)

% of votes, 2007 (2003)

Parti Québécois 28.3 (33.2)

Action Démocratique du Québec 30.8 (18.2)

Quebec Liberal Party 33.1 (46.0)

2007

2003

Others 7.8 (2.6)

Source: *The Economist*

icalizing the PQ "would be a recipe for marginalization, or even extinction."

The real surprise was Mario Dumont's conservative and moderately nationalist ADQ, which surged to within seven seats of Charest's minority government: it leapt from 5 to 41 seats and from 18.2% to 30.8% of the votes. A 36-year-old economics graduate from Concordia University, Dumont had led a walk-out from the Liberal party in 1992 because the party did not favor an independent Quebec. However, after the failed referendum in 1995, in which he gave lukewarm support for sovereignty, he shifted his position between the extremes of federalism and hard-line separation.

According to a 2009 poll, three-fourths of Quebecers did not believe sovereignty would ever happen, and 54% were against the idea entirely. In the wake of the fabulously successful Vancouver Winter Olympic Games in February 2010, fewer than a third of Québécois supported the notion of having their own Olympic team. That is wonderful news for Canadian unity. Even the province's youth, once the hotbed of nationalist sentiment, seem uninterested. Support for sovereignty is at its lowest ebb in nearly four decades.

Election year 2008 reflected this in Quebec. In the October federal elections the Bloc Québécois won the most seats in Quebec, but saw its vote decrease by 4%, the second lowest in its history, after a campaign in which it did not say a single word about independence. It was the Liberals, not the Conservatives, who gained from the BQ's losses. Prime Minister Harper blunted his ability to reach out to francophones in Quebec by aggressively attacking the BQ and by sneering at cultural subsidies in Quebec.

In Quebec's December provincial elections only seven weeks later, in which the economy was the main issue, the PQ, led for the first time by Pauline Marois, Quebec's first female leader, did better than predicted. One reason was that sovereignty was banished from her campaign. She noted in an interview: "We might well have a referendum some day. I'm keeping the door open." Her party captured 35.15% of the votes and 51 seats, while the

ADQ crashed to only 16.35% of the votes and a mere seven seats.

Pauline Marois's cold feet about advocating concrete steps and timetables toward sovereignty made the PQ ranks restive. She got a 93% endorsement as leader in the party's April 2011 national congress in return for allowing the hardliners to put language and sovereignty front and center again. If they get their way, Bill 101 would be expanded to post-secondary schools, and businesses with fewer than 50 employees would have to obey the French Language Charter. This is tricky terrain for the PQ: polls in 2011 indicated that two-thirds of Quebecers think parents should have the right to school their children in the language of their choice. These objectives also became grist for the May 2, 2011, federal elections, when the Bloc Québécois was practically wiped out in Quebec, losing all but four of its 49 seats.

Jean Charest became the first Quebec premier since the 1950s to win three terms in a row. He got the majority he was seeking, winning 42% of the votes and 66 of the 125 seats. However, his government is beset by scandal in the construction industry. Montreal seems unable to deal with an endemic culture of corruption and organized crime that is driving more and more citizens into the suburbs and more and more businesses out of the province.

However, when *Maclean's* published a cover story on October 4, 2010, calling Quebec "The Most Corrupt Province in Canada," Charest condemned such "Quebec bashing" and demanded an apology to Quebecers. The House of Commons expressed its "profound sadness at the prejudice displayed and the stereotypes employed by *Maclean's* magazine to denigrate the Quebec nation." Nevertheless, *La Presse* termed the claim "undeniable." This was supported by political columnist Vincent Marissal, who noted that "every Quebec media outlet has drawn similar conclusions."

Despite Charest's abysmal 13% approval rating, the lowest in Canada, he faces no revolt in his Liberal party. The success of the province's economy is the reason why he rules unchallenged. He is

a survivor and a fierce campaigner, so he can be expected to remain in power.

ONTARIO: Ontario has traditionally been Canada's political pivot and economic motor, despite the growth of the West, the ambitions of the Maritimes and the assertiveness of Quebec. It has 38% of Canada's population and produces about a third of Canada's wealth. Former Premier David Peterson was once asked if he was uncomfortable about Ontario's becoming wealthier while other regions were suffering. He answered: "One of the things that keeps this country together is that everybody hates Ontario, and what keeps Ontario together is that everybody hates Toronto, and what keeps Toronto together is that everybody hates Bay Street" (Canada's Wall Street).

But its preeminence is being challenged by Canada's new economic power centers: Alberta, British Columbia, oil- and resource-rich Saskatchewan and Newfoundland and Labrador. Ontario does not play the kind of leadership role in Canada it once did. Although it is by no means a poor province, its economy has been performing sluggishly for a decade or so, and much of the troubled auto industry is within its borders. In the decade from 2001 its per capita GDP remained virtually unchanged. The surging West's combined GDP surpassed that of Ontario for the first time in 2008. Ontario now embarrassingly receives equalization payments as a "have-not" province.

Toronto's status as the country's premier city is being challenged for the first time in a century: this time by Calgary. The city has budget and infrastructure problems, and its manufacturing sector is in bad shape, having shed 100,000 jobs in the five years to 2008. But it continues to attract 40% of all immigrants to Canada; 44% of its residents are foreign-born, well above the province's 27%. It also remains the country's financial center. Private wealth is pouring into art galleries, theaters and new museums. It tries hard to retain its image as a "city on the rise."

Canada's largest province is not officially bilingual. However, the government

Premier Dalton McGuinty

tive with nearby American states, and started paying down the provincial debt.

In 1999, a reform compressed high school from five to four years and stressed more math and science. Since 2000, pupils are subject to a code of conduct that includes reciting the Oath of Citizenship and pledging allegiance to the Queen. It is hoped that the oath and code will instill respect for Canada and make schools safer. In 2001 he offered vouchers granting tax credits to parents who send their child to a private school.

For many voters the pace of the changes was too fast. In 1997 the provincial gov-

ernment stepped into a political minefield by introducing Bill 103. This unified the Toronto area's six municipalities and created a regional government of Metropolitan Toronto for a city of about 4.6 million. The idea was to eliminate inefficient redundancy in urban services and reduce the public payroll. Suddenly signs reading "Vote No to megacity" appeared everywhere, and three-fourths of voters opposed the merger in separate referenda in the six municipalities. Nevertheless, the cost-cutting government vowed to ignore the results and enact the reform, which it did.

extends French-language services to Ontario's half million francophones (about 5% of the total population). When an Ontario court ruled that under the Charter of Rights francophones are entitled to an education in French, the province quickly complied. Toronto is the most ethnically diverse city in North America. In 2002 Ontario received its first Aboriginal lieutenant-governor in Canada: James Bartleman, a Minjikanig Indian and former Canadian ambassador to the EU.

After the 1995 provincial elections, Tory leader Mike Harris, who heralded a "common sense revolution," became premier. Never ducking a fight, he took on almost every established group in the province. He undertook the 1990s' most radical alteration of government in Canada. In fact, in his six and a half years in power, he changed Ontario more than any other premier in the preceding 50 years. His calls for tax reductions and balancing budgets resonated throughout Canada. He also changed Ontario's relationship with Ottawa and the other provinces. Before him, Ontario's role in Canada had been as national builder and national conciliator, putting the country's interests ahead of those of the province. Instead, he forcefully advanced Ontario's interests with Ottawa. His Ontario-first stance temporarily changed the balance of power in federal-provincial relations.

By 1997 he had eliminated 10,600 civil service jobs, saying: "government's role is not to see how many people we can employ." He pared social assistance payments by a fifth while instituting a workfare program for recipients. He ordered the closure of dozens of hospitals by the end of the century, and he battled doctors over health care costs. He revamped environmental and labor laws to make them more business-friendly. He cut the provincial income tax rate by 30% over three years. With a hefty budget surplus in 2000, the government cut personal taxes, halved corporate taxes over six years in a bid to lure businesses and make Ontario more competi-

Toronto's Rogers Centre (formerly SkyDome), one of the most modern sports facility in the world
Photo: Ian Steer

113

Canada

Portage Avenue looking east to Main Street, Winnipeg   Photo: Henry Kalen

Public opinion experts noted a profound change in Ontarians' values in the 1990s: there is less reliance on government and more self-reliance. Harris depended on this. In the 1999 provincial elections, he and his Tory party achieved a come-from-behind victory, becoming the first sitting government in Ontario since 1967 to win back-to-back majorities. In 2002 he stepped down, leaving the party trailing far behind Dalton McGuinty's Liberals, which won power emphatically in October 2003. Promising not to increase taxes but to roll back tax breaks promised by the Tories and to reinvest that money in schools and hospitals.

No sooner was McGuinty in power than he discovered a staggering $6 billion deficit despite the Tories' campaign talk of balanced books. The Liberal government felt forced to take such belt-tightening measures as revoking corporate tax cuts and looking for ways to give private firms a larger role in building and operating hospitals and other public services. To help clean up the air, his government in June 2004 banned smoking in all bars and restaurants.

Voters reelected his party in October 2007 with 42% of the votes and 71 of 107 seats. The Conservatives, led by the aptly named John Tory, won 31.6% and 26 seats, while the NDP garnered 16.8% and 10 seats. In a referendum, voters also turned down the proportional representation electoral system. The low turnout was a new record for the province: 52.8%. The election's defining issue was the funding of religious schools. Ontario is the only province that pays the whole cost for attendance to Roman Catholic Schools (reflecting the fact that a third of its residents are Catholic), but it covers none of the expenses for schools of any other religion. John Tory's proposal to extend free education to all faiths raised the specter of taxpayer-financed Islamic *madrassas* to train terrorists.

McGuinty also seeks to strengthen the province's finances by demanding from Ottawa some of the $23 billion excess in what Ontario pays into the federation and what it gets out of it. He argues that this money is needed at home for his top priority—education. He knows well, however, that because of the historically ingrained anti-Central Canada sentiments across the

Hon. Greg Selinger

country, no other provinces would support Ontario in a fight with Ottawa.

Perhaps he should be more worried about the unity of his own province. There are renewed rumblings in the northwestern part of Ontario, comprising 60% of the territory but only 2% of the population, for secession from Ontario and joining neighboring Manitoba. Given the economic distress caused by the downturn in the paper and pulp industry, the citizens there feel neglected by distant Toronto.

MANITOBA: Manitoba was traditionally one of the few Canadian provinces in which there were real ideological differences between the two main parties that alternate in power: the NDP and the Conservatives. The divisions were created in the Winnipeg General Strike in 1919. Manitoba enjoys one of the country's highest economic growth rates and the lowest unemployment rate (5.2% in 2011, vs. 7.6% in Canada). It has Western Canada's most diversified economy. It is increasingly shifting away from agriculture (which constitutes just 5% of its economy) and food-related industries and into other forms of manufacturing, financial services, transportation, and mining and petroleum production. This makes it well-equipped to deal with economic downturns. Manitoba is sharing in the West's economic renaissance.

Among the few negative things to happen to Manitoba in recent years occurred in 1997 when it experienced its worst flood of the century along the Red River's 100-mile run from the U.S. border to Lake Winnipeg. The raging waters temporarily drove 25,000 inhabitants from their homes, 8,000 in the outskirts of Winnipeg. The center of Winnipeg was spared disaster. An $800-million expansion of the Red River floodway is designed to minimize this danger in the future. But disaster struck again in May 2011, when the Manitoba government declared a state of emergency to deal with "unprecedented and historic" flooding of the Assiniboine River. About 2,000 people were displaced, and 800 soldiers were sent to top up existing dikes, fortify unprotected properties and deploy mobile flood protection equipment.

Despite a good economic situation, voters decided to change horses in 1999, and a new premier, Gary Doer of the NDP, was sworn in on October 5. A self-confessed "recovering workaholic," whom *Chatelaine* magazine had proclaimed one of Canada's 12 sexiest men in 1990, Doer had been working hard for a decade and a half to give his party a more moderate image. Preferring the label "social democrat" to "socialist," he stated, "I believe in a mixed economy. Some of the old debates about business versus labour are outdated." Doer rode high in the polls by showing a knack for negotiating a middle way between entrenched business and labor interests. His toil and a series of defeats paid off when the NDP was twice reelected. In 2007 his NDP won 48% of the votes and 36 seats, the Conservatives 37.9% of 16 seats, and the Liberals 12.4% and only two seats.

On October 19, 2009, Doer passed the premiership to Greg Selinger, MLA from St. Boniface since 1999 and former minister for both finance and French language services. He received a Bachelor of Social Work from the University of Manitoba, a Masters in Public Administration from Queens University, and a PhD from the London School of Economics. He will lead the NDP in the next provincial election on October 4, 2011. Doer was named as Canada's ambassador to the United States, a post that will benefit from his well-developed negotiation skills and the fact that he had been in the U.S. more than any other premier. He personally knows all four former governors in President Barak Obama's cabinet.

The capital city of Winnipeg, where 60% of the province's population lives, is experiencing a worrying loss in population, especially by the young, educated and well-trained. In 2005 alone, 22,000 left Manitoba, the highest number since 1990, despite relatively low unemployment. It is the only western province experiencing a net out-migration. Enrollment has dramatically fallen in some neighborhood schools. Winnipeg also has the highest crime rate of any large Canadian city, double the national average. Manitobans' disposable income lags $2,400 behind that of Saskatchewan and $10,000 behind that of Alberta.

The question of extending francophone language rights in Manitoba has been an enduring problem and has a long and bitter history. In the 1870 Manitoba Act that brought Manitoba into the Confederation, the use of French in the courts, legislature and law was guaranteed. However, the percentage of anglophones climbed steadily, and in 1890 the provincial government declared that English was the only official language. The once vibrant francophone population became gradually assimilated until, by the late 1970s,

Wheat fields and town of Minnedosa, Manitoba.   Photo: Henry Kalen

only about 50,000 (or approximately 5% of the total population), remained, scattered in 30 communities across the province and conducting most of their daily affairs in English. Only in tiny Ste-Anne, near Winnipeg, did French survive as the main language. Because of immersion schools, adult language education, and offspring of marriages between anglophones and francophones, the number of French speakers doubled to over 100,000 by the end of the century.

In 1979 the federal Supreme Court ruled that the 1890 law was unconstitutional. This ruling raised serious questions about the validity of 4,500 provincial laws that had been passed only in English. The then Conservative government in Manitoba began translating some of the laws. But the issue reached center stage in 1981 when a francophone lawyer from Winnipeg, Roger Bilodeau, challenged the constitutionality of a speeding ticket written in English only. Faced with the mind-boggling threat that a court might declare most of the province's laws to be invalid, the government worked out a deal with the *Societé Franco-Manitobaine:* 400 laws would be translated into French (at the federal government's expense), and some French language services in government agencies would be expanded. The government put the substance of this agreement into legislation and introduced it into the assembly.

The Conservatives in Manitoba were willing to allow the translation of 400 laws, but they fought against any constitutional recognition of French as an official language in the province. Their opposition and a deafening anglophone outcry against the legislation prevented it from being enacted. Francophone activists vowed to continue the long struggle in the courts. The situation was most uncomfortable for ex-Prime Minister Brian Mulroney, a bilingual Quebecer, whose firm support of French language rights was essential to his Conservative party's electoral chances in Quebec. He went to Winnipeg and argued strongly in favor of francophone rights, a move which alienated many Manitoban Tories.

The year 1985 brought a dramatic turn-around in Manitoba. The Canadian Supreme Court ruled unanimously that all laws enacted in the province since 1890 were invalid. To head off legal chaos, the government engineered an agreement on a timetable for translating the existing laws. As a result, the entire French-language controversy wilted in importance and ceased for the time being to plague the province's political life. In 1988 it reappeared with a vengeance in response to Quebec's decision to disregard a Supreme Court ruling permitting English-language signs. Manitoba's government immediately announced that its support of the Meech Lake accord would be rescinded, a move that ultimately killed the accord. In 1992 the Supreme Court ordered the creation of a Manitoba-wide all-francophone school district, in which 75% of the instruction would be in French. Perhaps a retired liquor board manager best captured the mood of more and more Westerners when he said: "Bilingualism is a bunch of horse manure. I don't accept this business of us being bilingual and Quebec being French only."

Canada

SASKATCHEWAN: Only 60 years ago, this province, which is the size of Texas, depended almost entirely upon a one-crop economy. One of its few claims to fame was that all Royal Canadian Mounted Police are trained at a depot founded on a creek crossing known originally as Pile of Bones. It was made the capital of the Northwest Territories and soon thereafter renamed Regina after Queen Victoria.

Today Saskatchewan accounts for 40% of all cultivated land in Canada. Its average farm size has risen from 400 to 1,152 acres since 1936. It produces 60% of Canada's wheat (80% of its durum), a third of its oats and barley and about a third of its oil seeds. But by 2005 agriculture represented only 7% of the province's GDP, down from an earlier 50%.

It also has impressive mineral resources, which now contribute more to its economy than does farming. It has oil, including bitumen-like oil sands in the northwest, which are part of the same geological formation as those found in neighboring Alberta. Oil-sands Quest from Calgary had by 2008 invested $160 million in exploration of Saskatchewan's oil sands. The province is now the ninth biggest supplier of oil to the U.S. although America's Energy and Independence Act may limit purchases of

Regina, with the Legislative Building (upper portion) set in beautiful Wascana Park
Government of Saskatchewan

Brad Wall
Premier of Saskatchewan

pollution-producing oil from the sands. The U.S. buys more oil from the province than from Kuwait.

Saskatchewan possesses natural gas and low-grade brown lignite coal. It possesses the world's largest carbon sequestration project near Weyburn. Six thousand tons of carbon dioxide emissions from a synthetic fuel plant in North Dakota are piped across the border each day and pumped underground. It has the world's largest recoverable supply of potash (over 40%), which is used for fertilizer. Backed by the federal government in 2010, Premier Wall blocked the hostile takeover of Potash Corporation of Saskatchewan (PCS), which had been privatized in 1989, by the Anglo-Australian mining giant, BHP Billiton. This would have been Canada's biggest-

ever corporate takeover. BHP Billiton is already building the world's biggest potash mine near the village of Jansen, 100 miles (150 kilometers) east of Saskatoon. However, this site will not yield ore until 2015 at the earliest.

It has some of the globe's highest grade uranium deposits and produces more than one-fourth of the world's supply. Premier Wall boasted: "We are the Saudi Arabia of uranium." But it cannot enrich uranium since Canada is not one of the few countries permitted by international treaty to do so. Saskatoon-based Cameco, the world's largest uranium processor, began in 1997 to process nuclear material from former Soviet warheads as part of an international accord to reduce atomic weapons after the Cold War ended.

Its dependence on the prices of grain and other commodities such as oil, potash and uranium, means that its economy booms when prices are high and suffers when they are low. Prices were low for a long time, and this necessitated government overspending and a large deficit, which the government had to confront by slashing public spending and jobs, freezing wages, and selling off some of the province's largest publicly owned corporations, including Potash Corporation of Saskatchewan and the gas utility, SaskEnergy.

Saskatchewan had always been fertile ground for the NDP, which grew out of radical farmer movements that bloomed during the Great Depression. It had ruled off and on for over a half century. The province was shaken in 1988 by its decision to repeal a law requiring the use of both French and English in the courts and provincial assembly and the translation of all past and present laws into French. This upset Saskatchewan's francophones, who constitute 2.3% of the total population. Voters meted out cruel revenge on the *Tories* in the 1991 provincial elections. The NDP won by a landslide and ruled for the next 16 years.

By 1995 Saskatchewan boasted a budget surplus and became the first province to balance its budget. For a while, the NDP ruled over a prospering province. Its population was growing and stood at over one million. Its agriculture was more diversified than ever. The number of oil and gas wells drilled rose steadily, and its potash sector did well. However, the subsequent collapse of commodity prices especially hurt Saskatchewan.

For a while, it was in deep trouble. After 1986 the number of small farms dropped by more than 20,000 due to shrinking farm subsidies, forfeitures and drought. Many were bought up by large, intensive farm operations with hired management. The rural population was leaving the villages in droves and moving into Regina, Saskatoon and neighboring Alberta. The overall population fell from 1,134,000 in 2002 to only 994,843 in 2003. One saw abandoned buildings all along Saskatchewan's highways.

But by 2008 the population had risen again to over one million, and it has the fastest population growth and lowest unemployment rate of any province. A commodities-fueled boom has brought greater prosperity to the entire province and has reversed the decades-long population exodus. Investments are pouring in. Perhaps most unexpectedly, Saskatchewan joined Alberta, BC and most recently Newfoundland as a "have" province, no longer entitled to federal equalization payments. Ontario slipped to embarrassing "have-not" status and now has a per capita GDP lower than Saskatchewan's.

The inner city of Regina was in particular trouble. It is one of the poorest areas in urban Canada, with almost a third of residents dependent on government aid. Its poorest people are Aboriginals, who are fleeing reservations and now constitute 42% of North Central Regina's population. While Statistics Canada reports that Aboriginals are doing better in most urban centers, Regina remains a conspicuous exception. However, there were noticeable improvements by 2008. A new sense of optimism had taken hold in the city, as new funding was found for youth employment and skills training programs and other initiatives. There is also greater interaction between city hall and the aboriginal community. Creeland Mini-mart, the downtown reserve's first business, began pumping gas and selling snacks.

The last NDP premier was Lorne Calvert (NDP), a United Church minister, who grew up in a working-class neighborhood of Moose Jaw. He led his party to a narrow victory in 2003. His allegation that the opposition would sell the province's crown corporations was a key factor in his victory.

He tried this tactic again in the 2007 elections, but to no avail. He faced a much strengthened Saskatchewan Party, which had been created in 1997 by many Tories and joined by some Liberals. It had become the dominant conservative alternative to the NDP. Its first leader, Elwin Hermanson, is a farmer who pursued a tax-cutting, government reduction agenda. He had come within a whisker of becoming premier. He stepped down as party leader after a second defeat and was replaced by Brad Wall, a young lawyer who moderated the party.

In 2007 Wall's Saskatchewan Party gained 10 seats for a total of 38, with 50.9% of the votes, while Calvert's NDP dropped an equal number of seats for a total of 20, with 37.2% of the votes. In 2011 Wall was the most popular premier in Canada, enjoying a 63% approval rating.

Commenting on the province's rising fortunes, Jim Marshall, chief economist at the Saskatchewan Institute of Public Policy, said "we're not your father's Saskatchewan. It's a different place, and that's not well known." Perhaps it was a positive omen that Regina's professional football team, the Roughriders, won the CFL's 2007 Grey Cup for the first time in 18 years. As good neighbors, they ceded the cup the following year to the Calgary Stampeders. In 2009 they blew the Grey Cup by having 13 players on the field for a key play. In Canada that is only one too many, but it was a championship loser nevertheless.

Saskatoon brought glory back to the province the next year by being named Canada's second-"smartest" and second-

"most cultured" city (after Victoria and right above Regina) in *Maclean's* third annual ranking of Canadian cities. In terms of "social engagement," it topped the list. Thus, the city that has long been the brunt of jokes for being a hick town in the middle of nowhere emerges as a leading center of learning and culture.

ALBERTA: This province, named for Queen Victoria's husband, enjoys the fruits of its oil and gas wealth. Oil revenues swelled the province's treasury and the Alberta Heritage Savings Trust Fund, which is to be used toward the long-term development of the province and toward lightening Albertans' tax burden. Alienation and resentment in western Canada, so familiar in the nation's history, survives. But it is weaker now that an Albertan is Canada's prime minister. There is little support for secession from Canada at this prosperous time despite a 2006 poll in the *National Post* showing that a third of Western Canadians (and 42% of Albertans) thought the western provinces should explore setting up their own country. Basically Albertans want the federal government to leave them alone.

In 1992 Ralph Klein, a former folksy environment minister and mayor of Calgary, became premier. He was one of the most colorful figures in Canadian politics. A one-time high school dropout, he became a celebrated local TV reporter in the 1970s, known for his talent in getting stories from the street level. He cultivated contacts with biker gangs, prostitutes, and Indian groups. Sometime called "Red-neck Ralph" because of his undiplomatic language, he benefited considerably from his image as an extroverted down-to-earth man of the people. He launched to "Ralph's Revolution." His Albertan agenda dominated Canadian political debates. He demonstrated that governments can cut costs deeply and quickly and still post impressive victories.

He was determined to resolve the financial crisis without raising taxes, and he made reductions in almost every kind of government service. By 1997 he had re-

Canada

Hon. Ed Smelmach

Hon. Ralph Klein

duced government expenditures by 20%, cut thousands of positions from the civil service, closed hospitals and slashed welfare rolls. Alberta led Canada in deregulation and privatization. Car licensing, liquor retailing and electricity distribution are in private hands.

Klein pushed through a law mandating a balanced budget and requiring that three-quarters of any budget surplus be used to pay off debt. In 1995 he could announce Alberta's first budget surplus in a decade, and a decade later the province had a surplus of over $10 billion, the country's highest economic growth and lowest unemployment (3.4% in 2007, up to 5.4% in 2009). As energy prices climbed, so did royalties from C$3.2 billion between 1993–99 to C$7 billion in 2004; until the recession commenced in the fall of 2008, they were expected to top C$12 billion by 2010. With the world's second-

largest oil reserves (175 billion barrels) after Saudi Arabia, those Albertan royalties and budget surpluses were thought to keep rising. It has the lowest provincial personal tax rates (a flat-tax of 10.5%, Canada's first), and it is the only province without a provincial sales tax.

In 2005 Alberta paid off its debt, the only province to do so; the average debt burden in the other nine provinces is about 30% of provincial GDP. In 2006 the government sent each of its 3.2 million citizens a "resource rebate" of $400, dubbed "Ralph bucks." With all that wealth, no wonder Ontario Premier Dalton McGuinty called Alberta "the elephant in the room" when the 10 provincial premiers meet.

In the fall of 2008, oil and natural gas prices plummeted by two-thirds, while the world fell into recession. Alberta produces two-thirds of Canada's supplies of both energy sources. Sixty per cent of

its crude oil is derived from tar sands, but these sources are under increasing scrutiny by its main customer: the United States. It is feared that the 2007 Energy Independence and Security Act, which includes a ban on the U.S. government purchasing alternative fuels that produce more carbon emissions than conventional petroleum, could apply to the oil sands, whose production is indeed much more polluting. Greenpeace succeeded in putting the oil sands on the green radar screen, and some European companies are considering selling their investments in the sands.

Albertans dismiss these threats and say that if the Americans and Europeans do not want their oil, Alberta will build a pipeline to the west coast and ship it to China. Indeed, in 2009 state-owned Petro-China purchased a majority stake in two tar-sands projects. However, there are local objections, especially from Aboriginal groups, to such a pipeline to the West Coast. The preferred pipeline is the Keystone XL, which would take oil all the way from Alberta to Texas and to refineries along the way. Since it would cross the U.S. border, the Secretary of State must give the green light.

Albertans had suffered an economic bust in the 1980s and were experiencing it again. For the first time in almost two decades, its budget is in deficit—by $6.9 billion. The Heritage Fund shrank to $15.8 billion by 2009, and no contribution was made. Many Klein-era perks were pruned. As the country's economic engine, the province's bad luck negatively affects the rest of Canada.

Alberta's economy is helped in bad times because it has become increasingly diversified. By 2001 the energy sector represented only 21% of the province's GDP, down from 40% in 1985. The manufacturing, technology, service and wholesale trade sectors are burgeoning. New industries are pouring in. Buoyed by a prosperous farm economy and rising oil and gas prices until late 2008, the province outperformed the Canadian economy in every year since 1990 except one. It has the highest per capita disposable income, the highest GDP per capita, and the highest rate of job creation in Canada. With all that money pouring in, the provincial government temporarily put aside much of its earlier fiscal discipline. In Klein's final years, spending rose by 10% per annum.

The most visible sign of Alberta's dynamic economy is Calgary, which is the country's wealth magnet. It is second only to Toronto as a corporate head-office center. The Ontario capital has 10 of the largest 20 Canadian companies' head offices, while Calgary has six, all oil and gas firms. Office space is the country's most

The exciting Chuck Wagon Race during Calgary's once-a-year (July) celebration of the Old West called The Calgary Stampede

expensive, and fossil fuel companies and those that do business with them occupy three-fourths of it. Until the recession, the residential housing market was red hot. It has the lowest unemployment rate of any major city.

It also boasts Canada's third most ethnically diverse population and the greatest number of post-high school degrees per capita. In 2010 Calgary voters elected the first Muslim mayor of a major Canadian city, Naheed Nenshi. Born of immigrant parents, he graduated from the University of Calgary and did his graduate work at Harvard. The dynamic economy makes Calgary a magnet for immigrants (ahead of Montreal), and almost a fourth of the residents are visible minorities. *Maclean's* ranked it third among Canada's "smartest" cities in 2010.

Alberta has built the finest public education system in Canada, with its children regularly outscoring pupils from other provinces (and other countries, according to the 2007 PISA results) on standardized tests. In *Maclean's* annual college rankings in 2006, Alberta's sole university was rated number one in all of Canada (third in 2010). It needs another university. Albertans increased their tax-deductible charitable giving by more than 15% in 2006, thereby helping transform Calgary into an intellectual and cultural center, as well as a business one. However, it is still one of the few North American cities of over a million residents that does not have an art museum.

But the province faces serious problems. Canadians are pouring into Alberta at the rate of 100,000 each year, enough to create a medium size town. Its net migration in 2006 was 62,000, compared with Ontario's net loss of 34,000. This puts severe strains on housing, government services and infrastructure, and the labor market. For example, the shortage of bar staff was so critical around St. Patrick's Day in 2007 that the government briefly considered allowing children as young as 12 to work in bars. Calgary passed the one million mark in 2006, causing rush-hour traffic to slow to a trickle.

Fort McMurray, where the oil sands are located, needs new water and wastewater treatment plants, a new landfill, better and more roads and bridges and more nurses and doctors. The locals were wary of the boom all around them. One summed up the town's problems: "Too many single men, too much time, too much money, too much trouble." High wages also attract drug dealers: drug abuse in the northern oil area is four times the average in the rest of the province. About 40% of oil workers test positive for cocaine or marijuana in job screening or post-accident tests. Economic hard times have befallen the city and lessened the intensity of these problems.

Klein temporarily scaled back his health-care reductions because of festering unease about government spending cuts, dramatized by hospital workers' repeated walkouts. But then his government introduced Bill 11, which drew particularly sharp criticism. In order to reduce waiting lists and relieve pressure on the public health system, the legislation allows private clinics to perform all cataract surgery and many hernia, foot, ear, nose and throat operations. The expenses are fully covered by the provincial health-care plan. He made a cross-country tour in January 2005 to promote this "third way." Critics contended that Klein was, in effect, creating private hospitals, which are illegal in Canada, and was paving the way for American-style two-tiered health care. According to a 2006 survey, Alberta and BC offer the best health care in Canada.

Klein easily won a fourth mandate in 2004. After 32 consecutive years in power, no one doubted that the Tories would win by a landslide. This is typical in the province's unique political culture. Oppositions are always weak, and governments are routinely reelected by huge majorities. Alberta celebrated its 100th birthday in 2005. During its entire existence, it has experienced only four changes of government. Each time an established ruling party was replaced by a new upstart.

At the September 2006 leadership contest to decide on his successor, a dark horse won: Ed Stelmach, a quiet farmer. He had grown up on the same farm his Ukrainian grandparents had homesteaded, and he did not learn English until he entered school. Even though two-thirds of Albertans live in cities, Stelmach, who assumed the premiership in December 2006, appointed only three of his 19 ministers from Calgary and one from Edmonton.

His critics said his focus was too rural. But he argued that Alberta was not getting its fair share of the oil boom, including from the oil sands, which provide about half of the province's total oil and gas output. Within a year he was able to raise the oil and gas royalties for the provincial government by 20% from 2010. He ignored industry threats to pull out and saw his popularity rise when the companies vowed to retaliate. The royalties are still less than the world average of 68% for similar deposits and are below the fees companies are required to pay for Alaskan oil.

Stelmach was less popular than was Klein. His position was temporarily strengthened by his March 2008 surprise landslide victory over the Liberal opposition, led by Kevin Taft. The Tories snagged 73 of Alberta's 83 ridings, up from 60, and reduced the Liberals' seats from 16 to only nine. Turnout of 41% was the lowest in Alberta's history. The Liberals had promised a "war on carbon" by putting the brake on developing the oil sands deposits. The voters' message was clear: full steam ahead with oil production, despite the consequences.

However, by 2010 Stelmach and his party were in free fall. Six out of 10 Albertans believed the province was moving in the wrong direction, and his $6.9 billion government deficit and his adjustments to oil and gas royalties had become unpopular. Citizens felt they have lost their "Alberta Advantage," that combination of low taxes and abundant opportunity.

Taking up the slack is another fast-growing fledgling conservative party that has grown out of a protest movement, the

Convention Centre, Edmonton, Alberta

119

Canada

Wildrose Alliance. It is led by the talented former journalist and broadcaster Danielle Smith. With other parties nipping at its heels, the Conservative caucus decided that Stelmach was leading the party to disaster. He wanted to balance the budget gradually, without deep cuts in services. Others, led by then Finance Minister Ted Morton, a political science professor at the University of Calgary, wanted to balance without delay. Rather than fight for his leadership, Stelmach announced in January 2011 his eventual resignation despite his huge parliamentary majority. Months later his successor had still not been named. No elections need to take place until March 2013.

In January 2005 Normie Kwong, who had overcome racial prejudice to help the Edmonton Eskimos and Calgary Stampeders professional football teams win four Grey Cups, was appointed lieutenant-governor.

BRITISH COLUMBIA: Since the 1970s this province of 3.8 million inhabitants has sometimes been referred to as "Lotus Land" because of its economic opportunities and relaxed and experimental lifestyles. In Canada it conjured up images of a California in the North. It is the third largest province in size and people after Ontario and Quebec. About two-fifths of its people live in greater Vancouver. Facing Asia, its economic reach extends to the Orient.

In 1999 Glen Clark became the third B.C. premier in succession to be driven from office by scandal. Since 1983 no premier had completed a full term of office. After a brief transition, he was succeeded by the B.C. attorney general, Ujjal Dosanjh. A Sihk born in the Punjab state of India, he was the first non-white to head a provincial government. He left India at age 17 for England. After four years there, he came to B.C. in 1968 and got a law degree. Canada's 400,000-strong Sikh community, concentrated in B.C. and Ontario, has produced an impressive list of leading Canadians. They include ex-Federal Fisheries Minister Herb Dhaliwal and figure skater Emanuel Sandhu.

Because of their religion, some Sikh men have won the right in court to wear their beards and turbans while pursuing careers as Mounties or as boxers. Many, like Dosanjh, do not do that. In 1985 Dosanjh was attacked and beaten with an iron pipe by religious extremists angry because he had condemned their terror-based campaign for Punjabi independence. BC is plagued by bloody Sikh gang warfare over drugs, money and women in which most victims are Sikhs themselves. They are Canada's most murderous gangs.

In 2003 a Sikh separatist was jailed in Vancouver for five years after being the first to admit guilt in making the explosives for the 1985 bombing of Air India Flight 182 off the Atlantic coast of Ireland killing all 331 persons aboard, most of them Canadian. The dreadful deed, the worst terrorist act in Canadian history, was committed in revenge for the Indian army's storming of the Sikhs' holiest shrine, the Golden Temple, a year earlier. The publicity about this bloody behavior helps explain why only 30% of Canadians said in a 2009 poll that they had a positive view of Sikhism.

In April 2003 the trial of two other Sikh nationalists began in the BC Supreme Court. This was the culmination of one of the most exhaustive criminal investigations in Canadian history, hampered by mysterious deaths of witnesses and the unwillingness of Sikh immigrants to cooperate with investigators. This longest, most complex and most expensive trial in Canadian history came to an end in March 2005 when the court allowed the two to walk free, concluding that the prosecution had not made its case. The verdict caused a public uproar when it was revealed that Canadian intelligence services had destroyed vital evidence. The government thereupon ordered further inquiries, first conducted by former Ontario premier, Bob Rae, and then by a retired Supreme Court judge. The inquiry released more documents that showed that Indian officials and Air India had given frequent threat assessments in advance, but they were treated with suspicion and were ignored.

In the 2001 provincial elections Dosanjh's NDP were driven from power in one of the biggest election sweeps in Canadian history. Gordon Campbell's Liberals won 76 of 79 legislative seats based on 57.5% of the votes. Voters on the left drifted to the Greens (12.4%) and the Marijuana Party (3.2%). Pledging "dramatic" tax cuts and a referendum on treaties negotiated with aboriginal peoples, Premier Campbell, former mayor of Vancouver, assumed the reins of a majority government.

Campbell wasted no time in introducing corporate tax breaks and a 25% provincial income tax cut. Thus the tax rate

fell from the second-highest in Canada to the second-lowest. He slashed government spending by 25%, trimming the fat in government departments, cutting 12,000 civil service jobs, throwing 100,000 off the welfare roles and reducing legal aid. He said: "one thing is clear. We will have to downsize our provincial government."

Election day May 17, 2005, was a historic occasion: it was the first serving government in Canada to go to the polls on a date fixed by the legislature almost four years earlier. Henceforth regular elections in BC are conducted every four years, depriving the governing party of the advantage of calling a vote at the most favorable time. Campbell was BC's first premier in 22 years willing or able to seek re-election.

Citizens were also asked to vote on a complicated new electoral system, the single transferable method used in Ireland, which allows voters to rank all the candidates in their riding regardless of party. Those who end up with the most votes win. The measure barely fell short of the required threshold of 60% approval, winning 57%. Voters are excused for being somewhat baffled by their choice among 45 parties that registered for the elections. They included the Work Less Party of BC, the Sex Party, the BC Marijuana Party, the People of British Columbia Millionaires Party and two separatist parties.

Campbell faced the May 12, 2009, provincial elections with justified confidence. He and his Liberals won a historic third straight victory, garnering 46% of the votes and 49 seats. The NDP got 42% of the votes and 36 seats. No other party won a seat even though the Greens captured 8% of the votes. Turnout was disappointingly below 50%. In a referendum at the same time, the complicated single transferable voting system was again rejected. The method is simply too complicated for voters.

Like all of his predecessors, the Dartmouth-educated Campbell suffered a serious lapse of judgment in December 2002. While in Hawaii on vacation, he was arrested for drunk driving after an evening with friends; his blood-alcohol reading was twice the legal limit. His night in jail was probably the first such for a senior Canadian politician, and his mug shot was a godsend for opposition campaign posters. The entire affair was a reminder that the BC premier's job always comes with a built-in curse.

In November 2010 Campbell became the latest in a long line of BC premiers to be driven out of office in disgrace. In July 2010 he had approved of a harmonized sales tax (HST) that linked the provincial and federal sales taxes. This sparked a tax revolt that prompted 17 members of his Liberal caucus to threaten desertion if

Campbell did not step down. His approval rating ultimately fell to 9%, making him the most unpopular leader in Canadian history. It did not help him that economists applauded his fiscal policy, and the Fraser Institute named him the country's most fiscally responsible premier.

He was replaced as premier by Christy Clark, a former talk radio host, who won Campbell's upscale Point Grey riding in Vancouver by a whisker in a by-election. She had been a scrappy former deputy premier, earning such descriptions as "pit bull" and "acid-tongued Liberal hellcat." But she left politics for six years to be a good mother to her son. Exuding confidence, she faces a referendum on HST in June 2011 and probably an early election in the fall. Her Liberals will face an NDP, led by Adrian Dix, which is reenergized after its spectacular surge in the May 2011 federal elections.

The British Columbian dream has always had two Achilles heels: its dependence upon natural resources and exporting. Although the province has experienced a transformation from a resource-based economy (now only 17% of its GDP) to a more service- and manufacturing-based economy, it is still not fully prepared for today's global competition. Operating costs are high, which reflects elevated wages, living costs and personal tax rates. Labor laws are restrictive, and governmental regulation of the economy is excessive by North American standards. However, taking pages from the success of neighboring Alberta's government, the government is pursuing tax cuts and privatizations. BC and Alberta agreed in 2006 to drop their interprovincial trade barriers and recognize each other's standards in more than 60 professions. This

Trade, Investment and Labour Mobility Agreement, called TILMA, is meant to save money and create jobs. Saskatchewan joined TILMA.

Thanks to China's insatiable appetite for natural resources, BC is experiencing an economic upsurge, with investment rising and unemployment falling. Chinese imports have saved the coal industry in BC, which has 25 billion tons of proven reserves. Three new mines have opened, bringing the total to nine in 2005. Copper, zinc and molybdenum mining is booming, as is gas and oil production. Its lumber industry has found a new market in China. This resource boom brings prosperity to some of the province's poorer areas. BC is well positioned for the future as North America increasingly looks toward Asia and as Ontario's manufacturing prowess is waning.

One export crop that is booming is B.C.'s marijuana, which is reputed to be three to five times more potent than Mexican or Caribbean varieties. This includes a popular variety called "B.C. bud." It is reported to be the province's most lucrative export crop, by 2008 worth from $5 billion to $7 billion each year, almost as much as the value of the province's tourist industry. It is estimated that the marijuana industry employs more people than do traditional sectors like forestry. Police estimate that there are about 20,000 growing operations in houses across the province. U.S. border officials estimate that marijuana smuggling increased tenfold from 1997 to 1999 and blame the upsurge partly on the leniency of B.C. courts. By the end of 2007, however, Quebec had overtaken BC both in terms of marijuana production and popularity among American consumers.

In July 2005 police shut down an elaborate 360-foot tunnel from a shed in Canada to a living room 300 feet inside the U.S. border in Washington state. It was being used to smuggle drugs. Although numerous tunnels have been discovered along the Mexican border, this was the first along the Canadian one. Responding to requests by American investigators, Canadian authorities also raided the headquarters of the BC Marijuana Party and arrested its leader, Marc Emery, who had been operating a thriving mail-order business selling marijuana seeds over the Internet.

Much is distributed by brutal immigrant gangs from India and elsewhere. More than half of their trade is inside the U.S., where they often exchange drugs for cocaine, firearms and cash. They have also tapped the Japanese market. Vancouver's seaport is a point of entry for heroin and cocaine. The province has become a key hub in international organized crime, in

part because Western Canada is positioning itself to be North America's most important commercial corridor to Asia. This is ideal for criminal gangs' operations.

Gang warfare in Vancouver goes beyond Sikh and Indian circles. In 2008 it was estimated that about 950 gangs were fighting over drug turf and about 135 over the illegal gun trade. Because the police department is undermanned, there are few arrests and prosecutions. A surprising new development is that more and more women are gang members and involved in criminal activities. In all of Canada, they now make up about 6% of gang membership, 12% in British Columbia. Perhaps it is not surprising that when *Maclean's* looked at Canada's most dangerous cities, 11 of the top 20 were in British Columbia. Police authorities now rank Vancouver on a par with Los Angeles and New York in terms of being in the grip of crime syndicates. Their activities amount to about 7% of BC's economy. Vancouver experiences 3.6 times as many break and enters as New York, measured per 100,000 inhabitants.

The lamentable neglect of the Eastside was the focus of the 2002 city elections, won by former drug-squad officer with the Mounties and chief provincial coroner, Larry Campbell. He headed a coalition of community activists, unionists, pragmatic leftists and New Democrats, known as the Coalition of Progressive Electors (COPE). COPE also captured most seats on the city council and the school and park boards. Voters decided that they had had enough of people dying of overdose, disease and murder in the Eastside. The new city leaders moved to create "safe injection sites," where intravenous heroin users can inject drugs bought elsewhere without the threat of arrest under the supervision of public health care workers who would offer them safe needles and counseling to change their lives.

In 2005 Vancouver launched North America's first trial of heroin main tenance: giving addicts free heroin on condition that they enter treatment. The battered Eastside remains the most concentrated pocket of poverty and crime in Canada, with up to 1,800 homeless in the summer. Most critics blame the Liberal government's social-service cuts in its drive to eliminate the province's debt. Sam Sullivan, Vancouver's mayor elected in the fall of 2005, continues to support maintenance and treatment programs. Vancouver became the first Canadian city to legalize marijuana as a part of a growing movement advocating a more lenient approach to drugs. That was in line with Canadians' attitudes about recreational marijuana; a 2006 poll indicated that 63% favor it. The city and province had promised in their winning bid for the

Canada

2010 Winter Olympics that they would build new housing and provide more services for the poor and homeless, but they later confessed that insufficient funds have been budgeted for those.

British Columbians are statistically Canada's healthiest people. A mere 12% (9% in Vancouver) are obese. Only 16% smoke, and BC leads a group of provinces seeking to penalize the large tobacco companies for the health damage their products cause. Healthy living is a cultural trademark of the west coast.

One of the government's major challenges was environmental. It approved continued logging in two-thirds of Clayoquot Sound on the Pacific coast of Vancouver Island. Since this is one of the world's last remaining rainforests, this decision infuriated conservationists all over the world. Blockades and arrests along the logging roads kept the issue on the front pages until a government plan was announced to restrict logging and create new parks. The government finds itself caught in the middle between the logging industry's demands for reducing some of the requirements of the province's Forest Practices Code, and environmental groups, who find the code too lax to protect the forests. A new code was enacted to reduce the size of the blocks of trees cut during harvest, to force stricter environmental practices, and to increase the fees paid by forestry companies. This satisfied nobody, and protests continued. In 1998, 17% of forestry jobs disappeared, but forest products still account for 1 in 17 jobs.

To try to stimulate the logging industry, the B.C. government slashed logging royalties. The industry's new focus is the vast, largely undisturbed mid-coast forest between Vancouver Island and southern Alaska. It contains a quarter of the world's remaining temperate rain forest. But loggers face a collision with Indian villages, a cross-border alliance of environmentalists, and the tourist industry, which greets a half million tourists each year, most from the U.S.

By contrast, almost everybody approved of the creation in 1997 of a 10 million acre Muskwa-Kechika wilderness preserve in the northern Rockies. This was one of the largest conservation initiatives in Canadian history. Many North American environmentalists greeted this as an essential piece in a possible unbroken seam of protected land running from Yellowstone Park in the South through the Yukon Territory in the North (thus "Yellowstone to Yukon" or "Y2Y").

In 2000 four major BC logging companies and key environmental groups reached a landmark truce with regard to the Great Bear Rainforest, a remote temperate wilderness of thousand-year-old

Hon. Christy Clark

cedar trees, fjords, inlets, islands, glacial mountains, grizzly bears and wolves. It is considered to be the world's largest unlogged temperate rain forest. Logging activity was postponed until an unusual alliance of loggers, environmentalists, native groups and the BC government agreed in 2006 to create Great Bear Rainforest, a park along the Pacific coast from the mid-point of Vancouver Island to the Alaska border, twice the size of Yellowstone. It will remain off-limits to logging.

In 2007 the BC government unveiled a program to make the province "the continent's greenest spot." It would close down coal-burning energy plants and help create a Pacific Coast grouping of states and provinces to deal with climate change without waiting for their respective federal governments to act.

BC's economic problems created an uproar over offshore oil and gas development. Muted for decades by moratoriums, a panel of experts concluded in 2004 that restrictions are now unnecessary. Exploi-

Aboriginal guide in UBC Museum before "Big Raven"

tation could be a bonanza for BC's Liberal government.

Another challenge stems from 47 native claims to most of BC's land. It was the only province officially to ignore a 1763 directive by the British Crown requiring land treaties to be signed with aboriginals. It never signed treaties with the approximately 160,000 aboriginal inhabitants, leaving legal title to most of the area in dispute. The BC government joined with the federal government to try to reach a settlement. The 60 BC bands have joined the negotiation process.

There is widespread nervousness, even anger, among white British Columbians when the Indian bands begin tallying their losses in modern terms. One band, the Musqueam, claims all of downtown Vancouver and most of its suburbs, where their ancestors had hunted and fished. In 1999 it won court backing for a 74-fold increase in the land-lease rates it collects from householders in a Vancouver suburb. Residents say they face ruin. As such rulings engender opposition from non-aboriginal groups, bands ponder whether they might win more of their claims in court than in negotiations. Canada's Supreme Court came to the rescue of the 73 leaseholders in 2000 by ruling that they pay an annual rent of $10,000, rather than the $23,000 the band had demanded. Band members were outraged.

In 1998 an agreement was reached with the Nisga'a band, involving 772 square miles in the breathtakingly beautiful Nass Valley on BC's northwest coast just south of the Alaskan panhandle. In return for relinquishing claims eight times that size, the 5,000 members received $190 million and extensive powers of government: taxation, land use, family, social and health services, police, courts, schools, language and culture. Amid a storm of protest that the terms were too generous, the treaty was approved by the BC legislature in April 1999 and by the federal parliament at the end of the year. Another agreement that month awarded the Sechelt Indians 2,000 hectares of land 50 kilometers northwest of Vancouver and a $42 million "prosperity fund."

BC's Liberals oppose the model of self-government won by the Nisga'a in the 1998 treaty, and ex-Premier Campbell committed himself to put the native treaty process to a vote. In a July 2002 referendum an overwhelming percentage of voters gave the government a strong mandate to enter a "new era of reconciliation with First Nations." However, private property should not be subject to negotiation, parks should be maintained for all British Columbians, and an inherent right of self-government is not on the table. Any aboriginal self-government should have the "characteristics of local government with powers delegated from Canada and BC." Only 36% of eligible voters participated in the referendum.

In December 2009 the Nisga'a decided to break with their tradition of holding their land in common and to permit band members to own private property. Under Canada's Indian Act, aboriginals on reserves are usually given certificates of possession for their houses, which they rent, but they do not own them. They cannot even use them as collateral for loans. This Nisga'a decision could have revolutionary implications.

The Canadian government hopes that the basic principles of BC's prior agreements can be applied to negotiations not only with other BC bands, but with such groups as Inuit in northern Quebec and the Algonquin band, which claims the land in Ottawa on which the Canadian parliament sits. To create a better atmosphere for negotiations, the BC government, through its annual Throne Speech in 2003, apologized for its past treatment of indigenous peoples and vowed to resolve unfinished land treaties. BC's institutions had "failed aboriginal peoples across the province." Campbell even admitted later that he had been wrong on Nisga'a, and he announced in 2006 "A New Relationship with B.C. First Nations." The federal government of Stephen Harper joined the BC government to sign treaties with the Tsawwassen and Maanulth First Nations that will set a pattern for settling future land claims. They will phase out reserve-based tax exemptions. Progress is being made on the huge backlog of other unresolved treaty claims.

The business community blames such native-lands claims for the fact that BC attracted only half as much investment as Alberta during the 1990s. But native leader Stewart Phillip asserts that this is an unavoidable reality: "If any development does not enjoy the support of aboriginal people, then it's not going to happen."

A dispute over salmon fishing brought the BC and Canadian governments into direct conflict with the United States. After a 1985 treaty regulating the size of catches by American and Canadian fishermen expired in 1992, BC claimed that Americans were catching too many salmon in U.S. and international waters and thereby preventing them from spawning in BC rivers. To underscore its indignation, the government announced that BC would cancel a seabed lease to a navy weapons-testing base at Nanoose Bay used by American submarines for torpedo practice. Finally, he suspended BC's participation in about 50 agreements with neighboring American states on various topics.

In response, the U.S. Senate voted 81 to 19 for a resolution calling on the president

Legislative Assembly, Victoria

to send the U.S. navy to protect American ferries. Before this was seriously considered, though, the Canadian government announced that the U.S. would not be forced from the testing base. By 2005 the number of salmon spawning in the Fraser River had fallen to about five million, fewer than half the expected number because of higher ocean temperatures, overfishing, the destruction of spawning habitats, and, most controversially, diseases that are spread from open-pen salmon farms. The numbers continue to decline. This prompted federal officials to stop sockeye fishing. The Harper government announced in 2006 an inquiry into the collapse of the Fraser River salmon fishery and its opposition to "racially divided fisheries programs."

One-fourth of BC's population are immigrants. Some British Columbians are worried about an in-pouring of rich Chinese from Hong Kong, who were resettling their families and fortunes before mainland China assumed control of the colony in 1997. Canada actively tried to lure rich foreigners into the country in order to benefit the economy. But Vancouver's Chinese population jumped precipitously from 30,000 in the 1960s to more than a quarter million today. Ethnic Chinese comprise a fifth of Vancouver's population; 61% of the children in the public schools speak English as a second language.

In the 1990s Hong Kong Chinese were entering at the rate of more than 100 per day. Even though migrants from other Canadian provinces outnumbered those from Hong Kong by eight to one, a backlash began against the Chinese (whom some refer to as "Hongs"). Many natives accuse them of buying up BC's prize real estate, such as the site of Expo 86, and driving up prices for Vancouver's land and housing. The city's 600,000 residents

(two million in the entire urban area) pay Canada's highest prices for property: the average home in 2006 cost US$466,000.

BC's former lieutenant governor was wealthy Vancouver businessman David See-Chai Lam, who was Canada's first citizen of Chinese descent to occupy a vice-regal office. Lam, who donates up to $5 million to charitable causes each year, was an ideal man to help deal with this delicate and emotionally-charged issue. By 1999 the influx had slowed dramatically, as the number of immigrants dropped by about 30%. Also the composition changed from wealthy Hong Kong investors to small business owners and young factory workers from Taiwan and China.

In February 2010 Vancouver and the nearby Whistler resort hosted the Winter Olympics. Nervous organizers had to borrow money, import snow, look for ways to scale back on expenses, and make the event a little less spectacular than they had hoped. There were some miscalculations. One was the assumption that the 737 apartments in the Olympic Village, later named Millennium Water, could be sold without loss after the games were finished. Given the economic recession, only half were sold at the expected prices, and for a while the entire village had the air of a ghost town. The city had to assume the loan and sell the remaining apartments for about half the original prices, leaving taxpayers with a $200–$300 million loss. It is usually hard to lose money in Vancouver real estate; in 2011 the city was again named by *The Economist* as the most livable city anywhere.

However, from the moment three billion viewers tuned in to the opening ceremonies, it was clear that these Games would be among the best in history. Vancouver was the scene of spectacular Canadian athletic triumphs and an outpouring of Canadian pride.

Canada

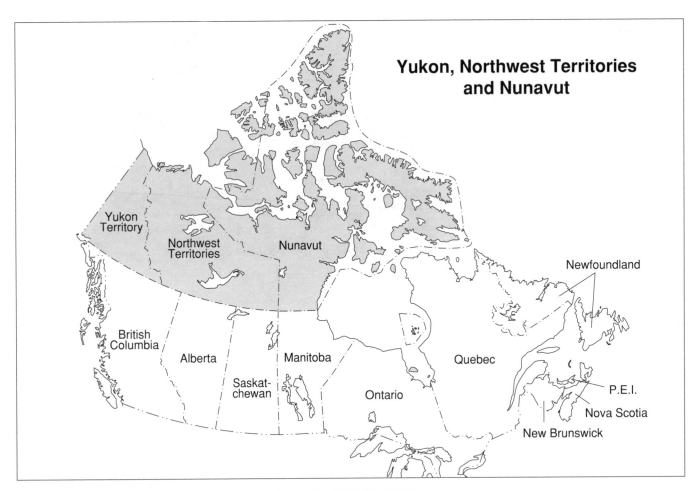

YUKON, NORTHWEST TERRITORIES AND NUNAVUT

The 34,000 Yukoners, 41,000 residents of the Northwest Territories (NWT), and the 32,200 inhabitants of Nunavut have taken impressive steps toward self-government since the early 1970s. However, they lack provincial status and cannot unilaterally amend their constitutions, which are acts of the Canadian parliament. Only the federal government can change them. Since the British ceded control in 1880, Ottawa controls most public land. The federal power over land use and non-renewable resources embraces most of the North.

Northerners are becoming increasingly assertive, and this makes disagreements wider and more numerous. There are many unsettled land and mineral rights claims being made by native groups in the Yukon and Northwest Territories. As a condition for the separation of Nunavut from the NWT in 1999, all aboriginal claims were settled in Nunavut. Since the federal government receives lucrative royalties for resource extraction in the North, it is not easy for Ottawa to relinquish this power. All three depend on federal subsidies, which amount to C$2 billion annually and which account for 60% of budget revenues in the Yukon and Northwest Territories

and close to 90% in Nunavut. Aboriginal groups also benefit from a host of other federal programs, such as exemption from taxes (although Inuit have to pay them).

All three territories have developed *de facto* responsible government. This means that the commissioners (formally the chief executive within the area appointed by Ottawa and answering to the Minister of Indian Affairs and Northern Development) accept the decisions made by the members of elected assemblies. Leaders, who call themselves "premier," are selected by their legislative assemblies, and then they are formally appointed by the commissioners. The commissioners behave like provincial lieutenant governors in that they do not overrule decisions made by the legislative assemblies.

Yukon Territory

Self-government along the Canadian model proceeded fastest in the Yukon Territory. The construction of the Alaskan Highway in 1942 brought thousands of immigrants into the Yukon, making the native population a minority. Since there are three times as many non-natives as Indians and Inuit in the Yukon, the demand

for Canadian institutions was greatest there. In 1978, party politics replaced a system of loose alliances, and party discipline enables the legislative system to operate more or less like any provincial government in Canada. Of course, it is no simple matter practicing democracy in a territory larger than France, with only 16,000 registered voters, scattered in 17 ridings with as few as 158 voters in the smallest (Old Crow), many of whom are reachable only by airplane or dogsled, and in temperatures as low as minus-50 degrees centigrade on election day.

The NDP first upset the Tories in 1985 and then repeated the performance in 1989. The NDP government sought to revive the declining mining industry while at the same time stimulating tourism—presently the Yukon's main industry, drawing 300,000 each year—and diversifying the economy. Gold production is only a tenth of what it was in its heyday. More distressing was the closure in 1997 of the lead-zinc mine at Faro, which had contributed a fifth of the Yukon's $1 billion GDP. No diamonds have been found.

The social and economic challenges are daunting: Almost a third of the workforce

**Hon. Dennis Fentie
Government Leader,
Yukon Territory**

resources, education and health. In 2003, after 10 years of negotiations, Ottawa granted it control over its natural resources, one of the final steps on the road to provincehood.

Disproportionately high levels of family breakdown and alcohol and drug abuse plague the Yukon. Even former Liberal leader Roger Coles was imprisoned in 1986 for cocaine trafficking. The capital city of Whitehorse has a homicide rate 355% higher than the Canadian average.

In 1992 the Tories, who had renamed themselves the Yukon Party to break ties with their unpopular federal counterpart, regained power. But in 1996 they had to relinquish it to the NDP. The 2000 elections completed the game of musical chairs. For the first time since party politics was introduced to the Yukon in 1978, the Liberals won, and their leader, Pat Duncan, formed the government. In November 2002 she handed the reins of power to Dennis Fentie, leader of the Yukon Party, who had defected from the NDP. As a young man he had been convicted of drug trafficking and served 17 months in penitentiary.

Northwest Territories

In contrast to the Yukon, native people constitute about 48% of the overall population in the Northwest Territories (NWT), a plural name that is likely to be changed in the future. The various ethnic groups are not spread evenly over this gigantic region extending about 500,000 square miles and located mainly above the tree line. Its population consists of 52% non-aboriginal, 28% Dene, 9% Métis and smatterings of other

Inuit boy in Nunavut
Courtesy: Michael J. Hewitt

aboriginals, speaking nine official languages—North Slavey, South Slavey, Cree, Chipewyan, Dogrib, Gwich'in, Inuvialuktun, English and French. One tenth are Inuvialuit (Western Inuit), who face daunting challenges in life. Their life expectancy is 10 years shorter than the Canadian average, the youth suicide rate is eight times higher, tuberculosis rates are 17 times as high, and dropping out of school is far more common than getting a diploma.

In 2003 a landmark agreement was reached with the 4,000 Dogrib Indians, who call themselves the Tlicho First Nation. Fol-

is employed by one of the three levels of government, and seasonal unemployment is high. As is true everywhere in the North, prices of products shipped in from the South, including food, are very expensive. The Yukon has only about 160 working farms.

Although it is heavily dependent upon Ottawa financially, the Yukon is gradually taking over more federal powers, such as

Aerial view of Whitehorse, capital of the Yukon and home for two-thirds of the Yukon's inhabitants. In the foreground is the S.S. Klondike, a national historical site, which saw regular service from the 1930s until the early 1950s, carrying passengers and freight on the Yukon River between Dawson City and Whitehorse.

Canada

lowing the treaty with BC's Nisga'a, this was only the second agreement that grants the inherent right to self-government to aboriginals. They gained ownership of an area of 15,000 square miles almost as large as Switzerland around Yellowknife between Great Slave Lake and the Great Bear Lake together with its natural resources. Abutting a diamond industry from which it gains 2% of the royalties (and all from any future mines), the Tlicho could become one of the richest First Nation groups in North America. They make and enforce laws, collect taxes, levy royalties on mines, and regulate land use, education, family and traditional medicine.

The NWT is a land rich in diamonds, oil and gas. It now has three operating diamond mines with many more planned. Diamonds now make up more than half of NWT's economic output. The last exhausted gold mine closed in 2005. To facilitate traffic to and from mines, exploration sites and remote communities, authorities build a thousand miles (1,450 kilometers) of winter roads each year. The busiest runs about 280 miles (420 kilometers) northeast from Yellowknife, over more than 30 frozen lakes. Others run into neighboring Nunavut. An increasing problem is that global warming is shortening the time that trucks can cross ice. This can leave the mining operations short of the necessary huge construction equipment and vast quantities of supplies and fuel, which must then be flown in at great expense. Without the full use of these winter roads, the NWT's economic lifeblood is threatened. Of course, global warming also creates problems for the Inuit: they must deal with unpredictable sea ice that can be fatal, snowmobiles must take longer routes, and their buildings are weakened by melting permafrost.

It is more self-sufficient and economically healthier than is Nunavut. The separation of Nunavut from the NWT in 1999 caused some economic suffering for the Northwest Territories' gritty frontier capital, Yellowknife (population 17,275). It lost about 500 federal and territorial government jobs and some of its much-needed transfer payments from Ottawa. It suffers from a chronic shortage of doctors and nurses. Aggravated assault in the capital of Yellowknife is more than 350% higher than the average in Canada. But in the 21st century tourism, especially among Japanese, is thriving. Yellowknife's economy is robust, thanks in large part to the mining boom. In 2008 it enjoyed a phenomenal 13% economic growth rate. Tiffany has established a cutting and polishing factory in the town. But housing remains tight, and drugs and crime are problems.

The prospect of uranium deposits in the north has attracted even more interest in the NWT. To protect their territory and its

Boreal Forest, a huge green swath across North America that is crucial for wildlife, native groups and the Canadian government agreed to move toward preserving an area four times the size of Yellowstone Park from diamond and uranium mining interests.

In the NWT's non-party system, the Legislative Assembly has the chance to review government leaders every two years. Since February 2011 the premier is Floyd Roland. He replaced Joe Handley, who in 2004 had succeeded Stephen Kakfwi, an aboriginal from the Dene band. Roland was first elected to the Legislative Assembly in 1995 and has held most major political posts on his path to become premier.

By tradition, it is only one of two legislatures in all of Canada (the other being Nunavut) that reaches decisions by consensus, rather than by party politics and majority votes. There is no formal opposition in the NWT legislative assembly, which is temporarily housed in an addition to The Yellowknife Inn. The chamber is adorned by native art, and the speaker and pages are dressed in native clothing. During sessions, members use their own languages, with all remarks being translated into the other official languages from interpreter booths. For the time being the NWT retains its name and territorial government. A new territorial constitution is being written, and possible changes in the political system are being studied.

Nunavut

The Inuit ("The People," singular: Inuk, called "Eskimo" in Alaska, a term meaning "meat-eater" that these people resent) comprise 85% of the people in a definable area to the northeast of the NWT. The Inuit Tapirisat of Canada (the national Inuit organization) asked in 1976 that the former Northwest Territories be split in two. The ultimate result was the establishment of a new eastern Arctic territory named *Nunavut* ("Our Land") on April 1, 1999.

The Inuit disliked sharing power with people who have nothing culturally in common with them. Nunavut is much more homogeneous than the NWT. The Inuit, a gentle maritime people, have a different temperament than the NWT's mixture of "frontier mavericks and fractious aboriginal groups," as *Maclean's* described them. Inuit found many Canadian institutions alien, and they considered Yellow knife to be too far away and too Canadian for their taste. For instance, one Inuit school supervisor in the Baffin region, located 2,500 kilometers and two time zones from Yellowknife, argued that the capital "is so far distant that I don't think they realize the impact of their de-

Hon. Floyd Roland
Premier, Northwest Territories

cisions on our communities." The Inuit persuaded the territorial government to carry out a referendum in the NWT in 1982 to determine whether there was popular support for such a division. The concept was supported by 56% of the voters. Inuit leaders made the division of the NWT the major item on their political agenda.

The breakthrough was made in 1992 when 54% of NWT voters accepted an agreement with the Canadian government. With a population of only 32,200, Nunavut's predominantly (85%) Inuit extend over 772,000 square miles in the Eastern Arctic, almost entirely above the tree line. They are settled in 26 communities, which can be reached only by plane or ship. There are no road connections. Perhaps the largest peaceful land settlement in history, the new territory comprises a fifth of Canada's land area, two-thirds of its coastline, and traverses three time zones. It is the size of California and Alaska combined. In Canadian terms, it is equivalent to BC, Alberta, and the Yukon combined, or twice as large as Ontario.

Inuit received legal title to 136,000 square miles, mineral rights to 14,000 square miles, and $1,148 billion over 14 years. In return, the Inuit had to renounce their claim to another 640,000 square miles of ancestral terrain, possibly containing rich gas and oil fields, which remain Crown land. Nevertheless, they receive a share in federal royalties from gas, oil, and mineral deposits on Crown lands, as well as hunting and fishing rights over all of Nunavut. As one participant in the negotiations put it, "We're a small people, but we have big ambitions."

In a plebiscite to determine their capital, the Inuit selected Iqaluit (pronounced ee-KA-loo-eet), formerly called Frobisher Bay, a modern community on the southern tip of Baffin Island. Iqaluit is Canada's fastest-growing capital, with 6,800 inhabitants in 2009. It is so small that there is no need for street names. Buildings simply have numbers.

The town launched the first Internet web site in the Inuktitut language, the first language for 70% of the territory's people. Along with English and French, it is an official language and the one that is used as much as possible in government. Increasingly English is the language of choice among young Inuit. Fearing that Inuktitut will slowly die in the capital, Premier Okalik ordered senior bureaucrats to learn the language if they want to keep their jobs. Laws are being drafted to make it Nunavut's working language by 2020. Television broadcasting is available in both Inuktitut and English. In Iqaluit one hears more English than Inuktitut, but the latter predominates in the 24 smaller communities. There is a local newspaper called the *Nunatsiaq News*.

Public school instruction is offered in Inuktitut, but parents may opt for English schooling. That has become a matter of concern. Instruction is given in Inuktitut until grade 3 or 4. Then it tapers off and English is favored. Only 18% of pupils said in a 2006 poll that they speak more Inuktitut than English in school. Part of the problem is a severe shortage of Inuktitut-speaking teachers. Only about a fourth of Inuit children graduate from high school.

Nunavut Arctic College offers some academic courses in both English and Inuktitut, training teachers as well as instructing Inuit artisans who desire to diversify their products. In 2005 a joint effort of the College and University of Victoria trained 11 law graduates in order to give the territory more professional expertise rooted in native culture. In 2009 work began on an Inuit cultural school in Clyde River, which will have satellite campuses teaching cultural programs in Baker Lake and Igloolik. When completed in 2011 it will provide full scholarships for 26 students 18 or over. The school's name is *Piqqusilirivvik*, which in Inuktitut for "a place that has those things important to us."

The NWT and Nunavut each send one MP to the House of Commons in Ottawa, and a new Senate seat is being created for them. Nunavut has an Inuit-controlled government with its own legislature, cabinet and court system. It represents North America's boldest experiment to give a native group so much self-determination. In elections to their legislative assembly, many of the ballots have to be dropped by plane into remote settlements. In the vote for the first legislature, held on February 15, 1999, 88% of eligible voters participated.

Hon. Eva Aariac
Premier, Nunavut

Under their nonpartisan political system, in which there are no parties and decisions are made by consensus, the 19 newly elected members meet for days after an election in order to choose their government leader. Their 19 seats are in a circle, not divided by an aisle to separate right and left, government and opposition. They are surrounded by symbols of their unique environment. The first item one sees upon entering the premier's office is a huge polar-bear rug. The upholstery in the legislative chamber one floor below is of seal skin. The door handles are made of walrus tusk, and the shaft of the ceremonial mace that symbolizes legitimacy is the tusk of a narwhal, a small Arctic whale.

The premier has to consult with all the Members of the Legislative Assembly (MLAs), not just with the cabinet, which the MLAs, not the premier, select. They have become more comfortable with Westminster traditions, such as addressing all comments to the speaker. But there have been some critics of government without parties and a loyal opposition. They contend that

there is no mechanism for accountability, that deals involve too much pork-barrel politics, and that there is no way for voters to "send a message" to the government. But supporters argue that the nonpartisan, consensual system is the Inuit way and that it allows the most talented people in the entire legislature to form the government.

The one female and 18 male deputies selected lawyer Paul Okalik as premier. Easily reelected in 2004, his vision was "that we achieve the same standard of living as other Canadians and at the same time preserve our culture and language." Okalik had personally experienced the troubles that afflict his entire Inuit people. He was young enough to be the only premier in Canada still paying off his student loans when he took office. He ruled a young region, with the continent's highest birth rate and where 40% of the population is under age 15 and half under 22; it is young men aged 15 to 29 who commit two-thirds of the crime. He had also personally been through alcoholism, a term in prison, and a brother's suicide. In November 2010 Eva Aariak was chosen to succeed Okalik as premier.

The rate of heavy drinking in Nunavut is three times the Canadian average, and a quarter of all babies are born with fetal alcohol syndrome. The head of Nunavut's RCMP said the root of all crime is "alcohol, alcohol, alcohol." Even in places where citizens have voted by plebiscite to prohibit alcohol, these decisions are undermined by bootleggers. This helps make the territories the most dangerous parts of Canada.

The suicide rate is seven times the Canadian average. Young men are almost 30 times more likely to commit suicide, and young women aged 15 to 24 are 36 times more likely to take their own lives than other Canadian women. Teacher Sheila Levy admitted: "suicide touches everyone here." In an attempt to combat this tragedy, a new mental health center was created in Iqaluit.

Drug addiction is epidemic. The lowest form of substance abuse—solvent sniffing—is 26 times more prevalent than in

Inuit camp, Baffin Island, Nunavut   Courtesy: Michael J. Hewitt

Canada

Canada as a whole; 20% of the people admit doing it. Aggravated assault is 1,033% higher, and sexual assaults are 1,270% more likely than in the rest of Canada. The rate of sexually transmitted disease is 15 times the national average. The high-school graduation rate is only 27%, and Nunavut has the lowest literacy rate in Canada.

A shocking dimension of this horrible crime rate is that some of the territory's political leaders show such bad examples. Levi Barnabas was given a cabinet post despite being convicted for sexual assault while he was Speaker of the House. James Arvaluk became education minister even though he had served prison time for rape and assault, having beaten a former girlfriend so brutally that she needed 18 stitches to sew up her mouth and sustained permanent nerve damage. Lorne Kusugak was unanimously appointed to a cabinet post two months after being charged with sexual assault and trying to strangle his victim.

A major contributor to these lamentable social problems is the lack of work. The official unemployment rate in 2004 was 30% among Inuit. But if one includes those who have given up looking for a job, the figure increases to an estimated 37% of Inuit. Because of the extremely high birthrate, many children will never find future jobs. By contrast, unemployment among the non-Inuit minority was only about 4%. Of the 2,789 jobs created in the territory's new public service by 2006, 45% went to Inuit, short of the stated goal of 50%. Unemployment is especially serious since Nunavut has Canada's highest cost of living and lowest per capita income—$11,000 in 1999, a third of that in the NWT. In 1999 a liter of milk cost $5 and a loaf of bread $3. It is small wonder that some provide for their families by going outside the wage economy and engaging in hunting and fishing. A third of the residents receive welfare, more than three times the Canadian average.

Most of the jobs are related to government spending, which accounts for more than half of Nunavut's employment. What little private sector work there is often depends directly on government projects, such as construction. Only five communities exist in Nunavut where getting a job is a viable option. Not including the land-claim payments, Ottawa sends Nunavut 90% of the territory's revenues. Per capita handouts amount to $21,622 each year in addition to $40,000 per person in "compensation" payments.

Nunavut has a very small tax base. It gets about five times as much revenue from tobacco taxes as from corporate income taxes. Lodging is a serious problem and is very expensive: 83% live in government-subsidized housing. This situation stems from the 1950s when the federal government forced the nomadic Inuit to resettle in permanent communities, resorting to such brutal measures as shooting their dogs. In 1992 the Canadian government formally apologized to more than a hundred Inuit who had been forced in the 1950s to move from their northern Quebec homes to the desolate high Arctic settlements of Resolute Bay and Grise Fiord. The purpose had been to assert Canadian sovereignty over the area, where a U.S. military outpost was located.

Prospects for economic development are not encouraging. Nunavut has fewer developed resources than the NWT. The best hope for broadening the tax base is mining although extraction costs of many of its resources are prohibitively high. By century's end, three mines were producing lead, zinc, gold and silver. The first diamond mine opened—Jericho—just south of the Arctic Circle. Jerico is largely responsible for Nunavut's economic growth rate in 2006 of 5.8%, second only to oil-rich Alberta. Ottawa takes 95% of the revenue on mining riches, and all three northern premiers want a bigger share.

A 1993 land claims settlement requires outside investors to draw up "impact benefit agreements" with local communities. There are only about 20 miles of paved highways connecting towns. Mobility must be by air. This creates obstacles in developing the tourist industry. The federal government is committed to creating three new national parks in the territory, and eco-tourism is rising. But with round-trip air tickets from Ottawa to Iqaluit costing over $2,000, tourism in Nunavut is for the well-to-do.

Perhaps the highest level tourists came to town in early February 2010: the fi-

Inuit hunter (aalluk), Gjoa Haven, Nunavut
Courtesy: Michael J. Hewitt

nance ministers of the Group of Seven, the world's leading developed nations. Canada's choice of location was inspired by the wish to assert Canadian sovereignty in the Arctic and to take a stand against the European Union's ban on seal products. The ministers were invited to a "community feast" and served seal meat, caribou, char jerky and musk-ox. They were also given souvenirs of sealskin mittens and waistcoats. In August 2009 Prime Minister Harper had brought the entire cabinet to Iqaluit for a meeting as a part of a five-day visit to the Arctic. While in Iqaluit, they ate raw seal meat to take a swipe at the EU and to make a gesture of solidarity with the Inuit. Governor General Jean had also eaten raw seal heart in order to make the same gesture.

Most Canadians must experience the extraordinary light and sweep of the Arctic through films. The first Inuit-language feature in history, *Atanarjuat* (The Fast Runner), a film about an epic tale of love, jealousy, murder and revenge, directed by Zacharias Kanuk, was greeted by rave reviews at the 2001 Cannes film festival. Award-winning Canadian filmmaker John Houston, who grew up in the Arctic and speaks fluent Inuktituk, has also turned his artistic talent to Nunavut. His *Songs in Stone*, about his Inuit art collecting parents in the North, opened in 1999. In 2001 he followed up with a documentary, *Nuliajuk: Mother of the Sea Beasts*, about a legendary sea deity by that name. No one can view these works without experiencing fascination for the Inuit imagination.

Dog team on the ice, Simpson Strait, Northwest Territories

THE GLOBE AND MAIL

CANADA'S NATIONAL NEWSPAPER ■ FOUNDED 1844 ■ GLOBEANDMAIL.COM ■ WEDNESDAY, JUNE 16, 200

Leaders split deeply on rights as campaign endgame begins

Former Opposition Leader Stephen Harper debates ex-Prime Minister Paul Martin in Electoral Campaign 2004   Photo: J.M. Carisse

PARTIES AND ELECTIONS

Like any modern democracy, the Canadian political system could not function without parties. They recruit and select candidates, define issues which are important, educate voters about them, finance and fight electoral campaigns, put up governments which rule at all political levels, and provide well organized opposition parties, which continually remind the electorate of the governments' shortcomings. For the government, the party is an essential tool for maintaining a parliamentary majority, and for the individual politician it is the ladder to power. For the political activist it is an important means for putting his ideas into practice, and for the voter it is an indispensable label for the set of politicians, policies, sympathies or interests.

Canadian parties emerged even before Confederation and were originally named and modeled after the two major British

parties in the 19th century, the Conservatives and Liberals. For a while, they were loose coalitions of various factions with little discipline and almost no organization outside of parliament. By the end of the 19th century, though, they had changed considerably to conform to the nature of the Canadian state and society. They now have several distinctive characteristics: first, they are decentralized, which is exactly what one would expect in such a federal state. At the bottom is the local poll organization, and above that is the riding (district) organization, which selects the candidates for parliamentary elections.

Unlike in the United States, it is not necessary in Canada for a candidate to reside in the riding in which he runs. It is a fairly strong tradition, however, that the candidate be from the constituency. Occasionally higher party officials will ask a riding to allow a certain person to run in that

electoral district. This is usually a party leader or cabinet member who desperately needs a parliamentary seat in order to be in a government or be a leader in the parliamentary opposition. An example of this was Brian Mulroney, who had never held an elective office before he was selected as Conservative party leader in 1983. In order to lead his then opposition party in the House of Commons, an MP from Nova Scotia agreed to give up his seat so that Mulroney could win it in a by-election. Since Mulroney had lived in the area as an undergraduate at St. Francis Xavier University, and since the riding organization calculated that it would doubtlessly benefit in the long run by lending a helping hand to a person who was likely to become the country's prime minister, it agreed to the move. However, the point must be reiterated: higher party bosses cannot simply "parachute" out-

Canada

siders into ridings whenever they wish to do so. If the riding organization says "no!", then that is the answer.

Parties also have regional and provincial associations. Most major parties maintain permanent provincial headquarters, which help the federal parties conduct campaigns during federal parliamentary elections. At the top is the national headquarters. Except for the headquarters in Ottawa and the provincial capitals, most of the lower party organizations more or less hibernate between elections. They remain ready to spring into action at a day's notice to wage electoral campaigns. The dates for these are never known long in advance. They are almost always determined by premiers and prime ministers to take place at their party's advantage. Provincial elections are never timed to coincide with federal elections. The national headquarters has a staff to support the party in a variety of ways. They hire issue consultants and pollsters, print literature and posters, and order campaign paraphernalia. They also plan party conventions, and generally serve the parliamentary party organizations in any way they can.

Party headquarters help raise money for campaigns. Elections have become very expensive, although Canadian candidates do not yet spend as much as their American counterparts. In 1963 Quebec became the first province to pass spending limits for campaigns. Some other provinces later followed suit and have a variety of spending ceilings. In 1974 the Trudeau government placed limits on federal election expenses. For example, in the 1988 elections, Canadian candidates were limited to spending a total of $6.6 million during the 51-day campaign, whereas American candidates spent $140 million in a campaign lasting two years.

Subsequent 2003 legislation also grants tax deductions for political contributions. Candidates who win more than 10% of the votes in their ridings recoup 60% of their expenses from the government. Parties that receive at least 2% of the votes receive a subsidy of $1.95 per voter. In addition, the federal government provides to candidates from recognized parties a certain amount of free broadcasting time. These contributions from state coffers have helped all the parties, particularly the NDP, which, unlike the Liberals and Conservatives, always had difficulty obtaining contributions from well-to-do individuals or corporations. It has had to rely more on dues from party members and affiliated labor unions than have the other two parties.

The volatility of public election finance was demonstrated in 2008, when a Tory budget provision that would have eliminated it almost brought the newly re-elected minority government down. This seemed blatantly partisan since the Conservatives were in good financial condition while the other parties' finances were desperate. The measure was withdrawn. But in 2011 reductions in the maximum campaign contribution from $5,000 to $1,000 went into effect. This change prevented Liberals from fully tapping their stable of big donors.

Broadcasters are usually prohibited from announcing the results of federal elections in provinces where the polls have not yet closed. Thus western Canadians would not be influenced in their voting by knowing how their eastern countrymen had voted. That rule was set aside by the Supreme Court in 2004 on the grounds that it is an infringement on the freedom of speech. Of course, the internet makes it impossible to black out results from being disseminated anywhere in Canada. But in 2004 and 2006 western Canadians could watch the returns in the east before deciding whether or how to vote.

Despite a kind of party structure that appears to be hierarchically organized from top to bottom, there are no powerful, country-wide parties that can hold the disparate governmental and party elements together and facilitate compromise or smooth out regional differences. No parties are powerful in all parts of the country; all have their fortresses and deserts. After 2006 the Liberals were weak in the West, the NDP had barely a toehold in the Maritimes, and until 1984 and again after 2006 there was almost nothing more depressing than being a Conservative (Tory) in Quebec. Also, regional parties can differ greatly from the national parties that bear the same names.

Although the overall organization is loose *outside* of legislative assemblies, the *parliamentary parties* are tightly bound and led. MPs or MLAs vote against their party leaders only at risk to their political careers. Unlike their American counterparts, they seldom refuse to support their leadership, either for reasons of conscience or to serve better the interests of their constituents in the ridings. Individual MPs make the concerns of their constituents known in their parliamentary caucuses, committees or debates in the whole House; they also serve their constituents in a variety of other ways. But they usually do not vote with the wishes of the folks back home uppermost in mind.

The reason is that parliamentary democracy is practiced at every level in Canada; governments stand or fall based on the legislative nose-count. The stakes are therefore too high for a party to be indifferent to how its representatives vote. Such party discipline has been loosening over the years. When a government has no majority in parliament, as was the case for seven years after the 2004 elections, there is a lot of wheeling and dealing to win votes from other parties. Members of Parliament find themselves courted for their vote, and this can strengthen their political influence in parliament. Since the advent of multi-party politics after the First World War, Canada has had 12 minority governments compared with 15 majority ones. Some of those minority ones have been successful governments under such prime ministers as Mackenzie King and Lester Pearson and in the 21st century under Stephen Harper. The requirement to vote as the party leaders demand is lifted on votes of conscience, such as one on whether to legalize same-sex marriage.

A second major characteristic of Canadian parties is that they are democratic in at least two ways: they willingly relinquish power when they lose elections, and the selection of their leaders is decided upon at national leadership conventions of delegates representing party organizations throughout the country. Only about a tenth of adult Canadians actually belong to a political party. But any member who wishes to be active in his local, regional or provincial party organization has the chance to influence the outcome of the leadership race. He or she can speak with aspirants for the national party leadership, who travel around the country soliciting support. The caucus pollings are a bit like primary elections among party activists.

At the party conventions, the candidates make speeches, and the voting is by secret ballot based on the majority principle. The first candidate to win a majority of the delegates' votes (a process that usually takes several rounds of balloting) wins. In each round of voting a candidate is eliminated. The losing candidates often openly symbolize their support for one of the stronger candidates by actually going over to that person's section in the stands to shake hands or embrace. Sometimes such gestures pay handsome political dividends. For instance, the first contender to cast his support to Brian Mulroney after the first ballot in 1983 was Michael Wilson, who later became finance minister. In 2006, he was named Canada's ambassador in Washington. The purpose of party conventions is not only to select new party leaders, but also to serve as pep rallies to boost party morale. They bring the party elite together with the grass-roots. Sometimes they also draft or adopt party programs or platforms, which are usually statements of what the party would like to achieve in the best of all worlds.

Such conventions have a certain American air about them. Permeated with the smell of hot dogs and hamburgers and awash with Coca Cola and beer, they are noisy, colorful affairs, with a rainbow of

Sir Wilfrid Laurier

hats, scarves, buttons and signs, and big bands playing such songs as "When the Saints Come Marching In" and "Glory, Glory Hallelujah." Before the candidates deliver their crucial speeches (invariably mixing French and English), their enthusiastic supporters march in carefully orchestrated parades around the convention floor, accompanied by bands playing such unlikely political tunes as "Chariots of Fire" (for the underdog, of course). Bono and Canadian singer Paul Anka performed at the Liberals' 2003 convention. The supporters of Stéphane Dion, who won the Liberals' leadership contest at their December 2006 convention in Montreal, pranced around the arena wearing green T-shirts with his name on them and reminding everyone of Dion's special expertise on the environment.

There are also plenty of unabashed expressions of patriotism, such as "this beautiful country," "the most fortunate cluster of people on the face of the globe" and *Vive le Canada!* In dizzying rounds of expensive receptions, dances (with plenty of rock music for the one-fourth to one-third of the delegates who are under age 25), barbecues and "chuck-wagon breakfasts", candidates have the opportunity to meet delegates directly. One major difference with American conventions, though, is that one does not always know for sure whom the Canadian delegates will select.

Programs and platforms seldom bind the party leaders, who must seek votes and make policy. The reason for this is related to a third characteristic of Canadian parties: they are mass, non-ideological coalitions of many diverse groups. From the beginning, their goals are to win elections and divide the spoils of victory. Thus, they are pragmatic, practical and flexible.

Minor or regional parties in Canada usually began outside of legislatures as protest movements and therefore tend to be more ideological in their programs and orientation. The federal system, which fragments the political process, helps such parties to arise and provides them with smaller arenas that are less heterogeneous than Canada as a whole. In such smaller units with fewer groups to appease, it is more feasible to take a more partisan approach. A closer look at each of the major parties will help elucidate the differences that do exist among them.

The Liberal Party

The Liberal Party, which in its earliest days was called the Reform Party, was Canada's most successful federal party in terms of years in power. Indeed, this party's history is in many ways the history of Canada itself. It originally began as a combination of agrarian interests in Western Ontario, anti-clerics from Quebec and reformist elements from Nova Scotia and New Brunswick. The dominant Ontario group lent the entire party its nickname as "Grits," a term which derived from one of its founders, who reportedly said that the party wanted candidates who were "all sand and no dirt, clear grit all the way through."

Sir Wilfrid Laurier was the party's first great leader. By standing firmly against conscription during World War I, he was able to convert Quebec into a powerful pillar of the Liberals. Laurier succeeded in persuading many *Québécois* that Canadian-style liberalism was not as stridently anti-clerical as the European variety. He was thereby able to synthesize Canadian liberalism with French Canadian support. This synthesis has been one of the great strengths of the party. Liberals have traditionally appealed to Roman Catholics, Jews and other ethnic minority groups, and they generally have been more successful in patching together diverse groups and interests. As Christina McCall-Newman wrote in her book, *Grits,* the party forged powerful "alliances of elites," which was a "marvelously adaptable institution." In every generation, the Liberals succeeded in giving Canadians what they thought they wanted. The party also led Canada into the welfare era. In its Kingston policy conference of 1960, it pledged such innovations as universal medicare, minimum wages, old-age pensions, measures which all major Canadian parties have come to support.

In the 1970s, the party began to stumble because of some important changes in Canadian society. Its base in Quebec was eroded by the struggle over separatism; in the eyes of many *Québécois*, the party no longer was the best vehicle for their aspirations. Clashes with the western provinces almost entirely eliminated the Liberal presence in that increasingly powerful region. The social welfare net was predicated upon the assumption that the economy would continue to grow and that the federal government would always have handsome surpluses at its disposal. When the worst recession in 50 years began in the early 1980s, that basic assumption was wiped away. More and more Canadians began to wonder if liberalism was a viable economic doctrine any more.

Trudeau let the party machinery and base wither and seemed to become increasingly aloof and insensitive. He had greatly invigorated the party after 1968, but he became more and more unpopular and a growing liability for his party. The party was in the doldrums and needed a fresh start.

The Liberal Party had dominated federal politics for most of the 20th century, after Sir Wilfrid Laurier created a seldom beatable majority in 1896. By election year 1984 it had ruled all but 22 years in that century. Ruling parties suffer from the declining popularity of leaders, whom a party cannot dismiss gracefully after many years of good service. "Trudeaumania" had long-since disappeared.

Many Canadians still admitted that Trudeau had been, in some important ways, good for Canada after becoming prime minister in 1968. He was a highly intelligent, learned, flamboyant and intriguing man. A completely bilingual Quebecer, he effectively confronted the specter of Quebec separatism by extending French language rights throughout Canada. The Liberal Party suffered in the West for this policy, but Canada's unity as a country was preserved. Trudeau's last government nationalized the constitution so that Canadians no longer have to request the British parliament to change it. He was also a very visible figure in the world arena. Some Canadians would say that he "put Canada on the map."

Rt. Hon. Jean Chrétien, former Prime Minister

Canada

At the same time, many Canadians came to view him as aloof, arrogant, and condescending, a reputation that began to rub off on his party. Also, many saw him as an unpredictable politician who sometimes behaved childishly in public. His banister slides or public displays of "the finger" were neither widely applauded nor appreciated. Finally, he seemed to ignore his party's need for effective organization of sound finances. He stepped down in June 1984 and lived in active retirement in Montreal until his death in October 2000.

His passing ignited an outpouring of grief that his countrymen had never before experienced. Parliament adjourned, the Supreme Court closed its doors, and normally reserved Canadians wept openly. He had clearly retained a hold on the imagination and loyalties of millions at home and abroad. People from all over Canada waited in line at Parliament Hill in Ottawa to see and touch his casket. They left red roses, which he had always worn in his lapel. His coffin was loaded into a hearse, a 19-gun salute was fired, and it was put on a train to Montreal. Along the way it slowed in small towns, and people waved and threw red roses. His body lay in state again in Montreal's City Hall. The doors were left open until 4 AM, when the last mourners left. Eight Mounties dressed in scarlet carried his coffin to his grave.

All Canadian prime ministers have mountains named after them when they die. The only exception is John Diefenbaker, who had a lake in Saskatchewan named for him. When Jean Chrétien, who admired Trudeau as his own mentor, decided to change the country's highest mountain, Mount Logan, to Mount Trudeau, an immediate outcry was heard. William Logan had been a famous geologist who in the mid-19th century had overseen the first comprehensive geological survey of Canada.

John Turner replaced Trudeau in June 1984. The former served as prime minister for 80 days before leading his party in a disastrous electoral defeat in September 1984. The 1984 leadership convention pitted Turner against his chief rival in the party, Jean Chrétien of Quebec. Chrétien was an extraordinarily versatile politician, having held virtually all the major cabinet posts. The 18th of 19 children (only nine survived), he grew up in an economically struggling family in Belgoville in northeast Quebec. After graduating from Laval University law school and practicing law in Shawinigan for a while, he went to Ottawa in 1963 as an MP who could barely speak English. He not only mastered the language, but he developed a good sense of humor. A childhood illness had left him able to move only one side of his mouth.

But he shrugged this off, saying that unlike many politicians, he could not speak out of both sides of his mouth.

He became party leader in 1990. Chrétien's appeal for Canadian unity was popular in anglophone Canada, but he faced hostility in his native Quebec, where his brand of "renewed federalism" found little resonance. Seldom in history had the Liberals' fortunes been so low in Quebec.

Chrétien led his Liberal Party into the 1993 federal elections ahead of all other parties. No one could have anticipated how massive the Liberal victory would actually be. It won 41.2% of the votes and 177 of 295 seats, all but exterminating its traditional rivals. Chrétien became the first Liberal prime minister ever to win office without a majority of seats in Quebec, where it captured only 19 of 75. This was particularly remarkable considering the fact that Chrétien himself is a *Québécois*.

He entered the June 1997 elections both as the most popular prime minister since polling began a half century ago and as the first federal leader to reduce the budget deficit in modern times. Although his Liberals declined from 174 seats (and 40% of the votes) to 155 seats (and 38%) in the House of Commons, his government was able to hang on to a narrow majority.

The Liberals had expected to win the 2000 elections, but the magnitude of victory was especially gratifying: they captured 173 seats (up from 155) based on 41% of the popular votes. This provided Chrétien with a comfortable majority in parliament and the honor of being the first leader to form three straight majority governments since 1945.

In 2000 Liberals found themselves divided. Finance Minister Paul Martin and his followers made it known that they had waited long enough to take over the party's reins. Martin's and Chrétien's differences went back to their bitter leadership contest in 1990, which Martin lost, and to the Meech Lake controversy, which Chrétien opposed and Martin supported. Martin had always been more accommodating to Quebec nationalists. The result was profound distrust between the two leaders. Chrétien resisted being pushed out.

By 2002 the party could no longer bear the public feuding. After Chrétien fired Martin in June, the Liberal caucus in parliament put enormous pressure on the prime minister to declare his intentions. He stepped down in December 2003. Martin assumed leadership of the party in the November 2003 convention.

In the June 28, 2004, elections the Liberals failed to capture their fourth parliamentary majority in a row and had to settle for a minority government. They captured only 36.7% of the votes and lost 37 seats, falling from 173 to 135. They did well in Atlantic Canada, fell far behind the *Bloc Québécois* in Quebec, saw their stranglehold in Ontario broken even though they still won the most seats, and did better than expected in the West.

The 2006 elections were a disaster for the Liberals, who were consigned to the opposition for the first time in a dozen years. They fell to 30.2% of the votes and only 103 seats. To no small extent, the outcome was as much a rejection of Martin and the Liberals as an acceptance of Harper and the Conservatives. A defeated Martin resigned as party head, leaving the Liberals leaderless and in disarray. They faced the dual task of choosing a leader and rebuilding their fractured and directionless party.

Its leadership convention took place in Montreal December 3, 2006, following a campaign that lasted almost a year. The most interesting contender was Michael Ignatieff. He is the grandson of Tsar Nicholas II's last minister of education, whose son landed in Montreal as a refugee in 1928. Michael, like his friend Bob Rae, was the son of a top-ranking Canadian diplomat, including an assignment as ambassador to the UN. He spent much of his youth abroad.

After graduation, he left Canada for three decades, earning a PhD in history at Harvard, writing 14 books, including his family memoir that won the Governor General's Award, and gathering seven honorary doctorates. He lectured on genocide and ethnic violence in Britain and the U.S., ending up in a professorship of human rights at Harvard from 2000–5. In 2006 he won a seat in Toronto as a Liberal.

However, he proved to have serious skeletons in his closet. In countless articles in leading American newspapers, he had displayed what became known as the "pronoun problem": using the words "we" and "us" when referring to Americans. Many Canadians did not like that. He had supported the U.S. invasion of Iraq in 2003, and he continued to favor military action in Afghanistan. That left him in Canada with a reputation as a "hawk."

Often compared with Trudeau because of his scholarly nature and unusual path into politics, he lacked parliamentary and cabinet experience, and that showed. He made many gaffes in the campaign. His loss to Stéphane Dion on the fourth ballot 55% to 45% was as much a protest against the Harvard alien carpetbagger as a vote for Dion. The Conservatives soon picked up on this theme by running TV and Internet ads saying "Just Visiting" and contending that Ignatieff has no interest in Canada unless he can rule it.

For more than a century, every elected leader of the Liberal Party eventually became prime minister. History did not repeat itself. Dion came off as a cerebral wonkish ex-professor whose strong suit is not political organization, who speaks mangled English, and who does not connect well with people. He had failed both as a party organizer and parliamentary leader; under his stewardship the party had gone from $5 million in the bank to $6 million in debt. The Liberal performance in the October 2008 elections was a disaster. Its share of the popular vote fell to 26%, the lowest since the party's founding in 1867. It dropped from 103 to 76 seats.

Dion insured his demise within weeks of the election. When the Harper government tried to end public funding of parties, Dion entered a conspiratorial coalition with the Bloc Québécois (which seeks the destruction of Canada as a unified country) and the NDP (which attacks the Liberals at every opportunity) to bring down the Tory government in a vote of confidence. Harper prevented that by persuading the governor general to prorogue Parliament until late January 2009 while he prepared a new budget. Dion's bumbling into this half-baked effort to unseat the Tory government provoked a backlash against Dion within his own party. Deputy chairman Ignatieff knew that such a strange coalition could only fail, that it would leave the Liberals both weaker and unable to govern, and that the party's finances would not permit a renewed election effort. He therefore led the party in supporting the new budget and in replacing the inept leader.

Dion agreed to go. Ignatieff's only serious rival was his former roommate at the University of Toronto, Bob Rae, but Rae dropped out without forcing a vote. Rae became the unofficial Liberal shadow foreign minister and was named by *Maclean's* in 2010 as the best orator in parliament. He speaks freely and can compel the room to his attention like few others. Ignatieff's four years in Parliament burnished his speaking skills, including mastering the art of the sound bite in both English and French. He ran a disciplined and coherent

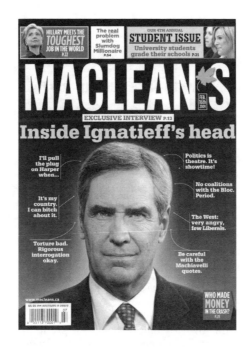

opposition leader's office, and he spent nearly a year on the road meeting voters.

The May 2011 federal elections were such a calamity for the Liberal Party that some observers wonder if it will ever recover. Ignatieff triggered the election in March 2011 by joining the NDP and separatist BQ in bringing about a vote of no-confidence against the Conservative minority government over an issue that voters seemed to care little about: contempt of parliament in concealing the true cost of prisons and new jet fighters. A February poll found that 51% of voters viewed him unfavorably, while only 25% had a positive view. The Conservatives branded him as a carpet-bagging elitist, who had

Rt. Hon. Charles Joseph Clark

no clue about the struggle of ordinary Canadians. They were ready and itching for an election, but the Liberals were not.

By the time the votes were counted, the party and the nation were dumbfounded. The Liberals had fallen to less than 20% of the votes and a mere 34 seats. This was their worst result ever and the first time they were not among the top two parties. It had turned to the left in desperation, but its voters gravitated to the Tories and New Democrats, who occupied the center. It lost big in Quebec because it could no longer pretend to be a bridge between the province and the rest of Canada. It is dead in the West and lost much of its foothold in Ontario. It had to relinquish to the NDP its position as official opposition in parliament. Ignatieff lost his own seat in Toronto and immediately resigned as party chairman to return to the classroom at the University of Toronto.

The party is left to ponder its continued relevancy and to face the many questions about its future and purpose. It selected Rob Rae as interim leader of the Liberal caucus in parliament. It must then choose an official party leader sometime in 2013. That leader will have to be bilingual, know how to maneuver the party back into the political center and have a clear idea how to fend off talk of a left-wing merger with the NDP. Bob Rae is hailed as a potential beacon of stability for the much-diminished party. He recalled the wisdom a former mayor of Toronto had imparted to him when he was just entering politics: "Bobby, in politics, you don't get what you deserve, you get what's coming to you."

The Conservative Party

Until 2004 two parties of the right had offered the Liberals three federal election victories on a platter because they split the opposition vote. For example, in 2000 they won a combined total of 38% of the votes (to the Liberals 41%), but because of the effect of the single-member electoral system, they received a combined total of only 78 seats to the Liberals' 172. They were cutting each other's throats. But "uniting the right" was difficult because the Progressive Conservative Party (PC) and the Canadian Alliance had grown out of different traditions, appealed to different kinds of Canadians, and had much bad blood between them. A look at both pillars of the new Conservative Party shows why their merger in 2004 was difficult but necessary.

Progressive Conservative Party

The Progressive Conservative Party (PC), under the leadership of Sir John A. Macdonald and his Quebec partner, Sir George-Etienne Cartier (then "The Conservative Party"), had dominated Cana-

Canada

dian politics for most of the first three decades of confederation. The Conservatives (Tories) suffered devastating political setbacks in the 20th century because of their support of a military draft during the First World War and because they were in power when the Great Depression struck in the early 1930s. At times it seemed almost as if they had been condemned to permanent opposition in federal politics. They traditionally drew much support from Protestants of British ethnic origin, but they needed to broaden their base.

In 1968 their exclusion from Quebec was prolonged by the emergence of the *Parti Québécois* and its antagonist, Pierre Elliott Trudeau. To polish the party's image by underscoring its moderate course and acceptance of Canada's social welfare net, they changed its name to Progressive Conservative, words which are not a contradiction in terms. They did not allow the Liberals either to outdo them in welfare spending by very much or to shove them to the right on the political spectrum. In 1978 Trudeau said that the Liberal position was the "radical center." Six years later, the PC leader defined the position of his own party as "the extreme center."

In the late 1970s the PC's opportunity to regain power in Ottawa had come. The Liberals had been driven out of power in every Canadian province, and the PC captured control of most provincial parliaments. In 1976 Joe Clark, a young Albertan in his 30s, who had buckled down to learn fluent French, came from behind to capture the party leadership. In 1979 he led his party to victory in the federal parliamentary elections. However, his minority government made some cardinal blunders that ensured that it would be short-lived. Despite the fact that the PC had failed to win a majority of seats in the House of Commons, Clark decided that his government would rule *as if* it had a majority. In other words, he decided upon a bold political course, which included such controversial stands as moving the Canadian embassy in Israel from Tel Aviv to Jerusalem, delaying the opening of parliament, and driving a very hard bargain with Conservative-governed Alberta in setting oil prices.

In an important budget vote, he failed to count noses carefully and lost the vote. He thereby prompted a new election in 1980, only eight months after the last one. An electorate that was most unimpressed with Clark's leadership gave the Liberals a new lease on life and voted the Conservatives out of power. Constantly nipped at the heels by critics within his own party, Clark decided to silence them by calling for a new leadership conference in June 1983. The result revealed the magnitude of his miscalculation: he lost on the fourth ballot to his challenger, Brian Mulroney.

Although Mulroney had had a passion for politics since his youth, he had never held elective office before becoming party leader. The oldest son of an Irish working-class family, Mulroney was born in the mill town of Baie Comeau, a predominantly French-speaking community located 265 miles north of Quebec City. His father was an electrician who had to hold down two jobs to make ends meet for a family with six children. He was the first offspring of a working class family ever to become prime minister in Canada.

The biggest asset he derived from his family background was that he grew up speaking French with his friends and English at home. Thus, he had acquired that indispensable advantage of being completely bilingual from childhood. This lingual ability, combined with a deep understanding and sympathy for their concerns and fears, enabled him to break through the distrust that many Quebecers had borne toward anglophones for two centuries.

Rt. Hon. Brian Mulroney

Mulroney became prime minister in 1984. In 1988 he was the first Tory prime minister since 1891 to receive back-to-back majority governments and the first prime minister of any party in 35 years to win two consecutive victories. The Tories won 43% of the vote (down from 49.9% in 1984) and 169 seats (down from 211).

In many ways Mulroney was a success. He changed Canada more profoundly than most of his predecessors because of his free trade, tax, and constitutional policies. As a party leader he held together a fractious mix of anglophone westerners and francophone Quebecers, with only a few defections. He was effective in foreign policy. But his popularity dropped to the lowest of any prime minister in a half century. He was widely mistrusted and disliked, partly because of his manner, which seemed affected and insincere.

His reputation was not helped by scandals after leaving office in 1993. He faced allegations that he had received money from Airbus to lobby the government and Air Canada to buy the European planes. He sued the government and won an apology and $2.1 million payment. But in a sensational House of Commons ethics committee inquiry in December 2007, he admitted that he had indeed received between $225,000 to $300,000, probably Airbus money, from a disreputable jailed dispenser of bribes, Karlheinz Schreiber, a German arms industry lobbyist. The cash was slipped to him in envelopes in hotel rooms, and he issued neither invoices nor receipts. Nor did he pay taxes on the money at the time, but sensing trouble he paid them later. He went to great lengths to cover up the payments. In his testimony to the committee, he admitted that he had shown an "error in judgment" and had made the biggest mistake of his life. A government enquiry found in 2010 that he had acted inappropriately by accepting the cash.

He was also disliked because of unpopular policies, such as the Free Trade Agreement, Meech Lake, high interest rates, and the federal 7% goods and services tax (GST), which went into effect in 1991. He faced the twin threats of regional alienation and Quebec nationalism. The rejection of his constitutional reform in October 1992 forced him to make an unpleasant decision in the interest of his party.

Bowing to his bleak electoral prospects, Mulroney announced in 1993 that he would step down after almost nine years as prime minister. He cleared the way for Kim Campbell, a former justice and defense minister from Vancouver, to take his place in June as party leader and prime minister and to lead the Tories in the October federal elections. Promising to "change the way we do politics in this country," she offered a refreshing candor in public, and her approval rating initially soared. In August, 51% of respondents approved of her performance as prime minister. This was the highest rating for any prime minister in 30 years.

But she was an inept campaigner and committed so many gaffes that one cruel reporter wrote that she rarely opened her mouth except to change feet. Although it would have been very difficult for any Tory to have succeeded, given the Mulroney legacy which had spawned severe cynicism in voters' minds, she led her party to the worst defeat in the history of any Canadian party. A group of 25 Canadian historians judged her in 1996 to have been the worst prime minister in Canadian history. After lecturing at Harvard and writing her autobiography, *Time and Change,* she accepted the post of Canadian consul general in Los Angeles. In 2010 she tried her hand at comedy by appearing in promotional clips for a VisionTV sitcom, "She's the Mayor."

The PC experienced a meltdown from 154 to *two* seats in the House of Commons, on the basis of 16% of the votes. The former pillars of Mulroney's strength, Quebec and Western conservatives, crumbled, as voters there streamed to the *Bloc Québécois* and the Reform Party, both protest movements committed to remaking the federal system.

.Campbell relinquished leadership to the perfectly bilingual Quebecer, Jean Charest, whom she had narrowly defeated for the leadership in June and who was one of the two Tories to win a seat. During the 1995 Quebec referendum campaign, he displayed far more guts and effectiveness in pleading the federal case than did Prime Minister Chrétien and was the only federal politician who advanced his status during that painful struggle.

The party, which is called the Yukon Party in that territory and the Saskatchewan Party in that province, retained parliamentary influence only in the Senate. Their desperate situation gave rise to black humor: "Why did the Tory cross the road? To meet the other Tory!" Even one longtime Tory strategist remarked: "At least now we know the real meaning of the Conservative ad that said, Think Twice." Under the leadership of the most popular pro-federal politician in Quebec, Jean Charest, the PC fought its way back to respectability in the 1997 elections, winning 19% of the votes and 20 seats, and emerged as the strongest party in the Atlantic provinces.

In 1998 Charest resigned to become the Liberal Party leader in Quebec; in 2003 he became Quebec premier. He was replaced by ex-Prime Minister Joe Clark, who had yearned to return to politics. Since the debt-ridden party could not afford a leadership

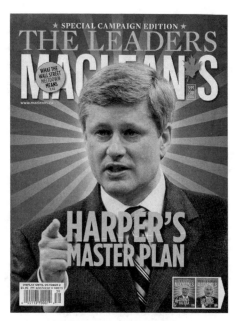

Rt. Hon. Stephen Harper

convention, its 87,000 members were invited to cast ballots. With half voting, he garnered 77% of the second-round votes.

He watched in 2000 as many Tories left the party to join the new Canadian Alliance that grew out of the Reform Party. The Tories were able to win a disappointing 12 seats in the House of Commons, based on 12% of the votes. This was the third consecutive devastating defeat. In only seven years the party had fallen from a majority government to a fifth-place party. It could no longer make its once-proud claim of being a truly national party able to speak for all Canadians in all walks of life. In 2002 Joe Clark told his party to select a new leader, and on June 1, 2003, it chose Peter MacKay in a dramatic convention. In 2006 MacKay became foreign minister and later defense minister.

The Canadian Alliance

The second pillar of the new Conservative Party is the Canadian Alliance, which had grown out of the Reform Party of Canada (RPC), led until 2000 by Preston Manning. Founded in 1987, this party viewed itself as carrying on the tradition of earlier western populist movements and promised to integrate its conservative philosophy with a commitment to the disadvantaged. It championed the cause of western Canada without advocating separation. It sought such constitutional changes as an elected Senate with equal regional representation and the possibility of recalling MPs whose performance is questionable to voters. It opposed bilingualism and special treatment for Quebec. Manning spoke about "One Canada," meaning that Quebec should decide whether it wishes to be a part of Canada as an equal province; if it does not, it

should leave. An anti-statist party, it sought a reduction in taxes, the size of government, and immigration. It also demanded more direct democracy in the form of referenda, recalls, and initiatives. Some observers saw its momentum as the "revolt of the middle classes."

It was so successful in exploiting western dissatisfaction that the party decided in 1991 to compete in elections everywhere but Quebec. Manning explained the party's momentum: "People are saying yes to Senate reform, . . . yes to a fair language policy and no to forced bilingualism, yes to candidates responsible to their ridings, no to central Canadian parties that tell their MPs how to vote." An avid student of the American Civil War, he saw the situation in his own country as similar to the U.S. before 1861. An insoluble problem leads to a totally new realignment of parties and the country. And it is an outsider, a "man of the people" from the West, who comes in and picks up the pieces. Whom might Manning have had in mind as Lincoln's Canadian equivalent?

The Reform Party demonstrated in the 1993 elections that it had become a major political force in Canada. It won 18.7% of the votes and 52 seats, narrowly missing becoming the official opposition in Ottawa. All its seats were from the West. One of its difficult challenges was to expand into eastern Canada. Manning was a folksy, mild-mannered man who sought more decorum in the House of Commons and modestly sat in the second row even though he had front-bench privileges. One of his first motions was to amend official bilingualism. Not surprisingly, the Liberal government and the separatist *Bloc Québécois* handily defeated this. Manning was not an effective parliamentarian.

The BQ and Reform Party actually had much in common, as Manning noted after meeting Lucien Bouchard over pancakes one morning: "I said we were discontented and wanted to reform the system, he said they were discontented and didn't think the system was reformable." In 1995 he told a gathering of conservatives in Washington: "The emerging political axis is: are you a traditionalist defending old systems . . . or are you a system changer? I would put us at the changing end. In Canada I would put the traditional parties on the system-defending end." The party capitalized on English Canada's frustration following the 1995 referendum on Quebec independence.

In the 1997 federal elections, it dominated the western provinces, winning 60 seats (19% of the votes nationwide) and becoming the official opposition in parliament. Manning showed that he has become a force to be reckoned with in Canadian politics. The Liberal government's

Canada

deficit cutting and law-and-order policies, as well as its tough approach toward Quebec, were influenced by Manning's popular appeals. His key political objective—to supplant forever the Tory party on the political right—was problematic, not least because Joe Clark adamantly rejected it. The Tory leader refused to attend Manning's "unite-the-right" convention in Ottawa in February 1999, calling it a "media event." No one denied the damage the two parties did to each other by competing in constituencies for the same voters. By fielding separate candidates, they cut each other's throats. But Manning wanted to change central Canada from the outside. Clark wanted to work with the center; he said: "I didn't grow up with the sense, ever, that the rest of the country was against me."

Manning became convinced that Reform was destined to permanent opposition if it remained trapped in the West and if Canada's conservatives remained divided. He was painfully aware that Reform and the Tories together had received as many votes in the 1997 federal elections as had the victorious Liberals (38%). But by competing with each other, they had won only 80 seats to the Liberals' 155. Therefore, in January 2000 his party invited all interested Tories to join them at a conference to discuss unification. By a 75%–25% margin, the delegates voted to create a new, broader party, called the Canadian Alliance. It promised to make some concessions to the center, such as accepting Canada's official bilingualism. It actively raided Tory ranks, and by the middle of the year it had surged to 19% in the polls, leaving the panicked Tories behind at 9%.

Stockwell Day, Alberta's former treasury minister, was elected party leader in July 2000, defeating a stunned Manning by a crushing 2-to-1 margin. He had undergone a dramatic transformation since his days as a marijuana-smoking college dropout who worked as a fisherman, hearse driver, auctioneer, and butcher in a meat packing plant. He became a born-again Christian with a social agenda so conservative that *Maclean's* magazine put his photo on the front cover with the title, "How Scary?" He pledged to reduce the role of government.

In the 2000 elections, the Alliance was all but vanquished in Ontario, winning only two rural seats. This was especially disappointing for Day, who had figured that if Alliance and Conservative voters could unify under one banner in Ontario, a powerful challenge to the Liberals' unassailable federal dominance could be made. That hope was dashed. The Alliance captured 64 seats from Manitoba to British Columbia. Although the Alliance, under Day's leadership, consolidated its hold on the West and its position as official opposition in Ottawa, it did not emerge as a national party that could serious threaten Liberal dominance in federal politics, despite its capture of 66 seats and a fourth of the popular vote nationwide.

In 2001 Day resigned, but he did not disappear. In 2006 his replacement, Stephen Harper from Alberta, who was only 43 years old at the time, put him in charge of the sprawling Department of Public Safety, the Canadian equivalent of the Department of Homeland Security. This had been created by the former Liberal government after September 11, 2001, to give a single minister control over everything from the RCMP and Canadian Security Intelligence Service, to running federal prisons and managing the border with the United States. He is praised for his frontbench survival skills.

An intelligent former policy adviser to Manning, Harper grew up in Toronto the middle-class son of an accountant. He moved to Alberta to do graduate work and has always lived a middle-class life in Calgary suburbs driving ordinary cars and earning a modest salary. He was not only a brilliant student, but he is a walking encyclopedia for hockey trivia. He claims to be writing a book on the subject. He wrote much of the party's early platform. He is an articulate campaigner in both official languages, a fiscal conservative, sure of his convictions, and an evangelical Christian without Day's public displays of born-again Christianity.

He demonstrated his negotiating skill throughout 2003 by building a bridge between the two rival parties on the right and then merging them to create a credible alternative to the Liberals. He persuaded the more centrist PC leader, Peter Mackay, that union was their only hope for electoral success. The two parties made the decision to form the Conservative Party in December 2003. The Alliance gave almost unanimous backing for the merger, but PC members had a more difficult time accepting it.

In March 2004 Harper defeated a neophyte politician—telegenic multi-millionaire heiress and Magna CEO, Belinda Stronach, who switched to the Liberal Party in May 2005—and former Tory health minister in Ontario, Tony Clement, for the new party's leadership. He declared: "My goal is not only to win an election. It's to create a natural Conservative majority in this country." He admitted that Quebec would be his party's toughest long-term challenge. There were defections, and fault-lines in the new party remained. Some prominent Tories refused to join. For example, Joe Clark not only refused to run for parliament again, but he hinted that he might support Paul Martin, "the devil we know." Many disgruntled Tories gravitated to the Liberals.

It takes a new party time to gel, and the Conservative Party was not yet a sturdy union when Prime Minister Martin called for new elections in June 2004. It was thrust into an election campaign without a full debate over policy. It still spoke with many contradictory voices. But the Conservatives performed reasonably well, showing in many ways more cohesion than the Liberals, who were licking deep wounds from Martin's bloody unseating of his old rival, Jean Chrétien. They captured 29.6% of the votes (down from the PC-Alliance combined total of 38% in 2000), but received 99 seats in the House of Commons, up from a combined 78. Most important, the Conservative Party now represented a viable political alternative for Canadians. In March 2005 Harper easily won a leadership review, receiving the support of 84% of the delegates at the party conference.

In the January 2006 elections the Conservatives won an impressive victory, securing 124 of 308 seats in the House of Commons on the basis of 36.3% of the votes. They won big in the West, where they got more than half of their seats, and all the seats in Alberta. Harper proudly proclaimed: "The West is now in." They broke the Liberal stranglehold on Ontario, winning 40 of its 106 seats. However, it was shut out in Toronto, Montreal and Vancouver.

Most dramatically, the Conservatives picked up 10 seats in Quebec, capturing 24.6% of the votes (up from 9%). Harper's openness to *Québécois* concerns, his budgetary gifts to the province, his talk of more flexible federalism, his frequent consultation with Quebec's Premier Charest, and his practice of beginning practically every speech in Ottawa in French, which he commands confidently, offer the prospect of even greater gains in Quebec. According to a 2007 poll, Harper got a good rating on his French from 81% of francophones.

The Conservatives rose steadily to almost 40% in the polls, but its numbers still did not translate into a parliamentary majority. He had to hang on to power in order to have a chance to achieve his real goal: to transform his party into a force capable of replacing the Liberals as the country's natural governing party due to their claim that only they can balance the interests of Quebec and the rest of Canada.

Nevertheless, Harper found himself in an agenda-setting position in Canadian politics. His disciplined control over the party left little room for sentiment or tolerance for failure. He is said to enjoy a comfortable family life that has changed little since they and their two children moved into the prime minister's residence. He is an accomplished amateur piano player who is a huge Beatles fan. When in 2009 his wife Laureen was the honorary chair for a benefit at the National Arts Center in Ottawa, she turned to him for the starring role. He grudgingly agreed to wear a leather vest and cowboy hat and to accompany himself on the piano while he sang *With a Little Help from my Friends* and *I Need Somebody to Love.* The black-tie crowd loved it.

Since ceremonial duties are performed by the Governor General, a prime minister's wife has no official role. She is not officially the "first lady." In fact, Laureen Harper's only public cause is fostering homeless cats for the Humane Society. However, the fact that she is more outgoing than her husband is a political asset for him.

Ensconced in their sprawling new campaign headquarters in an Ottawa industrial park and with a winning election team intact after the 2004 and 2006 campaigns, Harper and his party were itching for an election fight. By September 2008 he decided to ignore his own law fixing parliamentary terms and to call new elections for October 14. He failed to win his majority, but his party did increase its popular vote to 37.6% and win 19 additional seats. Disappointingly, it made no gains in Quebec, winning only 22% of the votes.

Through daring, Harper survived an opposition attempt to unseat his government through a vote of confidence shortly after the elections. That would have created an unworkable three-headed government that would have offered neither stability nor popular legitimacy. There was outrage throughout Canada over the prospect that separatists, the BQ, might get their hands on the levers of power in a deal concocted with no respect for the ballot box. Harper instinctively knew this, and polls showed upwards of 60% of the public hostile to the coalition taking power.

The Conservatives continued to rule via a somewhat stronger minority government. However, his large lead in the polls at least temporarily evaporated when he prorogued (sent home) parliament a second time for two months until the throne speech on March 3, 2010. This was a very unpopular decision. Although Harper claimed he needed time to "recalibrate" the budget, it appeared that he was preventing embarrassing documents relating to the treatment of detainees in Afghanistan from being discussed in a parliamentary committee. It seemed the government had something to hide.

Perhaps he was saved politically by the Winter Olympics in Vancouver. He was the chief fan for the victorious Canadian men's and women's hockey teams and basked in the glow of the thrilling sud-

Jack Layton
Source: *Maclean's*

den-death 3-2 victory of the Canadian men over their American rivals in the last event. Polls showed that he had widened his personal approval ratings over Michael Ignatieff during the Games, and shortly before the hockey final, 37% of voters said they favored the Conservatives compared with 29% for the Liberals. Only in Canada could this happen.

The Tories and Prime Minister Harper ruled for more than five years as Canada's longest-serving minority government. When the three opposition parties won a no-confidence vote in parliament on March 25, 2011, by a vote of 156 to 145, Harper jumped at the opportunity to call new elections in May that, he hoped, would give his government a stable parliamentary majority. He is a brilliant tactician who, in the words of the *Globe and Mail,* is "nasty, brutish—and competent." He correctly predicted that the Liberals and New Democrats would split the vote on the left, and the Tories would dominate the center.

He was not disappointed. The results of the May 2011 elections transformed Canadian politics. Voters responded to his argument that parliament had become dysfunctional and that his government needed a majority to stop the "socialists and separatists" (New Democrats and Bloc Québécois) from endangering the economic recovery and the nation's security. He framed the election as a simple choice between a stable Conservative majority in parliament or a "reckless coalition" of Liberals, New Democrats and Quebec separatists. He steered away from social issues, such as abortion and gay marriage, which are controversial and polarizing vote-losers. He focused on the economy, lower taxes, stronger defense and tougher measures against crime.

The Tories captured 167 seats out of 308, based on 39.6% of the votes. Only seven Tory incumbents lost their seats, com-

pared with 82 from other parties. Although its votes fell below 40% in all of Canada, they totaled 50% in two-thirds of the country. That is a formula for long-term success by the dominant party.

This was not just a victory. It was a realignment that could make the Conservatives the natural governing party in Canada, as the Liberals once were. Their traditional Liberal opponent was crushed. The Tory dominance of the West was strengthened: it won 54% of the votes in Manitoba, 56% in Saskatchewan, 67% in Alberta and 46% in BC. This was an average of 55% in the West, up by 9%.

But what was most stupefying were the Conservatives' gains in Ontario. In 2000 they captured two seats; in 2011 they got 73 seats and 44% of the votes. This was the first time since 1984 they carried this most populated province. They even won 30 seats in greater Toronto, including Ignatieff's. Although they lost ground in Quebec, the Tories made inroads into the influential immigrant community, especially South Asians and Chinese. Thus there is a new governing coalition: the West plus Ontario. That has never existed before, and it will grow as those two regions get about 30 more seats in the coming redistricting (the Tories' redistribution bill). The West now begins at the Ottawa River. The Conservatives have become Canada's dominant party.

The New Democratic Party

The most ideologically oriented Canadian party is the New Democratic Party (NDP), which is an offspring of the Cooperative Commonwealth Federation (CCF). The CCF was a protest party born in the prairies during the Great Depression that frontally attacked capitalism, "with its inherent injustice and inhumanity." Its famous Regina Manifesto of 1933 declared: "No CCF government will rest content until it has eradicated capitalism and put into operation the full program of socialized planning which will lead to the establishment in Canada of the co-operative commonwealth."

The party has never been revolutionary in the sense that it would take power by force; it was always democratic and sought change by means of the ballot box. Since it always sought votes, it has watered down its program throughout the years. In 1961 it changed its name to the New Democratic Party in order to broaden its appeal to non-socialists. However, tension remains between the impulses toward reform and toward electoral victory. It belongs to the Socialist International and remains the only successful social democratic party in North America.

The NDP found most of its support in urban areas in Ontario and the West. It also

Canada

does well in rural western areas, where it pays attention to farmers' wants. It succeeds in labor union circles, which are a declining reservoir of voters. More men than women give their votes to the NDP. It was vulnerable to Liberals, who sometimes picked up the NDP's ideas, such as medicare, and wrote them onto their own banners. It is very vulnerable to surges of populist conservative parties. In the late 1950s, the Diefenbaker landslide wiped the CCF out nationally. Until the May 2011 elections, the NDP had always been disadvantaged by the single-member district electoral system. This prevented it from having as high a percentage of seats in the House of Commons as its overall popular vote.

In 1989 it chose the first woman ever to become leader of a national political party of any size in North America—Miss Audrey McLaughlin, a former social worker from the Yukon. She inherited a divided and aging party perceived as being adrift on policy and in serious danger of being shunted to periphery of Canadian politics. The western wings of the NDP moved towards the right to capture mainstream voters, but this disappointed many party members who viewed this pragmatic move as a betrayal of cherished social democratic goals.

In the 1993 elections it captured only 6.8% of the votes and eight seats. It won seats only in the west. McLaughlin admitted that in the rest of Canada, "what we have been putting forward has not struck a chord with a large number of people. That's quite self-evident." The elections were the worst performance since the NDP's founding in 1961. Its Ottawa headquarters were sold, and most of its staff was laid off. While the buzzards circled, a new leader was selected in 1995: Alexa McDonough, a popular former social worker and 14-year leader of the tiny Nova Scotia NDP. Her selection followed a series of primaries among party members all over Canada intended to revitalize the party. She was chosen because she promised to unify the party's left and right.

Gilles Duceppe. Clever election slogan: A "clean" party in Quebec or Its "own" party in Quebec

In the 1997 elections it increased its voter harvest to 11% and 21 seats, mainly in the West. At its 1999 national convention delegates backed McDonough's demands by a 2 to 1 majority to move the party toward the political center. In the 2000 elections, the NDP won 8% of the votes and 13 seats, barely qualifying as an official party in Ottawa. McDonough was replaced in 2003 by Jack Layton, a charismatic PhD, fluently bilingual Toronto city councilor and former head of the Federation of Canadian Municipalities. He had a more ideological edge than his predecessor and was not above playing on latent anti-Americanism in Canada.

Layton reenergized the NDP and in the 2004 elections led it to its best result in a decade. Doing well in Ontario and the west, it more than doubled its votes nation-wide to 15.7% and jumped to 19 seats. Its platform called for increased government spending on healthcare and daycare, opposition to Canadian participation in America's missile defense, and especially the adoption of the proportional representation electoral system.

The NDP was the only party other than the Conservatives to improve its standing in the 2006 federal elections. Under the leadership of Jack Layton, who prefers the term "New Democrats" to the NDP acronym, it captured 17.5% of the votes and 29 seats. The NDP picked up a dozen seats in Ontario and 10 in BC. As usual, it was locked out of Quebec. It also had problems appealing to Asians and to other business-friendly immigrants. It did well in the 2008 elections, increasing its votes from 17.5% to 18.2% of the popular total and its seats from 29 to 37.

The NDP prepared well for the May 2011 elections. Party leader Jack Layton had just undergone prostate surgery and limped with a cane after hip surgery. But his party's campaign was anything but lame. In his eight years in charge, he had overhauled the NDP and sharpened its electoral focus by throwing overboard policies that had cost the party votes in past elections. It no longer spoke of a moratorium on new oil sands development or marijuana decriminalization, and it called for tax cuts for certain businesses. He greatly improved the party's technical and fund-raising capabilities, and the party bought a downtown property in Ottawa for its headquarters.

To woo Quebec voters, it advocated the separatists' view of the Canadian constitution as unfinished business. It supported a referendum standard for separation of 50 percent plus one vote. It proposed extending French-language protections to federally regulated industries. But the party's biggest drawing card in Quebec was Layton himself. He was born in Montreal in 1950 and grew up in Hudson, Quebec. He studied at McGill in Montreal, where he perfected the kind of relaxed, colloquial French that enabled him to perform best in the leaders' French-language TV debate. He emerged as a likeable street-smart Montrealer. He also shined in the English-language debate.

Canadians were left reeling when the election results came in. The NDP captured 31% of the votes and 103 seats, 58 of which in Quebec (up from one in 2008). It won seats in eight provinces. For the first time in its history, it became the official opposition in Ottawa and the dominant federal party in Quebec. In fact, Layton was the first anglophone leader of a national party to win in Quebec when a franco-

Fortunately, here, it's the Bloc

phone was heading another party (in this case Gilles Duceppe of the BQ). Quebec voters have frequently demonstrated massive swings in elections. Thus one should not regard as durable and lasting this dramatic rush to the NDP, a party that has never had a firm foothold in the province.

After the celebrations on election night were over, the party had to think hard how it would manage such a diverse and largely inexperienced group of MPs that included 58 Québécois, four McGill students (one of whom 19 years old), an ex-communist, teachers and activists, with very few seasoned politicians among them. One new NDP MP, Ruth Ellen Brosseau, was working in an Ottawa student bar when a party desperate for candidates from Quebec asked her to run in a Quebec riding. She said yes, but she did not set foot in the riding during the entire six-week campaign. Instead she spent some of her time in Las Vegas celebrating her 27th birthday. Never mind, she cruised to victory over the incumbent by 7,000 votes. She displayed rather good French skills when she visited her riding after the election.

The NDP caucus also contains a previous unapologetic advocate of an independent Newfoundland that could tear up the 1968 contract that awarded Hydro-Quebec cheap Churchill Falls power: Ryan Cleary. He unseated the Liberal incumbent in St. John's. A former editor of the *Independent* newspaper and an open-line radio host, he had earlier referred to the NDP as a bunch of "losers" and a "small pocket of aging granolas and artsy-fartsies." He now assures voters that "I do not consider myself a separatist. That's not what people want, and that's not what I want."

The NDP has nothing to do with two long-established parties miles to the left of it, which do consistently poorly throughout Canada. They are the Communist Party of Canada and a Maoist off-shoot called "Marxist-Leninists." The last Communist MP was elected in 1945, but his parliamentary career ended a year later when he was convicted of espionage.

Bloc Québécois

Until the 2011 federal elections, the political landscape was complicated by the *Bloc Québécois (BQ)*, composed originally in 1990 of a break-away group of nine Conservative and Liberal MPs from Quebec. Its first leader was Lucien Bouchard, formerly Canada's ambassador to France. The BQ captured 54 of the 75 seats in Quebec, the only province in which it competes. As the second-largest party in the House of Commons, the BQ became the official opposition. But Bouchard signaled the impermanence of his party in Ottawa by refusing to reside in Stornaway, the mansion at the disposal of the opposition

leader. "We don't intend to settle in Ottawa. The presence of the *Bloc* in Ottawa is by definition temporary," he declared.

Most of its MPs were new to Ottawa: 48 of 54. Many spoke no English. As a group, the BQ caucus members have little in common other than their commitment to separation from Canada; they range from left-leaning union activists to moderate lawyers and conservative business owners. They were quick to learn how to operate in Parliament.

Bouchard was an eloquent and passionate speaker in both languages. While leader of the opposition, he made official visits to Paris and Washington to explain his party's separatist agenda. These caused outrage in the rest of Canada; the *Edmonton Sun* described his Paris trip as a "one-finger salute to the country." In 1994 he nearly died from a flesh-eating disease that cost him a leg. Rising from doom, he enjoyed considerable sympathy for his personal courage and support for his milder form of Quebec separatism that allowed for continued economic ties with Canada.

The day after the failed 1995 referendum on Quebec independence, Jacques Parizeau announced his resignation as premier. Bouchard agreed to leave his post as BQ leader and replace him as Quebec's premier in 1996. Gilles Duceppe, a former hospital attendant, Maoist union organizer in his youth, and son of a famous Quebec actor, took over leadership of the BQ. He attributed his separatist leanings partly to having had to hear as a boy "God Save the Queen" played before hockey games. Duceppe guided the divided party into the 1997 federal elections. It declined from 75 seats to 44 and only 40% of the province's vote, down from 49% in 1993.

The BQ lost six seats in the 2000 federal elections to the national Liberals, who won as many seats in Quebec as the BQ: 37. Quebec nationalist sentiments had weakened considerably since the 1995 referendum, and Quebec sovereignty and constitutional reform had been put on the back burner. In April 2003 the PQ, on whom the BQ relies for organizational support, was ejected from power in Quebec. These developments hurt the BQ, a one-issue left-leaning party.

Its prospects looked dim until the 2004 elections gave it new life. After less than a year in power, the Quebec Liberal government under Jean Charest had become very unpopular. Then a government audit in Ottawa found that the federal government had since 1995 dished out about $75 million to advertising companies friendly to the Liberals to make anti-separatist propaganda in Quebec. Although most of the money had been simply pocketed with little or no work done, *Québécois* were deeply

offended. After having cleaned up much of the corruption in their province, this "sponsorship scandal" had been perpetrated by hypocritical federalists in Ottawa.

The results were stunning. The BQ won 50% of the votes, compared with 33% for the Liberals (and 19 seats), 9% for the Conservatives and 5% for the NDP. Its 54 seats matched the party's best performance in 1993. Even Jean Chrétien's old riding was picked off by a BQ candidate. The *Bloc* elected its first visible minority (black) MP and aboriginal MP. The party's slogan was clever: "*Un parti propre au Québec*," meaning either "a clean party" or "its own party" for Quebec.

Duceppe said repeatedly during the campaign that a vote for the BQ was not necessarily a vote for independence, but after the election he declared: "*Québécois* form a nation. We haven't decided tonight to make Quebec sovereign, but we can say that Quebec has shown it has confidence in sovereigntists." In the run-up to the January 2006 federal elections, he argued that an independent Quebec should have its own army and intelligence service, and he reminded Canadians in the televised debates: "Everyone common in Quebec knows Quebec is quite different from the rest of Canada. Not better, not worse. Plain different."

In those 2006 elections, the *Bloc Québécois* fell short of a majority of votes in Quebec, winning only 42% and slipping from 54 to 51 of the province's 75 seats. Not reaching the magical 50% mark, the BQ offered no prospect of a successful independence referendum any time soon. In 2007 Duceppe suffered a self-inflicted wound by announcing that he would return to Quebec to take over the *Parti* Québécois only to change his mind within 24 hours. In the October 2008 elections, the PQ did not campaign under the banner of Quebec independence, and partly for that reason it was able to block any Conservative advance in the province. It lost one seat for a total of 50.

The BQ experienced near annihilation in the 2011 elections, plunging from 47 to a mere four seats, too few to qualify as an official party in parliament. It remains as a powerless rump group. Gilles Duceppe, the longest-serving leader on the federal stage, immediately resigned. Only the most militant advocates of Quebec sovereignty stuck with the BQ, while soft sovereignists and federalists switched to the NDP. Clearly many Quebecers are tired of the BQ and seriously ask themselves if they really want to be represented in Ottawa by a party that is in perpetual opposition. Many want to play a more constructive role in federal politics. The fact is that in its two decades of existence, the BQ failed to make a contribution to

Canada

achieving the goal of separatist destiny. That is why it is a spent force.

It is doubtful that the NDP will be able to defend its dramatically enhanced presence in the province. Quebec has experienced many such surges, but they seldom last especially when much of it is attached to the personality of the leader, in this case NDP head Jack Layton.

The Greens

One new party, the Greens, took heart from the ecological protest movement in Germany. In 1983 it formed a movement that views "economic growth as a problem, not as a solution." In 2004 it made its best showing, winning a respectable 4.3% of the votes, up from only .8% in 2000. This was too few to win a seat but enough to qualify for federal financing of $1.75 per vote. Rejecting the labels of "right" or "left," the party combines traditional environmental positions, such as banning nuclear power and genetically modified foods, with calls for corporate and income tax cuts. But it has gotten a gust of wind in its sails from the rise of climate change to the top of Canadians' list of concerns.

The party's combative leader, Elizabeth May, is an American activist who left Smith College and accompanied her parents to Nova Scotia in 1972 in protest against the Vietnam War. She became a Canadian citizen in 1980, studied law at Dalhousie (and is now adding a masters in theology), and headed the Sierra Club of Canada for 17 years. The party has never been more popular since being led by May, who describes herself as an "eco bitch." She is earthy and quick-witted. It more than doubled its membership to 11,000 in only one year.

However, Green support has not traditionally translated into votes, in part because the party lacks effective organization. May has not been able to cure the party's backbiting, infighting and defections, and members have differing opinions on whether they belong to a party or a social movement. "Deep greens" suspect all power and are committed to shaking up the status quo. May prefers to work with those in power. For example, she cooperated closely with the formerly ruling Liberals to get the Kyoto Protocol ratified, even though the Sierra Club had ranked the Liberals fourth on environmental issues in both 2004 and 2006.

By helping to put the environment at the center of Canadian politics, May has spurred all parties to show more ecological commitment. However, electoral success did not quickly materialize. In 2008, the Greens garnered only 6.8% of the votes and not a single seat. Spurned by voters in Ontario and Nova Scotia, May moved to Saanich-Gulf Islands, British

Elizabeth May

Columbia, to win her long-coveted seat in the House of Commons. Nobody worked harder to win one. She knocked on countless doors and handed out packages of sunflower seeds, the international Greens' symbol. Her efforts paid off, and she won the party's first and only seat.

THE 2000 FEDERAL PARLIAMENTARY ELECTIONS

In 1993, Canadians experienced *three* prime ministers, matched only in 1896 and 1984. Peter C. Newman was right: "Governing Canada in the 1990s is a balancing act—like juggling wet fish while standing on a slippery diving board." The October 1993 elections had brought the biggest political upheaval in Canadian history. Turning against the Tory party of Brian Mulroney and his successor, Kim Campbell, the Conservatives fell to a humiliating two seats in the House of Commons. Rising from the debris were two new parties, the *Bloc Québécois* and the Reform Party. Both were committed to remaking Canadian politics and the country itself. They battled each other in Ottawa over their sharply different visions of Canada's future.

Put in charge was the Liberal Party of Jean Chrétien, who had held every major portfolio during the Trudeau era. He became the first francophone Quebecer ever to win a majority in the House of Commons without taking a majority of seats in Quebec. This was repeated in 1997, when Liberals captured only 26 seats in Quebec. Chrétien barely hung on to his own seat in his paper mill hometown of Shawinigan against a fiery Quebec separatist. Against the advice of his aides, he had called new elections for June 2, 1997, after

only three and one-half years. The party squeaked through with a 155-seat majority in the newly expanded 301-seat House of Commons. This was the first time since 1953 that a Liberal prime minister had won back-to-back majorities. With the BQ and the Reform Party winning votes by presenting radically conflicting views of Canada, it was difficult for Chrétien to develop a national accord on Quebec. The cracks in the Canadian federation appeared to be wider than ever.

Most Canadians, including members of Prime Minister Jean Chrétien's own Liberal Party, were surprised when he called new elections for November 27, 2000, after only three and one-half years. His decision was widely criticized, but the results proved that it had been an astute one. The economy was strong, and both the prime minister's and his party's popularity were at their highest level since 1993. The aftermath of an emotional outpouring in the wake of Trudeau's death seemed to indicate that the time was propitious.

The major opposition party to the Liberals, the Canadian Alliance, had just been created in 2000, and its fresh and energetic leader, Stockwell Day, was untested in national politics. He had just won a seat in the House of Commons and was planning to spend the winter parliamentary session to raise money and his profile for the next election. He also needed to do much work in Ontario to expand his new party's presence there in order to break the Liberal stranglehold that had delivered to Chrétien 101 seats in 1997. Finally, Chrétien's role as party leader was being challenged from within by popular Finance Minister Paul Martin, who was visibly impatient for his turn to be prime minister. By calling a snap election, Chrétien caught Day off guard and forced Martin to demonstrate loyalty in the heat of battle. Winning big, Chrétien silenced calls for him to step down in favor of Martin. "I'm elected and I intend to serve my term," he said.

It was an acrimonious campaign, with personalities playing a more important role than policies. The Liberals succeeded in painting the witty and telegenic Day as a political radical who harbored a secret agenda to endanger important Canadian institutions, such as state-funded one-tier health care, gun control, no capital punishment, and a woman's right to have an abortion under certain circumstances. Even his fundamentalist Christianity, including his belief in creationism, was scorned. Faith is normally considered out of bounds in Canadian elections, but former Ontario Premier David Peterson remarked on TV that Day's creationist views brought his intelligence into question. Such comments made Day a subject of ridicule. Even Conservative leader Joe Clark, who was generally credited with having conducted the best campaign, asked publicly: "Do you trust Stockwell Day's agenda?"

Day turned the heat on the prime minister by accusing him of criminal conduct for securing a loan for a friend in his Quebec constituency. Day rejected Chrétien's characterization of his intervention as a "normal operation" that a representative performs for his constituents and called it "moral rot." Chrétien was cleared of these ethics allegations five days before the election, but the whiff of scandal hung in the air. All participants demonstrated acrimony. Chrétien suggested that the Alliance was out to "destroy Canada." Day once charged that the prime minister put the rights of pedophiles over those of children. Even NDP leader Alexa McDonough compared Day to a cockroach, while the Tories ran negative ads on TV accusing Chrétien of being a "serial liar." It is little wonder that many voters lost interest, and voter turnout fell from 67% in 1997 to 62% in 2000, one of the lowest in Canadian history.

The Liberals had expected to win the elections, but the magnitude of victory was especially gratifying: they captured 173 seats (up from 155) based on 41% of the popular votes. This provided Chrétien with a comfortable majority in Parliament and the acclaim of being the first leader to deliver three straight majority governments since William Lyon Mackenzie King accomplished that feat in 1935, 1940, and 1945. The victory also came embellished with some remarkable gains. In Quebec, where the prime minister was often dismissed as an unpopular federalist, the Liberals increased their seats from 29 to 37, all at the expense of the BQ, which fell from 44 to 37 seats.

These gains and the fact that Chrétien's unity-oriented party won as many seats as did the separatist BQ lent credence to the Chrétien government's hard-line policy toward Quebec separatism. The Liberals retained their rock-solid domination of Ontario in federal elections by winning an overwhelming 100 seats, down only one from 1997. They also gained eight extra seats in the Atlantic Provinces.

The performance of the Canadian Alliance demonstrated the gaping divide between the East and West in Canada. It was all but vanquished in Ontario, winning only two rural seats. The party calculated that if only its and the Tories' voters could unify under one banner in Ontario, a powerful challenge to the Liberals' unassailable federal dominance could be made; that hope was dashed. The Alliance captured 64 seats from Manitoba to British Columbia, leaving only 14 to the Liberals.

Such an outcome again raised the question about national unity and western alienation. Although the Alliance, under Day's leadership, consolidated its hold on the West and its position as official opposition in Ottawa, it did not emerge as a national party that could seriously threaten Liberal dominance in federal politics, despite its capture of 66 seats and a fourth of the popular votes nationwide.

Both the Conservatives and the NDP narrowly escaped extinction and barely won the required dozen seats needed for official recognition as parliamentary parties. Only by winning nine seats in the Atlantic provinces, four fewer than in 1997, were the Tories able to secure a disappointing 12 seats in the House of Commons, based on 12% of the votes. This was the third consecutive devastating defeat. In only seven years the party had fallen from a majority government to a fifth-place party. It could no longer make its once-proud claim of being a truly national party able to speak for all Canadians in all walks of life. The NDP also faced the prospect of spending the next few years on the fringes of Canadian politics. McDonough held on to her Halifax riding, but her party's seats in the Atlantic provinces dropped from seven to four. Over-

all, the NDP won 8% of the votes and 13 seats, barely qualifying as an official party in Ottawa.

The election campaign was rancorous and personal, with too little serious discussion of issues of importance to Canada's future, such as how the country could remain competitive in the world economy, what to do about the declining value of the Canadian dollar and how to fix the health-care system. Noting that the wrangling about counting votes in Florida had diverted Canadians' already low interest in their own vote, David Rudd, director of the Canadian Institute for Strategic Studies, remarked dejectedly: "Even Mexico is more exciting than we are. I suppose that is what you get when you are a country that is at peace with itself and with its neighbors."

THE 2004 FEDERAL PARLIAMENTARY ELECTIONS

For a decade Paul Martin had worked to become prime minister and to assemble a formidable political war machine to accomplish his goal. His ruthless unseating of Jean Chrétien in 2003 created a deep

Canada

THE GLOBE AND MAIL

CANADA'S NATIONAL NEWSPAPER ▪ FOUNDED 1844 ▪ GLOBEANDMAIL.COM ▪ TUESDAY, JUNE 29, 2004

The election: A last-minute revival in central Canada propels the Liberals to a minority. But the nation is deeply split, with the largely Conservative West still waiting its turn and Quebec in the Bloc's hands

Ontario rescues Martin

BY HEATHER SCOFFIELD
AND JEFF SALLOT
IN OTTAWA

Voters returned the Liberals to power yesterday with more seats than even their own party had expected, but only with a minority in the House of Commons that will likely force Paul Martin to turn to the New Democratic Party for support.

It will be a return to a 1972 situation where Pierre Trudeau's Liberals had to negotiate on a daily basis with the NDP to maintain a majority in the House.

While the Liberal win is a far cry from the 172-seat majority that Jean Chrétien scored in the 2000 election, it's a far stronger result than public opinion polls, or even Liberal insiders, had projected past 48 hours ago.

Ontario and Quebec were key to the victory, as the Liberals lost far fewer seats than expected in both provinces.

For weeks, the election has been too close to call, and many Liberals were bracing for a Conservative minority backed by an ad hoc co-operation with the separatist Bloc Québécois.

Instead, the next government

Paul Martin replaces Chrétien in 2004

rift in the party, and his turfing out and ostracizing of the former prime minister's loyalists added to the bad blood. His heavy-handedness alienated many local Liberal officials and volunteers and left the party vulnerable to a newly united Conservative Party.

Shortly after he gained his coveted top spot, a scandal came to light revealing that $75 million of federal taxpayer money had been funneled to Liberal cronies' advertising firms to be used to undermine the separatist cause in Quebec. As Chrétien's former finance minister, Martin could not escape unscathed. The *National Post* called the scandal "the mother of all Achilles' heels." An Ipson-Reid poll in May 2004 found that 61% of voters considered the Liberals corrupt, and only 36% believed their party deserved to be reelected. There was a strong feeling that the Liberals had been in power too long. *Québécois* were furious, and many western Canadians saw it as proof that the Liberals are a profligate party.

Martin's half-year in power had been largely directionless and ineffective, with no overarching new policy agenda. Nevertheless, strongly desiring his own personal mandate, Martin decided to call new elections for June 28. Although many of his advisers thought he had made a mistake, he feared that the scandal might cause even more damage to the party. His poll ratings were falling continually. Also for the first time in over a decade, there was a credible alternative to Liberal rule taking shape in the form of the newly merged Conservative Party. He could have waited another 16 months to call

new elections, but the longer he hesitated, the more organized and prepared the new Conservatives would be. For the first time since 1993 Canada had a federal election whose result could not be predicted.

What followed was an ill-tempered and divisive campaign that produced a fractured parliament. There was a heavy dose of negative advertising. Harper tried to swing his new party toward the political center. But the outspoken social conservatism of some of his candidates and advisers fueled charges that Harper had a "hidden agenda," perhaps involving attempts to end abortion rights, alter the sacred medicare, abandon environmental treaties (especially the Kyoto Protocol on global warming) or align Canada more closely with U.S. foreign policy. It is impossible to disprove a "hidden agenda."

Harper fueled these suspicions in the final days of the campaign when he suppressed but refused to apologize for a press release from his party headquarters suggesting that Martin supported child pornography. Until the final week, Martin ran an incompetent and lethargic campaign, and the opinion polls showed the race as neck-and-neck. All three anglophone candidates speak tolerable to good French, and the general impression after the French- and English-language televised debates was that the Conservative leader, Stephen Harper, had done the best.

In the final days of the campaign Martin threw everything he had into the race, flying on the last day from coast to coast and dipping his feet into both oceans. When the votes were counted, the Liberals had succeeded in retaining power, but

with a minority of seats in the House of Commons. One out of five voters changed his mind on the last day and decided not to take a chance on Harper's new party. Only 60.5% of voters decided to go to the polls, by far the worst turnout ever in federal elections. The Liberals captured 36.7% of the votes and 135 seats, twenty short of a majority. In general, the Liberals dominated Canada's bigger cities, while the Conservatives did well in smaller communities.

The Conservatives overall won 29.6% of the votes (vs. a combined total of 38% in 2000) and a respectable 99 seats (compared with 78 in 2000). They broke the Liberal stranglehold on Ontario by winning 24 of 108 seats. Atlantic Canada proved to be a Liberal stronghold. Conservatives were disappointed not to have dominated the west, especially BC, more than they did. The NDP made spectacular gains, more than doubling its votes and winning 19 seats.

The biggest surprise was the strong showing of the separatist *Bloc Québécois* in Quebec. It is ironic that a shady financial tactic designed to weaken separatist sentiment in Quebec had precisely the opposite effect. The BQ captured half the votes and 54 of 75 seats, leaving only 19 for the Liberals. The vote was more a protest vote against the Liberals rather than a show of support for Quebec sovereignty. Nevertheless, separatists felt wind again in their sails.

A chastened but relieved Paul Martin admitted, "The message was unmistakable: Canadians expected, and expect, more from us as a party, and as a government we must do better, and we will." Without a parliamentary majority Liberals had to proceed carefully. He rejected

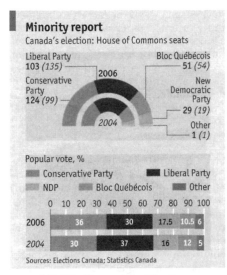

Minority report
Canada's election: House of Commons seats

Liberal Party 103 *(135)* — 2006 — Bloc Québécois 51 *(54)*
Conservative Party 124 *(99)* — New Democratic Party 29 *(19)*
2004 — Other 1 *(1)*

Popular vote, %
■ Conservative Party ■ Liberal Party
■ NDP ■ Bloc Québécois ■ Other

0 10 20 30 40 50 60 70 80 90 100

2006	36	30	17.5	10.5 6
2004	30	37	16	12 5

Sources: Elections Canada; Statistics Canada

2006 Parliamentary Elections
Source: *The Economist*

CONSERVATIVES		LIBERALS		BLOC QUÉBÉCOIS		NEW DEMOCRATS		INDEPENDENTS	
SEATS	POPULAR VOTE	SEATS	POPULAR VOTE	SEATS	POPULAR VOTE	SEATS	POPULAR VOTE	SEATS	POPULAR VOTE
122	36.5%	105	30.3%	50	10.4%	30	17.3%	1	0.6%

*LEADING AND ELECTED AS OF MIDNIGHT EST. FOR COMPLETE RESULTS, VISIT globeandmail.com

THE GLOBE AND MAIL

CANADA'S NATIONAL NEWSPAPER ■ FOUNDED 1844 ■ GLOBEANDMAIL.COM ■ TUESDAY, JANUARY 24, 2006

HARPER'S THIN BLUE LINE

Tories win slim minority, Martin steps down, pizza Parliament looms

BY MURRAY CAMPBELL
AND HEATHER SCOFFIELD

Voters put an end to 12 years of Liberal government yesterday but left the victorious Conservatives under Stephen Harper with a very tenuous hold on government.

Helped by a dramatic breakthrough in Quebec and a slide of Liberal fortunes in Ontario, the Conservatives eked out a minority government that will make Mr. Harper, a 46-year-old economist, Canada's 22nd prime minister.

Liberal Leader Paul Martin said he would not fight another election although he would remain as an MP. He promised to consult his new caucus and the party leadership "in the coming days" to ensure an orderly transition to a new leader.

"We are Liberals," he told supporters in Montreal. "We will not lose faith, we will not lose hope or resolve."

Canadians appeared to be saying they were tired of the scandals that had plagued the Liberals under Mr. Martin during his 26 months as prime minister and were ready to give a tentative embrace to a Conservative Party that pledged to clean up government while cutting taxes and cracking down on crime.

"This has been a difficult and challenging day at the end of a long and challenging campaign," said Finance Minister Ralph Goodale, who was re-elected in Regina.

Even though he was denied a majority, the election represented a significant victory for Mr. Harper who was given little chance of success when he took over the Conservatives more than two years ago after a merger of the Canadian Alliance and the Progressive Conservatives.

And for the 67-year-old Mr. Martin, the results will kindle a debate

Laureen Teskey and her husband, Stephen Harper, leave for Calgary yesterday morning. Last night, the Conservative Leader became prime-minister-designate.

TOM HANSON/CANADIAN PRESS

the option of forming a coalition government, something that Canada has not had since the First World War. He chose instead to lead what he called a "stable" minority government, seeking parliamentary votes from different parties for different issues. The last minority government had been formed in 1979 and lasted only eight months. No minority government in Canadian history has survived more than two years, and the average is 18 months. This was to be the fate of the Martin government.

THE 2006 FEDERAL PARLIAMENTARY ELECTIONS

The outgoing Liberal government of Paul Martin was dogged and ultimately dealt a fatal blow by the ever worsening "sponsorship scandal" in Quebec. This involved federal funds directed to Quebec advertising agencies with close ties to the Liberal Party in order to weaken the separatist movement. When the official

Gomery inquiry began hearing testimony in Montreal, the information was explosive. Advertising agency executives admitted to kickbacks, payoffs and payroll padding. One head of a firm received $30 million in government contracts and in return paid a "commission" of 17.5% in the form of false invoices and fake bills. Another ad executive secretly kicked back nearly a half million dollars to Liberal Party accounts. He told how he made payments in envelopes left on restaurant tables and put party operatives on his pay-

Canada

Liberal government runs out of wind

Source: *Globe and Mail*

roll, including relatives of former Prime Minister Chrétien.

These revelations were a political bombshell and a death sentence for the Liberal government, especially in Quebec. Then opposition leader Stephen Harper asked publicly: "How can we continue to prop up a government that is under criminal investigation and accusation of criminal conspiracy?"

The Gomery inquiry explicitly exonerated Prime Minister Martin in November 2005 of any blame. The same was not the case for Chrétien and his aides, who were cited for "omissions" and "insufficient oversight" by allowing the slush-fund scheme to be set up and operated under his watch. A beleaguered prime minister ordered his Liberals to repay about $1 million in party contributions and sent the 686-page report to the RCMP for possible criminal investigations. The damage from this sleaze debilitated the Liberal Party and haunted Martin. The then opposition leader Stephen Harper gained enormous credibility for his call: "We have to clean things up."

Martin was forced to focus on survival instead of a clear direction for his government. A successful finance minister, Martin proved to be a disappointing prime minister. Dependent upon the demanding and big-spending NDP for its continuation, Martin departed from his decade of

careful financial management and doled out public funds with abandon. His minority government nevertheless lost a vote of no-confidence 171 to 133, and new elections were called for January 23, 2006. This was the first winter election in 25 years, and at 56 days, the campaign was long by Canadian standards.

Tory leader Stephen Harper would not allow himself to be painted again as a dogmatic social conservative. He presented an effective blend of traditional conservatism and reassuring moderation. He moved pragmatically toward the political center, and he skirted around emotional social issues. He pledged to uphold Medicare, ruled out any change in the abortion law, and tempered his party's opposition to gay marriage and the Kyoto climate protocol. He focused on such things as cracking down on crime, reducing the sales tax, shortening waiting times for health care, giving parents money for child care and boosting defense spending.

He avoided foreign policy issues except for promising to improve relations with the United States, which he called "our best friends." This matter did provide some temporary excitement in an otherwise unexciting campaign. The U.S. ambassador to Canada, David Wilkins, lost patience hearing Martin lecture the U.S. on the subject of greenhouse gas emissions when it was public knowledge that

the U.S. was decreasing such emissions, while Canada's were growing. Wilkins made the untimely, if correct, statement: "It may be smart election-year politics to thump your chest and constantly criticize your friend and your No. 1 trading partner. But it is a slippery slope, and all of us should hope that it doesn't have a long-term impact on the relationship."

Martin, who in 2004 had campaigned for a "more sophisticated" relationship with the U.S., jumped on this intrusion into Canadian electoral politics and talked tough against the Yankees: "I'm not going to be dictated to," and "I'm going to call them as I see them." This flap bumped up Martin's poll numbers for a few days, and then they continued on their downward trajectory. When election day arrived, it was no longer a question of whether Harper's Conservatives would win, but whether they would be able to form a majority government.

Voters ended over 12 years of Liberal rule but brought in the country's second minority government in a row. The Conservatives won an impressive victory, securing 124 (up from 99) of 308 seats in the House of Commons on the basis of 36.3% of the votes (up from 29.6% in 2004). Thanks to a defection of a former Liberal minister from Vancouver, David Emerson (who later became foreign minister), the Tories actually command 125 seats.

The Liberals could hardly afford to lose any seats, having declined since 2004 to 30.2% of the votes (down from 36.7%) and only 103 seats (down from 135). To no small extent, the outcome was as much a rejection of Martin and the Liberals as an acceptance of Harper and the Conservatives. A defeated Martin resigned as party head, leaving the Liberals leaderless.

What was remarkable about this comeback was that Harper's party made gains in all parts of this diverse country and became a national party again for the first time since 1993. Canada returned to a competitive system of two national parties.

They won big in the West, where they got more than half of their seats, and all the seats in Alberta. Harper proudly proclaimed: "The West is now in." The election gives another nudge to the westward shift of Canada's political center of gravity. The Conservatives broke the Liberal stranglehold on Ontario, winning 40 of its 106 seats. However, none was in Toronto or Ottawa, nor in Montreal or Vancouver; it was shut out in these big cities. Its gains in Atlantic Canada were modest, but the post of foreign minister (later the defense ministry) was given to Peter MacKay to raise this region's visibility in the government. In fact, Harper gave his new cabinet geographical balance, even appointing his party co-chairman, Michael Fortier of Montreal, to the Senate so that he could have someone from Montreal in his cabinet.

Most dramatically, the Conservatives picked up 10 seats in Quebec, capturing 24.6% of the votes (up from 9%), ahead of the Liberals, who with 20.7% (and 13 seats) experienced one of their worst performances in Quebec since Confederation in 1867. It was headline news that many of those Conservative votes were won in nationalist strongholds in the eastern part of Quebec. The *Bloc Québécois* fell short of a majority of votes in Quebec, winning only 42% and slipping from 54 to 51 of the province's 75 seats. Not reaching the magical 50% mark, the BQ offered no prospect of a successful independence referendum any time soon.

Harper's openness to *Québécois* concerns, his talk of more flexible federalism, and his practice of beginning practically every speech in Ottawa in French, which he commands confidently, offers the prospect of even greater gains in *la belle province*. After becoming prime minister, he showered Quebec with attention, promising to recognize "the unique place of a strong, vibrant Quebec in a united Canada." His party was rewarded for this: within three months as prime minister, polls showed Tory support in Quebec reaching 34%, ahead of both the BQ and the Liberals.

The only other party to improve its standing was Jack Layton's New Democrats, which captured 17.5% of the votes and 29 seats (up from 19). The NDP picked up a dozen seats in Ontario and 10 in BC. As always, it was locked out of Quebec. Despite this strengthening, the NDP does not command the balance of power in Commons it did after the 2004 vote.

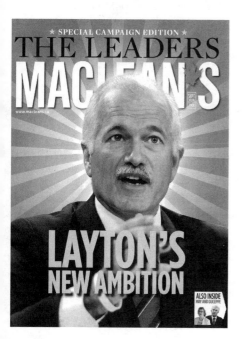

Normally a strong economy helps re-elect incumbent governments, but that rule did not apply in 2006. Voters opted for a government that had not tarnished itself with corruption and not endangered its perceived moral right to govern in a democracy. They liked Harper's humility, self-deprecation, moderation and willingness to listen and learn. His first words as prime minister designate were: "Tonight, our great country has voted for change."

THE 2008 FEDERAL PARLIAMENTARY ELECTIONS

In September 2008 Stephen Harper took stock of his two and one-half years in power at the head of a minority government. He had demonstrated considerable skill in managing the House of Commons. He had been an innovator on Quebec's nationhood. His government had been relatively free of scandals. He had put a dramatically new face on Canada's foreign policy. Analysts were writing that it had been a generation since Canada had had such an effective, ambitious and young leader. And the Liberal Party had just elected an ineffective leader, Stéphane Dion. Opinion polls indicated that no major aspect of his agenda bothered the voters and that a majority was within the Conservatives' reach.

Harper's ambition is for the Conservative Party to be the natural governing majority in the country. He felt confident in declaring elections for October 14, despite the law he himself had sponsored to have parliamentary elections at fixed times—thus not until a year later—and despite the fact that this would be the third time in little more than four years voters were called to the polls.

For the first three weeks, things went well for Harper's party, which maintained a steady 10-point lead. Then the situation turned sour. The global financial crisis that had begun in the United States changed the mood in Canada overnight to one of foreboding. Canada's economy was relatively good compared with most other rich nations, but suddenly voters doubted Canada's ability to cope with the world downturn. A bewildered Harper came off as insensitive and out-of-touch when he argued that the crashing stock market offered "good buying opportunities." He mentioned no government spending to stimulate the economy and save jobs. The polls eroded, and the Conservatives found themselves fighting for their lives.

On election day only 59.1% of registered voters turned out, the lowest in history. The Conservatives increased their share of the popular vote slightly to 37.3%. This

translated into 19 additional seats. This meant a somewhat stronger minority government, but not the hoped-for majority. The Tories consolidated their western base and picked up seats in suburban Ontario and the Maritime provinces. The Reform Party elements can be satisfied with the steady, incremental progress, slowly advancing eastward from British Columbia and Alberta election after election, now winning seats in suburban Ontario and the Maritime Provinces. They see a majority in the future.

Their biggest disappointment was Quebec, where they won only 22% of the votes and finished third behind the BQ and Liberals. The prime minister had made a serious misstep by making a snide remark about artists who receive government grants. Since many Québécois consider their culture to be the cornerstone of their nation, that was an insult with major symbolism. This rare Harper mistake prompted him immediately after the election to open the Francophonie Summit in Quebec City declaring himself "heir" to Samuel de Champlain and with a pledge of more funding for the international Quebec channel TV5. The *Bloc Québécois* made virtually no mention of Quebec sovereignty during the elections and was able to blunt any Conservative advance. It sacrificed one seat to win 50 of the 75 total Quebec seats.

Disaster befell the Liberals whose share of the popular vote plunged to 26.2%, their lowest since the foundation of the party in 1867. This was the third consecutive election in which their popular vote dropped. Their number of seats dived by a fourth from 103 to only 76. These included a mere seven seats in the entire West, while they lost their dominance of Ontario. The Liberal Party has become largely a Montreal-Toronto party with enclaves in Atlantic Canada. These results raise the serious question about whether it can even be con-

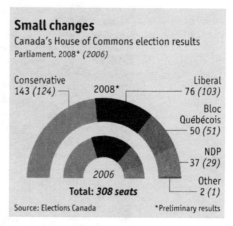

Small changes

Canada's House of Commons election results
Parliament, 2008* *(2006)*

Conservative 143 *(124)*   2008*   Liberal 76 *(103)*

Bloc Québécois 50 *(51)*

NDP 37 *(29)*

2006

Other 2 *(1)*

Total: 308 seats

Source: Elections Canada   *Preliminary results

2008 Parliamentary Elections
Source: *The Economist*

Canada

sidered a national party. This is a bitter realization for a party that had ruled Canada 55 of the previous 73 years.

Stéphane Dion had chosen to conduct a campaign based on an environmental plan called "Green Shift," that would include a carbon tax, just when Canadians were worrying primarily about the economy. The party's poor performance, along with Dion's clumsy attempt to defeat the government in a vote of no-confidence and take over the prime minister's role himself a few weeks after the election, cost him his leadership. Michael Ignatieff, whose popularity rivaled that of Prime Minister Harper, took the party's reins. Perhaps the only bright spot for the Liberals was the election of Justin Trudeau, son of the former prime minister, in a suburban Montreal riding.

Canada now had a five-party system. The NDP finished no higher in the popular vote than it had in 2006. It did climb from 29 to 37 seats, but it remained as far as ever from its professed goal of replacing the Liberals as the government-in-waiting. The Greens, led by the hard-charging Elizabeth May, fell far below their inflated expectations. But they increased their electoral support by 41%, winning 940,000 votes, or 6.8% of the total. This translated into no seats.

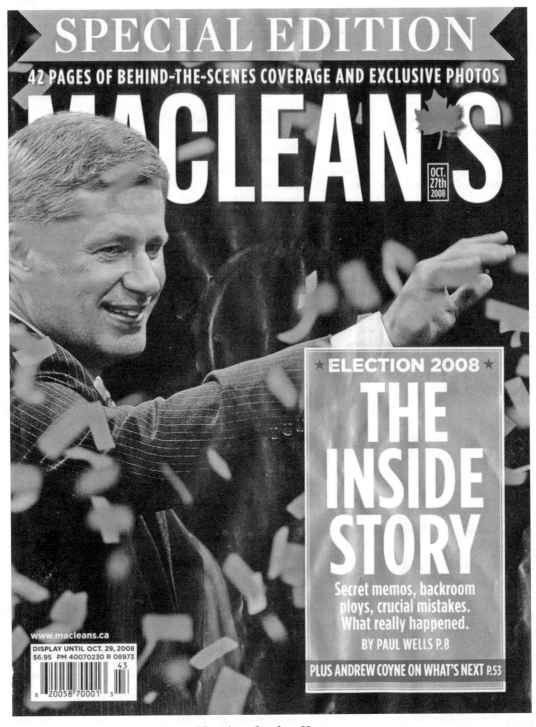

Victorious Stephen Harper

The 2011 Federal Parliamentary Elections

In one of the most dramatic federal elections in Canadian history, Canada returned to a three-party political system. The Tories and Prime Minister Stephen Harper had ruled for more than five years as Canada's longest-serving minority government. When the three opposition parties won a no-confidence vote in parliament on March 25, 2011, by a vote of 156 to 145, Harper jumped at the opportunity to call new elections in May that, he hoped, would give his government a stable parliamentary majority. He is a brilliant tactician who, in the words of the *Globe and Mail*, is "nasty, brutish—and competent." He correctly predicted that the Liberals and New Democrats would split the vote on the left, and the Tories would dominate the center.

He was not disappointed. The results transformed Canadian politics. Voters responded to his argument that parliament had become dysfunctional and that his government needed a majority to stop the "socialists and separatists" (New Democrats and Bloc Québécois) from endangering the economic recovery and the nation's security. He framed the election as a simple choice between a stable Conservative majority in parliament or a "reckless coalition" of Liberals, New Democrats and Quebec separatists. He steered away from social issues, such as abortion and gay marriage, which are controversial and polarizing vote-losers. He focused on the economy, lower taxes, stronger defense and tougher measures against crime.

The Tories captured 167 seats out of 308, based on 39.6% of the votes. Only seven Tory incumbents lost their seats, compared with 82 from other parties. Although its votes fell below 40% in all of Canada, they totaled 50% in two-thirds of the country. That is a formula for long-term success by the dominant party.

This was not just a victory. It was a realignment that could make the Conservatives the natural governing party in Canada, as the Liberals were in the 20th century. Their traditional Liberal opponent was crushed. Tory dominance of the West was strengthened: it won 54% of the votes in Manitoba, 56% in Saskatchewan, 67% in Alberta and 46% in BC. This was an average of 55% in the West, up by 9%.

But what was most stupefying were the Conservatives' gains in Ontario. In 2000 they had captured two seats; in 2011 they got 73 seats and 44% of the votes. This was the first time since 1984 they carried this most populated province. They even won 30 seats in greater Toronto, including that of Liberal leader Michael Ignatieff. Although they lost ground in Quebec, the Tories made inroads into the influential immigrant community, especially South Asians and Chinese.

Thus there is a new governing coalition: the West plus Ontario. That has never existed before, and it will grow as those two regions get about 30 more seats in the coming redistricting (the Tories' redistribution bill). The West now begins at the Ottawa River. The Conservatives have become Canada's dominant party.

The elections were such a calamity for the Liberal Party that some observers wonder if it will ever recover. Ignatieff had triggered the election in March 2011 by joining the NDP and separatist BQ in bringing about a vote of no-confidence against the Conservative minority government over an issue that voters seemed to care little about: contempt of parliament in concealing the true cost of prisons and new jet fighters. A February poll had found that 51% of voters viewed him unfavorably, while only 25% had a positive view. The Conservatives branded him as a carpet-bagging elitist, who had no clue about the struggle of ordinary Canadians. They were ready and itching for an election, but the Liberals were not.

By the time the votes were counted, the party and the nation were dumbfounded. The Liberals had fallen to less than 20% of the votes and a mere 34 seats. This was their worst result ever and the first time they were not among the top two parties. It had turned to the left in desperation, but its voters gravitated to the Tories and New Democrats, who occupied the center. It lost big in Quebec because it could no longer pretend to be a bridge between the province and the rest of Canada. It is dead in the West and lost much of its foothold in Ontario. It had to relinquish to the NDP its position as official opposition in parliament. Ignatieff lost his own seat in Toronto and immediately resigned as party chairman to return to the classroom at the University of Toronto. The party is left to ponder its continued relevance and to face the many questions about its future and purpose.

The NDP prepared well for the May 2011 elections. Party leader Jack Layton had just undergone prostate surgery and limped with a cane after hip surgery. But his party's campaign was anything but lame. In his eight years in charge, he had overhauled the NDP and sharpened its electoral focus by throwing overboard policies that had cost the party votes in past elections. It no longer spoke of a moratorium on new oil sands development or marijuana decriminalization, and it called for tax cuts for certain businesses. He greatly improved the party's technical and fund-raising capabilities, and the party bought a downtown property in Ottawa for its headquarters.

To woo Quebec voters, it advocated the separatists' view of the Canadian constitution as unfinished business. It supported a referendum standard for separation of 50 percent plus one vote. It proposed extending French-language protections to federally regulated industries. But the party's biggest drawing card in Quebec was Layton himself. He was born in Montreal in 1950 and grew up in Hudson, Quebec. He studied at McGill in Montreal, where he perfected the kind of relaxed, colloquial French that enabled him to perform best in the leaders' French-language TV debate. He emerged as a likeable street-smart Montrealer. He also shined in the English-language debate.

Canadians were left reeling when the election results came in. The NDP captured 31% of the votes and 103 seats, 58 of which in Quebec (up from one in 2008). It won seats in eight provinces. For the first time in its history, it became the official opposition in Ottawa and the dominant federal party in Quebec. In fact, Layton was the first anglophone leader of a national party to win in Quebec when a francophone was heading another party (in this case Gilles Duceppe of the BQ).

Quebec voters have frequently demonstrated massive swings in elections. After the celebrations on election night were over, the party had to think hard how it would manage such a diverse and largely inexperienced group of MPs that included 58 Québécois, four McGill students (one of whom 19 years old), an ex-communist, teachers and activists, with very few seasoned politicians among them.

The BQ experienced near annihilation in the 2011 elections, plunging from 47 to a mere four seats, too few to qualify as an official party in parliament. It remains as a powerless rump group. Gilles Duceppe, the longest-serving leader on the federal stage, immediately resigned. Only the most militant advocates of Quebec sovereignty stuck with the BQ, while soft sovereignists and federalists switched to the NDP. Clearly many Quebecers are tired of the BQ and seriously asked themselves if they really wanted to be represented in Ottawa by a party that is in perpetual opposition. Many want to play a more constructive role in federal politics. The fact is that in its two decades of existence, the BQ failed to make a contribution to achieving the goal of separatist destiny. That is why it is a spent force.

Spurned by voters in Ontario and Nova Scotia, Green leader Elizabeth May moved to Saanich-Gulf Islands, British Columbia, to win her long-coveted seat in the House of Commons. Nobody worked harder to win one. She knocked on countless doors and handed out packages of sunflower seeds, the international Greens symbol. Her efforts paid off, and she won the party's first and only seat.

Canada

Situated halfway between the White House and the Capitol, the splendid Canadian Embassy is the only foreign mission permitted on Pennsylvania Avenue.

Courtesy: Embassay of Canada

FOREIGN POLICY

Canada is the upper half of the North American continent and shares a 5,335-mile border (including Alaska) with the United States. This fact makes each country vital to the other. It tries to expand its trade with Asia, and it views its own security as linked with the security of Europe. But Asia and Europe are located far away. Canada's shared values, economic well-being and proximity to the United States require that it focus much of its foreign policy attention on its southern neighbor.

Canada is involved in innumerable forms of cooperation with the United States. They jointly administer the St. Lawrence Seaway, and their International Joint Commission (IJC) has objectively and far-sightedly dealt with many environmental issues for years. Following a bilateral agreement in 1972, it helped facilitate the cleanup of the Great Lakes, which contain 21% of the world's fresh water. A Permanent Joint Board on Defense coordinates the two countries' security relationship, and they are allies in the North Atlantic Treaty Organization (NATO) and in the North American Aerospace Defense Command (NORAD).

Polls have indicated that Americans are more willing to defend Canada in case of attack than they are to defend any other foreign country. In 2004, 84% supported their troops being sent to help Canada if attacked, and 75% of Canadians said the same about deploying their troops to defend the U.S. From 1984 to 1994, the top leaders of the two countries met each other at least annually, and the U.S. secretaries of state and Canadian ministers of foreign affairs met four times per year. By tradition, the first foreign leader with whom a new president should meet is the Canadian prime minister.

It was unusual that Bill Clinton waited almost two years to visit Ottawa in 1995. It was even more unusual that George W. Bush visited Mexico first after his inauguration in January 2001. After Paul Martin became prime minister in December 2003, he first invited UN Secretary-General Kofi Annan to visit Ottawa before extending an invitation to the American president. Martin and Bush first met in January 2004 during a multilateral meeting in Monterey, Mexico. Bush also met Martin's successor as prime minister, Stephen Harper, for the first time at a three-country summit in Mexico in March 2006.

After his re-election Bush finally made his first bilateral visit to Canada (his third visit to Canada overall) on November 30, 2004. It was billed as an official, not state, visit. Breaking with precedence, Bush declined the invitation to address a joint session of parliament. Instead he delivered his main address in Halifax, Nova Scotia, in order to be closer to those Canadians who had helped thousands of American air passengers stranded after the September 11 terrorist attacks.

Each country is the other's most important trading partner and target for foreign investment. Every day close to US$2 billion in trade and travel pass over the border. The U.S. conducts more trade with the single province of Ontario than with either Japan or the entire European Union (EU); Canada trades more with California than with Japan. In fact, more international trade passes over the Ambassador Bridge that connects Detroit and Windsor than either the U.S. or Canada conducts with any other country in the world. Every province (except two in the Maritimes) has more trade with the United States than with other Canadian provinces.

There are always disagreements in the economic and trade field. In Washington there is a reservoir of good will toward Canada, even though there is often a need for American leaders to be reminded of what Canadians want. Although the term is not used often any more, especially after former Prime Minister Chrétien's election in 1993, there is indeed a sort of "special relationship" between the two neighbors. If there were not, then Winston S. Churchill would not have been able to speak of "that long frontier from the Atlantic to the Pacific Oceans, guarded only by neighbourly respect and honourable obligations." It is now the world's longest thinly defended border.

Nevertheless, there are differences and difficulties. Former Prime Minister Trudeau once said that 70% of Canada's foreign policy involves its dealings with the U.S. Far less of America's foreign policy attention is focused on Canada. Some observers have called that kind of relationship "asymmetrical" since Canada is more dependent upon the United States than vice versa. The United States has ten times as many people and is economically and militarily more powerful and influential in the world than is Canada. Canada is a "middle power;" the United States is a "superpower." Canadians have problems getting their larger neighbor to pay attention to their concerns.

The Arctic and the Northwest Passage

This was indicated by the uproar over the American Coast Guard icebreaker *Polar Sea's* voyage in the summer of 1985 through the Northwest Passage without Canada's permission. The U.S. has long held that those are international waters, whereas Canada's position is that they are territorial waters. At the 1987 summit meeting in Ottawa, Mulroney asserted unmistakably that Canada owns the northern waters "lock, stock and icebergs."

A compromise was reached in 1988. The Arctic Cooperation Agreement permits the U.S. and Canada to increase their collaboration in the region without prejudicing the legal position of either country. It acknowledges American's (and the EU's, Britain's, Russia's and all other nations') rejection of Canada's claim that the waters are within Canadian sovereignty. No country questions that Canada owns their resources or that Canada is sovereign over its Arctic islands. However, by requiring Washington to obtain Ottawa's consent for passages through the waters (and that consent is always given), it hopes to prevent future incidents such as that caused by the *Polar Sea*. Canada and the U.S. agree that neither icebreakers nor nuclear submarines need permission to pass.

When the U.S. announced in 2000 that its new polar icebreaker, *Healy*, would sail through the passage that summer, a team of Canadian navigators and pollution experts went along.

Shipping routes at the top of the world

Source: *Maclean's*

The passage is not yet a reliable commercial route, and transit is limited chiefly to research or military craft. But the U.S. Navy estimates that the North Pole will be ice-free by 2035. If that happens, the Bering Strait between Russia and the U.S. could rival the Persian Gulf and the Strait of Malacca in shipping importance. In 2008 Prime Minister Harper announced stricter registration of ships sailing through the Northwest Passage; all ships are required to report to Nordreg, the Canadian Coast Guard agency. In general, it is tricky for Canada to determine whether to regard its southern neighbor as a friend or rival in the Far North.

Former U.S. Ambassador to Canada, Paul Cellucci, once said he agreed with Canada's position on the passageway, he was quickly corrected by his successor, David Wilkins, who restated American insistence that the passage is an international strait. In 2006, Wilkins himself then slipped and called the passage "neutral waters," and the Canadian government jumped to correct his mistake. His description was indeed at variance with the official American position, supported by the UK and others, that the waters are a "strait for international navigation."

A State Department official stressed that the U.S. prefers not to make a "big deal" of the navigation issue. The two partners agree to disagree about its legal status. But as a December 2007 *Maclean's* poll reveals, 55% of American respondents consider the Northwest Passage to be Canadian waters. This makes Americans the only people in the world besides Canadians

(66%) to believe this. It is important for Canadian politicians to be seen on the right side of this sovereignty issue.

Hours before calling a new election in the fall of 2008, Prime Minister Harper took several members of his cabinet to the far North for three days to demonstrate his commitment to defend "Canada's Arctic sovereignty." In fact, after becoming prime minister in 2006, Harper made the Far North one of his signature issues, and he travels there to inspect the military and its "Op Nanook" exercises. He even held a rally in Yellowknife, Northwest Territories, during his 2011 election campaign.

In the summer of 2010 about 160 reserve soldiers were sent north to train near Yellowknife in "Exercise Sovereign Grizzly." They helped set up the first reserve unit north of the 60th parallel. This is part of the 20-year Canada First Defence Strategy, announced in 2008, emphasizing domestic defense, especially in the Arctic. He justifies this as "use it or lose it."

His point is to demonstrate to the world that Canada's military forces can operate anywhere on Canadian territory. During the Second World War, the American ally had already demonstrated that it was possible to do that: in 1943 there were more Americans—33,000 military and civilians—in the Canadian North than Canadians.

In 2009 he took the entire cabinet to the Nunavut capital of Iqaluit for a cabinet meeting and even required all the members to join him in eating raw seal meat to show solidarity with the locals. He also hosted a Group of Seven meeting of finance ministers in Iqaluit in February 2010

Canada

to underscore Canada's presence in the North. In fact, all Arctic powers are boosting their northern presence. Norway moved its operational command north of the Arctic Circle, and Russia is upgrading its northern fleet, which already includes 18 icebreakers.

Canadians fear that the issue of sovereignty could become more important since global warming continues to melt the ice to such an extent that thousands of ships from all nations could routinely traverse the ecologically vulnerable waterway. This is especially worrisome because 90% of all goods in the world, measured by tonnage, are transported by sea. China's and India's rapid economic growth promises to increase the overcrowding of existing routes. In the 20th century, Arctic temperatures had risen twice as fast as those in the rest of the world. If melting continues at its present rate, there will be no ice cover during the summer by the middle to end of the 21st century. Another powerful magnet is that the region is estimated to contain a quarter of the world's undiscovered oil and gas.

The five various routes are a meandering set of channels through the Northwest Passage. They would offer a shipping channel between Europe and Asia 4,350 miles (7,000 kilometers) shorter than the route through the Panama Canal. For example, a ship traveling from Rotterdam to Yokohama would take 29 days to go around the Cape of Good Hope, 22 days via the Suez Canal, but only 15 days across the Arctic Ocean. Two other Arctic shipping routes are also inviting: the Northern Sea Route along the northern coast of Russia (which is already open part of the year) and the Arctic Bridge from Murmansk in Russia, around the southern tip of Greenland and into the Hudson Bay to Churchill, Manitoba. The shrinking ice cap also makes mineral deposits more accessible.

A U.S. Navy study in 2002 reported that the ice cover has been shrinking by 3% per year and that commercial shipping could begin as early as 2015. This assessment was supported by an international team of scientists in 2004. As sea ice continues to melt, it can no longer deflect the heat away from land and water. This speeds up the warming process. This scares Canadians, especially the Inuit, who urge Ottawa to assert its sovereignty over the waters of the Arctic archipelago. Canadians already claim that the Law of the Sea Convention gives them the right to regulate this area, but the U.S. did not ratify that agreement although it respects it in practice and intends to ratify it. The Canadian government ordered neither the promised powerful all-season ice-breaker nor the nuclear submarines needed to monitor the Northwest Passage. It has no search-and-rescue helicopters permanently based in the North, and it disbanded the one military unit capable of dropping onto the ice.

To underline its claims to sovereignty, it occasionally sends a coastal patrol boat into the passage during the summer, and every summer the Canadian Forces conduct joint army, naval and air exercises (called Op Nanook) in the Far North. Following the practical principle of Arctic sovereignty, "use it or lose it," the Harper government promised to build three armed icebreakers, a deep-water port and a military training center in the Arctic. However, the number of icebreakers was scaled down to one, but eight patrol vessels designed to operate in ice no more than one meter thick are on order. None would be completed before 2013.

While the ships are on hold, permafrost was broken at an abandoned mine in Nanisivik at the northern tip of Baffin Island near the entrance of the Northwest Passage to build a deep-water harbor that would allow Canada to refuel its military patrol ships. At Pangnirtung (population 1,300) on the east coast of Baffin Island, a harbor for the small Inuit fishing fleet is being constructed. It also made plans to re-

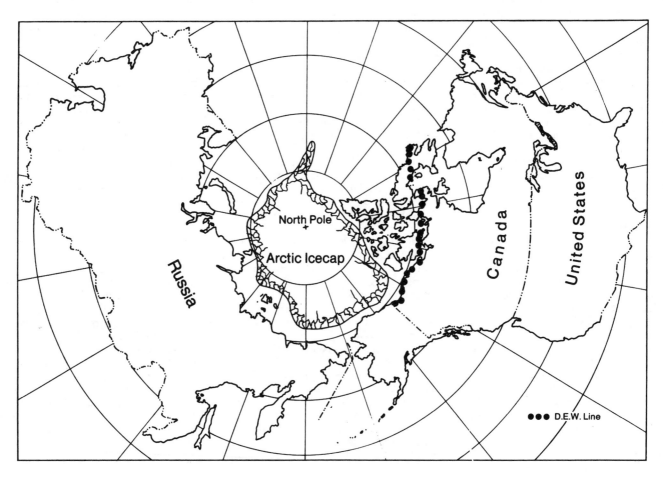

furbish an army facility in Resolute Bay in Nunavut to train soldiers year-round. Canada has only 400 soldiers to look after a northern region the size of Europe. These two bases would provide more resources to monitor traffic in the Passage. At Iqaluit the housing stock is being increased, and a research institute with a polar vessel is being constructed. An additional problem is that the maritime boundary between Alaska and the Yukon extending northward into a sliver of the oil-rich Beaufort Sea in the western Arctic has never been agreed. Canada protested when the U.S. sold leases for this disputed area.

In 2005 Canada became embroiled with Denmark over ownership of Hans Island, an uninhabited square-mile (1.6 kilometer) patch of Arctic rock of no strategic or economic value and of no influence on the maritime boundary between Greenland and Canada's northeast. Although largely self-ruling now, Greenland still falls under Danish sovereignty. Both Canada and Denmark claim the minuscule island, which at one point is only 14.5 miles from Canada.

Reflecting how closely the rock could be related to other Arctic jurisdiction issues, Canadian troops followed by the then defense minister himself, Bill Graham, visited the rock to plant the flag and erect an Inuit stone marker. The Danes responded by sending a warship to back up their sovereignty over the island; they also planted their flag. Ottawa responded by dispatching a frigate to keep an eye on Danish fishermen. The two countries soon called a truce and agreed to disagree over its possession. In an act of reconciliation, scientists from both countries proposed in 2007 that a joint weather station be built on the island. Fortunately Hans Island is the only Arctic land under dispute.

In the Arctic two prominent trends are the speed with which development is going forward and the huge number of political, legal and technical questions that remain unresolved. Unlike the treaty-bound Antarctica, which is a land continent and not an ocean like the Arctic, there is no supranational body in the Arctic. The starting gun for a scramble to claim chunks of the region was fired in August 2007 when Russia, using a mini-submarine, planted its flag on the ocean floor four kilometers below the ice of the North Pole. This daring move carried echoes of the Soviet launch of the first satellite, Sputnik, in 1957.

What is driving the polar countries (which also include the U.S., Norway and Denmark) is that according to the 1982 Law of the Sea, which is intended to regulate almost all human uses of the high seas, countries can claim an economic zone up to 200 nautical miles from their coast or even further if they can prove that the area in question is the extension of

Une carrière militaire c'est différent!

The career with a difference

LES FORCES ARMÉES CANADIENNES THE CANADIAN ARMED FORCES

their own continental shelf. That is the kind of claim being made by Russia with regard to the Lomonosov Ridge, which extends 1,800 kilometers (about 1,200 miles) from the Russian coast to Greenland (belonging to Denmark) and Canada's Ellesmere Island.

The terms of the Law of the Sea require a country to make a claim within a decade of ratifying it. Russia's deadline is 2009, Canada's 2013 and Denmark's 2014. Many leaders in Washington are talking about finally ratifying the law so that the U.S. can also make a claim. In several ways Canada has little to worry about. No country is actually threatening to invade Canada's North. There is also no large or serious overlap of its claims in the Arctic and those of the other four contenders. But Canada must be aware of potential conflict with its Inuit population, who claim much of the Arctic coast as their traditional territory. They are not against development. But they insist it be on their terms, meaning that it respect the environment and provide them with a share of the benefits. They also have banded together in the Inuit Circumpolar Council (ICC), created in 1977 to strengthen their interests and demands.

Canadians are sensitive about maintaining their sovereignty and independence in the world, a sensitivity that is sometimes hard for Americans to understand. Despite all their resemblances, Canadians are *not* Americans and do not think like Americans in all matters of foreign and military policy. The two peoples' activities in world affairs are compatible, but they are also distinct.

International Organizations

There are several reasons for such differences. Canada is active in certain political arenas in which the United States is not. One is the British Commonwealth of Na-

tions. Canada maintained close ties with Britain while it gradually cut the apron strings with the mother country. It was Canada's push for greater sovereignty as much as anything else that led to the Statute of Westminster in 1931. That important act eliminated all pretenses that Great Britain made the foreign and defense decisions for the dominions (white-settled colonies). Canada actually helped shape the kind of relationships with Britain that loosely bind together all Commonwealth countries.

Canada also is a leading member in the French Commonwealth of Nations, which loosely binds 49 countries that use French as their first or second language. This is dedicated chiefly to the survival of the French language. Canada's major purpose for supporting *La Francophonie* is to gain another forum for making its foreign policy presence known, as well as to indicate to the world Canada's bilingual character. Because of their bilingual status, the provinces of Quebec, New Brunswick, Ontario and Manitoba also have the right to send delegations. Another arena of special Canadian activity has long been francophone Africa, where Quebec has sought a more active Canadian role.

A further reason for differences is that Canada is a "middle power." It can neither project military power nor influence international politics, to the extent that the U.S. can. Therefore, Canadians are more inclined to focus on non-military or long-term economic developmental solutions to problems than are Americans, who despite the limits to their power can still project military force to many parts of the globe. Being a medium-sized power does not mean that Canada is of no consequence in world politics. On the contrary, it is far more important than one might expect for a country of only 33.2 million people.

Canada

Canada is a very active participant in international organizations. It was a founding member of the United Nations and is deeply involved in all aspects of the UN's work. With the largest combined coastline in the world, it took a strong interest in the law of the sea conferences. In 1997 the UN appointed a Canadian, Maurice Strong, to help coordinate the much needed administrative reform of that world body. In 1998 Canadian diplomat Louise Frechette was named the UN's first deputy secretary general in charge of reform issues. In 2004 Louise Arbour quit the Canadian Supreme Court to serve as UN High Commissioner for Human Rights until 2008. The head of the International Criminal Court (ICC) in 2005 was Canadian.

For the sixth time, Canada assumed a two-year term on the Security Council in 1999. However, it was rejected in 2010 for the first time since the UN's founding. The two western seats went to Germany and Portugal. It did not help that then opposition leader, Michael Ignatieff, said publicly that Canada had not earned such a prestigious position. Many member states do not like Harper's foreign policy, which gave outspoken support for Israel's right-wing government, closed embassies in Africa, and dragged its heals on climate change. Polls indicated that Canadians were rather indifferent to this setback: 38% said it did not matter, 42% that "it's humiliating and proves we're headed in the wrong direction," and 20% that "it's disappointing, but it shouldn't impact our policies."

The government had hoped that 2010 would be a year in which Canada would play an important role on the international stage. It is an important actor in the many international agencies that attempt to create and maintain global economic stability. It aids the World Bank, the International Monetary Fund (IMF) and the World Trade Organization (WTO). In 2000 Donald Johnston, a former Liberal cabinet member, was reelected to a second five-year term as secretary general of the Organization for Economic Cooperation and Development (OECD). He was the first non-European to hold the post.

Because of American insistence, Canada was in 1976 included in that select "group of seven" (G7) advanced industrial nations to meet periodically in "summit meetings" to discuss global economic issues at the highest level. When Russia participates, it is called the G8. In the 21st century that forum was enlarged to include major developing countries like Brazil, China, India and China, called the G20.

In the summer of 2010, Canada hosted both the G8 and G20 summits in Toronto. As always at such gatherings, thousands of anarchists, thugs, and advocates of myriad causes protested, and some turned violent, smashing shop windows, burning police cars and pelting the police with anything that can hurt. Toronto, which has always prided itself as a tolerant city, was shocked by the wanton criminality and destruction in the streets. There was an outcry in Canada about the $1 billion bill for security and clean-up and for what some viewed as overreaction by the police: about 1,100 demonstrators were arrested, including many bystanders, and 278 were ultimately charged.

In 1985, Canada hosted the first meeting in North America of the Organization of Security and Cooperation in Europe (OSCE), to monitor the progress of the so-called Helsinki Accords, signed in 1975 by 33 European nations and the U.S. and Canada. Its role in these accords indicates its interest in and importance for Europe. Then Minister of Foreign Affairs Joe Clark said in opening the conference, "Canada remains firmly convinced that a safe, prosperous and humane Europe is a cornerstone of a safe, prosperous and humane Canada."

Latin America

During the Cold War Canada was less likely than Americans to see the Soviet Union's hand in most Third-World conflicts. This meant that the United States had to do without Canada's support in dealing with such countries or regions as Grenada, Central America, or Cuba.

Canada never broke diplomatic and trade relations with Cuba. The Caribbean island has long been a sort of foil for Canada to demonstrate its foreign policy independence from the U.S. It is Cuba's largest trading partner, doing about a half billion dollars of trade each year, not including the sizable revenues from a steady stream of Canadian tourists. Canada is the island's largest source of foreign tourists. With a half billion in investments, it is also Cuba's largest foreign investor after Spain. In 1997, Canada reached an agreement with Cuba on a broad range of cooperation, including protecting human rights, combating drug trafficking and terrorism, and providing Cuba with food and medical aid. This was the broadest commitment yet by a major U.S. ally to work with the Castro regime. The House of Commons also signed an agreement with the Cuban parliament to exchange information and delegations.

Always sensitive to any American attempts to place limits on its sovereignty, Canada strongly opposes the Helms-Burton Act, which denies travel rights in the U.S. to companies and individuals that benefit from expropriated property in Cuba. Ottawa dismisses Washington's preference for isolating Cuba, arguing that Canada's policy of engaging Cuba is the best way of achieving human rights and democracy in the long run. To strengthen such "constructive engagement" in 1998, Chrétien became the first leader of a major Western country to visit Castro in Cuba in more than a decade. He made a personal appeal for the release of four prominent dissidents. When they were sentenced 11 months later, the prime minister felt betrayed and ordered a review of Canada's relations with Cuba.

Not until 1989 did Canada join the Organization of American States (OAS), and it has still not signed its collective security agreement, the Rio Treaty. For many years Latin American governments had encouraged Canada to join the OAS in order to mitigate Washington's pervasive influence on the organization. But Ottawa had feared that full membership could limit its independence of action in the region and create a greater risk of putting its foreign policy at odds with positions taken by an OAS dominated by the U.S.

In 1989 Canada accepted a leading role in supporting a UN peacekeeping force in Central America. When the U.S. withdrew its peacekeeping troops from Haiti in 1996, Canada assumed command of the UN force through 1997. Its 750 troops were the key personnel in maintaining peace, training a police force, and improving the judicial system. In 2004 it sent peacekeeping forces to Haiti once again.

When Port-au-Prince, the capital of Haiti, was devastated by a powerful earthquake in January 2010, Canada's response was fast and generous, providing an emergency hospital, air transport and a wide variety of supplies. Its financial assistance was the largest per capita of any nation and the second largest in total dollars after the United States. The number of troops it deployed to help was nearly as many as it had fighting in Afghanistan. Successfully coordinating its effort was a new secretariat in the Foreign Affairs Department called START (Stabilization and Reconstruction Task Force), which is charged to make sure that all parts of the Canadian government work together in a crisis. Canada's close historical and cultural ties to Haiti center on the large Haitian immigrant community, especially in Quebec. Former Governor General Jean was the most prominent Haitian refugee.

Canada hosted the third Summit of the Americas in Quebec in April 2001, where it supported creation of a Free Trade Area of the Americas (FTAA). It sponsored a "democracy clause" for FTAA that would penalize undemocratic regimes. However, little progress has been made for the FTAA. Prime Minister Harper's July 2007 trip through Latin America was a high-profile bid to intensify hemispheric development and trade. While Canada is increasing its two-way trade with Latin

America, it amounts to less than 5% of total Canadian trade or 15% of that portion that does not involve the United States.

Through NAFTA Canada's ties with Mexico were significantly tightened. In 2005 it forged with the U.S. and Mexico the Security and Prosperity Partnership of North America (SPP). Its purpose was to facilitate closer cooperation to maximize the flow of goods and services across their borders while minimizing the passage of terrorists and illegal migrants. It aimed to continue North American integration where NAFTA left off. The "Three Amigos," the top leaders of all three member states, were to meet annually.

It achieved little beyond giving rise to countless conspiracy theories about a future "continental union" of all three countries. Of course, North America lacks the historical impetus that the Second World War had on European integration. Also international terrorism, immigration and the violent drug war in Mexico have prompted Canada and the U.S. to strengthen their border enforcement. Canada imposed visa restrictions on Mexican visitors in 2009, a move that infuriated the Mexican government. The Obama and Harper governments found SPP too rigid and had little enthusiasm for it. They shut down its 20 working groups and cancelled the summits in 2010 and 2011.

Arms Control

Canadians push hard for arms control talks, and they once created a cabinet post in charge of disarmament affairs. In 1984, the government founded the Canadian Institute for International Peace and Security. This was created on the crest of strong public pressure for disarmament and a highly publicized and popular junket by Pierre Elliott Trudeau during his last year in office to several world capitals in an unsuccessful attempt to stimulate greater support for the arms control process. Trudeau won the Albert Einstein Peace Prize for this, but his efforts were not appreciated in Washington. American officials saw this as a public relations gimmick to revive his party's declining popularity and as a hindrance to their own efforts to persuade the Soviet Union to negotiate seriously. The Mulroney government later killed the institute.

In 1997, Canada spearheaded the diplomatic campaign to negotiate an international ban on anti-personnel landmines, which kill more than 2,000 non-belligerents each month. In this "Ottawa Process," as the crusade was known, the government tapped a humanitarian tradition in Canadian foreign policy and endorsed the work done by Nobel Peace Prize winner Jody Williams and other private advocates, such as Princess Diana. It found

huge support in world opinion. An American senator nominated Foreign Minister Axworthy for the Nobel Peace prize even though the U.S. did not support the ban. The Canadians detonated the remnants of their own stockpile, which had not been used since the Korean War and had long since ceased serving a tactical need for their armed forces.

On December 3, 1997, delegates from about 100 countries met in the Canadian capital to sign the treaty. This was an example of Canada's "value-added" diplomacy that permits Canada to play a visible role in world affairs despite acknowledged limits on its resources. Axworthy explained: "With the new fluidity taking place [since the end of the Cold War], there is room for value-added diplomacy. We made a choice that other middle powers have not. We decided to stay global." The view of some Canadians that their country is a kind of "moral superpower" inevitably creates friction with the superpower to the south.

Quebec and France

In any country, domestic political factors strongly influence foreign policy. In Canada, the particularly fragile unity of the country has created difficulties. It has always made Canadians especially wary of what they might interpret as American threats to their sovereignty. Also, the threat of Quebec separatism revealed a potential Achilles heel. It forced Canada to turn its attention even more inwardly than before and to look nervously abroad to see how other countries, especially France and the United States, would respond to Quebec claims of independence.

In 1967, French President Charles de Gaulle had given public support to separatism by saying in a speech in Montreal, "Vive le Québec libre" ("Long live free Quebec") which infuriated his host, Prime Minister Pearson. For a while it seemed as if the French government might even grant Quebec full diplomatic status in Paris, and, in some ways, it did indeed give Quebec's representatives, who outnumber Ottawa's diplomats, the trappings of such status. Such games were played as whose flag could be flown where, and there was some bickering over the titles which Quebec's representatives should be permitted to have. But France concluded, especially after Quebecers rejected sovereignty in 1980, that it should support a unified Canada and has subsequently done so.

In 1985 France's former Prime Minister Laurent Fabius, went to Canada on his first official visit abroad as head of government. He assured the Canadian government that while relations with Quebec were of great importance, "our ambition is vaster and aimed at all Canadians." He even offered a toast designed to undo the

damage done in 1967: *Vive le Canada; vive la France!* The French government also turned a cold shoulder to the 10,000 Canadians of French ancestry who submitted a request for dual citizenship in 1989 on the occasion of the 200th anniversary of the French Revolution.

In 1994 *Bloc Québécois* leader Lucien Bouchard, who had once been Canadian ambassador to France, made an official visit to Paris. He wanted to demonstrate to Quebecers that independence would not leave them international pariahs. His visit was not reported at all in the French media, and a reserved French foreign minister reminded him that France's position on the Quebec issue is "non-indifference but non-interference."

In 1997, Bouchard returned to the French capital as Premier of Quebec with a bevy of Quebec ministers and received a mixed report: President Jacques Chirac told him, in Bouchard's words, that "whatever road Quebec chooses, France will accompany it." However, ex-Prime Minister Lionel Jospin, who regarded Canada as an important ally in countering American cultural dominance in the world, was less enthusiastic, noting that any decision to recognize Quebec would have to take into account the Canadian government's assessment of the post-referendum situation.

At the 1999 Francophonie summit in New Brunswick, Chirac was also restrained. He stressed that France and Canada are partners and that Paris has no wish to interfere in other countries' affairs. But a gaffe made by one of France's presidential candidates in 2007, Ségolène Royal, who said in a speech that Quebec should have the right to self-determination, demonstrated that there remains some ambivalence in Paris concerning Quebec's future in Canada.

Upon his return to Canada, Bouchard found himself in a firefight over a proposed agreement between the province and France to enforce child support settlements. Since Canada's constitution limits provincial governments' foreign relations to culture and commerce, Ottawa scuttled the deal because of the contractual language that treated Quebec as a sovereign country.

Even in the cultural sphere Ottawa resists any gesture that seems to treat Quebec as a sovereign state. In March 1999, Canada angrily pulled out of an international meeting of culture ministers in Paris after the French government issued a direct invitation to Quebec. "Only the government of Canada has the right to decide on the presence and representation of Canada and its constituent parts in our relations with other foreign states."

Quebec also tried hard to gain some form of special recognition from the United States, but American leaders and diplo-

Canada

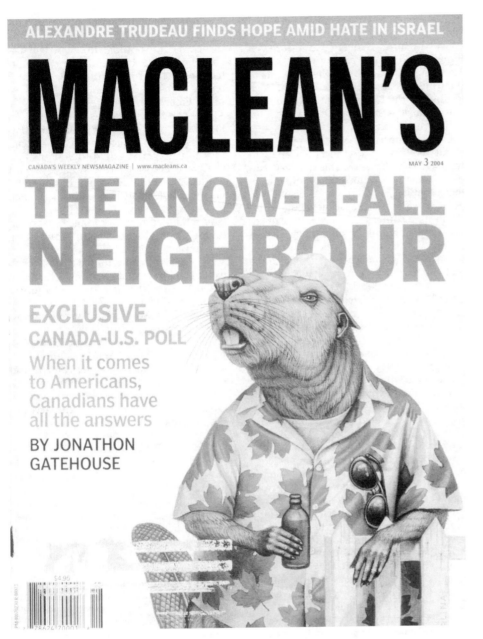

ALEXANDRE TRUDEAU FINDS HOPE AMID HATE IN ISRAEL

MACLEAN'S

CANADA'S WEEKLY NEWSMAGAZINE | www.macleans.ca

MAY 3 2004

THE KNOW-IT-ALL NEIGHBOUR

EXCLUSIVE
CANADA-U.S. POLL

When it comes
to Americans,
Canadians have
all the answers

BY JONATHON
GATEHOUSE

$4.95

mats were careful always to stress that the United States would deal only with Ottawa on diplomatic matters. They prevented Quebec from opening a kind of "embassy" in the U.S. and permitted only trade missions. Quebec has more than 25 representative offices throughout the world.

The consistent American view is that there should be only *one* Canada, not two. This was politely reiterated to Bouchard during his 1994 visit to Washington. It was expressed more bluntly to a former American political officer and later ambassador at the U.S. embassy in Ottawa, David T. Jones, who wrote in a 1997 article in the *Washington Quarterly* that the U.S. could "live with" an independent Quebec. The State Department publicly called this statement "an outrageous, undisciplined act."

To shore up Canada's relationship with France in 2000, the former prime minister appointed his nephew, Raymond Chrétien, as ambassador in Paris. Quebec's Liberal Premier, Jean Charest, maintained much more cooperative relations with his fellow Liberal government in Ottawa after his election in 2003. At the same time he traveled to Paris, flying the Quebec flag and acting like the government leader of a sovereign state. He initiated discussions to obtain for Quebec a greater presence in the international arena, especially in trade negotiations. "What we are aiming for is to be at the negotiating table with the federal government if the topic of discussion affects Quebec's competence. . . . As French speakers representing 2% of the population of North America, we have always felt the need to maintain external rela-

tions." Quebec did secure a seat in the UN Economic Social and Cultural Council (UNESCO), and it announced its desire for more such international memberships.

Charest returned to Paris in July 2007 to meet with new French President Nicolas Sarkozy, who is openly pro-Canadian. He discovered that nobody talks about separation anymore. But this time he was working closely with the federal government to stimulate Europeans' interest in a transatlantic, Canada-EU free trade agreement. In April 2008, France's leading right-leaning newspaper, *Le Figaro*, described the PQ as "an empty shell" that has "sold its soul" by resigning itself to ruling only a Canadian province, not its own country.

In 2008 there was an unprecedented number of contacts between Canadian and French politicians due to the celebrations surrounding the 400th anniversary of Quebec City's founding. Immediately after the October 2008 elections, Harper raced to Quebec City to open the Francophonie Summit declaring himself "heir" to Samuel de Champlain and pledging of more funding for the international Quebec channel TV5.

The prestigious French daily, *Le Monde*, lauded Governor General Michaëlle Jean, the great-great-granddaughter of French-owned Haitian slaves, during a May 2008 visit to Paris as an "almost Queen." Quebec nationalists fumed that she was being feted in France instead of Quebec Premier Jean Charest. President Sarkozy antagonized them again in February 2009. After ceremoniously awarding Charest the Legion of Honor medal, Sarkozy added: "Do you believe the world, as it faces an unprecedented crisis, needs more divisions?" He favors "deepening in every domain the unique relation that links France to Quebec," but the best way to do that is "in harmony with the relation that France maintains with all of Canada." Quebec nationalists were stunned at such "lack of respect" and "contemptible epithets." PQ leader Pauline Marois was dumbfounded: "What are you talking about, Mr. President?"

Complex Relations with the United States

The Canadian domestic political system is complicated. The provinces are very powerful and can sometimes place limits on Ottawa's power. Of course, American states also have the power to act on their own in many matters. Therefore, both countries experience some difficulties in settling bilateral affairs, when state and provincial capitals manage to get into the act.

Canada's parliamentary system simplifies the conduct of foreign policy. Responsibility is clearer, and once the federal government establishes policy, there are fewer obstacles to its implementation than in the U.S. Canada's parliamentary committees in the House of Commons and Senate debate policy and hold hearings. They may also suggest amendments. But Parliament cannot thwart a policy to which the government has committed itself. No majority government that has negotiated a treaty needs to worry about whether Parliament will ratify it.

The American political system works quite differently. As in Canada, power is divided in a geographic sense. However, unlike in Canada, power is also separated in Washington, and this can create diplomatic nightmares for both American and Canadian leaders. Foreigners have every reason to be mystified by America's large, highly decentralized institutions, which wield power of their own and which often seem to be hostile to each other. Separation of powers is particularly troublesome for foreign policy: it is often impossible for a president to produce what he promises to foreign leaders.

The complicated and extensive interagency bargaining in Washington confuses many Canadians although they expend a greater effort to understand the U.S. system than Americans do the Canadian. The American political system enables relatively unknown persons of various professional backgrounds to rise to the highest national political offices through a painfully long and complicated electoral system, largely unfathomable to Canadians (and to many Americans as well). A newly elected president may have little experience in foreign affairs and yet have the power to select a multitude of foreign policy advisers, secretaries and agency chiefs, many with little or no foreign policy background. Such a presidential "team" appears often to operate in an uncoordinated way, frequently sending off widely differing signals. This inevitably creates and fuels doubts about American leadership capabilities and the continuity of U.S. foreign policy. In 1996–7 it took 15 months for the Clinton administration finally to name a new ambassador to Canada, Gordon Giffin, who had lived most of his youth in Montreal and Toronto, and a couple months more for the Senate to confirm him.

Canadians are particularly frustrated by the powerful U.S. Congress. It has undergone significant changes: the seniority system has weakened, and the number of committees and subcommittees has proliferated. Also, the workload has become so demanding that congressmen and senators are retiring earlier. Therefore, an increasingly high percentage of the legislators are new in Congress. At the same time, committee and personal staffs have

grown enormously. What these changes have done is to take much of the power that used to be concentrated in a few key figures and to disperse it within Congress.

In this more decentralized (or, more positively, "democratized,") Congress, legislative work has become much more complicated. For instance, more than 40 congressional committees and subcommittees deal with the defense budget alone. In the absence of strong party discipline as in Canada, American congressmen and senators are more protective of their constituents' interests and can safely vote against their party leaders or the president if an issue of great interest in their districts or states is at stake. In December 2000, ex-Foreign Minister John Manley said that it would be easier to work with the new American President George W. Bush than with Congress: "It's always easier for Canada to deal with the United States when the administration has the strength to deal with issues and can expect congressional support."

Since senatorial approval (by a two-thirds vote) is needed for all treaties, the American upper house can even veto the most painstakingly crafted international agreement. Canadian governments have experienced how this fact can affect their bilateral relations with the United States. The East Coast Fisheries Agreement of 1979, the Tax Treaty of 1980 and the Pacific Salmon Treaty of 1983 were all victims of senatorial opposition. Also galling to Canadian diplomats and governments is the fact that after already making all the concessions it could to secure the president's or State Department's agreement, a president or secretary of state might come back to them and say that yet more concessions are needed in order to secure senatorial approval. Thus, Canada must sometimes go farther than halfway to get a ratified agreement, and that favors the United States.

In an attempt to get around this problem, Canada began to lobby directly in Congress in order to compete with the interest groups that were seeking to stymie agreements important to Canada. Allan Gotlieb was ambassador to the U.S. in the 1980s and wrote in *The Washington Diaries* that "Americans just do not see us as different from themselves. When we do something different, Americans feel betrayed. They don't see us as foreigners but as perverse Americans."

He changed the earlier standard practice of working only with the State Department and took his country's concerns directly to Congress and its powerful staffers. When calling on members of Congress, he remembers: "One always feels as though he is begging. One is. The challenge: how to beg and keep one's dignity."

He noted that diplomatic disputes often arise not as a result of White House decisions but from the rulings of unknown bureaucrats at federal agencies, which Canadian diplomats must not neglect. He also worked with journalists: "I would never have dreamed of how important journalists are in Washington. My views were shaped by 20 years in Ottawa dealing with the semi-educated press corps there." He concluded that his country has no friends in Washington, only interests. That might be changing: in 2006 a new congressional "Friends of Canada" caucus was created to focus on shared concerns.

In 2004 a new public advocacy and legislative secretariat was created in the Canadian Embassy, which includes provincial representatives, to lobby Congress more effectively. Alberta, which exports close to $90 billion in goods (mainly energy and food) to the U.S. annually, is the only province that runs a trade office out of the embassy. Quebec and Manitoba have their own lower-profile representatives to lobby on issues of interest; other provinces will no doubt follow. Quebec also has a tourism office elsewhere in Washington.

Former Ambassador Michael Wilson commented in 2007 that Canada's and Alberta's joint effort to influence the American government is good. He wanted to demonstrate that the bilateral relationship goes much farther than merely dealing with a few irritants and rises to the level of a global "partnership." This struck a positive note with an American diplomat: "It's exactly what we have wanted from Canada: a partner who will work with us together on the 96 per cent of international issues where our goals are the same: defeat terrorism, advance and consolidate democracy and good governance, prevent the proliferation of WMDs, promote economic development through open trade and development."

Canadians also rely on U.S. governors to advocate shared concerns in Washington. Gottlieb said "these governor relationships really matter because the states matter—that is increasingly where the problems come from. And if the governor is our friend, then we are closer to solving them." One governor who was certainly a friend is Vancouver-born Canadian citizen Jennifer Granholm of Michigan. One of the oldest relationships is the Conference of New England Governors and Eastern Canadian Premiers. A major asset of former Manitoba Premier Gary Doer, who was appointed to replace Michael Wilson as ambassador to the U.S. in 2009, was that he had spent much time in the U.S. and knew personally all four former governors in President Obama's cabinet. Of course, mayors and city councils on both sides of the border work closely together.

Canada

It also began to try harder to influence the American public directly. In one case, the Canadians produced a film on acid rain to help educate Americans on its consequences for Canadian fish, trees, lakes and public monuments. Some American officials bristled at this attempt by a foreign country to go over their heads in an important diplomatic issue and appeal directly to the American people. They temporarily banned the film, a move that predictably heightened Americans' interest in it and spurred them to jam halls in which the film was later shown.

Americans and Canadians have lots of practice in settling their disputes peacefully. When they cannot, they have taken their disputes to the International Court of Justice, agreeing in advance to abide by its decision. In 1984, the court rendered a long-awaited decision on a disputed maritime boundary in the Gulf of Maine, giving Canada jurisdiction over about one-sixth of the rich Georges Bank fishing grounds. Canadians were unhappy with this decision. Both countries worked out an agreement as to what should be done to manage the fish stocks that cross the boundary and are caught by both countries' fishermen.

The U.S.-Canadian Border

Even before the September 11, 2001, attacks, there was congressional clamor to tighten up controls along the U.S.-Canadian border. An Algerian with a fake Canadian passport was arrested at the border in December 1999 with enough material in his car to make four powerful bombs. Two other Algerians and a Canadian woman were picked up at the border to Vermont five days later with traces of explosives that sniffer dogs detected. All were identified as members of a violent Algerian organization called the Armed Islamic Group (GIA).

Charges were made in Congress that Canada was "soft on terrorism." Months of intense diplomatic and political activity were necessary before a deal could be reached dropping the proposed requirements for Canadians to fill out time-consuming entry forms at the border like all other foreigners. Nevertheless, the U.S. added 600 new customs and special agents along the border, bringing the number to 1,800.

The September 11 attacks changed the way many Americans look at their borders, and it raised the urgency to secure them. Officials set out to apply technology to create a "smart border" to tighten security and thwart terrorists while keeping the 49th parallel open for the world's largest trading relationship. The longest undefended border became a bit more defended and more complex to traverse.

The challenge is daunting: a truck crosses the Ambassador Bridge between Detroit and Windsor every six seconds. This bridge is the cornerstone of the two neighbors' trade, especially that of Canada's export-dependent economy. Even a temporary closing of the 555-meter-long bridge (with an accompanying tunnel) would be devastating to the two countries' $500 billion annual trade relationship and to Canada's economic future.

About 70% of Canada-U.S. trade travels by truck, with 37,000 trucks crossing the border every day; 58% of these cross at only five border crossings—Ambassador Bridge, Sarnia, Fort Erie, Lacolle, and the Pacific Highway. Eight out of ten top crossing points are either bridges or tunnels and have become bottlenecks with long waits. Speed is increasingly important because of growing "just-in-time delivery." Trucks loaded with goods bound for either country are pre-cleared and sealed with electronic sensors that allow them to cross the border in fast lanes. The "Nexus" system of allowing "pre-approved frequent travelers" across the frontier was improved and reintroduced.

Before September 11, half the 126 official crossings were unguarded at night, but they are all manned 24 hours now. The U.S. Coast Guard stops all boats that cross the maritime border in the Great Lakes and escorts all oil and gas tankers. When U.S. Coast Guard vessels in American waters installed machine guns and conducted periodic live-fire exercises in 2006, an outcry was heard all around the lakes. Armaments in the Great Lakes are supposed to be limited, according to an 1817 treaty. Eighty American and Canadian mayors demanded that the shooting stop.

Although the border has become more secure, it is not as open as it was before September 11. The number of Americans who cross the border dropped by 22% between 1999 and 2005. This hits Ontario the hardest, whose tourist trade is 95% dependent upon Americans. BC and Alberta depend more on Asian visitors, and Quebec on Europeans. In the other direction, the opening in Canada of large American retail outlets like Wal-Mart, Best Buy, Pottery Barn and Home Depot, as well as growing internet purchasing, have contributed to the reduction of Canadian day-trippers into the U.S.

Canadian consumers have complained loudly about the fact that although their loonie has reached parity with the U.S. dollar, prices for American goods are still higher in Canada than across the border. One can see this in the two prices on book covers: the American price is always lower. The price difference is especially grating for automobiles: in 2007 a Lexus

RX350 sold for $52,000 in Canada, but only $37,000 in Canada.

The stronger Canadian dollar and high Canadian gasoline prices helped drive many Canadians southward across the border for shopping. There they can visit certain chain stores, such as Target, Lord & Taylor, Macy's, Saks Fifth Avenue, J.Crew, Kenneth Cole, Anthropologie and Bath & Body Works, that have not expanded to Canada. They can generally buy products there for lower prices than they would have to pay at home. However, if they buy too much, they may be required to pay sales taxes and other duties when they reenter Canada. The greatest fear on both sides of the frontier is that the $1.6 billion daily two-way trade will be affected. Already old-style warehousing of goods is being reintroduced in many places to replace the efficiency of just-in-time delivery.

The main factor for slower border crossings is the fear of terrorist attacks; 44 government agencies on both sides have some jurisdiction over border matters, and that means slower crossings. Eight Canadian ministries alone have responsibility for some part of the border. The sprawling Department of Public Safety, the Canadian equivalent of the Department of Homeland Security, was created by the former Liberal government after September 11, 2001, to give a single minister control over everything from the RCMP and Canadian Security Intelligence Service, to running federal prisons and managing the border with the United States. In 2004 the U.S. began demanding fingerprints and photos at its borders for non-Canadian citizens between the ages of 14 and 80.

From January 2007 all airline passengers arriving in the U.S. had to show a valid passport. For the first time in history that was extended to land and water passengers on June 1, 2009, when the Western Hemisphere Travel Initiative came into effect. The disruption this requirement caused was reportedly modest even though there was a sharp drop in cross-border travel. However, relying on passports is a problem since only an estimated 34% of Americans over age 18 have one, compared to 54% of Canadians.

Where there is real worry, however, is that fire trucks and ambulances are delayed at the border, thereby hampering community-level cross-border cooperation. That already happened in 2008 when Quebec volunteer firemen speeding to a hotel blaze in upstate New York were held up so long on the border that the building had burned to the ground by the time they arrived on the scene. Nobody knows what may happen elsewhere in places like Stanstead, Quebec, and Derby Line, Vermont, which are, in effect, a single community. Not only do streets continue unguarded into the other country, but the joint opera house and library building is shared. Most of the interior is in Canada, but one can only enter the building from the United States. A black line on the floor runs through the library demarcating the two lands.

In the *Maclean's* 2003–04 year-end poll, 61% of Canadians approved of the idea of a North American perimeter. Prime Ministers Martin and Harper agreed that one of Canada's main challenges is to keep the American border open. After all, four-fifths of its exports head across the U.S. border, accounting for 52% of Canada's GDP. Given the facts that a truck crosses the Canada-U.S. border every 2.5 seconds and that every minute more than US$1 million in trade passes across it, trade must be kept unimpeded.

Bilateral cooperation has been stepped up, with a growing exchange of intelligence information and criminal records (allowing U.S. law enforcement agents to retrieve records from the Canadian Police Information Centre), consultation on visas (Canada requires no visa for 52 countries, while the U.S. exempts only 32), and collaboration at foreign embassies to stop people smuggling from overseas. At the time of the September 11 attacks, only Canadians worked at the RCMP headquarters in Ottawa. Now Americans from four agencies are based there. Cooperation is reported to be "pervasive." The two countries have acted in concert to plug a hole at St-Bernard-de-Lacolle along the Quebec border with New York. It is now more difficult to arrive in New York with fraudulent passports and then scoot across the border to claim refugee status.

The Mexican and Canadian borders are still different. Whereas the Mexican border is normally divided by walls, the Canadian frontier is in most places no more than a ditch or a cleared area in a forest. By 2007 the U.S. stationed only 950 border patrol agents along the Canadian border, compared with 10,200 along the shorter boundary with Mexico. But the U.S. is creating border security bases like it has along its border with Mexico. Each equipped with two helicopters, an airplane, a high-speed boat, and a staff of about 70, the first will be located at Bellingham (Washington) and Plattsburgh (New York), followed by bases near Detroit, Grand Forks (North Dakota) and Great Falls (Montana).

President Obama's homeland-security secretary, Janet Napolitano, wants controls along the Canadian border to be brought in line with those on the Mexican frontier. She says she wants everybody to realize that "this is a real border." Her department plans to install heat-detecting sensors and additional cameras along the

border. The U.S. also now uses unmanned surveillance drones to patrol parts of the frontier.

Both countries are targeting potential terrorists and smuggling. The latter includes marijuana from Canada and cocaine and weapons from the U.S., as well as large amounts of cash in both directions. To deal with the dangers of such cross-border criminality, the 4,800 officers of the Canada Border Services Agency will be armed with guns over the decade until 2017. The first 80 were issued in 2007. The ultimate aim of such cooperation is an even more open and safe U.S.-Canada border. In order to help spot persons crossing the border illegally or avoiding ports of entry, the U.S. began in 2009 mounting unmanned aircraft patrols from Grand Forks using Predator B aircraft.

Water Resources and Acid Rain
In 1909 the two countries signed and ratified the Boundary Waters Treaty to preserve the quality and quantity of their shared water. An International Joint Commission was set up to arbitrate disputes. In its century of existence, it has worked well; of 53 joint references, 51 were resolved by mutual agreement. Nevertheless, the two countries seem always to have on-going disagreements over use of North America's water resources.

For decades American governments have been interested in a project to divert the waters of the Garrison River in order to direct water from the Missouri River basin into 250,000 acres of parched lands in northwestern North Dakota for irrigation purposes. North Dakota long wanted

to drain millions of gallons of water from Devil's Lake, which has no natural outlet and is located 60 miles south of the Manitoba border, in order to prevent the rising lake from continuing to flood the surrounding countryside. The problem is that the spill-off waters might carry unwanted invasive species, parasites, disease, and the high concentrations of sulphates, arsenic, phosphorus and other pollutants from Devil's Lake via the Sheyenne River into the Red River across the Canadian border into Lake Winnipeg. From there they could ultimately pass through Canadian rivers (most of which flow northward) into the Hudson Bay watershed.

Although the projects had actually been started, the determined efforts of environmentalist groups on both sides of the border, as well as the Manitoba provincial government, prevented for a while the projects from getting complete approval. Nevertheless, there continued to be support in Congress for them. After devastating floods along the Red River in North Dakota and Manitoba in 1997, the two countries agreed to work together to minimize future flooding. In 2000, the North Dakota governor traveled to Manitoba to see firsthand the province's concerns and promised to consult with provincial leaders. A few months later the Manitoba premier and the governors of Minnesota and North Dakota met for the first time and reached an agreement to protect all citizens from Red River flooding. In the same year, Canada sent 200 firefighters to help weary Americans battle a hundred wildfires out of control across the Western United States. For the first time, the U.S. put a foreigner, a Canadian, in command of a unit battling a blaze.

Ultimately patience ran out in mid-2005. North Dakota officials, who had resisted Canadian requests to refer the issue to the commission, announced that the draining of Devil's Lake would begin. This kind of unilateral action could lead to difficulties for both neighbors. Half the 300 transboundary rivers flow southward into the United States. In 2005 Montana challenged BC's plans to mine coal under a vital riverbed. Good will can run thin. In a landmark cross-border pollution case, a Canadian company in BC, Teck Cominco, voluntarily agreed in 2006 to pay for any harm done to Americans or wildlife

Canada

by the waste products its zinc smelter had dumped into the Columbia River and traveled downstream into the U.S.

With ten times Canada's population, the United States is in much greater need of water resources, and American eyes have often looked to Canada's supply as a long-range solution. Canada has always resisted the large-scale transfer of its water resources, though. Its leaders have noted that even though the Canadian Shield has abundant lakes and streams, its water is not easily replenishable. The fact is that the flow of rain, spring water and snowmelt that goes through Canadian waterways represents 7% of the world's renewable water supply. Of Canada's 18 principal watershed systems, 15 provide less than 10% of their annual renewable supplies to human usage. Canadians have also opposed large-scale diversion of water from the Great Lakes, which are shared by both countries. Although they have occasionally studied the possibility of siphoning off that water, the Great Lakes states agreed not to initiate any such scheme without Ontario's permission.

In 2002 the International Boundary Waters Treaty Act went into effect banning the bulk removal of water from basins that straddle the border, particularly the Great Lakes. Actually, researchers who have searched for examples of economically viable ideas for bulk-water exports from Canada have found none. There are neither serious proposals nor realistic prospects for such exports to the U.S. Although NAFTA says nothing about water, ex-Foreign Minister Pierre Pettigrew, made clear: "Water is not a [tradable] good, it is a resource that needs to be managed."

One of the most stubborn problems of both countries was acid rain—pollution caused by the burning of fossil fuels and released into the air via high smokestacks. It mixes in the atmosphere with nitrogen oxide from automobile emissions to form

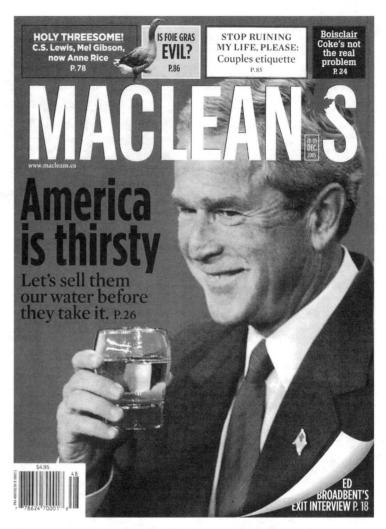

Source: *The Economist*

an acid moisture. This unhealthy combination sometimes is then carried hundreds of miles before being brought back to earth by rain, killing trees, fish and other animal life and eating away at stone buildings and monuments. For a country whose people are rightly proud of its natural beauty and 10% of whose work force depends upon tourism, this is a catastrophic ecological and economic problem.

Much of Canada's acid rain stems from plants in the U.S., particularly in the Midwest. Therefore, any solution to the problem must be an international one. American administrations tended to buy time by calling for "more research" on acid rain. Because of the salience of this issue in Canada, its leaders could not accept this and pushed for more concrete steps. The acid rain issue, which became a sort of litmus test for the two countries' relations, severely tried Canadians' patience.

In 1991 the two signed a landmark accord committing the two countries to curb emissions that cause acid rain and to reduce other pollutants. By 1995, acid rain levels had dropped significantly, and sulfur dioxide emissions had declined in the

East by 40% since 1980. There is still work to be done on both sides. In 2000, the New York attorney general asked the president to put pressure on the Ontario government to clean up coal-burning plants on the Canadian side that are destroying forests and causing respiratory problems in Buffalo and other border areas.

Prime Ministers and Presidents

Brian Mulroney came into office in 1984 determined to improve Canada-U.S. relations. Not since Lester Pearson and John F. Kennedy were in power in the early 1960s was there such a warm personal relationship between the leaders of these two neighbors and allies. Regular summit meetings forced Washington to confront Canadian issues promptly, instead of consigning them to the back burner. The invitation of Mulroney to address the U.S. Congress and to dedicate the newly completed Canadian embassy in Washington, the only foreign embassy to be permitted on Pennsylvania Avenue, demonstrated the two countries' good relations.

Mulroney had to pay a domestic political price for his relationship with Reagan and Bush. He reaped criticism for seeming too eager to please and to impress American presidents even though he was not afraid to say "no" when Canadian interests were at stake: he refused to withdraw from UNESCO, favored tough economic sanctions against South Africa, permitted Nicaragua to open a trade office in Toronto, and refused officially to endorse the Strategic Defense Initiative, or SDI. In fact, he publicly broke ranks with the U.S. more frequently than did either Pearson or Trudeau (whom President Nixon considered to be an "asshole," according to Watergate tapes). Mulroney merely concluded that a confrontational approach toward the U.S. is less effective than a more conciliatory style.

Former Prime Minister Chrétien decided that his approach toward the U.S. would be less enthusiastic and more formal. He had scorned Mulroney's pledge always to give the Americans the benefit of the doubt, joking that Mulroney would answer the phone from the president before it rang. He also announced after his election that, unlike Mulroney, he would

not be going fishing with the president, fearing that he might end up as the fish. He played golf with Clinton, but he winced in 1997 when the president introduced him in the Rose Garden by saying that "I don't know of any two world leaders who played golf together more than we have." Chrétien had said in 1992: "Mulroney cares more about getting others to like him than about getting the things that Canada needs. Me, I understand that in politics there is no room for friendship."

He also knew that Canadian voters do not like overt reverence for the U.S. They have ambivalent feelings toward the U.S. and are alternately drawn to and repelled by American might. They prefer what the *Globe and Mail* called "affected standoffishness" toward Washington. Chrétien expresses that ambivalence well. A 1994 poll showed that 53% of respondents approved his management of the relationship with America, compared with 25% for Mulroney in 1992. He established comfortable rapport with President Clinton, meeting discreetly with him 16 times lead-

Ambassador Gary A. Doer

ing up to an official visit to Washington in April 1997, his first since taking office in 1993.

He described that rapport as "good—and not cozy," and he treated Clinton as an equal, not as the ranking world leader. He felt free in 1997 to expound to the leaders of Belgium and Luxembourg that Clinton's views on NATO expansion are "not for reasons of security" but "for short-term political reasons to win elections." As one Canadian political commentator noted, Chrétien's assertion that American foreign policies are driven by domestic interests are about as shocking as the reality that the same is true for Canada.

Chrétien offered swift support for important American policies, and he appreciated Clinton's pitch for a united Canada during the president's 1995 visit to Ottawa, repeated at the time of the Quebec referendum: "A strong and united Canada has been a wonderful partner for the United States and an incredibly important and constructive citizen throughout the entire world." But when he introduced Clinton to Parliament, he said: "The Americans are our best friends—whether we like it or not." And he went out of his way in Washington in 1997 to underline the differences between the two countries, stressing the way Canada values such things as universal health care and gun control.

In Chrétien's words, "it's nice to have a big client like the United States, but you can't have just one. It wouldn't be a good business position." Nevertheless, the two countries' close economic ties and cordial relations remained essentially unchanged. Chrétien's foreign policy had been less

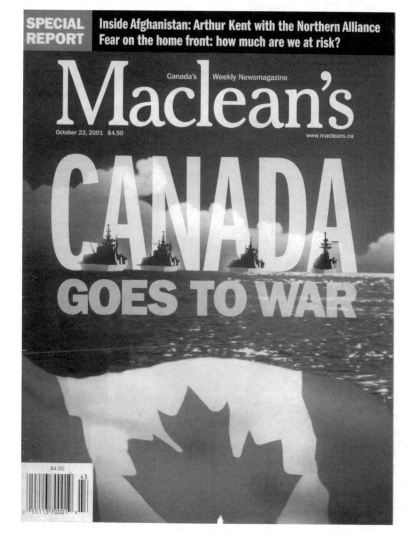

Canada

outspoken about human rights, more aggressive about promoting Canadian exports and economic interests, and less generous with foreign aid (which it cut to only .34% of GDP by 2007 (the world's 15th highest, ahead of the United States' .22%).

Ex-Foreign Minister Axworthy crusaded visibly and energetically on the world stage under the banners of "soft power" and "human security" that emphasize values and human need. He stepped down in 2000 and was replaced by John Manley, who proclaimed that his first priority was to enhance Canada's privileged relationship with the United States. In September 2003 the government announced that seven new consulates would be opened in the U.S., and two consulates would be upgraded to consulate generals. Twenty honorary consuls would be appointed. Thus representation in the U.S. grew from 15 to 22. Most new locations were in the Southeast, Southwest and Midwest. This reflects the government's concern about the shift of American political and economic power to the "Sunbelt" away from the northern states adjacent to Canada.

Prime Minister Paul Martin promised the same thing upon taking power in December 2003 and even created a cabinet committee with himself as chairman to explore ways to improve relations with Washington. The business lobby in Ottawa, as well as many other Canadian leaders, encouraged Martin to continue in this direction. He appointed a heavy hitter as ambassador to the U.S.: Frank McKenna, former premier of New Brunswick. Despite serious disagreements with the American government over issues like Iraq, there was unease about being estranged from the United States without the backing of a rising regional block like the European Union. If one adds to this an inadequacy of military power, fewer funds for foreign aid, and a declining share of America's imports, Canada was worried about its influence in the world.

Martin shifted the locus for making important decisions on the Canada-U.S. relationship from the Department of Foreign Affairs and International Trade to the Privy Council Office (PCO). His proposal to create a new Department of International Trade, separate from the Department of Foreign Affairs, was rejected by parliament in 2005. The Harper government decided in 2006 to keep the two together, thereby emphasizing the importance of trade with the U.S. After the September 11 terrorist attacks, responsibility for the bilateral border was transferred to the PCO.

Martin ordered major policy reviews in both foreign affairs and defense. In April 2005 the results, entitled "Now is the time to rebuild," were unveiled. The government pledged to bolster its diplomatic corps, beef up the military, and overhaul foreign aid in an attempt to reverse Canada's diminishing influence in foreign affairs. The prime minister asserted: "You cannot have a robust foreign policy if all you're prepared to engage in is empty moralizing." Concrete proposals included raising military spending by Can$10 billion over five years, increasing the size of the armed forces by 5,000 to 67,000, instituting a central command, strengthening the special operations forces, purchasing more equipment, such as helicopters and ships, and creating a new emergency response team capable of dealing with disasters anywhere.

After his reelection in 2004, President George W. Bush seized the opportunity to reach out to Canada and to improve the tone of the relationship. With only two weeks' notice, he accepted Martin's invitation to Canada. In his December 1, 2004, speech in Halifax, he thanked all those Canadians who "came out to wave—with all five fingers—for the hospitality." He also expressed belated gratitude to those who had taken in stranded American passengers after the September 11 terrorist strikes in New York and Washington. He admitted that "it's not always easy to sleep next to the elephant," but he spoke a language Canadians like to hear: building multilateral institutions and making international cooperation a top priority. He and his Canadian counterpart displayed the warmest personal relationship at the top in over a decade.

Martin's successor as prime minister, Stephen Harper, publicly resisted any opposition efforts to paint him as a Canadian Bush, and he stuck up for Canadian interests whenever they were challenged, such as in the Arctic. But he vowed throughout his leadership of the Conservative Party to transform a bilateral relationship that had turned sour. Noting that Canada's access to the highest governmental circles in Washington had persistently eroded, he named as ambassador investment banker and former finance minister in the Mulroney government, Michael Wilson. The

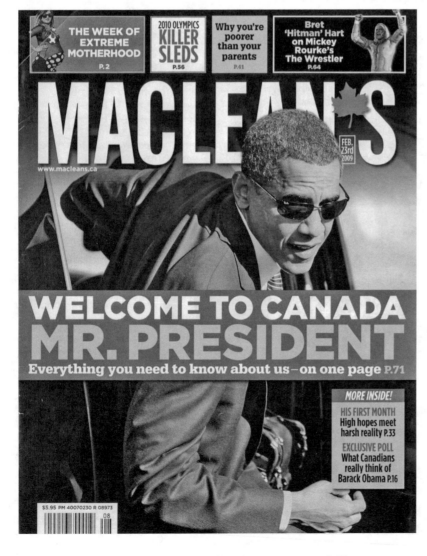

new ambassador promised a respectful but firm approach: "America is a neighbor. You don't throw snow on his driveway." When he left his post in the autumn of 2009, he noted that his best calling card in Washington was the fact that Canadian soldiers were fighting shoulder-to-shoulder with Americans in Afghanistan. "It was highly appreciated and highly admired." He was replaced by former Manitoba Premier Gary Doer.

Doer's American counterpart in Ottawa also took office in 2009: David Jacobson, a Chicago-based corporate lawyer and top fund raiser for President Obama. Like most American ambassadors, he knew little about the country when he was appointed. But in order to understand this huge land, he embarked on an 8-week coast-to-coast road trip across Canada, avoiding airplanes and getting the feel of the terrain. He met all the premiers and as many Canadians as he could.

Harper sent some positive signals to Washington: "Canada intends to be a player" and will advance "our shared values." He promised and delivered a large increase in defense spending, and he pledged to strengthen border and port security, renew NORAD, and continue his predecessor's policy of bolstering his country's efforts against the Taliban in Afghanistan. He embraced the American-led war on terrorism and asserted Israel's right to protect itself. He dared to incur Turkey's ire by calling the killing of Armenians in the First World War a genocide, something his American counterpart, Barack Obama, did not dare do as president. He discusses human rights with the Chinese to little avail. In fact, China's leaders lambasted him for his "disgusting conduct" in meeting the Dalai Lama in October 2007. Nevertheless, a 2007 poll revealed that a quarter of Canadians consider China the most important country to their interests.

Although he had seldom traveled outside Canada before becoming prime minister, Harper showed a wide-ranging interest in international affairs. He quickly acquired the confidence to handle foreign policy himself without depending on career diplomats. He enjoys having no subordinate on foreign policy.

He re-energized relations with Washington. He has his public's support in this. A survey published at the time he entered office showed a slim majority (54%) of Canadians wanting a foreign policy that would bring Canada closer to the U.S. But pollster Michael Adams says this message comes with a warning: "The minute you look like you're kowtowing, as far as we're concerned, you're toast."

The Canadian government is acutely aware of the traditional ambivalence many Canadians show toward too extensive co-operation with the U.S. Ex-Foreign Minister Manley noted: "There are two rules in Canadian politics. The first is: don't be too close to the United States. The second is: don't be too far from the United States." In the aftermath of the September 11 attacks, Canadians wanted their leaders to emphasize the second rule.

That was not the case in 2003 when the U.S. led a coalition to end Saddam Hussein's rule in Iraq. Emotions were high, and three-fourths of the Canadian public favored the government's decision to stay out of the war. The media do make a difference, however. Canadians who get most of their news from U.S. television were three times more likely to support the war effort in Iraq. In a 2004 poll, 66% of Canadians said their attitude toward the U.S. had worsened since 11 September; 76% said this was because of their dislike of President Bush. Only 16% of Canadians would have voted for him. Half saw the U.S. as arrogant, bullying or dangerous, and two-thirds thought America's global reputation had worsened over the past decade. Americans did not reciprocate these negative feelings: 74% said their opinion remained unchanged after four years, and 12% said they had improved.

American diplomats in Canada revealed some mild irritation of Canadian attitudes in cables that were publicized by Wikileaks. One is the American perception that Canadians "always carry a chip on their shoulder," apparently because of their feeling that Canada "is condemned to always play 'Robin' to the U.S. 'Batman'." Another is "moral outrage, a Canadian specialty." One diplomat described "soul searching" in Canada about its "decline from 'middle power' status to that of an 'active observer' of global affairs, a trend which some Canadians believe should be reversed." The Americans marveled that "despite the overwhelming importance of the U.S. to Canada for its economy and security," candidates for parliament rarely mention anything about relations with the U.S. The U.S. is like the "900-pound gorilla": "overwhelming but too potentially menacing to acknowledge."

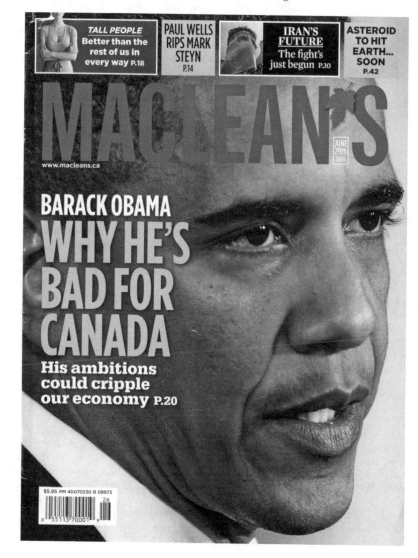

Canada

Thousands of Canadian fans booed the American national anthem before two Montreal Canadiens hockey games. Even a pee wee hockey team from Boston was booed and heckled. Such insensitive treatment of young Americans was so appalling to some Canadians that the team was invited back to Fredericton, NB, and treated with touching love and respect.

A stream of insults came from Canadian officials and MPs. The prime minister's communications director, Francine Ducros, called President Bush a "moron," a slip that cost Ducros her job. A Liberal MP was overheard to decry the "damn Americans, I hate those bastards"; Carolyn Parrish later apologized for that remark. However, a year later she lapsed into another anti-American tirade by stomping on a Bush doll during a nationally televised satire show. For this she was ousted from the Liberal parliamentary caucus. Another MP was reproached for declaring that the U.S. was leading "the coalition of the idiots" in Iraq. An NDP MP called Bush a "war criminal."

Some Canadians who actually met with President Bush had more complimentary memories of him. He was said always to have been well briefed. Former Liberal cabinet member, Anne McLellan, remembered that "he was a person easy to deal with. There is no artifice. He tells you exactly where he is coming from. There are not a lot of surprises—and there are benefits to that." No back-channels were needed to clarify statements or inferences.

Bush's commitment to NAFTA was never in doubt. By contrast, the Democratic Congress was more protectionist. During her campaign Democratic presidential candidate and later Secretary of State Hillary Clinton called NAFTA her husband's "mistake." Barack Obama sought electoral college votes by suggesting that it should be renegotiated. He dropped that pledge after his election, advocating only that the side agreements on labor and the environment should be brought into the main text of the treaty to ensure enforcement. As president he repeatedly emphasized his commitment to open trade between the two northern neighbors.

President Bush was a more consequential president for Canada than were most of his predecessors. For instance, he created the Department of Homeland Security after September 11, 2001, spurring Canada to reorganize its own government by creating the equivalent Department of Public Safety. He rearranged North American defense by creating a Northern Command. This prompted Ottawa to create its own Canada Command.

Canadians hated Bush's infamous "axis of evil" term. Few were aware that it had been coined by David Frum, a Canadian author and pundit who spent 13 months as a speech writer for the American president. Perhaps even fewer know that one of America's hardest-hitting neo-conservative columnists, Charles Krauthammer, also hails from Canada.

In November 2008 Americans elected a president whom many Canadians greeted as the near-perfect political leader: Barack Obama. They celebrated his inauguration on January 20, 2009, with an outpouring of enthusiasm not even shown to a Canadian prime minister for decades. Busloads of admirers made the nine-hour trip from Toronto and Ottawa to witness his swearing in, and some Canadian schools interrupted their classes to enable pupils to watch the ceremony. For the eight years of the Bush presidency, Canadians felt a kind of moral superiority to Americans, but that almost completely changed with his successor.

By February 19, 2009, when he made his first foreign trip as president—to Ottawa—Obama enjoyed an approval rating in Canada of 82%, higher than in the U.S. (64%) and much higher than that of Prime Minister Stephen Harper (38%) and then opposition leader Michael Ignatieff (42%). He is more popular in Canada than Harper will ever be.

From the time he stepped off Air Force One in Ottawa, he commanded nonstop TV coverage during his six and a half hours in the country. Canadians clustered on overpasses and along the road to get a glimpse of him, and he greeted 2,500 of them who had gathered outside the Parliament in freezing weather. His welcome by Canada's first black governor general, Michaëlle Jean, was a historic moment for both nations.

Obama's charm never faltered, and he revealed a special attachment to Canada: that he has a brother-in-law who is Canadian and that two of his key staff people are from Canada. "And I love this country and think that we could not have a better friend and ally." It remains to be seen whether this affection will last and bear diplomatic fruit. An opinion survey at the time revealed that 41% of Canadian respondents desired greater ties with U.S., while 45% thought Canada should maintain the same level of relations. Only 9% wanted the country to distance itself from its southern neighbor.

Within months, many Canadians expressed disappointment that the new American president appeared to be unresponsive to Canada's needs, soft on protectionism and supportive of legislation pending in Congress that could prevent Canadians from selling the oil gained from their western sands in the U.S., the destination for half of it. The president eased some concerns when in August 2009 he approved a pipeline called the Alberta Clipper to carry 800,000 barrels of oil sands fuel a day to the U.S. But perhaps expectations had been too great. Magazine headlines began to read: "Canada's Biggest Problem: America" or "Barack Obama. Why He's Bad for Canada." *Maclean's* reminded its readers that, though unpopular, "Bush was in fact a strong and committed supporter of many causes dear to our national interest, including trade, open borders and energy."

Response to September 11 Terrorist Attacks

The terrorist attacks against the World Trade Center and the Pentagon gave Americans and Canadians a shared sense of vulnerability. Their feeling of security between two wide oceans disappeared. Foreign Minister John Manley, who became deputy prime minister and was named to lead a powerful new cabinet committee on national security, stated: "The towers in Toronto are just as vulnerable. Canadians want to be safe, too." Not only did Manley show his solidarity with New Yorkers by signing up to run the New York marathon. He led his colleagues in assuming an unapologetic pro-American stance.

President George W. Bush's gaffe in failing to include Canada among 13 other countries he thanked in his September speech to Congress did not alter this. An embarrassed president later explained that the U.S. considers Canada a brother and saw no need to thank family. His ambassador to Ottawa, Paul Celucci, told the 100,000 Canadians who had gathered on Parliament Hill to honor the victims: "You are truly our closest friends." In 2004 President Bush awarded this secretive elite commando unit a Presidential Unit Citation for "extraordinary heroism in action against the enemy" in rooting out Taliban fighters from caves in Afghanistan. It was the first time since the Korean War in the early 1950s that Canadian soldiers received this rare and prestigious recognition. The 2002 annual *Maclean's*/CBC poll revealed that only a tenth of Canadians accept Bush's description of the relationship as "like family." The most frequent description (47%) was "friends but not particularly close"; 23% agreed with the formulation, "the best of friends"; 18% chose "cordial but distant," and only 1% described it as "openly hostile."

Canada's foreign policy shifted in the wake of the attacks from a primary preoccupation on trade and economics to fighting international terrorism. Prime Minister Chrétien vowed a few days after the attacks that Canada would "go every step of the way" with its American neighbors. His people seemed to agree: 84% of Canadians supported joining the U.S.

Canada

fight against terrorism although only 23% wanted to see their troops directly involved in the fighting. A third favored closer ties with the U.S., compared with only 23% in March 2001. Manley captured the mood: "On the Hill when we had the memorial service, and people had their Canadian and American flags and tears running down their faces, you realized that when it comes to an event like that, forget the border. There is no border in the sharing of that experience."

Canada's assistance to its hard-pressed southern neighbor included a military contribution to the war effort in Afghanistan. It dispatched the largest fighting flotilla the country sent to sea since the Korean War to join American and British war vessels: three frigates (the HMCS Halifax, the HMCS Charlottetown and the HMCS Vancouver), a destroyer (HMCS Iroquois), one of its two supply ships (HMCS Preserver) plus Sea King helicopters. They were manned by more than 1,000 sailors. It dispatched 100 commandos from the secretive Joint Task Force 2. The air force sent three Hercules transport planes, one Airbus and two Aurora maritime patrol planes. Its airmen also served on NATO Airborne Warning and Control System (AWACS) crews that patrolled the American east coast. This was the first time since the Revolutionary War that the U.S. needed protection by foreign troops on its soil. A Canadian pilot could scarcely believe what he was doing: "I never, ever imagined that we'd be here. This place in the world that we're now trying to defend has always been the biggest boy in town. It has always been the U.S. protecting everyone else."

Few Canadians or Americans knew at the time that in the minutes before the first hijacked airplane slammed into the World Trade Center, it was senior Canadian officers on duty at NORAD headquarters that morning who gave permission to U.S. Air Force base commanders on the east coast to intercept the aircraft in terrorists' hands.

The neighbors introduced important steps to shift the overall protection of their territory to North American "perimeter security." The Canadian public supported these cooperative measures as long as they did not challenge their country's sovereignty or capacity to act independently.

Both populations support efforts to stop terrorism. When asked in a 2005 poll, 74% of Canadians and 86% of Americans favor closer collaboration to deal with this threat. They also favor a more integrated system of military and emergency responses in the event of a catastrophic attack or natural disaster, like hurricane Katrina in 2005. In 2005 the two governments organized a panel of 20 Americans and 20 Canadians to study the two partners' pre-

Canadian Soldiers in Afghanistan

paredness for such crises. They were shocked by what they found. The protocols (most in paper and in only one copy) were scattered and out of reach of commanders. All plans but those of NORAD are hopelessly out of date, focusing on the earlier Soviet threat, often referring to agencies that no longer exist, and never having been practiced by those who would have to execute them. They concluded that it was irresponsible wishful thinking to depend on the ad hoc goodwill of both neighbors to help each other in an emergency.

Canada is not interested in creating a jointly managed North American perimeter with a common approach to customs, trade, immigration, security and defense, and it worries about talk in the U.S. of registering all travelers entering and leaving the country, including Canadians. However, it agreed in 2002 to allow U.S. troops to cross its border in the event of terrorist attacks or natural disasters, and Canadian troops have the same right to cross into the U.S. When that happens, U.S. forces would serve under Canadian command while in Canada, and Canadian soldiers would be commanded by Americans while on U.S. soil.

In 2002 the United States created a new Northern Command to defend North America and coordinate military relations with Canada and Mexico. A joint task force called the "Planning Group," based at NORAD's Colorado Springs headquarters, was created with Canada to work on

contingency plans to defend North America. Canada is also discussing a new command structure to match this Northern Command. It calls for the integration of the army, navy and air force into six regional commands answering to a single Canada Command headed by an admiral. A new expeditionary force would be created to respond to calls to intervene in failed states, and counter-terrorist special forces would be strengthened.

The common border is not quite the way Canadian diplomat Hugh Keenleyside defined it in 1929: "It is physically invisible, geographically illogical, militarily indefensible, and emotionally inescapable." It is more guarded today. Nevertheless, this frontier still has only one Border Patrol agent for every 16 miles, compared with the border with Mexico, which has enough agents assigned for one every 1,100 feet.

There is more intelligence sharing. For the first time ever, the FBI provides the RCMP access to its digital fingerprint database; no other foreign police force is granted such information. American law enforcement officers can now gain access to criminal records in the Canadian Police Information Centre. The Canadians introduced more tamper-proof passports and check background references more carefully before issuing travel documents. The partners ended "asylum shopping." They created a common set of standards for asylum and a common list of countries whose citizens must obtain visas before

163

Canada

entering either country. Would-be refugees must apply for asylum in the first country they enter and cannot reapply in the other if they are rejected.

Ottawa moved swiftly to erase any impression south of the border that Canada was tolerant toward terrorism. Its intelligence agency identified more than 50 terrorist groups that operate and raise money in Canada. The government allotted $4.2 billion to fight terror and steered a vigorous anti-terrorist act through both houses of parliament that makes it illegal "to harbor a terrorist" or to collect money to carry out terrorism. Police were granted authority to use electronic surveillance against terrorists and to arrest and detain suspected terrorists without warrants. Former Justice Minister Anne McLellan answered the objections of civil liberties groups by arguing that "reasonable limits" on citizens' rights "are justified in a free and democratic society." In February 2007 Parliament voted 159 to 124 to allow two anti-terrorism measures to lapse since they had never been used. A week later the Supreme Court gave Parliament a year to fix a law allowing foreign terrorist suspects to be detained indefinitely without trial while awaiting deportation.

Canada acted energetically in detaining immigrants suspected of involvement in terrorism. In August 2003 it arrested 19 men who could have links with al Qaeda. Its spy agency, the Canadian Security Intelligence Service (CSIS), conducts only domestic security operations, relying on "liaison officers" to gather foreign intelligence from friendly governments. It does no spying overseas. It handed over to the U.S. an alleged al Qaeda operative accused in a plot to blow up the American and Israeli embassies in Singapore. These actions keep alive the debate about how the fight against terrorism can be made compatible with the Canadian ideals of tolerance, inclusion and the belief that immigrants should have the same rights as Canadian citizens. But Prime Minister Harper underscored Canada's vigilance on terrorism during President Obama's first visit in February 2009: "I just want to make this clear to our American friends. The view of this government is unequivocal: threats to the United States are threats to Canada."

That terrorism is no idle threat to Canada was dramatically demonstrated in June 2006. Working closely together, the RCMP and CSIS uncovered a deadly plot by 18 homegrown Muslim terrorists in the Toronto area to launch a wave of truck-bomb attacks against the Toronto Stock Exchange, the Toronto office of CSIS, an undisclosed military base, and Parliament in Ottawa. They intended to capture politicians and beheading the prime minister if

he refused to order the withdrawal of Canadian troops from Afghanistan. Those charged came from a variety of Muslim countries, especially South Asia. Most were born in Canada, and the oldest plotter was an imam (clergyman) who reportedly spewed hatred of Canada in his sermons.

The operation began with police monitoring of internet chat rooms. Soon 400 intelligence and law-enforcement officers were involved in Canada's largest counterterrorist operation since the often reviled Anti-Terrorism Act was adopted after the September 11, 2001, attacks. The powers the act granted to the police were crucial in foiling the plot. The RCMP paid two civilian informants $4.4 million to help execute the successful sting operation. One, who received $300,000, was a young, charismatic Muslim with a taste for cocaine. The other, a Muslim businessman, was paid $4.1 million and is in the witness protection program. The authorities moved in when the group acquired three tons of ammonium nitrate fertilizer, one-third of the amount used in the 1995 Oklahoma City bombing. A Toronto mosque was burned in a backlash. But the roughly 2% of Canada's population that is Muslim, half of whom were born in the country, could be relieved that such a tolerant country did not blame them for the ghastly project of a small minority.

In 2008 charges were dropped against seven of the defendants. The evidence seemed to show that the group was more like a youth gang that loved inflammatory chatter, but knew little about the means and methods of pulling off an effective attack. Some Canadians had begun to wonder if this entire incredible conspiracy had been fact or fiction. Subsequent testimony and convictions eliminated any doubts that it had been real and dangerous. In September 2008 a young man who had been only 17 years old at the time of his arrest was found guilty of knowingly participating in a plot to behead the prime minister. He was the first to be found guilty of terrorism since the anti-terrorist laws had been enacted in 2001.

In 2009 four more were tried for conspiring to ignite three explosions in southern Ontario. Three of them pleaded guilty, including the 24-year old ringleader of the group, Zakaria Amara. His testimony revealed shocking incompetence. He underestimated the Canadian police, grossly exaggerated his chances for success, and placed faith in the wrong people, including two RCMP informants supported by numerous wiretaps. At his sentencing hearing in January 2010, he apologized to Canadians and especially his fellow Muslims for his "naïve and gullible" interpretation of Islam. He faces a life sentence since Canada has no capital punishment.

DEFENSE

Both the United States and Canada were blessed with oceans that insulated them from European and Asian conflicts and with a border between themselves that has not had to be defended for more than a century and a half. Therefore, military concerns were never paramount in either country until well into the 20th century. But two world wars forced very different roles on them. With Europe in shambles and near poverty, and with the emergence of the Soviet Union as a dominant force in Europe and Asia, the United States was compelled to play a role as financial, military and political leader of the free world. This role brought increased military responsibility to the United States, and security concerns became very important in its body politic.

Canada's military role remained minor, compared to that of the United States. Therefore, security issues have been much less important in Canadian politics. This low salience was reflected in Canada's low defense budgets, amounting to little more than 1% of GDP, the lowest in the Atlantic Alliance except Iceland and Luxembourg. The Harper government promised and produced in 2006 a hefty increase in defense spending that included US$13 billion in equipment purchases. By the May 2011 election, he had raised defense spending by 27%, falling back to 1.5% annually after the election. His countrymen have supported this unprecedented increase, which was intended to "revive Canada's leadership in the world."

As in political and economic affairs, Canada is linked with and dependent upon the United States in defense. Its close cooperation was first formalized in the Ogdensburg Agreement of 1940, before the U.S. had entered World War II. The Canadian government realized that Britain might be conquered and would therefore be unable to defend Canada. The American government was concerned that the approaches to the North American continent might not be secure if Britain were indeed defeated. Therefore, Prime Minister King met with President Roosevelt to sign a permanent defense agreement. As with all good and lasting treaties, this one was firmly based upon mutual interest. A year later at Hyde Park, FDR's New York estate, they agreed to pool their military production. The two countries' wartime cooperation was excellent.

Both nations sacrificed thousands of lives in the bitter global struggle. But they were spared the destruction of their own homelands and emerged from the war intact and richer than before. They both were among the very few countries in the world that could positively contribute to the reconstruction of war-torn Europe. Both shared the view that the Soviet Union posed a threat to the democracies of Western Europe. Canada agreed that its own security was linked to that of Western Europe. Additionally, it wanted to forge military ties with Western Europe in order to counterbalance its necessarily tight defense links with the United States. Canadian leaders were the first to make public statements about the need for a postwar Atlantic Alliance, and Canada became a founding member of NATO.

It is characteristic of the Canadian understanding of the world that its diplomats insisted on the inclusion of article II of the treaty, which underscored their conviction that the Atlantic Alliance had to be more than a military alliance. This became known as "the Canadian article" and called for a pledge by members to strengthen free institutions and to encourage economic cooperation.

Canada never provided the personnel and equipment to which it had committed itself at NATO's birth. In 1969, the Trudeau government reduced its troop strength in Europe from 10,000 to 5,000, a decision that angered Western European allies, especially Germany. The fact is that Trudeau, who was despised by many soldiers, spent more on defense than any other prime minister since. His federal budget allotted 13.3% to the Department of National Defence (DND), compared with 8.7% under Harper until 2011. The Mulroney government raised the Canadian contingent in Europe to 7,800 troops.

The end of the Cold War prompted Canada to announce in 1992 the withdrawal of all its troops and airmen from Europe and the closure of its bases in Lahr and Baden-Soellingen. This was completed in 1994. Canada hosted German air force units that trained in Goose Bay, Newfoundland, and army artillery and armor units outside of Winnipeg. The Germans announced in 2004 that they were moving out of Goose Bay.

At home Canada maintains three land combat groups. It also maintains two squadrons of aircraft that could be flown quickly with aerial refueling to Europe for close support of NATO forces. Part of its naval forces is also occupied in protecting the North Atlantic approaches. Canada regards NATO as a key part of its defense policy and earmarks 10,000 combat troops for NATO service. Ottawa confirmed at NATO's Prague Summit in November 2002 that it would take part in the alliance's new 21,000-strong rapid-response force deployable to all parts of the globe to combat terrorism and contain outlaw regimes.

In 2006 a Canadian general, Ray Henault, occupied the key post of chairman of NATO's military committee; this was the highest NATO post ever held by

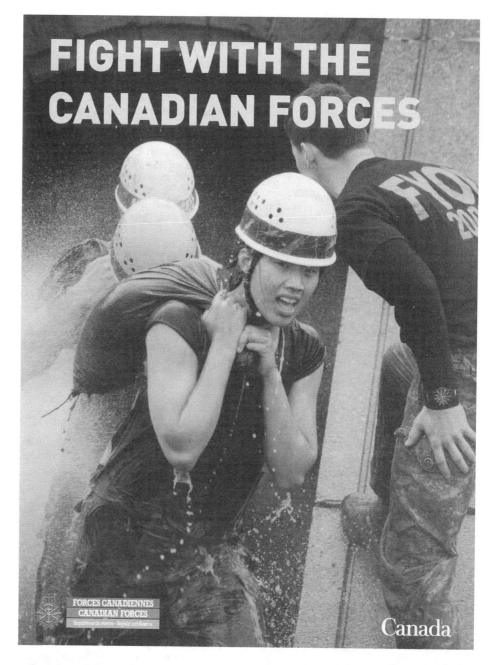

a Canadian. In April 2009 Defense Minister Peter MacKay was on the short list to become secretary-general of NATO. Although he lost out to Danish Prime Minister Anders Fogh Rasmussen, MacKay's near success demonstrated that a Canadian could one day occupy NATO's highest political office.

In all, its navy consists of 11,025 sailors plus 4,554 civilian Coast Guard. This includes about 2,800 women, who can serve on all ships but submarines. In December 2007 Commodore Jennifer Bennett, who heads an Ontario private school, was given command of the country's 24 naval reserve divisions, a position her father had held when she first joined the naval reserves 33 years earlier. She is the first

woman to lead a Canadian naval formation The navy sails four destroyers, 12 modern frigates, seven support ships, 14 patrol and coastal combatants, one diving support vessel and, until it was decommissioned in July 2000, a diesel-powered submarine. With 49 ships in 2010, the Canadian navy is proportionate to the British fleet of 84 and the U.S. navy of 313 ships. It has no anti-mine or year-round icebreaking capability and is widely considered to be incapable of adequately protecting the huge Canadian coastline.

The submarine was to be replaced by four Victoria-class conventional submarines from the UK. However, in October 2004, after three years of refitting and maddening cost overruns, one of the subs,

Canada

the HMCS Chicoutimi, caught on fire during her maiden voyage, and the first Canadian seaman in 49 years died of smoke inhalation. All four subs were promptly docked until the cause of the tragedy could be determined. The inquiry cast no blame, but part of the subsequent $10–$15 million in repairs was devoted to making the electrical cables much more waterproof. Critics were quick to react, claiming that Canada had bought the outdated subs mainly to engage in cat and mouse training exercises with American nuclear submarines in the North Atlantic. Why, they asked, was $750 million (mainly in trade for the use of Canadian airspace to train British pilots) squandered when Canada could not afford to field armed forces capable of defending the country?

Canada has no reliable naval helicopters or submarine surveillance planes. By 2004 a dozen of its Sea King helicopters had self-destructed, killing 10 crew members. One crashed in February 2003 while trying to take off from the deck of the HMCS Iroquois, a destroyer that was heading for the Persian Gulf. The navy could not find a replacement, so the ship had to leave without it. Finally in July 2004 the government selected an American-led consortium (with Canadian participation) to build 28 new Sikorsky H92 Superhawk maritime helicopters for a price tag of Can$3.2 billion (US$2.4 billion). They will be able to fly from the navy's frigates and can be used for anti-submarine, patrol, rescue and transport tasks. All forces will benefit from the purchase in 2009 of 15 Chinook heavy-lift helicopters built by Boeing. Delivery is scheduled to begin in 2013. Canada had already received six used Chinooks from the Americans for use in Afghanistan.

The land and air forces are slightly better off. In 2010, Canada had 65,722 men and women in all its armed forces (an increase of 3,722), of whom 34,775 are army. There are more Canadians trying to get into the all-volunteer military than there are open slots. The result is that the military personnel are carefully selected and well trained. The main problem is in retaining experienced soldiers, not attracting raw recruits. In 2002 the Canadian Forces raised the mandatory retirement age from 55 to 60 in order to head off a manpower shortfall. Among its 19,922 air force personnel (including 1,700 women and plus 2,344 Primary Reservists integrated within the air force structure) are some of the best pilots in the world.

They fly the aging CF-18 fighter. The number of planes is a problem. By 2010 it had 79 CF-18s, which must defend the airspace and coastlines of the world's second-largest country. They were used in 2011 to support NATO's no-fly zone over Libya along with the warship HMCS Charlottetown. But the Harper government decided to purchase 65 F-35 (Joint Strike) jet fighters from Lockheed Martin. There was criticism about the sophistication of the plane, the increasing cost ($16 billion) and the wisdom of purchasing a one-engine plane for use in the remote Arctic region.

To save money, the air force had to retire an entire fleet of electronic warfare aircraft. When it decided in 1999 to send peacekeeping forces to East Timor in Indonesia, it had difficulty transporting them there. It has so little transport capacity that it was compelled to use its only supply ship to service its entire Pacific fleet. The first of its aging transport planes was forced to turn back to base three times because of malfunctions with its compass and tail rudder. Another 34-year-old C-130 Hercules aircraft managed to make the trip, but only by flying below 10,000 feet because of a faulty cabin-pressurization system.

Canada is caught between the conflicting realities of declining defense budgets and increasing military conflict around the world. This was apparent in August 2000 when armed Canadian commandos in a dramatic high-seas seizure had to be dropped from a Sea King helicopter onto the deck of a private American freighter to take control of the ship that was transporting 590 military vehicles and 440 containers of small arms, ammunition, communications and surveillance equipment being shipped back on contract from Kosovo. The shipping company had refused to unload it in Canada until a private debt was settled. The capture was flawless, but the embarrassing thing was that the cargo amounted to about 10% of the Canadian army's entire supply of such equipment. A Canadian defense expert,

David Rudd, remarked: "There is a definite mismatch between Canada's desire to remain a player on the world stage and the ability of the armed forces to carry it out. They are over-stretched everywhere."

The air force is acquiring new search and rescue helicopters. To hone its search and rescue capabilities in the Arctic, Canada hosted joint exercises with American and Russian soldiers in 1995. It was the first time in 50 years that Russians trained on Canadian soil. NORAD had a joint exercise with Russia in 2010.

In 1993 it created a secret counter-terrorist force called Joint Task Force 2 (JTF2). Well-trained and well-equipped with the latest high-tech weaponry, this commando unit, numbering 1,500 in 2010, is considered to be on a par with the best of Britain's and America's special forces. It is especially trained for operations in extreme winter conditions, and in 2001 it was tapped for clandestine service in the Afghan war. It fights effectively alongside U.S. and other allied special operations forces. It was granted a prestigious unit citation by the U.S. president. The former commander of U.S. Central Command, Gen. Tommy Franks, praised the Canadian soldiers: "They've done an absolutely wonderful job." "We are in their debt. We recognize our friends."

Canada's land forces are good, but they number only 8,000 combat troops out of a total land force of 19,922 (including 1,600 women). They have 114 tanks. Because the White Paper designates peacekeeping as the Canadian Forces' main job in an unstable world, Canada acquired additional armored personnel carriers and other equipment needed for that commitment. It purchased 66 soft-armor Strykers, an 8-wheel troop carrier that is lighter and more mobile than tanks.

Public outrage over the murder of a Somali teenager and shockingly crude hazing rituals led to the disbanding in 1995 of the Canadian Airborne Regiment. It was replaced by three separate parachute companies, each serving as the nucleus for a new light infantry battalion. Canada is strained to maintain adequate units for peacekeeping. To reduce costs, headquarters staffs were slashed by 50% and the top officer corps by 25%. The civilian workforce was trimmed from 33,000 to 20,000. The three services consolidated their headquarters in Ottawa. In 1999 the defense department endorsed a plan to sell off as much as 10% of its property and buildings to raise funds for equipment.

There is an inadequate number of trained and organized manpower reserves. By 2010 there were 33,967 reservists. Of these about 22,000 are Primary Reserves, and 4,303 are native rangers who serve in the Arctic. They can never be forced to deploy for war or

Canada

peacekeeping; they must volunteer. About 13% of troops deployed abroad are reservists. The 2008 Canada First Defence Strategy calls for greater priority of domestic defense and an Arctic military presence.

Sovereignty over the Arctic is enforced by 60 soldiers stationed in Yellowknife, to be backed by a 100-soldier reserve unit in 2019. They are supported by four ageing Twin Otter bush aircraft. The main ground force is 1,600 Canadian Rangers, 80% of whom are Inuit. They are a reserve force based in 165 remote communities composed largely of Inuit and Indians (including women) who, transported by dog-sled and snowmobiles and armed with pre-First World War Lee Enfield rifles and a toll-free 800 number to report any trouble, perform surveillance duty in the Arctic. Their mission is to fly the Canadian flag and assert sovereignty over remote Arctic areas. They are the only arm of the military that uses its own transportation equipment, such as fishing boats and motorized canoes. They are organized in over 50 patrols in communities across the North, each limited to 30 members. They are widely admired, and there are waiting lists of Inuit hoping to join.

It is no surprise that Canada depends upon its alliance with the United States. It is engaged in many forms of military cooperation. There are 130 U.S. soldiers stationed in Canada. The two countries' security relationship is coordinated by the Permanent Joint Board on Defense. There is the Defense Production Sharing Agreement, which exempts Canada from duties and "Buy American" policies. By 2007 Canada had a $7 billion defense industry. Half of it came from sales to the U.S. military and 80% to all NATO allies. Much of the rest came from over 70 countries. In 2005 it was the world's ninth-largest seller of military weapons.

There is also cooperation in anti-submarine warfare (ASW). Since Canada is economically dependent upon trading, it is crucial that the seas surrounding it be safe in times of crisis. It does have several ASW destroyers and some long-distance coastal aircraft, but it needs American air cover and nuclear attack submarines to deal with an enemy submarine threat, especially in the Arctic Ocean.

Perhaps the closest form of military collaboration is in the North American Aerospace Command (NORAD), created in 1957 and renewed again for five years in 2006, with a new emphasis on global surveillance from space. It has a joint staff of American and Canadian officers. The only thing that distinguishes the Americans from the Canadians there is the patch on their sleeves. They formerly worked in a well-protected headquarters dug into Cheyenne Mountain in Colorado. But

NORAD announced in 2006 the transfer of its surveillance operations to an office building a dozen miles away at Peterson Air Force Base. The mountain facility, composed of 15 underground buildings centered on the war room, is kept on "warm standby," meaning that it could be reopened within hours in case of emergency.

NORAD was a response to the threat posed in the 1950s and 1960s that Soviet bombers could fly across Canadian territory and into the North American heartland. To meet this threat, two lines of radar installations were stretched across Canada. The outermost line was called the Distant Early Warning Line (DEW), consisting of 31 radar stations scanning the Arctic region. The second line, closer to the U.S. border, was the Pine Tree Line, consisting of 24 stations. Canada supplemented these radar lines with three all-weather fighter squadrons, which fly American F-18 aircraft, a training squadron, an electronic warfare squadron and space sensor units.

By the 1980s, these radar lines were obsolete. Low flying airplanes and cruise missiles could fly past them undetected. Also, the increasing importance of land- and submarine-based missiles (ICBM and SLBM), as opposed to manned bombers, made these radar defenses even less suited to present defense needs. The transition to missiles also made parts of NORAD's defense system, composed of interceptor aircraft and defensive missiles, obsolete. The collapse of the Soviet threat completed the process of obsolescence. The manned DEW stations were converted to unmanned ones.

Nuclear Weapons

The problems of creating a defense against potential air strikes from the Soviet Union were linked with a ticklish issue in Canada: the use of nuclear weapons. From the very beginning Canadians and their governments have been uneasy about any Canadian role involving atomic weapons. They assumed a commitment in the 1950s to arm their forces ear-marked for NORAD with such weapons for one major reason: in terms of destructive power, nuclear weapons are less expensive than conventional arms. Canadians hosted five kinds of U.S. nuclear weapons from 1950 to 1984: Mark IV air-dropped atomic bombs deployed for use by the Strategic Air Command bombers at Goose Bay; Bomarc surface-to-air missiles; Genie air-launched missiles on CF-101 VanDoo fighters; Falcon air-to-air missiles; and anti-submarine nuclear depth bombs at Argentia Bay, Newfoundland.

The Canadian government under John Diefenbaker stalled Canadian acceptance of nuclear weapons to be used with the military equipment it had purchased. He also hesitated to put NORAD forces (which still had no nuclear warheads) on alert during the 1962 Cuban Missile Crisis, thereby greatly aggravating his already strained relationship with President John F. Kennedy.

The leader of the opposition Liberal Party, Lester Pearson, put the issue squarely to the people by promising an end to Diefenbaker's wavering policy by "discharging the commitments [which Canada] has already accepted. . . It can only do this by accepting nuclear warheads for those defensive tactical weapons which cannot effectively be used without them but which we have agreed to use." By the skillful use of press releases that showed that the Canadian prime minister was not being entirely honest with his own people, Kennedy helped bring about Diefenbaker's defeat in

Cheyenne Mountain, Colorado. Canadian and American soldiers at NORAD.
NOTE: This operation was moved to nearby Peterson Air Force Base in 2006.

167

Canada

the April 1963 election. The vote was, in part, an expression of Canadians' desire to honor their defense commitments and military cooperation with the United States. At the same time, the entire debate was an early reminder of how unenthusiastic and ambiguous Canadians have been concerning their country's part in a defense based upon atomic arms.

In 1984, the Canadians deactivated their last nuclear warheads, replacing them with conventional ones. Canada still was linked with nuclear deterrence, however. Ottawa permitted experiments with a wide variety of nuclear-related weapons systems on Canadian territory, so long as they did not actually carry nuclear warheads. The most controversial result was that Americans were permitted to test unarmed cruise missiles over Canada. Such testing was actually proposed to Canada by Germany as a token gesture in support of the 1979 twin-track decision involving the deployment of medium-range nuclear missiles in Western Europe. Trudeau had committed himself in public to disarmament. However, he accepted NATO's request because he was aware that Canada relied upon nuclear deterrence for its defense and therefore had to accept some obligations because of that reliance.

These tests unleashed a loud debate and demonstrations throughout the country. A diverse "peace movement" began to gel. In 1994, the Canadian government grudgingly approved the continuation of U.S. cruise missile tests over Western Canada, but the U.S. announced that such tests are no longer needed. Canada still permits some forms of U.S. testing. In December 1999 it permitted the U.S. Air Force to test an unmanned aerial vehicle (UAV) called Global Hawk, which is used for intelligence purposes.

Remarks by former U.S. Secretary of Defense Caspar Weinberger on Canadian television during the Quebec summit meeting in 1985 to the effect that American nuclear weapons could possibly be sent to Canada during a crisis brought down a thunder of protest and prompted an official denial that there were any such plans. A similar outcry erupted over the question of whether Canada should participate in the Strategic Defense Initiative (SDI—dubbed "Star Wars"). Such participation promised hefty contracts to Canadian industries, but the fear that it could unleash a new round of arms competition made it a "hot potato." In 1985, Mulroney announced his government's decision not to participate in SDI, but to permit private Canadians to accept contracts for SDI-related research.

Former Defense Minister Art Eggleton sought in 2000 to lay the groundwork for some kind of limited Canadian participation. He argued that it fits within NORAD and that failure to take part would deprive Canada of important space research and harm Canada's defense relationship with the U.S. While Canada was prepared to assume a certain role as a partner in nuclear deterrence, its leaders stressed that Canada is a nuclear-free country. It is adamantly opposed by the NDP, whose support Martin's minority government needed on certain issues.

In 2004 the Martin government quietly agreed that the joint U.S.-Canada NORAD operations center in Colorado Springs could share incoming missile information with NORTHCOM, the American command that will control the 40 interceptor rockets planned for Alaska, California and at sea. Therefore, technically the Canadians are already in although the Americans do not ask them for land or money for the system. In February 2005 Ottawa announced that Canada would not take part in the planned North American ballistic-missile defense system. That is a decision that could be reversed in the future.

There are not many influential voices in Canada, outside the NDP, calling for with-

drawal from NATO or NORAD. These alliances are supported by a solid majority of Canadians. Besides, there has always been an uncomfortable awareness that if Canada did not contribute to its own defense, the United States might defend Canada in its own way in time of crisis. Some have called this possibility an "involuntary American guarantee."

It is doubtful that any enemy would ever consider Canada and the U.S. as totally separate entities, one neutral and one belligerent, in time of war. The two countries are linked so closely economically that no enemy could attack the United States without also affecting Canada's vital interests. Also, Canada's location is so strategically important to the U.S. that no country could attack Canada without the United States responding. Since this is the case, Canadian governments have always considered it better to cooperate in North American defense arrangements in order to be able to influence or shape that defense. Such a calculation has been gruesomely called, "no incineration without representation." One of Canada's most distinguished diplomats, J.H. Taylor, noted that though many Canadians find it hard to accept, they are "one of the most secure countries in the world . . . defended by the United States in the act of defending itself, whether we choose to defend ourselves or not."

Defense Spending

Responding to concern over sovereignty in the 1980s, the Mulroney government established a northern training center and five new fighter bases in the high Arctic. Canadians traditionally saw the primary threat to their *security* coming from the Soviet Union and its allies and the primary threat to their *sovereignty* coming from the United States. Both of these threats intersected in the Arctic. No longer is it true, as a Canadian officer said in the 1940s, "there's nowhere to go and nothing to do once you get there." It remains an unlikely theater for ground operations, but long-range aircraft and nuclear submarines posed major problems.

Located between both superpowers, the Arctic was the only ocean from which American nuclear subs could hit targets anywhere in the Soviet Union. The USSR was no less committed to the Arctic: half of its nuclear attack and missile-launching subs were deployed there. Soviet subs could trespass in Canadian waters to launch cruise missiles, to lay mines which could block sea access and exits from Canada, to ambush American submarines which might be moving through them (with or without Canada's consent), or to pass to the North Atlantic, over which Canadian reinforcements would travel in case of war in Europe.

The frightening thing for Canada is that it does not have a single ship capable of operating in the Arctic outside the summer months. It has neither all-season icebreakers nor minesweepers. It has no submarines capable of operating under the ice for more than a few days, even though a third of its territorial waters is covered by ice most of the year. Finally, it has no independent way of even knowing what is going on in the Arctic.

In 1989, the government announced budget cuts that canceled orders for more CF-18 aircraft, a new generation of frontline tanks to replace the aging Leopards, and the promised "Polar 8" icebreaker and fleet of nuclear-powered submarines capable of under-ice warfare. This stunning move led some critics to question the government's commitment to Arctic sovereignty. An exasperated Peter Newman wrote in *Maclean's*: "To have Arctic sovereignty protected by the only country [the U.S.] that challenges it means we have become squatters on our own land."

In 1991 Canada faced a dilemma about how to respond to Iraq's invasion of Kuwait. It was torn by conflicting traditions of participation in the Western alliance and of peacekeeping, and polls indicated that Canadians were unsure what to do. The Mulroney government decided that it had to support its allies militarily while assuring Canadians that its participation had not compromised its ability to be a peacekeeper. President George H.W. Bush declared: "The American people knew

from Day 1 where Canada stood. We are very, very grateful for that."

Canada sent its crack CF-18 Desert Cats fighter squadron to Bahrain; its 24 planes, refueled by a Canadian tanker based in Qatar, flew 2,700 combat missions. It also sent three ships to the Persian Gulf outfitted with weaponry cannibalized from half-completed replacement frigates. In all, 2,200 military personnel participated in the campaign, and for the first time in Canadian history, there was not a single casualty. Its Gulf operations captured the attention and admiration of a people normally indifferent to defense. As soon as the hostilities ended, the government dispatched hundreds of troops to the Iraq-Kuwait border as part of a UN peacekeeping mission.

In 1997, it won praise at home when it deployed 8,600 troops, three times the combined strength of Canada's UN peacekeepers in Bosnia, Haiti and the Golan Heights, to fight against the flooding Red River in Manitoba, which drove 25,000 Canadians from their homes. This was the country's largest single military endeavor since the Korean War. The military's image, tarnished by a series of embarrassments, was reversed by the sight of skilled helicopter pilots plucking desperate countrymen from their rooftops and of mud-caked troops standing in knee-deep water while tossing sandbags. In 1998, 11,000 troops were mobilized to help communities across eastern Ontario and southern Quebec, including Ottawa and Montreal, deal with a devastating ice storm and power blackout, called

Helping earthquake victims in Kashmir

Source: *Maclean's*

Canada

Prime Minister Harper visits troops in Afghanistan

the "Ice Siege of '98." Ex-Defense Minister Eggleton said: "This is by far the biggest deployment in our history to deal with a disaster in Canada."

In 1992 the armed forces lifted the ban against homosexuals in the armed forces, following a court ruling that exclusion violated the Charter of Rights and Freedoms. While there is still a diminishing stigma attached to being a homosexual in the forces, there was little resistance to the new rules. In fact, Pentagon officials had extensive consultations with their Canadian counterparts to discuss the relative success of this transition. Gay partners of Canadian soldiers get spousal benefits, and the first gay marriage at a Canadian Forces base took place in 2005. In 2008 a Canadian Forces recruiting booth was set up at Toronto's gay pride festival.

By 2004 Canada was spending only 1.1% of its GDP on defense, half the average figure for its NATO partners. Most shocking to many communities was the outright closure of 30 military bases in Canada. The government did not have to take the blame for the 1994 American closure of its naval base in Argenta, Newfoundland, where unemployment was already 20%. A crucial installation during the Second World War, when 20,000 Americans were stationed there, it, too, fell victim to defense cuts following the end of the Cold War. This closing brought to public attention conflicting visions of what the government owes civilian employees, who have claim to much higher severance pay than in the U.S. Since the employer of the 265 newly unemployed Newfoundlanders was the U.S. govern-

ment, they grudgingly had to accept a far smaller good-bye package than their Canadian counterparts elsewhere.

Canadians suddenly developed a renewed interest in military matters after the September 11, 2001, terrorist attacks in New York and Washington. In the 2002 and 2003 Maclean's/CBC polls, two out of three Canadians agreed that "we must substantially increase the amount of money we spend on the Armed Forces" although 57% believed that the main purpose of the military should continue to be peacekeeping. Eggleton argued: "The world is changing, and Canada must adapt its armed forces to the evolving military and security environment." However, a 2001 defense study by the Canadian Conference of Defence Associations concluded: "The Canadian Forces currently inhabit the worst of two worlds: conventional military capabilities are in decline; and new capabilities are unaffordable." Prime Minister Harper fulfilled his campaign pledge to raise military spending, with transport helicopters and planes as priority items.

Two military academies were closed: the Collège Militaire Royal (CMR) in St-Jean, Quebec, and the Royal Roads Military College in Victoria, BC, leaving only one military university, the bilingual Royal Military College (RMC) in Kingston, Ontario. The shutdown of the CMR was met by a thunder of protest in Quebec since it had been a major steppingstone for francophone Quebecers into the officer ranks. The government needed to reexamine not only its defense funds, but also its doctrine in a dramatically different world.

The Canadian Armed Forces underwent painful self-examination following a wave of bad publicity from peacekeeping missions in Somalia and Bosnia. In 1997 it was revealed that Canada's first female infantry officer, Captain Sandra Perron, had been the subject of discrimination, had perhaps been brutalized during training exercises, and had "never been totally accepted" despite her good performance record. In 1998, MacLean's published three lengthy reports about sexual assaults in the military that prompted many women to come forth with complaints.

The forces felt compelled to set up a sexual assault hotline and to join in encouraging female soldiers to tell their stories. They were swamped with charges of rape, including from 21-year veteran Deanna Brasseur, one of the first Canadian women to fly a CF-18 fighter. The Ministry of Defence released a damning report that described how women had faced assault, harassment and intimidation for the past decade. For the first time in its 40-year history, the renowned Snowbirds aerobatic squadron was assigned a woman commander, LTC Maryse Carmichael, in 2010.

Peacekeeping and Overseas Deployments

Canada used to be one of the world's most important sources of peacekeeping forces. In 1995 it opened the Lester B. Pearson Canadian International Peacekeeping Centre in Cornwallis, NS, to train soldiers in this kind of service. It was named after the former prime minister, who won a Nobel Peace Prize for his mediation efforts in the 1956 Suez Crisis. He proposed that forces from nations not involved in the conflict help separate the belligerents. Since that time Canada has supported every peacekeeping venture which the UN has sponsored. Canadians have served in Palestine, Korea, Cyprus, Egypt, India, Pakistan, New Guinea, the Congo, Yemen, Lebanon, Nigeria, West Irian, Cambodia, Iran, Iraq, Kuwait and East Timor.

In 2004 it had over 4,500 troops serving in a dozen trouble spots, including in Afghanistan and war-torn Bosnia, Kosovo, and the Ethiopian-Eritrean border. In 1997 Major General Lewis Mackenzie commanded all UN forces for four and one-half months in the former Yugoslavia. In 1993 Canada deployed 845 troops to Somalia to assist in a global rescue operation. In 1994 two Canadian generals commanded the UN peacekeeping contingent trying to create order in Rwanda's genocidal civil war. In 1996, Canada again took the lead in central Africa when the UN appointed the ex-Canadian ambassador to the U.S, Raymond Chrétien, as special envoy to deal with the war and refugee crisis. Ottawa sent 350 troops to prepare the mission. Its publicly visible peacekeeping operations were supported materially and diplomatically by the United States, a sign that they were in line with American interests as well.

Canadians solidly supported their country's involvement in the NATO bombing campaign against Yugoslavia in 1999 to try to bring a halt to ethnic cleansing of Albanians in Kosovo. It sent 18 CF-18 Hornets equipped with precision-guided munitions to fly missions. Canadian pilots flew about 10% of the initial NATO strike missions and commanded half the ones in which they participated. It left 800 troops in Kosovo to try to stabilize that traumatized land. It continued to deploy 1,200 troops in Bosnia, turning over its role there to European allies in 2005.

Canada dispatched 800 ground troops to Macedonia to help enforce an eventual peace settlement. This was in line with ex-Foreign Minister Lloyd Axworthy's policy, which he called the "human security agenda" to help suffering individuals. Ex-Prime Minister Chrétien asserted: "As Canadians, as world citizens, we could not sit and watch as people are displaced, their homes looted and burned, and lives taken away." Referring to peacekeeping, he added in 1999: "We are always there, like the Boy Scouts. Canadians love it."

Canada's peacekeeping experience in Somalia and the Balkans was sobering. The worst military scandal in Canada's post-1945 history occurred in Somalia, where a group of elite Canadian soldiers from the Airborne Regiment brutally tortured and killed a frail 16-year old Somali, who had entered their camp looking for food. At least 16 other soldiers heard his screams and pleas but did nothing. This seriously tarnished the country's positive self-image as a peacekeeper, as well as the public image of the Canadian Forces themselves. The Airborne Regiment involved in this crime, for which nine soldiers were court-martialed, was disbanded in 1995 when videos were released showing soldiers making racist remarks and engaging in grotesque hazing rituals.

The follow-up inquiry delved deeply into the subtleties of how leadership and organization may have created the atmosphere in which such beatings could occur. They also had to deal with a 1993 occurrence in Bosnia in which Canadian troops were caught engaging in drunkenness, sex, black marketeering, and patient abuse at a mental hospital they were guarding. Officers must now undergo special training in military law, human rights, ethics and public affairs before assuming command of their own units.

The challenges to peacekeepers have enormously increased. This is, in part, because of obsolete equipment. General

Mackenzie called his overworked, underarmed and outgunned troops "the poor cousins when it comes to the budget, and they deserve better when we send them abroad to do our dirty work." Also, the days are over when peacekeepers serve at the invitation of a host country to monitor an existing peace. They must deal with belligerents who still want to fight.

Alex Morrison of the Canadian Institute for Strategic Studies noted that today's peacekeeping "is not playing with toys in a sandbox. It's what our men and women in uniform would surely call war." There is an unofficial distinction today between "peacekeeping," which involves wearing a blue UN beret and keeping two groups separate that want peace, and "stabilizing operations," which involves troops who can coerce belligerents with overwhelming military power. In 2008 only 169 Canadian forces were committed to nine UN missions; the rest of the soldiers deployed overseas were in the more dangerous second category. Ex-Defence Minister (and former general) Gordon O'Connor observed in 2006: "It is a shock for many people in our country that we're involved in something that is not blue helmets and no rifles." Canada has become a warrior nation, not a peacekeeping one.

Peacekeeping and other more robust military deployments create problems that

Canada must confront. Repeated peacekeeping deployments pose severe hardships on soldiers and their families and produce burnout. This aggravates the problem of retention in the armed forces. At its peak in 1993 Canada deployed 4,641 peacekeepers worldwide. If one does not count its soldiers in Kosovo and Afghanistan, Canada had fallen by 2011 to 53rd place of 115 nations in terms of total number of troops, police and observers involved in UN peacekeeping operations. Most were in Haiti and Sudan, and 13% were women. The U.S. placed 71st.

In 2009 Canada was still the eighth largest contributor to the UN's total peacekeeping budget. Its foreign aid spending (.32% of GDP in 2011, compared with .19% for the U.S.) also ranks 16th in the world as a percentage of GDP (U.S. is 24th). This is among the lowest within the Organization for Economic Cooperation and Development (OECD) as a percentage of GDP. Its total aid of Can$3.7 billion is roughly equivalent to what the Bill & Melinda Gates Foundation gives away each year.

In 2004 it deployed 170 troops to Haiti to join with U.S., French and Chilean troops to restore order on that strife-ridden island. It left 66 police officers until July 2007 to train the Haitian National Police. It sent hundreds of soldiers and tons of supplies and an emergency hospital

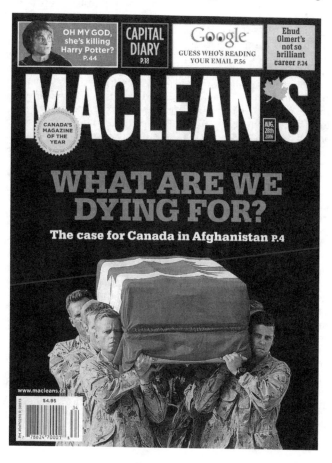

Canada

back to Haiti in January 2010 to help relieve the suffering after the catastrophic earthquake that devastated the capital of Port-au-Prince and killed tens of thousands of Haitians.

Canada maintains a temporary deployment of 2,830 soldiers in Afghanistan until the end of 2011, but it will leave up to 1,000 near Kabul to train Afghan security forces and police and to assist Canada's aid and reconstruction efforts. It permanently deploys 303 military personnel in the United States with Northcom and NORAD. It also maintains 287 troops in Germany and only 8 in Kosovo.

Iraq

Canadian diplomats had worked in vain to achieve a compromise in the UN Security Council that would have avoided war with Iraq. Two days before the bombing in Iraq began in March 2003, Prime Minister Chrétien announced that no Canadian troops would fight because the war was not backed by a UN mandate. Opposition leader Stephen Harper of the Canadian Alliance publicly apologized to Americans, writing: "For the first time in history, the Canadian government has not stood beside its key British and American allies in their time of need."

Nevertheless Canada left its more than 50 technicians and liaison officers at allied headquarters in Qatar, at sea with U.S. ships, and as exchange soldiers in U.S. units in Iraq. One was Major-General Walter Natyncyk, who had been seconded to the U.S. Third Armored Corps in Fort Hood, Texas, as deputy commander. When his unit shipped out to Iraq, Ottawa gave him the green light to go too. "The Canadian government sent me to Fort Hood, bottom line, to show in a tangible way the close affiliation between the U.S. and Canada." In fact, Canadian soldiers in Iraq under the cover of various "liaison" programs are more numerous than some of the contingents in the coalition of the willing. Thus, in a December 2007 *Maclean's* poll that determined that Americans know more about Canada than any other people, those half of Americans who thought Canadian soldiers were fighting on their side in Iraq were not entirely wrong.

Canadians still make up the largest contingent of foreign nationals serving in the American military, and probably hundreds of them are in Iraq. A Canadian commodore commanded a flotilla of a dozen American, British, French, Italian and other nations' ships, including two Halifax-class frigates and the HMCS Iroquois destroyer, in the Persian Gulf in case of "an emergency." Canada also trained Iraqi police and troops in Jordan. In 2009 it dispatched a warship, *Winnipeg*, to the Indian Ocean waters off the coast of So-

malia to be part of an international flotilla formed to combat down pirates.

Canada had delivered Can$215 (US$166) million in humanitarian and reconstruction aid to Iraq, and it distinguished itself as the fastest disburser of aid. This quiet effort was far more than that of most nations explicitly backing the war. This is why Canada was hurt by a U.S. decision to grant primary contracts in Iraq only to allies who were supporting the war effort, thereby excluding Canadian companies. This slight was rectified when President Bush assured ex-Prime Minister Martin that Canadian companies could bid on a new round of contracts. Ottawa announced that it would send troops back to Afghanistan, thereby freeing American soldiers for operations in the Persian Gulf.

Tempers gradually cooled. Chrétien called on his countrymen to respect the American decision. He tried to explain his stand in the least offensive way, saying that he did not support the war effort, but hoped for victory, that he did not support regime change in Iraq, but was glad Saddam was gone. His deputy, John Manley, made it clear that "at the end of the day, governments come and go, different people are in different offices, but at an institutional level we've got to make sure the continental relationship works." Quebec singer Celine Dion was flown to the USS Truman to sing "God Bless America" to the troops. In 2005 she donated US$1 million to aid Katrina hurricane victims, while her government offered whatever assistance the U.S. might need. American ambassador Paul Cellucci, who had earlier expressed his "disappointment" in Canada's lack of support, joined in the conciliation: "We are friends, we are allies, we are neighbors, and we are family. And nothing is ever going to change that."

Asked why Canada first sent troops to Afghanistan, General Rick Hillier explained: "As a way to relieve the pressure of saying no to the Americans on Iraq." The Afghanistan deployment was therefore of major political importance for the Canadians. It was their most conspicuous contribution to the "war on terror" and was therefore significant in Ottawa's attempt to rebuild its credibility in Washington after refusing to participate in the 2003 Iraq war. The Canadian Forces felt a strong need to do something significant for the United States.

Afghanistan

Its major overseas military commitment is to Afghanistan. Ottawa offered 1,000 troops to join the UN peacekeeping force there in 2002. In 2003 it sent a battle group of 1,900 soldiers back to Afghanistan for a further one-year tour of UN duty and assumed command of peacekeeping forces in

Kabul. By 2007 its 2,500 soldiers constituted the fourth-largest contingent within the overall peacekeeping force of 32,800 NATO-led troops in Afghanistan. Its contingent of 2,830 combat forces in 2011 is slated for withdrawal the end of the year. But up to 1,000 will be redeployed near Kabul to train Afghan security forces and police and to assist Canada's aid and reconstruction efforts. The Canadians were responsible for maintaining security in Kandahar, one of the most historically fractious and dangerous parts of the country.

In 2004 they were commanded by Canadian General Rick Hillier, who was appointed a year later as chief of the defense staff. He overhauled the structure of the Canadian military, restored its morale and prepared it for a new era of combat missions abroad before his retirement in July 2008. He appeared on TV regularly, gaining a level of fame theretofore unknown for a Canadian military officer. He regularly took ice hockey players to visit the troops in the field. He expressed his view of military power in a very un-Canadian way: "We are the Canadian Forces and our job is to be able to kill people." The outspoken General Hillier's experiences with the Taliban left him convinced that they are "detestable murderers and scumbags."

The Afghan engagement enabled Canada to play its part in the post-September 11 world without being at the beck and call of the American president. By taking part in and even commanding the NATO force, which is acting with a UN mandate in Afghanistan, it showed and improved its military competence in difficult anti-insurgency warfare. For Prime Minister Harper Afghanistan was the defining element in the new face for Canada in the world. He told troops at Kandahar Airfield: "Your work is also about demonstrating an international leadership role for our country."

But the government was careful not to imply that it is fighting in an "American war." It has interests that overlap with other Western nations and that are by nature global and threatened by a totalitarian ideology, represented by the Taliban. It was not easy for the Conservative government to make the point that its troops were serving under a UN and NATO mandate, not a U.S. one.

Its force is proving to be a workable alternative to the traditional blue-bereted UN peacekeeping missions. It is a display of what Ottawa calls "Three D" defense that also includes development and diplomacy. This engagement is Canada's dominant military commitment. Not since the Korean War has Canada been involved in such a large and dangerous wartime effort and suffered so many casualties—133 deaths (half by roadside bombs) and 800

Canada

wounded by the end of 2009. This is proportionally higher than those of other NATO countries, including the U.S. Only the U.S. and UK have suffered more casualties. But the effort has changed the public image of the Canadian Forces to an army engaged in full-scale combat and counterinsurgency warfare. It has given the military a chance to transform itself into an efficient fighting machine.

Tragically four Canadian soldiers were killed by friendly fire when an American F-16 pilot mistakenly dropped a bomb on them during a training exercise in Afghanistan. A high-level Canada-U.S. investigation concluded that the pilots had shown "reckless disregard" for the rules of engagement, but a subsequent American military hearing made a non-binding recommendation against court martial and criminal charges on the grounds that administrative punishment would better serve "the interests of good order and discipline." The U.S. army awarded each of the four soldiers a Bronze Star.

Regrettably this was not the last time. In 2006, Canadian troops called in air support during a fierce engagement with the Taliban. But the U.S. jets mistakenly strafed the Canadian soldiers, killing one and wounding 30. The dead soldier was Mark Graham, a former Olympic sprinter at the 1992 Barcelona Games.

The war placed unknown strains on many of the soldiers who fought in Afghanistan. While on patrol in Helmand province, infantry captain, Robert Semrau, spotted a suffering enemy who he judged to be "98% dead." To end his suffering, Semrau shot the man. But such mercy killing is a violation of the Geneva Conventions and the Canadian Forces Code of Conduct, which obligates soldiers to provide first aid to all casualties, friend or foe. He was the first Canadian soldier to be charged with battlefield murder. He was tried and convicted of disgraceful conduct, demoted and released from the army. But his case captured the sympathy of thousands of Canadians and of many rank-and-file soldiers.

It is one of the largest donors, providing CAN$650 million in aid through 2007 and pledging over $1 billion more. This makes Afghanistan by far the largest recipient of Canada's bilateral aid. This assistance is the largest Canadian aid commitment ever made to a single country.

The outgoing Liberal government decided in 2005 to deploy 2,500 troops to Afghanistan to strengthen the anti-insurgency effort in the province of Kandahar,

south of Kabul. They fought shoulder-to-shoulder with Americans, British, Dutch and other allies. In all, 37 allies contributed troops to the International Security Assistance Force (ISAF). In March 2006 it took command of the 6,000-strong multinational brigade that operated under aggressive NATO rules of engagement. This force included 100 elusive commandos from the elite Joint Task Force 2 unit. Canada paid for this deployment in lives because this was undeniably dangerous fighting. General Hillier called this "three-block war": humanitarian assistance, peace support operations and high-intensity conflict, all within a relatively small area.

By November 2010 Canada had suffered 152 battle fatalities. The highest ranking was Colonel Geoff Parker, who had been slated to become NATO's deputy commander in Kandahar. To put this in perspective, 211 Canadian police officers and firefighters were killed across Canada during the same period.

Polls from 2007 to 2010 revealed that half the Canadians thought the mission had failed and wanted it abandoned and their troops brought home. The end of 2010, 53% of respondents in one poll said "it's time to get out." Only 31.6% thought Canada should stay. Many are appalled by the casualties and the brutality: one captain was badly wounded in the head by a young man wielding an ax while attending a meeting of village elders.

One of the first political crises Prime Minister Harper faced in office was its return to the tradition of banning news media coverage of returning coffins from war and the flying of flags at half-staff to mark the death of troops. He argued that the families should be able to grieve out of the limelight, but critics accused him of not honoring the dead. He was forced to back down. Harper telephones the family of every soldier killed in action, so he is constantly reminded of the horror of that war.

The ensuing vigorous and emotional debate merely underscores Canadians' uneasiness over this enhanced role in Afghanistan and the government's nervousness about uncertain public support for the war. Some see an Iraq-like quagmire, the wrong cause in the wrong place. Canadians are debating what the appropriate global role is for their country and military.

Toward the end of 2009 the Harper government was embarrassed by allegations made by a former diplomat in Afghanistan, Richard Colvin, that in 2006 and early 2007 Canadian soldiers handed detainees over to Afghan authorities knowing that the lat-

ter use torture and that they did not follow up on the detainees' welfare. Colvin called this practice "un-Canadian, counterproductive and probably illegal." The Harper government allegedly ignored reports of this. When a parliamentary committee of inquiry demanded to see documents relevant to the case, Harper prorogued (closed) parliament for two months, while Canadians were distracted by the Winter Olympics. It seemed to many that the government had something important to hide. This scandal overshadowed the entire debate of Canada's military role in the country. It eroded further Canadians' fading support for the war effort.

Harper staunchly supported the war effort to which the previous Liberal government had committed the country. His first foreign trip after becoming prime minister was to visit Canadian troops in Afghanistan for two days. In April 2007 he defeated an opposition proposal in Commons to withdraw all Canadian troops. However, he could not extend the mission beyond 2011 without parliamentary approval, and all three opposition parties opposed that. There was a strong fear of an open-ended commitment. He did not need parliamentary approval to leave up to a thousand troops in Afghanistan to train Afghan security forces and to support humanitarian efforts.

Realizing that this war could go on for years, Harper ordered a substantial increase in military spending, to include the purchase of transport helicopters, three new support ships, transport aircraft and 2,300 supply trucks. His government, which had budgeted $20.6 billion for defense in 2010, wants to increase the full-time military force from 65,722 to 75,000 and add 10,000 more reservists (who constitute 13% of the fighting forces in Afghanistan).

The fact that three generals with experience in irregular warfare in the Middle East and Afghanistan—Chief of Defence Staff General Rick Hillier (who stepped down in July 2008 after more than three years at the top of the Canadian Forces), his chief of strategic planning, General Andrew Leslie (since 2007 Chief of the Land Staff), and General Walter Natynczyk (who replaced Hillier as Chief of the Defence Staff)—had risen to top positions within the Canadian forces brought fresh thinking about modern war-fighting and about the need to reform Canada's military to be fit for more robust requirements. They restored the forces' morale and prepared them for a dangerous new era of combat missions abroad.

Canada

ECONOMY

By world standards, Canada is a rich country. Measured in terms of gross national product (GDP—the total value of the goods and services a country produces annually), it ranks eleventh in the world, despite the fact that it has only 33.2 million inhabitants. As the visitor can easily see, the average Canadian has a standard of living as high as the average American. Enjoying the sixth highest per capita GDP in the OECD (often called a "rich man's club" of nations), Canadians live better than the Japanese, Germans and French. There is less visible poverty than in the United States. Canadians are well clothed, housed, fed, educated and cared for.

The UN Human Development Report consistently ranks Canada as among the world's best places to live based on standard of living, life expectancy, and educational attainment, usually slightly above the U.S. In 2010 it placed eighth. It also ranked first in equality for women in 2000. Because of its bountiful natural resources, many people have said that Canada was economically "a solution searching for a problem." However, there are occasional reminders that the large, complex Canadian economy has weaknesses as well as strengths.

Canada has a capitalist, free-market economy, although the state's hand in the economy is considerably greater than in the United States. Its natural beauty attracts millions of tourists each year, mainly from the United States although that has slowed since the September 11 attacks; a million Canadians (one out of ten jobs) earn their living from the tourist industry. It is a country richly endowed with natural resources of all kinds. Although only 5% of its total territory is arable, it possesses enough arable land to be one of the world's largest producers of food. For a long time, natural resources and agriculture were the pillars of Canada's economy. In the 18th and 19th centuries, it borrowed and attracted large amounts of capital from abroad, and it imported manufactured goods. It paid for imported goods with raw materials and grain.

In the 20th century, and especially after 1945, the Canadian economy changed considerably. Its services and manufacturing sectors now overshadow the resource and agricultural (primary) sector in terms of contribution to GDP and employment. Services provide 76% of employment and 69% of GDP while industry is responsible for 21% of the jobs and 32% of GDP, of which 21% is from manufacturing and mining. Only 3% of employment and GDP are derived from agriculture. This sparsely-populated country has a small domestic market of 33.2 million people. Canada must trade in order to maintain its prosperity; foreign trade with the U.S. alone generates 52% of its GDP, as opposed to less than 20% of the United States'. One out of three Canadian jobs is linked to trade. This dependence upon the international market makes Canada particularly vulnerable to world-wide economic trends and protectionism.

The problem of dependence is compounded by the fact that its international trade is practically dominated by one country: the United States. Every year Canada sells 77.7% of its exports to the U.S., and 52.4% of its imports must be bought from its only neighbor. Until 2008, it relied on its trade surplus with the United States to pay for its trade deficit with the rest of the world. The economic turndown in the U.S. from 2008 temporarily ended its surplus with its southern neighbor, but it was restored by 2010. In 2007 China overtook Canada to become the largest source of American imports, and it is now the U.S.'s second-largest overall trading partner after Canada.

Foreigners, especially Americans, own a large portion of its economy. The U.S. accounts for 64% of total foreign direct investment (FDI) in Canada and the European Union for only 29%. In 2000 Americans accounted for 75% of Canada's foreign ownership. Canadian FDI in the U.S. more than trebled between 1989 and 2002, growing to US$92 billion in 2002 and several times that by 2005. Half of its outbound foreign direct investment (FDI) goes to the U.S.

Because the Canadian and American economies are so tightly linked, when the U.S. sneezes, Canada catches pneumonia. *Maclean's* went even farther in 2008: "If the U.S. catches a cold, well, call up the undertaker." U.S. economic growth is too important and its ties to other economies too complex for the effects of an American downturn not to be felt beyond its borders. When the American economy slips into recession, the Canadian economy normally follows the same downward path, but it usually takes a little longer to recover. The good news is that when the U.S. economy booms, it can pull Canada along in its slipstream.

Lacking the size and diversity of the U.S. economy, Canada is normally not as resilient as the United States when faced with economic adversity. However, in the 21st century the high world demand for natural resources, especially oil, gas and mining, gave the Canadian economy much needed stability and predictability. In the 1970s and 1980s, the dependence upon the U.S. stimulated economic nationalism again, which has always been close to the surface of most Canadians. Yet, as reasonable as the calls for "Canada for the Canadians" are, they brought serious problems to the Canadian economy.

Geography has so closely linked the two countries' economies that cooperation, not conflict, is in their mutual interest. Also, Canada is too open a country, with too vulnerable an economy, to pursue a consistent policy of economic nationalism. The U.S. and Canada are each other's most important trading partners and form the world's largest bilateral trade relationship. Since the Free Trade Agreement (FTA) went into effect in 1989, the value of two-way trade had trebled by 2011, surpassing US$645 billion, making this the world's largest bilateral trading relationship. If services are added, the total is about $800 billion. Including the value of services, total trade equaled $1.6 billion each day in 2007. In the process, the FTA has reoriented Canada's economic axis from east-west to north-south and has reduced the number and importance of trade disputes to a trickle. However, since 2000 trade with non-U.S. partners grew faster than trade with the U.S.

Trade with Canada is of increasing importance for the United States; a fifth of America's exports and imports flow to and from Canada. One-third of all trans-border trade takes place within companies having a presence on both sides of the border. Cross-border trade supports 221,500 jobs in Michigan alone. The Canadian foreign ministry estimates that more than 7 million American jobs depend on Canada-U.S. free trade. America's trade with Canada is, in dollar value, about three times its trade with Japan. Canada's second largest partner is China, which provides 9.8% of Canadian imports. Canada runs a large trade deficit with it, and until the financial crisis of 2008 that was more than compensated by Canada's trade surplus with the rest of the world. By 2004, 400 companies had established a permanent presence in China, and in 2005 its trade with China soared by 40%.

The U.S. sells more to the single province of Ontario than to either Japan or *all* of Western Europe. Canada sells more to a single American company, Home Depot, than it does to all of France. Canada is the largest trading partner for 36 of the 50 American states, and Pennsylvania exports more to Canada than to its next seven markets combined.

Motor vehicles and parts represent 14% of Canada's manufacturing output and employ more than 150,000 Canadians. They account for about 25% of U.S. merchandise exports to Canada and about a quarter of imports. They constitute 23% of Canadian exports to the U.S., and 90% of the vehicles and automotive parts manufactured in Canada are shipped south. Thus, when the situation of the American automotive industry turns bad, as in 2008–9, this is shared by Canada, and production in Canada plummets. Windsor's jobless rate shot up to 14.4% during the recession, and two-thirds of the jobs lost were in Ontario, most of them in manu-

facturing. The second largest category of U.S. exports is electronics and telecommunications equipment.

Canada is the United States' largest supplier of imported energy—oil, uranium, natural gas and electricity. It sends 99% of its oil exports to the U.S. It supplies 21% of U.S. imports of crude and refined oil products (amounting to more than 10% of America's overall oil needs) and 94% of its natural gas imports, all through pipelines. Canada is the only country in the Group of Seven, except the UK, that is a net oil exporter. Both countries also suffer similar problems: high labor costs (although the unit cost of production is lower in Canada) and a decline of traditional industries.

The Primary Sector

After this brief overview of the Canadian economy, let us look more closely at its individual components and at the economic policies that the Canadian federal governments have pursued. Any treatment of the Canadian economy must always begin with the primary sector. Throughout the country's history, raw materials and agriculture provided the foundation for Canada's development. Today this sector accounts for only 5% of the workforce and less than 8% of its GDP, and the agricultural portion now amounts to 3% of the value of Canada's total output. In terms of employment, 3% of Canadians now make a living from farming, and the corresponding figure for mining, lumbering, fishing and other forms of primary extraction is only about 2%.

Yet these figures understate the importance of the primary sector for the overall economy. This element is the basis for much of Canada's manufacturing, such as wood and paper products, food and beverages and petroleum products. Even

more significant is its contribution to Canada's export trade: about 60% of the country's exports leave in raw or semiprocessed form, a high percentage for any developed country. Canada can be thankful for its natural wealth. A problem with heavy reliance on the export of raw materials, however, is that their prices fluctuate widely on world markets. Therefore, a country becomes excessively vulnerable to the ups and downs of outside market forces. Unfortunately, this has often been the case with Canada. Things go well whenever the voracious demand in the U.S. and developing countries, especially China, for raw materials keeps the prices for Canada's metals, minerals, lumber and oil up. Canada's economy thrives when the prices of natural resources, especially energy, are high, which has been the case most of the time in the 21st century; it is hurt when prices go down, as in 2008–9.

Fishing

Most of Canada's earliest European visitors had come to fish in the waters off its 241,402-kilometer (149,670 miles) coastline, and the success of early settlements in Canada depended greatly on the ability to maintain a subsistence fishery. Canada was once the world's leading exporter of fish and fish products. Canada's formerly rich fishing grounds, extending 200 miles off its coasts, contained 150 fish and shellfish species. It was able to maintain more than 900 fish processing plants, which employed over 100,000 persons. Most of these plants were located in the Atlantic provinces. In Newfoundland alone, about 15% of the inhabitants found employment in fishing or fish processing.

In 1989 Newfoundland's dependence on a fishing industry was devastated by over fishing and dwindling stocks. A 2005

Earlier days in Battle Harbour, Labrador.

Courtesy: Mike Earle

Canada

study concluded that stocks of adult cod off the North American coast had diminished by 96% since the fishing industry took off in the 1850s. In 1992 Ottawa slapped a moratorium on all northern cod fishing to allow stocks to replenish themselves. That provoked a clash with France. The French claimed the right to fish in the Gulf of St. Lawrence because of their tiny island outposts, St. Pierre (pop. 6,500) and Miquelon (pop. 600), located just 16 miles off the Newfoundland coast. Fishermen in both Newfoundland and the two French islands feared that French trawlers would further deplete codfish stocks in the Gulf. The feud was settled by treaty in 1995, a year in which Canada used its navy to see that earlier agreements would be respected. A further dispute between the two countries broke out in 2005 over rights to thousands of square miles of Atlantic seabed south of the islands.

The EU agreed temporarily to restrict fishing in the waters inside and outside the 200-mile zone in order to allow stocks to replenish themselves. When pirate fishermen from Europe, especially Spain, continued to overfish the dwindling stocks, the Canadians decided in 1995 to act. It sent a frigate, fired a shot over the bow of a Spanish trawler outside the 200-mile fishing zone, boarded the vessel and ordered it to St. John's. There it found illegal nets on board and doctored records proving that the fishermen had indeed violated international agreements. After much acrimony, a settlement was reached calling for closer monitoring and enforcement of fish catches. The UN International Court of Justice decided in 1998 that it lacked jurisdiction to settle the dispute. Canadians applauded the use of military force to support their national interests. In 2003 the federal government closed down most of the remaining Atlantic cod fishing industry.

Canada also was involved in a festering dispute with the U.S. over the fishing of fragile West Coast salmon stocks, which swim through Alaskan waters into Canadian waters to breed. Both sides accepted mediation, but those talks ended in stalemate in 1997. In June 1999 a landmark agreement was reached establishing a system of flexible catch quotas and a $140 million fund to protect spawning grounds. However, aquaculture threatens to make diplomacy irrelevant, despite the emotional tie that British Columbia has with wild salmon. More fish are produced on fish farms within the province than are caught in its waters. The number of wild salmon continues to decline, many from diseases contracted from salmon farms.

No beings overfish more than do seals. Bowing to foreign and domestic political pressure, Canada banned the unrestricted killing of seals thereby enabling the seal population to triple since the 1970s to about six million on the east coast. Each animal consumes an average of 45 pounds of fish a day. This, as well as overfishing, combined almost to destroy the fish stocks, especially cod.

To reduce the seal population to a manageable level, the federal government began in 1994 to support the price of seal meat, which is used for animal feed. Seal over-reproduction and the need for employment in outlying areas are the reasons why people from Quebec and Newfoundland living close to thawing ice floes in the Gulf of St. Laurence are permitted each spring to engage in the world's largest seal slaughter for a few weeks. For those living in rural regions where work is sporadic at best following the disappearance of cod stocks, the hunt supplements their meager winter incomes. One sealer who pocketed $5,000 in one week noted: "When you make $25,000 a year, that's a big boost."

About 6,000 people benefit from seal hunting, and by 1997 they had quadrupled the size of their annual catch, despite the protests of animal rights activists. The largest seal hunt in a half century took place in 2004, with more than 200,000 taken in the first 36 hours. The rest of the 350,000 maximum was hauled in by smaller operations. The quota for 2006 was 335,000 harp seals (not the whitecoat seals), a tiny percentage of the overall population. The 2008 quota was 275,000 harp seals and 8,200 hooded seals. The killing of baby seals remains outlawed, but critics claim that it still happens and that most of the seals killed are only one or two months old.

The business is fraught with dangers. In April 2007, nearly 100 fishing boats got trapped in thick ice caused by a sustained dry Arctic wind. The crushing ice destroyed or damaged some of the boats, and only the country's largest icebreakers could free the boats and rescue the 450 stranded hunters. Due to global warming there are fewer suitable seals to hunt; premature thawing of the ice causes seal pups to fall through the ice and drown.

The sealers are harassed each step of the way by animal rights activists, such as Beatle Paul McCartney, Pamela Anderson and Brigitte Bardot. They find such an animal cull cruel. Tempers flare as both sides do what they think has to be done. Opinion polls in 2009 revealed that most Canadians agree with them: 51% found seal hunting "cruel and inhumane and should be banned"; another 17% regarded it as "ugly and brutal, but that's no reason to ban it." Only 25% had no objections and 7% "don't care."

A major blow to commercial harvesting was delivered in May 2009 by the European Parliament, which banned the importing or sale of furs and other seal products. Cana-

dian officials immediately protested. They noted that European fur farms growing minks and foxes kill more animals every four or five days than the entire annual hunt does in a year. But a European animal rights spokesman called the ban the "final nail in the coffin." Products from subsistence hunts by Inuit and other indigenous peoples were exempted. To poke a thumb in the EU's eyes, the prime minister and his entire cabinet flew to Nunavut and nibbled appetisers of raw seal. Governor General Jean helped Inuit cut out the heart of a seal and then ate part of it raw. The parliamentary canteen in Ottawa even served seal meat for the first time ever.

Fur and Timber

Lucrative fishing possibilities had lured Europeans to Canada, who then established contact with Indians. These native Canadians had very valuable goods to trade—furs. With its cold climate and rugged timbered terrain, Canada provides a natural habitat for a wide variety of fur-bearing animals, including beaver, wild mink, Arctic fox, muskrat, otter, coyote, timber wolf, red fox, marten and Canada lynx. As we saw earlier, the fur trade dominated the Canadian economy from the early 1600s to the late 1700s, and it powerfully shaped the Canadian destiny. Unlike the fishing industry, which was restricted chiefly to the fringes of Canada, the fur trade directed European attention toward the north and the interior of the huge North American continent. It broadened the horizon of the early Canadians and provided the initial impetus to expand Canada "from sea to sea."

It was also an enterprise best conducted by huge trade monopolies, such as the Hudson's Bay and Northwest Companies. It therefore left in Canadians' mouths a good taste of large, state-sanctioned economic monopolies, which still differs somewhat from the American preference for purely private competitive firms. A negative consequence of the fur trade, though, was that for many decades it retarded both permanent settlement in the West and the development of Canadian manufacturing. Profits from fur could simply buy whatever foreign manufactures were needed. Although its significance for Canada's overall economy is minimal today, the sale abroad of raw Canadian furs continues. Despite protests by animal rights activists, the British army admitted in 2003 that it had failed after twenty years of searching to find an artificial substitute for the traditional bearskin head-dresses worn most famously by guards at Buckingham Palace. Only the pelt of the Canadian black bear can survive the 24-hour year-round onslaught of British weather.

An unintended consequence of the severe restrictions on the fur trade is that the traditional livelihood of many Aboriginals disappeared. They have had to replace their lost income by permitting oil, gas and mining into their previously unspoiled areas. This has contributed to environmental problems. Trappers once killed wolves to protect other animals in their traps. But the wolf population has soared, to the detriment of the caribou and buffalo herds. A national symbol, the beaver, has also multiplied dramatically to an estimated 20 million animals in Canada alone. In their avid pursuit of building dams, they have destroyed many trees and caused unwanted flooding of farmland.

Unlike the fur trade, the timber trade was favorable to settlement in Canada. Ships carrying timber to Europe had excess space for the return passage. Settlers could occupy such space very economically. Indeed, except during the American Revolutionary War, timber provided the first significant boost to the populating of Canada. Timber was also conducive to agriculture since logging operations left land cleared for agricultural use. As important in the long run was the fact that, unlike the fur business, timberwork stimulated manufacturing. Lumber had to be processed in sawmills, transported in vehicles larger than canoes and ultimately transformed into such goods as ocean-going vessels and furniture.

The timber trade also created a market for many kinds of metal tools. A fourth of Canada's territory is covered by forest. With 10% of the globe's total forest area, it is the world's premier exporter of timber and forest products and its third largest producer, with about 14% of the total world production. In a good year, almost 250 million trees are felled in Canada.

Four million trees are required to produce the newsprint for *The New York Times* in one year alone. Canada is the world's largest exporter of newsprint. A third of the world's newsprint comes from its forests. Unfortunately for the industry, declining newspaper sales world-wide, smaller newspaper formats, the transfer of many classified ads to the internet, and such modern practices as the "paperless office" have cut seriously into demand. So have the environmentalist policies of such publications as *Victoria's Secret*, which announced in 2006 that it would not print catalogues on paper manufactured from endangered Canadian boreal forests. Sales fell 8.5% in 2005 alone, and 31 pulp and paper mills in Canada (13 of them in Ontario) closed either entirely or partially.

The problem is that trees are being cut faster than they can be replenished. Also, mismanagement is so bad that millions of trees that are cut are never transported out

Largest grain elevator in North America, Thunder Bay, Ontario

of the forests and are left to rot. To make matters worse, Canadian forests have been ravaged in recent years by acid rain, by fires which have destroyed about six times more forest area than loggers harvested, and by such pests as the spruce budworm, which defoliated about 185 million acres in the eastern half of Canada, and the mountain pine beetle, which kills more trees in BC than wildfires or logging. The latter, which can kill a mature tree in one year, is threatening to cross the Rocky Mountains and sweep across the entire northern continent.

The gradual destruction of Canada's most lucrative natural resource is particularly dangerous because it is Canada's largest employer. It employs about 300,000 persons as loggers and as workers in sawmills and pulp and paper operations, primarily in outlying communities whose economic stability depends upon it. Another 700,000 jobs exist because of it. In British Columbia, which accounts for 60% of Canada's lumber production, one in four persons is at least indirectly dependent upon the forest industry. Thus, when this industry experiences hard times, as a result of a decline in the American construction industry, for example, the entire Canadian economy suffers. Canadians control about 75% of the country's total timber production.

For many years passions on both sides of the border were inflamed by a seemingly interminable dispute over softwood lumber. Canada consistently supplies about a third of the U.S. market. American companies claimed that Canadian producers receive illegal subsidies and should therefore be forced to pay countervailing duties (which amounted to 32% in 2001 and 10% in 2006). Canada retorts that it merely has a different system for granting rights to cut and that American producers are engaging in selfish protectionism. In a nutshell, 95% of the timber in the U.S. is privately owned and is sold by auction at market prices. In Canada, the prov-

inces own about 94% of the timber, and they set the harvest levels and stumpage fees. American producers contend that the fees are below market prices and therefore constitute a subsidy, which is forbidden. Canadians rejected this argument.

In 1996 the two countries signed an agreement granting selected provinces fee-free access to the U.S. market for a certain volume of wood but requiring Canada to collect fees on anything above that level. When the agreement expired in 2001, the two countries again found themselves at loggerheads, so to speak. While waiting for the World Trade Organization (WTO) to rule on the dispute, mills in British Columbia (which accounts for half of lumber exports) and Quebec had to close, and thousands lost their jobs.

In 2002 the U.S. imposed countervailing duties averaging 27% on Canadian lumber exports. Although these duties hurt, the Canadian lumber industry concentrated its production in its most efficient mills thereby lowering average costs and strengthening the industry economically. This unexpected Canadian response hurt both American producers, who faced stiffer competition, and consumers, who must pay higher prices for protected lumber.

In May 2003 the WTO determined that Canada's stumpage is not an unfair subsidy, and a NAFTA panel ruled in September that the U.S. had not proven that Canadian softwood exports threatened to injure American lumber firms. In December the two countries reached a tentative agreement lasting three years that would limit Canadian producers to 31.5% of the U.S. market. In another ruling in April 2004, the WTO rejected all of Canada's complaints against American anti-dumping duties on softwood lumber. Nevertheless, the deadlock continued, even after a NAFTA panel ruled yet again in September 2004 that Canada's softwood lumber exports are not subsidized, and the United States agreed to accept this ruling. A half year later the WTO established a dispute

Canada

panel to investigate whether the U.S. has complied with its rulings against tariffs on Canadian softwood lumber. Although Canada's annual softwood sales of $7 billion to the U.S. accounted for only about 3% of the trade relationship, the dispute took on oversized political symbolism.

Finally the 20-year dispute seemed to be resolved in April 2006, the first foreign policy success of Prime Minister Harper's government. The U.S. lifted a 10% duty on softwood lumber and agreed to refund $4 billion of the $5 billion collected since 2002, paying about a half billion of the remainder to American softwood lumber producers. However, Canada agreed that if the price of lumber fell below a threshold calculated by a complex formula, or if a surge in exports occurred, it would levy an export tax (to be retained by the Canadian provinces) or quotas on Canadian shipments, or a combination of the two. Although this settlement departed significantly from the principle of free trade, Canadians greeted it.

In April 2009 the new Obama administration reintroduced a 10% duty on some lumber imports, claiming that the Canadians had not made amends for violating the trade deal. In January 2011 American trade officials asked a London arbitration court to penalize exports from British Columbia arguing that the underpricing of timber from public lands was a subsidy. But BC shrugged this off because the U.S. is not its only market now. Its exports to China have increased tenfold since 2003. By 2011 its total sales to China and Japan exceed those to the U.S., which once bought two-thirds of BC's lumber. By 2011 that had fallen to only a third, thanks in part to its housing crisis.

Agriculture

Agriculture provided the livelihood for a large portion of settlers to Canada. When, toward the end of the 19th century, strains of wheat were developed which could thrive in the northern climes of the Prairie regions, settlement in the Western part of Canada was greatly stimulated. This produced a strong demand for metal implements and manufactured supplies and a powerful additional incentive to complete the East–West railway. Newcomers could easily enter farming; a federal governmental homestead policy provided any farmer with 160 acres of land, provided that he lived on it and worked it for five years.

Such family-owned and operated farms remain the backbone of Canadian agriculture, despite the continuing tendency for farms to grow in size and decline in number. The average farm in Canada today is 540 acres; in the Prairie provinces they average over 900 acres. About 7% of the country's total land area is devoted to farming; most is within 300 miles of the U.S. border and is concentrated in only three provinces: Saskatchewan (which has 40% of it), Alberta and Ontario.

The relative importance of agriculture has declined in Canada, although it remains important in its export sector. In 1900 approximately 75% of Canadians were engaged in agriculture; by 1946, this percentage had decreased to 29%, and today it is 3%. Its share in GDP has also declined dramatically, from 12% in 1951 to 3% by 2011. Nevertheless, agriculture remains important. About 40% of Canada's produce is exported, including about 85% of the wheat crop. Its major buyers are Japan, the U.S., the EU and China. In 2010 Canada sold three times more wheat to Asia than to EU countries.

Canada is the world's second largest exporter of wheat (behind the U.S.), and wheat (60% of which is grown in Saskatchewan) alone accounts for nearly half of all agricultural export earnings. Canada holds a fifth of the international market. Any precipitous fall in world wheat prices sends many Saskatchewan family farms into bankruptcy, as occurred at the turn of the century when the cost of production exceeded prices of grain. Also the widespread rejection in Europe of genetically modified organism (GMO) foods has narrowed Canada's market. Only in North American markets can GMO foods be readily sold. In 2003, Canada joined the U.S. to challenge in the WTO the EU's ban on GMOs. Some Canadian farmers are trying to keep their crops free of GMO pollen in order to be able to sell to non-GMO markets.

Because of its agricultural prowess, Canada is a net exporter of food. However, this fortunate situation is due chiefly to wheat production. Canada runs a deficit in fruit, vegetables, nuts, honey, sugar, tobacco and other products, which may in the future cause Canada to become a net importer of food. They face the same specter as do the American farmers: hard times at best, and bankruptcy at worst.

In 2003 cattle farmers, who sell $7 billion worth of beef each year, were shaken by North America's first case of mad-cow disease (BSE). A single cow in northern Alberta tested positive. The U.S., which normally accounts for three-fourths of all Canadian beef exports, and nearly 30 other countries temporarily sealed their borders to Canadian beef, causing severe financial loss to Canadian farmers. Herds in all three western provinces were quarantined and slaughtered. The next shock came in December 2003 when a cow in Washington State also tested positive for BSE. It turned out that it had come from an Alberta herd. In 2007 a 13-year-old beef cow from Alberta was confirmed to have the disease, the 11th case since 2003. Ottawa opted for a partial ban of U.S. beef that was much less restrictive than the one Washington had imposed.

During 2004, the U.S. slowly opened its doors to boneless processed Canadian beef from young animals. President Bush said before his visit to Canada in November 2004 that the ban should be lifted, but the wheels of bureaucracy grind slowly and mysteriously in Washington. Despite the fact that another Canadian cow was found in January 2005 to be infected by BSE, the American door to Canadian cattle under 30 months of age was to be opened in March 2005. But a federal judge in Montana ordered the border to remain closed. Two months later the U.S. Senate blocked the agriculture department's efforts to open the border and instead voted to block Canada's designation as a "minimal risk" region for BSE. In 2006 Bush vowed to end all BSE-related restrictions.

One product in which Canada does not run a deficit is beer. American beer drinkers have been thirsty for the Molson, Labatt, O'Keefe and Moosehead beers and ales. In 1992 agreements were reached not only eliminating barriers that prevented beer brewed in one province from being sold in another, but opening up the market to American beers. By 2004 the only Canadian-owned beer left after Labatt

ST. LAWRENCE SEAWAY

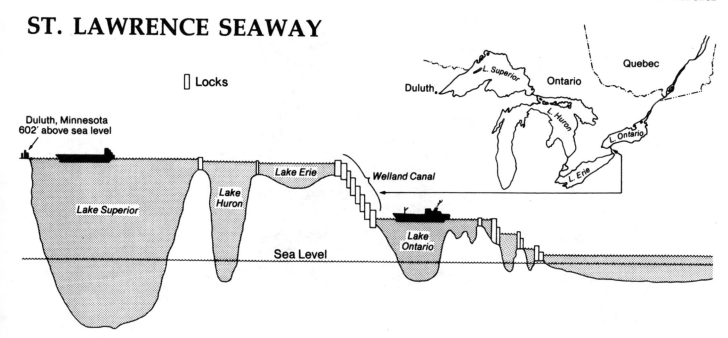

☐ Locks

Duluth, Minnesota
602' above sea level

Lake Superior

Lake Huron

Lake Erie

Welland Canal

Sea Level

Lake Ontario

Duluth. L. Superior Ontario Quebec
L. Huron
L. Ontario
L. Erie

was bought by Belgium's Interbrew was Molson, which has over 40% of Canada's beer market. But the beer that flaunted nationalism and came up with the rant, "I am Canadian," decided to merge with Coors, the third-largest brewer in the U.S. It had already brewed and sold Coors in Canada. Canadian beers in the U.S. face stiff competition from the 1,600 microbreweries that are multiplying fast and successfully challenging the old conventional wisdom that Canadian beer tastes better than the American variety.

Canadians purchase about half of California's exported wines. Canadian wines, 90% of which come from Ontario (particularly the Niagara area) and most of the rest from BC, have come into their own and have won hundreds of international awards. Canadian "ice wine" is an expensive dessert wine made from frost-bitten grapes of which Canada has become the world's leading producer. It has a national appellation, which enables it to be sold in the European Union. It faces stiff competition from another Canadian product—cider or "apple ice wine," a beverage with 12% alcohol from Quebec. The domestic market for wine remains somewhat restricted because Canadians are not big wine drinkers although that is slowly changing. They consume on average only 10 liters per year (one-sixth that in France and Italy), compared with 88 liters of beer.

As in other sectors of the Canadian economy, the state's hand has always been involved in agriculture. Since the Great Depression, marketing boards for various types of farm products have regulated markets. They have attempted to keep farm prices up (and staple food prices for consumers as much as 50% higher than in

the U.S.) in order to control the chronic problem of low and unstable agricultural prices. In the centralized "supply management" structure, dozens of federal and provincial government boards assign production quotas for dairy, poultry and other farm products.

Wheat growers typically have only one customer, the Canadian Wheat Board (CWB). It monopolizes the buying and selling of wheat and barley crops, as well as providing quality control. It fixes a guaranteed price, and the government covers any losses. Founded in 1935, it is the only marketer for Prairie grain destined for export or human consumption within Canada. It is one of the world's biggest grain exporters. Farmers elect the majority of its 15-member board of directors, and the federal government does not control or interfere in day-to-day operations. The Western Grain Stabilization and the Agricultural Stabilization Act Programs are federal projects designed to enhance stability. There are only limited sub-

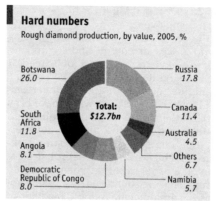

Hard numbers
Rough diamond production, by value, 2005, %

Botswana 26.0

South Africa 11.8

Angola 8.1

Democratic Republic of Congo 8.0

Russia 17.8

Canada 11.4

Australia 4.5

Others 6.7

Namibia 5.7

Total: $12.7bn

Source: *The Economist*

sidies to save Canadian farmers. For example, in 1998, for every $100 of income for a Canadian wheat farmer, $9 came from government subsidies. However, the American farmer received $38 and a Western European $57.

Nevertheless, the U.S. again launched a formal complaint at the World Trade Organization (WTO) in 2002 claiming that the Wheat Board is a monopolistic state trading organization that breaks global trading rules. It also objected to the federal government's policy of compensating farmers for any deficit in the board's pool. In 2003 it slapped a 3.94% tariff on Canadian wheat. In twelve previous investigations Washington had failed to prove any illegal subsidies or that the board deliberately underprices Canadian wheat to steal market share abroad. In 2004 the WTO accepted the Wheat Board's export practices. But in 2007 Prime Minister Harper announced plans to eliminate the board's monopoly, making good on an earlier election pledge. He believes farmers should be able to sell their crops freely. The Liberals oppose this move.

Governmental protection of agriculture is not as great as in the EU or Japan, but there has been a tendency over the years for it to grow in Canada. Thus, these efforts are perpetually surrounded by political controversy. American farmers resent high subsidies and tariffs up to 350% on dairy products. Other provinces ask why Quebec holds about half the dairy quota, and younger farmers resent having to pay hundreds of thousands of dollars to purchase a quota share when they go into business.

The potential Achilles' heel of Canada's agricultural breadbasket has always been transportation of grain from western sources to eastern markets or ports. West-

Canada

ern farmers are dependent on the railroads, which take their grain to the port of Thunder Bay on the northern shore of Lake Superior. There the grain is deposited in some of the largest grain elevators in the world, whence it is loaded into ships and transported through the elaborate locks of Sault Ste. Marie and into the St. Lawrence Seaway system.

Mining

Canada is one of the world's major storehouses for minerals. It ranks first in the world in mineral exports and third in the world in terms of mineral production, behind the United States and Russia. It is the world's largest producer of asbestos, zinc, silver, nickel and potash, and the second largest of gypsum, molybdenum and sulfur. It is also one of the world's major producers of uranium, titanium, aluminum, cobalt, gold, lead, copper, iron and platinum. Its export of potentially deadly asbestos mainly to poor countries has come under increasing criticism within Canada, especially Quebec, where ca. 1,000 persons still make their living from asbestos mining. In 1981 a huge body of gold ore was discovered at Hemlo in northwestern Ontario. With improved mining technology, Canada is now extracting more gold than ever before and is the world's third largest producer, after Russia and South Africa and tied with the U.S.

Diamond production in the Northwest Territories and Nunavut is increasing so dramatically that it has transformed that region into the world's third-biggest producer of high-quality diamonds with 11.4% of the world market, after Botswana (26%) and Russia (17.8%). The boom has generated commercial and political interest in the Canadian Arctic not experienced since the 19th century. Most diamonds are shipped to London and then to Belgium. A Tiffany diamond-finishing center was established in Yellowknife. Canada has the potential to threaten De Beers' century-old grip on the industry. For that reason, De Beers decided in 2004 to channel almost half its exploration budget to Canada. It signed joint ventures and partnerships, and more than four-fifths of its holdings are in Nunavut. It opened a mine in 2007.

Canada's mineral wealth is distributed over virtually the entire country. This brings both advantages and disadvantages. It brings some economic activity to regions, especially in the North, which would be otherwise almost completely locked out of the country's economy. On the other hand, the costs of extraction and transportation are very high in the North. Also, mining operations sometimes create unfortunate collisions between the interests of mining companies, on the one hand, and environmental groups and native groups, on the

Astronaut Julie Payette

other, whose lands and special rights are largely located in the North.

Industry and Services

For all of Canada's wealth in the primary (agriculture) sector, it must be remembered that Canada is no longer a rural society composed of farmers, trappers, lumberjacks and fishermen, but is instead a predominantly industrial, highly urbanized country. Four out of five Canadians live in cities, and the largest ten cities produce 51% of Canada's GDP. Only about 10% of the country's GDP comes from the primary sector, even though much of its manufacturing is centered on processing primary products. Industry accounts for 32% of GDP, of which manufacturing and mining constitute 20.4% of GDP. Industry creates 21% of employment. In terms of sales, the largest industry is petroleum and natural gas extraction and refining, followed by the manufacture of motor vehicles, pulp and paper, meat processing and iron and steel. The auto and paper and pulp industries are the leaders, as measured by employment. Over one million jobs depend on the resource sector, making it Canada's second-largest employer.

It is nevertheless true that the soaring world prices of energy and natural resources have turned part of Canada's economy on its head in the 21st century. Its engines of growth are no longer cars and high-tech industries, which have been hurt by the strong Canadian dollar and troubles in the North American auto sector, but energy and other natural resources, which by 2005 constituted more than 60% of its exports (when imported components are subtracted). The same applies to employment. Young Canadians in rural areas, where jobs are available in oil-

fields, mines, and forests, have an easier time finding work than youth in big cities. Since 2000 the number of blue-collar jobs has increased faster than white-collar ones. In oil-rich Alberta the unemployment rate is half that in the rest of the country.

A particular characteristic of Canadian manufacturing is that it is highly concentrated in several ways. First, it is mainly located in the two largest provinces: Ontario and Quebec. Second, it tends to be concentrated in the hands of rather few firms. For instance, almost all brewing is concentrated in one company, and the same is true of cane and sugar beet processing. Fifteen of the top 40 industries in Canada had concentration ratios in the hands of single firms of more than 50%. Third, an unusually high percentage of Canadian manufacturing is in the hands of foreign companies. A final problem is that much of Canada's manufacturing is done by industries that produce semi-processed primary products. Such industries are particularly vulnerable to competitors in developing countries, where labor costs are much lower.

This is not to say that Canada has no high-technology industries. In 2006 the World Economic Forum ranked Canada sixth in the world in terms of information technology; the U.S. was first. It produces such sophisticated products as guidance systems for missiles and "smart" weapons, space satellites, and robot arms for American space ships. "Canadarm" has been used on more than 50 shuttle missions, most spectacularly on the repair of the Hubble Space Telescope in 1993. In 1999 the company that produced Canadarm was sold to the American concern, Macdonald-Rotweiler. In 1987 it had become the first international partner to reach an agreement on participating in NASA's space station project. It supplied a sophisticated computerized manipulator arm, called "Canada Hand," that not only services spacecraft in the sky, but puts together sections of the orbiting space station after the U.S. has ferried them into space. In return, Canadian researchers are able to use the full range of capabilities provided on the permanently manned space station.

Canada provides astronauts, such as Chris Hadfield in 1995. The U.S. Navy Test Pilot of the Year in 1992, he became the first Canadian to be a part of a shuttle flight crew, as opposed to a scientific team. He commented: "For a Canadian kid, this was just an impossible dream." In 2001 he became the first Canadian to walk in space, doing so twice to help deploy Canadarm2 on the international space station. However, without warning the robotic arm froze and refused to function. This was a dramatic breakdown because the entire multibillion dollar space station depends on the Canadarm2. Fortunately it was a computer problem that was fixed a tense month later. In 2010 Hadfield was chosen to lead a NASA underwater mission, which uses the ocean floor to simulate exploration missions to asteroids, moons and Mars.

In 1997 a Canadian born in Iceland, Bjarni Tryggvason, took part in an 11-day space shuttle mission. In 1999 Julie Payette was the first Canadian to fly to the international space station, and she returned in May 2009. Canada has a mini "Silicon Valley" clustered mainly around Ottawa. Nevertheless, some Canadians are worried that their country's manufacturing activities revolve too much around low-growth industries.

As in most economically advanced countries, the fastest growing sector in Canada's economy is the service one, in which no physical object is produced. If one includes all persons involved in wholesale and retail trade, finance, transportation, recreation and in the wide range of government services (including health and education), then three-fourths of all Canadians are employed in this sector; they produce over two-thirds (69%) of GDP. According to the Economic Council of Canada, proportionally more people hold jobs in the civilian service sector in Canada than in any other economically advanced, western nation. It is this area in which most women who are moving into the employment market find jobs. It is also this sector that is unfortunately hit hardest by unemployment.

Every economically powerful country has its own peculiar problems, vulnerabilities and dependencies. There is no denying that most countries on this earth would be delighted to have the kinds of problems that Canada has. Still, one should not lose sight of the fact that Canada does confront some real challenges, which include its large size, the tensions which plague federal-provincial relations, labor unions which are far more confrontational and ideological than their American counterparts, and heavy economic dependence upon a single foreign country, namely the United States.

Energy

Among Canada's plentiful natural resources are copious energy reserves of all kinds. It is self-sufficient in energy. This is a particular blessing given the fact that Canada is one of the world leaders in per capita energy consumption, even higher than the U.S. Canada is blessed with large reserves of fossil fuels. In the 21st century energy in all forms is Canada's number one export, and it accounted for more than half its merchandise trade surplus with the U.S. It supplies 16% of America's natural gas needs and 22% of its oil (ris-

ing to a third of U.S. imported oil by 2030). Canada, with the world's second-largest oil and gas reserves, is by far America's most secure and reliable source of imported energy, considering that the next suppliers, each responsible for 11%–12% of U.S. imports, are Mexico, Saudi Arabia and Venezuela.

Canada possesses almost a quarter of the world's fresh water and 7% of the planet's renewable water supply. The Canadian government, backed by 69% of the people, according to polls, refuses to export any of it to the U.S., which is dangerously short of water in some regions. It is not surprising that Canada is a major producer of hydroelectricity, which now supplies about two-thirds of its own electrical power needs.

Since 1901 it pumps much leftover electricity into American grids. New Brunswick sells power from its Point Lepreau nuclear plant to Maine, and Hydro-Québec has major contracts with New York and New England states. Hydro-Québec took over New Brunswick's power generating plants in 2010 and plans to move into the American Midwest market of 66 million people, where electricity rates are three times higher than in Quebec. Manitoba sells ten times more electricity to its American neighbors than to Saskatchewan, and British Columbia exports electricity as far as California. Canadian electricity companies benefit from American federal legislation mandating electricity suppliers to increase their renewable energy sources by 20% by 2020. The country's vast clean hydroelectricity is in this category. Hydro-Québec is also investing heavily in wind power. Despite its green image, Quebecers are the second biggest energy consumers after Alberta, 31% of whose GDP is derived from oil and gas.

Canada is a major supplier of electricity to New York and Michigan. At peak times, especially in the winter, it also buys electricity from U.S. utilities. In fact, it was a problem in one of Ontario's relay stations

that caused the great blackout in 1965, which paralyzed the entire northeastern United States. In 1997 Ontario Hydro and Hydro-Québec were told by American regulators that they must open their markets or lose cross-border sales.

The U.S. and Canada have developed an interconnected power grid that is so tight that a problem at one power plant can cascade and cause a massive blackout. This happened August 14, 2003, when a breakdown in an Ohio power plant triggered automatic shutdowns of 100 generating stations (including 18 nuclear power plants) across Ontario and seven American states. It left 50 million Canadians and Americans, including 10 million in Ontario alone, without power. The blackout was six-times more extensive than the one in 1965. Officials on both sides of the border were left to confront estimates that up to $100 billion would be needed to modernize the North American power grid and increase its capability. In the decade preceding the blackout, American demand for power had increased by 30% while capacity had grown by only 15%.

Canada produces a fifth of the world's uranium; 15% of its exports go to the United States. In 2009 Canada had a total of 22 nuclear reactors, many of which are close to the end of their useful service. It had been two and a half decades since a new reactor had been commissioned in either Canada or the U.S. Until 1999 Ontario relied on nuclear power for 60% of its electricity, compared with 13% for Canada as a whole and 20% for the U.S. Ontario had earlier announced that eight of its 18 reactors would be shut down after an internal study documented widespread management problems and years of inadequate maintenance and safety practices. This was a severe blow to the CANDU reactors, which had been touted as more versatile, cheaper to operate and safer than its competitors. In 40 years CANDU was able to make only 11 sales.

Ontario, which dominates Canada's nuclear industry, is on the brink of an energy crisis. It has been in turmoil since an earlier Conservative government in 1998 broke up the now defunct Ontario Hydro, a long-standing monopoly. The province now has less generating capacity than it had in the mid-1990s. The problems with Ontario's crumbling power generating system can almost certainly only be solved with more nuclear power in the future. In 2005 it started up two reactors at the Pickering station east of Toronto and is working on restarting two more there.

Environmentalists predictably vow to oppose any plan to develop nuclear power further. Although Ottawa has no say in how provinces supply their power needs, the Harper government supports an ex-

Canada

pansion of the nuclear option. Atomic power emits almost no greenhouse gasses; only the upfront cost of $5 billion for each nuclear plant is daunting. By 2007 public opinion in favor of nuclear had risen to 44% overall and 63% in Ontario, where people remember the 2003 power grid failure. However, Harper wants the government out of the nuclear business. His government announced in 2009 that it would privatize the part of the state-owned Atomic Energy of Canada (AECL) that makes and services nuclear-power stations. This means the eventual extinction of CANDU.

Coal supplies only a tenth of Canada's overall energy needs. This is an environmental advantage. Canada is a net exporter of coal, selling more through Vancouver to Asia than it imports into eastern Canada from the nearby Appalachian fields in the U.S. Nova Scotia announced in 2001 that its last underground coal mine, the Prince colliery 25 miles north of Sydney, would shut down, ending a 280-year industry that had sustained a poor region. Ontario vowed to shut down its coal-fired power stations by 2009 although they provide a fifth of its electricity. Alberta is the only province still constructing coal-fired plants. However, Ottawa and it spend heavily on carbon capture technology.

Coal is a major contributor to global warming, a climatic phenomenon whose signs are obvious in Canada: droughts in the prairies and melting sea-ice and permafrost in the North. Coal is responsible for a fourth of all of Canada's greenhouse gas emissions, while only about 5% are produced by the oil sands. This amounts

to one-tenth of one per cent of global emissions. In 2002 parliament ratified the Kyoto Accord, which obligates Canada to reduce its greenhouse gas emissions by 6% of its 1990 levels. The federal government had to fight to win agreement among provincial premiers.

The opposition, led by Alberta and supported by the Conservatives, argued that Kyoto is a costly fiasco that would mean mass layoffs. The earlier Liberal governments endorsed Kyoto, but did almost nothing to meet its objectives. By 2009 gas emissions were 26% higher than in 1990, and natural gas and coal generation of electricity contributed 17% of Canada's greenhouse gasses in 2004. The government could offset this by purchasing emission credits from countries, such as Russia, that have exceeded their targets. But handing billions of dollars over to countries like that for this purpose would be hard to sell politically at home.

After assuming power in 2006 the Conservative government acknowledged the obvious fact that painful cuts in jobs and public spending would be necessary to achieve small benefit for the environment. It would also require wrenching life changes that many Canadians would not make. Canada uses more energy than any other developed nation in the world except tiny Luxembourg and Iceland. Like their southern neighbors, Canadians burn a lot of gasoline, which, although more expensive than in the U.S., is still half the price as in Europe. It does not help that global warming sounds good in a country that has long and bitter winters. Some growers, such as grape, maple, corn, wheat and soy-

bean farmers, would see their yields rise, and mining operations in the North would be easier and cheaper. Another bright note is that because of its low population Canada's overall emissions amount to only 2% of the world total.

The Harper government reduced funding for the protocol in 2006 and dropped the targets. He began looking for more effective and realistic alternatives. But the opposition passed a parliamentary resolution in 2007 requiring the Conservative government to meet the difficult Kyoto requirements. Seeing the issue rise to the top of voters' concerns, Harper had no choice but to take global warming seriously. The U.S. refused to ratify the original Kyoto Protocol, but it nevertheless managed to reduce its greenhouse gas emissions slightly after 1998.

Canada's problems stem in part from the fact that 28% of its increased carbon dioxide emissions come from its oil production, especially from the oil sands, which is responsible for 5% of it. Since Canada produces only 2% of global emissions, the oil sands are responsible for only .1% of them. This is important for the American goal of great energy independence. But Canadians fear that the 2007 Energy Independence and Security Act, which bans U.S. government purchases of alternative fuels that produce more carbon emissions than conventional petroleum, could apply to their oil sands.

In a sign that the U.S. had not yet decided to take that course, the Obama administration approved the construction of a 1,000-mile Alberta Clipper pipeline to carry 800,000 barrels a day of fuel from the vast oil sands into the United States. An existing Keystone pipeline runs from Alberta to the oil crossroads at Cushing, Oklahoma. Far more important is the fate of the proposed 2,000-mile underground Keystone XL pipeline, which would open new capacity for Alberta's crude oil by extending from Cushing to the Texas Gulf Coast with connections to a network of pipelines and refineries elsewhere in the U.S. Since this would cross the U.S. border, the final approval will be made by the U.S. State Department, which in 2010 issued a favorable draft environmental impact statement. Progress has been made in reducing oil sand pollution. For example, more than 80% of the water is recycled, and some tailing ponds (containing wastes) are being reclaimed as green land. But the proposed pipelint became a lightening rod for discontent about the oil sands in Alberta since a little over half of Canada's oil comes from those sands.

The oil sands have become a major political and diplomatic problem for the Conservative government, and Canada has become a pollution villain in the eyes of

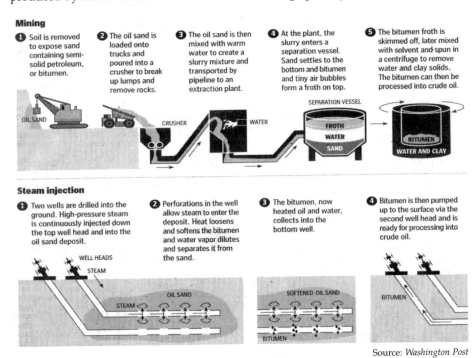

Mining

① Soil is removed to expose sand containing semi-solid petroleum, or bitumen.

② The oil sand is loaded onto trucks and poured into a crusher to break up lumps and remove rocks.

③ The oil sand is then mixed with warm water to create a slurry mixture and transported by pipeline to an extraction plant.

④ At the plant, the slurry enters a separation vessel. Sand settles to the bottom and bitumen and tiny air bubbles form a froth on top.

⑤ The bitumen froth is skimmed off, later mixed with solvent and spun in a centrifuge to remove water and clay solids. The bitumen can then be processed into crude oil.

Steam injection

① Two wells are drilled into the ground. High-pressure steam is continuously injected down the top well head and into the oil sand deposit.

② Perforations in the well allow steam to enter the deposit. Heat loosens and softens the bitumen and water vapor dilutes and separates it from the sand.

③ The bitumen, now heated oil and water, collects into the bottom well.

④ Bitumen is then pumped up to the surface via the second well head and is ready for processing into crude oil.

Source: *Washington Post*

many environmental groups. An international Climate Change Performance Index for 2009 placed Canada 59th, one rung higher than Saudi Arabia. Its adopted policy is to wait for Washington to figure out its own climate change legislation and then follow suit.

In the meantime, more than 900 American companies are suppliers to Canada's oil sands operations, and Canada is making plans to expand its Asian market for petroleum. Pipeline projects are underway to transport its oil westward to the Pacific coast for shipment to China and Japan. Disputes with aboriginal groups have complicated and delayed these efforts. In any case, Alberta's tar-sand oil will be produced and exported whether the U.S. buys it or not.

Canada is one of the few developed countries with the potential to be self-sufficient in both crude oil and natural gas. These two energy sources now supply about 60% of its current energy consumption. Natural gas accounts for about a fifth of Canada's total energy. Canada is not only self-sufficient in natural gas, but is able to export considerable amounts to the United States. In 1999 a natural gas pipeline was completed that transports enough gas from northwestern Canada to Chicago to heat a million American homes each day.

A massive offshore natural gas deposit, estimated to be equal in size to all of the country's known gas reserves, was discovered in 2002 about 120 kilometers (80 miles) west of Vancouver Island in BC. The fuel is frozen in a thick layer of ice, and environmental concerns could postpone extraction for decades.

Until recently, most of Canada's known oil and gas reserves and production were in Western Canada, mainly in Alberta and Saskatchewan. Today 11 of the 13 provinces and territories (Quebec and Nunavut being

the exceptions) are energy producers and have more of a stake in the energy industry than as mere consumers. Thus governments all over Canada have welcomed American investment in the Canadian oil and gas industries. During 2001 alone, more than $35 billion in Canadian assets fell into American hands. This brought foreign ownership to 48%, up from 33% in 1999, but below the 74% level in the late 1970s. Of course, energy investments flow both ways across the 49th parallel. Canadian oil and gas giants, such as PanCanadian Energy, Nexen, and Alberta Energy Company, have extensive holdings in the U.S.

Canada is the world's eighth largest oil producer. With a 10% share, it is America's largest foreign source of imported petroleum products by far (ahead of Mexico, Saudi Arabia and Venezuela). Oil furnishes almost 40% of Canada's own total energy needs. Now that it is able to extract oil profitably from oil sands (a molasses-type substance also called tar sands), it has the world's second largest reserves after Saudi Arabia. They are predicted to last for 40–50 years; according to industry forecasts, the oil sands will by 2015 account for over a fourth of North America's oil production. Investments in the petroleum and gas industries are pouring into Canada, not only from the U.S. but also from countries like China, India and France. Helped by tax and royalty breaks from the federal and Alberta governments, $51 billion in realized or promised investment in oil-sands development were made for the years 1996 to 2010.

The Athabasca oil sands in Alberta are the chief basis for Canada's energy optimism today. They are found in an area about half the size of Colorado in central Alberta, and the formation extends into neighboring Saskatchewan. The commercial center is Fort McMurray, in the northeastern corner of Alberta. Property values

in this boom town have shot up higher than in Toronto or Vancouver. They are estimated to contain the equivalent of some 300 times the known recoverable Canadian liquid oil reserves. Thanks to impressive technological advances in separating the oil from the sand, almost half (46%) of Canada's oil production comes from the sands. Huge investments are pouring in from Royal Dutch Shell, ExxonMobil and Total.

It presents a technological challenge to dig up raw oil sand using massive power shovels, or in a liquefied form using steam so that bitumen can be pumped to the surface. The process requires large quantities of water and natural gas to boil that water. The environmental cost is great. Each barrel of oil produced requires two to five barrels of water and enough natural gas to heat a home for one to five days. Four tons of earth are dug up, and the process emits lots of greenhouse gases. It produces two or three times as much carbon dioxide as does a normal well. However, progress has been made to reduce such pollution.

Oil sands production became profitable since the price of oil is over $50 per barrel. However, the profit margin is only about 15% compared to about 30% for conventional oil drilling. But there are advantages: oil from the sands involves no exploration risk since it is definitely there. Once up and running, it will flow for 30 years or more. The crude oil that is extracted in this way is shipped to refineries in the American Midwest and on to Oklahoma. It is a hugely valuable present and future resource for Canada and the rest of North America.

Other large potential reserves of oil and gas are believed to lie under the Arctic Ocean (especially Beaufort Sea) and under the Atlantic waters off the east coast of Canada. Prospecting and drilling off Can-

On the coast of British Columbia

Courtesy: Michael J. Hewitt

Canada

ada's coast is expensive and dangerous, as the capsizing of the oil rig Ocean Ranger, with 85 men aboard, demonstrated. It is also politically delicate, igniting serious disagreements between Ottawa and provincial governments over ownership and pricing of these resources.

Canada is encountering some difficulty in finding new, easily extractable gas reserves, as gas in western Canada is being depleted. The resulting squeeze has heightened interest in two ambitious long-term projects to transport natural gas from Alaska and the Canadian Arctic to the lower 48 states. The all-Canada route would link new gas fields in the Mackenzie River delta to pipelines in Alberta and could provide almost 2% of American consumption. An even larger one extending from Prudhoe Bay in northern Alaska through the Yukon to the Alberta pipelines would yield even more. Both schemes face numerous environmental, technical and financial obstacles.

In 1984 North America's first tidal power plant began to churn out electricity at Annapolis Royal on the Bay of Fundy (Nova Scotia), where the tides are among the largest in the world. Despite its long coastlines, immense forests and bountiful sunlight and wind, these kinds of renewable resources made up less than 5% of Canadians' energy consumption. It will be many years before these kinds of renewable energy sources will make a truly significant contribution to Canada's energy requirements.

Transportation

Canada is immense. However, given the distribution of its population, it should best be viewed as a snakelike country, more than 4,000 miles wide and only 75 to 100 miles deep. The major population clusters are separated not only by such physical barriers as the Gulf of St. Lawrence, the Great Lakes, the Canadian Shield, the Rocky Mountains and sheer distance; they are also separated by lingual barriers. Boston, New York City, Buffalo, Detroit, Chicago, Minneapolis and Seattle have always exerted an economic pull on Canadians as strong or stronger than that of other Canadian cities or regions. Therefore, Canada must expend enormous sums of money to bind that band of regions together that stretch east to west from coast to coast. From the beginning, constructing and maintaining roads and highways which cut through the Shield and the forests and which must withstand the hostile winter climate have been major undertakings. However, roads alone could never hold together the world's second largest country.

Canada was blessed with long coastlines and a fifth of the world's fresh water, all of which facilitated the cheapest

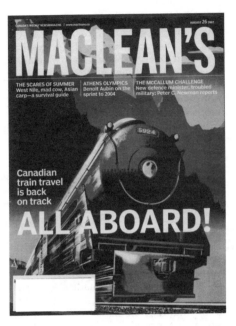

form of transportation: by water. Nevertheless, a complicated and expensive canal system was required to bind these natural waterways together. None was so significant as the St. Lawrence Seaway, a grandiose project that links 56 ports and was undertaken jointly by Canada and the United States. By means of seven locks, stepping from Montreal to Lake Ontario and eight locks along the Welland Canal, ships can now reach waters 183 meters (617 feet) above sea level and 2,300 miles (3,864 kilometers) from the Atlantic Ocean to the head of the Great Lakes. Containing a fifth of the world's non-polar fresh water, the five Great Lakes are governed by the Boundary Waters Treaty of 1909, implemented by an independent bi-national joint commission, which has functioned without dispute or political intervention. Due to successful cooperation between the two countries and among local governments around the lakes, they are much cleaner than they were in 1978, when the cleanup was launched.

By the 1980s the St. Lawrence Seaway was losing much cargo traffic to barges down the Mississippi River and container traffic by rail to large Atlantic ports in the U.S. and at Halifax. Maintenance problems and the drop in American steel production have further threatened its major role as a seasonal carrier of grain, coal and iron ore. The result has been severe financial losses. Nevertheless, this bilateral cooperative project, completed in 1959, was a welcomed change from the competition that had existed between the two neighbors from the beginning of the 19th century, with the United States always being a step ahead. The problems of proceeding by water from the St. Lawrence River into the Canadian West had been clear since the early

part of the 16th century, when Jacques Cartier was rebuffed by the turbulent Lachine Rapids just west of what is now Montreal, thereby frustrating his efforts to find a Northwest Passage to the Far East.

When the fur trade with the Northwest was diverted to the Hudson Bay in 1820, Canadian planners began to devise a way somehow to bring grain from both the U.S. and Canada through the Great Lakes to Montreal. These designs were temporarily foiled by the American construction of the Erie Canal in 1825, which enabled Midwestern grain to be shipped through the Great Lakes to Buffalo or Oswego and then along a relatively inexpensive, two-way, all-season canal through the flat terrain of upstate New York into the Hudson River to New York harbor. To build a competitive Canadian canal system required enormous support from governments in both Britain and Canada, and it also required solutions to daunting technical challenges. The first was to soften the abruptness of the 300-foot drop from Lake Erie to Lake Ontario. As demonstrated by numerous adventurers who have gone over the Niagara Falls in barrels, there are certain risks involved with navigating that treacherous watery precipice.

No sooner had this problem been solved by the construction of the Welland Canal in 1829 than the energetic southern neighbors presented yet another challenge: they expanded their railroads at a dizzying rate. By 1850 they had over 9,000 miles of track laid, compared with only 100 miles in Canada. This necessitated another Canadian mega project to carve railways, through hostile country from the Atlantic to the Pacific, that were so expensive that Canada was strapped with a huge debt even before it became a self-governing nation in 1867.

The government chartered what became the Canadian Pacific Railroad (CPR), bestowing ultimately on it 26 million acres of prime land, more than $100 million grants and loans and 700 miles of already-built railway in eastern Canada. Pierre Berton wrote in his books, *The National Dream* and *The Last Spike*, that the CPR tied Canada together "like a line of steel from coast to coast." "Our cities and towns popped up along it like beads on a string. Without it we would have developed vertically rather than horizontally. We became the nation we are because of the railroad."

The Canadian Rail Passenger Service is called VIA, which is heavily subsidized by taxpayers. Prior to establishing this service in 1977, rail passenger service had been provided almost wholly by the two Canadian systems, Canadian Pacific and Canadian National. Both are private since the government privatized CN in 1995. Most shares were bought by Americans and doubled their value in two years. To remain economically viable, CN shed 14,000 of its 36,000 employees and sold off a half billion dollars of real estate holdings, including the CN Tower in Toronto. It abandoned more than a quarter of its track. By 1996 it was earning a profit.

Seeking to cut costs, the CPR requested the government to take over its passenger operations (forgetting about the huge subsidies it had received from the government when it was built). The state's purchase of the passenger business left the CPR as one of the world's most profitable railways, with large holdings in the energy, shipping, trucking and hotel sectors. It moved its headquarters from Montreal to Calgary in 1996.

CP Rail and Canadian National (renamed CN North America, headquarters in Montreal) have entered the north-south freight market in a big way. CP Rail owns two U.S. railways (Soo Line in the Midwest and Delaware and Hudson in the Northeast). CN North America formed an alliance with the Burlington Northern railway in the West. CN also allied with America's largest long-distance trucking firm, JB Hunt. After NAFTA went into effect, trains started running from Canada through the U.S. into Mexico. In 2000 CN and CP agreed to share track in Canada and the U.S. CN gained access to CP's New York, New Jersey and Pennsylvania networks, while CP began operating on CN's busy Toronto-Chicago main line. This agreement was historic for such traditional rivals.

VIA was chartered and the passenger service was amalgamated into a single system calculated to save costs. However, as in the U.S., when it comes to determining the cost of passenger service, railroad accountants are highly imaginative. The system provides vital service to areas with no roads which otherwise would not be accessible. A few smaller lines supplement this service. Combined, they reach such remote points as Mosoonee on James Bay (where there may be snowstorms in June) and Churchill on Hudson Bay (where polar bears plague the local dumps and trash bins). In all, the system reaches 450 communities, but 85% of its revenues are generated in the Quebec City-Windsor corridor linking the major cities in Ontario and Quebec.

By 1989 the government had to face squarely the obvious problem that Via simply was not sustainable. Federal subsidies had risen steadily (totaling $1.6 billion from 1992–7 with an increase of $402 million in 2000), and ridership had declined from 55.4 million passengers in 1945 to 6.4 million in 1988, less than 5% of total intercity travel by all means of transportation. Half the track being used was originally built before 1914. Therefore, routes and subsidies were

slashed. More than half of Via's service disappeared in 1990, to about 9.5 million kilometers (down from 19 million). From 1990 to 1998, service had fallen from 810 trains per week to 396, and Via's job force had been slashed from 7,000 to 3,000. Some transcontinental service from Vancouver to Halifax and numerous regional routes, mainly in Central and Eastern Canada, remain. But its southern transcontinental route in the West on the Canadian Pacific was cancelled. Cuts created real hardships for travelers in many rural communities, where services disappeared entirely. However, healthy infusions of government money enabled a resurgent VIA in 2003 to offer 139 plush new passenger cars, 21 new locomotives, and renovated stations.

In addition to rivers, canals, lakes and railways, there is an air link, which is the only tie to many points in the extreme Canadian North. Two privately-owned airlines competed: Montreal-based Air Canada and Calgary-based PWA, parent of Canadian Airlines International (CAI). Both struggled to survive. After their merger in 1999, Air Canada carried 80% of Canada's air passengers and got 90% of airline revenues.

That changed dramatically, as no-frills discount carriers increasingly snatched market share. Air Canada's fell by 2004 to

51%, and Calgary-based WestJet, modeled on Southwest Airlines in the U.S., steadily increased its share by 2009 to 36%. It hopes to squeeze out Air Canada and control as much as half the domestic market one day. It also signed deals with international carriers to corner a greater share of the lucrative transborder business.

Several other low-cost carriers, such as Jetsgo in Montreal and Canjet Airlines of Nova Scotia, have grown rapidly and even started cutting into Air Canada's extensive cross-border network. All of these trends helped force Air Canada into bankruptcy protection in 2003 and into acrimonious litigation with WestJet over suspected industrial espionage. Victor Li, a Canadian citizen and son of a Hong Kong billionaire, acquired a 31% stake in Air Canada. In 2004 it emerged from bankruptcy. It flies smaller aircraft more frequently on domestic routes to compete with low-cost competitors, while expanding its more profitable international routes. America's stricter visa requirements for transit passengers encourage more international passengers to fly over Toronto, Montreal and Vancouver, thereby benefiting Air Canada, enabling it to return to profitability. The rejuvenated airline selected Céline Dion as its main advertising voice.

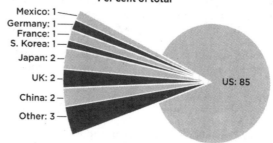

EXPORTS: Canada's exports by country, 2005.
Per cent of total

Mexico: 1
Germany: 1
France: 1
S. Korea: 1
Japan: 2
UK: 2
China: 2
Other: 3
US: 85

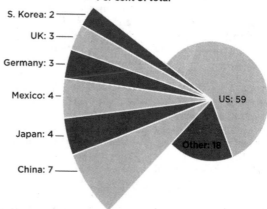

IMPORTS: Canada's imports by country, 2005.
Per cent of total

S. Korea: 2
UK: 3
Germany: 3
Mexico: 4
Japan: 4
China: 7
US: 59
Other: 18

THE U.S. REMAINS our dominant trade relationship, but to prosper, Canada has to focus more on the rest of the world

Source: *Maclean's*

Canada

In 1995 Canada and the U.S. signed an "open skies" agreement allowing their airlines access to any airport on the other side of the border at unregulated prices. For the first time in more than three decades, there is direct service between Washington, DC, and Canadian cities. In the five years after the agreement was signed, air passenger traffic between the two countries went up by two-thirds, as 24 U.S. cities began direct flights to Canada, and Air Canada tripled its American destinations to 45.

Federalism and Labor

A second major problem is the effect on the economy of federal-provincial controversies. Canada is a federal state, in which the provinces are more powerful than are American states. The boundaries of jurisdictions between the governments in Ottawa and in the provinces have not yet been as sharply drawn as in the U.S., and this overlapping of jurisdictions becomes very visible in economic disputes. This is made more difficult by the fact that the two levels of government have become much more economically interdependent since 1945.

In an attempt to even out the economic disparities among the various provinces and to demonstrate to all Canadians the benefits of being a part of Canada, no matter where in the country they might live, the federal government transfers some of its tax revenues directly to the provinces. These "transfer payments" are made on the basis of a hodge-podge of fiscal formulae, laws, regulations, subsidies and traditions, which support such activities as social welfare, health and education. The allocation formulae inevitably cause serious disagreements between Ottawa and the provincial governments, some of which depend on such payments for half their budgets. Saskatchewan, Alberta and BC receive nothing. Transfers to newly rich Newfoundland and Nova Scotia were supposed to be reduced by 70 to 90 cents for every dollar of provincial revenue for their huge offshore oil and gas reserves. However, the Newfoundland government retained some of its support. An embarrassed Ontario moved into the "have-not" category.

It is not clear that these transfer payments significantly improve poorer regions' basic economic structures; some of the Atlantic provinces remain relatively poor, and Alberta is still the economic leader despite being hard hit by the global recession in 2008–9. Nevertheless, these transfers sometimes spark criticism from the United States because the assistance to exporting industries smacks of export subsidies forbidden by GATT international trade agreements. There are very

few policy areas where only one government acts.

Intense intergovernmental arguments are raging over transfer payments. The negotiations and compromising necessary to coordinate economic policies greatly delays solutions. In an effort to reduce the federal government deficit, the Liberal government made serious cuts in the transfer payments to the provinces. Between 1990 and 1998 the total value of such payments fell by 5.4%, leaving the provinces to serve more people with less money. In response, they cut services, including in health care (8.7% 1985–95), universities (8% 1995–97), and welfare (4.7% 1994–96).

Social welfare is almost entirely a provincial responsibility, and Ottawa provides only 16% of health care costs. Cash transfers to the provinces constituted about 10% of federal program spending in 1997. In 1999 then Prime Minister Chrétien and nine premiers agreed on a "social union" that would provide a framework for more power sharing and cooperation on national social programs. Quebec's premier rejected the plan because it did not give Quebec the right to opt out of new federal programs and simply take its proportionate share of federal funding.

A third burden to the economy is the type of labor unions in Canada. Of course, employers' power in Canada needs the same kinds of organized employee checks as in other countries. Workers and civil servants have almost complete freedom to organize in Canada, and the unions perform an essential function of watching out for employee interests. Almost a third (30%, compared with less than a fifth in the U.S.) of all wage-earners are unionized (40% in Quebec), and 70% of members belong to unions affiliated with the Canadian Labor Congress (CLC). Private sector union membership in 2008 had declined to 16%, whereas 71% of public sector workers are unionized. As in the U.S., unions negotiate by workplace rather than across an industry. Canadian unions are a blend between American and British and have problems stemming from both connections. A further complication is that many union leaders in Quebec are nationalists who are willing to use their economic clout to further their separatist or provincial political goals.

About half of the Canadian labor movement belongs to unions whose headquarters are in the United States and are extensions of large American unions. The AFL-CIO affiliates give their Canadian branches considerable autonomy, but Canadian unionists are nevertheless subject to pressures from south of the border. After a 1984 strike against General Motors of Canada resulted in a settlement more fa-

vorable than that received by American workers, Canadian United Auto Workers (UAW) director Robert White decided to sever Canadian auto workers from the American-based UAW. White no doubt hoped that other Canadian unionized workers would follow, but Canadian members of the United Steelworkers refused in 1985 to break their ties with their Pittsburgh headquarters.

The more militant tendency reflects the other labor heritage which Canadian unions share: the British one. As in the United Kingdom, Canadian unions are organized along craft lines. This means that a company must usually deal with several unions, rather than with only one. Thus, if only one of several unions strikes, an entire plant closes down. Canadian unionists tend to regard their American counterparts as too cowardly and too accommodating to employers.

Another difference is the ties unions have to political parties. Although most American unions like to support the candidates of the Democratic Party, it is a moderate, middle-of-the-road party. By contrast, the CLC is directly supportive of the New Democratic Party, much as British unions are organizationally linked to the British Labour Party. The NDP writes class conflict on its banner, and, therefore, Canadian unions share a tempered spirit of class conflict. The CLC is always forced to deal with governing parties in Ottawa and most provinces that it is trying to put out of power. This makes for considerable tension.

The unions' political influence has declined, and their support by the general public is waning. They have shown themselves to be impotent in fighting unemployment. On top of their image problems, they are unable to attract white collar and service industry workers. As in the U.S., their traditional base—smokestack industries and mining—are losing jobs because of technological changes. An outgrowth of this more confrontational approach is that Canada has the third-worst strike record among western industrialized countries after Iceland and Spain. When Canadians strike, they tend to strike hard and long. The first national public-service strike in Canadian history almost paralyzed the country in 1991. The frequency of strikes, sometimes with the financial backing of hefty strike funds in the U.S., is one of several factors that make Canadian productivity lower than in the U.S. even though it outperforms the American neighbor in some sectors.

Economic Dependence

A fourth major economic problem with which Canadians have struggled since their inception as a self-governing people is their dependence upon the outside world, especially upon a single country—the United States. With a relatively small domestic market, Canada must trade heavily abroad in order to maintain its citizens' high standard of living. Fifty-two percent of its GDP is generated by foreign trade, and the bulk of that trade is with its neighbor to the south. In some sectors of Canada's economy, the dependence upon foreign trade is much greater. For newsprint, the proportion is 88%; for wheat 85%, and for zinc 61%.

In 1972 the Canadian government decided to try a "third option" to impossible self-reliance and excessive dependence upon the United States: to diversify its trade with countries other than the United States. Canadians vigorously sought trade with the EU and Asia. The EU is Canada's second-largest trading partner, accounting in 2011 for 7.5% Canadian exports and 12.5% of its imports. It is also Canada's second biggest source of investment after the U.S.

In 2009 Canada and the EU gave the green light to talks aiming at a trade agreement. Most trade between Canada and the EU are already tariff-free. What remains are farm products, which are the hardest to eliminate. The EU trades five times more with China than with Canada. Canadian efforts to expand trade in Asia bore some fruit. Japan is Canada's third largest trading partner, with China right behind and rising rapidly. However, its trade with Asia is little more than 10% of that with the U.S. From 2006–2009, Canada signed eight bilateral trade agreements with other countries in a further attempt to lessen its dependence upon trade with the U.S.

Vancouver, which is closer to Tokyo than to Halifax, NS, is North America's second busiest port (after New York) and handles more tonnage than all other Canadian ports put together. It is the seat of many banks. It aspires to become North America's gateway to Asia. Of course, the expansion of trade ties with Asia is a two-way street. The challenge to Canadian markets from China, South Korea, Taiwan and other Asian countries with low labor costs and aggressive marketing strategies is as worrisome to Canada as it is to the United States. This challenge from the Orient has given the two North American countries even more in common with each other and helped undermine the objective of the "third option."

Despite the efforts to diversify, Americans still buy and sell about three-quarters of Canada's exports and imports. American-Canadian trade constitutes the largest two-country trade relationship in the world. This trade tie is very important for the United States, about a fifth of its exports and imports, roughly the same volume of American trade with the entire European Union. According to Canadian government estimates, about 7 million American residents are employed, directly or indirectly in the export trade with Canada, and the border states of Michigan, New York and Ohio are particularly involved in such trade. Clearly, this vibrant trade relationship is mutually beneficial to both neighbors, even though American trade has an overall greater importance for Canada than *vice versa*.

Roughly two-thirds of Canada's $75 billion tourist trade depends on American travelers. Thirteen million American tourists annually and several million more from other countries provide jobs for one out of ten Canadians. Due to the rising value of the Canadian dollar, which has reached parity with the U.S. dollar, and a tightening of the border since the September 11 terrorist attacks, especially since passports are required since June 1, 2009, tourism from the United States slowed down.

Canadians are also ardent foreign travelers. At any given time during the winter, 5% of the Canadian population is vacationing in Florida. Two million Canadian "snowbirds" find their way there, and more than a million vacation in Mexico each year. Francophones have their own free newspaper, *Le Soleil de la Floride*. From early November until the first week in April, Monday through Saturday, all can listen to five-minute news broadcasts on about 20 Florida radio stations: "Canada Calling—the News from Home for Vacationing Canadians," anchored by long-time Toronto newscaster Prior Smith (website: www.canadacalling.com). He is kind to his American listeners by using inches, feet, Fahrenheit and "zee," not "zed."

Francophones tend to congregate on the Atlantic Coast, whereas anglophones prefer the Gulf Coast. In 1992 the Canadian Snowbird Association was formed, and since 1994 Canadians gather in the Florida State Fairgrounds for a couple days in January and flaunt their Canadianness in a "Snowbird Extravaganza," which offers entertainment and a trade show; 80,000 attended in 1997. The yearning for a warmer climate also helped persuade a million Canadians to settle permanently in the Los Angeles area.

A far more worrisome development than trade dependence, in the minds of many Canadians, has always been the high degree of foreign ownership of their country's economy. No other industrialized country has such a large portion of its economy in foreign hands, and certainly no other industrial country has such a great chunk of its wealth in the hands of *one* foreign nation. This is, of course, not a new problem. From the early 19th century on, investment capital, primarily British, poured into Canada to build canals and railways and to develop paper and mining industries. After World War I, the United States replaced Britain as the main source of capital.

John A. Macdonald's "National Policy," which had erected a tariff wall against foreign goods in order to encourage manufacturing within Canada, had the unforeseen effect of encouraging foreign producers to scale that tariff wall by creating branch plants in Canada itself. That way, foreign companies could sell in the Canadian market and also, for a long time, even gain favored access to markets in the British Commonwealth due to the British Preferential Tariff. Thus, the high Canadian tariffs had at least two effects: one, they increased foreign ownership. Second, manufacturing enterprises within Canada could relax behind the tariff shield, rather than strive for the kind of efficiency which would be required if they had been fully exposed to foreign competition.

In 1947 the discovery of oil in Alberta sparked huge foreign investments in the exploration and development of energy sources. Almost before Canadians realized it, foreign investments in Canada had increased by 800% between 1950 and 1975. At the same time, Canadians are investing more abroad, especially in the U.S., than foreigners are investing in Canada. Measured on a per capita basis, Canadian investment in the U.S. is *twice* as high as the American investment in Canada. In 1999 it owned 9% of total foreign direct investment (FDI) in the United States, making it the fifth largest foreign investor, with the United Kingdom as first.

Statistics Canada figured that in 2005 FDI in Canada, primarily from the U.S., was worth $390 billion. But boosted by a rising Canadian dollar, Canadian ownership of foreign companies—with the U.S. remaining the most popular place for Canadians to invest—was growing at an even faster rate, now worth $452 billion. In some sectors, such as machine manufacturing and metals, Canadians are already the leaders. Lured by many American chambers of commerce, Canadians are attracted by the political stability, the tax incentives, and the size and proximity of the world's largest market. Such Canadian giants as Alcan, Northern Telecom, Seagram, Bombardier and Magna International bought companies in the U.S.

Some Canadians cynically refer to their country as a "branch-plant economy," the most important decisions for which being made in a foreign country. They argue American companies are like parasites, drawing huge profits out of Canada, closing their Canadian subsidiaries whenever it pleases them, and hogging most of the research and development for their American headquarters and plants. The critics

Canada

frequently overlook the fact that these American companies created thousands of jobs in Canada which otherwise would not have existed, introduce much future technology into Canada, and pay staggering amounts of taxes to the federal and provincial governments.

FIRA and the National Energy Policy, 1960–1985

By the 1960s, the question of foreign control over the Canadian economy had become an important and widespread political issue in that country. "Economic nationalism" exercised a formidable influence on Canadian politics from the late 1960s into the 1980s and became a considerable bone of foreign political contention between these two large neighbors. These fears prompted the creation of the Foreign Investment Review Agency (FIRA) to screen investment proposals by foreigners. Such an agency actually came into existence in 1974.

FIRA was a red flag waved in the faces of foreign (mainly American) investors. Although about 90% of all proposals were ultimately approved (a figure that climbed by 1983 to 97%, a fact that irritated many Canadian nationalists), applications were so expensive and time-consuming that many potential investors decided not even to submit them. In general, applicants had to be able to demonstrate that the American company's presence in Canada would be of "substantial benefit" to the Canadian economy. Also, approval often came with numerous conditions, known as "performance criteria." These could include a minimum of jobs to be created or of money to be invested. Or they could require foreign companies to purchase supplies in Canada, a requirement which, upon American prompting, was declared impermissible by the General Agreement on Tariffs and Trade (GATT), now enforced by the World Trade Organization (WTO). These "performance criteria" would not apply to Canadian companies, so a double standard was created.

FIRA and other economic nationalist policies did succeed in the sense that foreign control over the assets of all corporations in Canada did fall from 37% in 1971 to 16% by 1981. On the other hand, foreign investors found FIRA excessively intrusive and began to fear that the Canadian government might change the rules of the game after they had placed their money in Canada. Foreign investments began to dry up. At the same time, inflation and unemployment began to climb. In other words, FIRA coincided with the worst recession in Canada since the 1930s, and unlike in the U.S., Canadian nationalism always tends to become weaker in times of economic distress.

FIRA became a major target of the conservatives, who were not ideologically opposed to such regulation of foreign investment, but who concluded quite realistically that such restrictions seriously threatened Canadians' high standard of living. Therefore, within weeks of becoming prime minister in 1984, Mulroney renamed the agency "Investment Canada" and gave it a mandate to encourage, not discourage, foreign investment. He assured Americans that "there shall be one game—building Canada—and one set of rules. These shall not be changed after the game has started to the detriment of any of the players."

Investment Canada screened only those direct foreign takeovers of firms with more than $5 million in assets. The government continued to watch very closely any foreign investments in the cultural sector, though. Almost all Canadians, of whatever political persuasion, are very sensitive to any threat of foreign control over Canadian culture.

Energy was also a sector of Canadian concern. In 1980, at the peak of Canada's lucrative production of oil and gas, the Canadian government made its most far-reaching economic move, designed to take control of at least 50% of its oil industry by the 1990s. The National Energy Policy (NEP) was a series of legislative acts that, through grants, tax write-offs and various incentives, favored Canadian owned or controlled companies. There were several odious aspects of the NEP, from the standpoint of foreign investors. It operated retroactively to confiscate some of the foreign oil companies' profits. This lowered the book value of the companies and therefore made them prime targets for being bought out by favored Canadian firms.

American businesses that felt forced to sell out did not receive what they considered to be a fair market price. Perhaps worse, the NEP contained a "back-in" clause. This required the transfer to the government-owned oil company, Petro-Canada (PETROCAN—created in 1976 with its headquarters in Calgary), of up to 25% of the value of an oil or gas well after a find had been made on federal lands; indeed, all land in the Arctic region is owned by the federal government. This clause took no notice of the exploration costs of finding the oil or gas in the first place.

By world standards, the NEP was rather gentle. The nationalization of all foreign energy assets was never considered, even though Canadian provinces earlier had taken over direct control of certain other raw materials: Quebec took control of most of the asbestos industry, while Saskatchewan did the same with the potash within its borders. However, the NEP did represent a changing of the "rules of the game" by violating the principle that dis-

criminatory changes in rules should not be applied to foreign investments already in place. This is a dangerous practice for any country that is so dependent upon foreign investment, as Canada has always been. Both the FIRA and the NEP also moved Canadian-American relations into the spotlight and stimulated intense irritation in the minds of many Americans who had barely thought about Canada before. It added tension to the two countries' dealings. As Andrew Malcolm observed, "it signaled the end, if a formal conclusion was needed, of the quiet old boy network of handling bilateral relations."

The basic objective of the NEP—to "Canadianize" the bulk of Canada's own energy resources—was and remains popular in Canada. In fact, one of the reasons why the Tory Prime Minister Joe Clark was thrown out of office in 1980 was the fact that he wanted to return PETROCAN to private ownership. In one respect, the NEP was succeeding: by 1983, the percentage of the oil industry belonging to Canada had already risen to 35%, an impressive step toward the goal of 50%. However, the timing of the policy could not have been worse. In the years leading up to the NEP, oil and gas prices steadily increased, but by the early 1980s, they declined significantly on world markets. This meant that the holdings and profits of PETROCAN and private Canadian oil companies also declined. The government had calculated that rising oil and gas prices would provide the revenues to buy back much of the foreign-owned oil industry. Instead, those prices fell, and interest rates rose to the stratospheric level of 21%.

Canadian oil companies found that they had created serious problems for themselves by going deeply into debt to buy foreign companies at what seemed at the time to be bargain prices. They were thrown into a serious economic crisis. The most celebrated case of a Canadian oil company that went on a wild spending and borrowing spree was Dome Petroleum. By 1982 it was on the verge of becoming such a financial disaster that it could have undermined confidence in the country's entire financial system if the federal government and the banks had not given it large amounts of aid to keep it from going bankrupt. By 1983 Dome had to take huge losses to sell assets in a depressed market in order to remain solvent. The lowered price of oil, combined with foreign investors' fears of losing any more money in Canada, caused drilling operations in the country to dry up for a while, and it diverted much of that activity to the United States. The resulting bust severely hit Alberta's economy and temporarily created the first *eastward* shift of population in many years.

The economic costs of the NEP and FIRA brought a political reaction as well. Their introduction roughly coincided with Canada's worst recession in a half century, during which unemployment climbed into double figures. These measures exacerbated Canada's economic woes and actually discouraged the achievement of self-sufficiency. More and more Canadians became convinced that they were more damaging than helpful to Canada in the long term. The debate that ensued did not revolve around matters of principle; Canadians by and large accepted the federal government's right to seek the objectives which FIRA and NEP sought. Indeed, no people can be faulted for wishing to gain control over their own economic resources, and thereby over their own destiny. Instead, the debate involved the question of what is prudent and necessary for Canada.

In Canada, protectionist sentiment is usually strongest in times of economic prosperity, and the years leading up to FIRA and the NEP were boom years. In times of economic adversity, Canadians are more likely to look for ways to facilitate the international trade and the inflow of foreign capital upon which their prosperity has always depended. In the United States, the opposite is true: protectionist sentiment tends to be strongest during threatening economic times and weakest during good times. In Trudeau's final years as prime minister, FIRA's provisions began to be slackened and streamlined, and more attempts were made to assuage the fears of foreign investors. The *Conservatives* pointed directly at these nationalist measures as villains partially responsible for Canada's hard times.

The Mulroney government moved quickly to dismantle the two programs since the Liberal government had designed them. Most of the teeth were pulled out of FIRA's mouth, and the thrust was reversed to encourage, rather than discourage, investment. FIRA was renamed "Investment Canada" and, in the words of one of its advertisements in foreign magazines, "the Canadian Government has placed the welcome mat out to foreign investors." By 1985 the Montreal and Toronto stock exchanges had opened electronic trading links with the stock exchanges in Boston, New York and Chicago, facilitating the sale of a number of Canadian stocks to American investors.

In 1985 Mulroney signed an "Atlantic Accord" granting Newfoundland control over its offshore energy resources. He also signed a "Western Accord" with the premiers of British Columbia, Alberta and Saskatchewan that largely freed the Canadian oil industry from federal regulation. In a third step the government adopted a frontier energy policy known

as the Canada Petroleum Resources Act, which meant less government intervention in federally-controlled northern and offshore areas. Finally, it deregulated the natural gas market.

Government controls on the exporting and pricing of oil and natural gas have been abolished, and discrimination in tax treatment of exploration spending between Canadian and foreign firms was ended. These accords effectively spelled the end of the NEP. Canadian ownership in its oil industry had declined by 1989 to 42.1%, down from 47.9% in 1985. In 1991, 15% of PETROCAN's shares were sold to the public, and in 1995 the Chrétien government announced the sale of its remaining 70% stake and eliminated the 25% limit on foreign investment in PETROCAN. In 2004 the Martin government expressed the intention to put the state's final 18.7% share on the auction block. However, it fell from power in January 2006, and not until March 2009 was it acquired by Suncor Energy, which had pioneered the development of Alberta's oil sands.

In 2010 a rare rejection of foreign investment in Canada took place. BHP Billiton, an Anglo-Australian mining company, made a $39 billion hostile takeover bid for PotashCorp of Saskatchewan. Premier Brad Wall called on Prime Minister Stephen Harper and his fellow Canadians to "stand up for Canada" by opposing this purchase. Canada possesses 53% of the world's reserves of potash, a strategic resource vital to food production. PotashCorp alone accounts for about a third of the world's supply of this food nutrient. They stopped the deal.

Out of 1,600 reviewed foreign purchase requests in the preceding 25 years, this was only the second time one had been turned down. Canada is among the world's most open countries to foreign investors. But there are some sectors that remain off-limits to foreigners: banks, publishing, broadcasting, cable television systems, telecommunications, airlines and one of Canada's two major railways. In 2011 the largest banks and pension funds launched a rival bid to prevent the London Stock Exchange from buying the Toronto stock exchange (TMX), regarded by most Canadians as a strategic asset. The new merger would be branded "Maple."

Free Trade Agreement

By 1985 the old, controversial issue of free trade with the United States again moved into political center stage. This debate has existed as long as Canada has been an independent country. When the British adopted a policy of free trade in 1846, the colonies of British North America entered into a Reciprocity Treaty with the United States. This treaty facilitated

free trade for many manufactured goods until the United States unilaterally abrogated it in 1866. This American move divided Canadians on the question of free trade with the U.S. for the next century and a quarter. After all attempts to reach some kind of agreement had failed, John A. Macdonald declared his National Policy of trade protection in 1878, asserting that "no great nation has ever arisen whose policy was free trade."

In the early 20th century the Canadian government had second thoughts about this. Prime Minister Laurier reflected upon President William Howard Taft's question: "Canada is at the parting of the ways. Shall she be an isolated country, as much separated from us as if she were across an ocean, or shall her people and our people profit by the proximity that our geography furnishes and stimulate trade across the border?" Laurier decided that his country should seek free trade, but Canadian voters had different thoughts and voted him out of power in the 1911 election, which was fought on that issue. The *Conservative* slogan, "No Truck or Trade with the Yankees!" was a potent one. The arguments for or against free trade have not basically changed since that time.

Two world wars greatly intensified the trade ties between the two countries, and after the Second World War they entered *sectoral* free trade agreements with each other. In 1959 they created the Canadian-United States Defense Production Sharing Arrangement, which permits unfettered trade in military products. To the chagrin of Canadian peace groups, the government and industries seek to increase their contracts with the Pentagon in order to have a larger share of American defense spending.

The second milestone in sectoral free trade was the 1965 Canadian-United States Automotive Trade Agreement, which required that the Big Three U.S. automakers build as many cars in Canada as they sell there. It is responsible for the fact that a third of Canada's exports to the United States and more than a fourth of its total exports are in the form of finished vehicles and automotive parts. Auto ownership in the U.S. has reached an astonishing 99.8% in the U.S. (compared with 68% in Canada), and 85% of all vehicles assembled in Canada are sold in the U.S. Ontario produced more vehicles than Michigan for the first time in 2004.

The Canadian Autoworkers Union announced in 2005 that 57,500 Canadians were directly employed by carmakers, 10,000 fewer than in 1998; 85% worked for the Big Three. The auto pact did not provide for free trade in replacement parts, tires, batteries and used cars. In 2000 the World Trade Organization (WTO) accepted

Canada

Japan's and the EU's argument that the auto pact violates international trade guidelines. The Canadian government unsuccessfully appealed the ruling. Canada's auto industry was responsible directly or indirectly for more than a million jobs in Canada, 11% of the full-time work force. When the Big Three fell into crisis in 2008–9 and Chrysler entered bankruptcy protection in April 2009, many Canadian autoworkers found their employment terminated or curtailed. But the government came to the rescue and acquired Chrysler stock that Fiat is eager to buy.

The Mulroney government was more interested in free trade. Radically reversing the position which John A. Macdonald had taken a century ago, Mulroney asserted in 1984 that efforts to control trade and investment "ignored the basic lesson of our history, namely that free and unfettered access to world markets has been a boon to strong and dynamic economic growth." No doubt the massive Canadian surplus in the trade account with the U.S. helped change some Canadians' minds.

Canadians have always been afraid that free trade with the U.S. would kill their weaker, less efficient manufacturing companies. However, this fear was less justified in an era when Canadians are able to sell more manufactured goods to the U.S. than vice-versa. It also makes less sense at a time when both countries face their greatest trade challenges from Japan, China, and certain third world countries, whose lower labor costs help them to undersell American and Canadian products in those two countries' home markets. These challenges give the U.S. and Canada a strong incentive to join efforts to tighten their own trade ties with each other.

The business community is almost unanimously in favor of it. The Liberal Party opposed completely free trade. Some provincial premiers, especially in Ontario, were fearful that an agreement could prevent them from subsidizing or otherwise favoring companies within their boundaries in order to save jobs. Organized labor, supported by the NDP, feared that free trade could destroy the jobs of many Canadian workers. Finally, cultural nationalists argued that such cornerstones of Canadian culture as filmmaking and book production would be killed by free trade.

To assuage all these fears, Mulroney announced that essential Canadian economic, political, cultural and social features were not negotiable. In a speech in Chicago he said: "Our political sovereignty, our system of social programs, our commitment to fight regional disparities, our unique cultural identity, our special linguistic character—these are the essence of Canada."

Mulroney argued that "the deal is a must for Canada," and he proceeded to negotiate and sign the Free Trade Agreement (FTA) on January 2, 1988. The 12 months that followed saw one of the most furious debates and outbursts of nationalism ever to grip Canada. It pitted proponents, who argued that the agreement would protect Canada against American protectionism, keep economic nationalism within Canada in check, and create jobs, against opponents, who feared that Canadian industry and culture would be crushed.

As the smaller European members of the EU or EFTA have seen, distinctive cultures can indeed survive within free trade organizations. Also, some sensitive areas of the economy were exempted from the agreement, such as water, east coast fish, most agricultural products, and the "cultural industries." Free Trade was the crucial issue in the 1988 elections. The fact that Mulroney's Tory government was returned to power was an important sign that Canadians had largely shed their economic inferiority complex toward the U.S. In 1988 both houses of parliament approved of FTA amidst uproarious attempts to show who was the most patriotic: opposition members sang "O Canada," while Tories waved the Canadian flag. The pact went into effect in 1989.

Although the value of bilateral merchandise trade jumped by 42% in the first four years of FTA's existence, criticism persisted that it brought job losses to Canada. The issue of subsidies continues to be an explosive matter. But cross-border trade and investment boomed. In 1994 some shoppers were induced to stay in Canada by a lowering of Canadian taxes on cigarettes, as well as by the opening of 136 Wal-Mart stores, purchased from Woolworth Canada. Each has a McDonald's restaurant inside and the trademark low prices, customer service "with a smile," and "greeter" at the door. Wal-Mart promised that 60% of the products in these stores would be produced in Canada. This was necessary at first because of the requirement that every package in Canada be labeled in French and English.

The retailing giant had to learn some hard lessons about doing business in Quebec. It distributed thousands of flyers in English only and sent letters to its middle managers in English, which were violations of the province's language laws. Another problem is the way its name sounds in Quebecers' ears. A columnist for *Le Journal de Montreal* claimed that "even uttering the word [Wal-Mart] is disgusting, like chewing an old Kleenex that was forgotten in the pocket of a winter coat." It found itself in another legal thicket in 1997 when, fearing American legal action, it took a line of pajamas off its shelves pro-

duced in Cuba. This action was a violation of a Canadian law that forbids companies in Canada from complying with the American trade embargo against Cuba, with which Canada conducts normal relations. This incident merely demonstrated again how sensitive Canada is concerning its sovereignty *vis-à-vis* the U.S; Wal-Mart restocked the pajamas.

The Ontario Labor Relations Board ordered the company's store in Windsor to become the chain's first to have union employees. This did not happen, but in 2004 the Quebec Labour Relations Board approved the United Food and Commercial Workers (UFCW) union's bid to represent the 180 Wal-Mart employees in Jonquière, 250 miles northeast of Montreal. Wal-Mart responded a year later by closing the store, allegedly for economic reasons. Few people believed that explanation, and the union continued to recruit support from a dozen of the 44 stores in Quebec and at twice that number elsewhere in Canada.

In 2006 it faced a union showdown in St. Hyacinthe, 40 miles outside of Montreal, which is the only Wal-Mart store in North America with broad union representation. In April 2009 a Quebec government arbitrator awarded employees at the store a labor agreement that included a grievance process and seniority rights. Its struggle is greatest in Quebec, where about 40% of the workforce is unionized, the highest percentage in North America.

Despite such problems of adaptation, Wal-Mart had by 2005 captured about 52% of the discount market. It not only took business from other department store giants, such as Kmart (which has disappeared), Canada's traditional leader but now American-owned, Zellers (28% of the market share), and "The Bay," a struggling dowdy department and discount chain that was sold in 2006 to an American company. But by offering an 8% reduction in the price of a standard basket of department store goods and by winning customer loyalty through friendly service, it helped force Eaton's, a national institution, to seek bankruptcy in 1997, from which it emerged wounded later in the year; Eaton's market share had dwindled to 7% by 1999.

This was a bitter blow to many Canadians, who for generations had grown up mail-ordering from the Eaton's catalogue and staring at the company's magical Christmas season displays. Eaton's, which French language police had earlier forced to drop the English possessive from its signs in Quebec, failed to adjust to a new age of retail competition. In 1999 Sears Canada bought Eaton's corporate entity and 18 of its stores. These included six downtown stores and the flagship Toronto Eaton Center, which were renamed Eatons (without apostrophe) and reopened in 2000 after an upscale makeover. The rest were turned into Sears stores. However, this business plan failed. In 2002 five of the remaining stores were converted to Sears outlets, and two were closed. Eatons is no more.

Though vilified on both sides of the border, Wal-Mart's success is related to what it offers to areas, consumers and employees. Most Canadian communities with an outlet reached out to it and embraced it. Thousands of small suppliers compete to get their products on Wal-Mart's shelves, and new stores receive six to ten applicants for every available job. A 2004 survey by the Canadian Imperial Bank of Commerce of more than 1,800 small-business owners in Canada revealed that only 16% of them claimed to have been hurt by competition from large retailers like Home Depot and Wal-Mart, and 5% said they had benefited from them. The overwhelming majority contended that their presence had little or no impact on their businesses.

The American chains keep coming. Target announced plans to take over hundreds of Zellers stores in 2013, its first expansion over the U.S. border. Other American businesses hoping to make up for declining sales at home by expanding to Canada are J.Crew, Kohl's and Marshalls.

Canadian firms, seeking lower tax rates, lower wages in anti-union states, and especially market penetration, are the fifth-largest purchaser of American assets, with 9% of the total foreign holdings. Canada's international competitiveness is enhanced by the fact that it is one of the cheapest places in the industrialized world to do business. This is true despite its high corporate taxes. In 2000 federal corporate rates began to be reduced from 28% to 21% over three years, below the U.S. level. In 1999 the start-up and operating costs of a business were 7.8% lower in Canada than in the U.S. A World Bank/Harvard study in 2000 placed Canada at the top of the international list for the least amount of red-tape in setting up a business.

Canada's strengths are relatively high quality and inexpensive telecommunications, a good transport network, cheap fuel, low total business travel costs, and a lack of corruption. Housing prices used to be generally lower than in the U.S., but the average home in Canada in 2011 was $345,000, higher than in the U.S. However, one of its weaknesses is that its manufacturers are only about 80% as productive as their U.S. counterparts.

The pact has helped reorient Canada's economy north–south rather than along the historical east-west lines. British Columbia looks increasingly to Washington and Oregon, Quebec to New York, the Maritimes to the American Northeast. A former Ontario premier said: "We have a stronger relationship with Michigan than any other jurisdiction around."

NAFTA

In 1991 negotiations were begun to add Mexico to a North American Free Trade Agreement (NAFTA). They began as talks between the U.S. and its southern neighbor. Although only a tiny fraction of Canada's trade in goods and services is with Mexico (about 4%), Canada feared that if it remained on the sidelines, it could be adversely affected. Its preferential access to the American market could be eroded, and trade and investment could be diverted; therefore Canada joined the talks. A trilateral agreement extending from the Yukon to the Yucatan creates an open market of 435 million people with an economic output larger than that of the European Union. Proponents say that it increases growth and makes North America more competitive with Asian and European rivals. It could also be a step toward a Western Hemisphere free trade area.

The difficulty was to knit together three economies of vastly different sizes and stages of development and with huge disparities in per capita income (in 2007 about $41,640 in the U.S., $34,480 in Canada versus only $7,180 in Mexico). Negotiations were concluded in 1992, and the three countries' leaders signed NAFTA in December.

NAFTA took effect on January 1, 1994, and was phased in over 10 years. In its first year, Canada's trade with the U.S. increased by 12% and with Mexico by 21%. Because U.S.-Canadian bilateral trade doubled from 1988 to 1999, there are few people in Canadian political circles who criticize the principle of free trade. An EKOS poll in 2002 found that three-fourths of Canadians supported free trade with the U.S. (up from 30% in 1992). In 2003 two-thirds favored stronger economic integration with the U.S, and 57% even supported an economic union along the lines of the European Union (59% of Mexicans agreed while only 44% of Americans liked this idea).

However, the strains of globalization have cut away at Americans' liking for free trade. Asked in 2007 if America has benefited from foreign trade agreements such as NAFTA, only 15% of Democrats and 20% of Republicans agreed. Hillary Clinton said in her campaign that NAFTA had "hurt a lot of American workers." Barak Obama vowed immediately to call the "president [sic] of Canada to try to amend NAFTA." However, when one of his staff met a Canadian diplomat in Chicago and told him not to worry about such election rhetoric, the information was leaked and caused confusion in Canada. Both Prime Minister Harper and Mexican President Felipe Calderón made it clear that they would not support reopening the agreement. As president, Obama dropped the talk of reopening negotiations and limited his message to bringing side agreements on labor and the environment into the text of the treaty to make them more enforceable.

In the beginning many Canadians had feared that closer integration with the American economy could threaten their social-welfare model, but that has not happened. Canadians are willing to pay the higher taxes needed to finance their generous public services. Nevertheless, conflicts continued over cultural products, wheat, potatoes, fishing, lumber, beer, steel and other things. Most trade disputes between Canada and the U.S. involve sectors shielded from NAFTA. These disagreements test the willingness of both countries to live peaceably within the rules they had accepted.

In 1995, Chile was invited to join. In 1996, Canada signed free trade agreements with both Chile and Israel, with which it conducts a modest amount of trade annually (ca. a half billion dollars each). In 1997, former Prime Minister Chrétien called for more bilateral trade agreements with Latin American countries, beginning with Brazil. It entered formal negotiations with Costa Rica in 2000, followed very quickly by free trade talks between Canada and Guatemala, Honduras, El Salvador and Nicaragua. A trade deal with Costa Rica was ratified in 2002, and a bilateral free-trade agreement was forged with Colombia in 2009.

Canada also proposed a NAFTA-EU agreement, then a Canadian-EU pact. The EU turned this down in 1999, but it agreed in 2009 to begin talks. Discussions with Japan to forge a trade pact remained fruitless. The Canadian market is too small to tempt some non-North American partners. In April 2001, Quebec City was host to 34 Western Hemispheric nations to launch the creation of a Free Trade Area of the Americas (FTAA). Canada is one of FTAA's strongest advocates, and a 2003 poll found that 69% of Canadians supported it. But it had made little progress by the end of the decade.

It may be surprising that although Canada enjoys freer trade with its NAFTA partners, there are still sizable trade barriers between Canadian provinces. Such "balkanization" is cited as an important reason for sluggish productivity growth. Two of them—Alberta and British Columbia—became so frustrated with the lack of progress toward domestic free trade that in 2007 they created the Trade, Investment and Labour Mobility Agreement (TILMA). Within two years this should eliminate

Canada

Prime Minister Harper meets with Presidents Calderón and Obama in Guadalajara

most impediments to the free flow of trade, investment and labor between them. An example of obvious improvement is that a hay wagon from one province that crosses the border into the other will no longer have to have its bales restacked in order to comply with two different arcane transportation rules. The two neighbors are the country's fastest-growing region, with 7.7 million people and a GDP of CAN$400 billion. The agreement will create Canada's second-largest economic unit after Ontario.

Strong State Role

The territorial size, low population, and hostile geography of Canada have always necessitated a greater degree of state intervention in the economy than was the case in the U.S. Canadians have always been less receptive to the notion of a *laissez-faire* market (in which the government intervenes little) and more receptive to strong government control than have Americans. As Canadian economist Dian Cohen wrote in a column in *Maclean's*, "public policy and public enterprises to activate the policies in the absence of private initiatives are even more Canadian than the beaver and the Maple Leaf. It is ironic that we Canadians spend so much time looking for ways in which we differ from Americans but overlook the one crucial characteristic that has always set us apart—an almost blind belief in the virtues of public enterprise."

Even though they differ among themselves in matters of degree, all Canadian political parties are more supportive of a strong state hand in the society and economy than either the Democratic or Republican parties in the United States. During his electoral campaign, Mulroney stressed

the *Conservative* welfare tradition. Nevertheless, in its first economic policy statement the Mulroney government had to conclude that in Canada "government has become too big."

This can be seen in a variety of forms. First, it is visible in the large number of nationalized industries, or "Crown corporations," as they are called in Canada. They can be found in virtually every aspect of Canadian life: in culture (Canada Council or the CBC, which was founded on the cry: "It's the state or The States!"); trade (Canadian Wheat Board); housing; transportation (St. Lawrence Seaway Authority, National Harbors Board); utilities (Atomic Energy of Canada, Eldorado Nuclear); industry (Sydney Steel Corporation); development (Canada Development Investment Corporation). Whereas in the United States, utilities are privately owned, but regulated by public commissions, in Canada they are publicly owned and operated.

At the top of Canada's financial world are five banks: the Royal Bank of Canada, the Bank of Montreal, the Canadian Imperial Bank of Commerce, the Bank of Nova Scotia, and Toronto Dominion Bank. Among all North American banks, all five of these are in the top 15 in market value. Although Canadian banks were not immune to the global banking crisis in 2008–9, their value fell less than in the U.S. No bank failed. In 2008 the World Economic Forum picked the country's banking system as the healthiest in the world; U.S. banks were ranked 40th. Canada's big five control 93% of the assets of the 12 national banks. In 1998, the Canadian government blocked two proposed mergers among four of these giants, calling the links "an unacceptable concentration of economic power." It would have enabled

only two banks to control 70% of all bank deposits, especially since U.S. banks are prevented from entering the Canadian market.

In general, Canada has relatively few multinational companies. On the Fortune 500 list of the world's largest companies in 2004, Canada's top entry was George Weston Ltd. in 240th place. While Sweden has Ikea and Finland Nokia, Canada does not have a single global brand.

Some Crown corporations have existed for a long time and are known to some Americans, such as the CBC; 70% of them were created since 1960. Some make a profit, but some of them are perennial money losers and are kept alive chiefly to save jobs; in fact, many were taken over in the first place because they were not able to survive on their own.

Second, Canada has a higher percentage of its GDP in government hands than does the United States. Of course, defense spending is much greater in the U.S. although it rose in both countries. In 2011 it accounted for 1.5% of GDP in Canada, after going up 9% annually for three years. If one only looks at the civilian sector, then the differences between the two countries would be even greater. Canadians pay higher taxes and have fewer write-offs. They cannot write off the interest they pay on home mortgages, whereas this is perhaps the greatest tax "loophole" in the United States. Americans can even write off the charitable contributions they give to *Canadian* charities; Canada is the only country to which the United States extends this privilege.

The annual *Maclean's*/CBC polls from 1997 to 2002 revealed that Canadians were less inclined to look to the state to solve their economic problems than they once were: they accepted the message that government deficits must be reduced if the country's long-term prosperity is to be preserved. They are willing to tolerate fundamental changes in the social safety net: 61% accept the evolution of private universities; 53% are resigned to having the government hand over some social services to charities; and 47% find the emergence of a two-tier (state and private) health-care system acceptable. Upon leaving his job at ABC in New York in 2001, Canadian Broadcaster Kevin Newman recalled a difference that remains between the two peoples: 56% of American adults do some form of volunteer work every year, compared with 32% of Canadians.

The growing trend toward individualism was confirmed in the 2002 *Maclean's*/CBC poll: 81% (compared with 71% three years earlier) thought they themselves—as opposed to government, labor unions or business leaders—were best able to take care of their economic interests. In

1997 they had given former Prime Minister Chrétien his second majority in a row even after he had declared that Canadians "know that there is nobody who will have a magic wand and solve all the problems [just by] being there."

Health and Welfare

Third, Canada has a more extensive and expensive social welfare net than does the United States. It is an ironic fact that many democratic countries that have conservative, elitist political and social traditions also have developed broad nets of social welfare. This is the case with Britain, Germany and Sweden, and it is also true of Canada. In the United States, *equality of opportunity* for the individual was a supreme value, and this required a weaker state that could not place restrictions on the individual. Canada always had a strong state, and when it became democratized, citizens demanded that it intervene on behalf of all of them to secure more *equality of results*. That is, they demanded that the state redistribute the wealth of the country so that the differences in wealth among citizens would be diminished.

The Great Depression of the 1930s gave special impetus to this. As Keith Banting observed in his book, *The Welfare State and Canadian Federalism,* "during the last half century, the Canadian state has established a new set of social rights, a set of claims for protection from the insecurities of modern society. It is deeply embedded in the fabric of Canadian life." Social welfare spending in Canada now embraces such things as pensions, disability protection, unemployment insurance, child benefits, maternity welfare, subsidized housing and free medical care.

Under the Canada Pension Plan, every Canadian has the right to receive a government pension when he or she reaches retirement age. That pension includes an automatic entitlement, as well as supplemental benefits for those who can demonstrate that they need them. Almost all employed and self-employed persons are compelled to contribute to this plan, and the payments are financed from the contributions and interest of the invested funds. Like the U.S. social security system, it is a pay-as-you-go system, meaning that current contributions are used to pay current retirees. Unlike America's, it has been put on solid financial footing for at least the next three-quarters of a century. Under the Family Allowances Act of 1944, parents with children under age 18 living at home and with low enough incomes are automatically entitled to a monthly allowance of $29.95 (which is taxable) for each child.

Canada's Medicare system, paid largely from tax sources, provides health care to

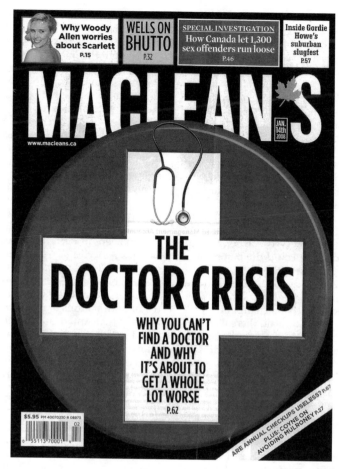

any Canadian who needs it. Patients choose their own doctors, who are not employed by the state, and they seldom see a large hospital bill. "Medically necessary" hospital treatment and doctor services are paid out of taxpayer dollars making up 71% of spending on health care in 2003. However, other medical goods and services, such as drugs dispensed outside hospitals, vision care, dental services and long-term care, are not always covered. About 30% of all health care spending comes from private pockets. Originally the federal government paid one half, but cuts greatly reduced that share to only 16% of its health dollars, with the provinces paying more and more. Health care now consumes 46% the provinces' spending (up from 35% in 1999, with prescription drugs the biggest driver of costs). This is a very expensive service. Within federal guidelines, the provinces operate their own health systems.

Canadians like this system in principle; in 2010, 69% said they were proud of their health care system. Former Governor General Adrienne Clarkson called Medicare "a practical expression of the values that define us as a country." In 2004 a television contest to determine "the greatest Canadian" picked Tommy Douglas, the earlier Saskatchewan premier who pioneered Medicare; a *Maclean's* poll a cou-

ple weeks later found that Pierre Elliot Trudeau is considered to be the greatest Canadian, either living or dead (with 22% of the votes).

Polling figures in 2002 showed that 85% of Canadians considered their health-care system better than America's, and 87% opposed making it more like that of the U.S. However, they argue about its problems and demand more funding. In 2006 the World Health Organization (WHO) ranked Canada 30th in the world, ahead of 37th-placed U.S., in terms of quality of health services. A 2010 comparative study of seven developed countries placed Canada last in terms of effective care and timeliness of care, behind the U.S. The level of government spending per capita on health care twice as high in the U.S.: $7,290 vs. $3,895 in Canada. As in the U.S., the costs of health care have ballooned; by 2005 they had climbed by a third over the past decade.

Canadians say that health care is one of their foremost worries. In 2005, 86% told pollsters that health care was a very or fairly serious problem. In the 2006 federal elections Prime Minster Stephen Harper did not propose a sweeping overhaul of Medicare, but one of his five chief campaign promises was to guarantee short waiting times for services to help the two

Canada

million Canadians on waiting lists. However, since this is a provincial responsibility, he has not been able to fulfill it.

Canada faces a crisis of spiraling health costs caused by higher pay and benefits for medical personnel, who constitute 7% of Canada's work force, soaring prices for high-tech medical equipment, and a growing number of older persons. To cope with the costs, hospitals everywhere have taken beds out of service, limited the operations performed, cut back on many services and purchases of high-tech diagnostic equipment, and reduced nursing and physician staffs. One result has been lengthening waiting lists and some highly publicized deaths of patients waiting for treatment or surgery. One exasperated patient claimed: "You could die before they know what's wrong with you!"

Asked in 2004 if their confidence in the health system was rising or falling, 6% of respondents said it was rising, and 47% said it was falling; 86% said there were not enough doctors and 81% not enough nurses. In 2005, only 23% of Canadians were able to see a doctor the same day they needed one. Five million Canadians had no family doctor in 2011. Emergency rooms were maxed out. Part of the problem is that the new generation of physicians is no longer willing to work the many hours their predecessors did. This is related to the large number of women in the healthcare profession, who must juggle work and families: 80% of the workforce is female, as are 52% of physicians under age 35.

More and more Canadians wonder if their country can afford the popular publicly funded universal system that offers one of the highest standards of health care in the world. Few Canadians, even doctors, look to the U.S. for a solution although many Americans turn to the Canadian system as worthy of imitation. Health costs in the U.S. are rising even faster, and Americans pay a higher percentage of their GDP (16%) for medical care than do Canadians (10% and rising), even though millions of Americans have no medical protection at all. Canadian doctors, who remain in the top 1% of all professional workers in terms of income, must devote a much smaller percentage of their earnings to malpractice insurance.

Canadians are seeing their drug medication prices rise because of a booming cross-border trade in pharmaceuticals. Drug prices are cheaper than in the U.S. because of the lower value of the Canadian dollar and because of price breaks from pharmaceutical companies negotiated by the Canadian government. Ottawa demands lower prices and threatens to strip away patent protection if the manufactures do not give in. Americans who need common medicines, which can often be half the price in Canada, flock across the border or use the internet to acquire at a discount the medications they need. Even many American city and state governments are turning to Canada to purchase drugs although dozens of Canadian internet pharmacies refuse to fill such bulk orders. Thus, medicines mostly produced in the U.S. but intended for Canadians are being resold at a profit in the higher-priced American market. This tightens supplies and increases prices for Canadians. Former Health Minister Ujjal Dosanjh proclaimed: "Canada cannot be the drugstore of the United States."

By almost any standard, the Canadian system keeps its citizens at least as healthy as does America's. A joint head-to-head survey in 2004 by Statistics Canada and the U.S. National Center for Health Statistics determined that the overall health status of both nations is remarkably similar. It found that Americans like their market-based health care system more than Canadians like their own Medicare, which costs less per capita. For-profit U.S. hospitals cost on average 19% more than publicly funded Canadian equivalents. Life expectancy at 79.2 for men (77.7 in U.S.) and 83.6 years for women (82.1 in U.S.) is the ninth highest in the world and slightly longer than for Americans. Infant mortality rate is 24% lower than in the U.S. Heart disease, the focus of much advanced American medical research, kills Canadians at a rate 20% lower than for Americans, despite similar dietary habits. Americans are more obese: 33% of women and 31% of men, compared with 19% of women and 17% of men in Canada; 36% of Canadians are merely "overweight," and 8% of kids are obese. At just over five feet eleven, the average Canadian-born male is nearly an inch taller than his American counterpart. More Canadians smoke regularly, but the disparities between the health of rich and poor are more pronounced in the U.S.

The Canadian approach to health care is that it cannot be left to market forces. In 2001 Canada became the first country to allow terminally ill patients to grow and smoke their own marijuana in order to alleviate their pain. All they need is a doctor's certificate. The government also began gearing up to supply patients and researchers. This did not extend to recreational use of the drug. Two-thirds (63%) of Canadians told pollsters in 2006 that they favored legalization. A government report revealed in 2004 that marijuana use in Canada had nearly doubled in the previous 13 years.

A basic principle in health care benefits, as well as in other benefits such as family allowances, is *universality*, meaning that *all* Canadians can receive them, regardless of wealth and/or income. During his 1984 electoral campaign, Mulroney called such universality "a sacred trust." The daunting costs of the social welfare system caused his government to reconsider after the election, but public pressure on the government was so great that Mulroney was forced to back off from any attempt to tamper with this fundamental principle.

The soaring costs and federal cuts sparked demands that fundamental changes be made in health care and the welfare system. In 1994, Ontario ended health coverage for thousands of foreign students and immigrants with temporary residence authorization. Some provinces refuse to cover bills for Canadians visiting from other regions of Canada. Provinces imposed three-month waiting periods before new residents can be covered, and coverage abroad was limited. Certain operations, such as vasectomy reversals, that were once paid, are no longer free. In 2004 Ontario imposed a new healthcare tax while removing coverage for physiotherapy, chiropractic and eye tests. In the same year Vancouver's St. Paul's Hospital contracted out 947 publicly funded surgeries to three private clinics. Private health care had already slipped into the door. In 2004, almost a third of all money spent on health care had been paid for out of private pockets. Private clinics were springing up everywhere.

The ground was thereby set for the kind of private services and insurance approved by the Supreme Court in a landmark ruling in June 2005. The justices struck down a Quebec law that banned private medical insurance and ordered the province to enact a reform within a year. It ruled that long waits for various medical procedures violate patients' lives and freedom and that prohibitions on private health insurance were unconstitutional when the public system failed to deliver "reasonable services."

This ruling generated calls for more private clinics and insurance in several provinces beyond Quebec, which already had about 50 private health clinics even before the court decision. There were dozens of such clinics in Alberta and BC. But they were primarily limited to services not covered by Medicare. Polls in 2004 had indicated that Canadians are very wary about their health-care system and are open to change as long as there is no resort to higher co-payments and personal wealth to get timely care. A year later 59% of respondents supported the Supreme Court ruling; a further 59% indicated their support for Alberta's proposal permitting payment out-of-pocket for service enhancements, like better prosthetic joints; and a majority believed that private insurance would reduce waiting times and have a positive effect on Medicare as a whole.

BC and Alberta were leading the way to more private care. The BC government is eying a system in which it would pay for essential treatment delivered in both public and private clinics and hospitals. Albertans are discussing legislation to permit doctors to practice simultaneously in private and public institutions and to permit the construction of private hospitals. Even the widely-read weekly newsmagazine *Maclean's* devoted an entire issue on May 1, 2006, to advising Canadians on all the private care offerings in their country.

The level of care varies from region to region and from city to rural locales. Attempting to eliminate the federal deficit, Ottawa took billions of dollars out of the system, amounting to an 8.7% reduction from 1985–95. This left the difficult decisions to the provinces, which passed many of them on to local governments. The federal government thereby abdicated its right to insist on maintaining national standards. In effect, there is no longer a national Medicare system.

Ottawa was under intense pressure to return to the provinces the money it had taken from health care, so in 2000 the federal budget boosted such spending by 25%. Seeking a legacy in his final year in office, outgoing Prime Minister Chrétien ordered in 2003 that over $9 billion more be spent over three years to improve diagnostic equipment, primary and home care, and drug coverage. Paul Martin's 2004 and 2005 budgets continued these increases.

The biggest health scare in 2003 was the spread of a mysterious respiratory disease, Severe Acute Respiratory Syndrome (SARS), to Canada. Because of its close links with China, Toronto became the population center most affected by the deadly virus outside of Asia. The WHO felt compelled to issue a travel advisory twice for Toronto, an embarrassing and economically damaging move the city's mayor called outrageous. Toronto accounts for 20% of Canada's economic growth and tourism is the city's second-largest industry after finance. SARS seriously blemished Toronto's image as a safe place to visit and live even though the city won praise for the way it handled the crisis. The illness claimed 31 lives in the city (44 in Ontario). An investigative commission issued a report in 2007 that the disease spread because of a shoddy public health system and inadequate safety practices. Almost three-fourths of the victims became infected in clinics and hospitals.

In 2004 British Columbia experienced an outbreak of an avian influenza, which was fortunately not the kind that could infect humans and animals. Nevertheless,

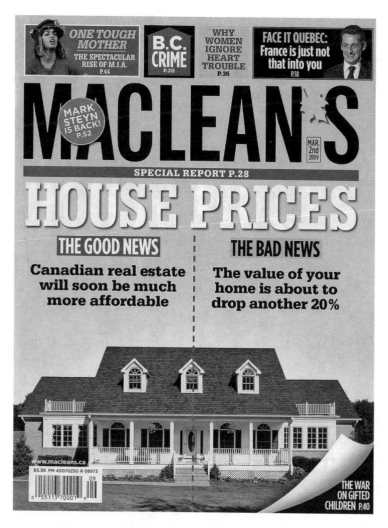

38 countries, including the U.S., imposed bans on poultry products from BC, and 19 million chickens, turkeys and other poultry had to be killed in order to prevent the flu from spreading.

The erosion of the Canadian health system shows the risks of making health care dependent upon taxes. When budget deficits have to be reduced, and political pressure makes tax increases impossible, health and welfare programs become targets for cuts. The earlier Reform and Alliance Parties' success since 1993 demonstrated the appeal in Canada of attacking government waste and abuse by overhauling social programs and holding the line on taxes. The rapid rise in taxes from 31.6% of GDP in 1980 to 36.8% in 1999 (compared with 29% in the U.S.) provoked a near tax revolt. The difference is particularly pronounced in income taxes: at middle-income levels, an American pays about half the income tax a Canadian pays. But 40% of Canadians pay no income tax at all, and the lowest rate is 15%. Those in the top income bracket pay from 39% in Alberta to 48% in Quebec, compared with a top of 37% in the U.S. The

high taxes have driven some wealthy Canadians, such as singer Shania Twain, billionaire Michael DeGroote and auto magnate Frank Stronach, to establish residency in lower tax jurisdictions, such as Bermuda or Switzerland. In 2008 the federal goods and services tax fell to 5%.

While Canadians remain devoted to their safety net, they are demanding that their governments end what seems to be a built-in incentive for Canadians to resort to welfare and unemployment. In 1999, Ottawa responded by providing a modest tax break. This was continued in 2000, when the federal government announced sweeping tax cuts, indexing tax brackets to inflation to eliminate "bracket creep," and increasing child tax benefits. Canadians often find welfare policy models in the U.S. In 2007 the federal government proposed a Working Income Tax Benefit to make work more appealing than welfare. This is practically a carbon copy of America's Earned Income Tax Credit.

There seems to be an emerging consensus that many social programs have failed to solve the problems of those who need them most, while bestowing benefits on

Canada

many for whom they were never intended. From 1981 to 1995 the number of Canadians on social assistance doubled. Some programs have perhaps even hurt those whom they were designed to help by fostering dependency. Inadequate retraining has been provided. Many provinces are clamoring for the right to introduce their own reforms while demanding more federal assistance to pay for them.

This, however, undermines a fundamental tenet of Canadian federalism—uniform standards of social services across the country. Since many Canadians regard their social security net as one of the country's hallmarks which helps define their national identity, any attempt to overhaul it arouses fierce opposition and intense struggles among competing interests. But with a half-trillion-dollar national debt hanging over their heads, politicians find it harder to sweep the problems under the rug.

Canada's social welfare system has not eradicated poverty. As in the U.S., the gap between rich and poor is widening in the new century. This development challenges deeply held assumptions about Canada as a place where U.S.-style extremes of wage and income distribution do not exist and where the safety net is adequate for all. The number of children living in 2010 below the poverty line (defined as a household in which income is half the national median) was 10%, a proportion that has remained steady over the preceding 15 years. The OECD in 2010 ranked Canada 22d of 31 rich countries in this regard, ahead of the U.S.

About 300,000 Canadians are homeless, including more families with young children. The number of people using food banks was 900,000 in 2010, a 9% increase in one year and 92% increase from 1991–2001. Single mothers are especially hard hit: a federal report in 2001 concluded that it took 75.4 weeks of work—the equivalent of 1.5 full-time jobs at an average wage—to cover a family's basic expenses. Specific goals announced in the 1980s to eliminate child poverty by 2000 are no longer mentioned.

The number of homeless persons who trudge with their few belongings from soup kitchen to hostel has doubled in Canadian cities since the 1980s. Observers estimate that 100,000 people lack shelter on any given day. Despite the magnitude of social welfare benefits and income guarantees, Canadians are still vulnerable to the ups and downs of the economy. Poverty has not been a major political issue in Canada, probably because it still does not have a high enough visibility to prompt the government to try to act on it.

The federal and provincial governments share responsibility for social welfare pol-

icy; it has therefore become a major source of conflict between Ottawa and the provinces. These issues have been at the heart of many a struggle concerning the distribution of power among the various governments of Canada. Social welfare spending was a major contributor to staggeringly high federal and provincial budget deficits. As the federal and most provincial governments balanced their budgets, welfare spending declined.

As in the U.S., there is a widespread fear that the economic rules are permanently and profoundly changing and that government is unwilling and unable to help. Fewer and fewer Canadians are optimistic about the future or believe that their lives will become steadily more prosperous, or that their children's wealth will surpass their own. They fear that their governments will no longer be able to fund their health care, pensions, and other social services that they now view as entitlements.

Transfer payments sustain public services in all "have-not" provinces. Only British Columbia, Alberta and more recently Saskatchewan and Newfoundland qualify as "have" provinces. Newfoundland has used some its new-found oil and mining wealth to reduce its poverty rate in half to 6.5%. Ontario slipped into the "have-not" category. Beginning in 1996 federal transfer payments to the provinces for social programs were converted into block grants and reduced by 4%. Provinces, most of which are also trying to balance their budgets, have no alternative to reducing their services.

Current Economic Situation

The accumulated national debt stands at 82% of GDP, sharply up from 65% in 2007 and the highest since 2007. Paying the interest on this debt is one of the federal government's largest single expenditures, greater than its spending on health care, family allowances, old-age pensions and social assistance combined. When the indebtedness of the 10 provinces (except largely debt-free Alberta) is added, the total debt is larger than the economy itself. This is high among industrialized nations, and from a third to half of that debt is in foreign hands. The government's spending cuts and rigorous budget deficit reduction left little room for new and expensive programs. Canada succeeded in eliminating its budget deficits after 1998, but in 2011 it stood at 3.4% of GDP, far below that of the U.S.

Due to the global financial crisis that began in the fall of 2008, the government was forced in the fiscal year of 2009–10 to end 12 years of budget surpluses. By 2009 the economy had shrunk by an annualized rate of 3.4%, a year later by 1.2%.

However, Canada's recession was the mildest downturn in three decades, and by 2011 growth was humming at 2.9%. Inflation rose to 3.3% in 2011, and unemployment declined to 7.6%, impressively lower than 9% in the U.S.

Home prices by 2009 had declined by 25% in the U.S., but only half as much in Canada. By 2011, while American housing was still in the doldrums, the Canadian housing market was soaring on low mortgage rates to a record high of $345,000 on average (up from $158,000 in 1999). Some economists believe house prices are almost as overvalued as they were in America at the height of the housing bubble. Vancouver, which *The Economist* selected in 2011 as the world's most livable city (with Toronto and Calgary also ranked in the top five), was the most expensive housing market, with a median house price of $540,900. Two-thirds (68.4%) of Canadians have their own homes, compared with 66.4% south of the border.

Some provinces, such as Alberta, faced serious labor shortages. However, youth unemployment (under 24 years) still was high, and regional joblessness was as high as 13% in newly oil-rich Newfoundland.

The temporary economic downturn in the U.S. following September 11, 2001, inevitably hurt Canada, but it did not drag the country into recession. This was the first time in a quarter century that Canada avoided being pulled down by America. Canadians had not invested as heavily in high-technology companies, and they had just 45% of their wealth in stocks before the bubble burst, while American households had 63% in the stock market. The result by 2003 was that household net worth in Canada was down just 6% from the peak, compared with a plunge of 27% in the U.S.

High world prices for oil and gas are a boon for the country with the world's second largest oil reserves and helped increase Canada's diplomatic and economic influence in the world. For instance, it elevates Canada to a higher priority in the eyes of the U.S. government. Canadians lead the world in internet use, with 48% of households connected, compared with 43% in the U.S. Recently, 85% of Canadians still believed their quality of life is superior to that of Americans. A 2007 poll revealed that 91% of Americans believed they would have a better quality of life if they moved to Canada.

Productivity is lower in Canada. In 2007 output per man-hour was 79% of America's, and there are reasons for this. In general the U.S. economy remains more productive in part because of its investments in technology and education. Canada spends less than half as much on research and development; business investment in R&D especially lags. It devotes much less on higher education and training; since 1993 the U.S. increased the annual spending on education by 3.3%, compared with .2% for Canada. Investment per worker in machinery and equipment, especially in information technologies, is only 60% of the American level.

The productivity gap is partly explained by the facts that the average Canadian works 157 fewer hours per year, amounting to a full month. He takes 3.9 weeks of vacation compared with two weeks for his American counterpart. He also retires earlier at age 61. In the World Economic Forum's annual rankings of most competitive countries, Canada has slipped from sixth in 1998 to tenth in 2008.

Measured in terms of per capita GDP, Canada's living standard is one fifth below that of the U.S. Using purchasing power parity, the gap is 13%. After adjusting for currency and purchasing power, the median Canadian household has a net worth of US$122,260, compared with US$93,100 south of the border. Canadians live in slightly smaller houses (2,000 vs. 2,434 sq. feet). Nevertheless, only 19% of Canadians thought in 2007 that Americans had a better standard of living than they did; 53% did not think that a gap would make any difference in their lives. An impressive 72% were satisfied with their living standard as it was.

That satisfaction did not necessarily extend into the future. In a 2007 poll, 45% of Canadians did not believe the next generation would be able to afford a better standard of living, and only 26% thought it would continue to get better. A slight boost for optimism came in December 2009 when the recession was officially declared to have ended. But not all Canadians felt like the recession has passed. In a 2011 poll, 35.4% of respondents pointed to the economy as the most pressing issue facing Canada; 21% said poverty, Afghanistan and national unity; 18.9% named the federal budget deficit, and 12.9% the aging population. In a subsequent RBC report, 45% said rising food and gas prices significantly impacted their budgets.

Canada tried to rebrand its economy in the 1990s as high-tech. But the contemporary foundation of its economy is a familiar one: natural resources, particularly oil and mining, albeit technologically sophisticated. When world, and especially Chinese, demand keeps commodity prices high, Canada will be able to look forward to a strong economy and currency.

FUTURE

A SES survey in 2005 revealed that, despite their political differences, Canadians and Americans think a lot more alike about important things and are, in fact, closer than one might think. They want to work closely with each other on such matters as counter-terrorism and still define their two nations more by their similarities than by their differences. Asked which country is most like their own in terms of human rights, Canadians picked the U.S. more than any other (43%), and 51% of Americans chose Canada. While 51% of Americans believed that self-interest should guide a country's decision making, 61% of Canadians held that view.

Canadians are as determined as ever to preserve their sovereignty and their independence of action. But they accept the need for greater security along the border, increased police cooperation with U.S. authorities, common policies on immigration and refugees, and even restrictions on some of their personal freedoms in order to meet the terrorist threat. Positive sentiments are stronger today, with President Barack Obama enjoying in February 2009 an approval rating in Canada of 82%.

Canadians have developed a certain boldness in social matters that sets them off somewhat from Americans. For example, more of them supported court-mandated same-sex marriage. In the 2006 *Maclean's* Canada Day Poll, 70% of women and 61% of men said they approved of homosexuality, and 56% and 39% indicated that they approved of gay marriage. Overall, 61% accepted or approved the idea of gay couples adopting children. The House of Commons voted gay marriage into law in July 2005.

This social liberalism points to an increasingly self-confident country. These social issues join gun control and health care in solidifying a Canadian sense of separateness from the U.S. However, in terms of health care, Canadians will continue to move progressively toward a dual public and private system.

Two dramatic changes have taken place in Quebec. The first is a young federal Conservative leader from the West, Stephen Harper, who speaks French confidently and often, and who has shown a genuine interest in the needs and concerns of Quebec. The second is that *Québécois* seem to accept Canada more than they used to. Only 2% of them considered national unity a major issue. As the most socially liberal Canadians, *Québécois* like the social experimentalism they see in Canada, such as gay marriage, abortion and legalization of marijuana: 69% endorsed the statement that they are proud of what Canada is becoming "because it shows what a socially progressive and diverse country we live in." The figure in the rest of Canada was 54%.

From being the most pro-American Canadians, *Québécois* have become perhaps the most skeptical of the foreign and social policies pursued by the United States— 60% said their attitude toward the U.S. had become more negative in recent years, compared with just under half of Canadians as a whole. The popularity of the current American president is bound to lessen this animosity.

A final reason for this unprecedented *Québécois* embrace of common Canadian values is the confidence *Québécois* now have that their language and culture are more firmly entrenched than ever before. In the May 2011 federal elections, the *Bloc Québécois* was wiped out in the province, winning only four lonely seats in the House of Commons, far short of the number required to constitute an official parliamentary party. In contrast, the PQ improved its standing in the December 2008 provincial elections because its new leader, Pauline Marois, put the independence issue into the deep freeze. To attain party unity in 2011, she promised the faithful to speak more about language protection and eventual sovereignty although she did not dare name a time for a referendum on the issue. Quebec separatism remains in deep slumber.

By federal election day, May 2, 2011, Canadians were tired of five years of minority governments and gave Stephen Harper's Conservatives the parliamentary majority he had always wanted: 167 of the total 308

Prime Minister Stephen Harper

Canada

parliamentary seats. By linking the West with Ontario, he has brought about a durable party realignment. The surprise dark horse was the New Democratic Party (NDP), which under the able and genial leadership of Jack Layton, captured an astonishing 103 seats (up from 37), including 58 in Quebec (up from only one). For the first time, the NDP assumed the position as official opposition. But it will face a major challenge in maintaining cohesion and common purpose among 103 vastly diverse members of parliament, most of whom had never set foot in the House of Commons.

The Liberal Party suffered the worst defeat in its history and declined to an embarrassing 34 seats (down from 77). It failed to win one out of five voters, and was unceremoniously ejected from Quebec, one of its prior strongholds. Party leader Michael Ignatieff immediately resigned leaving the party rudderless as it faces an uncertain future. Former Ontario Premier Bob Rae will be a competent interim Liberal leader.

Harper has proven to be an astute leader with excellent political instincts. He plans carefully, displays and demands discipline, seeks constantly to expand his party's seats, and focuses on accomplishing a few promised goals rather than dozens of scattered objectives, as did his predecessor. He soft-peddles polarizing social issues, such as gay marriage, abortion or the death penalty.

With his new majority, he can be expected to honor his pledges to continue support of Alberta's oil sands industry, cut sales and corporate taxes (the latter from 21% to 15%), introduce a series of law-and-order bills he could not enact with a minority government, shut down a disputed registry for rifles, end government subsidies for political parties, pay down the federal debt and introduce a balanced business-friendly budget. One thing he will not try again is to change the wording of the national anthem, *O Canada*. Such a public outcry erupted when his government suggested this in 2006 that it beat a hasty retreat. Canada has done well under his economic stewardship. It suffered a milder recession and much lower unemployment than the U.S.

The country has benefited from a well-regulated banking system, growing Asian markets and high world prices for Canada's natural resources.

Harper cuts a statesman-like figure in summits, and he has gained visibility and respect in the United States and Europe. He is comfortable and confident in his management of Canada's foreign policy. He had already changed the tone in dealings with the United States, whom he calls "our best friend" even before President Obama's election and triumphant six-hour visit to Ottawa in February 2009. This is made easier by an American president more popular in Canada than Harper himself.

Both countries will realize in 2012 how much enmity they have overcome as they commemorate the bicentennial of the War of 1812. This conflict was tactfully mentioned by Governor General David Johnston in his first Throne Speech in early June 2012. He reminded his countrymen that the United States is Canada's most important trading partner and ally.

Harper pleased many Canadians and Americans alike by moving his government back toward a muscular foreign policy that truly reflects Canadian values and makes Canada a recognized player on the world stage. That involved a serious combat commitment to neutralize the insurgency in Afghanistan. A majority of Canadians oppose continued engagement in Afghanistan. The government will fulfill its promise to withdraw all Canadian combat troops by the end of 2011, leaving up to 1,000 to train Afghan security forces and assist with Canadian humanitarian missions. Its fighter jets and one frigate participate in NATO's enforcement of a no-fly zone over Libya. The government will continue persistently to assert Canadian sovereignty in the Arctic.

After proroguing parliament for two months until the throne speech on March 3, 2010, the prime minister's popularity suffered. Perhaps Harper was saved politically by the Winter Olympics in Vancouver. He was the chief fan for the victorious Canadian men's and women's hockey teams and basked in the glow of the thrilling sudden-death 3-2 victory of the Canadian men over their American rivals in the last event. Canada stunned the sporting world by winning more gold medals than any nation had ever won in the Winter Games. The world was treated to a rare glimpse of boisterous, flag-waving Canadian patriotism. Polls showed that Harper had widened his personal approval ratings during the Games. Shortly before the hockey final, 37% of voters said they favored the Conservatives compared with 29% for the Liberals. Only in Canada could this happen.

Web Sites and Bibliography of Key English-Language Books

WEB SITES

www.canoe.ca and www.Yahoo.ca (Canadian search engines.)

www.canadianembassy.org (This site is a key source containing a search engine, an issues menu, many links, a virtual reference desk and a virtual tour of the Canadian embassy in Washington.)

www.ambassadeducanada.org (All of the above functions in French)

www.usembassycanada.org (Site for US embassy in Ottawa with reports and information)

www.canada.gc.ca (General Web site for information on Canada from the Canadian government. See links.)

www.cbc.ca (Web site for the Canadian Broadcasting Corporation. This is an excellent current source for all aspects of Canadian news, with numerous links. See also www.cbc.ca/newsworld/)

www.ctv.ca (Broad Canadian reporting)

www.radio-canada.ca/nouvelles (French-language news)

www.elections.ca (election results. Phone: 1-800-463-6868)

www.pm.gc.ca (Web site for Canadian prime minister's office. By substituting the first letters of other ministries, access to other ministries' Web sites can be gained. See below.)

www.fin.gc.ca (Web site for Canadian Finance Ministry)

www.strategis.ic.gc.ca (Industry Canada)

www.dfait-maeci.gc.ca (Web site for Department of Foreign Affairs and International Trade)

www.cfp-pec.gc.ca (Web site of Canadian Centre for Foreign Policy Development. See many links. For peacekeeping, add: /peacekeeping/menu-e.asp. For additional links, add: /y2k. For magazine, add: /Canada-magazine)

www.cbsa.asfc.gc.ca (Canada Border Services Agency)

www.cic.gc.ca (Citizenship and Immigration Canada)

http://www.mapleleafweb.com/main.shtml (Central site for Canadian affairs)

www.canschool.org (Web site for many aspects of Canadians in the World)

www.citizens.ca (Site for information relating to who Canadians are; description of people)

www.gov.nu.ca (Site for Nunavut)

http://parkscanada.gc.ca (Parks Canada site)

www.travelcanada.ca

www.liberal.ca (Liberal Party site)

www.conservative.ca (Conservative Party site)

www.ndp.ca (National Democratic Party site)

www.bloc.ca (Bloc Québécois party site)

www.greenparty.ca (Green Party site)

www.un.org (Web site for United Nations. Many links.)

www.nato.org (Web site for NATO. Many links.)

www.chatelaine.com (Web site for *Chatelaine* weekly Canadian magazine. In English and French.)

www.macleans.ca (Web site for *Maclean's* weekly Canadian news magazine)

www.mh-education.com (*Maclean's* educational Web site. See links.)

www.GlobeAndMail.ca (Respected Canadian national newspaper)

www.nationalpost.com (Respected Canadian national newspaper)

www.torontostar.com (Respected Canadian national newspaper)

www.ottawa citizen.com (Respected Canadian national newspaper)

www.montrealgazette.com (Respected Canadian national newspaper)

www.winnipegfreepress.com (Respected Canadian national newspaper)

www.vancouversun.com (Respected Canadian national newspaper)

www.ledevoir.com (Respected Quebec French-language newspaper)

www.candacalling.com (Prior Smith's five-minute Canadian newscasts)

www.cyberpress.com (Canadian news)

www.iam.ca (Humorous Web site for Molson beer's Canadian nationalism commercial)

www.economist.com (Respected British news weekly with some coverage of Canadian affairs)

www.chicagotribune.com (Respected U.S. newspaper with some coverage of Canadian affairs. Named best overall US newspaper online service for newspapers with circulation over 100,000.)

www.csmonitor.com (Respected U.S. newspaper, *Christian Science Monitor*, with some coverage of Canadian affairs. Named best overall US newspaper online service for newspapers with circulation under 100,000.)

www.nytimes.com (Respected U.S. newspaper, *The New York Times*, with some coverage of Canadian affairs)

www.washingtonpost.com (Respected U.S. newspaper with some coverage of Canadian affairs)

www.washingtontimes.com (Respected U.S. newspaper with some coverage of Canadian affairs)

www.canada.plattsburgh.edu (The Center for the Study of Canada at the State University of New York Plattsburgh maintains the major Web site for Canadian Studies. E-mail address: CANADA-ACSUS@Plattsburgh.EDU. Search also for Association for Canadian Studies in the U.S.—ACSUS.)

philippe.premont@dfait=maeci.gc.ca (New-scan E-mail of Weekly Canadian news summaries)

I. GENERAL

Beach, Richard, ed. *O Canada, its geography, history and the people who call it home.* 2d rev. ed. Plattsburgh, NY: Center for the Study of Canada, 2000.

Berton, Pierre. *Why We Act Like Canadians. A Personal Exploration of Our National Character.* Toronto: McClelland and Stewart, 1982.

——. *Hollywood's Canada.* Nd.

Black, Peter. *Canada Matters: Chronicles of a Northern Neighbour.* Plattsburgh, NY: Center for the Study of Canada, 2002.

Ricker, Darrell and John Wright. *What Canadians Think.* Toronto: Doubleday, 2005.

Callwood, June. *Portrait of Canada.* Garden City, NY: Doubleday, 1981.

The Canadian Encyclopedia, 2d ed., 4 vols. Edmonton: Hurtig, 1988.

——. *The Canadian Pocket Encyclopedia.* Vancouver, BC: CanExpo, annual edition.

Center for the Study of Canada. *Occasional Paper Series.* See also its annual *Teaching Canada.* Its 2002 volume (21) is entitled *Canada & The World.* Plattsburgh: State University of New York. (Phone: 518-564-2086).

Crowley, Jason Clemons and Niels Veldhuis. *The Canadian Century. Moving Out of America's Shadow.* 2010.

Dermer, Jerry, ed. *The Canadian Profile. People, Institutions, Infrastructure.* North York, Ont: Captus Press, 1992.

DePalma, Anthony. *Here: A Biography of the North American Continent.* New York: HarperCollins, 2001.

Gould, Karen, Jockel, Joseph T. and Metcalf, William, eds. *Northern Exposures. Scholarship on Canada in the United States.* Washington, D.C.: Association for Canadian Studies in the United States, 1993.

Hobson, Archie. *The Cambridge Gazetteer of the United States and Canada. A Dictionary of Places.* New York: Cambridge University Press, 1995.

Joyce, William W. and Richard Beach. *Introducing Canada. Current Backgrounders, Strategies, and Resources for Educators.* Washington D.C.: National Council for Social Studies, 1997.

Malcolm, Andrew H. *The Canadians.* New York: Times Books, 1985.

Mathews, Robin. *Canadian Identity. Major Forces Shaping the Life of a People.* Ottawa: Steel Rail Educational Publishing, 1988.

Metcalfe, William, ed. *Understanding Canada. A Multi-disciplinary Introduction to Canadian Studies.* New York: New York University Press, 1982.

Olive, David. *Canada Inside Out: How We See Ourselves/How Others See Us.* New York: Bantam, 1996.

Pryke, Kenneth G. and Soderlund, Walter C. *Profiles of Canada.* Toronto: Copp Clark Pitman, 1992.

Richler, Noah. *This is My Country, What's Yours?* Toronto: McClelland & Stewart, 2006.

Roste, Vaughn. *The Xenophobe's Guide to the Canadians.* London: Oval Books, 2004.

Sabin, Louis. *Canada.* Mahwah, NJ: Troll Associates, 1985.

Sherman, George. *O Canada. Its Geography, History and the People Who Call It Home.* Plattsburgh, NY: Center for the Study of Canada, 1994.

Taras, David, et al. *A Passion for Identity.* 2d ed. Scarborough, Ont: Nelson, 1992.

The 1997 Corpus Almanac & Canadian Sourcebook. Don Mills, Ont.: Southam Magazine & Information Group, 1997.

II. BIOGRAPHIES AND AUTOBIOGRAPHIES

Ayre, John. *Northrop Frye.* Vintage Books, 1990.

Boyden, Joseph. *Extraordinary Canadians: Louis Riel and Gabriel Dumont.* Toronto: Penguin, 2009.

Brown, R.C. *Robert Laird Borden: A Biography.* 2 vols. Toronto: 1975, 1980.

Cayley, David. *Northrop Frye in Conversation.* Donn Mills, Ont: Anansi, 1992.

Charlesbois, Peter. *The Life of Louis Riel.* Toronto: NC, 1975.

Chretién, Jean. *Straight from the Heart.* Toronto: Key Porter, 1985.

——. *My Years As Prime Minister.* 2007

Clarkson, Adrienne. *Heart Matters.* Toronto: Penguin, 2006.

Cohen, Andrew and J.L Granatstein, eds. *Trudeau's Shadow. The Life and Legacy of Pierre Elliott Trudeau.* Toronto: Vintage, 1999.

Creighton, Donald. *John A. Macdonald.* 2 vols. Toronto: Macmillan, 1968.

Delacourt, Susan. *Juggernaut: Paul Martin's Campaign for Chrétien's Crown.* Toronto: McClelland & Stewart, 2003.

Diefenbaker, John G. *One Canada.* 3 vols. Toronto: Macmillan, 1975–1977.

English, John. *The Worldly Years of Lester Pearson 1949–1972.* Toronto: Alfred A. Knopt, 1993.

Ferns, Henry and Ostry, Bernard. *The Age of Mackenzie King.* Toronto: James Lorimer, 1976.

Flanagan, Thomas. *Louis "David" Riel: Prophet of the New World.* Toronto: University of Toronto Press, 1979.

——. *Harper's Team: Behind the Scenes in the Conservative Rise to Power.* 2007.

Foran, Charles. *Extraordinary Canadians: Maurice Richard.* Toronto: Penguin, 2011.

Fraser, Graham. *PQ: Réne Lévesque and the Parti Quebecois.*

Garr, Allen. *Tough Guy: Bill Bennett and the Taking of British Columbia.* Toronto: Key Porter, 1985.

Gillen, Mollie. *Lucy Maud Montgomery.* Markham, Ont: Fitzhenry Whiteside, n.d.

Gwyn, Richard. *The Northern Magnus. Pierre Trudeau and Canadians.* Markham, Ont.: Paper Jacks, 1981.

——. *John A.: The Man Who Made Us.* (About John A. Macdonald). 2007.

Harcourt, Michael, with Wayne Skene. *A Measure of Defiance.* Vancouver, BC: Douglas & McIntyre, 1996.

Ignatieff, Michael. *True Patriot Love. Four Generations in Search of Canada.* Viking Canada, 2009.

Johnson, William. *Stephen Harper and the Future of Canada.* Toronto: McClelland and Stewart, 2005.

Lam, Vincent. *Extraordinary Canadians: Tommy Douglas.* Toronto: Penguin, 2011.

Lévesque, Réne. *Memoirs.* Toronto: Cross Canada Books, 1986.

McNaught, Kenneth. *A Prophet in Politics. A Biography of J.S. Woodsworth,* Toronto: University of Toronto Press, 1959.

MacDonald, L. Ian. *Brian Mulroney. The Making of the Prime Minister.* Toronto: McClelland and Stewart, 1987.

MacNeil, Robert. *Looking for my Country. Finding Myself in America.* Toronto: Vintage Canada, 2002.

Martin, Laurence. *The Antagonist: Lucien Bouchard and the Politics of Delusion.* Toronto: Viking, 1997.

Martin, Paul. *Hell or High Water.* 2008.

McIlroy, Thad, ed. *A Rose is a Rose: A Tribute to Pierre Elliott Trudeau in Cartoons and Quotes.* Toronto: Doubleday, 1984.

Morison, Samuel Eliot. *Samuel Champlain, Father of New France.* Boston: Little Brown, 1972.

Mulroney, Brian. *Where I Stand.* Toronto: McClelland and Stewart, 1983.

Neatby, H.B. *William Lyon Mackenzie King.* 3 vols. Toronto: 1963, 1976.

Manning, Preston. *The New Canada.* Toronto: Macmillan, 1992.

Pearson, L.B. *Mike: The Memoirs of the Rt. Hon. Lester B. Pearson.* vol. I, 1897–1948; vol. II, 1948–1957; vol. III, 1957–68. Toronto: 1972–75.

Pelletier, Gerard. *Years of Impatience.* New York: Facts on File, 1984.

Pickersgill, J. W. *My Years with Louis St. Laurent.* Toronto: 1975.

Pratte, André. *Extraordinary Canadians: Wilfrid Laurier.* Toronto: Penguin, 2011.

Radwanski, George. *Trudeau.* Agincourt, Ont: Signet, 1978.

Rae, Bob. *From Protest to Power: Personal Reflections on a Life in Politics.* Toronto: Viking/Penguin, 1996.

Richards, David Adams. *Lord Beaverbrook.* Toronto: Penguin Group (Canada), 2008.

Ross, Catherine S. *Alice Munro.* Toronto: ECW Press, 1992.

Saul, John Ralson. *Extraordinary Canadians: Louis Hippolyte LaFontaine and Robert Baldwin.* Toronto: Penguin, 2010.

Sawatsky, John. *Mulroney. The Politics of Ambition.* Don Mills, Ont: Stoddart, 1991.

Schull, J. *Laurier: The First Canadian.* Toronto: 1966.

Stanley, G. *Louis Riel.* Toronto: 1963.

Sweeny, A. *George-Etienne Cartier: A Biography.* Toronto: 1976.

Thomson, D. *Alexander Mackenzie: Clear Grit.* Toronto: 1960.

Thomson, D.C. *Louis St. Laurent: Canadian.* Toronto: 1967.

Urquhart, Jane. *Extraordinary Canadians: L.M. Montgomery.* Penguin Group (Canada), 2009.

Young, B. *George-Etienne Cartier: Montreal Bourgeois.* Montreal and London: 1981.

Penguin Group (Canada) launched in 2008 a three-year *Extraordinary Canadians* series, edited by Ralston Saul and composed of 20 Canadian biographies by notable Canadian novelists and authors. The biographies are lively and important stories told by talented writers, not ponderous academic works.

III. HISTORY

Allan, Ralph. *Ordeal By Fire. Canada, 1910–1945.* Toronto: Doubleday, 1961.

Anderson, Fred. *Crucible of War. The Seven Years War and the Fate of Empire in British North America, 1754–1766.* Toronto: Vintage Books, 2001.

Baldwin, Douglas and Odnyak, Emily. *Canada's Political Heritage.* Regina: Weigl Educational Publishers, Ltd., 1985.

Beal, Bob and Macleod, Rod. *Prairie Fire. The 1885 North West Rebellion.* Edmonton, Alb.: Hurtig, 1984.

Bercuson, David J. *Canada and the Burden of Unity.* Toronto: Copp Clark Pittman, Ltd. 1985.

Berger, Carl. *Contemporary Approaches to Canadian History.* Toronto: Copp Clark Pittman, 1987.

Bernier, Serge. *The Royal 22e Regiment, 1919–1999.* Montreal: Art Global, 2000.

Berton, Pierre. *My Country. The Remarkable Past.* Toronto: Seal Books, 1979.

——. *The Invasion of Canada 1812–1813.* Toronto: McClelland and Stewart, 1980.

——. *The Great Depression, 1929–1939.* Markham, Ont: McClelland Stewart, 1990.

——. *Marching as to War. Canada's Turbulent Years 1899–1953.* Toronto: Doubleday Canada, 2001.

Bird, Harrison. *Attack on Quebec: The American Invasion of Canada 1775.* New York: Oxford University Press, 1968.

Bothwell, Robert and Drummond, Ian, and English, John. *Canada Since 1945.* Toronto: University of Toronto Press, 1989.

Broadfoot, Barry. *The Pioneer Years 1895–1914. Memories of Settlers Who Opened the West.* Toronto, Garden City, NY: Doubleday, 1976.

Brown, Craig. *The Illustrated History of Canada.* Toronto: Lester, 1991.

Buckner, Phillip A. *The Transition to Responsible Government: British Policy in British North America, 1815–1850.* Westport, CT: Greenwood, 1985.

Bumstead, J.M., *The Peoples of Canada.* Vol 1: *A Pre-Confederation History.* Vol 2: *A Post-Confederation History.* Don Mills, Ont: Oxford University Press, 1992.

Canadian History. A Readers Guide. 2 volumes: *Beginnings to Confederation,* ed. by M. Brook Taylor, and *Confederation to the Present,* ed. by Doug Owram. Toronto: University of Toronto Press, 1994.

Butler, Rick and Carrier, Jean-Guy, eds. *The Trudeau Decade.* Toronto and Garden City, NY: Doubleday, 1979.

Canadian Broadcasting Corporation. *Canada: A People's History.* A 16-part film documentary series, 2001.

Careless, J.M.S. *Canada. A Story of Challenge.* Rev. ed. Toronto: Macmillan, 1970.

Carroll, Joy. *Wolfe and Montcalm. Their Life, Their Times, and the Fate of a Continent.* Buffalo, NY: Firefly Books, 2004.

Clarkson, Stephen and McCall, Christina. *Trudeau and Our Times. The Magnificent Obsession.* Vol. 1. Markham, Ont: McClelland and Stewart, 1991.

Cohen, Andrew. *Lester B. Pearson.* Penguin Extraordinary Canadians, 2008.

Conrad, Margaret and Finkel, Alvin, et al. *History of the Canadian Peoples.* 2 vols. Toronto: Copp Clark Pitman, 1993.

Constain, Thomas B. *The White and the Gold. The French Regime in Canada.* Toronto and Garden City, NY: Doubleday, 1970.

Cook, Ramsey. *The Voyages of Jacques Cartier.* Toronto: University of Toronto Press, 1993.

Dempsey, Hugh A., ed. *The CPR West. The Iron Road and the Making of a Nation.* Vancouver, BC: Douglas and McIntyre, 1984.

Douglas, W.A.B. and Greenhous, B. *Out of the Shadows: Canada in the Second World War.* Rev. ed. Toronto: Dundurn Press, 1993.

Finkel, A. *Business and Social Reform in the 1930s.* Toronto: 1979.

Flanagan, Thomas. *Riel and the Rebellion: 1885 Reconsidered.* Saskatoon, Sask.: Western Producer Prairie Books, 1983.

Francis, R. Douglas and Smith, Donald B. *Readings in Canadian History.* Vol. 1: Pre-Confederation. vol. 2: Post-Confederation. 4th ed. Toronto: Harcourt Brace, 1994.

Francis, R. Douglas, et. al. *Origins: Canadian History to Confederation. Destinies: Canadian History Since Confederation.* 2 vols. 2d ed. Toronto: Rinehard Winston, 1992.

——. *Readings in Canadian History.* Vol. 1: Pre-Confederation. vol. 2: Post-Confederation. 4th ed. Toronto: HBJ-Holt, 1994.

Fraser, Blair. *The Search for Identity. Canada: Postwar to the Present.* Garden City, NY and Toronto: Doubleday, 1967.

Gilbert, A.D., et al. *Reappraisals in Canadian History.* 2 vols. Scarborough, Ont: Prentice-Hall, 1993.

Gruending, Dennis. *Great Canadian Speeches.* Markham, Ont: Fitzhenry and White, 2004.

Hagan, John. *Northern Passage. American Vietnam War Resisters in Canada.* Cambridge, MA: Harvard University, 2001.

Hardy, W.G. *From Sea Unto Sea. The Road to Nationhood 1850–1910.* Toronto and Garden City, NY: Doubleday, 1970.

Harris, R. Cole and Warkentin, John. *Canada Before Confederation. A Study of Historical Geography.* New York: Oxford University Press, 1974.

Historica-Dominion Institute. *We Were Freedom.* Contains 65 gripping oral histories by Canadians in World War II. 2010.

The Illustrated History of Canada. Markham, Ont: Fitzhenry Whiteside, 1988.

Jasanoff, Maya. *Liberty's Exiles. American Loyalists in the Revolutionary World.* New York: Knopf, 2011.

Lanctot, G. *Canada and the American Revolution, 1774–1783.* Toronto: 1967.

Lussier, Antoine S., ed. *Louis Riel and the Métis.* Winnipeg: Pemmican, 1983.

Mackay, Donald. *The People's Railway. A History of Canadian National.* Vancouver: Douglas McIntyre, 1992.

Masters, Donald C. *A Short History of Canada.* Huntington, NY: Krieger, 1980.

McFadden, Fred, ed. *Origins. A History of Canada.* Markham, Ont: Fitzhenry Whiteside, 1988.

McInnis, Edgar. *Canada. A Political and Social History.* Toronto: Holt, Rinehart and Winston, 1982.

McNaught, Kenneth. *The Pelican History of Canada.* New York: Penguin, 1982.

Moore, Christopher. *The Loyalist Revolution, Exile, Settlement.* Toronto: McClelland and Stewart, 1994.

Morchain, Janet. *Search for a Nation.* Markham, Ontario: Fitzhenry and Whiteside, Ltd., 1984.

Morton, Desmond. *A Short History of Canada.* 5th rev. ed. Toronto: McClelland and Stewart, 2001.

——. *A Military History of Canada. From Champlain to Kosovo.* Toronto: McClelland and Stewart, 1999.

Morton, W.L. *The Canadian Identity.* 2d ed. Toronto: University of Toronto Press, 1972.

Neatby, Blair. *The Politics of Chaos: Canada in the Thirties.* Toronto: Macmillan, 1972.

Newman, Peter C. *The Canadian Establishment.* 2 vols. Toronto: McClelland and Stewart, 1975 and 1981.

Silver, A.I. *An Introduction to Canadian History.* Toronto: Canadian Scholars' Press, 1993.

Sherman, George. *The Canada Connection in American History. A Guide for Teachers.* 3d rev. ed. Plattsburgh, NY: Center for the Study of Canada, 1994.

Sprague, D.N. *Canada and the Métis, 1869–1885.* Waterloo, Ont.: Wilfrid Laurier Press, 1988.

Stanley, George F.G. *The War of 1812: Land Operations.* Toronto: Macmillan, 1983.

——. *The Birth of Western Canada. A History of the Riel Rebellions.* Toronto: University of Toronto Press, 1992.

Taylor, Charles. *Radical Tories: The Conservative Tradition in Canada.* Toronto: Anansi, 1982.

Thompson, John H. *Canada, 1922–1939. Decades of Discord.* Toronto: McClelland and Stewart, 1985.

Waiser, Bill and De Brou, Dave, eds. *Documenting Canada. A History of Modern Canada in Documents.* Saskatoon, Sask: Fifth House, 1991.

Weisbord, Merrily. *The Strangest Dream. Canadian Communists, the Spy Trials, and the Cold War.* Toronto: Lester Orpen Dennys, 1983.

Wise, S.F. and Brown, R.C. *Canada Views the United States: Nineteenth-Century Political Attitudes.* Toronto: Macmillan, 1976.

Zaslow, M., ed. *The Defended Border: Upper Canada and the War of 1812.* Toronto: 1964.

IV. POLITICS

Adams, Michael. *Fire and Ice: The United States, Canada and the Myth of Converging Values.* Toronto: Penguin, 2003.

Archer, Keith, and Alan Whitehorn. *Political Activists. The NDP in Convention.* New York: Oxford University Press, 1998.

Atkinson, Michael M. *Governing Canada. Institutions and Public Policy.* Toronto: Harcourt Brace, 1993.

Bell, David and Teppermann, Lorne. *Roots of Disunity. A Study of Canadian Political Culture.* Rev. ed. New York: Oxford University Press, 1992.

Bickerton, James P., Gagnon, Alain-G., and Smith, Patrick J. *Ties that Bind. Parties and Voters in Canada.* New York: Oxford University, 1999.

Bickerton, James P. and Gagnon, Alain-G. *Canadian Politics. An Introduction to the Discipline.* Peterborough, Ont: Broadview Press, 1994.

Blair, R.S. and McLeod, J.T., eds. *The Canadian Political Tradition. Basic Readings.* Scarborough, Ont: Methuen, 1987.

Boydell, Craig L., and Connidis, Ingrid Arnet. *The Canadian Criminel Justice System.* Toronto: Holt, Rinehart Winston, 1982.

Brodie, Janine. *Women and Politics in Canada.* Scarborough, Ont.: McGraw-Hill Reyerson, 1985.

Brooks, Stephen, ed. *Political Thought in Canada. Contemporary Perspectives.* Richmond Hill, Ont.: Irwin, 1984.

——. *Canadian Democracy.* 3d ed. New York: Oxford University, 2000.

Cairns, Alan C. and Williams, Douglas E. *Constitution, Government and Society in Canada.* Toronto: McClelland and Stewart, 1988.

Cairns, Alan C. *Charter Versus Federalism.* Montreal: McGill-Queens University Press, 1992.

Cameron, Duncan and Smith, Miriam, eds. *Constitutional Politics.* Toronto: James Lorimer, 1993.

Cheffins, Ronald I. and Johnson, Patricia A. *The Revised Canadian Constitution.* Scarborough, Ont: McGraw-Hill Ryerson Hill, Ltd., 1986.

Cairns, Alan C. and Williams, Douglas E. *Constitution, Government and Society in Canada.* Toronto: McClelland and Stewart, 1988.

Conklin, William E. *Images of a Constitution.* Toronto: University of Toronto Press, 1989.

Cook, Ramsay. *Canada, Quebec and the Uses of Nationalism.* Toronto: McClelland and Stewart, 1986.

Courtney, John C., ed. *The Canadian House of Commons.* Univ. of Calgary Press, 1985.

Dawson, R. MacGregor and W.F. Revised by Norman Ward. *Democratic Government in Canada.* Toronto: University of Toronto Press, 1989.

De Palma, Anthony. *Here: A Biography of the New American Continent.* 2001.

Doern, G. Bruce, Leslie A. Pal and Brian W. Tomlin, eds. *Border Crossings. The Internationalization of Canadian Public Policy.* New York: Oxford University Press, 1996.

Donaldson, Gordon. *Eighteen Men: The Prime Ministers of Canada.* Toronto: Doubleday, 1985.

Eagles, Munroe, et al, eds. *The Almanac of Canadian Politics.* 2d ed. New York: Oxford University Press, 1996.

Flanagan, Tom. *Waiting for the Wave. The Reform Party and Preston Manning.* Don Mills, Ont: Stoddart, 1995.

Forbes, Hugh Donald, ed. *Canadian Political Thought.* Don Mills, Ont.: Oxford University Press, 1985.

Franks, C.E.S. *The Parliament of Canada.* Toronto: Univ. of Toronto Press, 1987.

Gerecke, Kent, ed. *The Canadian City.* Montreal: Black Rose Books, 1993.

Gollner, Andrew B. and Salée, Daniel, eds. *Canada Under Mulroney. An End-of-Term Report.* Montreal: Véhicule Press, 1988.

Goldenberg, Eddie. *The Way It Works: Inside Ottawa.* 2006.

Granatstein, J.L., et. al. *Sacred Trust: Brian Mulroney and the Conservative Party in Power.* Toronto: Cross Canada Books, 1986.

Grant, George. *Lament for a Nation. The Defeat of Canadian Nationalism.* Ottawa: Carleton University Press, 1982.

Higgins, Donald J.H. *Local and Urban Politics in Canada.* Agincourt, Ont: Gage, 1986.

Jackson, Robert J. and Jackson, Doreen. *Politics in Canada. Culture, Institutions, Behaviour and Public Policy.* 4th ed. Upper Saddle River, NJ: Prentice-Hall, 1998.

Kealey, Linda and Sangster, Joan. *Beyond the Vote. Canadian Women and Politics.* Toronto: University of Toronto Press, 1989.

Kernaghan, Kenneth, ed. *Public Administration in Canada.* 5th ed. Toronto: Methuen, 1985.

Knopff, Ranier and Morton, F.L. *Charter Politics.* Scarborough, Ont: Nelson, 1991.

Landes, Ronald G. *The Canadian Polity: A Comparative Introduction.* 2d ed. Scarborough, Ont.: Prentice-Hall, 1987.

Langford, J. Stuart. *A Practical Guide to the New Canadian Constitution.* Toronto: Canadian Broadcasting Corporation, 1982.

Leach, Richard H., ed. *Reshaping Confederation: The 1982 Reform of the Canadian Constitution.* Durham, NC: Duke University Press, 1984.

Levine, Allan. *Scrum Wars. The Prime Ministers and the Media.* Toronto: Dundurn Press, 1993.

MacIvor, Heather. *Women and Politics in Canada.* Peterborough, Ont: Broadview Press, 1994.

Manfredi, Christopher P. and Rush, Mark. *Judging Democracy.* Peterborough, Ont.: Broadview Press, 2008. This is a comparison of the Canadian and American Supreme Courts.

Manfredi, Christopher P. *Judicial Power and the Charter.* 2d ed. New York: Oxford University, 2000.

McKenna, M.C. *The Canadian and American Constitutions in Comparative Perspective.* Calgary: University of Calgary Press, 1993.

McKercher, William R., ed. *The U.S. Bill of Rights and the Canadian Charter of Rights and Freedoms.* Toronto: Ontario Economic Council, 1983.

McMenemy, John. *The Language of Canadian Politics. A Guide to Important Terms and Concepts.* Rev. ed. Waterloo, Ont: Wilfred Laurier University Press, 1993.

McRoberts, Kenneth, ed. *Misconceiving Canada. The Struggle for National Unity.* New York: Oxford University Press, 1997.

——. and Patrick J. Monahan, eds. *The Charlottetown Accord, the Referendum, and the Future of Canada.* Toronto, 1993.

McWhinney, Edward. *Canada and the Constitution 1979–1982: Patriation and the Charter of Rights.* Toronto: University of Toronto Press, 1982.

Megyery, Kathy, ed. *Women in Canadian Politics.* Toronto: Dundurn, 1992.

Milne, David. *The New Canadian Constitution.* Toronto: James Lorimer, 1982.

Monahan, Patrick. *Politics and the Constitution. The Charter, Federalism and The Supreme Court of Canada.* Agincourt, Ont: Carswell, 1987.

Morton, Desmond. *The New Democrats 1961–1986.* Toronto: Copp Clark Pitman, 1986.

Morton, E.L. *Law, Politics and the Judicial Process in Canada.* 2d ed. Calgary: University of Calgary Press, 1992.

Pal, Leslie A., ed. *How Ottawa Spends 2000–2001. Redefining the Federal Role.* New York: Oxford University, 2000.

Pal, Leslie and Taras, David, eds. *Prime Ministers and Premiers. Political Leadership and Public Policy in Canada.* Scarborough, Ont: Prentice-Hall, 1988.

Pammett, J., et al. *The Absent Mandate: The Politics of Discontent in Canada.* Agincourt, Ont.: 1984.

Peacock, Anthony A., ed. *Rethinking the Constitution.* New York: Oxford University Press, 1996.

Penner, Norman. *From Protest to Power. Social Democracy in Canada 1900–Present.* Toronto: James Lorimer, 1993.

Perlin, George, ed. *Party Democracy in Canada. The Politics of National Party Conventions.* Scarborough, Ont: Prentice-Hall, 1988.

Romanow, Roy J. and Whyte, John D. *Canada . . . Notwithstanding.* Toronto: Methuen, 1984.

Russell, Peter H. *Leading Constitutional Decisions.* 3d ed. Ottawa: Carleton University Press, 1982.

——. *The Judiciary in Canada. The Third Branch of Government.* Scarborough, Ont: McGraw-Hill Ryerson, 1987.

——. *Constitutional Odyssey. Can Canadians Be a Sovereign People?* Toronto: University of Toronto Press, 1993.

Simpson, Jeffrey. *Faultlines. Struggling for a Canadian Vision.* Scarborough: HarperCollins, 1993.

Snell, James G. and Vaughan, Frederick. *The Supreme Court of Canada.* Toronto: University of Toronto Press, 1985.

The L-Shaped Party: The Liberal Party of Canada, 1958–1980. Toronto: 1981.

Wearing, Joseph. *Strained Relations. Canadian Parties and Voters.* Toronto: McClelland and Stewart, 1988.

Wells, Paul. *Right Side Up. The Fall of Paul Martin and the Rise of Stephen Harper's New Conservatism.* Toronto: McClelland & Stewart. 2007.

Whitehorn, Alan. *Canadian Socialism. Essays of CCF-NDP.* Don Mills, Ont: Oxford University Press, 1992.

Woods, Shirley E. *Her Excellency Jeanne Sauve.* Toronto: Cross Canada Books, 1986.

Wilson-Smith, Anthony. *Double Vision: The Inside Story of the Liberals in Power.* Toronto: Doubleday, 1996.

V. FEDERALISM, REGIONALISM, PROVINCIAL POLITICS AND NATIVE PEOPLES

Alfred, Taiaiake. *Peace, Power, Righteousness. An Indigenous Manifesto.* New York: Oxford University, 1999.

Anderson, Alun. *After the Ice: Life, Death and Geopolitics in the New Arctic.* Washington: Smithsonian (Virgin Books), 2009.

Archer, Keith, and Young, U., eds. *Regionalism and Party Politics in Canada.* New York: Oxford University, 2000.

Asch, Michael. *Home and Native Land: Aboriginal Rights and the Canadian Constitution.* Toronto: Methuen, 1984.

Banting, Keith and Simeon, Richard. *And No One Cheered. Federalism, Democracy and the Constitution Act.* Toronto: Methuen, 1983.

Banting, Keith. *The Welfare State and Canadian Federalism* 2d ed. Montreal: McGill-Queen's University Press, 1987.

Barman, Jean. *The West beyond the West. A History of British Columbia.* Toronto: University of Toronto Press, 1993.

Bennett, A., et al. *Inuit of the North.* Markham, Ont: Fitzhenry Whiteside, n.d.

Berger, Thomas R. *Northern Frontier, Northern Homeland.* Vancouver: Douglas McIntyre, 1988.

Bolger, F.W.P., ed. *Canada's Smallest Province: A History of P.E.I.* Charlottestown, P.E.I.: 1973.

Bone, Robert M. *The Geography of the Canadian North.* Don Mills, Ont: Oxford University Press, 1992.

Bothwell, Robert. *Canada since 1945. Power, Politics and Provincialism.* Toronto: University of Toronto Press, 1982.

Brym, Robert J., ed. *Regionalism in Canada.* Richmond Hill, Ont.: Irwin, 1986.

Careless, J.M.S. *Toronto to 1918. An Illustrated History.* Toronto: James Lorimer, 1985.

Cassidy, Frank, ed. *Aboriginal Self-Determination.* Lantzville, BC: Oolichan Books, 1991.

Coates, Kenneth. *Aboriginal Land Claims in Canada.* Toronto: Copp Clark Pitman, 1992.

Conway, J.F. *The West: The History of a Region in Confederation.* Toronto: James Lorimer, 1983.

Cox, Bruce Alden, ed. *Native People, Native Lands. Canadian Indians, Inuit and Metis.* Ottawa: Carleton Univ. Press, 1987.

Crowe, Keith J. *A History of the Original Peoples of Northern Canada.* Rev. ed. Montreal: McGills-Queens University Press, 1991.

Dickerson, Mark O. *Whose North? Political Change, Political Development, and Self-Government in the Northwest Territories.* Vancouver: University of British Columbia Press, 1992.

Dickason, Olive P. *Canada's First Nations. A History of Founding Peoples from Earliest Times.* Markham, Ont: McClelland Stewart, 1992.

Duffy, R. Quinn. *The Road to Nunavut. The Progress of the Eastern Arctic Inuit Since the Second World War.* Montreal: McGill-Queen's Univ. Press, 1988.

Elias, Peter D. *Development of Aboriginal People's Communities.* North York, Ont: Captus Press, 1991.

Ellis, Richard. *On Thin Ice: The Changing World of the Polar Bear.* New York: Knopf, 2009.

Forbes, E.R. and Muise, D.A., eds. *The Atlantic Provinces in Confederation.* Toronto: University of Toronto Press, 1993.

Francis, R. Douglas and Palmer, Howard, eds. *The Prairie West. Historical Readings.* 2d ed. Edmonton, Alb: University of Alberta Press, 1992.

Frideres, James. *Native People in Canada: Contemporary Conflicts.* 3d. ed. Scarborough, Ont: Prentice Hall, 1988.

Friesen, Gerald. *The Canadian Prairies. A History.* Toronto: University of Toronto Press, 1984.

Friesen, John W. *The Cultural Maze: Complex Questions on Native Destiny.* Calgary: Temeron Books, 1991.

Gallant, Melvin. *The Country of Acadia.* Toronto: Simon Pierre, 1985.

Gibbins, Roger. *Regionalism. Territorial Politics in Canada and the United States.* Toronto: Butterworths, 1982.

Giraud, Marcel. *The Métis in the Canadian West (Le Métis Canadien).* Translated by George Woodstock. Edmonton: University of Alberta Press, 1986.

Griffiths, N.E.S. *The Acadians: Creation of a People.* Toronto: McGraw-Hill Ryerson, 1973.

Hamilton, John David. *The Arctic Revolution. Social Change in the NWT 1935–1993.* Toronto: Dundurn Press, 1993.

Hiller, J. and Neary, P., eds. *Newfoundland in the Nineteenth and Twentieth Centuries.*

Ibbitson, John. *Promised Land: Inside the Mike Harris Revolution.* 1997.

Johnston, Wayne. *The Colony of Unrequited Dreams.* (Novel about Joe Smallwood and Newfoundland) NY: Anchor Books, 2000.

Lauritzen, Philip. *Oil and Amulets: Inuit—A People at the Top of the World.* St. John's, Newf.: Breakwater Books, 1983.

Lemon, James. *Toronto Since 1918. An Illustrated History.* Toronto: James Lorimer, 1985.

Little Bear, Leroy, et al, eds. *Pathways to Self-Determination. Canadian Indians and the Canadian State.* Toronto: University of Toronto Press, 1984.

Long, Anthony and Boldt, Menno. *Governments in Conflict? Provinces and Indian Nations in Canada.* Toronto: University of Toronto Press, 1989.

Melnyk, George, et. *Riel to Reform. A History of Protest in Western Canada.* Saskatoon, Sask: Fifth House, 1991.

Milne, David. *Tug of War. Ottawa and the Provinces under Trudeau and Mulroney.* Toronto: James Lorimer, 1986.

Molyneux, Geoffrey. *British Columbia. An Illustrated History.* Vancouver: Polestar, 1992.

Morley, J.T. *Secular Socialists: The CCF/NDP in Ontario, A Biography.* Montreal: McGill-Queen's University Press, 1984.

Morrison, R. Bruce and Wilson, C. Roderick, eds. *The Native Peoples.* McClelland Stewart, 1986.

Morse, Bradford W., ed. *Aboriginal Peoples and the Law. Indian, Métis and Inuit Rights in Canada.* Ottawa: Carleton University Press, 1984.

Morton, W.L. *Manitoba: A History.* 2d ed. Toronto: 1967.

Neary, Peter and Hiller, James, eds. *Twentieth Century Newfoundland: Explorations.* St. Johns: Breakwater, 1993.

Nikiforuk, Sheila Pratt and Wanagas, Don, eds. *Running on Empty. Alberta After The Boom.* Edmonton: NeWest Press, 1987.

Olling, Randy and Westmacott, Martin, eds. *Perspectives on Canadian Federalism.* Scarborough, Ont: Prentice-Hall, 1988.

Ormsby, M. *British Columbia: A History.* Toronto: 1968.

Palmer, Hans and Tamara, eds. *Peoples of Alberta. Portraits of Cultural Diversity.* Saskatoon, Sask: Western Producer Prairie Books, 1985.

——. *Alberta: A New History.* Markham, Ont: McClelland Stewart, 1990.

Patterson, E.P., III. *The Canadian Indian: A History since 1500.* Don Mills, Ont.: 1972.

Peterson, Jacqueline and Brown, Jennifer, eds. *The New Peoples: Being and Becoming Métis in North America.* Winnipeg: University of Manitoba Press, 1984.

Purich, Donald. *Our Land, Native Rights in Canada.* Toronto: James Lorimer, 1987.

——. *The Inuit and Their Land. The Story of Nunavut.* Toronto: James Lorimer, 1993.

Rasporich, A.W., ed. *The Making of the Modern West.* Calgary: University of Calgary Press, 1984.

Ray, Arthur. *I Have Lived Here Since the World Began.* General Publishing, 1996.

Riggs, A.R. and Velk, Tom. *Federalism in Peril.* Vancouver: Fraser Institute, 1992.

Robinson, J. Lewis. *Concepts and Themes in the Regional Geography of Canada.* Vancouver: Talon Books, Ltd., 1983.

Rocher, François and Smith, Miriam. *New Trends in Canadian Federalism.* Peterborough, Ont: Broadview Press, 1994.

Ross, Sally and Deveau, Alphonse. *The Acadians of Nova Scotia.* Halifax: Nimbus, 1992.

Saywell, John T. *The Office of Lieutenant-Governor.* Toronto: Copp Clark Pittman, Ltd., 1985.

Smiley, D.V. *Federal Condition in Canada.* Toronto: McGraw-Hill Ryerson, 1987.

Stelter, Gilbert A. and Artibise, Alan F.J. *The Canadian City. Essays in Urban and Social History.* Ottawa: Carleton University Press, 1984.

Taylor, John H. *Ottawa. An Illustrated History.* Toronto: James Lorimer, 1986.

Trudeau, Pierre Elliott. *Federalism and the French Canadians.* Toronto: Macmillan, 1968.

Tuohy, Carolyn J. *Policy and Politics in Canada. Institutionalized Ambivalence.* Philadelphia: Temple University Press, 1992.

Tupper, Allan and Gibbins, Roger. *Government and Politics in Alberta.* Edmonton: University of Alberta Press, 1992.

Weaver, R. Kent, ed. *The Collapse of Canada?* Washington, D.C.: Brookings Institution, 1992.

Webb, Melody. *Yukon. The Last Frontier.* Vancouver: University of British Columbia Press, 1993.

White, Graham. *The Ontario Legislature. A Political Analysis.* Toronto: University of Toronto Press, 1989.

——. and Levy, Gary, eds. *Provincial and Territorial Assemblies in Canada.* Toronto: Toronto University Press, 1989.

White, Randall. *Ontario 1610–1985. A Political and Economic History.* Toronto: Dundurn, 1985.

Wiseman, Nelson. *Social Democracy in Manitoba: A History of the CCF-NDP 1932–1977.* Winnipeg: University of Manitoba Press, 1984.

Woods, Jr., Shirley E. *Ottawa.* Toronto: Doubleday Canada Ltd., 1985.

Wotherspoon, Terry and Satzewich, Vic. *First Nations: A Struggle for Equality.* Scarborough, Ont: Nelson, 1992.

Zellen, Barry. *Breaking the Ice. From Land Claims to Tribal Sovereignty in the Arctic.* Lanham, MD: Rowman Littlefield, 2008.

VI. FOREIGN AND DEFENSE POLICY

Andrew, Arthur. *The Rise and Fall of a Middle Power: Canadian Diplomacy from King to Mulroney.* Toronto: James Lorimer, 1993.

Bercuson, David. *Significant Incident: Canada's Army, the Airborne, and the Murder in Somalia.* Markham, Ont.: McClelland & Stewart, 1996.

—— and J. L. Granatstein. *Dictionary of Canadian Military History.* Toronto: Oxford University, 1992.

Blanchard, James. *Behind the Embassy Door: Canada, Clinton and Quebec.* 1998.

Cellucci, Paul. *Unquiet Diplomacy.* Toronto: Key Porter, 2005.

Clarkson, Stephen. *Canada and the Reagan Challenge.* Toronto: James Lorimer, 1982.

Cohen, Andrew. *While Canada Slept. How We Lost our Place in the World.* Toronto: McClelland and Steward, 2004.

Cooper, Andrew F. *Tests of Global Governance. Canadian Diplomacy and United Nations World Conferences.* Washington: Brookings, 2004.

Cuff, Robert D. *Ties that Bind: Canadian-American Relations in Wartime from the Great War to the Cold War.* Toronto: Hakkert, 1977.

Curtis, Kenneth M. and Carroll, John E. *Canadian-American Relations. The Promise and the Challenge.* Lexington, MA: Lexington Books, 1983.

Cutler, A. Claire and Zacher, Mark W., eds. *Canadian Foreign Policy and International Economic Regimes.* Vancouver: University of British Columbia Press, 1992.

Dewitt, David B. and Kirton, John J. *Canada as a Principal Power. A Study in Foreign Policy and International Relations.* Toronto and New York: John Wiley, 1983.

Diubaldo, Richard J. *A Study of Canadian-American Defence Policy, 1945–1975: Northern Issues and Strategic Resources.* Ottawa: Department of National Defense, 1978.

Doran, Charles F. and Sigler, John H., eds. *Canada and the United States.* Scarborough, Ont.: Prentice-Hall, 1985.

Douglas, W.A.B., ed. *The Royal Canadian Navy in Transition, 1910–1985.* Vancouver: University of British Columbia Press, 1988.

Downton, Eric. *Pacific Challenge. Canada's Future in the New Asia.* Don Mills, Ont: Stoddart, 1986.

English, John and Hillmer, Norman, eds. *Making a Difference? Canada's Foreign Policy in a Changing World Order.* Toronto, Lester, 1992.

Flaherty, David and McKercher, William. *Southern Exposure.* Scarborough: McGraw-Hill Ryerson, Ltd., 1986.

Fox, William T.R. *A Continent Apart.* Toronto: University of Toronto Press, 1985.

Gotlieb, Allan. *Washington Diaries.* 2006.

Granatstein, J.L. *Canadian Foreign Policy. Historical Readings.* Rev. ed. Toronto: Copp Clark Pitman, 1992.

——. *Torwards a New World. Readings in the History of Canadian Foreign Policy.* Toronto: Copp Clark Pitman, 1992.

——. and Hillmer, Norman. *For Better or For Worse. Canada and the United States in the 1990s.* Toronto: Copp Clark Pitman, 1992.

Grant, Shelagh. *Polar Imperative: A History of Arctic Sovereignty in North America.* 2011.

Griffiths, Franklyn, ed. *Politics of the Northwest Passage.* Montreal: McGill-Queen's Univ. Press, 1987.

Gwyn, Richard. *The 49th Paradox: Canada in North America.* Toronto: McClelland and Stewart, 1985.

Haglund, David. G. and Sokolsky, Joel J. *The U.S.-Canada Security Relationship.* Boulder, CO: Westview Press, 1989.

Haycock, R.G. and Hunt, B.D. *Canada's Defence.* Toronto: Copp Clark Pitman, 1993.

Hillier, Gen. Rich. *A Soldier First: Bullets, Bureaucrats and the Politics of War.* 2009.

Holmes, John W. *Life with Uncle. The Canadian-American Relationship.* Toronto: University of Toronto Press, 1981.

Honderich, John. *Arctic Imperative. Is Canada Losing the North?* Toronto: Univ. of Toronto Press, 1987.

Jockel, Joseph T. *Security to the North. Canada-U.S. Defense Relations in the 1990s.* East Lansing: Michigan State University Press, 1991.

——. *No Boundaries Upstairs. Canada, The United States and the Origins of North American Air Defence, 1945–1958.* Vancouver: Univ. of British Columbia Press, 1987.

—— and Sokolsky, Joel. *Canada and Collective Security. Odd Man Out.* New York: Praeger, 1986.

Jockel, Joseph T. *Canada and International Peacekeeping.* Washington, D.C.: Center for Strategic and International Studies, 1994.

Keating, Tom. *Canada and World Order. The Multilateralist Tradition in Canadian Foreign Policy.* Markham, Ont: McClelland Stewart, 1993.

Kirton, John. *Canadian Foreign Policy in a Changing World.* 2007.

Laxer, James. *Stalking the Elephant: My Discovery of America.* New York: Viking, 2000.

Mahant, Edelgard E. and Mount, Graeme S. *An Introduction to Canadian-American Relations.* 2d ed. Toronto: Methuen, 1989.

Martin, Lawrence. *The Presidents and the Prime Ministers. Washington and Ottawa Face to Face: The Myth of Bilateral Bliss 1867–1982.* Markham, Ont.: Paper Jacks, 1984.

McQuaig, Linda. *Holding the Bully's Coat: Canada and the U.S. Empire.* Toronto: Doubleday, 2007.

Middlemiss, Danford W. and Sokolsky, Joel. *Canadian Defence. Decisions and Determinants.* Toronto: HBJ/Holt, 1989.

Molot, Maureen Appel, and Hampson, Fen Osler, eds. *Canada Among Nations 2000.* New York: Oxford University, 2000.

——, eds. *Canada Among Nations 1999. A Big League Player?* New York: Oxford University, 1999.

Morton, Desmond. *A Military History of Canada From Champlain to the Gulf War.* Markham, Ont: McClelland Stewart, 1992.

Munton, D. and Kirton, J. *Canadian Foreign Policy.* Scarborough, Ont: Prentice-Hall, 1992.

Nossal, Kim Richard. *The Politics of Canadian Foreign Policy.* 2d ed. Scarborough, Ont: Prentice-Hall Canada, 1989.

Orvik, Nils, ed. *Canada and NATO.* Kingston: Queen's University Press, 1982.

Pearson, Geoffrey A.H. *Lester B. Pearson and Crisis Democracy.* Ottawa: Carleton University Press, 1993.

Porter, Gerald. *In Retreat: The Canadian Forces in the Trudeau Years*. Ottawa: Deneau and Greenberg, n.d.

Preston, Richard A. *To Serve Canada. A History of the Royal Military College Since the Second World War*. Ottawa: University of Ottawa Press, 1991.

Reflections from the Past. Perspectives on Canada and on the Canada-U.S. Relationship. Plattsburgh, NY: Center for the Study of Canada, 1991.

Rosenblum, Simon. *Misguided Missiles*. Toronto: James Lorimer Company, 1985.

Shiels, Frederick L. *Ethnic Separatism and World Politics*. Lanham, MD: University Press of America, 1984.

Simpson, Jeffrey. *Star-Spangled Canadians: Canadians Living the American Dream*. New York: HarperCollins, 2000.

Stacey, C.P. *Canada and the Age of Conflict: A History of Canadian External Policies, 1867–1921*, vol. 1, and *The Mackenzie King Era, 1921–1948*, vol. 2. Toronto: Macmillan, 1977.

——. *Arms, Men and Governments: The War Policies of Canada, 1939–1945*. Ottawa: 1970.

Stein, Janice Gross and Lang, Eugene. *The Unexpected War. Canada in Kandahar*. Toronto: Penguin, 2007.

Thomas, David, ed. *Canada and the United States. Differences that Count*. Peterborough, Ont: Broadview Press, 1993.

Thompson, John Herd and Randall, Stephen J. *Canada and the United States. Ambivalent Allies*. Montreal: McGill-Queens University Press, 1993.

VII. QUEBEC

Arnopoulos, Sheila McLeod and Clift, Dominique. *The English Fact in Quebec*. Montreal: McGill-Queen's Univeristy Press, 1980.

Beach, Richard. *Alliance or Alienation. Québec & Canada as the Century Turns*. Plattsburgh, NY: Center for the Study of Canada, 2000.

Behiels, Michael D., ed. *Quebec Since 1945. Selected Readings*. Toronto: Copp Clark Pitman, 1987.

Bercuson, David. *Deconfederation: Canada Without Quebec*. Toronto: Key Porter, 1991.

Bernier, Luc. *From Paris to Washington: Quebec's Foreign Policy in a Changing World*. Washington, D.C.: Center for Strategic and International Studies, 1994.

Bourhis, Richard Y., ed. *Conflict and Language Planning in Quebec*. Clevedon, Avon, England: Multilingual Matters, 1984.

Center for the Study of Canada. *L'Americanité des Québécois*. Plattsburgh, NY, 2002.

Clift, Dominique. *Quebec Nationalism in Crisis*. Montreal: McGill-Queen's University Press, 1980.

Coleman, William D. *The Independence Movement in Quebec 1945–1980*. Toronto: University of Toronto Press, 1984.

Conologue, Ray. *Impossible Nation: The Longing for Homeland in Canada and Quebec*. General Publishing, 1996.

Dickinson, John and Young, Brian. *A Short History of Quebec*. 2d rev. ed. Toronto: Copp Clark Pitman, 1993.

Dodge, William, ed. *Boundaries of Identity. A Quebec Reader*. Toronto: Lester, 1992.

Drache, D. and Perin, R. *Negotiating with a Sovereign Quebec*. Toronto: James Lorimer, 1993.

Eccles, W. J. *The French in North America, 1500–1782*. Rev. ed. Markham, Ont: Fitzhenry Whiteside, 1998.

Fidler, Richard. *Canada, Adieu? Quebec Debates its Future*. Latzville, BC: Oolichan Books, 1991.

Fitzmaurice, John. *Quebec and Canada: Past, Present, and Future*. New York: St. Martin's, 1985.

Fournier, Pierre. *The Quebec Establishment. The Ruling Class and the State*. Montreal: Black Rose Books, 1988.

Ganon, Alain G., ed. *Quebec: State and Society in Crisis*. Toronto: Methuen, 1984.

Gilbert, Paula Ruth, et al. *Women Writers in Quebec. Essays in Honor of Jeanne Kissner*. Plattsburgh, NY: Center for the Study of Canada, 2002.

Griffin, Anne. *Quebec. The Challenge of Independence*. Cranbury, NJ: Associated University Presses, 1984.

Guindon, Hubert. *Tradition, Modernity, and Nationhood. Essays on Quebec Society*. Toronto: University of Toronto Press, 1989.

Hero, A.O., Jr. and Balthazar, Louis. *Contemporary Quebec the United States*. Lanham, MD: University Press of America, 1988.

Jacobs, Jane. *The Question of Separatism. Quebec and the Struggle over Sovereignty*. New York: Vintage Books, 1981.

Lachapelle, Guy. *The Quebec Democracy. Structures, Processes and Policies*. Toronto: McGraw Hill Ryerson, 1993.

Laczko, Leslie S. *Pluralism and Inequality in Quebec*. New York: St. Martin's, 1994.

Leonard, Jean-François and Leveillee, Jacques. *Montreal after Drapeau*. Montreal: Black Rose Books, 1988.

Lévesque, Réne. *My Quebec*. Toronto: Totem Books, 1979.

Levine, Marc. *The Reconquest of Montreal: Language Policy and Social Change in a Bilingual City*. Philadelphia: Temple University Press, 1990.

McRoberts, Kenneth. *Quebec. Social Change and Political Crisis*. 3d ed. Toronto: McClelland and Stewart, 1988.

Milner, Henry. *Politics in the New Quebec*. Toronto: McClelland and Stewart, 1978.

Moniere, D. *Ideologies in Quebec: The Historical Development*. Toronto: 1981.

Nardochhio, Elaine F. *Theatre and Politics in Modern Quebec. A History*. Edmonton: University of Alberta Press, 1985.

Nish, C. *The French Regime*. Scarborough, Ont.: Prentice-Hall, 1965.

Ouellet, Fernand. *Economy, Class, and Nation in Quebec*. Toronto: Copp Clark Pitman, 1991.

Parizeau, Jacques. *For a Sovereign Quebec*. 1997.

Poliquin, Daniel. *Extraordinary Canadians: René Lévesque*. Penguin Group (Canada), 2009.

Quinlan, Don. *Images of French Canada*. Markham, Ont: Fitzhenry Whiteside, 1988.

Reid, Scott. *Canada Remapped. How the Partition of Quebec Will Reshape the Nation*. Vancouver: Arsenal Pulp Press, 1992.

Richler, Mordecai. *Oh Canada! Oh Quebec! Requiem for a Divided Country*. Toronto: Penguin, 1992.

Robinson, Sinclair and Smith, Donald. *Practical Handbook of Quebec and Acadian French*. Toronto: Anansi, 1984.

Roussopoulos, Dimitrios I, ed. *Quebec and Radical Social Change*. Montreal: Black Rose Books, 1988.

Saywell, John. *The Rise of the Parti Quebecois 1967–1976*. Toronto: University of Toronto Press, 1977.

Shaw, William F. and Albert, Lionel. *Partition. The Price of Quebec's Independence*. Montreal: Thornhill, 1980.

Trofimenkoff, Susan Mann. *The Dream of Nation. A Social and Intellectual History of Quebec*. Toronto: Gage, 1983.

Vallieres, Pierre. *White Niggers of America*. Toronto: McClelland and Stewart, 1971.

——. *The Impossible Quebec. Illusions of Sovereignty-Association*. Montreal: Black Rose Books, 1988.

Wade, M. *The French Canadians*. 2 vols. Rev. ed. Toronto: 1975, 1976.

Walker, Douglas C. *The Pronunciation of Canadian French*. Ottawa: University of Ottawa Press, 1985.

VIII. ECONOMY

Anderson, F.J. *Natural Resources in Canada. Economic Theory and Policy*. Toronto: Methuen, 1985.

Armstrong, Muriel. *The Canadian Economy and Its Problems*. 4th ed. Scarborough, Ont.: Prentice-Hall, 1988.

Brodie, Janine. *The Political Economy of Canadian Regionalism*. Toronto: Harcourt Brace Jovanovich, 1990.

Caloren, Fred, ed. *Is the Canadian Economy Closing Down?* Montreal: Black Rose Books, 1988.

The Canada-U.S. Economic Relationship. Plattsburgh, NY: Center for the Study of Canada, 1991.

Crane, David. *The Next Canadian Century. Building a Competitive Economy*. Don Mills, Ont: Stoddart, 1993.

Doern, Bruce and Toner, Glen. *The Politics of Energy. The Development and Implementation of the NEP*. Toronto: Methuen, 1985.

Fallis, George. *The Costs of Constitutional Change*. Toronto: James Lorimer, 1993.

French, Richard and van Loon, Richard. *How Ottawa Decides: Planning and Industrial Policy-Making 1968–1983*. Rev. ed. Toronto: James Lorimer, 1984.

Fry, Earl H. *Canada's Unity Crisis. Implications for U.S.-Canada Economic Relations*. Washington D.C.: Brookings, 1992.

Globerman, Steven and Walker, Michael. *Assessing NAFTA*. Vancouver: Fraser Institute, 1993.

Hoebing, Joyce, et al. *NAFTA and Sovereignty*. Washington D.C.: CSIS Press, 1996.

Howlett, Michael, Netherton, Alex, and Ramesh, M. *The Political Economy of Canada*. 2d ed. New York: Oxford University, 1999.

Ismael, Jacqueline S., eds. *Canadian Welfare State. Evolution and Transition*. Edmonton: Univ. of Alberta Press, 1987.

Langdon, Frank. *The Politics of Canadian-Japanese Economic Relations, 1952–1983*. Vancouver: University of British Columbia Press, 1983.

Laxer, James. *Leap of Faith. Free Trade and the Future of Canada*. Edmonton: Hurtig, 1986.

Leslie, Peter. *Federal State, National Economy*. Toronto: Univ. of Toronto Press, 1987.

Levi, Michael A. *The Canadian Oil Sands: Energy Security vs. Climate Change*. Washington, DC: Brookings, 2009.

Muirhead, B.W. *The Development of Postwar Canadian Trade Policy*. Montreal: McGill-Queen's University Press, 1992.

Naylor, C. David, ed. *Canadian Health Care and the State*. Montreal: McGills-Queen's University Press, 1992.

Pomfred, Richard. *The Economic Development of Canada*. 2d ed. Scarborough, Ont: Nelson, 1992.

Pritchard, Robert S., ed. *Crown Corporations in Canada*. Toronto: Butterworths, 1983.

Rea, Kenneth. *A Guide to Canadian Economic History*. Toronto: Canadian Scholars' Press, 1993.

Safarian, A.E. *The Canadian Economy in the Great Depression*. Toronto: 1970.

Sarlo, Christopher A. *Poverty in Canada*. Vancouver: Fraser Institute, 1992.

Schott, Jeffrey J. and Smith, Murray G., eds. *The Canada-United States Free Trade Agreement: The Global Impact*. Washington, DC: Institute for International Economics, 1988.

Sitwell, O.F.G. and Seifried, Neil R.M. *The Regional Structure of the Canadian Economy*. Toronto: Methuen, 1984.

Vogt, Roy, et al. *Economics. Understanding the Canadian Economy*. 4th ed. Toronto: HBJ-Holt, 1993.

Watkins, M.H. and Grant, H.M.K. *Canadian Economic History*. Ottawa: Carleton University Press, 1993.

IX. CULTURE AND SOCIETY

Ashworth, Mary. *Children of the Canadian Mosaic. A Brief History to 1950*. Toronto: Oise Press, 1992.

Backhouse, Constance and Flaherty, David H, eds. *Challenging Times. The Women's Movement in Canada and the United States*. Montreal: McGills-Queens University Press, 1992.

Baker, Maureen, ed. *The Family: Changing Trends in Canada*. Scarborough, Ont.: McGraw-Hill Reyerson, 1984.

Balkind, Alvin, et al. *Visions/Contemporary Art in Canada*. Vancouver, B.C.: Douglas and McIntyre, 1983.

Berkowitz, S.D., ed. *Models and Myths in Canadian Sociology*. Toronto: Butterworths, 1984.

Berry, J.W. and Laponce, J.A., eds. *Multiculturalism in Canada. A Review of Research*. Toronto: University of Toronto Press, 1993.

Bibby, Reginald W. and Poterski, Donald C. *The Emerging Generation*. Irwin Publishing, Inc., 1985.

Bibby, Reginald W. *Restless Gods: The Renaissance of Religion in Canada*. Don Mills, Ont.: Stoddart, 2002.

Bird, Michael. *Canadian Folk Art. Old Ways in a New Land*. Don Mills, Ont.: Oxford University Press, 1983.

Bolaria, B. Singh, ed. *Social Issues and Contradictions in Canadian Society*. Toronto: Harcourt Brace, 1991.

Brannigan, Augustine. *Crimes, Courts, and Corrections: An Introduction to Crime and Social Control in Canada*. Toronto: Holt, Rinehart Winston, 1984.

Buchignani, Norman. *Cultures in Canada: Strength in Diversity*. Regina, Sask.: L.A. Weigl Educational Associates, 1984.

Burnet, Jean and Palmer, Howard. *Coming Canadians. An Introduction to a History of Canada's Peoples*. Markham, Ont: McClelland Stewart, 1988.

Burnett, David and Schiff, Marilyn. *Contemporary Canadian Art*. Edmonton, Alb.: Hurtig, 1983.

Canada in Film and Video. Plattsburgh, NY: Canadian Film Distribution Center (phone: 1-800-388-6784), annually updated.

Chacko, James. *Cultural Sovereignty: Myth or Reality*. Windsor, Ont.: University of Windsor Press, 1986.

Clandfield, David. *Canadian Film*. Don Mills, Ont: Oxford Univ. Press, 1987.

Colombo, John Robert. *Canadian Literary Landmarks*. Willowdale, Ont.: Hounslow, 1984.

——. *Contemporary Canadian Photography. From the Collection of the National Film Board*. Edmonton, Alb: Hurtig, 1984.

The Dictionary of Canadian Quotations. Don Mills, Ont: Stoddart, 1991.

Crean, Susan and Rioux, Marcel. *Two Nations: An Essay on the Culture and Politics of Canada and Quebec in a World of American Pre-eminence*. Toronto: James Lorimer, 1983.

Cross, Michael S. and Kealey, Gregory S., eds. *Modern Canada. 1930–1980s. Readings in Canadian Social History*. vol. 5. Toronto: McClelland and Stewart, 1984.

Driedger, Leo, ed. *The Canadian Mosaic. A Quest for Identity*. Toronto: McClelland and Stewart, 1978.

——. *Ethnic Canada: Identities and Inequalities*. Mississauga, Ont.: Copp Clark Pitman, 1987.

Elliott, Jean Leonard, ed. *Two Nations, Many Cultures. Ethnic Groups in Canada*. 2d ed. Scarborough, Ont.: Prentice-Hall, 1983.

Feldman, Seth, ed. *Take Two. A Tribute to Canadian Film*. Richmond Hill, Ont.: Irwin, 1984.

Forcese, Dennis and Richter, Stephen, eds. *Social Issues: Sociological Views of Canada*. Scarborough, Ont.: Prentice-Hall, 1982.

Forcese, Dennis. *The Canadian Class Structure*. Scarborough: McGraw-Hill Ryerson, Ltd., 1986.

Francis, Daniel. *The Imaginary Indian. The Image of the Indian in Canadian Culture*. Vancouver: Arsenal Pulp Press, 1992.

Friesen, John W. *When Cultures Clash. Case Studies in Multiculturalism*. Calgary, Alb.: Temeron Books, 1993.

Frye, Northrop. *Divisions on a Ground: Essays on Canadian Culture*. Toronto: Anansi, 1982.

Globerman, Steven. *The Immigration Dilemma*. Vancouver: Fraser Institute, 1992.

Haas, J., et al. *Shaping Identity in Canadian Society*. Scarborough, Ont.: Prentice-Hall, 1978.

Herberg, Edward N. *Ethnic Groups in Canada. Adaptations and Transitions*. Scarborough, Ont: Methuen, 1988.

Huang, Evelyn and Jeffrey, Lawrence. *Chinese Canadians*. Vancouver: Douglas McIntyre, 1992.

Joy, Richard J. *Canada's Official Languages. The Progress of Bilingualism*. Toronto: University of Toronto Press, 1992.

Kallen, Evelyn. *Ethnicity and Human Rights in Canada*. 2d ed. New York: Oxford University Press, 1995.

Kallmann, Helmut, et al, eds. *Encyclopedia of Music in Canada*. 2d ed. Toronto: University of Toronto Press, 1992.

Knowles, Valerie. *Strangers at Our Gates. Canadian Immigration and Immigration Policy, 1540–1990*. Toronto: Dundurn Press, 1992.

Kymlicka, Will. *Finding Our Way. Rethinking Ethnocultural Relations in Canada*. New York: Oxford University Press, 1998.

Link, Eugene P. *The T.B.'s Progress. Norman Bethune as Artist.* Plattsburgh, NY: Center for the Study of Canada, 1991.

MacNeil, Robert. *Burden of Desire.* A Harvest Book, n.d.

Marchak, M. Patricia. *Ideological Perspectives on Canada.* 3d ed. Scarborough, Ont: McGraw-Hill Ryerson, 1987.

Marchand, Philip. *Marshall McLuhan: The Medium & the Messenger.* Cambridge: MIT Press, 1998.

Miles, Angele and Finn, Geraldine, eds. *Feminism in Canada. From Pressure to Politics.* Montreal: Black Rose Books, 1982.

Morris, Peter. *The Film Companion. A Comprehensive Guide to More than 650 Canadian Films and Filmmakers.* Richmond Hill, Ont.: Irwin, 1984.

Murray, Joan. *The Best of the Group of Seven.* Edmonton, Alb: Hurtig, 1984.

Nemiroff, Diana, et al, eds. *Land Spirit Power. First Nations at the National Gallery of Canada.* Ottawa: National Gallery of Art, 1992.

Porter, John. *The Measure of Canadian Society: Education, Equality, and Opportunity.* Ottawa: Carleton Univ. Press, 1988.

Reid, Dennis. *A Concise History of Canadian Painting.* 2d ed. Don Mills, Ont.: Oxford University Press, 1988.

Rooney, John F., Jr., et al, eds. *The Remarkable Continent: An Atlas of the United States and Canadian Society and Cultures.* College Station, TX: Texas A&M Press, 1982.

Ross, Jeffrey Ian, ed. *Violence in Canada. Sociological Perspectives.* New York: Oxford University Press, 1996.

Shek, Ben-Z. *French-Canadian and Quebecois Novels.* Oxford: Oxford University Press, 1991.

Story, G.M. et al, eds. *Dictionary of Newfoundland English.* 2d ed. Toronto: University of Toronto Press, 2002.

Tippett, Maria. *By a Lady. Celebrating Three Centuries of Art by Canadian Women.* Toronto: Penguin, 1992.

Trofimenkoff, Susan Mann and Prentice, Alison, eds. *The Neglected Majority. Volume 2. Essays in Canadian Women's History.* Toronto: McClelland and Stewart, 1985.

Webber, James D. *Reimagining Canada. Language, Culture, Community, and the Canadian Constitution.* Montreal: McGill-Queen's University Press, 1993.

Webster, Judith. *Voices of Canada. An Introduction to Canadian Culture.* Burlington, VT: Assoc. for Canadian Studies in the United States, 1977.

X. FICTION LITERATURE

Atwood, Margaret. *Surfacing.* Toronto: McClelland and Stewart, 1972.

———. *Lady Oracle.* Toronto: McClelland and Stewart, 1976.

———. *Life before Man.* Toronto: McClelland and Stewart, 1979.

———. *Survival: A Thematic Guide to Canadian Literature.*

———. ed. *The New Oxford Book of Canadian Verse in English.* Don Mills, Ont: Oxford Univ. Press, 1982.

———. and Weaver, Robert, eds. *The Oxford Book of Canadian Short Stories in English.* Don Mills, Ont: Oxford Univ. Press, 1988.

———. *Alias Grace.* 1996.

———. *The Blind Assassin.* New York: Doubleday, 2000.

———. *The Year of the Flood.* Bloomsbury, 2009.

Carrier, Roch. *La Guerre, yes sir!* Trans. Sheila Fischman. Toronto: Anansi, 1970.

Davidson, Arnold E. *Coyote Country. Fictions of the Canadian West.* Durham, NC: Duke University Press, 1993.

Gustafson, Ralph, ed. *The Penguin Book of Canadian Verse.* Markham, Ont.: Penguin, 1984. Toronto: Anansi, 1972.

Hebert, Anne. *Kamouraska.* Trans. Norman Shapiro. Toronto: Musson, 1973.

Hemon, Louis. *Maria Chapdelaine.* Trans. W.H. Blake. Toronto: Macmillan, 1921.

Keith, W.J. *Canadian Literature in English.* Toronto: Copp Clark Pitman, 1985.

———. *Literary Images of Ontario.* Toronto: University of Toronto Press, 1992.

Leacock, Stephen. *Sunshine Sketches of a Little Town.* Toronto: McClelland and Stewart, 1970.

Lecker, Robert and David, Jack, eds. *The New Canadian Anthology: Poetry and Short Fiction in English.* Scarborough, Ont: Methuen, 1988.

Lee, Dennis. ed. *The New Canadian Poets. 1970–1985.* Toronto, Ont.: McClelland and Stewart, 1985.

MacLennan, Hugh. *Two Solitudes.* Toronto: Collins, 1945.

McCombs, Judith and Palmer, Carole. *Margaret Atwood. A Reference Guide.* New York: G.K. Hall, 1991.

Montgomery, Lucy Maud. *The Alpine Path. The Story of My Career.* Markham, Ont: Fitzhenry Whiteside, n.d.

New, W.H. *A History of Canadian Literature.* Chicago: Ivan R. Dee, 2000.

Norris, Ken. ed. *Canadian Poetry Now. 20 Poets of the '80s.* Toronto: Anansi, 1984.

Nowlan, Michael, ed. *A Land, A People.* St. John's, Newfoundland: Breakwater Books, Ltd., 1986.

Perkyns, Richard, ed. *Major Plays of the Canadian Theater 1934–1984.* Richmond Hill, Ont.: Irwin, 1984.

Roy, Gabrielle. *The Tin Flute.* Trans. Hannah Josephson. NCL, 1957.

———. Translated by Patricia Claxton. *Enchantment and Sorrow. An Autobiography of Gabrielle Roy.* Toronto: Lester Orpen Dennys, 1987.

Toye, William, ed. *The Oxford Companion to Canadian Literature.* Don Mills, Ont.: Oxford University Press, 1983.

Wagner, Anton, ed. *Contemporary Canadian Theatre. New World Visions.* Toronto: Simon Pierre, 1985.

Wasserman, Jerry, ed. *Modern Canadian Plays, Revised Edition.* Vancouver: Talon Books, 1986.

Weaver, Robert, ed. *Canadian Short Stories.* Fourth Series. Oxford University Press, 1985.

Wiebe, Rudy. *The Temptations of Big Bear.* Toronto: McClelland and Stewart, 1973.

———. *The Scorched-Wood People.* Toronto: McClelland and Stewart, 1977.

Arms of Canada